Writing Choices

◆ ◆ ◆ ◆ ◆ ◆ ◆ ◆ ◆ ◆ ◆ ◆

Shaping Contexts for Critical Readers

Kathleen Bell

University of Central Florida

Allyn and Bacon

Boston   London   Toronto   Sydney   Tokyo   Singapore

Vice-President, Editor-in-Chief, Humanities: Joseph Opiela
Editorial Assistant: Julia Hallett
Marketing Manager: Christopher Bennem
Text Design: Denise Hoffman, Glenview Studios
Editorial-Production Services: Tara L. Masih
Composition and Prepress Buyer: Linda Cox
Electronic Paging: Omegatype Typography, Inc.
Manufacturing Buyer: Suzanne Lareau
Cover Coordinator: Linda Knowles

Library of Congress Cataloging-in-Publication Data

Bell, Kathleen, 1946–
    Writing choices : shaping contexts for critical readers / Kathleen Bell.
      p. cm.
    Includes index.
    ISBN 0-205-29121-X (pbk.)
        1. English language—Rhetoric. 2. Criticism—Authorship.
    3. Critical thinking. 4. Academic writing. 5. College readers. I. Title.

    PE1479.C7 B45 2000
    808'.042—dc21   00–033173

Printed in the United States of America
10 9 8 7 6 5 4 3 2 1   05 04 03 02 01 00

ACKNOWLEDGMENTS

Introduction
    Gen. Colin L. Powell, "Everybody's Children," from *Time,* December 15, 1997.
Copyright © 1997 by Gen. Colin L. Powell. Reprinted by permission of author.
    Jodie Marion, "You've Got Mail." Copyright © 2000. Reprinted by permission
of the author.

Acknowledgments and copyrights are continued at the back of the book on pages
548–551, which constitute an extension of the copyright page.

contents

◆ ✦ ✦ ✦ ✦ ✦ ✦ ✦ ✦ ✦

8 Exploring Cyberspace   243

9 Making Health Decisions   303

preface
✦ ✦ ✦ ✦ ✦ ✦ ✦ ✦ ✦ ✦ ✦

Writing involves a series of choices, choices that writers consciously make to connect readers to the texts they create. Each text, of course, involves a different *rhetorical context* on which a writer bases his or her writing choices: the subject may change, the audience or reader may be more knowledgeable, the writer's purpose may be different. Each rhetorical context, then, requires writers to vary the strategy of the choices they make in order to connect readers to their texts. The purpose of *Writing Choices* is to develop students' understanding of the rhetorical context as a bridge between knowing what choices are involved in creating effective writing and actively using readings as resources for analyzing and making those choices in their own writing.

Becoming a Critical Reader

When my writing students and I read an essay, we read in different ways. They read to understand content; I analyze how the content is composed and presented to evaluate the effectiveness of the writing. They ask *what,* and I ask *how* and *why.* Together these two ways of reading illustrate the process of becoming a critical reader, that is, *using a writer's lens to read.*

The first step to developing that critical writer's lens involves the reader identifying her or his connection to the content: *What do you already know about the subject?* What related experiences do you have? What reading knowledge? What is your attitude toward the subject? Forming a personal context with the subject brings the reader closer to discovering the writer's purpose: why the writer wants to connect the reader to the subject. This discovery begins the interactive dialogue between the writer and the reader. The process of using a writer's lens to read, illustrated in the Introduction, reveals how writers and readers work together to make meaning. One extended example in this section shows one student's process of discovering a connection to the content and the writer's purpose.

The next level involves understanding how the rhetorical context influences the writer's choices. A second example in the Introduction illustrates the thinking that underlies the choices one writer makes in designing a specific rhetorical context to connect with a particular audience. The writer explains in detail how her own connection to the subject, the occasion for writing, led to her choice of audience and purpose. From this context the writer plans a strategy for making writing choices by examining the relationships of writer to reader, reader to subject, and writer and reader to purpose. To emphasize how the rhetorical context provides the foundation for writing decisions, every reading in the text includes a defined context.

Analyzing the actual choices writers make to complement their rhetorical context and to stimulate interaction with their readers is the next level in developing critical readers. The choices that organize the text—point of view, structure, voice, and credibility—follow a sequence that emphasizes how the choices work together to create meaning for readers. The extended example in the Introduction reveals that the process of making those choices is neither linear nor formulaic. To simplify the analysis in the example, each choice category appears under a separate heading to correlate with the Part One chapters. Students can then use this example as a reference when analyzing essays or drafting their own. The actual chapter for each writing choice demonstrates how the use of that choice shapes the writer's ideas and develops a relationship between the reader, the writer, and the subject. Students can follow the effects of each choice in a fully annotated example and test their understanding by annotating another selection from the same context.

Part One: "The Writer's Choices" is devoted to developing students' critical reading abilities. It focuses on the global decisions involved in essay design and on the language and structural features that navigate ideas to fulfill that design. The emphasis is on using the rhetorical context as the foundation for discovering the possibilities and potential problems in creating a dialogue with a wide range of specific audiences in a variety of contexts: how to take readers from *what they already know* to *what they need to know*. This focus intends to complement instruction presented in a guide to writing and a handbook by serving as a bridge between knowing *what* choices need to be made to understanding *how* and *why* those choices are effective in different contexts. To help students internalize this process of analysis, each chapter includes the following common features:

- ❖ **Rhetorical Context:** The relationships between writer, reader, subject, and purpose serve as the basis for discussing and analyzing the writing choices in each chapter.

- ❖ **Question Format:** Questions based on the relationships between writer, reader, subject, and purpose form a heuristic framework for internalizing the possibilities for making choices.

- ❖ **Process:** The process of using the question framework to make choices is demonstrated in several brief examples representing a variety of contexts.

- ❖ **Exercises:** Following the sample process are brief exercises intended to give students general familiarity with the terms and process.

- ❖ **Sample Analysis:** The sample analysis begins with a full description of the rhetorical context of the essay and a projection of the intended audience's expectations. The essay is then annotated, to point out what choices the writer made related to the chapter focus. An analysis of the effectiveness of those choices with respect to the rhetorical context follows the essay. Each chapter focuses on a different context.

- ❖ **Application:** The "On Your Own" section presents students with an essay written to the same audience as the sample analysis essay. Using the same basic rhetorical context allows the sample analysis to serve as a reference for students' practice application.

The writing choices selected for each chapter and the sequence in which the chapters appear attempt to capture the organic, recursive nature of shaping an essay to connect the writer with his or her intended readers. Each chapter builds on the previous one but also involves a reanalysis, and often a revision, of previous decisions.

Chapter 1, "Framing the Context," explores each of the foundational relationships that serve as the basis for making writing choices: writer to subject, writer to reader, reader to subject, and writer and reader to purpose.

Chapter 2, "Determining Point of View," demonstrates how the writer's familiarity with the subject and relationship to the audience affect the writer's visibility and the angle from which the writer presents information: subjective, objective, or merged.

Chapter 3, "Shaping Ideas," examines how purpose influences the writer's choice of arranging content in connecting the reader to the subject and purpose. Choices include chronological, sequential, and spatial arrangements.

Chapter 4, "Choosing a Voice," explains how the voice a writer chooses reflects the writer's attitude toward the subject and the reader in fulfilling the purpose and complementing the point of view. The focus is on level of formality as conveyed through diction, sentence features, and punctuation.

Chapter 5, "Establishing Credibility," demonstrates how the writer's choice of documentation—personal experience, professional authority, primary sources, secondary sources, and shared authority with the reader—establishes credibility in specific contexts. How to access sources, determine a search strategy, evaluate sources, and incorporate sources are demonstrated in a full range of point of view and voice combinations.

Together the chapters in Part One demonstrate how to use the writer's lens in analyzing the effectiveness of writing choices. This process is the basis for responding to the readings in Part Two and, ultimately, for students to make choices in their own writing.

Evaluating Writing Choices

Part Two, the "Readings" section, presents students with seven themed chapters, each containing ten readings for analysis and evaluation. Each theme represents a topic or field undergoing changes in the way people view it.

Choosing Heroes: As our country has developed has our need for heroes changed? Who are our heroes? Why do we have them? What criteria determine hero quality?

Finding Community: How does the image we have of ourselves contribute to the identity we seek in a community? Where do we go to find community and how do we gain membership?

Exploring Cyberspace: How do we use what we already know to experience and test this new frontier? What are the risks and the rewards?

Making Health Decisions: The availability of information makes health decisions considerably more complex. How do you determine when you need information and what sources to use?

Re-Viewing Media: New forms of media appear at an increasingly fast rate. How do those changes affect our daily lives? What do those changes reflect about our culture?

Defining Environmental Ethics: Can one person make a difference in saving the environment? What does it mean to make an ethical commitment?

Speculating on the New Century: How real and how virtual will your future be? Will some of our problems finally be solved? Will we become more or less in control of our lives?

In addition to stimulating students' interest in these topics and providing captivating issues for writing, these readings have a responsibility to continue the development of students' critical reading abilities—their ability to read with a writer's lens—begun in Part One. To strengthen that ability, each group of themed readings contains the following features:

❖ A wide range of rhetorical contexts, from students' classroom-based assignments, general interest news articles, and on-line organizational and commercial material to documented professional and academic selections, to demonstrate a diversity in choices in point of view, voice, arrangement, and use of sources;

❖ A range of sources and genres, from literary essays, journalism, speeches, and narratives to academic research and editorials, to increase students' versatility in determining the context and the value of the information presented.

To get students as close as possible to the text of each reading, to ensure that their interaction with the text increases their awareness of how the writer's choices shape the context for readers, the pedagogical apparatus in each chapter follows the framework established in Part One:

> *Rhetorical Context:* The headnote for each reading outlines the rhetorical context, identifying how the writer's level of expertise, the year of publication, the occasion for writing, the intended audience of readers, and the writer's purpose might influence the readers' expectations and the writer's choices.
>
> *Follow-up Questions:* The questions on each reading follow the sequence of writer's choice chapters in Part One: framing the context; determining point of view; shaping ideas; choosing voice; establishing credibility. The repetition of this emphasis helps students to internalize the relationship between the rhetorical context and making wrting choices, thus strengthening their ability to perceive not only how and why choices are made but also to detect where possibilities and problems or constraints may exist in their own writing.
>
> *Writing Suggestions:* As an extension of the conversation formed by the ten diverse readings in each chapter, the writing suggestions on each theme focus on issues raised by the readings and create specific contexts for students to demonstrate their understanding of making effective choices. Learning to view their work contextually puts the student writer in control of decision making and shifts the reason for revising from merely pleasing the instructor to pleasing the writer in establishing a dialogue with the intended reader.

Reading through a writer's lens requires a great deal of practice, but once students internalize the questions they need to ask about making writing choices they will become not only more critical in their reading but also more confident in making those choices in their own writing.

Acknowledgments

During the last few decades of teaching writing and directing writing programs, I have listened to students' incessant query, "How can reading make me a better writer?" Though I'm still not convinced that they really wish to read, *Writing Choices* is my latest attempt to make the connection between reading and writing more tangible for students. So I begin by thanking those students who have convinced me that they sincerely want to know the answer to that question. Ideas do not become texts, however, without a strong commitment from an experienced publisher, so it is with deep gratitude that I thank the following people at Allyn & Bacon: my editor, Joe Opiela, whose sustained belief in this project and years of experience have made it a reality; my production manager—and permission sleuth extraordinaire, Elaine Ober; and editorial assistant Kristen Desmond, who was forced to bring order to chaos on more than one occasion. Finally, I would like to thank the following reviewers whose recommendations and cogent questions helped me to practice what I preach: Chris Burnham, New Mexico State University; Martha Henning, Pacific Northwest Community College; Richard Batteiger, Oklahoma State University; Clyde Moneyhun, Youngstown State University; John M. Clark, Bowling Green University; Linda Bensel-Meyers, University of Tennessee; Joseph Petraglia-Bahri, Georgia Institute of Technology; Ellen Andrews-Knodt, Penn State Abington; Meg Morgan, University of North Carolina–Charlotte; Paul Heilker, Virginia Technical University; and Lisa J. McClure, Southern Illinois University.

—Kathleen Bell
University of Central Florida

Connecting Readers and Writers

The relationship between readers and writers depends on a willingness to explore ideas together. Writers stake out a territory to explore, provide maps designed for discovery, and invite readers to join the expedition. Readers, in turn, survey the invitation and weigh the possibilities for discovery before making a commitment to the journey. The next time you're in a bookstore or library, you can observe these negotiations in action. Watch how readers peruse a book or periodical; how they closely read the front and back cover, skim the table of contents and index, flip through the text, read the opening. What convinces readers to check out or buy the text, or to place it back on the shelf? What choices do writers make to form the initial relationship with readers and to maintain that relationship? Determining what those choices are and how to make them is the purpose of *Writing Choices*.

Understanding the Reader's Role

"All writing depends on the generosity of the reader," states Alberto Manguel in his book *The History of Reading*. He explains this statement by describing the relationship between the writer and the reader:

> *While the writer remains present, the text remains incomplete. Only when the writer relinquishes the text, does the text come into existence. At that point, the existence of the text is a silent existence, silent until the moment in which*

a reader reads it. Only when the able eye makes contact with the markings on the tablet, does the text come to active life. (179)

What is the "able eye" Manguel refers to, and how does its "generosity" activate a piece of writing?

An "able eye" implies not only the training to decode language symbols into meaning, but also an ability to activate the intentions of the writer. In other words, readers who develop an "able eye" *expect* to interact with the writer and know how to follow the map of the writer's intentions. The "generosity" that ignites and maintains that interaction assumes certain conditions about the reader-writer relationship: (1) that the writer has something significant to say; (2) that the writer is credible; (3) that the writer and reader share a mutual respect for discovery; and (4) that the road to making discoveries involves reading *with* the writer and *against* the writer, testing assumptions, agreeing and disagreeing.

A reader who assumes this participant role constructs his or her *own* meaning from the text. By actively responding, such as by writing in the margins or in a response journal, the reader taps a reservoir of knowledge, experiences, and concerns that blended together create a personally constructed context for understanding the writer's ideas. In this way, you and I can read the same essay, and while we might agree on the facts presented, we will each construct our own meaning. For example, if a writer compares the fate of an object to that of an eight-track tape player, you and I both understand the writer's intention to identify the object as a short-lived fad, but the way we construct that meaning differs because of our ages. You know the eight-track from old television shows and movies while I, unfortunately, actually bought and used one. In this way the writer's choice of comparison allows us both to interact with the text using different personal levels to understand the idea.

To discover the choices writers make to interact with readers, readers first must identify *when* and *how* they are involved with the text. If you are reading *with* the reader, what choices does the writer make to establish that connection with you? Is it the writer's personal voice, the familiar experiences, the authoritative information? If you are reading *against* the writer, what writing choices produce that tension? Is it lack of details, unsupported claims, inappropriate tone, a leap in logic? Identifying the choices that provoke your involvement and reveal the writer's intentions in a specific work immediately activates the text and allows the reader to begin a dialogue of discovery with the writer.

Sample Interactive Reading

The Rhetorical Context   Writers compose their writing for a specific purpose and with specific readers in mind. The article below appeared December 15, 1997, on the last-page essay section of *Time,* a weekly news magazine read by the general, educated public ages eighteen to eighty-plus. Their purpose for reading is to keep up with the impact of current events, both national and international. Some readers will know more about individual subjects than others will, but all will be reading to be better informed, not for entertainment.

The Reader's Interaction   The person responding to the article is a first-year college student. In the right-hand column she notes her personal level of involvement, both *with* and *against* the writer. Notice how her level of interaction responds to the writer's choices identified in the left-hand column. In paragraph five, where she begins to respond *against* the writer, the reader questions the writer's choices and in doing so realizes what the writer's purpose is. This point of tension is where the reader's personal context merges with the writer's intention to create new meaning.

Reading the Essay   As you read the essay, use an "able eye" to examine how the annotations in both columns work together to produce the interaction with the text. You may find that your personal context differs from that of the student responder. If so, note those differences to discuss after the reading.

◆ ◆ ◆

Everybody's Children

General Colin L. Powell

1   One of the most frightening scenes in Charles Dickens' *A Christmas Carol* occurs when the Ghost of Christmas Present reveals to the yet unredeemed Ebenezer Scrooge two ragged and

Writer's Choices

Identifies with the readers: Powell uses literature familiar to most readers to form an immediate connection, evoke associations, and identify neglected children as the problem.

Connects reader to his purpose: Nurturing can make children productive members of society; nurturing is everyone's responsibility.

Connects reader closer to the writer and the subject: Identifies self as director of America's Promise; makes an emotional appeal to the reader to be involved.

Connects reader to the subject with background information on America's Promise: purpose; goals.

wolfish children—a boy and a girl, cowering in the folds of his robe. Even flint-hearted Scrooge is intimidated by the sight of them: "Where angels might have sat enthroned, devils lurked, and glared out menacing."

2   "Spirit," he asks, "are they yours?"

3   "They are Man's," the ghost replies. "And they cling to me, appealing from their fathers. This boy is Ignorance. This girl is Want. Beware them both, and all of their degree, but most of all beware this boy, for on his brow I see that written which is Doom unless the writing be erased."

4   Children can be angels or devils, depending, on the kind of nurturing they receive from others. They can grow into responsible and contributing members of society, or they can become its dependents, predators and outcasts. And because they are "Man's" children, they are everybody's children. The whole society has a stake in their destiny and a duty to help them grow up strong and confident.

5   As chairman of America's Promise—The Alliance for Youth, I see angels enthroned and devils lurking every day that I deal with this country's young people. I never cease to be amazed at how little it takes to turn one into the other. In a land as richly blessed as ours, it is indeed tragic to reflect that for want of a little guidance and encouragement, a child may drop out of school, turn to drugs or crime, or create new life before he or she is mature enough to assume the responsibilities of parenthood. Yet as many as 15 million American youngsters are at risk of falling prey to these or other social scourges of our time.

6   America's Promise was created to give these kids a better chance at life. By the end of the year 2000, we aim to provide at least 2 million of them with five basic resources we believe they need to make it in today's America. These are: an ongoing relationship with a caring adult; safe places and structured activities from which to learn and

Reader's Personal Context

Every holiday season this story emerges, usually in a contemporary version; the haves versus the have nots.

Angel and devil. I was both as a kid, but I turned out okay. I'll probably have kids someday in the future.

That's a lot of kids who are in trouble. I wonder how that figure was calculated.

I thought we already had lots of programs to take care of these problems.

grow during nonschool hours; a healthy start and a healthy future; a marketable skill through effective education; and an opportunity to give back through community service.

Stimulates dialogue with readers by posing a question to them.

7   The logic of the first four resources is immediately obvious; the logic of the fifth is less so. If youngsters lack basic needs, does it make sense to ask them to give?

Asking people to give back after you've helped them? I never heard of using that approach before.

Connects reader closer to subject with benefits of volunteering.

8   Paradoxically, the answer is yes. Young people—like adults—usually find that when they make a real effort on behalf of others, they get back more than they contribute. Many youngsters report that volunteering in their communities has helped them understand people who are different from themselves, has opened up new career possibilities to them and has enlarged their horizons. According to one poll, more than half of teenage respondents said that their grades improved as a result of volunteering. In Maryland, which has a "service-learning" requirement that students must fulfill to graduate from high school, one initially reluctant volunteer later wrote a first-person account for the Washington *Post,* in which she confessed that her experience in community service was generally positive and actually added value to her résumé.

I remember "service" being a category on my college application; I didn't have any.

Connects reader to purpose with specific example of success.

9   Even youngsters from disadvantaged backgrounds find that they are enriched by giving of themselves. The Corporation for National Service (AmeriCorps) has some very uplifting stories to tell of young people whose lives have been transformed by serving others. A 20-year-old victim of a drive-by shooting in Los Angeles went on to counsel other youths on how to settle conflicts peacefully. Another AmeriCorps volunteer, a former gang member and drug dealer in Milwaukee, Wis., later founded an organization that helps teenagers break away from gangs.

Do we have a local AmeriCorps group? I've never read about them. What percentage of those helped then work as volunteers?

Connects reader to purpose with personal testimony from volunteer.

10   Recently, I attended a rally for America's Promise in San Antonio, Texas. One of the speakers was a young man who had dropped out of

high school at age 15. But his experience as a volunteer inspired him to earn his graduate-equivalency diploma, which set him on the road to college. "Because of community service," he told a hushed crowd of several thousand people, "my life has changed like night and day, and in the process I have made a difference in other people's lives."

Connects reader to purpose with examples of commitment others have made to America's Promise.

11   Time and again I have been heartened by the willingness of so many young people to embrace an ethic of citizenship that includes service to community and nation. In response to the call issued by America's Promise, the Boy Scouts and Girl Scouts of America have pledged millions of additional hours in service projects, as have the youth affiliates of the Kiwanis and Rotary clubs. Not long ago, the Boys & Girls Clubs of America presented me with a "promise book" of commitments made by Boys & Girls Clubs all across the nation. That book is two inches thick!

These groups need to find projects. When would I find the time, what with work, college, and studying?

Connects writer, reader, subject, and purpose using "we" and returning to the holiday spirit and opening sad images from Dickens.

12   Giving, to our youth, and helping them learn the joys of giving back, could literally transform America, if we were all willing to involve ourselves in this effort. At this time of year, more than any other, it behooves us to ask ourselves honestly if we are doing enough for "Man's" children. If not, Ignorance and Want will dog our steps and dampen our holiday cheer until we do.

The holiday spirit does inspire me to help, but I don't see how I could sustain the commitment.

The author is chairman of America's Promise—The Alliance for Youth. Those interested in volunteering should call 888-55-YOUTH.

This reader's responses read both *with* the writer and *against* the writer: While the reader appreciates the problem and the need to volunteer, she also questions what other help is available and the level of time commitment expected. Her *personal context* does not include the experience in volunteering necessary to visualize the work required behind the success stories Powell presents. Reviewing the writer's choices in the left-hand column, it's clear that Powell did not think it necessary to include that information.

When the reader discovers there is a difference between her expectations and the information presented, she asks, "Why didn't

Powell include this information?" At this point she must reconsider Powell's purpose for writing the essay, and in doing so, she understands his purpose is primarily just to motivate the reader to volunteer. He assumes his readers will not oppose helping a person in need. Making this discovery allows the reader to reread the essay using a writer's lens to better understand the writing choices Powell made. Instead of asking, "What is this essay about?" she can focus on Powell's purpose by asking, "Does he convince me to volunteer?" If she is convinced, she can call the number at the end of the article for more information.

Understanding the Writer's Role

Writers write for others to read, even when those readers are themselves. Once they develop their own connection to a subject, they explore ways to share that connection. The first level of problem-solving the writer faces, then, is to determine what readers *already* know about the subject and what they *need* to know in order to share the connection. Reviewing Powell's essay, we can clearly see what assumptions he made about his readers' knowledge and needs:

What *Time* readers already know:

who Gen. Colin L. Powell is

the story of Dickens's *A Christmas Carol*

children require nurturing

many children who live in deprived environments need help

we are all members of the same society

What *Time* readers need to know:

what America's Promise—the Alliance for Youth stands for

what Gen. Powell's connection to the organization is

the act of giving benefits both the giver and the receiver

people who receive help are more likely to give help in return

others have already made a commitment to the organization's goals

a united effort will produce results

What helps us to understand these assumptions Powell makes is the quantity and quality of information he presents at various points in the essay. For example, only the first four paragraphs of the essay address what Powell assumes the *Time* readers already know. If Powell's assumptions are correct, then those introductory paragraphs will successfully connect the readers to the subject. Following the introductory paragraphs, Powell devotes two paragraphs to establishing the goals of America's Promise and his role as chairman. This role and Powell's reputation as a national leader allow him to use a well-informed, authoritative *point of view*. Also, his experiences in developing the program make his use of personal *voice* appropriate for presenting the information.

The remaining six paragraphs focus on specific examples illustrating the benefits of volunteering to the giver, the recipient, and society. Note that the two recipient examples contain the most concrete details, including a quote from a recipient who then became a volunteer. The quantity and quality of information in this section establish layers of *credibility* to connect readers with the potential success of the program. This sequence of writing choices illustrates how Powell deliberately designed a strategy to respond to what the *Time* readers need to know if they are to be motivated to join America's Promise.

The writer's role begins with the writer's connection to the subject. However, to present that connection in writing, the role of the writer also includes analyzing the reader's connection to the subject. This relationship between writers and readers begins the problem-solving process of writing.

The Process of Making Choices

Writers who want to connect with their readers know that at some point in the composing process they need to consciously shape their writing in order to ignite that connection. When this conscious effort begins depends a great deal on the writer's individual composing process. For example, if you choose to write about a subject on which you are already well informed, you may begin drafting quickly with an audience in mind. But if you begin with only a strong opinion on a subject, you may need to conduct research to find supporting information and the opinions of others. This research can help you to discover the audience with whom you would like to connect.

Once you do decide who your intended audience is, you can begin to shape your writing to connect with that reader, to create a dialogue that allows the reader to participate in the text.

One Writer's Choices

In the following example you can follow along with writer Jodie Marion as she explains how she developed her essay from the discovery draft stage generating content to a revised draft in which she consciously shapes her essay to create a dialogue with a specific group of readers. Marion, a native of the Indian River region in Florida, earned her master of fine arts in literature at the University of Central Florida. She is an experienced freelance writer for community publications and now devotes her time to pursuing a master of fine arts in poetry. As an experienced writer she pays close attention to what choices she makes, how those choices convey meaning, and how those choices promote interaction with her readers. Still, the complexity of this process is difficult to explain.

You may be unfamiliar with some of the terms Marion uses to explain her choices. The headings used to identify her choices—rhetorical context, point of view, shape, voice, and credibility—correspond to the chapters in Part One so each will be explained in detail. When you study those chapters and when you analyze the readings in Part Two, you might find it helpful to return to this example as a reference.

Finding a Subject

Initially, I wanted to address the <.com> sign, to examine it as a "sign of the times"—a springboard for a discussion about how impatient we are as a society, how it sometimes seems that we buzz, blip, and hurry our way through life. I wanted then to arrive at this grand conclusion: that simply by slowing down, by relying less on technology, and by contemplating our fate in the electronic age, all would be well. A lofty goal. However, after a few pages of trying to work with the topic, it became apparent that the subject was too broad and that I was not able to write with a fair, balanced tone; I'm simply not well versed enough in the fields of media studies and communication to present a balanced, yet brief, essay on that original subject. So, I then tried to focus on an emblem that I could use to illustrate a smaller facet of our engagement with technology. I settled on the phrase "You've got mail" because it involves a pervasive part of modern life (e-mail), a subject about which I can present more than one angle and prompt questions for the audience to consider.

I came into this essay wanting to resist the praising of e-mail, wanting to find reason to argue for a resurgence of letter writing. And while part of me still feels nostalgic about hand-penned letters that make individual journeys from real places to real places, I admit that I've come to embrace the wonders of electronic communication and find that there are two distinct arenas for communication. Had I not written this piece, I wouldn't have discovered all the remarkable and lamentable facets of e-mail. Had I not gone through this process, I wouldn't have realized that there is certainly room for both kinds of communication—it just depends on the purpose for writing.

My Rhetorical Context *(See Chapter 1)*

- ❖ *Subject:* E-mail and traditional forms of written communication—how they compare and why we should consider their similarities and differences.

- ❖ *Occasion:* My motivations for exploring this subject involve both personal and public concerns. Publicly, as a global community, we are undergoing a massive shift in our communication practices and increased reliance on computers; therefore, it is useful to consider how these changes affect our society. On a personal level, because I am a writer, words—how we manipulate, rely on, and value them—are always worthwhile as a subject to explore, and I admit that I'm always looking for ways to encourage people to become more aware of language.

- ❖ *Audience:* The audience is very broad: I expect my readers to know what e-mail is and suppose that a majority actively uses an e-mail account. However, those readers who may have never considered how communication is drastically changing also comprise a primary audience for the piece. (This essay can also encourage those who are suspicious of electronic correspondence that it has its merits.) I assume that most readers will buy my assumptions in the first paragraph about our loss of patience and increased reliance on computers. And though I do not expect all of the readers to share my infatuation with language, I also assume that they will indulge the topic because everyone is connected in some way to written language and many to e-mail.

- ❖ *Purpose:* I want my audience to consider what their relationships are with printed language and how these relationships can be altered depending on the kind of communication they choose. It's important that my audience realize that they have options not only in the words they choose to write, but also in how they send them. I hope the essay prompts my readers to ask questions like the following: So what? Why does it matter that there are different ways to send written messages? How different can e-mail and snail mail be, anyway? I want the readers to challenge my conclusions by reflecting on their own patterns of written communication.

◆ ◆ ◆

You've Got Mail

Jodie Marion

The limits of my language mean the limits of my world.
—Ludwig Wittgenstein, *Tractus Logico-Philosophicas* (1922)

1   Like millions of other people, the soft glow of a computer screen and the electric hum of its hard drive have become a permanent presence in my home—an integral part of my daily routine. And computers have become pervasive in the workplace too, affording many the luxury to work out of the home, blurring the boundaries between "home" and "work." We've welcomed the computer into our lives, but some would contend that the transition has been a bit too quick, that we're hurling ourselves gracelessly into an age that demands computer savvy and speed in all our transactions, business and personal.

2   Patience, that once noble virtue, is out of vogue these days. So, it follows that our patterns of correspondence have had to acclimate to these changes. One obvious emblem of these changes is electronic mail, or "e-mail," a system created for practical purposes, not only to decrease paper waste in communication but also to increase efficiency by eliminating office phone tag. But the system is now part of our personal lives, too, and this merits some investigation. It seems worthwhile and essential that we (as individuals and as a society) stop, for at least a moment, to consider how our increased reliance on e-mail affects us—because e-mail means more than just "speedy" communication: it has created new opportunities in written communication and new levels of intimacy, though it has also

overshadowed some of the unique, irreplaceable characteristics of traditional written communication.

Permanence and impermanence: these words describe the most elementary differences between the new and the old forms. For example, think about junk mail . . . disposing of it is more satisfying in the virtual world. One button and the undesired mail is vaporized (impermanence), whereas getting rid of a real letter involves some guilt—another piece destined for the landfill (permanence). However, a more significant distinction must be made between the levels of commitment held by the readers of e-mail versus letters. There's a greater connection between a letter and its reader than a screen and its observer. Letters are more visceral. An envelope confirms that the letter—that the act of writing itself—has a permanent, fixed place in our world. Letters come with stamps that prove they've been in *real,* physical places like San Francisco, California, or Peoria, Illinois. Each letter *is* its own universe; each is housed in its own self-contained, unique package. Maybe the stationery is personalized, maybe it is even scented like the sender. Handwritten words are also markers of individuality. And finally, the greatest biological marker of individuality of all, DNA, belongs to a letter—the sender's saliva used on the seal.

E-mail, on the other hand, calls our notion of place into question. Although it's not a physical place, the mail center exists as a "place" on the Web, a site. And rather than just a receptacle for electronic messages, like my real mailbox is a receptacle for many individual letters, I see the site of my e-mail account as a kind of forum where the different voices I know congregate, each chiming in about our shared interests, our points of intersection. This creates a community not easily accessed with traditional pen and paper. And what a strange composition! People who may very well scratch one another's eyes out in person coexist peacefully side by side in my e-mail account, and I can send messages to all of them with a few simple commands. It's as if I have a captive audience twenty-four hours, seven days a week.

But I didn't always feel such possibility and optimism about e-mail. I used to have separate accounts for work and for my personal life, just like I have a real mailbox at home and a mailbox in my office at work. I had the impression that e-mail was efficient for the perfunctory tasks of work. For example, the department coordinator sends quick messages to find out when we can hold our next committee meeting: "Send best times for next meeting. Thanx, NM." No niceties, no chit-chat, just bare bones communication, which seems fine for painfully tedious administrative tasks, but when used for personal messages, is it the right medium? Thoughtful enough for intimate contact with friends and family? I'm beginning to think that it can be. What potential does e-mail have to enhance our personal lives? It seems possible that the element of spontaneity and interactive quality of e-mail communication can be just as useful in our personal relationships, if not more so, as in letters.

6   It's comforting to know I can check my mail at 7:00 P.M., stew on it for a few hours (if I choose), answer it at 2:00 A.M., and have a response by the next afternoon. Aside from convenience, the exchanges between the parties remain fresh, like a telephone conversation, but better, because there's more time to be deliberate and thoughtful about the words chosen. If you've just had disagreeable words on the phone with your partner, you can fire off an e-mail and avoid calling him or her during the wee hours of the night; the computer screen provides a *distance*, a buffer that allows you to vent emotions without having to worry about tripping over your words or being unnerved by someone's physical presence. You can take your time and be deliberate, unlike face-to-face communication. Writing gives you that opportunity, and with e-mail you get the immediate effects of a spoken conversation, but you also get the chance to monitor and shape what you want the listener to remember for posterity.

7   Unlike the ephemerality of the spoken word, written language is enduring—you can revisit it and see exactly what was communicated rather than guessing at what was said. And fine writing, that with unmistakable clarity and sincerity, depends entirely on which words are chosen and the syntactic grace with which they are arranged. Typed or handwritten, that remains constant. If you can create an engaging voice with a pen, that voice will certainly translate in cyberspace.

8   Thinking back to the epigraph, I see that Wittgenstein was definitely onto something: one of the primary functions of language is to create more options, more ways of describing, more ways of solving problems, more ways to develop our (hopefully) expanding consciousnesses. In other words, language dismantles "limits." Whether inked onto personalized stationery or distributed through a mass electronic mailing, language—words—do create the parameters of your universe. We cannot exchange concepts or ideas without having codes (words) for them. Words are pacts we make with one another, places where we agree on meaning—and places where we

challenge existing meaning. So is it supremely important *how* the written language is transmitted? Not *that* important. What seems more crucial is a writer's ability to communicate succinctly, genuinely, and with grace. We do not have to choose between handwritten letters or the computer. In fact, it's a great relief to have one more medium where these challenges can transpire.

✦ ✦ ✦

Reflecting on My Writing Choices

Point of View *(See Chapter 2)*   Once I figured out where I stood with the subject, I had to decide how close or visible I wanted to be to my readers—the point of view I wanted to use. This didn't prove difficult because I knew that the subject was relatively familiar to most people these days, and that shared base of knowledge gave me the chance to use a merged point of view. I made the assumption that my readers and I have shared cultural experiences concerning my topic and that they would value my experience as a prompt to consider their own experiences in relation to the subject.

The merged point of view begins immediately as I align my experience (the visual and aural image of the computer in my home) with that of "millions of other Americans," but I had to be careful not to use an entirely subjective approach: just because my readers share a common experience doesn't mean they share my concerns. This is where I tried to mediate with an objective statement we could consider together. The epigraph, for example, is an outside source that my readers and I can keep focused on, rather than looking at me and my experience for the whole essay. I try not to be in the forefront, and when I am, I try to include the reader, too, as found in the concluding paragraph with the persistent use of "we."

Shape *(See Chapter 3)*   This proved to be a difficult task. In choosing a structure I had to first determine what my reader already knew—something I had considered when playing with points of view. Although I was fairly confident that no one would be alienated by the subject matter, my primary concern was that my readers would recognize why they should bother thinking about the function of e-mail in their personal lives. I knew that before I introduced my subjective experience I would have to build common ground—

that's what I think the first two paragraphs accomplish. In this way, I see the structure as sequential; that is, the first two paragraphs show how e-mail has become a pervasive element in our public and private lives, how the significance of my concerns came to be. This sequential structure assured me that my assumptions would be apparent to the readers, that they would probably concede, "Okay, I know where she's coming from," and hang on until I arrive at the focal point at the end of paragraph 2 where I introduce the ideas about how e-mail gives us new ways to communicate.

Then, I had to consider which sequence might work best to prompt my readers to ponder their own experience with the subject—that's the function of this essay, not to provide "answers," but to provoke discussion. I just kept writing and paring down my ideas, not sure which sequence would work best. After numerous false starts, I began to feel most comfortable with the idea of showing my readers how I "came around," how I became comfortable with the role e-mail was developing in my personal life. And in this way, by enabling readers to see my path of discovery, the sequence unfolded as a trip sequence. Though abstract, the sights I visit include a discussion of the tangibility of letters and a visit to my experience with e-mail. It's a trip of considerations. And as with most trip sequences, the discovery comes at the end when I make the larger connection with language's role in this discussion. This is the most difficult part, I think, about shaping an essay. For me, it involves an obscene amount of process, but it seems to be the only way. Incidentally, I also purposely avoided many potentially provocative subjects—like privacy and e-mail accounts, the possibility of on-line chatting, and the loss of penmanship—so that there would be plenty of discoveries for the readers after they finished reading.

The epigraph gives the essay a frame and helps develop closure because it gives me a point in history to refer to at the end of the piece. Ideas about technology and language do not exist in a vacuum, and I wanted to demonstrate the importance of the subject by connecting with someone legitimate in history

Voice *(See Chapter 4)*   What kind of voice would complement the merged point of view? That is the primary question I had to resolve. Because my purpose is to encourage questions and discussion from the reader, I simply had to concentrate on maintaining a voice that didn't slip into a lecture, but one that would also encourage the reader to ask questions regarding language and communication media; a balance between formality and informality was in order. The trip sequence gave me an opportunity to merge levels of formality. Early in the essay I present a kind of emotional rejection of e-mail, and my voice is relatively informal. However, as I begin to come to a rational understanding of its role, my voice becomes increasingly formal.

I tried to avoid too many structural complexities without developing a monotonous rhythm—managing a mediation between formality and informality. A good percentage of my sentences fall into the subject-verb-object pattern (plain enough), although there are several variations of it, usually via a string of parenthetical elements to add specificity and emphasis. My sentences are full of seams; that is, they are often more a collection of details stuck to one or two subjects rather than structurally complex patterns. And the sentence structure is designed to never let the reader get too comfortable with the rhythm—to insist on an interactive reading. The last sentence in paragraph two is a healthy example of this attempt: the parentheses clarify "we"; the commas around the prepositional phrase "for at least a moment" adds pause, or thoughtfulness; the dash focuses attention on the "because," or the "why the reader should care" part of the essay; and the colon harnesses the dash's momentum so that the reader prepares adequately for the upcoming list. Quite a lot of responsibility for the reader. The rhetorical questions in paragraph five also provide an opportunity for interactivity. And for more structural diversity, there's an exclamatory sentence—something I rarely include in an essay, simply because I think prose should be able to convey surprise or excitement without the obnoxiousness of an exclamation point. In this essay, though, I think it works because I use the exclamatory sentence as a way to balance formality of the previous sentences involving "forums" and "communities."

Similarly, the infusion of parenthesis, dashes, colons, semicolons, and ellipses is designed to push, pull, slow down, and speed up the reader. I really had to temper my use of dashes, and although there are still nine of them in the piece, I don't think they lose their effectiveness. Again, because I chose a sentence structure that privileges detail, parenthetical elements—especially dashes—affirm that emphasis. Part of my intended interactivity, the merged point of view, also involves occasional direct address of "you" and the development of "we" in the first and last paragraphs. The ellipses in paragraph two are another invitation for the reader to consider ideas: they pause after I suggest "thinking about" junk mail.

However I tried to compromise the structural complexity of my prose; I didn't try to do the same with word choice. It's relatively elevated, but I do not see that as a barricade for the reader, since I give my readers a quote by Wittgenstein that encourages expansion of their universes by increasing their knowledge of language. I would be a hypocrite to compromise or limit my word choices. So, words like "acclimate," "perfunctory," "impermanence," "visceral," and "ephemerality" weren't edited out and coexist nicely, I think, beside the playful punctuation to create a merged voice that unifies writer and reader while prompting readers to explore in their own fashion after the reading.

Credibility *(See Chapter 5)*   This voice, I hope, has developed a fairly strong sense of ethos; even if the readers arrive at entirely different conclusions, they will still be able to acknowledge my point of view as one of concern. I intentionally did not seek outside sources because my topic deals with a personal understanding of a subject rather than an expert opinion designed to persuade. Therefore, my credibility must come from my prose: the appropriateness of my point of view, my voice, and the high level of detail comprise the primary ways in which I earn the readers' trust. For example, using thorough examples for both kinds of e-mail communication (business and personal) as well as a detailed description of a letter's tangibility prove to my readers that I've done more than just think vaguely about the topic. But I do have one concession to an outside source: the framing quote by Wittgenstein. I wanted the reader to know that there was a "bigger picture," that my brief exploration of two forms of communication serves some higher purpose. If language is the ultimate focus of the piece, then what better way to illustrate that than by a careful exercise of it? Ethos, then, is demonstrated in the prose rather than listed on a Works Cited page.

✦ ✦ ✦

"A piece of writing is never finished. It's just taken out of the typewriter to meet a deadline." These words of wisdom from Donald Murray, veteran journalist for the *Boston Globe* and a writing teacher always willing to examine his own writing choices, capture the possibilities for revision that exist in Jodie Marion's reflections on her writing choices. When you use this reflection process during a peer response workshop or in a conference with your instructor, you can test how your decisions promote interaction with your intended readers. Writing well requires close attention to how one writing choice affects another.

As a reader of "You've Got Mail," you may agree with Marion that her choices provoked your interaction with her ideas, or if you do not fit her audience profile, you may find the essay too abstract to involve you. Once you have carefully studied the writing choices in Chapters 1–5, return to this writer's reflections to see if your awareness of writing choices changes your response in any way.

Reading as a Writer: The Challenge

Reading with a writer's lens requires "an able eye" and lots of practice. Each reading selection has a slightly different context requiring fine distinctions, even in the same publication. Part One of this text guides you in developing that "able eye" by examining the thinking process behind the choices writers make, how they think about the ways in which they can connect with the reader and to the subject— each choice producing a different effect. Part Two gives you practice in using that "able eye" to analyze the choices writers have made in a variety of contexts, to discover how they solved the problem of connecting writer, reader, and subject.

◆ ✦

part one

Writing Choices

In this section you will find five chapters that focus on the major decisions writers make to connect their intended readers with the subject and purpose of the writing. These decisions begin with how the writer designs the **rhetorical context:** the subject, the occasion for writing, the intended readers or audience, and the purpose for writing to particular readers about a subject. Every piece of writing you read and every piece you write *has* a rhetorical context. Understanding how the rhetorical context influences how you interact with what you read and how the choices you make as a writer stimulate the involvement of your readers is the purpose of the five chapters in Part One: "Framing the Context," "Determining Point of View," "Shaping Ideas," "Choosing a Voice," and "Establishing Credibility."

Each chapter uses a series of questions based on discovering the relationships between the writer, the reader, the subject, and the purpose. By applying these questions to what you read, you will see *why* and *how* writers make choices to connect readers to their ideas. A sample annotated reading in each chapter demonstrates how writers make those choices and the effects those choices have on readers. And you can practice your understanding of this process by annotating another reading written to the same audience of readers. The readings included in the first five chapters also focus on the themes presented in Part Two, so they can be used as resources for your own writing. A better understanding of the conscious decisions writers make can make you a more critical reader and a more effective writer.

Chapter 1

✦ ✦ ✦ ✦ ✦ ✦ ✦ ✦ ✦ ✦

Framing the Context

Writing involves a series of choices, conscious choices with the power to convey our ideas. Ideas, however, are not easy to control. They live in a network of associations in our minds, constantly forming connective relationships, new thoughts. Fortunately, the physical act of writing requires that we slow down our thinking in order to move our fingers across the keyboard or to move a pen across paper to form words and sentences. We simply can't write as fast as we think. This slowing down allows us to control our ideas, to make deliberate choices. The problem is where do we start? How do we begin to make choices?

Experienced and professional writers begin by *framing the rhetorical context.* By defining the main elements of communication involved in a specific writing situation—subject, occasion, audience, purpose—writers establish the frame or boundaries for making their writing choices.

✪ **Subject:** Whether self-selected or assigned, writing usually begins with a subject: the causes of a candidate's defeat; a trip to Venice; the reaction of one chemical on another; the effective use of black-and-white flashbacks in a film; the value of changing speed-limit laws. The more specific the definition of the topic is, the more specific the writing choices become.

✪ **Occasion:** The occasion for a writing situation includes two considerations: (1) the writer's connection to the subject and (2) the writer's impetus for writing about the subject. For example, the writer's impetus for writing may be an assignment, such

21

as writing a weekly column for a newspaper or preparing a lab report for biology, but the writer's connection to the subject relates more specifically to what the writer knows about the subject and how the writer came to that understanding. For example, a student under the stress of high credit-card debt might feel strongly about warning others about the hazards of owning a credit card.

⬧ **Audience:** The specific person or group of people with whom the writer hopes to create a dialogue. A well-defined audience helps the writer to select and present information clearly and convincingly. Audiences not familiar with the subject may require more background information while those familiar with the subject may need more in-depth material.

⬧ **Purpose:** The primary purpose is the relationship the writer wants to establish between the reader and the subject: the writer wants to inform the reader on how weather patterns affect housing costs; the writer wants to convince the reader to defeat the bill to raise taxes; the writer wants to demonstrate to the reader the need to use caution in viewing the solar eclipse.

The diagram below shows how these rhetorical elements interrelate to frame the writing context:

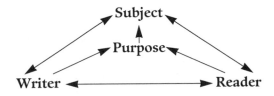

Each of these four rhetorical elements, when specifically defined, form a map for guiding writers in making deliberate choices. Let's examine more closely how these rhetorical elements influence those decisions.

The Writer's Relationship to the Subject

Asking questions about the subject helps you to discover what connections will inform your writing. Questions jog your memory, stimulate associations, and generate issues related to the subject. The questions below provide direction *before* you begin writing.

1. What do you *already* know about the subject and *how* did you come to know it?

Questions	Possible Sources
How is it defined? Classified?	personal experience
What is its history?	observations
What people are involved?	views of respected
How does it work? How is it used?	authorities
	primary documents
What are its strengths and weaknesses?	secondary documents
	general media coverage
How do others view it?	generally accepted
How does it influence others of its kind?	knowledge

2. What do you *need* or *want* to know about the subject?

   To answer this question, look for knowledge gaps in your responses to the first question. Then, determine how you can search for that missing information.

Here is an example of how one writer assigned to write an essay on the effects of television used these questions to discover his connection to the subject.

Subject: Television

Question Responses	Sources of Knowledge
defined as creating "the global village"	Marshal McLuhan (sociology class)
introduced into homes in late 1940s, but don't know when it was invented	general knowledge; *Happy Days* reruns
has developed from a bulky box with a small screen and black-and-white limited programming to color, eighty-plus cable channels packaged in slim wall-size units that can interface with computers	personal experience

it works via satellite and fiber optics, but I don't know the actual process	general knowledge
used primarily for entertainment and news; includes sports, arts, education, science, travel, weather	personal experience
people involved include FCC, owners, sponsors, programmers, technicians, actors, viewers	general knowledge
it has stimulated the advancement of technology by merging audio and video—satellite dishes, camcorders, Internet(?)	general knowledge
strengths: access, affordability, variety in programs; weaknesses: inactivity (couch potatoes), addictive, commercialism, show ratings, stereotypes	personal experience
TV has always been a part of my life, from *Sesame Street* to MTV to championship playoffs to home movies. Between work and school, I don't have much time to watch it now. Mostly it's a form of relaxation and inexpensive entertainment for me.	

This writer's responses and sources of knowledge reveal that his connection to television is based on personal experience and general knowledge. Knowing this basic connection can lead the writer to establish a more specific focus and a receptive audience related to this personal-experience point of view. In this case, the writer might choose an audience of readers who share his experiences and would appreciate his insights, or he might use his personal-based experience as a supportive example in an essay for a sociology course. However, if he wanted to write on the effects of television viewing on young children, the influence of television on the development of technology, or how television programs increase prejudicial views, he would need to conduct considerable research to fill the gaps in his knowledge base in order to establish a credible dialogue with his readers.

Discovering your knowledge base on a subject and determining what gaps exist not only define your connections to a subject, but also help you to find a focus and a potential audience.

The Writer's Relationship to the Reader/Audience

Consider the last time you learned an interesting fact, or how to do something new, or even some juicy gossip. Who did you share that information with—a best friend, someone who needed the information to make a decision, someone who knows the subject well? And why did you decide to share the information with that person—to entertain, to inform, to impress, to persuade? The person you chose and the reason for sharing the information implicitly reveal your connection to that person. For example, forwarding a virus alert you received on e-mail to members of an organization you belong to reveals your concern for people you regularly communicate with.

A similar process takes place in writing. After writing a draft or two to test your understanding of the subject, the connections you make on a personal level will lead you to a variety of potential audiences with whom you would like to "speak to," people who can benefit by what you know. In order to choose that audience, you first need to examine how you relate to each other. Here are some questions that will help you to determine that relationship.

Does the reader know me personally or identify me as being a type of person?

What attitude does the reader have toward me?

What are our shared experiences, attitudes, interests, values, prejudices?

Will our differences present barriers to communication?

What role do I expect the reader to play in the dialogue?

What role can I assume in the dialogue with this reader?

If the student writing on the subject of television had narrowed his focus to "how television viewing has shaped my interests," he might consider an audience of college students in his own age range as potential readers for his experienced-based knowledge. Answering the questions listed previously will help him to determine how appropriate that relationship might be to presenting his views. Here are some possible responses to these questions:

Does the reader know me personally or identify me as a type of person?
A general audience of college students will not know me personally, but they are likely to view me as similar to them in age and educational goals.

What attitude does the reader have toward me?
The reader's attitude will probably be at least neutral but more likely positive because of our similar age and educational environment.

What are our shared experiences, attitudes, interests, values, prejudices?
In general, we share a sense of history from growing up during the same time period, and we all value education enough to pursue a college degree. But the differences in our socioeconomic and cultural backgrounds could present some distinct differences in interests, values, and prejudices.

Will our differences prevent barriers to communication?
As kids we probably shared many of the same media-driven experiences, such as toys and clothes, and many of our educational experiences were similar. But differences in family backgrounds and culture could produce different ways of interpreting and valuing those experiences. I can't assume we were all affected the same way. Even gender can make a difference.

What role do I expect the reader to play in the dialogue?
Our similarities should be strong enough to form a partnership of shared experience. The reader should have strong associations to contribute to understanding my reflections and views.

What role do I expect to assume in the dialogue with this reader?
I should be able to assume a personal, friendly role based on our shared sense of history and experience.

This writer's responses to the questions reveal a strong supportive relationship with the potential reader. But the responses also reveal a possible difference in family background and values that he needs to consider

When writers explore their relationship to intended readers, they discover ways to focus on their subject more specifically and the possibilities for shaping both tone and content.

The Reader's Relationship to the Subject

People who have worked together for a fair amount of time or who are accustomed to participating in the same activities together learn to anticipate each other's actions. They know what to expect because they share similar knowledge and skill. For instance, I once knew a father and son who enjoyed playing chess regularly. The first time I watched them play, I was amazed to see them set up the chess board several moves into the game. It was obvious that they had played together for years and had decided to begin the game at a point where their thinking was really challenged.

The same anticipation guides writers when they select the content and arrangement for the information they want to present. Basically, writers ask the same questions they ask themselves when forming their connection to the subject: What does the reader already know about this subject and how did the reader gain this knowledge? What does the reader need to know about this subject?

By exploring the reader's relationship to the subject, writers can determine what to assume about the reader's contribution to the dialogue. Here are some specific questions to help writers to discover that relationship.

How much does the reader know about what I want to say?

How did the reader gain this knowledge?

What opinion does the reader have about my subject?

How strong is that opinion?

How willing is the reader to act on that opinion?

Why does the reader react this way to the subject?

The writer in our previous example who wants to write to other college students about how viewing television shaped his interests might answer these questions in the following way:

> *How much does the reader know about what I want to say?*
> I expect other college students to have basically the same level of knowledge. Most of them probably haven't thought consciously about how television has shaped their interests.

> *How did the reader gain this knowledge?*
> These readers gained their knowledge in the same way I did, through personal experience.

> *What opinion does the reader have about my subject?*
> The readers have probably wasted as much time watching television as I have, and they probably haven't thought seriously about its influence. Their attitude is likely positive and even defensive about its harmful effects.

> *How strong is that opinion?*
> Their positive attitude is probably strong because television is still a source of entertainment that they share with their family and friends. But they probably haven't formed a strong opinion about its influence on their own interests.

> *How willing is the reader to act on that opinion?*
> The readers' positive attitude should make them willing to reflect on the subject with me.

> *Why does the reader react this way to the subject?*
> Since the readers have years of television viewing experience and fond memories of favorite shows, they should enjoy reflecting on those experiences. But interests that inspire people to attend college are probably based more on "real life" experiences.

From these responses, the writer knows that he can anticipate the readers' strong, nostalgic associations to the names of specific television shows that were broadcast from their childhood years through high school. This shared knowledge establishes a strong beginning point and a firm foundation for making references throughout the essay. But these responses also make clear that the writer has discovered the main problem he faces: How can he get the readers to discover the influence those years of television viewing had on shaping their interests?

Examining the reader's relationship to the subject defines for writers what assumptions they can make about the reader's contribution to the dialogue and what the reader *needs* to know to understand fully the writer's view on the subject.

The Relationship of the Writer and the Reader to the Purpose

The writer's purpose is the spark that ignites the dialogue between the reader and the writer. The connections they make to each other and the subject create that spark. By analyzing those relationships—writer to subject, writer to reader, reader to subject—writers discover what readers *need* to know and *why* they need to know it. When this relationship between the reader and the subject is expressed as a question, then writers more clearly understand the problem they need to solve with their writing. Solving this problem, then, becomes the writer's purpose.

The essay exams, lab reports, position papers, and research investigations assigned in college usually require students to write on a prescribed topic to the instructor as audience. These academic assignments have an implied general purpose: to demonstrate how well students have synthesized the course material. The instructor needs to know how well students have connected with what they are learning. The problem for students, then, is to determine what question they can pose about the assigned subject that will help them to demonstrate the full extent of what they know.

Let's say, for example, that an art history student has been assigned to analyze how abstract paintings convey meaning. From this assignment the student can assume that her instructor needs to know not only what the abstract paintings she selects to analyze mean and how that meaning is conveyed, but also how their meaning fits into the larger context of the art history studied in class, in this case the theory of abstract art in the twentieth century. To meet the implied purpose of the assignment, the student needs to pose a question about her subject that when answered will demonstrate her full understanding of the abstract movement in art. For this particular assignment the student's question might be: How do Kandinsky's *Tempered Elan* and Miro's *Personnages rythmiques* address the issue of whether abstract art is a self-contained whole or an open form? The choices the student makes in answering this question establishes the organizational structure of the essay. The question poses the problem underlying the purpose (what the instructor needs to know about the student's learning), and the answer—the organizational structure used to ignite the dialogue between writer and reader—resolves the problem. (Chapter 3 discusses these choices in detail.)

In the example we have been following in the previous sections of this chapter, the writer's personal context for writing requires the same question/solution approach to establishing a complete purpose for the writing. After analyzing the relationships between writer, reader, and subject, the writer discovered that his intended readers, other college students, probably haven't considered how their television viewing experiences have shaped their interests. What the readers need to know, then, is that reflecting on those experiences is worthwhile. In response to that need, the writer must frame a purpose question that when answered will stimulate the reader's need to reflect. One possible question might be: If it's true that by the time students graduate from high school they have spent more hours watching television than they have going to school, then how valuable was the experience of watching television? This question poses a substantial problem for the reader to become involved in the dialogue, to reflect on his or her own experience in the same way the writer chooses to do.

The purpose writers hope to accomplish lies at the heart of their writing. Framing that purpose in the form of a problem stimulates the involvement of the reader in solving the problem. The questions below will guide you in defining your problem/solution framework:

> Why do I want to have a dialogue with this particular reader or group of readers?
>
> What do these readers still need to know about this subject?
>
> Why do these readers need to know what I have to present?
>
> How can the ways by which I have discovered the significance of this purpose inform my organizational structure?

The student writing the personal essay on television viewing responded to these questions in ways that helped him to clarify the significance of his purpose.

Why do I want to have a dialogue with this particular group of readers?
I want other college students to experience the same sense of discovery.

What do the readers still need to know about this subject?
They need to know that they probably spent more hours watching television than anything else, except sleeping.

Why do readers need to know what I have to present?
They will learn something new about the influences in their lives and the value of devoting time to something important.

How can the ways by which I discovered the significance of this purpose inform my organizational structure?
I can begin with the statistics from the magazine article on witnessing violent acts on television that inspired me to reflect on my television viewing experience. Then I can demonstrate how I calculated the time I spent watching different kinds of programs— the same programs many of them watched. When I present the results of these calculations, I hope the readers will already be using the same process to calculate their own results. Then together we can reflect on how we spend our time.

This writer might revise this organizational structure in some ways, but for now he has found a way to begin solving his problem with a clear sense of purpose.

✦ **E X E R C I S E**   To understand the process of framing the context, choose two of the subjects below (or two of your own choice), and explore the four relationships presented in this chapter by answering the questions presented in each of the following sections: Writer to Subject, Writer to Reader, Reader to Subject, Writer and Reader to Purpose.

the V chip	cloning	assisted suicide
theme parks	tattoos	school uniforms
exercise	e-mail	terrorists

✦ READING CRITICALLY
The Rhetorical Context

Every January, *Ms.* publishes its "Women of the Year" issue. The excerpt below features one of the eleven women from 1997 profiled in the January/February 1998 issue. The article on Jody Williams, a Nobel Peace Prize winner, was written by Kathleen Burge, a correspondent for the *Boston Globe*.

Understanding how a writer frames the rhetorical context for a piece of writing can help you to understand how the writer's purpose is intended to involve you or others as readers. The annotated selection that follows illustrates how the rhetorical context shaped the writer's choices.

Rhetorical Context

◆ **Subject:** Jody Williams, Nobel Peace Prize recipient 1997; coordinator of the International Campaign to Ban Landmines

◆ **Occasion:** *Ms.* "Women of the Year" issue; an opportunity for the writer, Kathleen Burge, to advance her reputation as a writer and to convey her admiration for another woman's work

◆ **Audience:** *Ms.* readers; primarily politically informed women concerned about women's rights, status, representation, and recognition

◆ **Purpose:** To convey the qualities in Jody Williams that earned her the Nobel Peace Prize and to inspire readers to do work that can, in the editor's words, "make a difference."

Readers' Expectations   Readers will know who Jody Williams is from general news coverage, but they will not know many specifics about how she came to work for the organization, the difficulties she met in achieving success, and how her personal background prepared or inspired her to meet the challenge. They will expect both a political and personal focus. *Ms.* readers read to be informed, not entertained, so the writer needs to use an informative tone and to include both qualitative and quantitative information within the space limitations for the article.

✦ ✦ ✦

Jody Williams

Kathleen Burge

1   When Jody Williams won the Nobel Peace Prize last fall along with the organization she coordinates, the International Campaign to Ban Landmines, she saw the award as her biggest megaphone yet in a dogged campaign to rid the world of these vicious weapons. She tried to deflect the glare of media scrutiny from herself onto President Clinton, the most conspicuous holdout on an international ban treaty she helped negotiate. Calling Clinton a "weenie" for his recalcitrance, she noted that he hadn't phoned her yet with congratulations—and by the way, it wasn't too late for him to sign that treaty.

Begins with what the reader already knows and sets a strong political tone for relating to the subject.

2   Williams is less a thorn in Clinton's side than a two-by-four over his head. It's a style that's been characteristic of her since she took on the daunting task of leading the movement to ban landmines in 1991. Within a mere six years, she has built the campaign into a coalition of 1,000 nongovernmental organizations in 60 countries that has had remarkable impact. At press time in December, 122 nations signed a ban—a staggering accomplishment for a grassroots political organization of the type that usually toils for decades in obscurity.

Expands the reader's understanding of Williams's work with specific facts, numbers, and quotes; establishes reasons for shared admiration.

3   An estimated 100 million mines lurk beneath the ground in 68 countries, maiming or killing at least 26,000 people a year, and Williams is an eloquent witness to their horror. "Once the soldier walks away from the weapon, the weapon cannot tell the difference between a soldier, a woman, a child, a grandmother going out to collect firewood to make the family meal," she says. "Once peace is declared, the landmine does not declare peace. The landmine is eternally prepared to take victims."

4   Thousands of activists around the world have fought against mines—including Princess Diana, who comforted victims in Angola and Bosnia—but Williams is now the campaign's most visible crusader. She is famous for her

Increases reader's knowledge of how Williams's energy gains the results that earned the award.

rapid-fire communications, an important component of the campaign's swift success. Early on, she believed the urgency of faxes would energize groups abroad, making them feel a vital part of the campaign. These days, she is the queen of e-mail, relying so heavily on electronic messages that colleagues are sometimes startled when she phones. For years, Williams began her day at 4 A.M., a habit born from waking up in the middle of the night and worrying about work. "I think she does the work of 30 people," says Susan Walker, U.S. director of Handicap International, an early supporter of the campaign.

Writer establishes credibility of her knowledge on the subject by relating on-the-scene details.

The Nobel prize and its $1 million award, which   5 Williams and the campaign share, was announced on October 10, the day after her forty-seventh birthday. The first reporters beat the morning light to her house at the end of a dirt road in Putney, Vermont. Camera crews chased her around the yard as she threw sticks for her German shepherd, Stella. Men in dark suits skulked at the edge of the lawn, speaking Norwegian into cell phones. Williams, a nonsmoker with the gravelly voice of a nicotine addict, greeted the world barefoot, wearing jeans and a short tank top that occasionally exposed a sliver of belly. "What you see is what you get," said her younger brother, Mark, to reporters. "She's not going to fake anything, ever."

Begins to establish a new relationship between the reader and the subject by introducing Williams's family.

Sometimes even her family seems baffled by Williams.   6 Her mother once asked why, with her two graduate degrees, she didn't get a job that paid real money. But Ruth Williams learned long ago it's no use trying to change her eldest daughter's mind. "When she sets her sights on anything, that's all she sees," she says. The day the Nobel was announced, Mark Williams shook his head when he heard the "weenie" remark. "Is she saying that again?" he groaned.

Builds the new relationship between the reader and the subject by using childhood experiences to develop Williams's character.

Williams grew up in Brattleboro, Vermont, where her   7 parents supported five children by running a vending machine business. One of Williams' early motivations to speak out against injustice came in elementary school, when other kids mocked her older brother, Stephen, born deaf and later diagnosed as schizophrenic. Stephen couldn't hear the taunts, but his sister did. She became his voice, defending him and rebuking his tormentors. "If she got a chance, she would push them around physically," her mother remembers. "Then she would defend the kids that the other kids would pick on."

8   Later, in the early days of the Vietnam war, Williams fought some battles at home, over dinner with her father. He supported the war; Williams was adamantly opposed. The rest of the family, she remembers, "sat there in tense silence, wishing we'd just shut up and eat." After college and a master's degree in teaching English as a second language, Williams taught in Mexico for a few years. Fluent in Spanish, and armed with another master's from Johns Hopkins School for Advanced International Studies, she headed to Central America in 1981, working first for a group that led delegations to Nicaragua and Honduras, and later as associate director of Medical Aid to El Salvador.

9   After 11 years in Central America, as the various civil wars that had consumed the area were winding down, Williams began looking for something new to do. When her friend Robert Muller, a paraplegic Vietnam veteran who heads the Vietnam Veterans of America Foundation, offered her $24,000 a year to start his group's anti-mine campaign, she quickly agreed. "I had done so much hands-on work in Central America that I wanted to step back a bit and look at larger issues of war and peace," says Williams. "The landmine is a graphic summary of all that." From the beginning, the campaign's mission was concise: beyond banning mines, it hoped to increase resources for mine victims and for the removal of weapons from the ground. "Jody has helped to keep the issues focused on what is achievable," says Susan Walker. "A lot of movements get lost in being too diffuse or too sidetracked."

> Writer amplifies reader's knowledge of Williams's growing passion for justice with detailed political and educational background; addresses what the reader needs to know about the choices that led to Williams's involvement with the organization.

10   Williams began with a flurry of faxes she sent around the world to recruit organizations that would develop local campaigns. Her strategy was twofold: form or work with already existing grassroots organizations to lobby their individual governments, while mounting international pressure for a mine ban. In countries that produced mines, she found activists who felt angry about their nation's role. In countries littered with mines, she sought victims as well as activists. As long as the local groups informed the campaign

> Writer tightens the focus on the strategies Williams used to unite the organization's efforts; the reader now moves from knowing the *what* and the *why* of Williams's achievement to the *how*.

of their work, Williams said, they could decide how to lobby their governments. The 1,000 groups that now fight mines under the campaign's aegis range from relatively small domestic groups in Angola and Afghanistan—two of the world's most mine-littered countries—to large, established organizations like the American Medical Association and Human Rights Watch. On the international level, Williams turned to the U.N.'s Convention on Conventional Weapons (CCW), signed in 1980, which restricted but did not ban the use of mines. Working the hallways during a CCW session, Williams buttonholed diplomats, seeking to get them to agree to ban mines outright. The effort failed, but the campaign succeeded in uniting countries that supported a ban.

In this final section, the writer allows the reader to share the details of the actual moment of the organization's greatest success; this creates an emotional crescendo for the reader in understanding Williams's feat.

In 1996, at another international meeting to revise the CCW, Williams and her colleagues invited top government leaders to a series of lunches. Over soup and salad, the campaign discovered a forceful ally in Canada. The Canadians offered to sponsor an international conference in October 1996. Fifty countries—including the United States—participated; another 24 observed. On the final day of the conference, Canadian Foreign Minister Lloyd Axworthy stunned world leaders by challenging them to reconvene in a year to negotiate a ban treaty. It was the campaign's single greatest leap forward. Williams and the other activists stood up and cheered. 11

Last September, the negotiations took place in Oslo. Activists worried that the U.S., arguing that mines were essential to protect troops in the divided Korean peninsula, would derail the treaty. "They thought they'd be able to go in and slap people upside the head the way they always have," Williams said. "Fortunately, the world retained its stiff spine and kept saying 'no' to the U.S. It was pretty amazing." In December, the countries met in Ottawa to sign the treaty, which will take effect once it is ratified by 40 nations. 12

Williams celebrated the Nobel prize and her birthday Vermont-style: her parents, siblings, their spouses, significant others, and children piled into Williams' house to chow down on homemade lasagna. And then she got right back to work. There are conferences to plan—in Japan, Hungary, Russia, Korea, and India, all by year's end. 13

14   For Williams, the personal spotlight has been the one liability of winning the world's most prestigious humanitarian award. In November, the campaign's steering committee met in Paris. As board members zipped through the city in a taxi, one of them tipped off the driver that he was ferrying around the most recent winner of the Peace Prize. The driver turned around to ask for her autograph. "Jody was totally embarrassed," said Susannah Sirkin, deputy director of Physicians for Human Rights. "She doesn't enjoy all this attention."

By returning the focus to Williams as a person in the conclusion, the writer finalizes the reader's personal relationship to the subject and fulfills the purpose to gain the reader's complete admiration for Williams as the recipient of the Nobel Peace Prize.

✦ ✦ ✦

This article clearly illustrates how to make writing choices that are responsive to the rhetorical context. The writer's relationship to the subject keeps the focus on Williams's character: her energy, her passion, her humility—all conveyed through specific details and quotes with implicit admiration. Yet out of respect for the readers' needs, the writer maintains an informative tone, keeping the content she presents anchored in the details of Williams's work and achievements. Notice also how the writer chooses to organize the profile by beginning with information the readers already know and leading to a behind-the-scenes view that anticipates questions readers might ask: How did Williams celebrate this extraordinary honor? What did her family think about it? How will winning the Nobel Prize affect the cause? What will Williams do next? Anticipating and answering these questions not only allows the reader to participate in the dialogue but also fulfills the writer's purpose to inspire others to make a difference with their work.

✦ ON YOUR OWN
Analyzing the Writer's Choices

The following profile appeared in the "Women of the Year" issue of *Ms.* with the previous essay on Jody Williams. The rhetorical context is exactly the same in audience, purpose, and occasion; only the subject is different. On a separate sheet of paper, describe the choices Emily Gest, who writes for the *New York Daily News,* makes in each of the nine paragraphs to connect the reader to the subject, Donna

Shirley, and to fulfill her purpose. After describing the writer's choices, write a paragraph analyzing the effectiveness of those choices in addressing the framework of the rhetorical context.

✦ ✦ ✦

Donna Shirley

Emily Gest

Perhaps no planet has piqued the curiosity of people around the   1
world the way Mars has. We've created movies, written books, and conjured up "Martians"—all attempts at understanding the mysterious red planet. In 1997, we took a giant leap forward in space exploration and got to see Mars through the eyes of Sojourner, a 25-pound robot dreamed up by a team led by Donna Shirley, manager of the Mars Exploration Program at NASA's Jet Propulsion Laboratory (JPL). Shirley not only created and managed the project that made it possible to drive, on Mars, the first autonomous robot in space, but she also took the time to explain to a science-wary public how we got there.

The path to such achievement wasn't easy or quick. In the late   2
1980s, Sojourner wasn't even a concept. At the time, JPL had been designing rovers the size of pickup trucks to go to Mars, collect samples, and give them to a rocket to bring back to earth. But at an estimated cost of $10 billion, nobody was willing to fund the project. Shirley, however, thought there must be a way to build an inexpensive robot to explore Mars, despite her colleagues' skepticism. Meanwhile, a group at JPL had been developing a small mobility system to traverse very rugged terrain, and another had been developing an indoor rover with artificial intelligence that mimicked the sensory ability of insects. By putting the brain of the indoor rover inside the body of the mobility rest vehicle, Shirley created an early model of the spacecraft she now calls her "baby."

Sojourner, named after the 19th-century feminist abolitionist   3
Sojourner Truth, looks like a gold box on six wheels with a table on top. The box acts as a high-tech thermos bottle that keeps the electronics within it from freezing. And the tabletop is a small solar panel that provides all the electricity for the unit. It's simple in concept but not in construction. The robot had to be built inexpensively ($25

million) and be able to survive at least a week on Mars. "[It] sounds like a lot of money, but it's not, considering it was for the complete rover; it was the first autonomous robot in space; it was the smallest ever flown; and it had to operate under the harshest environment," Shirley rattles off in one breath. In the end, she spent two years on the project, which came in $1 million under budget, and kept Sojourner on Mars for three months, taking pictures and collecting valuable data about the only planet in our solar system thought to have once sustained life.

4   After a seven-month voyage to Mars aboard the Pathfinder spacecraft, Sojourner relayed her first satellite pictures back to earth in early July. Elated, Shirley spent hours giving interviews filled with pithy anecdotes to newspapers and television shows. Countering the image of scientists as a pocket-protector-wearing set, she said her group was acting "like a bunch of kids" who were "going bananas" about the data the rover had retrieved. Sojourner, she said, had eyes and a brain.

5   Shirley's ability to boil down complex scientific concepts into tangible sound bites has helped her pick up where Carl Sagan left off—making the field more accessible and interesting to a populace intimidated by science. She wants people to apply it to their daily lives. "If you don't know where your sewage goes, how will you vote intelligently on bond issues for building new sewers? If you don't know where electricity comes from, how will you be able to question your electricity rates?" she asks.

6   The problem lies, she feels, with those instructing future teachers. "We need to get teachers not to be afraid to teach science," she says. To get kids interested in Mars, she organized an essay contest to pick the rover's name that garnered more than 3,000 submissions from kids all over the world. Also, her program is developing Mars-related course materials that are being distributed to as many interested teachers as her budget allows. And she'd particularly like to find ways to keep girls interested in science past the third, fourth, and fifth grades.

7   When Shirley first joined JPL in 1966, the lab was a man's domain. While the numbers have improved—several other women worked with her on Sojourner—she is the only woman outside human resources to hold a high-level management position. Last July, Hillary Rodham Clinton wrote in her newspaper column that

"Shirley's vision should inspire everyone interested in science" and that she hoped it would have "particular resonance for girls, who traditionally have participated less in science than boys."

"I'm astonished by how hungry people are for role models," Shirley responds. "There ought to be thousands like me who are role models that people are getting excited about." 8

One of Shirley's gravest concerns is that the Mars Exploration Program budget will be cut. Funding is vulnerable to public approval, she says. "There's no real downside to exploring space," she adds passionately. "There's a little pollution from the launches, but we're not killing off animals or hurting people. The earth-orbiting satellites that are able to predict hurricanes have saved thousands of lives." 9

"We are like the cathedral builders of the Middle Ages. It's not something that's going to be finished in anybody's lifetime or have an instant rate of return, but for hundreds of years, people will look at these things and be uplifted." 10

Chapter 2

✦ ✦ ✦ ✦ ✦ ✦ ✦ ✦ ✦ ✦ ✦

Determining Point of View

The pine and juniper forests have a light accumulation of snow, but the trails into the canyon remain open.

Kaibab squirrels scamper among the blue spruce and fir, while 5,700 feet below, the Colorado River flows steadily for 61 miles.

Centuries after the first European recorded viewing the canyon in 1540, Maj. John Wesley Powell led the first expedition to explore the length of the canyon in 1869.

Descending the Bright Angel Trail 4,460 to the river, we shed layers of clothing to accommodate the thirty-degree change in temperature on the desert floor.

Each of these *vantage points* or *angles* presents the Grand Canyon from a different geographical point of view, a physical location that invites the reader to enter the scene:

View 1: Top of the South Rim: Characterized by the type of trees, depth of snow, and open winter trails

View 2: Top of the North Rim: Characterized by the type of squirrel, trees, and height

View 3: Historical: Characterized by the undefined pristine state

View 4: Cliffs of the South Rim: Characterized by the name of the trail, the height, and the top to bottom view

But each geographic point of view also conveys a view of the writer, that is, where the writer is in relationship to the scene. The distance writers establish between themselves, the reader, and the information they present defines their *rhetorical stance,* the angle from which they choose to write. Those angles generally fall into three basic categories:

Subjective: The writer, as a directly involved participant or spectator, is highly visible.

Objective: The writer chooses not to be visible at all; the entire focus is on the subject.

Merged: The writer maintains a focus on the subject but is occasionally visible through the personalization of details.

Applying these angles to the four views of the Grand Canyon, we can see that View 4 has a subjective angle; the writer, "we," is directly involved and visible in the scene. View 3 has an objective angle; the writer is not visible and all focus is on the factual history. Views 1 and 2, however, include some details that give us the sense that the writer actually visited those scenes, even though the writer is not clearly visible in the scene. In this way, Views 1 and 2 have a merged angle.

The Problem

What is the most appropriate distance to establish between you and your reader? How visible do you need to be in order to involve the reader in dialogue with your writing? The solution to this problem depends primarily on the writer's relationship to the reader with respect to the subject. By questioning the closeness and distance of that relationship, you can determine an appropriate level of visibility to establish.

Writer to Reader

Does the reader know me personally or by reputation?
Does or will the reader respect my experience with this subject?
Will the reader find my personal views refreshing or insightful?

If you answer Yes to any of these questions, then using a subjective or merged point of view will create a comfortable relationship with the reader. But if you find no immediate personal connection to the reader, then an objective point of view may be more appropriate.

What experiences, attitudes, and values do we share on this subject?

The stronger your shared experiences, the more visible your point of view can be using a subjective or merged point of view. But if you have little in common or if the readers are highly diversified, an objective point of view will be more appropriate.

Is there anything in the reader's background that will prevent the reader from accepting my views as valid?

On the surface, you and the reader may seem similar, such as being born in the same year. But if you were raised in different regions of the country, your views on some subjects may vary. An objective point of view might work better to maintain the focus on the subject rather than on you.

What authorities does the reader respect?

If the reader respects you as an authority, then any one of the three points of view will meet the reader's expectations. If the reader does not view you as an authority, then an objective or merged point of view is more appropriate.

On what level do I want the reader to participate in this dialogue?

If you expect the reader to respond on an academic or professional level, then an objective or merged point of view is appropriate to maintain a focus on the subject. A subjective point of view will invite the reader to respond on a more personal level.

The answers to these questions generate a range of choices for determining the point of view best suited to the relationship you want to establish with your reader. The following passages demonstrate how writers, in answering those questions, use different point-of-view choices to shape their relationship with their readers.

Passage 1: *Subjective Point of View*

I learned from the age of two or three that any room in our house, at any time of day, was there to read in, or to be read to. My mother read to me. She'd read to me in the big bedroom in the mornings, when we were in her rocker together, which ticked in rhythm as we rocked, as though we had a cricket accompanying the story. She'd read to me in the dining room on winter afternoons in front of the coal fire, with our cuckoo clock ending the story with "Cuckoo," and at night when I'd got in my own bed. I must have given her no peace.

—Eudora Welty, *One Writer's Beginnings*

The autobiographical nature of this passage tells us that Welty believes readers respect her and view her as an authority. Consequently, readers expect the writer to be an active participant. Still, Welty needs to do more than report her remembrances if she wants the reader to actually enter the scene and experience the influence of her mother reading to her. To create that close, personal relationship, she incorporates familiar, concrete sensory details—rocking chair, cricket sound, cuckoo clock, specific rooms, time of day—to evoke shared memories in her readers.

Passage 2: *Objective Point of View*

To ask "What is literacy?" is to ask, most of all, how literacy is to be understood. For some, literacy is a technology; for others, a cognitive consequence; for still others, a set of cultural relationships; yet for others, a part of the highest human impulse to think and rethink experience in place. Literacy is a complex phenomemon, making problems of perspective and definition inevitable. Literacy is also something of real value, making struggle around it unlikely to end.

—Deborah Brandt, *Literacy as Involvement:*
The Acts of Writers, Readers, and Texts

The focus in this passage clearly emphasizes the subject: literacy. The writer is not visible to the reader, but the distance of the writer from the reader does not prevent the reader from entering the scene. First, the writer poses a question to immediately involve the reader in seeking the answer. Then, to convey respect for the experiences, values, and disposition the readers may bring to the text, she acknowledges a variety of perspectives that may be used to answer the question. Unlike Welty, Brandt does not reveal her personal perspective, but she identifies several levels of connection that involve the reader directly with the subject. By presenting her research study from an objective point of view, Brandt allows the readers to interpret the findings from their own perspective instead of directly antagonizing differences in their views toward literacy.

Passage 3: *Merged Point of View*

Over the last decade an estimated $2 billion has been spent on more that 2 million computers for America's classrooms. That's not surprising. We constantly hear from Washington that the schools are in trouble and that computers are a god-send. Within the education establishment, in poor as well as rich schools, the machines are awaited with nearly religious awe. An inner-city principal bragged to a teacher friend of mine recently that his school "has a computer in every class-room . . . despite being in a bad neighborhood!"

—David Gelernter, "Unplugged," *The New Republic*

From the first sentence the reader knows the subject is the influence of computers on education, and by the second sentence, in which the writer offers a personal response, the reader senses the presence of the writer. With the writer's choice of "we" in the third sentence, the relationship between the writer and reader becomes merged. This merged connection conveys an assumed shared experience and background with respect to the subject and establishes a mutual interest and authority. Even when presenting the direct quote in the last sentence the writer chooses to maintain a measured distance. Instead of focusing on his participation as a reporter by saying, "I interviewed a teacher friend of mine who told me . . . ," Gelernter keeps the emphasis on the influence of computers in the classroom. Although Gelernter, a professor of computer science at Yale University, has the expertise to use a subjective point of view, he chooses to be less visible in his relationship to the educated and well-informed readers of *The New Republic*. The merged point of view allows the writer and reader to explore the subject together.

Creating Levels of Distance

Point of View	Content Characteristics	Writer's Visibility
Subjective	personal; participant or on-site; familiar, concrete details; sensory; emotional; use of "I" or "we"	high; close to reader

Point of View	Content Characteristics	Writer's Visibility
Objective	emphasis on subject; factual; well researched; multiple views; convincing but not emotional	not apparent; far from reader
Merged	shared authority; emphasis on subject; some personal comments or observations; common use of "we"	integrated; moderate to low presence

The writer's relationship to the reader becomes a creative force in determining point of view. Exploring those possibilities as a writer will help you to better understand what relationship you want to establish and how to select information to involve the reader in your thinking.

✦ **EXERCISE**   Choose a paragraph from a magazine, professional journal, or book that interests you. Write a paragraph analyzing the point of view—subjective, objective, or merged—from which that paragraph is written. Then, rewrite the paragraph from the other two points of view. Explain in what ways the two different points of view are or are not appropriate for establishing a relationship with the intended readers.

✦ **READING CRITICALLY**
Determining Point of View

Writers choose a point of view specifically to establish a relationship with the reader that will bring the reader closer to knowing and understanding the subject. In reading the annotated article that follows, study carefully how the writer uses point of view choices *in each paragraph* to develop a relationship with the readers of *Civilization,* a magazine published every two months by the Library of Congress. The article "Neo-Toys" appeared in the October/November 1998 issue. The writer, Paul Saffo, is the frequently quoted director of the California-based Institute for the Future, a nonprofit foundation that

provides strategic planning and forecasting services to major corporations and government agencies.

Rhetorical Context

- ⬍ **Subject:** Cyber, techno-toys

- ⬍ **Occasion:** The writer, Paul Saffo, has professional credentials
  as a technology forecaster. On the basis of his reputation he was
  invited to contribute an essay to this special issue on Technology versus Humanism.

- ⬍ **Audience:** Readers of *Civilization* are college-educated people
  aged thirty and above who are interested in how our culture—
  its art, literature, history, and creativity—defines our civilization.

- ⬍ **Purpose:** To question the effect techno-toys will have on the
  future of our civilization, especially the effects on children's
  imagination and socialization.

Readers' Expectations   Readers will have a general knowledge of
techno-toys based on print or televised advertisements, and if they are
parents, grandparents, teachers, or "techies," they may have personal
experience with electronic toys. Since these toys are new to the culture, the readers probably have not yet formed a permanent opinion
on their effect. Their interest in culture makes them open-minded to
new developments as well as historical comparisons. Their purpose
for reading is to stay informed and to stimulate their thinking.

✦ ✦ ✦

Neo-Toys

Paul Saffo

1   My mother disliked batteries and detested the toys that
required them. The electrically induced racket and kinet-
ics struck her as cheap distractions, unwelcome intrusions
into the free exercise of childhood imagination. Like TV,
these gizmos rewarded passivity, and the fragility of their

Writer uses a
subjective point of
view to establish his
connection to the
subject. His personal
experience evokes
the readers' childhood
associations with toys
and parents; close
visibility.

circuits guaranteed broken hearts and frequent contributions to the local landfill. Not that Mom was against technology. She admired, for example, the industrious ethos of
PCs, and like today's parents, she probably would have
both marveled at and fretted over the impact of the Internet on teenagers. But she would be positively horrified by
what is on the horizon.

The younger siblings of "screenagers" (adolescents   2
raised on the Internet) are welcoming something newer,
cuter and more insidious than e-mail and web sites into
their playpens and rec-rooms—primitive electronic life-
forms. The first of these new companions, Tamagotchi, an
egg-shaped key chain created by Japanese toymaker Bandai,
became a huge hit in 1997 and has already spawned myriad
imitations. The Giga Pet from Tiger Electronics, Baby Byte
from TrendMasters, Nano Baby from Playmates and the
generically named Virtual Friend from Disney all feature the
same basic design as Bandai's original. Owners administer
to their toy's lifelike needs—for food, or medicine, or sleep,
or love—by pressing little buttons, listening for beeping
alarms, and monitoring the primitive graphics of the liquid-
crystal interface. New, more advanced critters are also appearing on toy-store shelves, including ActiMates Barney.
This computer-controlled incarnation of the friendly purple dinosaur interacts with its human playmate while they
both watch Barney videos or Barney CD-ROMs. And for
the under-two set, it's rumored that an interactive Teletubby
will soon be seated beside diapered tots nationwide.

The animating force behind these life-forms is cheaper   3
than a disposable lighter, smaller than a Necco wafer and
far more sophisticated than a AA battery. Once, microprocessors entered our lives exclusively in big, expensive PC
boxes. Now, computer chips, vastly more powerful and affordable, are sneaking into everything, including toys. Just
as Intel cofounder George Moore predicted, the capabilities
of microprocessors—and the gizmos that use them—are re-
doubling at an astonishing rate.

Already, electronic life-forms threaten to change child-   4
hood reality as fundamentally as TV did in the early 1950s.
Not only do Tamagotchis disrupt classrooms and attention

Margin notes:

Writer shifts to a more objective angle to provide background on the subject; continues to use concrete details to keep reader close to subject.

Writer continues background on how new toys emerged but uses "our" to signal merged point of view.

spans with their beeping, they are far more fragile than real pets, more fragile even than the disposable battery-powered toys I grew up with. The only difference is that, after a pair of pixilated angel wings flutters across their screens, their lives can be restored. Since schools have begun banning the toys, distraught parents now find themselves babysitting key chains—taking them to work and waking up to feed them in the middle of the night—all to protect their children from a first-hand knowledge of simulated death.

> Writer maintains merged point of view with audience to study the problem together; uses "I" to merge personal with background information.

5   And with the arrival of ActiMates Barney and his interactive brethren, preschoolers now take it for granted they can have nonbiological buddies that a power button brings to life, no imagination required. As they grow up, they may seek ever more capable lifeforms to accompany them on life's journey. Long before today's neocompanions are ready for the landfill, they will be swept away by waves of successively more capable and seductive contrivances. Instead of raising a single creature, children will nurture pocket-size worlds. And the descendants of Barney will not just talk, they will also listen and understand simple speech. After that, who knows? Walking companions that toddle after their child pals, homework buddies that help with algebra, cyberjocks that fill in when dad can't play catch: all are possible within a reasonable time frame.

> Writer develops the problem for the readers to consider possible effects; implied personal projections.

6   It's still too early to determine the long-term effects these toys will have on their owners, but one can't help wondering. What does a child learn about life and death by nurturing a Tamagotchi? Certainly the virtual death of a software life-form is preferable to the sacrifice of turtles, rats and brine shrimp "sea monkeys" by earlier generations; but does a Tamagotchi death reach the virtues of interdependence? Or imply that death has no consequence, that, instead of grieving, one can simply push the reset button? Will these devices provide a healthy simulation—training wheels for eventual interaction with the real world—or an unhealthy retreat from messy everyday reality?

> Writer uses a series of questions to draw readers indirectly into the dialogue; use of "ode" implies a merged point of view—reader and writer need to answer the questions together

7   The lessons from earlier technologies are deeply ambiguous. Television is a potent discovery tool, but an even more potent time-sink, serving up parent-fretting violence and vapid contentless drivel. Meanwhile, the vast wasteland

Writer forecasts
answers to the
questions; uses "we"
to maintain merged
relationship with
readers.

of TV threatens to be overwhelmed by the vaster wasteland of cyberspace—an Internet landscape of awesome educational and social power that is also a convivial environment for criminals, pornographers and scam artists. Technologies mirror the cultures that create them, so it is no surprise that the Internet reflects both what we desire and what we detest in our society. The coming world of electronic life-forms will likely be no different.

Although it will be decades, if ever, before these life-   8
forms actually are "intelligent," they've already joined TV and the Internet in the gallery of parental nightmares. Of course, it's possible that the only thing parents really need to worry about is their own peace of mind. In spite of all the wizardry inside these neocompanions, kids find them only slightly more mesmerizing than Betsy Wetsy and Teddy Ruxpin, their analog ancestors. Even as toy stores display ActiMates Barney in a special showcase decorated with hype, only a few feet away last season's interactive companions litter overcrowded shelves marked CLEARANCE and REDUCED. This year's nightmarish novelty will likely be next year's remaindered anachronism. After all, back when my mother was herself a child, parents were alarmed over trashy dimestore novels. And unlike novels, at least these electronic life-forms are easy to stop dead in their tracks— just sneak up behind them and yank out the batteries.

Writer uses a series
of comparisons to
toys from different
generations keeping
readers closely
involved; personal
reference to his
mother frames the
essay with parental
responsibility focus.

✦ ✦ ✦

Saffo's reputation as a professional technology forecaster gives him the credibility to write from an authoritative point of view, but instead of distancing himself from the readers, he chooses to use a merged point of view throughout most of the article. For this particular rhetorical context, the merged point of view works well. Since the subject is relatively new to the reader and the writer's purpose is to explore the effects of techno-toys on culture, the merged point of view allows the readers and the writer to discover an answer together. The merged point of view has the advantage of keeping the emphasis on the subject while permitting the reader and writer to share authority as they form their own opinions.

✦ ON YOUR OWN
Analyzing the Writer's Choices

The following essay also appeared in *Civilization*. The audience is the same as described for the previous selection, but the subject and purpose are different. The subject of this essay is rituals of violence and renegotiation; the article appeared in the "Civility" section of the December 1999/January 2000 issue. The writer, Hannah Nyala, is a freelance writer who has also published two novels, *Point Last Seen* and *Will's War.*

On a separate sheet of paper, describe the choices the writer makes in establishing point of view in each of the four paragraphs. Identify the techniques the writer uses and how those techniques establish the writer's relationship to the reader and the reader's relationship to the subject. After describing the writer's choices, write a paragraph analyzing the effectiveness of those choices in addressing the framework of the rhetorical context.

❖ ❖ ❖

Revenge and Reconciliation
Hannah Nyala

1   A few years ago, in part to escape the violence of our own culture, my children and I went abroad to live among the Ju/'hoansi Bushmen in the Kalahari Desert. As the plan quickly came unraveled, we learned some unexpected, and perhaps universal, lessons about violence. The morning after arrived in our first bush camp, I was startled awake by loud, angry voices moving in our direction in a hurry. Elbowing my way up from between my two sleeping children, I charged out of our tent half-clothed, glasses askew, to see about 25 men and women coming toward us, wielding pots and pans, sticks and skillets, knives and spears. I clumsily splayed out my arms and legs and planted my feet in the sand, intending if nothing else to block their access to Ruth and Jon.

2   By the time I straightened my glasses, the crowd had neatly split in two, gone around our tent, and disappeared. One man was chasing another, a poisoned arrow set in his bow, shouting what I later learned

was roughly "I kill you! I will kill you!" Everyone else was simply lend-ing moral support (backed up by a tool) to one party or the other. The impending violence had nothing to do with my children or me. I'd just posed half nude in front of all these strangers for nothing.

Not ten minutes later, the crowd came filtering back out of the   3
bush, talking quietly and easily among themselves. I was impressed by their calm in the wake of homicide, and would have said so, had I known the words in Ju/'hoan. But then the two men reappeared—grinning, talking, strolling along with their arms slung around each other's shoulders. I never again saw them exchange a sour look or cross word. This wasn't just impressive; it was stunning—and truly outside my experiential pasture.

I'm from the United States, after all, where we do violence of   4
every hue, and reckon that much of it is justified on some level. Vio-lence is one of our unspoken truths, a kernel deep enough inside each of us that most people don't have to acknowledge it (and don't, unless forced). Yet each new terrifying, public act of mayhem flails us open and offers another glimpse of this truth.

Less than 15 years ago, we could soothe ourselves with the com-   5
pelling myth that only the angry poor or disgruntled postal workers were likely to run amok. Now, we're not so sure. We worry about staring up a gun barrel toward a demon wearing the ruddy, freckled face of the kid next door. No wonder we're gating our communities, buying more guns, adding 911 to the speed dial.

Is it any wonder, either, that some of us, smitten with a quasi-   6
anthropological form of nostalgia, are tempted to turn people like the Ju/'hoansi into paragons of moral decency—civility, if you will—possessors of rituals of fierce social conscience that we collectively seem to have lost?

The temptation does make some sense. Popular films like *The*   7
Gods Must Be Crazy and books like *The Lost World of the Kalahari* reprise the familiar narrative of Rousseau's noble savage, in which people like the Bushmen are seen to exist outside of time, outside the ugly effects of competition and corruption. They are wise enough to re-ject everything that has corroded modern life, especially its violence and greed—everything that we are perverse enough to embrace. Yet this idyllic storyline—however often it appears, however potentially redemptive it sounds to us—has no factual basis whatsoever.

The Ju/'hoansi, like the rest of us, have no direct line to the di-   8
vine to help them navigate the treacherous shoals of rage. Anthro-

pologists have been documenting for decades how the effects of war, apartheid, and Western culture have caused a storm of personal and social upheaval among the Bushmen; few of their quarrels end quickly or definitively. They live in smaller communities and carry far fewer guns, yes, but their strife is no less real, no less pitched to the death than ours.

9   And despite our ready reverence for it, the myth of the gentle premodern is precisely that. Archaeologists are continually uncovering evidence of cannibalism, mass sacrifices, infanticide, and warfare across the globe; ethnographers and historians have documented violence in every known society. Of course, they have also uncovered what we have lost: the rituals that contain the violence. Today, however, the effectiveness of those rituals is an open question just about everywhere—just as it was in the Kalahari that morning.

10   The Ju/'hoansi are not our wise ancestors; to suppose they are is to miss the traits and troubles we share in an increasingly global society. My encounter with the Ju/'hoansi could have been rendered as a lighthearted account of ritualized street theater—noisy, flamboyant playacting posing no real danger to those involved. But not a soul outside our tent that morning thought the two men were acting. Among the Ju/'hoansi, even the mention of a poison-tipped spear or arrow in an argument raises the stakes, and bringing out such a weapon during a physical confrontation raises them to life and death.

11   Nor were the rest of the Ju/'hoansi simply cheering supporters, since fights between individuals rarely stay confined to the combatants alone. Violence among them is a public act, one in which the entire community has a well-guarded stake. Finally, the quick, apparently decisive end to this conflict was largely an illusion. True, I did not see these men exchange another cross word, but soon afterward one of them moved away to another village and didn't return, following a longstanding Ju/'hoansi tradition of relocating rather than risking continued hostility.

12   The man's departure, however, did not provide closure. Instead, everyone in the camp tackled the incident with the most ordinary, most powerful, and indeed, most transformative weapon. They talked about it. The morning's confrontation got rehashed time and again in the months to follow. Young and old folks discussed it; they laughed and snarled about it. Fury met compassion.

13   In the process, the conflict's ability to undermine the community or harm its members was destabilized considerably as everyone

learned more about what had actually happened. Laying blame wasn't the point; talking about the discord was. Violence itself was not obliterated; rather, it was tightly linked to a continuous thread of small, nonviolent acts in which everyone participated to some degree. The oppositions stood side by side, and everyone collaborated in their negotiations.

So what's "traditional" or "premodern" about that? The whole 14 sequel reminded me of nothing so much as home, except that here our talking tends to get overrun by "experts" offering sound bites— excruciatingly simple answers or blame nailed so narrowly that the rest of us skate free. We cannot afford this detachment. The talk itself is a crucial part of the process.

Perhaps it is time for us not simply to do away with notions of 15 premodern ritual versus modern violence. Perhaps we should rethink our notions of violence entirely and ask whether our concepts themselves are part of the problem. To do this, we will need to talk harder and longer—and with more people—than we ever have. Crippling oppositions don't disappear overnight. We have to learn to feel their weight, put a name to them, and then move on.

Chapter 3

✦ ✦ ✦ ✦ ✦ ✦ ✦ ✦ ✦ ✦ ✦ ✦

Shaping Ideas

As readers we have come to expect much of what we read to be structured in predictable ways: directions, letters, news stories, recipes, travel guides, classified ads, announcements, memos. This is what we call *functional* or *transactional writing*—writing to get things done. We need that predictable structure to provide clear direction, so we can apply first aid, program our VCRs, complete an assignment, or fulfill a contract.

Writing that requires us to think about ideas and opinions, however, requires a personalized structure—a shape that brings meaning and coherence to each individual writer's ideas. In essays these shapes often follow familiar structures, ways of knowing that as writers and readers we are accustomed to, such as the historical development of an idea or the process of how something functions. Experimenting with these structures helps writers to know their subjects better and guides them in choosing the structure that best builds a meaningful relationship between the reader and the subject. For example, readers who *do not know* very much about the subject may need a historical framework or structure to connect with the subject; readers who *already know* the subject well will look for a different or inventive way of viewing the subject.

Choosing a Structure

The structure of an essay has two responsibilities: (1) to convey the writer's special way of seeing an idea, and (2) to establish a new relationship between the reader and the subject. In this way, the external structure or shape of an essay functions as a bridge connecting writer, reader, and subject. Let's play with the idea of a bridge, for a moment, to understand how to choose the best design for making connections.

The basic purpose of a bridge is to connect one land mass with another land mass. The distance between those two land masses and the reason or purpose for making the connection determine the design of the bridge. For example, when hiking a trail, you expect to find merely logs, rock formations, or a plank of some kind to get you from one side of a stream to another. But as the distance and height increase, such as when crossing a river, you expect a structure with greater support, maybe a wider wooden, steel, or concrete bridge with railings to keep you balanced.

The same principles of distance hold true for choosing structures to convey your ideas:

> When the distance between your ideas and the reader's ideas is short and close, the shape of the connecting structure you choose can be familiar or innovative with little reinforcement.

> When there is greater distance between your ideas and the reader's ideas or when you view the idea from a different height or angle, the shape of the connecting structure you choose needs stronger support and reinforcement.

The second principle of bridges, the purpose or reason for crossing from one land mass to another, also affects the shape of the structure. The reasons for hiking across a stream or a river, for instance, might be for the pleasure of communing with nature or the challenge of an adventure in new territory. These travelers don't mind exploring different kinds of bridges to achieve their purpose. But travelers whose purpose is more urgent, those under the stress of time or weather conditions, need reassurance that the strength of the structure will get them safely to the other side. Similarly, in choosing the shape of a structure for readers to follow the reasoning of your ideas, the purpose of taking the journey affects the risks you can take in designing the structure. Some general guidelines you can follow are:

> When the writer and reader share a similar purpose for exploring an idea, the structure for presenting the idea can be more open and take more risks or different paths of discovery.

When the writer and reader differ in their purpose for exploring an idea, when the reader may be apprehensive or skeptical of the journey, the structure for presenting the idea needs to be clearly fortified and take fewer risks in reaching discovery.

Each individual rhetorical situation, of course, requires a design of its own. A close analysis of what your intended audience already knows about your subject and how close their reasoning is to the idea you want to convey will lead you to several workable structures. Although the range of available structures is as varied as the rhetorical situations, most of the frameworks used to develop ideas logically fall into three main categories: *chronological, sequential,* and *spatial.*

Chronological Structures

Any organization that follows the order in which events occur or have occurred is *chronological.* Time order, used in narrative to tell stories and in presenting the history of ideas and events, is probably the most familiar and most comfortable structure for both writers and readers. Whether you choose numerical time frames, such as centuries, weeks, and hours, or conceptual time frames, such as childhood and adolescence, your reader will have a clear understanding of your beginning point and each point that follows in that system of order. That shared understanding of progressing from point to point both orders and clarifies meaning. In the following example, notice how the writer, Todd Gitlin, incorporates both numerical and conceptual time order to introduce his book *The Sixties: Years of Hope, Days of Rage.*

> On New Year's Eve, as 1958 slipped into 1959, I wasn't especially aware I was living in the dead, dreary Fifties. I was a high school senior about to turn sixteen. I had little sense of living in any kind of "Fifities" at all; I wasn't old enough to think in decades. I was simply living my life: striving for grades, wondering about sex, matching my exploits against those—real and imagined—of my rivals, watching the tides of adolescence rip through me. The only threshold I thought about was the one I would cross later that year, on the way to college. I was not living in history, but in biography.

As readers, we expect the subject, the decade of the sixties, to be presented in a chronological structure. The general public audience for whom the book was written shares a common knowledge on the subject and will feel comfortable with this structure. But Gitlin also chooses to use the chronology of his personal experience as the primary structure for presenting his ideas. In this way Gitlin alerts the reader that his linear retelling of history will be a personalized time order of the decade. This choice adds a new dimension to what the audience already knows and increases the potential for discovery.

By experimenting with different forms of chronological structure, both numerical and conceptual, you can use familiar shapes to develop a new focus.

Sequential Structures

The sequence in which one thing follows another certainly involves the element of time to some degree, but time is not the main principle for ordering the sequence. Instead, writers use sequence to establish the significance of their ideas—a framework for showing how that significance developed. The two most frequently used sequential structures are the *function sequence* and the *organic sequence.*

The *function sequence* orders elements to show how things, people, or systems function or came to be. For example, a function sequence would capture how a person decides to *become* a taxidermist, not how to *be* a taxidermist; not how to build a skyscraper, but why skyscrapers exist. The sequence, then, is determined by the significance the writer sees in the function. In the excerpt below, Laura Green introduces us to the function of "stoop-sitting."

> If baseball is the American pastime, then "stoop-sitting," as they call it in Chicago, is the neighborhood pastime, a pleasure as simple as music. If there is one event, one tradition that turns a block into a community, sitting on the stoop is it.
>
> On our block, stoop etiquette was as rigid as a tea ceremony. We met on one stoop only, the steep wooden steps of a woman who grew up in one of those tight xenophobic Chicago neighborhoods that gave birth to stoop-sitting as a balm for life in the factories and stockyards. Her house was on the east side of the street, where the stoop caught the late afternoon sun. Because she was the owner and not a tenant, it was okay for the rest of us to ease our tired hams on her wooden steps. We met there and nowhere else. We congregated only at certain times of the day and only if she was already there.

In the first paragraph Green tells us that the significance of stoop-sitting is to build community. As readers we can expect that the sequence of stoop-sitting events that follow will in some ordered way develop the sense of community Green experienced. Readers who have no stoop-sitting experience may have difficulty predicting exactly what events will follow, but Green's description of a familiar neighborhood scene bridges the gap in experience.

The *organic sequence* uses the inherent qualities of the thing, person, or system to order events. The most familiar organic sequences involve the biological, chemical, and physical nature of things. But the writer's purpose is not to explain those natural processes; instead, the writer uses the organic nature of the subject to develop a significant point in the same way the function sequence is used. For example, a writer who wants to make a point about the significance of controlling water in producing electricity may trace the flow of a particular body of water from its calm body of origin to the surging force of a waterfall. In this way the organic sequence captures the natural force of the water, allowing the writer to develop the point of significance at each stage of the sequence—both the water and the point develop force.

In the excerpt below, Marie De Santis uses the organic sequence of salmon spawning to explain how water management programs have seriously eroded the salmon's traditional means of spawning and have led to hatchery-bred salmon.

> In a stream so shallow that its full body is no longer submerged in the water, the salmon twists on its side to get a better grip with its tail. Its gillplate is torn, big hunks of skin hang off its sides from collisions on rocks, there are deep gouges in its body, and all around for miles to go there is only the cruelty of more jagged rocks and less and less water to sustain the swim. Surely the animal is dying!
>
> And then the salmon leaps like an arrow shot from a bow; some surge and will and passion ignores the animal body and focuses on the stream.
>
> Of all the extremes of adaptation to the ocean's awful toll on the young, none is more mythic in proportion than the salmon's mighty journey to the mountain streams.

In this introduction, De Santis begins the organic structure at the end of the sequence. The image she presents of the salmon at the end of the journey immediately engages the reader in discovering why the salmon is in such a battered condition, thus creating a reason for tracing the organic sequence. The lines below, taken from the first sentence from each paragraph of the sequence De Santis uses, demonstrate how she uses the organic sequence to shape the essay:

> On every continent of the northern hemisphere . . .
> As soon as the ice melts on the Yukon, . . .
> The salmon gets to spawn once in life, . . .
> The salmon arrives battered and starved . . .
> Soon the banks of the stream . . .
> The young salmon arrive in the estuary . . .
> Then one day, the youngsters do not return. . . .
> So accessible is the salmon's life . . .
> But once the salmon enters the sea . . .

Fully understanding the instinctive nature of the salmon brings the reader closer to realizing the significance of water management programs to the salmon's life. Because few readers are likely to know the details of this organic sequence, this choice of structure works well in bridging that gap in knowledge.

Another type of organic sequence is the *trip structure,* a sequence that reflects the path of discovery. Like most trips, this type of organic sequence has a strong time element, but the path is rarely a straight line. The writer uses the trip structure to slowly build each sequential piece of making the discovery. It's usually not until the end of the sequence that the significance of the discovery is realized.

A good example of the organic trip sequence is William Least Heat-Moon's *Blue Highways.* As the title suggests, the organic sequence is based on America's "blue highways," the backroads that criss-cross across the country. The book is divided into chapters representing the direction of his journey. Below are the openings to the beginning sections in the first chapter, "Eastward":

1

Beware thoughts that come in the night. They aren't turned properly; they come in askew, free of sense and restriction, deriving from the most remote of sources. Take the idea of February 17, a day of canceled expectations, the day I learned my job teaching English was finished because of declining enrollment at the college, the day I called my wife from whom I'd been separated for nine months to give her the news, the day she let slip about her "friend"—Rick or Dick or Chick. Something like that.

That morning, before all the news started hitting the fan, Eddie Short Leaf, who worked a bottomland section of the Missouri River and plowed snow off campus sidewalks, told me if the deep cold didn't break soon the trees would freeze straight through and explode. Indeed.

That night, as I lay wondering whether I would get sleep or explosion, I got the idea instead. A man who couldn't make things go right could at least go. He could quit trying to get out of the way of life. Chuck routine. Live the real jeopardy of circumstance. It was a question of dignity.

The result: On March 19, the last night of winter, I again lay awake in the tangled bed, this time doubting the madness of just walking out on things, doubting the whole plan that would begin at daybreak—to set out on a long (equivalent to half the circumference of the earth), circular trip over the back roads of the United States. Following a circle would give a purpose—to come around again—where taking a straight line would not. And I was going to do it by living out of the back end of a truck. But how to begin a beginning?

2

The vernal equinox came on gray and quiet, a curiously still morning not winter and not spring, as if the cycle paused. Because things go their own way, my daybreak departure turned to a morning departure, then to an afternoon departure. Finally, I climbed into the van, rolled down the window, looked a last time at the rented apartment. From a dead elm sparrow hawks used each year came a high *whee* as the nestlings squealed for more grub. I started the engine. When I returned a season from now if I did return those squabs would be gone from the nest.

3

A pledge: I give this chapter to myself. When done with it, I will shut up about *that* topic.

Call me Least Heat-Moon. My father calls himself Heat-Moon, my elder brother Little Heat-Moon. I, coming last, am therefore Least. It has been a long lesson of a name to learn.

To the Siouan peoples, the Moon of Heat is the seventh month, a time also known as the Blood Moon—I think because of its dusky midsummer color.

4

The first highway: Interstate 70 eastbound out of Columbia, Missouri. The road here follows, more or less, the Booneslick Trail, the initial leg of the Oregon Trail; it also parallels both the southern latitude of the last great glacier in central Missouri as well as the northern boundary of the Osage Nation. The Cherokee and I had skirmished its length in Missouri and Illinois for ten years, and memory made for hard driving that first day of spring. But it was the fastest route east out of the homeland. When memory is too much, turn to the eye. So I watched particularities.

Item: a green and grainy and corrupted ice over the ponds.

Item: blackbirds, passing like storm-born leaves, sweeping just above the treetops, moving as if invisibly tethered to one will.

5

The rain came again in the night and moved on east to leave a morning of cool overcast. In Well's Restaurant I said to a man whose cap told me what fertilizer he used, "You've got a clean little town here."

"Grayville's bigger than a whale, but the oil riggers get us a mite dirty around the ears," he said. "I've got no oil myself, not that I haven't drilled up a sieve." He jerked his thumb heavenward. "Gave me beans, but if I'da got my rightful druthers, I'da took oil." He adjusted his cap. "So what's your line?"

"Don't have one."

"How's that work?"

"It doesn't and isn't."

He grunted and went back to his coffee. The man took me for a bindlestiff. Next time I'd say I sold ventilated aluminum awnings or repaired long-rinse cycles on Whirlpools. Now my presence disturbed him. After the third tilt of his empty cup, he

tried to make sense of me by asking where I was from and why
I was so far from home. I hadn't traveled even three hundred
miles yet. I told him I planned to drive around the country on
the smallest roads I could find.

Notice how Least Heat-Moon uses the first few opening sections to set the stage: when and why he began the trip—the occasion; the season at the time of his departure; his first route and the
level of observation that will inform the trip—a mixture of "particularities" and personal associations. Within minutes, then, the readers are on the road with the writer. Most readers probably have not
traveled the backroads bordering the perimeter of the United States,
but knowing that those roads actually appear on a map creates a
sense of security and direction in accompanying the writer on the
adventure. The trip sequence, then, provides a low-risk structure
that also allows for discovery. And much like reading a travel journal
after you return from a trip, the real discovery comes at the end when
the journey is complete.

Spatial Structures

Spatial structures can also contain strong elements of time and sequence, but the organizing principle of spatial structure depends on
the distribution of objects or features in *physical* space. For example,
you might write about the significance of a building by your order of
walking through it, or from the outside—top to bottom before entering. If an entire landscape is involved, you might structure the
view from the foreground to the horizon line. Other orders might include left to right, large to small, most to least conspicuous. By focusing on visible materials and movements, writers use spatial order
to lead the reader to a point of significance.

In the following passage from *Mary: An Autobiography,* Mary
Mebane writes about the backyard of her childhood in rural North
Carolina. Notice how she uses spatial order in the introduction of this
section to establish a structure for the reader to view her experiences:

> My name is Mary.
> When I first opened my eyes to the world, on June 26,
> 1933, in the Wildwood community in Durham County, North
> Carolina, the world was a green Eden—and it was magic. My fa-
> vorite place in the whole world was a big rock in the backyard

that looked like the back of a buried elephant. I spent a lot of time squatting on that rock. I realize now that I probably selected it because it was in the *center* of our yard, and from it, by shifting ever so slightly, this way and that, I could see *everything*. I liked to look. Mama must have told me several thousand times that I was going to die with my eyes open, looking.

When I sat on the rock with my back to the house, the fields were in front of me. On the left was another lot that we called the Rock Pile, and to the right was an untended strip of land, strewn with rocks but cleared enough to be plowed sometimes. The Rock Pile, full of weeds and tall trees, was a place of mystery. It had so many rocks and some of them were so large that it was left uncleared with just a path through it. Behind me I could overhear voices coming from the back porch and kitchen. I could see who was chopping or picking something in the garden and I could see who was coming through the Rock Pile.

After introducing her childhood backyard and placing the rock as the center from which she views life around her, Mebane gives the reader specific anchor points: left, right, front, and behind. As the narrative of her childhood continues, Mebane structures the reader's introduction to new characters and activities with family members by using those same anchor points. In this way the familiarity of the spatial structure puts the reader at ease when a new ingredient to the scene is added.

Another form of spatial structure is the *extended metaphor.* Metaphors suggest a likeness or similarity between two objects or actions; the sense of one is transferred to the other in the comparison. For example, if someone said, "Help is only a heartbeat away," then you would know that help will arrive quickly. When the comparison is maintained throughout the piece of writing, it is called an extended metaphor, in essence a spatial structure. In the short essay below, entitled "At Harvesttime," Maya Angelou uses an extended metaphor to convey what she has learned about the consequences of her actions.

There is an immutable life principle with which many people will quarrel.

Although nature has proven season in and season out that if the thing that is planted bears at all, it will yield more of itself, there are those who seem certain that if they plant tomato seeds, at harvesttime they can reap onions.

Too many times for comfort I have expected to reap good when I know I have sown evil. My lame excuse is that I have not always known that actions can only reproduce themselves, or rather, I have not always allowed myself to be aware of that knowledge. Now, after years of observation and enough courage to admit what I have observed, I try to plant peace if I do not want discord; to plant loyalty and honesty if I want to avoid betrayal and lies.

Of course, there is no absolute assurance that those things I plant will always fall upon arable land and will take root and grow, nor can I know if another cultivator did not leave contrary seeds before I arrived. I do know, however, that if I leave little to chance, if I am careful about the kinds of seeds I plant, about their potency and nature, I can, within reason, trust my expectations.

By comparing her treatment of people to the planting process, which yields a harvest, Angelou captures visually for the reader the abstract value she has learned about her own behavior. The familiar harvest-time metaphor structures that understanding for the reader. In addition to making the abstract more concrete, an extended metaphor can make the complex or unfamiliar clear, such as comparing economic theory to the moves in a chess game or sport, and it can generate new possibilities for viewing the familiar, as in a comparison of getting a college degree to taking a ride in a hot-air balloon.

A more complex spatial structure used frequently by experienced writers is the *mosaic structure*. In a mosaic, each tile or piece of the essay appears separately with no apparent central structure. But as each piece is added, a pattern begins to emerge. Not until the final piece is put into place does the meaning of this structure become clear to the reader. Writers who choose to use this structure must be sure that their readers are patient people who enjoy a sense of mystery.

Writers who incorporate many quotes and sources, often with conflicting views, use a mosaic structure as a process of gathering data for the reader to consider before reaching a conclusion. Others skillfully use narratives from different time periods in their lives to reach a new understanding from the cumulative effect of weaving in and out of different events. In the excerpt below from the book *Silent Dancing*, Judith Ortiz Cofer uses a mosaic structure, incorporating scenes from a "silent" home movie, presented in italics, in between sections of her narrative reflections of her childhood after moving from Puerto Rico to Paterson, New Jersey.

We have a home movie of this party. Several times my mother and I have watched it together, and I have asked questions about the silent revelers coming in and out of focus. It is grainy and of short duration, but it's a great visual aid to my memory of life at that time. And it is in color—the only complete scene in color I can recall from those years.

We lived in Puerto Rico until my brother was born in 1954. Soon after, because of economic pressures on our growing family, my father joined the United States Navy. He was assigned to duty on a ship in Brooklyn Yard—a place of cement and steel that was to be his home base in the States until his retirement more than twenty years later. He left the Island first, alone, going to New York City and tracking down his uncle who lived with his family across the Hudson River in Paterson, New Jersey. There my father found a tiny apartment in a huge tenement that had once housed Jewish families but was just being taken over and transformed by Puerto Ricans, overflowing from New York City. In 1955 he sent for us. My mother was only twenty years old, I was not quite three, and my brother was a toddler when we arrived at *El Building,* as the place had been christened by its newest residents.

My father could have passed as European, but we couldn't. My brother and I both have our mother's black hair and olive skin, and so we lived in El Building and visited our great-uncle and his fair children on the next block. It was their private joke that they were the German branch of the family. Not many years later that area too would be mainly Puerto Rican. It was as if the heart of the city map were being gradually colored brown—*café con leche* brown. Our color.

The movie opens with a sweep of the living room. It is "typical" immigrant Puerto Rican decor for the time: the sofa and chairs are square and hard-looking, upholstered in bright colors (blue and yellow in this instance), and covered with the transparent plastic that furniture salesmen then were so adept at convincing women to buy. The linoleum on the floor is light blue; if it had been subjected to spike heels (as it was in most places), there were dime-sized indentations all over it that cannot be seen in this movie. The room is full of people dressed up: dark suits for the men, red dresses for the women. When I have asked my mother why most of the women are in red that night, she has shrugged, "I don't remember. Just a coincidence." She doesn't have my obsession for assigning symbolism to everything.

Cofer's use of the mosaic structure documents her remembrances in a personalized spatial order. But the reappearance of characters and the accumulation of details—food, colors, dress, language—lead the reader through this weaving of associations to an understanding of what Cofer calls "the flavor of Puerto Rico."

Strategies for Choosing Structures

Structures connect what the writer *already* knows to what the reader *needs* to know. The key to choosing that connecting structure depends first on determining how much distance exists between what the writer and the reader know about the subject. The questions below help to gauge that distance.

Reader to Subject
How much does the reader know about the subject?

Readers like to learn something new or different about subjects they are already interested in, so you don't want to use a structure that repeats too much of what the reader already knows. The closer you and your reader are in your knowledge on the subject, the more personal, familiar, and innovative the structure can be. Readers who know little about the subject will benefit from the background that historical time order and sequential function structures provide.

How did the reader gain knowledge on the subject or what prevents the reader from knowing about the subject?

The source of a reader's knowledge may be closely aligned to a structure. For instance, a reader may know about a country only from reading travel guides or seeing films. If you want to establish a new relationship between the reader and the country, you would choose a different structure for shaping your ideas. Knowing if the reader has personal experience with the subject, an academic foundation, or is limited to general media coverage of the subject can guide you in choosing the structure with the best fit for involving the reader in a new way.

What opinion or disposition does the reader have on the subject?
How strong is that opinion? How different or similar is it to my view?

When readers share your opinion on a subject, you have a good deal of flexibility in choosing a structure, especially an innovative one, such as an extended metaphor, that can generate new insights or a conceptual time order or trip structure to heighten their experience. But when readers are opposed to your opinion, the decision is more difficult. When this is the case, choose a structure that builds on the points you can agree on.

Obviously, there is no perfect formula for choosing a structure to shape your ideas, but a careful analysis of the distance between what you know and what the reader already knows can point the way. And once you do choose a structure, make sure it complements the point of view you want to use. More than likely answering the questions presented in Chapter 2 on the writer's relationship to the reader and answering the questions above on the reader's relationship to the subject will lead to a point of view and structure that match. But the greater the distance between you and the reader in knowledge of one another and the subject, the more problematic the choice will be. For example, if you wanted to convince parents that requiring school uniforms will inhibit their children's creativity, then the distance between your experience and the parents' concerns is likely to present a problem.

Your immediate source of knowledge for this context is probably your own experience, but because parents prefer to view their children as "special" individuals, your experience may not be convincing. In this case, a subjective point of view or chronological narrative structure will not establish an appropriate relationship. If you choose a merged or objective point of view to decrease your visibility, then a functional structure or an extended metaphor structure will complement your need for lower visibility and also clarify your points. There are other possibilities for matching point of view with structure for this rhetorical context. The key point to remember is that investing more time in analyzing and planning your structure will result in a design that connects you with the reader in a meaningful way. Let the following four points guide you in making your final structure choice. Readers need (1) to have the focus clearly defined; (2) to understand their connection to the subject; (3) to know the reasoning that informs your opinion; and (4) to have confidence in the writer as a provider of information.

✦ **EXERCISE**   Several different structures may be appropriate for a particular rhetorical context. To determine which structure is best for your purpose, it's a good idea to experiment with several plans first. This invention strategy will help you to select the best fit for your audience and purpose. Select one of the topics below (or one of your own). Identify a potential audience and purpose for the topic you select. Then, outline three possible structures for that rhetorical context. Choose a structure from each of the three categories covered in this chapter: chronological, sequential, and spatial.

women's sports	house music	glaciers
SUVs	censorship	space exploration
credit cards	computer games	xenophobia

✦ **READING CRITICALLY**
Shaping Ideas

In the following essay, William Gibson, an award-winning science fiction writer and author of the novels *Neuromancer, Count Zero, Mona Lisa Overdrive,* and *Idoru,* presents his view on the value of the Internet. His audience, the readers of the *New York Times* Sunday magazine, know Gibson's reputation and more than likely use the Internet, so they will be motivated to read the essay. As you read the annotations to study how Gibson structures the essay, keep in mind the close relationship Gibson and his audience share.

Rhetorical Context

◆ **Subject:** The Internet

◆ **Occasion:** The opportunity for the writer to address a large audience with the novelty of his view and to promote his reputation as a writer.

◆ **Audience:** Well-educated professionals who enjoy reading. The Sunday *New York Times* is a ritual for most of these readers; they read the magazine leisurely and for pleasure.

◆ **Purpose:** To offer a fresh view on the value of the Internet.

Readers' Expectations   The *New York Times* Sunday Magazine readers will expect the essay to be thought-provoking, enjoyable, and well written. Their primary purpose for reading is pleasure, so they expect to be closely involved in the dialogue with the writer. They also will expect Gibson, as a science fiction writer, to forecast the future in some way. The irony conveyed in the title will pique their interest and prepare them for a view opposite from what they would expect.

◆ ◆ ◆

The Net Is a Waste of Time . . . and That's What's Good About It

William Gibson

Begins with a subjective point of view to introduce himself and his use of the Net; introduces central focus of staring into space and browsing.

I coined the word "Cyberspace" in 1981 in one of my first fiction stories and subsequently used it to describe something that people insist on seeing as a sort of literary forerunner of the Internet. This being so, some think it remarkable that I do not use E-mail. In all truth, I have avoided it because I am lazy and enjoy staring blankly into space (which is also the space where novels come from) and because unanswered mail, E- or otherwise, is a source of discomfort.   1

Builds on the staring into space focus by linking it to the test pattern device used in early television; identifies staring at technology as a group activity.

But I have recently become an avid browser of the World Wide Web. Some people find this odd. My wife finds it positively perverse. I, however, scent big changes afoot, possibilities that were never quite as manifest in earlier incarnations of the Net.   2

I was born in 1948. I can't recall a world before television, but I know I must have experienced one. I do, dimly, recall the arrival of a piece of brown wooden furniture with   3 sturdy Bakelite knobs and a screen no larger than the screen on this Powerbook.

4   Initially there was nothing on it but "snow," and then the nightly advent of a targetlike device called "the test pattern," which people actually gathered to watch.

5   Today I think about the test pattern as I surf the Web. I imagine that the World Wide Web and its modest wonders are no more than the test pattern for whatever the 21st century will regard as its equivalent medium. Not that I can even remotely imagine what that medium might actually be.

6   In the age of wooden television in the South where I grew up, leisure involved sitting on screened porches, smoking cigarettes, drinking iced tea, engaging in conversation and staring into space. It might also involve fishing.

7   Sometimes the Web does remind me of fishing. It never reminds me of conversation, although it can feel a lot like staring into space. "Surfing the Web" (as dubious a metaphor as "the information highway") is, as a friend of mine has it, "like reading magazines with the pages stuck together." My wife shakes her head in dismay as I patiently await the downloading of some Japanese Beatles fan's personal catalogue of bootlegs. "But it's from Japan!" She isn't moved. She goes out to enjoy the flowers in her garden.

8   I stay in. Hooked. Is this leisure—this browsing, randomly linking my way through these small patches of virtual real-estate—or do I somehow imagine that I am performing some more dynamic function? The content of the Web aspires to absolute variety. One might find anything there. It is like rummaging in the forefront of the collective global mind. Somewhere, surely, there is a site that contains . . . everything we have lost?

9   The finest and most secret pleasure afforded new users of the Web rests in submitting to the search engine of Alta Vista the names of people we may not have spoken aloud in years. Will she be here? Has he survived unto this age? (She isn't there. Someone with his name has recently posted to a news group concerned with gossip about soap stars.) What is this casting of the nets of identity? Do we engage here in something of a tragic seriousness?

Marginal annotations:

[¶4] Makes an analogy between the test pattern and surfing the Web; predicts Web is a test pattern for the next generation of technology; establishes the staring-test pattern-surfing relationship as the central focus for understanding his view of the subject.

[¶7] At this point the reader knows that Gibson has chosen a *spatial sequence* for structuring his information.

[¶8] Gibson adds the concept of leisure to convey the attitude he has toward staring/surfing and adds "variety" to the spatial dimension.

[¶9] Shares a specific experience to show his surfing/staring leisure enjoyment; internal spatial dimension.

Compares staring/watching as a leisure activity in television, film, and the Web to show how the entertainment value eventually fades so we need to access new technology. The readers' associations with these events involves them closely in the dialogue with the reader.

In the age of wooden television, media were there to entertain, to sell an advertiser's product, perhaps to inform. Watching television, then, could indeed be considered a leisure activity. In our hypermediated age, we have come to suspect that watching television constitutes a species of work. Post-industrial creatures of an information economy, increasingly sense that accessing media is what we do. We have become terminally self-conscious. There is no such thing as simple entertainment. We watch ourselves watching. We watch ourselves watching Beavis and Butthead, who are watching rock videos. Simply to watch, without the buffer of irony in place, might reveal a fatal naïveté. 10

But that is our response to aging media like film and television, survivors from the age of wood. The Web is new, and our response to it has not yet hardened. That is a large part of its appeal. It is something half-formed, growing. Larval. It is not what it was six months ago; in another six months it will be something else again. It was not planned; it simply happened, is happening. It is happening the way cities happened. It *is* a city. 11

Toward the end of the age of wooden televisions the futurists of the Sunday supplements announced the advent of the "leisure society." Technology would leave us less and less to do in the Marxian sense of yanking the levers of production. The challenge, then, would be to fill our days with meaningful, healthful, satisfying activity. As with most products of an earlier era's futurism, we find it difficult today to imagine the exact coordinates from which this vision came. In any case, our world does not offer us a surplus of leisure. The word itself has grown somehow suspect, as quaint and vaguely melancholy as the battered leather valise in a Ralph Lauren window display. Only the very old or the economically disadvantaged (provided they are not chained to the schedules of their environment's more demanding addictions) have a great deal of time on their hands. To be successful, apparently, is to be chronically busy. As new technologies search out and lace over every interstice in the net of global communication, we find ourselves with increasingly less excuse for . . . slack. 12

Builds to his final, ironic point that the technology intended to give us more leisure has actually intensified our work. So, "we" should "waste time" on the Web during its infancy before its future arrives.

13   And that, I would argue, is what the World Wide Web, the test pattern for whatever will become the dominant global medium, offers us. Today, in its clumsy, larval, curiously innocent way, it offers us the opportunity to waste time, to wander aimlessly, to daydream about the countless other lives, the other people, on the far sides of however many monitors in that postgeographical meta-country we increasingly call home. It will probably evolve into something considerably less random, and less fun—we seem to have a knack for that—but in the meantime, in its gloriously unsorted Global Ham Television Postcard Universes phase, surfing the Web is a procrastinator's dream. And people who see you doing it might even imagine you're working.

✦ ✦ ✦

Gibson meets the readers' expectations by using his "cyberspace" reputation to project how the future of the Web affects our behavior. Because his audience is familiar with both him and the Web, he chooses a subjective, personal point of view and a complementary spatial, metaphoric structure to establish a new relationship to what they *already* know. The element of time plays a significant role in understanding Gibson's main idea, but rather than use a historical chronological structure, he chooses to use the *before/after, then/now* spatial sequence. And, to make his point more entertaining and vivid for the readers, he chooses to incorporate the test pattern as an extended metaphor. The metaphor generates concrete associations for the readers, thus increasing their participation in the dialogue.

✦ ON YOUR OWN
Analyzing the Writer's Choices

Max Frankel's essay, "Let's Be Chromatically Correct," also appeared in the *New York Times* Sunday Magazine. The rhetorical context is exactly the same as it is for the previous essay by Gibson except for the subject. On a separate sheet of paper, describe how each paragraph fits into Frankel's choice of structure. Complete your analysis by writing a paragraph analyzing the effectiveness of Frankel's structure on establishing a new relationship between the reader and the subject.

✦ ✦ ✦

Let's Be Chromatically Correct

Max Frankel

Americans who are simplistically called people of color seem to 1 have had none of the difficulty felt by the allegedly uncolored in absorbing the evidence that Thomas Jefferson sired at least one of Sally Hemings's children. "Everybody knew that already," Fareed Thomas told a *Times* reporter, referring to his like-minded African-American classmates in a Los Angeles high school.

The reporter, Don Terry, readily accepted this testimony and in- 2 serted a charming autobiographical note. He said that adult African-Americans, too, have never doubted that Jefferson and many other of their ancestors practiced miscegenation freely.

"They believed it every time they traced the black and white 3 branches of their own family trees," Terry wrote. "They believed it every time they held a family reunion, and Aunt Wakara, her skin the color of coffee with cream, showed up along with dark-skinned Uncle Noah, espresso-colored cousin. Henry, brown sister Julie and baby Nia, who was smack dab in the middle."

Without even a wink of irony, Terry went on to quote Fareed's 4 teacher, Fahamisha Butler: "Look at the black people in this class. We are the color of the rainbow. Our ancestors didn't come over from Africa this way."

They sure didn't. But neither did they ever call the rainbow 5 black. Or white, for that matter. The Terry dispatch suggests that a faster way to escape some of America's racial and ethnic muddles may be for all of us to sharpen our vision and make our speech chromatically correct.

The police and the news media could help by becoming much 6 more discriminating about skin color. Just as they have always distinguished among people's black, brown, red, yellow, gray or white hair and their blue, brown, green, gray or hazel eyes, let them offer a rich array of skin shades. What a boon to social harmony and effective police work if we all shed the sloppy habit of identifying achievers and miscreants as merely blacks or whites, and instead called them ebonies, chocolates, cocoas, coffees, lattes and creams on the one hand, and pinks, ivories, taupes and eggshells on the other.

7   Think how liberating it would be to read, "The gunman, a six-foot ocher, fired twice at the frail, russet shopkeeper before two elderly neighbors, one buff, one milky, wrestled him to the ground." Or, "Muhammed Jefferson Akeem, the first umber ever elected to the House of Representatives, is being actively wooed by both the Melanic and Earthtone caucuses." And how helpful it would be to detectives if police artists rendered their portraits of wanted suspects in truly descriptive shadings.

8   An even larger social benefit could be achieved in the national census in 2000. America's mating habits have confused and distorted the decennial population counts since Jefferson's time because the racial classifications have forced so many inhabitants to make an intolerable choice between "black" and "white."

9   At the least, the census should have provided a registry long ago for "mulattoes" and "quadroons," and for their descendants—as "octonegral" and "octocaucasal" or some such. In still later generations, of course, this would lead to a wholly unpronounceable nomenclature, without clearing up the additional confusions created by the remaining census racial categories—American Indian, Eskimo and Aleut and Asian and Pacific Islander. Worse, the Census Bureau then divides all these arbitrary racial groupings into Hispanic and non-Hispanic subsets, looking to document racial and ethnic strength rather than facial coloration.

10   Whatever may be the residual political and sociological value of these categories, they should not dominate our thought and speech. They cry out for refinement in the next century. Modern printing and computer technologies would make it easy for all of us to be given a new census form that includes a vivid color chart depicting the planet's full range of skin shades. That chart would be held up against every face to determine the closest match.

11   Such a supplementary survey would finally produce a record that looks like America. The results could be filed and published both graphically and in a new vocabulary of designer colors: mahogany, saffron and zinc, among others. Barring any change in our mating habits, what may still strike conservative minds as facetious

in 2000 will, I think, appear not only sensible but also downright necessary by 2100.

As we correct our speech and thoughts chromatically, why not 12 begin to clean them up historically, too? Unvarnished color consciousness requires that we abandon African-American, Hispanic and Caucasian as anachronistic exaggerations or falsehoods.

Jefferson, who believed that the starkest sort of race mixing pro- 13 duces a "degradation of human character," obviously judged Sally Hemings as sufficiently pale (i.e., un-African) to bear his child, but still dark enough (African) to remain his slave. Most of his American contemporaries probably saw no contradiction in such bifurcated reasoning. Even a man of great intellect and democratic conviction could love and own a woman simultaneously. Nowadays, we ascribe that attitude to a "timebound" racism—not unlike the timebound sexism that we blame for preserving the ideal of wifely obedience into our century's marriage vow.

Finding this dusty furniture in the mind's attic can be both 14 shocking and illuminating. Just as we now wonder how otherwise enlightened people could trade in dark-skinned bodies or demand and accept female subservience, future generations are bound to marvel at how so many of their forebears could routinely feast while others went hungry, or how some ancestors could amass fortunes while others went begging. Like slavery and male domination in their time, the inequalities of our day are justified even in the most progressive circles as not only tolerable but also actually essential to economic growth and social harmony.

Our descendants will shake their heads in disbelief. But in that 15 distant time, like Jefferson, we will surely want it said that things were never so black and white.

Chapter 4
♦ ✦ ✦ ✦ ✦ ✦ ✦ ✦ ✦ ✦ ✦

Choosing a Voice

Voice is something we grow up learning to use without an instruction book. As speakers, each conversational situation we add to our experience from childhood to adulthood builds our intuition on how to use our voice effectively in relating to others in specific situations. From the informality of family and social situations with friends to more formal academic and work-related situations, we accumulate an understanding of how others respond to our voice. This range of experiences also reveals that each of us has *more than one* voice to contribute to a conversation. For example, a person's expertise on a subject might result in a confident, professional voice when speaking to colleagues in that field but a modest, humorous voice when explaining a similar concept to listeners unfamiliar with the field. The same person might have a quiet, retiring voice in social conversations.

As speakers, our direct contact with the audience, either face-to-face or voice-to-voice, allows us to judge immediately the clarity and credibility of our words and ideas. In response, we can repeat our statements, raise or lower our voices, add more information, increase the persuasiveness of our tone when the audience indicates a specific need. As writers, however, we don't have the advantage of that direct contact. Instead, writers must determine in advance what relationship they want to establish with their readers (point of view) and then choose the right balance of stylistic features to construct an appropriate voice for that relationship.

Stylistic Features Affecting Voice

Style refers to the choices a person makes in using language. Public speakers and well-known writers are often characterized by a particular style they developed over years of making similar or habitual choices in using language for similar purposes and to reach similar audiences. Presidents, novelists, short story writers, and essayists fall into this category. We look forward to their work, or avoid it, because of their style. But for those of us who have not yet gained such public recognition of our style, each new rhetorical situation challenges us to make conscious stylistic choices. These choices fall into three basic categories of language features: (1) sentence patterns, length, and variety; (2) word choice and placement; and (3) punctuation.

Combinations of choices in these categories can result in distinct and varied voices. Of course, no exact rules exist to produce any one voice, so writers have to experiment with different combinations to capture just the right fit for the relationship they want to establish with readers. Below is an example illustrating how a writer might experiment with these choices to create different voices and relationships with readers (based on Richard Eastman's *Style,* 3rd ed., Oxford UP, 1984, 104–107). Notice how even a change in pronoun creates a totally different voice and relationship with the reader.

Original

We think we learn from teachers, and sometimes we do. But the teachers are not always to be found in school or in great laboratories. Sometimes what we learn depends upon our own powers of insight. —Loren Eiseley, *The Unexpected Universe,* 1969

Analysis: The standard subject-verb-object/complement sentence pattern, similar sentence length, general vocabulary, and conventional punctuation create a voice with no particular emphasis. However, Eiseley's use of "we" establishes a partnership with the reader, inviting the reader to reflect with him. This choice gives the voice a friendly tone and makes the writer visible to the reader.

Version 1

I thought that **I** learned from teachers, and **I** sometimes did. But **my** teachers were not always to be found in school or great laboratories. Sometimes what **I** learn depends upon **my** own powers of insight.

Analysis: By changing "we" to "I" the voice in this version becomes solitary, autobiographical. The sentence patterns, length, and word choice have not changed, but the writer's relationship to the reader has. The writer is visible but no longer in direct partnership with the reader. Still, the personal emphasis promotes intimacy with the reader through the informal tone.

Version 2

You think **you** learn from teachers, and sometimes **you** do. But the teachers are not always found in school or great laboratories. Sometimes what **you** learn must depend upon **your** own powers of insight.

Analysis: Replacing "we" with "you" personalizes the writing for the reader. In some cases addressing the reader directly as "you" can place the writer above the reader, as in "You would do well to heed my advice." But in this passage, the writer and "you" are aligned as one, similar to the "we" relationship in the original but less direct and more informal in tone.

Version 3

People think **they** learn from teachers, and sometimes **they** do. But the teachers are not always to be found in school or in great laboratories. Sometimes what **people** learn depends upon **their** own powers of insight.

Analysis: This version no longer directly addresses the reader ("we"; "you") or directly invites the reader to join the writer in personal ("I") reflection. By shifting to an objective point of view using "they," the writer *indirectly* asks the reader to join in reflecting on learning as an abstract issue. The personalized experience is no longer visible; the voice of the writer becomes more formal and distant.

Version 4

Only sometimes do **students** learn from teachers. **The fact is that genuine instruction is** not always to be found in school or in great laboratories. Sometimes what **you** learn **must** depend upon **your** own powers of insight.

Analysis: In this version the writer assumes a position of authority *above* the reader. The words "only," "the fact is," and "must" convey that authority and separate the writer's knowledge on the subject from the reader's knowledge. The "you" in this version does *not* include the writer. Also, changing the pattern of the first sentence from compound to a direct statement of fact indicates that the writer's authority makes the writer clearly visible. If the reader perceives the writer to be a legitimate authority, this voice can work effectively to establish a relationship with the reader.

Version 5

It is commonly thought that people learn from teachers, and **maybe** that is sometimes true. But **perhaps** the teachers are not always found in schools or in great laboratories. **Isn't it possible that learning** may sometimes depend upon **one's** own powers of insight?

Analysis: The boldfaced changes in wording, "commonly thought," "maybe," "perhaps," and the conversion of the final sentence into a question convey a tentativeness that places the authority of the writer *below* the reader. The use of passive voice in the opening sentence ("It is commonly thought" by whom?) and the depersonalized "one's" in the last sentence further distance the writer from the reader. The overall effect is the voice of a writer who defers to the knowledge of the reader. In a situation in which the writer wishes to convey respect for the readers' experience (age, status, authority), this voice may establish an effective relationship.

Version 6

You know, people are always saying they learn from teachers! **Okay, so they** do, sometimes. But **what I want to get across is this—you don't** always find **your** teachers in school or in **labs either. No, sir!** Sometimes **you find the teacher right in your** own **eyes and ears and brains. That's where it's at!**

Analysis: The writer is clearly visible in this version, but the overuse of exclamations to convey emphasis and tone, and the use of slang expressions create a voice with little credibility or concern for establishing a relationship with the reader. In daily conversation this version might convey a closeness to the listener, but in writing it indicates a lack of thoughtful consideration for language and the reader. This level of informality is rarely appropriate except when quoting from an interview.

Version 7

Although learning is judged to require teachers (and sometimes **indeed it does), the real instructors may** be found **not so much** in school or in great laboratories **as in the student's** own powers of insight.

Analysis: This version conveys more of a literary formality in its phrasing and word choice ("Although learning is judged"; "indeed it does") and in the complexity of the sentence structure. By reshaping the thoughts from three sentences into one long sentence, the writer implies a sophisticated understanding of language on the part of the reader—a shared relationship. The parenthetical phrase decreases the formality and reveals the writer's voice more directly.

Creating a voice to reveal the point of view (Chap. 2) you plan to use requires conscious choices. The number of combinations of stylistic features is equal to the number of rhetorical situations you address, so the best resource you can use is your handbook. Here are some specific choices to consider in each stylistic feature category:

Sentences: Pattern, Length, and Variety

Types of sentences:	declarative; interrogative; exclamatory; imperative
Level of complexity:	simple; fragment; compound; complex; compound-complex
Rhythm:	repetition; parallelism; periodic structure; rhetorical question

Word Choice and Placement

Range of choice:	general to specific; abstract to concrete; denotation to connotation; euphemism; cliché; jargon
Rhythm and sound:	monosyllabic; polysyllabic; alliteration; assonance; onomatopoeia; contractions; personal or impersonal pronouns; active or passive verbs

Word Choice and Placement (cont.)

Emphasis and position: cataloging; climactic sequence; repetition; parallelism; figurative lan-
guage: simile, metaphor, personification, hyperbole, allusion, oxymoron,
antithesis

Punctuation

parentheses; dashes; ellipses; colons; semicolons; direct and indirect quotations; italics

Choosing a Voice to Reveal Point of View

Sometimes the immediacy of your need to write begins with a voice—
you're outraged, amused, skeptical, grateful, supportive. That underlying motivation connects you directly with a specific audience,
readers whom you believe need to hear your views. At other times you
write *into* a voice. As your knowledge of and attitude toward the subject grow and develop, your voice begins to take shape and your idea
of the readers that you want to hear what you say begins to form. As
Chapter 2 explains, once you determine your relationship to the subject and the readers who will benefit from what you know, you need
to choose a point of view or an angle for the readers to examine the
subject. That point of view, in turn, determines how visible your role
is in presenting the information and how audible your voice is. The
process follows a closely integrated sequence:

Rhetorical Context	*Process Sequence*	
Subject and occasion	writer's relationship to the subject	+
Audience	readers' connection to the writer and subject	+
Purpose	point of view to examine subject	= **Voice**

Here is an example of how that process might lead to constructing a writing voice. Let's say that Kyle, after changing from a

fast-food diet to a vegetarian diet, feels that he is healthier and more energetic. Although he knows that other factors might contribute to his improved health, he believes that the vegetarian diet makes a significant difference. He wants to share his discovery with other college students who will benefit from a change in diet. Assuming that these readers will be as skeptical as he was initially and admitting that he is no expert, Kyle decides to use a subjective point of view based on his personal experience. But what voice should he use to reveal that point of view? If he is too informal, the readers may not take his views seriously, but if he is too formal, they may not be interested or think he is overstepping his level of expertise. Kyle decides to align himself *with* the reader as a "typical" busy college student by using the pronoun *we*. In this way he can balance the informal nature of a common lifestyle with the formality of his concern for health and still maintain a subjective point of view.

Constructing Informal and Formal Voices

Writing voices ranging from informal to formal are appropriate for all points of view depending on the context of the rhetorical situation. Slight adjustments to the combination of stylistic features can add either a touch of informality or formality to your voice—the fine tuning needed to reveal the point of view and establish the desired distance in your relationship with the reader. The examples below illustrate how stylistic features can be used to construct both informal and formal voices for each point of view.

Subjective Point of View: Writer's Visibility Is Close to the Reader

Informal

About four years ago I let anger consume me. It was a seething, festering anger directed toward a woman who had done me wrong. The situation was complex, laced with gossip, lying, and betrayal. Looking back, I realize the events weren't that deserving of rage, but resentful thoughts swirled through my head all day long. I couldn't stand how I felt, but neither could I shake the negativity.

—Jill Kramer, "Dialing Up Angels" in *Natural Health* (see page 350)

Voice Analysis: The use of relatively short simple and compound sentences coupled with the general vocabulary of everyday speech produces a comfortable, informal voice. Also, the use of "I" in most sentences personalizes the informal voice and creates a close relationsip between the writer and the reader. Notice how the sequence of terms in sentence three—"gossip, lying, and betrayal"—generates the tension of the situation.

Formal

I am up to my waist in a basin of cool, acid-clear water, at the head of a box canyon some six hundred feet above the Colorado River. I place my outstretched hands flat against a terminal wall of dark limestone which rises more that a hundred feet above me, and down which a sheet of water falls—the thin creek in whose pooled waters I now stand. The water splits at my fingertips into wild threads; higher up, a warm canyon wind lifts water off the limestone in a fine spray; these droplets intercept and shatter sunlight. Down, down another four waterfalls and fern-shrouded pools below, the water spills into an eddy of the Colorado River, in the shadow of a huge boulder. Our boat is tied there.

—Barry Lopez, "Gone Back into the Earth"
in *Crossing Open Ground* (see page 452)

Voice Analysis: The "I" used in the subjective point of view is used sparingly in this excerpt, keeping the writer close to the reader but shifting the emphasis to what the writer sees and experiences. The sensory images focusing on the passage of the water as it travels down the canyon walls is captured in the structure of the long, flowing sentences in the middle of the paragraph (sentences by word count: 27, 40, 30, 26, 5). Using figurative language such as metaphor and personification—"the water splits . . . into wild threads" and "droplets intercept and shatter sunlight," the writer achieves a literary, more formal relationship between the reader and his personal experience.

Merged Point of View: Writer Has an Integrated, Moderate to Low Presence

Informal

The Year of the Ocean is a wake-up call: a reminder that the riches of the ocean cannot be taken for granted; that we are all stewards of this strategic resource; and that the health of the ocean depends on each one of us. We are hoping that this message reaches every man, woman, and child in this country—and beyond.

—William M. Daley, "Environmental Heroes," awards presentation (see page 160)

Voice Analysis: Speaking to a gathering of Key West citizens, U.S. Secretary of Commerce William M. Daley chooses to use a series of simple, direct statements and familiar vocabulary. While the emphasis is on the environment, Daley uses "we" and "our" to merge his relationship with the local audience. Notice that the "we" in the first sentence refers to Daley as a U.S. citizen just like his audience but that the "we" in the second sentence refers to Daley as a member of the U.S. Commerce Department. The voice is educated but open and friendly.

Formal

Back when I used to watch Saturday morning cartoons, a public-service ad ran regularly in which an animated cat, wearing a pirate's hat and squinting into a spyglass, would urge his young audience to read. His pitch was that books would take us anywhere we wanted to go—"Just read a book!" he cried, prancing about as various exotic scenes flashed in the background. That cat introduced me to the notion that reading a book—in particular a novel—transports us elsewhere, and moreover that we readers embark on a kind of voyage: We don't simply go alone to a strange place and do nothing; we accompany an orphan boy arriving in a strange city, or a woman deserting her husband.

—Karen Olsson, "Adrift on the Digital Sea" in *Civilization* (see page 244)

Voice Analysis: Writing to a sophisticated, educated reader, the writer uses longer complex sentences and, in places, an elevated vocabulary, such as "transports," "notion," "moreover," and "accompany." The use of dashes, which can be perceived as informal, interrupt the long sentences with additional information that could make comprehension more difficult for less experienced readers. Still, Olsson uses "I" and "we" to define the merged point of view, thus minimizing her presence but preventing her voice from becoming too formal.

Objective Point of View: Writer's Presence Not Apparent; Distanced from Reader

Informal

In the dessicated climate of New Mexico's San Juan Basin, a land of red sandstone mesas peppered with piñon trees, water is so precious that Navajo tradition regards it as a living entity. Survival here has long depended on the health of underground pools and streams that feed wells and the occasional surface spring. That's why Billy Martin is worried. The water supply to his tiny town of Crownpoint (pop. 2,500) is threatened, he says, by moneygrubbers who don't understand water's importance to Native American culture. It sounds like a familiar story . . . until you realize that Martin, 69, isn't upset with white businessmen. He's talking about his Navajo brethren.

—Dan Cray, "Navajo vs. Navajo" in *Time* (see page 433)

Voice Analysis: Time readers read quickly to keep up with the news, so this writer chooses stylistic features such as simple sentence structure, average length sentences, contractions, and general vocabulary to create an objective but informal voice. These informal stylistic features, including an indirect quote, ellipses, and addressing the audience with the familiar pronoun "you," keep the focus on the information, not the writer, and make reading easy.

Formal

Environmental policies have improved steadily and substantially in the United States since Americans celebrated the first Earth Day in 1970 to demonstrate their growing concerns about the environment. But geographic areas inhabited chiefly by racial minority groups still are more likely than mostly white areas to experience serious air, water, and soil pollution from industries such as oil refineries and chemical plants. Low-income and minority communities also are more likely to house waste-treatment facilities, incinerators, and toxic-waste dumps. And children in minority communities face a higher-than-average risk of lead poisoning because of lead-based paint in their homes.

—Bailus Walker, Jr., "Toward Environmental Equity: Colleges and Universities Can Help Find Solutions" in *The Chronicle of Higher Education* (see page 418)

Voice Analysis: In introducing the subject to his highly educated readers, the writer keeps an objective focus on the subject by not using any personal pronouns to address the audience directly. Although the vocabulary is not elevated nor the sentences highly complex, the length of the sentences and the inclusion of several hyphenated terms and strings of prepositional phrases create a serious formality with no rhythmic breaks.

Each of the writing voices illustrated above was constructed to meet the demands of a specific rhetorical situation, but together they show that there are general guidelines you can follow in combining stylistic features to complement the point of view you choose and the level of formality that defines the relationship you want to achieve with your readers.

Informal Voice	*Formal Voice*
simple and compound sentences	frequent use of complex sentences
short to average length sentences	longer, embedded sentences
general, familiar vocabulary	elevated, literary, hyphenated vocabulary
familiar word order, sometimes varied	varied word order in sentence openings
frequent use of contractions	infrequent use of contractions
addresses audience directly	occasional use of direct address
punctuation familiar, sometimes varied to clarify or convey emotion or emphasis	punctuation more varied and complex; often used to embed information
relaxed, comfortable readability	slower, more challenging readability

The better you understand your connection to the subject, who your readers are and their relationship to you and the subject, and why you are addressing these readers, the clearer your choices will be in

constructing your writing voice. Just be sure to allow experimenta-
tion time during your composing process.

✦ EXERCISE

1. For each sentence below, write one version in a more formal
   voice and one version in a less formal voice.

   The fears, however, persist.
   I've always felt in a hurry to get things done.
   Why can't you try harder to do better?
   Amazing facts filled every page.
   Under the bed the dog shivered at the sound of thunder.

2. Choose two of the voice samples presented on pages 83–86, one
   informal voice and one formal voice, and rewrite each to illustrate the opposite level of formality.

✦ READING CRITICALLY
Choosing a Voice

On January 11, 1999, *Time* devoted its entire issue to "The Future of
Medicine." In the essay below, James D. Watson, who along with
Francis Crick won the Nobel Prize in 1953 for their discovery of the
structure of DNA, presents his personal viewpoint on the future of
genetic engineering. Watson's reputation in the field gives him greater
flexibility in choosing a voice than most writers would have. Read the
annotations carefully to consider the effect of Watson's choices.

Rhetorical Context

⬥ **Subject:** Genetic engineering

⬥ **Occasion:** An invitation for Watson to share his expertise and
predictions

⬥ **Audience:** *Time* readers, ages twenty-five to eighty-plus; educated, critical readers who want to stay informed on national and
global news events. All are familiar with the basic concept of genetic engineering and related issues, such as in vitro fertilization,

DNA chromosome intervention, and test-tube babies. These readers know they will have to make choices in the future about genetic engineering.

❖ **Purpose:** To convince the readers to support using genetic engineering to advance our scientifc understanding of who we are

Readers' Expectations   Most *Time* readers will recognize James D. Watson by reputation, though few will be knowledgeable in the field. Some may already have faced decisions in fertility-related issues. Since Watson's discovery has made genetic engineering more accessible, readers will expect Watson to support its future development. They know Watson is a scientist, but they don't know how moral issues affect his judgment. The one-page length of the essay in the publication gives readers the opportunity to read slowly and thoughtfully.

✦ ✦ ✦

All for the Good

James D. Watson

1   There is lots of zip in DNA-based biology today. With each passing year it incorporates an ever increasing fraction of the life sciences, ranging from single-cell organisms, like bacteria and yeast, to the complexities of the human brain. All this wonderful biological frenzy was unimaginable when I first entered the world of genetics. In 1948, biology was an all too descriptive discipline near the bottom of science's totem pole, with physics at its top. By then Einstein's turn-of-the-century ideas about the interconversion of matter and energy had been transformed into the powers of the atom. If not held in check, the weapons they made possible might well destroy the very fabric of civilized human life. So physics of the late 1940s were simultaneously revered for making atoms relevant to society and feared for what their toys could do if they were to fall into the hands of evil.

Opening sentence conveys an unexpected informal tone with the phrase "lots of zip."

Continues informal voice by using familiar vocabulary ("with each passing year"; "all this wonderful") and average-length sentences.

Uses "I" to identify his involvement in the sciences when the powers of the atom were developed.

An indirect, understated use of authority to present the good versus evil analogy.

Uses a familiar, nontechnical vocabulary to make the analogy between discovering the power of the atom and discovering the power of DNA.

As the paragraph progresses, the sentence structure becomes more complex (information embedded in parentheses).

Uses a rhetorical question to address the audience directly through implied "you."

Use of an informal dash to indicate change in tone, one of disapproval.

Continues to use general vocabulary to maintain an informal voice: "got into the hands of"; "itching"; "Happily"; "doomsday scenario." These words also express his frustrated emotions as a participant in this history.

Asserts personal view directly with the phrase "to my knowledge" to emphasize the safety of experiments.

Directly asserts the "moral" conclusion that informs his overall view. His use of "I" is in keeping with his informal voice, but is also authoritative.

Uses "we" in one sentence to align himself with the audience as a member of society. But in the next sentence he uses "we" ambiguously. Is it "we" members of society or "we" the scientists?

Such ambivalent feelings are now widely held to- 2
ward biology. The double-helical structure of DNA, initially admired for its intellectual simplicity, today represents to many a double-edged sword that can be used for evil as well as good. No sooner had scientists at Stanford University in 1973 begun rearranging DNA molecules in test tubes (and, equally important, reinserting the novel DNA segments back into living cells) than critics began likening these "recombinant" DNA procedures to the physicist's power to break apart atoms. Might not some of the test-tube-rearranged DNA molecules impart to their host cells disease-causing capabilities that, like nuclear weapons, are capable of seriously disrupting human civilization? Soon there were cries from both scientists and non-scientists that such research might best be ruled by stringent regulations—if not laws.

As a result, several years were to pass before the 3
power of recombinant-DNA technology got into the hands of working scientists, who by then were itch-ing to explore previously unattainable secrets of life. Happily, the proposals to control recombinant-DNA research through legislation never got close to enact-ment. And when anti-DNA doomsday scenarios failed to materialize, even the modestly restrictive governmental regulations began to wither away. In retrospect, recombinant-DNA may rank as the safest revolutionary technology ever developed. To my knowl-edge, not one fatality, much less illness, has been caused by a genetically manipulated organism.

The moral I draw from this painful episode is this: 4
Never postpone experiments that have clearly defined future benefits for fear of dangers that can't be quan-tified. Though it may sound at first uncaring, we can react rationally only to real (as opposed to hypotheti-cal) risks. Yet for several years we postponed important experiments on the genetic basis of cancer, for exam-ple, because we took much too seriously spurious ar-guments that the genes at the root of human cancer might themselves be dangerous to work with.

5   Though most forms of DNA manipulation are now effectively unregulated, one important potential goal remains blocked. Experiments aimed at learning how to insert functional genetic material into human germ cells—sperm and eggs—remain off limits to most of the world's scientists. No governmental body wants to take responsibility for initiating steps that might help redirect the course of future human evolution. These decisions reflect widespread concerns that we, as humans, may not have; the wisdom to modify the most precious of all human treasures—our chromosomal "instruction books." Dare we be entrusted with improving upon the results of the several million years of Darwinian natural selection? Are human germ cells Rubicons that geneticists may never cross?

Equal-length sentences convey equal importance to each sentence.

Defines use of "we" as "humans" indicating clear shared relationship with the readers as a member of society and "our" to convey his respect for the individual.

Poses two questions using references that might separate him from some of his readers: (1) "Darwinian" will alert the Creationists and (2) the allusion to "Rubicons"—point of no return—may be unfamiliar to many readers. The writer is slightly above the readers at this point.

6   Unlike many of my peers, I'm reluctant to accept such reasoning, again using the argument that you should never put off doing something useful for fear of evil that may never arrive. The first germ-line gene manipulations are unlikely to be attempted for frivolous reasons. Nor does the state of today's science provide the knowledge that would be needed to generate "superpersons" whose far-ranging talents would make those who are genetically unmodified feel redundant and unwanted. Such creations will remain denizens of science fiction, not the real world, far into the future. When they are finally attempted, germ-line genetic manipulations will probably be done to change a death sentence into a life verdict—by creating children who are resistant to a deadly virus, for example, much the way we can already protect plants from viruses by inserting antiviral DNA segments into their genomes.

Uses "I," a contraction, and "you" to return to his informal voice.

In trying to reduce any fears the readers might have, Watson uses references to science fiction terms "superpersons" and "denizens" to downplay fictional predictions. He also appeals emotionally to the reader by using children as an example of genetics reversing "a death sentence to a life verdict."

7   If appropriate go-ahead signals come, the first resulting gene-bettered children will in no sense threaten human civilization. They will be seen as special only by those in their immediate circles, and are likely to pass as unnoticed in later life as the now grownup "test-tube baby" Louise Brown does today. If they grow up

Continues using informal vocabulary ("go-ahead signals") and a familiar example (test-tube baby) to create an acceptable analogy.

Predicts possible outcomes using impersonal "they" to create distance from the reader.

healthily gene-bettered, more such children will follow, and they and those whose lives are enriched by their existence will rejoice that science has again improved human life. If, however, the added genetic material fails to work, better procedures must be developed before more couples commit their psyches toward such inherently unsettling pathways to producing healthy children.

Continues to incorporate informal vocabulary ("faint at heart"; "up to the job"; "most unfair") and personal pronouns "we" and "our" to instill shared support for genetic engineering.

Moving forward will not be for the faint of heart. But if the next century witnesses failure, let it be because our science is not yet up to the job, not because we don't have the courage to make less random the sometimes most unfair courses of human evolution.

8

✦ ✦ ✦

Watson's reputation allows him to write in a formal authoritative voice, but instead he chooses to use an informal voice to reveal his subjective point of view from a less intimidating point of view. The informal voice helps the reader to view Watson as a concerned member of society as well as an expert scientist. Watson may not have convinced all of his readers to have the "courage" to experiment with "our" scientific knowledge, but by using an informal voice to create a shared relationship with the readers, he established mutual respect.

✦ON YOUR OWN
Analyzing the Writer's Choices

The following essay also appeared in "The Future of Medicine" issue of *Time*. The audience and subject are the same as those described for the Watson essay, but the writer's purpose and choice of voice are different. Robert Wright is a regular contributing writer to *Time* who has earned his own byline but who has no scientific credentials in the field of genetic engineering.

On a separate sheet of paper, describe the choices Wright makes in constructing a voice to reveal his point of view and relationship with the audience *in each paragraph*. Identify the stylistic feature choices he makes to convey a formal or informal voice. After describing the writer's choices, write a paragraph analyzing the effectiveness of those choices in responding to the rhetorical context.

✦ ✦ ✦

Who Gets the Good Genes?

Robert Wright

1   In the 1932 novel *Brave New World,* Aldous Huxley envisioned future childbirth as a very orderly affair. At the Central London Hatchery and Conditioning Center, in accordance with orders from the Social Predestination Room, eggs were fertilized, bottled and put on a conveyor belt. Nine months later, the embryos—after "decanting"— were babies. Thanks to state-sponsored brainwashing, they would grow up delighted with their genetically assigned social roles—from clever, ambitious alphas to dim-witted epsilons.

2   Ever since publication of Huxley's dystopian novel, this has been the standard eugenics nightmare: government social engineers subverting individual reproductive choice for the sake of an eerie social efficiency. But as the age of genetic engineering dawns, the more plausible nightmare is roughly the opposite: that a laissez-faire eugenics will emerge from the free choices of millions of parents. Indeed, the only way to avoid Huxleyesque social stratification may be for the government to get into the eugenics business.

3   Huxley's scenario made sense back in 1932. Some American states were forcibly sterilizing the "feebleminded," and Hitler had praised these policies in *Mein Kampf.* But the biotech revolution that Huxley dimly foresaw has turned the logic of eugenics inside out. It lets parents choose genetic traits, whether by selective abortion, selective reimplanting of eggs fertilized in vitro or—in perhaps just a few years—injecting genes into fertilized eggs. In Huxley's day eugenics happened only by government mandate; now it will take government mandate—a ban on genetic tinkering—to prevent it.

4   An out-and-out ban isn't in the cards, though. Who would try to stop parents from ensuring that their child doesn't have hemophilia? And once some treatments are allowed, deciding where to draw the line becomes difficult.

The Bishop of Edinburgh tried. After overseeing a British Medical Association study on bioethics, he embraced genetic tinkering for "medical reasons," while denouncing the "Frankenstein idea" of making "designer babies" with good looks and a high IQ. But what is the difference? Therapists consider learning disabilities to be medical problems, and if we find a way to diagnose and remedy them before birth, we'll be raising scores on IQ tests. Should we tell parents they can't do that, that the state has decided they must have a child with dyslexia? Minor memory flaws? Below-average verbal skills? At some point you cross the line between handicap and inconvenience, but people will disagree about where.

If the government does try to ban certain eugenic maneuvers, some rich parents will visit clinics in more permissive nations, then come home to bear their tip-top children. (Already, British parents have traveled to Saudi Arabia to choose their baby's sex in vitro, a procedure that is illegal at home.) Even without a ban, it will be upperclass parents who can afford pricey genetic technologies. Children who would in any event go to the finest doctors and schools will get an even bigger head start on health and achievement.

This unequal access won't bring a rigid caste system à la *Brave New World*. The interplay between genes and environment is too complex to permit the easy fine-tuning of mind and spirit. Besides, in vitro fertilization is nobody's idea of a good time; even many affluent parents will forgo painful invasive procedures unless horrible hereditary defects are at stake. But the technology will become more powerful and user friendly. Sooner or later, as the most glaring genetic liabilities drift toward the bottom of the socioeconomic scale, we will see a biological stratification vivid enough to mock American values.

Enter the government. The one realistic way to avoid this nightmare is to ensure that poor people will be able to afford the same technologies that the rich are using. Put that way, it sounds innocent, but critics will rightly say it amounts to subsidizing eugenics.

State involvement will create a bioethical quagmire. Even if everyone magically agrees that improving a child's memory is as valid as avoiding dyslexia, there will still be things taxpayers aren't ready to pay for—genes of unproven benefit, say, or alterations whose downsides may exceed the upside. (The tendency of genes to have more than one effect—pleiotropy—seems to be the rule, not the exception.) The question will be which techniques are beyond the pale.

The answers will change as knowledge advances, but the arguments will never end.

10   In *Brave New World,* state-sponsored eugenics was part of a larger totalitarianism, a cultural war against family bonds and enduring romance and other quaint vestiges of free reproductive choice. The novel worked; it left readers thinking that nothing could be more ghastly than having government get into the designer-baby business. But if this business is left to the marketplace, we may see that government involvement, however messy, however creepy, is not the creepiest alternative.

Chapter 5

✦ ✦ ✦ ✦ ✦ ✦ ✦ ✦ ✦ ✦

Establishing Credibility

"Consider the source" is advice parents like to give their children, advice we learn to depend on as adults, especially as our decisions become more important and as more sources of information become available. For example: What sources do you consult before buying a car, a CD player, new software? Whose advice do you seek on student loans, your career, your health?

No doubt you can easily list a minimum of three sources to consult for each item named in the above questions, sources ranging from counselors and family physicians to consumer guides and the Internet. With the abundance of sources available, how can you determine which one offers the best information for *your* purpose? What quantity and quality of resources do you need to make a decision?

Writers face these same questions in choosing sources their readers will respect. If readers trust the writer's information, then the writer has established *credibility* or *ethos*. *Ethos*, a Greek word for *character,* is present in every act of communication. What we say and how we say it creates an impression of who we are, and that perceived impression—favorable or otherwise—establishes a level of trust in the reader or listener. In face-to-face situations with people we do not know, we usually judge character by the person's command of the subject, tone of voice, body language, and reputation or how others respond. If the person appears knowledgeable, fair, and sincere, we tend to trust that person. In writing situations, readers use the same qualities to judge character and determine trust, but they have more time to look for and consider those qualities. Writers, then, must carefully construct their ethos if they expect readers to trust what they write.

Choices in Creating Ethos

Point of View   The distance you establish between you and your readers is the first choice you make in creating your ethos as a writer. As Chapter 3 explains, the closer you position yourself to the reader, the more personal your relationship. The closer the relationship, however, the more the reader must rely on the writer's particular expertise and relevant personal experience to accept the information. In this way, the subjective, merged, or objective point of view you choose introduces your character to the reader. If the point of view you choose does *not* match your authority on the subject, the readers are likely to perceive a "credibility gap" in accepting the ideas you want to convey.

Voice   The voice you choose to complement your point of view (see Chap. 4) plays an important role in establishing your credibility with the intended readers. Because voice conveys the level of formality and your attitude toward the subject and reader, the word choices and sentence complexity you use to create your writing voice work together to establish a trustworthy relationship with the reader. Most critical readers have a built-in detector that alerts them when a writer's voice oversteps its authority or tries to convince using false flattery. Whether you choose an informal voice or a formal one, readers expect an honest presentation of information and a genuine interest in their well-being. In other words, the reader needs to trust in the sincerity and authority conveyed through your voice. When your own level of expertise lacks proven authority, then you must incorporate sources your readers will respect.

Sources   In judging the sources that writers use, readers ask two important questions: (1) How does the writer know this information? and (2) How does this information support my values? In response to these questions, writers need to select sources that convey authority, fairness, and ethical principles recognized by the community to which the readers belong. The choice of sources, then, reflects the trust and goodwill writers need to establish if they expect readers to respect the information they present.

Constructing Credibility

The process of constructing credibility begins with *accessing sources:* What sources are available and how do you locate them? Now that we have evolved from the Industrial Age to the Information Age, there are a vast number of sources to consider. To determine where to start your exploration, you will need a search strategy. Once you have located the sources you think will best serve your purpose, you can move to step two: *evaluating sources.* This step involves generating the criteria for verifying the authority and credibility of the source, and also for determining how useful the source will be in fulfilling your purpose. Finally, after selecting the most authoritative and purposeful sources you can move to step three: *incorporating sources.* At this point you decide how the different ways of presenting sources (i.e., direct quotes, paraphrase, statistics, charts, personal experience, etc.) can best be used to establish your credibility with the reader.

Accessing Sources

A vast array of sources exists today from which you can establish your credibility as a writer. So before you begin your search, consider these primary locations and the types of resources available in each:

Library Resources
Books
Articles in magazines and newspapers
Articles in scholarly journals
General and specialized reference works
Government documents
Primary sources such as letters and diaries
Special collections
Audio/visual materials

Field Resources
Interviews
Opinion surveys; questionnaires
Guest speakers
Literature from organizations

Observations; experiments

Documentaries; films

Internet Resources

Web search sites (directories and indexes)

Newsgroups and listservs

Reference works

Government documents

News articles

Electronic texts

MUDs and MOOs

E-mail

Each of the sources listed above provides different kinds of information, some you may need to increase your credibility with your intended audience, and some you may not need. To determine which kinds of sources you need, you must answer these questions:

1. What level of expertise on the subject do I have and how did I achieve that expertise?

   Considerations

   Personal experience—as a participant; as a spectator

   Historical background—from reading, course study, interviews

   Current knowledge—from reading, experience

   Specialized knowledge—from professional experience, scholarly research, acquaintances in the field, observation, experiments, length/duration of personal experience

2. What kinds of sources do my readers respect as authoritative?

   Considerations

   Experts recognized by the general media

   People with titles—Dr., General, Rev., CEO, President

   Authors of current books

   Classical literature

   Reference works—encyclopedias, dictionaries, manuals

   Government documents and officials

Laws; statistics; surveys

Periodicals

Internet

Personal testimony, experience

When you know the answers to these questions, you can begin to design a search strategy to access the kinds of sources needed to build the credibility between what you already know and what the audience needs to respect the information you present. For example, if your on-the-job experience delivering the local newspaper for the past five years convinces you that there is a decline in the number of people who rely on newspapers as their source for news, but your intended audience respects the verification of surveys and statistics, then your search strategy should include those sources as potential supportive evidence. And, if that intended audience values the currency of material presented on the Internet, then you should search that resource for the most current statistical information. Of course, once you access that information, the next step is to establish the credibility of the source.

Evaluating Sources

Selecting a source to use in your writing involves two levels of evaluation:

1. Does the source establish credibility for me? Do I trust the writer's character and the information he or she presents?
2. Will my intended readers value this source? Will using it increase my credibility as a writer?

To determine the answer to the first question you can use the rhetorical context of the source as a guide for generating criteria or standards for credibility. The criteria outlined below are appropriate to written sources you find in the library or on the Internet.

◆ Author

What are the writer's credentials as a writer?
years of experience; genre of writing; publication record

What are the author's credentials related to the subject?
education; training; personal experience; previous publications

Is contact information provided?
e-mail or snail mail address for the writer or publisher

(In some cases an organization, such as Planned Parenthood, may be the author.)

◆ Occasion

How timely is the source?
breaking news; update on previous knowledge; reflection on previous events; dated material published during the early history of the subject

Is there any quality control?
self-published; reviewed by editorial board or professional peers; part of a recognized/unrecognized organizational Web site

What reason did the writer have for publishing this material?
job or class assignment; researcher in field; increase reputation

◆ Subject

What does the title reveal about the subject?
broad coverage; historical; narrowly defined

How complex is the presentation of information?
length; use of headings, illustrations, charts; length of paragraphs

What types of supporting evidence does the writer include?
personal experience; expert testimony; interviews; statistics; general news reports; scholarly research; in-links, out-links

How appropriate are the sources used to the focus and audience?
relevance; timeliness; level of formality; fairness (balanced or one-sided); representative (statistics; surveys); range and variety

◆ Audience

What does the writer assume the reader already knows about the subject?
history; theory; general knowledge; personal experience

What attitude does the writer assume the reader has toward the subject?
supportive; oppositional; ambivalent

Are you a member of the intended audience?

◆ Purpose

What does the title reveal about the writer's attitude toward the subject?
supportive; oppositional; neutral

What point of view does the writer use?
subjective; merged; objective

Does the writer's voice complement the point of view?
level of formality: word choice, sentence complexity, paragraph density; fairness or bias; appropriate distance to the reader

How appropriate is the point of view and voice to the types of sources used?
same level of formality; above or below distance established

Do the sources used reflect the values of the audience?
conservative, moderate, liberal

(Keep in mind that your readers will ask the same questions about *your* writing.)

To answer the second question, "Will my intended readers value this source and will using it increase my credibility as a writer?" you will need to generate criteria specific to the rhetorical context of your writing. These criteria follow the same line of reasoning you use in determining your search strategy.

Sample Source

"The American Freshman: National Norms for Fall 1998"

A statistical report published by The American Council on Education and the University of California at Los Angeles Higher Education Research Institute.

The statistics are based on survey responses of 275,811 freshmen entering 469 two-year and four-year institutions in the fall of 1998. Reported annually.

Student Writer's Rhetorical Context

◆ **Subject:** Required volunteer service course for graduation

◆ **Audience:** Faculty Senate General Education Program Committee

✦ **Purpose:** To convince the committee members that requiring volunteer service as a graduation requirement should not be mandated in the form of a course.

✦ **Occasion:** The student, who works part-time, takes a full load of courses, and commutes to campus, would like different options for fulfilling the new requirement.

Evaluation of Using Source to Construct Credibility

Questions	*Responses*
Writer's perception of self to the subject:	
What is my level of expertise?	Limited volunteer experience in high school service club; agree with the benefits
Writer's perception of self to audience:	
Does the audience recognize me by reputation?	No, I am one of many students. We do agree on the value of the requirement, but we differ in how we must allocate our time on a daily basis.
In what ways are we similar? Common values, knowledge, experience, attitude toward subject?	
In what ways do we differ?	
Reader's perception of writer to subject:	
Does the writer have the authority to inform me on this subject?	Faculty do respect students' views in class, but they do not see us as authorities in designing curriculum or requirements.
Reader's perception of self to writer:	
What assumptions does the writer make about my knowledge, experience, and values? Is the writer concerned for my well-being?	I assume the faculty want what is best for students to be fully educated. They are well informed, but with respect to their well-being, I question if they want to teach another course.

Analysis

The faculty will respect the source because the survey was conducted by two institutions of higher learning, researchers equal in knowledge, experience, and values. Although the data are limited to the views of freshmen, the report still reflects college students' views. This source will build my credibility beyond the singular voice of one opinion.

This process of evaluating sources requires thoughtful, sometimes time-consuming, analysis, but the effort in choosing the best sources for your purpose makes the difference between the audience merely reading your essay and respecting your ideas.

Incorporating Sources

The methods you choose for incorporating sources also contribute to your credibility. By choosing methods to complement the point of view and the voice you use, you maintain both the distance and level of formality you want to establish with your readers. Imagine the effect of using a parenthetical citation in an informal personal essay:

> I fought often with my parents that summer, and, of course, I always felt guilty afterward (Johnson 182). But after two weeks on the road, we finally worked out our differences.

Why would the writer need to document feeling guilty in relating a personal experience to the reader? The citation not only interrupts the flow of the narrative but also makes evident the writer's insecurity in developing a relationship with the reader. The result creates a definite credibility gap.

Each combination of point of view and voice establishes a different distance and level of formality. The closer the writer is to the reader, the more the reader will rely on the writer as an authority; the greater the distance between the writer and reader, the more the reader will rely on the sources the writer incorporates. The following examples, most from the readings in Part Two, illustrate how writers incorporate sources to construct credibility for the point of view and voice they choose to relate to the intended audience.

Subjective Point of View

Informal Voice

acknowledgment phrase

A co-worker suggested I contact Renée Swisko, a spiritual healer from Marina Del Rey, Calif.

indirect quote

At certain points, Swisko asked if I felt energy moving through me. To be honest, I didn't feel much on a physical level—only an occasional tremble—but I did notice a growing sense of lightness and peace.

—Jill Kramer, "Dialing Up Angels"

Formal Voice

Statistics with no source cited. Readers must accept her expertise as credible to trust the data.

In Kenya, as in so much of the African continent, 80 percent of the farmers—and the fuel gatherers—are women.

Writer uses specific facts and details from her personal knowledge and experience.

We receive much of our support from abroad, mostly from women all over this world, who send us small checks. And the United Nations Development Fund for Women gave us a big boost, $100,000 in 1981. We also received support from the Danish Voluntary Fund and the Norwegian Agency for International Development. In the U.S. we are supported by the African Development Foundation, which helped us to make a film about the Green Belt Movement in 1985.

—Wangari Maathai, "Foresters without Diplomas"

Merged Point of View

Informal Voice

Informal use of undocumented but believable statistics.

From April 22–28, various anti-media groups will be sponsoring "TV Turnoff Week," a challenge to the 98 percent of Americans who own at least one television to switch it off and find something better to do.

Selects and summarizes results of a study without naming the study or the researchers.

It's no wonder then that a study done on teenagers ages 13 to 17 showed that only 25 percent could name the city where the U.S. Constitution was written, while 75 percent knew where you would find the zip code 90210.

—Corbett Trubey, "The Argument Against TV"

(The list of resources at the end of the article leads the reader to assume that the informal references above can be located in the sources listed.)

Formal Voice

"If you were a 16-year-old and you wanted to make music, you picked up a guitar and made music," says Mika Salmi, founder of Atom Films and former talent scout who discovered Nine Inch Nails.

Direct quote with acknowledgment phrase.

A page on www.dfilm.com, a traveling and online festival of digital films, boasts an inspiring quote from Francis Ford Coppola (mix his media though he does): "One day . . . "

Description and attribution of source to introduce quote.

"There's a real gap between the two [markets]," agrees Norm Meyrowitz, president of Macromedia Products, who adds that the company plans to keep it that way.

Direct quote.

Indirect quote.

> —Greg Lindsay, "Hey Kids, Let's Put on a Show"

Objective Point of View
Informal Voice

Stephen Roach, chief economist at Morgan Stanley, seems to admit as much when he says downsizing, wage stagnation, and a short-sighted corporate efficiency mania have drastically changed the work environment to the detriment of the worker. "It has certainly raised questions of cynicism, loyalty, perceived sense of worth and career aspirations," he says, neatly summarizing the traumas at Dilbert's unnamed yet universal employer. On the other hand, surveys show that a lot of us are fairly satisfied with our jobs. A *Newsweek* Poll conducted last summer indicated an impressive majority—87 percent—considered their workplace a "pleasant environment."

Paraphrase.

Direct quote.

Summary of poll results.

There's even a Web site devoted to such horror stories—www.myboss.com.

Resource to consult.

Historical reference.

Ever since Apple's Macintosh development team in the mid-1980s wore T shirts proclaiming 90 HOURS A WEEK AND LOVING IT! high-tech companies have figured out it's good business to coax triple-time work out of single-salary employees . . .

.   —Steven Levy, "Working in Dilbert's World"

Formal Voice

Literary reference.

American writers such as Sinclair Lewis and John O'Hara satirized small towns as insular, claustrophobic places, inhabited by petty, mean-spirited people.

Paraphrase with citation.

Summary.

In a typical case, the U.S. Supreme Court ruled that the Sierra Club has no legal standing to argue for the preservation of parkland as a community resource (Glendon 112). Rather, if the Sierra Club wished to show standing, it would have to demonstrate that particular individuals were harmed.

Direct quote with citation.

Gans further noted that "for most West Enders [in Boston] . . . life in the area resembled that found in the village or small town, and even in the suburb" (*The Urban Villagers,* 14–15).

Additional source recommendation.

They form political clubs and are a force in local politics. (Jim Sleeper's *Closest of Strangers* provides a fine description of these New York City communities.)

Statistics.

In 1950, 14.4 percent of those sixty-five years of age and older lived alone (Monk 534); by 1990 the percentage stood at nearly 31 percent (U.S. Bureau of the Census, Table L, 12).

—Amitai Etzioni, "The New Community"

From these examples we can make some generalizations about what techniques are used to incorporate sources and how they build credibility.

Techniques	*Constructing Credibility*
concrete, sensory and factual details from personal experience	A high level of detail and emotions convinces the reader of your participation and encourages involvement with your ideas.

values statement	Whether direct or indirect, these statements assure the readers of the beliefs and concerns that inform your ideas.
field-specific knowledge	Knowing the terms, history, and people particular to a field conveys concern for informing the reader through expertise, education, or both.
acknowledgment phrase	Identifying authorities or the people involved shows concern for the readers' understanding and need for authority.
summary	Summarizing another's views can be helpful and show concern for the reader by providing background information.
paraphrase	Rephrasing an authority's words in your own language can maintain your voice and still convey authority; include an acknowledgment phrase and, in formal contexts, a citation.
indirect quotes	Indirect quotes provide a sense of authority—you heard it or read it; using an acknowledgment phrase or citation can increase authority for some readers.
direct quotes	Carefully selecting exact words from authorities adds life and expertise to your ideas. Used with an acknowledgment phrase and, in formal contexts, a citation, direct quotes demonstrate your research efforts and sincerity for informing the reader.
statistics; polls, surveys	Many readers have learned to mistrust statistics, so be sure to identify the source, date, organization

	who conducted the study, and the size of the sample to establish trust.
literary and historical references and allusions	These sources, unless explained, assume a well-educated reader who will acknowledge the extent of your learning and goodwill; if readers are not familiar with the sources, they may be intimidated and distrust you.
additional recommended sources	Readers are likely to accept these recommendations with goodwill if you have established a clear level of credibility.

With the exception of using an informal personal voice and sources in formal contexts, or formal citations in informal contexts, most techniques for incorporating sources can be used to build your credibility. A careful analysis of your audience, allowing others to read your drafts, and reading your work as a reader, not a writer, will help you to make the appropriate decisions.

◆ EXERCISE

1. The survey on American freshmen cited on page 99 included the following statistics:

Political Orientation	Total	Men	Women
Far left	2.7%	3.5%	2.1%
Liberal	20.8	19.0	22.3
Middle of the road	56.5	55.2	57.6
Conservative	18.6	20.1	17.2
Far right	1.5	2.3	0.7

   Make a list of sources (two source minimum) each group will respect. Identify any differences in gender in responding to those sources.

2. Analyze the ethos you look for in others' writing. Choose two subjects, one of personal interest and one universal concern. Make a list of eight sources you respect as authoritative for each subject. Include sources from all three access locations listed on page 100.

✦ R E A D I N G   C R I T I C A L L Y
Constructing Credibility

It doesn't take long to access sources on the Internet, but finding quality sources to construct and reinforce your credibility in an essay or research paper may take longer than you expect. The selection below, which appeared in a search for articles on "skin cancer," was located at Prevention.com, a magazine affiliated Web site accessed through Women.com, a network of eighteen sites providing "content, community, commerce, and services that serve the diverse needs of the online woman today." The Prevention.com homepage includes full credentials for all the health column writers, full contact information for the publication, the main features in the current print version of the magazine, and an archive of the special reports issued over the past several years. The following special report, published on June 29, 1999, does not identify an author, so the reader must assume that the information presented was compiled by the editors from the many sources they have available. The author, then, is the organization, *Prevention* magazine. At the bottom of each screen/page of the report appears the following disclaimer: "Prevention.com is intended to heighten awareness of health information and does not suggest diagnosis or treatment. This information is not a substitute for medical attention. See your health-care professional for medical advice and treatment."

Rhetorical Context

◆ **Subject:** Skin cancer; melanoma

◆ **Occasion:** An increase in skin cancer cases

◆ **Audience:** Although the article is available to anyone using the Internet, this special report is intended for readers concerned with and responsible for their health. People sixteen-plus can easily read the article. Most will have a specific reason for focusing on the issue of skin cancer.

◆ **Purpose:** To inform the readers of the most current findings on detecting skin cancer

Readers' Expectations   The readers will have general knowledge of the effects of sun exposure on causing skin cancer and the need for using sunscreen from media coverage, personal experience, or both. The subject of detecting skin cancer, however, is probably less familiar. Readers will expect this report to guide them in obtaining accurate information from their doctor. Although no author is identified, readers should expect the information to be based on the views of authorities in this well-established consumer health publication.

✦ ✦ ✦

The Cancer Your Doctor May Miss

Prevention.com

Concrete personal experience.

1   When the freckle on Lisa Burton's upper arm started to change, she went to her family doctor. He said it was nothing. A few years later, when it became one of the warning signs of cancer (a sore that never healed), another doctor told her she had eczema.

Statistics from unnamed source.

2   It wasn't until eight years later, when she saw a dermatologist and insisted on a biopsy, that Lisa learned that her freckle was actually a melanoma. Every year, more than 41,000 people are diagnosed with melanoma and 7,300 people die from it.

3   Miraculously, even though more than a decade had passed since her symptoms first appeared, the diagnosis came in time to save Lisa's life. For that, she credits her own persistence.

4   It's a recipe that can work for you too. To beat melanoma, consider the following suggestions:

Get Checked

Talk to Your Dermatologist

The ABCD Rule

Evaluate Your Risk

1. See a Dermatologist

Summary of unnamed studies.

Statistics from unnamed source.

5   Studies have shown that dermatologists can identify melanomas with greater accuracy than nondermatologists. Yet only 40% of us take our skin complaints to these highly trained specialists.

6   Even doctors themselves recognize the problem. In a survey of 355 family physicians in the Toronto area, 56% said they lacked the confidence to identify melanoma, nearly 80% said they'd have trouble recognizing early or subtle lesions, and a shocking 72% didn't even know that an itchy mole can signal a malignancy *(Journal of the American Academy of Dermatology, Dec. 1997)*.

Cited study from professional journal.

7   You should see a dermatologist for a full-body screening at least once every three years between the ages of 20 and 40; annually if you're 41 or older.

Recommendations possible from cited study.

2. Do Self-Checks Regularly

8 About half of all melanomas are initially discovered by the patient. It's been estimated that regular skin self-examinations reduce death from melanoma by 63%.

Statistics from unnamed source.

9   Fact is, when confined to the upper skin layer, melanoma has a nearly 100% cure rate. Since melanoma can take anywhere from a couple of months to several years to grow deeper, take advantage of that window of opportunity by regularly checking your skin.

10   It's also important to listen to your gut feelings. If you have a suspicious mole that your doctor thinks is nothing, get a second opinion—fast. A good dermatologist can help you catch a melanoma in its curable stages.

General reference.

An Ideal Dermatologist Will

11 . . . have 10-plus years of experience. As expected, dues-paying pays off. In a recent study, dermatologists who had 10 or more years of clinical experience showed an accuracy rate of 80% in diagnosing melanoma, higher than that of senior and junior trainees *(British Journal of Dermatology, Feb. 1998)*.

Cited study from professional journal.

12   . . . ask these questions: Have you noticed any new moles or a change in the size, color, shape, or sensation of a preexisting mole? Is there a history of skin cancer in your family?

13   Do you tend to burn? What is your history with sunburns? Few or many? Severe or mild?

14   . . . check every inch. Melanoma can occur on any part of your skin, including areas that rarely see the sun, such

Summary of unnamed studies.

as the scalp and the bottoms of your feet. Studies have shown that patients who undergo full-body skin exams are 6.4 times more likely to have a melanoma detected than those receiving partial exams.

An Ideal Dermatologist Will

Acknowledged professional authority.

... use the ABCD rule. The American Academy of Dermatology's ABCD checklist is the suggested tool for determining if a lesion is malignant. Moles with any one of these features have melanoma potential: 15

> Asymmetry: one-half doesn't match the other
>
> Border: irregularity (ragged, notched, or blurred edges)

Paraphrased material.

> Color: variation (shades of tan, brown, and black—or even red, blue, or white!)
>
> Diameter: greater than ¼-inch—the size of a pencil eraser

A recently proposed amendment to this rule includes "E" for elevation or enlargement.   16

General reference.

Other warning signs can include itching, bleeding, tenderness, or crusting of the mole's surface.   17

Melanoma can occur on any part of your skin, including areas that rarely see sun, such as the scalp and the bottoms of your feet.   18

Are You at Risk?

You may be susceptible to melanoma and not even know it. Here's an easy way to find out. This memory device—   19

Acknowledgment phrase for professional expert.

created by Thomas Fitzpatrick, MD, professor emeritus of dermatology at Harvard Medical School in Boston—spells out (Malignant) Melanoma's RISK factors: Consider each a red flag.

> Moles that are atypical (just one doubles your risk)
>
> Moles that are numerous
>
> Red hair or freckles
>
> Inability to tan

Sunburns (particularly severe ones before age 14)

Kindred (family history of melanoma)

Melanoma Prevention Checklist

20 Avoid sun as much as possible between 10 am and 4 pm.

Wear a waterproof sunscreen with an SPF of at least 15   Summary.
and full UVB/UVA protection.

Check your skin regularly.

Know your family history.

Know the warning signs of melanoma.

See a dermatologist at least once every three years for
a thorough head-to-toe skin check (annually if you're
41 or older).

Related stories:

21 Sun Smarts   Additional sources.

Vitamins for Sunburn

Skin Care Resource Center

Soothe Sunburn Naturally

Preventing Age Spots.

✦ ✦ ✦

Evaluating an Internet Source:
"The Cancer Your Doctor May Miss"

✦ **Author** No one person is identified as the author, so readers
must assume the editors of *Prevention* compiled the information
from available sources. The credentials of the publication's writers, available on the Web site, indicate that they have degrees and
expertise in their fields. Readers can assume the information is
based on authority. An e-mail address is included if readers want
to contact the editors about the article.

✦ **Occasion** Each page contains the date the article was published
and the date of access so readers can verify the currency of the

information. The publication wants to keep readers well informed and continue their reputation as a credible source.

◆ **Subject** *Title:* By announcing that this cancer may be undetected by doctors, the title immediately involves the reader in discovering why there is a problem.

Complexity: The article is relatively short but full of information clearly presented by the use of headings, numbers, and a list of guidelines on each page so readers can easily navigate forward or back for quick reference. Lots of active white space between paragraphs is used for high readability.

Supporting Sources: The report includes a balance of sources cited from professional journals and authorities with summaries of data from unnamed studies. No direct quotes are used. At the end of the report links to related stories that appeared in *Prevention* are listed for readers to consult.

◆ **Audience** *Assumptions:* The editors who compiled the report assume that the readers have a general knowledge of the subject and an interest in living a healthy lifestyle. The editors and the readers share a concern for being aware of health problems and being well informed when consulting health-care professionals.

◆ **Purpose** *Title:* The editors express concern in the title that immediately involves the readers in identifying the problems with detecting skin cancer. The informative, conversational tone puts the reader at ease—a sign of goodwill when discussing health issues. On each page/section of the report there is a tool for sending that page to a friend—the opportunity to inform others.

Point of View and Voice: The editors use an objective point of view and an informal voice. By directly addressing the audience with "you," they maintain the informal voice created by average-length sentences, familiar word choice, occasional direct questions, and contractions. The focus is on the subject and material to inform the readers.

Sources and Audience Values: The editors incorporate a variety of sources, from personal experience and summarized data from unnamed studies to authoritative citations from professionals. The effect is one of balance that maintains the objective point of view and informal tone and appeals to the readers' need for greater awareness. If readers want a higher level of information, they can consult the professional journals cited in the report; if they want more general information, they can link to the related stories.

Overall, the report establishes a comfortable credibility with the reader and encourages the reader to be informed before consulting a health-care professional. The citations from the professional journals provide excellent starting points for locating more extensive explanations and bibliographic materials to conduct more in-depth research.

✦ON YOUR OWN
Analyzing the Writer's Choices

The following article also appeared on the Internet. The article, which appeared in a subject search for "alcohol and health," was found on the Presbyterian Church USA Web site (www.pcusa.org), which includes links to external news sources. The following article, published November 16, 1998, was indexed in the "Action Alert" section. The Washington Office of the PCUSA General Assembly issued this "Action Alert" for the purpose of informing the regular readership on the argument underlying the proposed new labeling on wine and to urge the readers to take action.

Use the evaluation scheme on page 115 to determine how the organizational author establishes credibility. Summarize your evaluation in a paragraph and identify in what context it would be appropriate to use this source to construct credibility.

✦ ✦ ✦

Proposed New Labeling Implies Wine Has Health Benefits

p c u s a . o r g

1   **ISSUE**   The Bureau of Alcohol, Tobacco and Firearms, part of the U.S. Treasury Department, is again considering a proposal for new labels for wine bottles that will imply to consumers that there are

health benefits to be had from drinking wine. These labels would state: "To learn the health effects of moderate wine consumption, send for the Federal Government's Dietary Guidelines for Americans." IF YOU DISAGREE WITH THE PROPOSAL TO USE SUCH A LABEL, write to the Treasury Department and to the Bureau of Alcohol, Tobacco and Firearms asking that they reject the wine labels that make health claims.

BACKGROUND   Over the past several years, the alcoholic beverage with the fastest growing consumption is wine. Of all alcohol drunk with a meal, 50 percent is wine, 35 percent is beer and 15 percent is hard liquor. Much of that growth has come as a result of an ongoing campaign by the wine industry to convince people that drinking wine will improve one's health. 2

This campaign has been based on a variety of scientific studies that show that the consumption of a moderate amount of alcohol may reduce the chances of a heart attack for some people. At the same time, however, there is overwhelming evidence that for many others, any drinking may be unhealthy or risk-laden. Even for people who might benefit from moderate drinking, the risks outweigh the benefits as consumption increases. 3

More than a year ago, the Wine Institute went to the Bureau of Alcohol, Tobacco and Firearms for permission to allow wineries to make indirect "health claims" for drinking wine. Advocacy efforts by those who oppose alcohol abuse have so far stymied plans to sell wine as a health food. The label application is now on "indefinite hold." 4

ACTION   Write to the Treasury Department and to the Bureau of Alcohol, Tobacco and Firearms, asking that they reject the proposed wine health claim labels. 5

Secretary Robert Rubin
U.S. Department of Treasury
1500 Pennsylvania Ave., NW
Washington, DC 20220

Mr. John W. Magaw, Director
Bureau of Alcohol, Tobacco and Firearms
650 Massachusetts Avenue, NW
Washington, DC 20226

TALKING POINTS

6   **1.** The existing mandated warning labels currently caution that alcohol consumption during pregnancy may lead to birth defects. IT IS IMPORTANT NOT TO UNDERCUT THIS MESSAGE.

7   A recent study by the federal Centers for Disease Control and Prevention found that drinking by pregnant women, the cause of fetal alcohol syndrome, is increasing. The authors of that study suggested that " . . . exposure to recent reports on the health benefits of moderate drinking may have contributed to the recent increase in alcohol consumption."

8   **2.** The current version of the Dietary Guidelines was released in 1995. Since then, new research has become available linking "moderate" drinking, particularly by pre-menopausal women, with an increased incidence of breast cancer. The studies indicate that the risk of breast cancer begins to increase at consumption levels as small as one drink per day. The 1995 Dietary Guidelines do not warn women of this risk, and so any label referring to those guidelines would neglect that critical information.

9   **3.** Last spring, as part of the initial consideration of the Wine Institute's request, the Bureau of Alcohol, Tobacco and Firearms asked the Center for Substance Abuse Prevention (CSAP) to conduct a study of how consumers might react to the proposed labels. That study found that 88 percent of existing wine drinkers would not drink more in response to the new labels. This study is now being used as evidence that the proposed labels would not trigger a public health problem.

10   That CSAP study has two major shortcomings:

- It only tested people who were already wine drinkers. Representatives of the wine industry have been quoted in various industry publications as saying that they hope that the information about "health benefits" will attract new wine drinkers. The CSAP study excluded any look at whether or not proposed health claims would persuade non-drinkers to begin drinking wine.

- The study found that few consumers would heed the suggestion of the proposed label and actually consult the Dietary Guidelines to see what the document said.

4. The proposed label refers to "moderate wine consumption." It 11
   does not define the word moderate. In general it has been found
   that most people define "moderate consumption" as whatever
   they already do. In essence, the term "moderate" has no specific
   meaning.

5. When people consume more than one to two drinks of alcohol 12
   a day, they are at risk for other health problems. The U.S. Dietary
   Guidelines warn that "higher levels of alcohol intake raise the
   risk for high blood pressure, stroke, heart disease, certain cancers, accidents, suicides, birth defects, and overall mortality. Too
   much alcohol may cause cirrhosis of the liver, inflammation of
   the pancreas and damage to the brain and heart." One or two
   drinks a day and interaction with medication may result in a potential health risk.

GENERAL ASSEMBLY GUIDANCE The 1986 General As- 13
sembly adopted a report on "The Social and Health Effects of Alcohol Use and Abuse." Included in the section on "Why Focus on
Alcohol Alone and on Public Policy?" is that a previous General Assembly had requested the focus and that alcohol is a legal product.

This comprehensive report states: ". . . The General Assembly 14
encourages and supports personal decisions to abstain from alcohol.
For those who choose to drink and can do so without becoming
dependent, the General Assembly urges a pattern of moderate and
responsible drinking behavior. Finally, the General Assembly rec-
ommends and supports a comprehensive public policy approach to
regulate the availability and use of alcohol in a manner consistent
with its special character and the potential risk to persons and society inherent in its use and it continues to recommend and support
appropriate treatment of all who are affected by alcohol-related
problems."

General principles include: "moderate drinking in low-risk situ- 15
ations should not be opposed" and "effective public policy measures
designed to make alcohol less readily available and less attractive,
particularly to vulnerable groups or in high-risk situations, should
be encouraged and supported."

FOR YOUR INFORMATION The National Institute on Alco- 16
hol Abuse and Alcoholism and the Center for Substance Abuse Prevention have launched a long-term program to study the effects of

alcohol advertising on underage youth. Alcohol producers maintain that their advertising efforts do not encourage underage drinking, despite the clear appeal of the Budweiser frogs and the Miller penguins to adolescents and children.

17   Congress has also required the Federal Trade Commission to investigate the advertising of alcohol to young people. The Commission recently issued groundbreaking special orders to major alcohol producers requesting information about their youth advertising practices.

18   In response to a surge of reported alcohol problems on college campuses, the Higher Education Act was changed to provide incentives for college administrations to combat binge drinking.

19   Despite these victories, there are still challenges ahead. The White House Office of National Drug Control Policy has launched a major anti-drug youth media campaign which almost totally ignores alcohol—despite the reality that alcohol is the leading drug of abuse and leading drug killer among young people in this country. Also the U.S. Department of Health and Human Services should be urged to focus more attention on alcohol issues, ranging from developing media spots to de-glamorize underage drinking to responding publicly to industry propaganda regarding moderate drinking and health.

20   Additional information can be obtained from:

Alcohol Policies Project
Center for Science in the Public Interest
1875 Connecticut Avenue, NW, Suite 300
Washington, DC 20009–5728
Tel. (202) 332-9110, ext. 385
E-mail: alcproject@cspinet.org
www.csinet.orgi/booze

If you have any questions, please contact Bernadine Grant McRipley at (202) 543-1126 or by e-mail at bmcripley@ctr.pcusa.org.

part two

◆ ◆

Readings

In this section you will find seven chapters of readings, each on a topic undergoing changes in the way people view them: "Choosing Heroes," "Finding Community," "Exploring Cyberspace," "Making Health Decisions," "Re-Viewing Media," "Defining Environmental Ethics," and "Speculating on the New Century." These readings serve two purposes.

First, the diverse opinions and experiences the writers present in each chapter form a conversation on the topic intended to provoke your participation as a reader. Reading with an "able eye," as illustrated in the Introduction, encourages you to read both *with* and *against* the writer, to know more about what you think and how you form your own opinions.

Second, the questions following each reading direct you to read the selections as a writer. By closely examining the choices writers make, you will gain practice in making decisions in your own writing. The diversity in audience, purpose, and occasion in the readings provides different rhetorical problems to solve in choosing the point of view, shape, voice, and credibility needed to establish an interactive relationship with the intended readers. The chapters in Part One of this book will guide you in identifying and analyzing those choices.

Finally, at the end of each chapter you will find writing suggestions designed to combine the two purposes: expressing your views on a topic and making deliberate writing choices in presenting those views to different audiences and for diverse purposes.

Chapter 6

Choosing Heroes

Heroes have always been a part of the American way of life, or so it seems. A walk through a city park or even a small town square will produce a statue or plaque commemorating the actions of someone who contributed significantly to that specific geographic location, the region, or the nation. Biographies provide another source for identifying heroes. Our elementary school years generally introduce us to the lives of famous inventors, explorers, and presidents—all people no longer living. As adults, we find the biographies and autobiographies of "the living" competing for our attention; record-breaking feats in sports, overcoming personal tragedy, or achieving box office fame can inspire hero worship today. Some would argue that our choice of heroes has changed, that as our country has developed as a nation so, too, has our need for heroes.

The readings in this section raise many questions about heroes: who they are, why we have them, what criteria determine hero quality. To begin the chapter, Edelstein lays a foundation for understanding how changing social conditions affect our need for certain kinds of heroes; then Reynolds and Melendez examine the mythological dimensions underlying popular culture heroes; Ehrenreich questions how society's ideology excludes the selection of women as heroes; Bernstein, Peterson, Didion, Daley, and Hagedorn analyze character issues; and Truth exemplifies heroism through word and deed.

These readings represent a diverse range of contexts: academics, students, journalists, and politicians conveying their ideas to a variety of audiences. Each context requires the writer to make specific choices in point of view, structure, voice, and sources to establish credibility. The questions that follow each reading will help you to examine the choices these writers make and to determine how effectively those choices connect the readers to the writers' ideas.

Read each selection with an "able eye," paying close attention to how the writer's choices influence the way in which you interact with the text. Remember that as a reader, you are an integral part of the writer's decisions. Read *with* and *against* the writer to determine where and why your ideas differ. At the end of the chapter you will find Writing Suggestions for responding to the ideas presented in the readings.

No More Heroes

Alan Edelstein

✦ ✦ ✦

Alan Edelstein, associate professor of sociology at Towson State University, makes a bold claim in the title of the book from which this excerpt is taken: Everybody Is Sitting on the Curb: How and Why America's Heroes Disappeared. *To prove his point, Edelstein presents a 250-page study of the changing social conditions and social systems in America that he believes have altered Americans' values, aspirations, and expectations. In the excerpt below from the first chapter of the book, Edelstein lays the foundation for defining the qualities a person must achieve to become a national hero and the conditions that undermine the possibility.*

Introduction

The United States has run out of heroes. "Hero" refers to a national hero, a Universal American around whom we all would rally if called. The hero is the man—rarely the woman, a point to be considered later—who inspires children and adults, who reflects the finest qualities of the American people, and who is recognized by the American people as an inspiration and as someone who reflects those qualities. It is not just that the hero represents most if not all Americans; it is that most if not all Americans are happy to have him as their representative. That is the man who is gone from our lives—and permanently.

Nor are there any arenas from which a modern American hero can arise. Quite the contrary, many of the fields from which Americans drew their past heroes are gone, and the structures of other fields that were once sources of American heroes have been altered to the point of obstructing the creation of new heroes.

The argument here is not that there aren't heroic people in the United States anymore. Americans perform heroic acts every day. A glance at any local newspaper testifies to that assertion. "Ordinary" men and women in this country regularly perform extraordinary feats of courage and self-sacrifice. As a matter of course members of local police and fire departments save lives while risking their own. Federal agents who place themselves in danger combatting drug traffickers, the men and women of our armed forces, and the people who work in emergency rooms of big city hospitals are only some of the Americans who routinely perform actions that can only be called heroic.

4   But these heroic actions do not necessarily make them heroes. They are performed as a function of the job and in that sense they are not extraordinary. More important, these heroic actions, brave and self-sacrificing as they may be, are generally acknowledged locally, not nationally. To be a hero is to be a national hero, and to be a national hero is to have national recognition. If this were not the case the "American hero" would be defined by a small number of people, by a few individuals living within a limited geographical area. The American hero would be reduced to idiosyncratic and compartmentalized whim.

5   To avoid this possibility, the respect and admiration of people throughout the United States is a requisite for status as an American hero. The only way to become a national hero is to accomplish something that demands and receives national recognition. But that doesn't seem to happen anymore. It is difficult to recall the last ticker-tape parade for an individual American hero. Ticker-tape parades these days celebrate groups: freed hostages, winning ball teams, returning service personnel. Even those who courageously helped in the rescue of the people trapped after the explosion of the Federal Building in Oklahoma City were admired collectively. The individual American hero has vanished.

6   Americans generally agree that we no longer have any heroes, that the giants that once dominated our history in various arenas no longer exist, and that no new heroes have risen in their place. That is one reason why Americans today look backward for their heroes. Tales of politicians and military men, gunfighters and sports figures, gangsters and adventurers, idols and celebrities of not so recent history, are constantly relived in movies and on television, and the images of past heroes are regularly shown on calendars and posters. We recall our past heroes with great enthusiasm because there aren't any contemporary heroes of equal stature to take their place.

7   So uncertain is the status of hero in the United States today that even some of our traditional heroes have come into question. In part this is because of "political correctness," but in part it is because of a diminishing reverence for and increasing cynicism toward heroes generally. A list of America's heroes who are under attack include

Columbus, perhaps the easiest example, who has gone from being "the discoverer of America" to being a butcher of innocents, a cruel and inept conqueror, a symbol of genocide. Since his assassination John Kennedy has been idolized, but he has also been vilified to the point where Douglas Brinkley regards some of the attacks on his memory as approaching a "vendetta." Albert Einstein, the twentieth century's symbol of intellectual greatness, has been accused of being "an adulterous, egomaniacal misogynist." And Walt Disney, who made his reputation by making wholesome films for the whole family to enjoy, was, according to a biography—an "unauthorized" one, obviously—impotent, anti-Semitic, and an alcoholic. Further, he "never actually drew Mickey Mouse."[1]

There have been attacks on George Washington, a slave owner; on Thomas Jefferson, a racist and slave owner (Washington freed his slaves, Jefferson didn't); on Paul Revere, who never did reach Concord (and the celebrated midnight ride may have been a sham); on Abraham Lincoln, who, in addition to telling stories that were racist, knowingly dealt with dishonest politicians; and on the defenders of the Alamo, who were at best liars and at worst cowardly. 8

None of the efforts at demythifying the heroes of America's past has succeeded as of yet, and it is unlikely that the images of idols such as Washington, Jefferson, or Lincoln, to select the most obvious examples, will be destroyed. Still, the efforts to harm their memories do exist, and there can be no doubt that the legends of some of America's past icons will suffer. Future generations will have fewer traditional heroes to admire, if they have any at all. 9

There is ample proof, both anecdotal and substantive, that the United States no longer has any heroes, nor has the ability to produce new ones. Numerous people have gone on record suggesting that the American hero has vanished. Both historian Arthur Schlesinger, Jr., and political scientist Larry Nachman, for example, argue that we live in an era that is void of heroes. Our lives are no longer filled with and controlled by great men. Kenneth Clark, the noted psychologist, argues that regardless of the field, the time of the national hero is past. Others agree that we no longer create heroes in the United States. Daniel Boorstin dislikes those who today are feted but who are simply " manufactured" heroes of our time, and Kim McQuaid calls his study of the Vietnam/Watergate Era a "history without heroes."[2] 10

11   People as diverse in attitudes and personality as Tom Wolfe and Jimmy Carter, Norman Mailer and Mike Royko concur: there is today a paucity of heroes in the United States—virtually none. Royko argues that today's role models are no match for those of America's past and Mailer suggests that there's no one left to "capture the secret imagination of a people and so be good for the vitality of his nation." Jimmy Carter has noted that ours is "an age of few heroes." Tom Wolfe agrees, adding that the situation is not going to improve in the foreseeable future. Russell Baker in his *New York Times* column has suggested that "heroes are pretty well all washed up in America these days," while Walter Turett Anderson, writing in the *UTNE Reader*, asked have we "outgrown the age of heroes?" A *Newsweek* magazine article is titled "In Search of Heroes." The author of the article, Peter H. Gibbon, is not optimistic about the success of the search. Writing in *The New Yorker*, Bill Buford notes that "ours is not a time of heroes," and a play by Sam Shepard has one character noting the rapid death of our heroes; the reason: "it's a sign a' the times."[3]

12   Another indication that people are aware that the American hero has vanished is discernible from contemporary literature. An amazing number of books and articles published in the United States, both fiction and nonfiction, are titled or subtitled "the last hero," an obvious indication that the authors believe that there are no heroes left in the country, that the subject of the book or article was or is America's final hero. An equally impressive number of books and articles wonder where America's heroes have gone. Some call attention to individuals the authors believe should be regarded as national heroes but who are unknown to most people. There are writers who come right to the point. Edward Hoagland, Joshua Meyrowitz, Don Wycliff, and Daniel Walden all ask the same question: What has happened? Where did America's heroes go?[4]

13   Most important of all, the American people do not think that the United States has any heroes. This attitude on the part of the people is of special significance because a hero, and especially an American hero, is a social creation. The American hero is, and can only be, a consequence of the attitudes of the American people: a hero is a hero only because the people say he is. The denial of the existence of an American hero by the American people, then, is critical because their denial is the final statement about the subject.

14   And they do deny the hero. A survey published in *Time* magazine pointed out that only two men were regarded as heroes to people be-

tween the ages of 18 and 44, Robert Kennedy and Martin Luther King, Jr., both dead more than twenty years at the time the survey was taken. That may be why President Clinton evoked their memories in a speech in May 1994. They were the last people who could be celebrated by the nation. In the years since the *Time* survey was taken no one has been elevated to the status of Kennedy or King in the eyes of the American people. A more recent *Time*/CNN poll indicated that younger Americans cannot agree upon a hero. On a broader level, one study revealed that fully 70 percent of the people—seven out of every ten Americans—believe that we no longer have any living heroes. That percentage is unlikely to improve in time. If anything, the number of Americans who believe in an American hero will diminish. Because the American hero is a product of the beliefs of the American people, and as Americans believe that we no longer have American heroes, ipso facto, we no longer have any American heroes.[5]

Arthur Schlesinger, Jr., is incorrect in suggesting that our age "objects" to heroes (as well as to hero worship). It doesn't object to heroes, it just can't find any. The United States still searches for heroes, still seeks them out. On occasion the search borders on the frenetic. In fact, the public demand for heroes is so extensive that there are advertisements for them. *Parade* magazine asked people to nominate an unsung hero so that he might receive national recognition, and *Newsweek* magazine ran an advertisement from *America's Awards* asking people to "send us a story of your hero." The cover of an earlier issue of *Parade* magazine featured a picture of John F. Kennedy's children; the accompanying article had them asking the public to "Help Us Find A Hero."[6]   15

The Carnegie Hero Fund located in Pittsburgh, Pennsylvania, is dedicated to identifying, locating, and rewarding individuals throughout the country who have performed heroic deeds. The fund has specific criteria to determine who qualifies as a hero and stipulates that those whose "vocations require them to perform [heroic] acts" are ineligible to receive the award. There are exceptions to the rule however: those who perform acts of courage that are "clearly beyond the line of duty" may be regarded as heroes. A second organization, The Giraffe Project based in Washington, D.C., also recognizes heroes, specifically "local heroes who stick their necks out to make the world a better place." Although more subjective in its judgment than the   16

Carnegie Hero Fund and limited geographically because it looks for local heroes, the idea is the same: seek out and recognize heroes.[7]

17 The media are doing their part to find contemporary American heroes. One television program (on the Arts & Entertainment network) was in fact called "Heroes" and ABC has its "Person of the Week," a weekly segment of ABC's national news broadcast designed to demonstrate to us that we still are capable of producing heroes, people of consequence. It is not at all unusual for a "Movie of the Week" or for television magazine shows (or print magazines, for that matter) to tell the story of an unheralded individual who accomplished something praiseworthy. Newspapers also contribute to the effort to find and to call attention to potential national heroes. Sunday supplements regularly include stories detailing the exploits of an unknown individual who risked life and limb for a significant purpose. This is all fine and the individuals considered here surely deserve their place in the sun. But as heroic as their efforts are, and as noble as the efforts of the media are to celebrate those efforts, they cannot hide the fact that the United States no longer has any heroes.

Notes

Abbreviations

NYT—*New York Times*
NYTM—*New York Times Magazine*
NYTBR—*New York Times Book Review*
NYRB—*New York Review of Books*
BES—*The (Baltimore) Evening Sun*
TBS—*The Baltimore Sun*

1. *NYT*, October 6, 1991, p. H 2; *Insight*, October 21, 1991, pp. 11–17. *NYTM*, October 31, 1993, p. 33 and *Newsweek*, July 26, 1993, p. 44. *NYT*, March 29, 1994, p. A 10. *NYTM*, October 31, 1993, p. 33. *Newsweek*, July 26, 1993, p. 44.
2. Schlesinger, "The Decline of Heroes," in *Heroes and Anti-Heroes*, ed. Harold Lubin (Scranton, Pa.: Chandler Publishing, 1968), p. 341; ibid., p. 322. Clark is cited in Don Wycliff, "Where Have All the Heroes Gone?" *NYTM*, July 31, 1985, p. 23; Boorstin, "From Hero to Celebrity," in Lubin, p. 327; Nachman, "Thoughts on Heroism," *The World and I*, February 1988, p. 547. McQuaid, *The Anxious Years: America in the Vietnam-Watergate Era* (New York: Basic Books, 1989), p. ix.
3. Wolfe, in *Time* magazine, February 13, 1989, p. 90; Mailer, in Richard Schickel, *Intimate Strangers: The Culture of Celebrity* (New York: Double-

day & Company, 1985), p. 172. Royko, in *BES*, July 2, 1993, p. 2 A; The *UTNE Reader*, May/June, 1993, p. 95; President Carter, in Peter N. Carrol, *It Seemed Like Nothing Happened* (New York: Holt, Rinehart and Winston, 1982), p. 172. See also *Newsweek* magazine, January 18, 1993; the quote from the Shepard play is given in an article by Marilyn Stasio, *NYTBR*, October 14, 1990, p. 1. Bill Buford, in *The New Yorker*, June 26/July 3, 1995, p. 12.

4. Hoagland, in *NYTM*, March 10, 1984; Meyrowitz, in *Psychology Today*, July 1984; Wycliff, in *NYTM*, July 1, 1985; Walden, "Life in America," *USA Today*, January 1986.

5. *Time* magazine, May 9, 1988, p. 46 and *Time* magazine, July 16,1990, p. 23. James Patterson and Peter Kim, *The Day America Told the Truth: What People Really Believe about Everything That Really Matters* (Englewood Cliffs, N. J.: Prentice-Hall, 1991) p. 207.

6. Schlesinger, in Lubin, p. 343. *Parade* magazine, March 15, 1992, p. 6 and February 25, 1990; *Newsweek* magazine, February 17, 1992, p. 27.

7. The quote explaining the criteria for awards from the Carnegie Hero Fund comes from their 1991 *Annual Report;* data on the Giraffe Project from *The Giraffe Gazette*, vol. 2, no. 1 (Winter 1991).

✦ ✦ ✦

✦ Framing the Context

1. Edelstein begins his introduction with a bold claim and definition. What relationship is this approach likely to establish with his intended educated, academic audience? Explain why.

2. Based on paragraphs 1–5, how would you state Edelstein's purpose?

✦ Point of View

3. Although Edelstein uses the pronoun "we" twice in paragraph 6, what point of view dominates this introduction to Chapter 1? Cite examples of the characteristics that indicate his point of view choice.

4. In what ways is Edelstein's choice of point of view appropriate to the intended readers' relationship to the subject of lost heroes?

✦ Shape of Ideas

5. At the end of paragraphs 5, 10, and 14, Edelstein inserts additional space between paragraphs. How does this strategy fit his framework for connecting the readers to his purpose?

6. From the shape of information Edelstein presents, particularly in the layers used in paragraphs 10–17, what can you surmise Edelstein assumes his readers *need* to know?

✦ *Choosing Voice*

7. In what ways does the formality of Edelstein's voice match his chosen point of view? Cite examples in his use of language that indicate this relationship.

8. At the end of paragraphs 5, 9, 14, and 17, Edelstein concludes with a similar statement. How does this repetition and positioning contribute to Edelstein's voice, and what effect does it have on the intended readers?

✦ *Credibility*

9. In paragraph 10, Edelstein identifies the profession of his first three references, but in the remainder of that paragraph and in paragraphs 11 and 12 he does not identify the people to whom he refers. What assumptions does Edelstein make about his readers' background and how do these assumptions affect his credibility?

10. Social scientists often cite their sources by placing superscript numbers at the end of a paragraph that includes many sources and explaining those sources in the "Notes" section at the end of the text. Examine Edelstein's use of this system and explain how it is likely to affect his credibility with the intended readers.

A Long Time Ago in a Galaxy Not So Far Away

Alexander Melendez

✦ ✦ ✦

Does the classical view of the hero still influence our image of the hero today? To answer this question, Alexander Melendez explores the parallels between Achilles, hero of The Illiad, *and Luke Skywalker, hero of* Star Wars. *In this documented position student essay written for his freshman composition course, Melendez illustrates the similarities between the two heroes in an effort to understand why that classical image endures.*

A cloud of dust billows in the distance. The great Trojan Hector stands at the gates of his home citadel awaiting the chariot of the mighty Greek hero Achilles. Achilles charges toward his arch nemesis with unshakable resolve. Athena appears before him and fuels his rage by saying, "At last our hopes run high, my brilliant Achilles . . . We'll kill this Hector, mad as he is for battle" (*Illiad* 22.256–260)!

Achilles pursues Hector around the walls of Troy. Hector runs, determined not to face Achilles' lethal wrath. He continues to run until the goddess Athena appears to him as his brother. Hector stops to speak to him and Achilles takes advantage of the situation. A mythic battle ensues. Swords clash, spears fly, armor is pierced and flesh is rent asunder. In a final fit of passionate rage, Achilles impales Hector's throat upon his spear, irrevocably snuffing out his life. Achilles stands alone before the gates of the soon to be ruined Troy.

Now, shift the image to the unforgiving cold of space. A huge spherical battle station, the Death Star, capable of annihilating an entire planet in the blink of an eye, looms over a battle amongst the stars. The Imperial forces are protecting the station as the Rebel Alliance, a small band of dissidents opposing Imperial rule, attempts to destroy it. Star fighters blaze to and fro, destroying one another with reckless abandon. In one of the Rebel fighters sits Luke Skywalker, a young hero who is among the last of the mighty Jedi Knights, preparing to make a final run on the Death Star in an attempt to destroy it. Directly in front of him is the sinister Dark Jedi, Darth Vader, lord of the Imperial forces, in a ship far superior to Luke's. Darth Vader's ship fires bolts of wicked green energy at Luke's ship, scorching its surface. Young Skywalker enters the immense trench running through the middle equator of the Death Star, and initiates his targeting computer. At his rear is Darth Vader, who is targeting Luke and preparing to destroy him with a blast from his laser cannons. A laser beam blasts out from nowhere and strikes Vader's ship, knocking it off course and sending it careening out of control. It is Han Solo, in his ship the *Millenium Falcon*. Over the communications link, Han shouts to Luke, "Come on kid, let's blow this thing and go home!" (*Star Wars: A New Hope*, 1977).

4   Tensions are riding high, and Luke hears the voice of his dead mentor, slain by Darth Vader, the Jedi Master Obi-Wan Kenobi through the void between this world and the next, beckoning him to trust his senses, and not the computer in front of him, "Use the Force, Luke!" (*Star Wars: A New Hope*, 1977).

5   Luke turns off his targeting system and reaches out with the mysterious power of the Force. He closes his eyes and presses a button on the ship's console. Two gleaming red photon torpedoes stream from Luke's ship and strike their target, causing a chain reaction within the Death Star, destroying it. Luke's ship floats alone amidst the debris of the once grand battle station. Darth Vader is nowhere to be seen.

6   There is an unmistakable similarity in these two seemingly detached examples. Homer's epic poem *The Illiad* reaches through time. It tells us a story of a hero who was a cut above the rest, blessed by the gods, a stalwart warrior who was able to overcome insurmountable odds and bring victory to his cause. The *Star Wars* trilogy tells us a similar story of a hero who was more than an average man, attuned to the mystical energies of the Force, yet another warrior who overcomes insurmountable odds and brings victory to his cause. *The Illiad* provides a literary base for the plot and characters of *Star Wars* in the aspects of the heroic elements portrayed by both Achilles and Luke Skywalker, locations that are undeniably corresponding, such as the Death Star and the citadel of Troy, in the respect that the two are both areas of immense power contained in relatively small areas, and the value placed heroism by both the Greeks and our contemporary society.

7   In order to comprehend most clearly how contemporary writers use Achillean motifs to animate their own heroes, it is necessary to have a thorough understanding of how these motifs function in the

Illiadic portrait, which became archetypal because of Homer's great authority (King 3). The task is therefore to set forth these motifs—many of which for centuries had the power to instantly evoke Achilles in the reader's mind—and to discuss them in the context of Homer's conception of his hero.

There are four elements to the Homeric paradigm for the literary hero. The first of these is swiftness (King 3). The speed of Achilles is impressed upon us over and over throughout the course of the epic. Three epithets are constantly used to refer to his speed. He is thirty-one times, twenty-one times, and eleven times—"swift footed Achilles" (King 3). We are told that no one man can rival Achilles in running (*Illiad* 13.324–325). Achilles' great speed is what assists him in his lethally efficient warcraft in books XXI and XXII when Achilles chases the stampeding Trojans nearly to the gates of Troy and when Hector, even with the help of Apollo, cannot outrun his maddened pursuer and escape to the protection of the city walls. This is paralleled in *Star Wars* in Luke Skywalker's natural attunement to the energies of the Force. In *Star Wars: A New Hope*, Obi-Wan Kenobi and Luke are aboard the starship the *Millenium Falcon,* training in the ways of the Force. As a Jedi Master, Obi-Wan Kenobi takes it upon himself to show Luke all of the skills a Jedi knight needs to master in order to become one with the Force. In the training exercise they are engaging in, a small spherical object about the size of a fist looms over Luke's head, firing minuscule laser beams at him. Luke, with his lightsaber, the weapon of a Jedi knight in hand, attempts to deflect the little bolts of energy while blindfolded, using only the shimmering blue blade of energy. The unit fires one, two, and three bolts, and Luke, reaching out with the Force, slicing the air with his lightsaber, blocks all three of the blazing laser strikes in less than a second. Luke used physical prowess and the power of the Force to complete his training, just as Achilles used physical prowess and the grace of the gods to complete the tasks he had at hand.

The next element in the Homeric paradigm is physical attractiveness. In the *Illiad,* we know Achilles is attractive because we are told it over and over again throughout the text. There even seems to be one character, Nireus, whose sole purpose seems to be to mark Achilles' extraordinary beauty (King 3). The first we hear about Achilles' beauty is, oddly enough, the first time this character appears: "Nireus came beneath Illium the most beautiful man of all the Danaans after the flawless Achilles" (*Illiad* 2.671–674).

8

9

10   Because the relative attractiveness or unattractiveness of a person is subjective, one must refer to a set of standards set forth by society in order to judge whether or not the hero in question meets the standard of physical beauty. According to fashion designer Enrico Fendi, the ideal male is six feet in height, slender and well-defined, not overly muscular, with light hair and dark eyes. The question now is does Luke Skywalker fit the contemporary paradigm of physical attractiveness for a male. Luke Skywalker is six feet tall, slender and well-defined, not overly muscular, with blonde hair and deep blue eyes. If we base the premise of physical beauty on the above paradigm, Luke fits the bill perfectly. Both Achilles and Luke Skywalker meet the second element of the Homeric paradigm for the literary hero.

11   The third element in the Homeric paradigm is youth. When Achilles left for war, he was, according to the character Phoinix, "a child, inexperienced in battle or assembly, where men become distinguished" (*Illiad* 9.440–441).

12   Nine years, twelve sacked cities, and presumably many "assemblies" later, Achilles firmly takes his place among men as the "'speaker of words and doer of deeds' that Phoinix was sent to teach him to be" (*Illiad* 9.442–443).

13   In the *Star Wars* trilogy, Luke Skywalker is consistently referred to as "young," whether it is by his mentor Obi-wan Kenobi, or by his arch nemesis Darth Vader. Luke's youth is akin to Achilles' youth because both are a surprise to enemies and mentors. Just as Phoinix was surprised at Achilles' success in war, Darth Vader was shocked by young Skywalker's battle prowess. Near the end of *Star Wars: The Empire Strikes Back,* Darth Vader and young Skywalker are dueling with lightsabers. Luke, an excellent swordsman with little practice behind him, deflects blow after vicious blow from the glimmering blood-red blade of the skilled warrior. After a few frustrating exchanges, Darth Vader breaks off his assault and comments, "Impressive. The Force is with you, young Skywalker, but you are not a Jedi yet" (*Star Wars: The Empire Strikes Back,* 1980).

14   Luke Skywalker earns the respect of his most hated enemy by being proficient in the art of battle at a very early age. Comparatively, Achilles earns the respect of everyone around him and his teacher Phoinix by being successful in his military campaigns.

15   The final element in the Homeric paradigm of the hero is complexity. Achilles is not just a cold and ruthlessly efficient killing machine. He has multiple facets that make him a well-rounded man.

The first of Achilles' many talents are healing. When Machaon, physician son of Asklepios (*Illiad* 4.194, 11.518), is wounded near the beginning of the Great Battle, he is quickly taken back to the ship, because "a healer is a man worth many others, for cutting out arrows and sprinkling kindly drugs" (*Illiad* 11.514–515).

Five books later, Machaon is brought back to the ship where Achilles is viewing the battle, and is attended to by Achilles himself. While this is going on, Patroclus makes a comment that describes the magnitude of Achilles' healing talent: "The healers, on one hand, work to heal the wounded; you, on the other hand, work to heal the healers" (*Illiad* 16.28–29). This serves to make Achilles' gift of healing truly great, because he is the healer of the healers (King 9). [16]

Another skill Achilles has is the gift of the bard. In book IX of the *Illiad,* Achilles sings tales of dead friends and battle (*Illiad* 9.186). Both of these make Achilles more human and easier to envision, creating a stalwart warrior with a lion's heart and a gentle touch. [17]

Luke Skywalker's complexity lay in his extraordinary connection to the powers of the Force, or the energy that binds the universe and all life together in the *Star Wars* Universe. He is unique, he has dreams and aspirations, and he wants to go out and be a hero among the stars. In a sense, he wanted to fulfill a destiny he did not know existed, and this manifested itself in his desire to leave home; a fantastic version of the American West's romanticized concept of what American historians have termed "Manifest Destiny," or the desire to move on to greater places and newer challenges. [18]

The character of Luke Skywalker fits neatly into the Homeric paradigm for the archetypal literary hero that Homer created in his character Achilles. However, the similarity of these two integral characters is not the only element the *Star Wars* trilogy borrowed from the *Illiad.* Two locations and two characters from both stories correspond in a most interesting manner. [19]

In the *Illiad,* the Trojan War is perpetuated over a woman, namely Helen of Troy. Two men from Troy and Greece quarrel over Helen, and the whole Mediterranean world falls into a miserable conflict that lasts ten years and costs uncounted millions of lives. In *Star Wars: A New Hope,* major conflicts begin when Leia Organa, the Princess of the High Alderranian council of the Republic, is racing toward the planet Tatooine in search of the Jedi Master Obi-Wan Kenobi. She is attempting to deliver the small droid (robot with advanced artificial intelligence) Artoo-Detoo (R2-D2) to him. Within [20]

Artoo's memory banks are the technical readouts for the Death Star battle station. Princess Leia hopes that Obi-Wan can take the technical readouts to the Rebel Base on the planet Yavin Four, so they might be analyzed and a weakness in the battle station found and exploited. En route to Tatooine, the Princess's transport ship is besieged by the flagship of the Imperial Navy, the ISD (Imperial Star Destroyer) Dominance. Darth Vader takes the Princess prisoner just as she jettisons the droid Artoo-Detoo. The Rebel Alliance responds violently to the Empire's abduction of the princess, and an intergalactic war ensues. Therefore, Leia is Helen's counterpart in a galaxy far, far away.

21   In both stories, there exists an area of immense power. In the *Illiad,* this area is called Troy. Historically, Troy is a city that sits on the plateau of Hissarlik in the plains of Troy (Schliemann). There are approximately fifty-seven hundred feet of walls that envelope the city. The actual interior boundaries of the city extend for close to four hundred feet at its widest parts, declining to as little as one hundred feet in some parts (Schliemann appendix). In short, Troy was no major metropolitan area. And this is what makes Homer's story so incredible. The fact that a city so small could carry on, and almost win a ten year war that rivals both World Wars in scope and bloodshed, with the entire nation of Greece, suggests that the city in question is unfathomably superlative.

22   Comparatively, in *Star Wars,* the Imperial's terrible battle station, the Death Star, is a relatively small area capable of mass destruction (thus the name "Death Star"). According to the *Star Wars* mythology, the Death Star is a spherical construct one thousand-forty kilometers in diameter, and has a mass that is one–one hundredth that of the earth. Granted, this seems large when pictured, however, when compared to a planet the size of our earth, it is really quite small. The fact that it has the potential to obliterate an entire world the size of the earth in the blink of an eye demonstrates its position as a small area with superior power.

23   When George Lucas imagined the *Star Wars* trilogy, he did, in essence, create a modern-day *Illiad*. He rekindled the spirit of the archetypal hero. He reaffirmed the contention that heroes dwell among us, and these people are more than special. They create role models for us all, and stimulate the imaginations of people the world over. Just as the *Illiad* is an ancient epic of heroic deeds, the *Star Wars*

trilogy is a contemporary epic of heroic deeds—it is the mythic epic of the twentieth century. It gives people a renewed hope in the tradition of humanity, and reaffirms the contention that we, as a people, as long as heroes like Achilles and Luke Skywalker exist, shall not perish from the earth.

Works Cited

Homer. *The Illiad.* NY: Knopf, 1996.

King, Katherine Callen. *Achilles: Paradigms of the War Hero from Homer to the Middle Ages.* London: U of CA P, 1987.

Schlieman, Heinrich. *Troy and Its Remains.* NY: Arno P, 1976.

Star Wars: A New Hope. Dir. George Lucas. 20th Century Fox, 1977.

Star Wars: The Empire Strikes Back. Dir. George Lucas. 20th Century Fox, 1980.

Star Wars: Return of the Jedi. Dir. George Lucas. 20th Century Fox, 1983.

✦ ✦ ✦

✦ *Framing the Context*

1. Writing the essay as a course assignment, Melendez has two primary audiences: the instructor who will evaluate his writing and readers who are interested in the content. How does he use the introduction (paras. 1–4) to form a relationship with both readers?

2. What assumptions does Melendez make about what the readers already know about the subject and what they need to know?

✦ *Point of View*

3. What features in paragraphs 4, 5, 6, 7, and 15 identify Melendez's point of view? Name the point of view he uses.

4. How does this point of view establish a relationship with the readers that brings them closer to knowing and understanding the subject?

✦ *Shape of Ideas*

5. Identify the framework Melendez uses to structure his essay. Explain how this structure creates a clear path of discovery for the readers to understand Melendez's purpose.

6. How do Melendez's comparisons of *The Illiad* and *Star Wars* complement that structure?

◆ *Choosing Voice*

7. Use the language features in paragraph 4 to identify the formality level of voice Melendez chooses to use.

8. How would you characterize the difference in Melendez's voice in the opening narrative scenes? Is the same level of formality used?

◆ *Credibility*

9. How does Melendez's choice of sources establish credibility with the readers? What other sources might he have used to establish his credibility?

10. In what way do the methods used to incorporate sources contribute to Melendez's ethos?

Living in the New Middle Ages

Richard Reynolds

✦ ✦ ✦

The same Batman, Superman, Spider-Man, and Wonder Woman who starred in our childhood memories now populate the pages of academic study. In his analysis of the endurance and evolution of these superheroes from their birth in the Action Comics *of 1938, Richard Reynolds, whose books on popular culture include the topics of computer animation, electronic movie stars, and progressive talk radio, argues for the legitimacy of the superhero as a cultural icon whose persona and exploits chronicle the changes in America's ideology. The following is a chapter from his book* Super Heroes.

Superhero narratives clearly give substance to certain ideologi- 1
cal myths about the society they address: the USA. A narrative such
as Thor confronts ideological myth making very directly: it places
the traditional hero or God on the stage of American society. Thor's
heroism and integrity become a barometer by which can be mea-
sured the character of those he encounters. Other remarkable beings
such as the Silver Surfer (an alien), Doctor Strange (Master of the
Mystic Arts) or the Spectre (a ghost) function in the same way: apart
from providing a magnificent set of heroic qualities, they also examine society through the window of their own very peculiar viewpoint.
The odd thing about Superman is that he doesn't provide such an
angle of view: culturally, Superman is completely American.

This strategy of viewing the world through the eyes of a re- 2
markable outsider makes a very clear statement of how most superhero narratives view their host culture. Far from being as 'escapist'
as is claimed, most superhero comics are intensely grounded in the
normal and everyday. There is a constant delight in showing the
mundane nature of daily life. In part, this is a strategy to build up
suspense and contrast: a supervillain like Doctor Doom or Magneto
can be made to seem so much more threatening against a background of recognizable reality. But there is another reason as well.
Superheroes are by and large not upholders of the letter of the law;
they are not law enforcement agents employed by the state. The set

143

of values they traditionally defend is summed up by the Superman tag of 'Truth, Justice and the American Way'. Sometimes the last term has been interpreted in a narrowly nationalistic sense; superheroes have on occasions become uncritical supporters of US foreign policy. But far more often the third term has stood for the ideals enshrined in the US Constitution. Superheroes have been better Americans—as the founding fathers would have understood the term—than most of America's modern political leaders.

3   Captain America—inescapably a patriotic icon—was forced to go through an agonizing readjustment of his political outlook in a series of Steve Englehart stories written in the aftermath of the Watergate scandal. Disgusted by corruption within government circles, he abandoned the Captain America identity to become plain Steve Rogers, then made a tentative superhero comeback as the Nomad— one who does not have a home. During this long-running storyline from 1974–75, Steve Rogers battled a couple of false Captain Americas who stepped in to fill his vacant shoes, and was encouraged to return to his Captain America identity by his black superhero partner The Falcon.

4   In *Captain America* 177 the Falcon tries unsuccessfully to persuade Steve Rogers not to throw in the towel. Getting a negative response, he vows from that moment on to go it alone:

> *You taught me to play the super-hero game, so I'm gonna play it . . . and I'm not lookin' back! Goodbye and good luck!*
>
> *Sam! . . . Is this the way it's going to be now? Follow my conscience . . . and lose my friends . . . lose everything except my self-respect? Lord, I hope not!*[1]

At the word 'Sam!' The Falcon flies away, and Steve is left speaking the remaining words to himself. Cap's recovery of his full identity and costume is abetted by the Falcon's loyalty to a particular version of the American Dream. As embodied by Captain America, the American Dream equals self-improvement—Steve Rogers, once a skinny weakling, was transformed by the power of science into a super-soldier and patriotic symbol. The Englehart/Watergate stories involved turning the Captain America legend inward on itself—did post-Watergate, post-Vietnam America still deserve its heroes?

5   But the Captain America iconography can be used in contrasting ways. Take, for example, the cover of the Captain America special of 1990, 'Captain America goes to war against drugs.' The comic

was produced in co-operation with the FBI, and contains on the inside cover a list of government departments which have reviewed its contents, as well as a list of 56 FBI offices which have a 'Drug Demand Reduction Coordinator'.

The story shows a young baseball player, Mitch, a star pitcher, who is offered cocaine by an alien space monster to help him relax before a game. Captain America solves Mitch's problems, mainly through providing moral support. The cover, however, doesn't show a scene from the story inside. Instead, it depicts an allegorical scene in which Captain America throws his red, white and blue shield at the word 'DRUGS', while a multi-ethnic, multi-gender group of teenage kids look on and cheer. The kids' clothes and accessories show them to be personifications of American urban youth—placed against a smooth, green background which is further universalized by the high angle of view.

The ideological strategy of this cover is to say: 'We're on the same side'. A comic-book narrative or cover design can effortlessly draw conflicting elements into a visual relationship, thus apparently resolving any contradictions which might have seemed to exist. There seems to be only the one way to decode this image: Captain America and American youth are on the same side, have the same agenda, are fighting for the same ideals.

Continuity, and the ability of sequential art to resolve contradictions simply by including them in the same panel, has made it difficult for black superheroes to inscribe any ideological values of their own. But it certainly couldn't be said that black superheroes haven't become numerically stronger as the years have gone by: The Black Panther, Power Man, The Falcon, Storm of the X-Men, Cyborg of the Teen Titans, and the black incarnations of Captain Marvel and the Punisher have all established themselves since the late sixties. Yet it is one thing to decree black superheroes, quite another to inscribe a plausible ideology for them.

A key ideological myth of the superhero comic is that the normal and everyday enshrines positive values that must be defended through heroic action—and defended over and over again almost without respite against an endless battery of menaces determined to remake the world for the benefit of aliens, mutants, criminals, or sub-aqua beings from Atlantis. The normal is valuable and is constantly under attack, which means that almost by definition the superhero is battling on behalf of the status quo. Into this heroic matrix one can insert representatives of any race or creed imaginable, but in order to be functioning superheroes they will need to conform to the ideological rules of the game. The superhero has a mission to preserve society, not to re-invent it.

10   The most effective form of social comment in superhero narratives is therefore satire. It has always been possible to use the satirical method from inside the political consensus or status quo in order to denounce the outstanding follies and abuses of the age—without suggesting or accepting that there is anything fundamentally wrong with the status quo's ideology. The Falcon became an effective vehicle for this kind of satire during his membership of The Avengers from *Avengers* 181 to 194. Drafted into the team against the wishes of some members (chiefly Hawkeye) as a quota representing minorities, The Falcon was under pressure to prove himself to the rest of the team—despite support from his erstwhile partner Captain America. The Falcon finally comes good in a battle with the Grey Gargoyle (*Avengers* 190–191) but then quits the team three issues later;

> *What I mean is that the main reason I joined the Avengers was to fill a government quota—and that quota no longer exists . . . so I'm handing in my walking papers. Maybe that'll ease some of the tension I seem to have brought in with me.*

Captain America replies:

> *I . . . don't think anyone really noticed, Falcon. But if you've made your decision, we'll honor it.*[2]

The script by Dave Michelinie manages to satirize the situation pertaining to black superheroes: they are present in effect to fill up a quota, without offering anything different or unique which challenges the superhero status quo. Oppositional readings of certain comics may, however, throw up a different ideological perspective. For example, the whole theme of the X-Men—the isolation of mutants and their alienation from 'normal' society—can be read as a parable of the alienation of any minority. The original Magneto and his Brotherhood of Evil Mutants,[3] who disdained to cooperate with homo sapiens, could be read as an example of a minority grouping determined to force its own place within society. Such oppositional readings of the X-Men are possible—gay readings of the mutant subtext have been fairly common in the letter columns over the years.[4] But such exercises seem to be little more than efforts to wrench the subtext of the comic into a desired oppositional reading, rather than a fully engaged exploration of the open possibilities of the text—and of the nuances and subtleties which function as irony and satire, and therefore debunk or defang any absolutely oppositional reading.

This leads to the even more vexed subject of gender and of 11 women superheroes. How can women who dress up in the styles of 1940s pornography be anything other than the pawns or tools of male fantasy? There has certainly been a sufficient quantity of powerful women superheroes—back to Wonder Woman in 1941, the Good Girl heroines of the late 1940s, the Batgirl and Supergirl offshoots, the various Marvel superheroines from the Scarlet Witch and the Black Widow to the She-Hulk and the new (black) Captain Marvel. But any feminist critic could demonstrate that most of these characters fail to inscribe any specifically female qualities: they behave in battle like male heroes with thin waists and silicone breasts, and in repose are either smugly domestic (the Invisible Woman, the Wasp) or brooding and remote—a slightly threatening male fantasy (Wonder Woman, or the Scarlet Witch).

It's easy to look at superhero comics and list the issues they fail 12 to address. The relationship between the Vision and the Scarlet Witch, as it developed from *Avengers* 100 or so onwards, is a good example of how a mainstream Marvel title has mythologized the sex life of its characters over a considerable period of time. The Scarlet Witch, generally aloof in her manner, is an extremely powerful heroine, able to affect reality in unpredictable ways with her Hex power, which is a combination of magical and Mutant abilities (she was once a member of Magneto's Brotherhood of Evil Mutants, and is in fact Magneto's daughter). She has a voluptuous figure, shown off only too effectively by her red 'bathing costume' outfit and long trailing cloak. Cool in a crisis, her powers have many times saved the day against some of the Avengers' most formidable foes. The Vision likewise is a severe prospect for any supervillain. A synthetic android robot with an artificial 'human' personality, he has the ability to increase or reduce his body density to an unlimited extent. The Vision can become insubstantial or infinitely heavy and hard. He can also project destructive heat rays from his eyes, and has advanced computer-like intellectual faculties—a perfect example of the 'science as magic' motif discussed in chapter one. Over the years, these two became lovers, and eventually husband and wife. The Scarlet Witch's brother, himself the mutant superhero Quicksilver, has often shown disapproval of the marriage, disgusted that his sister should have wed a 'soulless machine'.[5]

13   There is clearly a pornographic subtext to this relationship, of the kind discussed in chapter two. But the Scarlet Witch's sexuality is presented blatantly the more firmly to deny it: no member of the Avengers has ever been known to remark on her revealing costume and sexy appearance. Such remarks just don't get made: the frisson of fetishistic sexuality is adduced with one hand only to be dismissed with the other. Sexuality is simultaneously presented—from the male point of view—in all its tempting erotic trappings—and then controlled, or domesticated, by a simple denial of its power and appeal.

14   Yet none of these adolescent contradictions might be seen to apply to a character like the Vision—cool, calculating and robotlike. If anyone can ignore or see past the Scarlet Witch's surface sexuality, it must be him: the 'soulless machine', who is immune to all temptations of the flesh. In fact, the robotic Vision is only a slightly more extreme version of the typical straight-laced superhero character, and his relationship with the Scarlet Witch an example of the reconciliation of opposites which is the stock-in-trade of the ideological subtext of many-superhero comics. The mythology has moved on a little from the sado-masochism of William Moulton Marston's alluring woman a man is 'proud to submit to.' Instead, the myth could be described as an unearned state of post-feminism, and carries the message for both male and female readers: 'You can have your cake and eat it'. For women, the subtext might be read as 'You can dress sexy and still be taken seriously and hold a position of power'. For men: 'Just because you like her to wear sexy clothes doesn't mean you're degrading her status and equality.'[6] This is clearly a comfortable and comforting myth which can be found expressed rather differently in any issue of *Cosmopolitan, New Woman* or any of the other post-feminist women's magazines. Yet it could be argued that the superheroes arrive at this comfortable position via a slightly tougher route. The male superheroes embody a correspondingly exaggerated and kinky form of macho sex appeal, which puts them, in the fetish stakes, on a par with many of the superheroines.

As superhero comics have been and largely still are an art-form conceived with an adolescent audience at least partly in mind, it is wise to refer these issues of gender politics back to the viewpoint of an adolescent. It's also significant to bear in mind how deeply the Oedipus myth is embedded in the mythology of many of the key male superheroes. In their simultaneous offering and denying of sexuality, plus their cool strength and determination in battle with supervillains, the superheroines offer a reconciliation of all the conflicting demands of adolescent male sexual desire. Sexuality is domesticated (i.e. made safe) and yet remains exceptionally exciting. Women are visually thrilling, and yet threatening and dangerous only to outsiders and strangers.

The mythologizing of sexuality is a potential key to the ways in which superhero myths address the questions of power and justice within the societies they depict and/or reflect. Superheroes are always moving between extremes, and the greatest superhero artists excel at giving these contrasts a visible form. Murky film noir interiors cut to the wide open spaces above the rooftops; the splendour of New York from the air contrasts with the squalor at street level. Goodness and corruption co-exist. This must be so, because of the continuity of the stories: menaces can never be finally defeated, and the episodic, soap-opera plots support the notion that all victories are temporary.

After a serious menace has been cleared up, which may involve the termination of plots and subplots stretching back for a year or more, a subsequent issue will often begin with a deliberate 'clean slate' panel or panels. Often the 'clean slate' panel involves the superhero looking down at a bird's-eye view of a calm and peaceful city. Such panels may occur on the last page of the issue concluding a plot-line, or the first page of the following installment. Either way, it seems for the moment that things are working out—evil has finally been brought under control. But a fully engaged reader knows it's only an illusion: new menaces will be popping up before long. The heroes need to triumph in the short term, but they can never be said to live happily ever after.

Society is constantly in transition, nothing will stay where you put it. This is an aspect of the superhero myth which has undergone considerable change over the lifetime of the genre. The comics of the 1940s and 1950s are set against a background of greater stability, and the heroes battled menaces which were either abnormally-motivated products of their society (The Joker, Lex Luthor), or else external menaces. Within the last 30 years, all this has changed. The normality which the superhero sees as so valuable seems to be constantly in a state of siege. The situation in superhero continuity is becoming an image of society as pictured by Umberto Eco in his essay 'Living in the new Middle Ages'.

19   Eco argues that contemporary society is coming to resemble or reconstruct the middle ages, and that the perceived breakdown of the Pax Americana is a modern equivalent to the collapse of the Roman Empire.

> *What is required to make a good Middle Ages? First of all, a great peace that is breaking down, a great international power that has unified the world in language, customs, ideologies, religions, art, and technology, and then at a certain point, thanks to its ungovernable complexity, collapses. It collapses because the 'barbarians' are pressing at its borders; these barbarians are not necessarily uncultivated, but they are bringing new customs, new views of the world. These Barbarians may burst in with violence, because they want to seize a wealth that has been denied them, or they may steal into the social and cultural body of the reigning Pax, spreading new faiths and new perspectives of life.*[7]

Eco is speaking of Western or global culture, but his remarks are intended to apply to the US itself, the instigator of the Pax Americana. Superhero comics had relatively little to do with the mythologizing of the Cold War,[8] yet many see manifest in the superhero cult the qualities of individualism and the collective identity of WASP America which went on the offensive in the McCarthyite and Cold War period. Eco's perception of the new middle ages involves the recognition that cultural space is permeable, that—unlike the watertight 'Empire'—the host culture is subject to influences from outside itself that are beyond its control. *The Dark Knight Returns* and *Watchmen* are two comics which seem to take this cultural 'permeability' as their starting point for their reconstruction of superhero ideology.

20   This, it could be argued, is where the superhero acts out his role in the game of cultural semiotics. Like most important signs, the superhero supports a varied and contradictory battery of readings. He is both the exotic and the agent of order which brings the exotic to book. His costume marks him out as a proponent of change and exoticism, yet he surprises us by his adherence to an almost archaic code of personal honour. As with superhero sexuality, the unpredictable nature of contemporary culture is adduced through a play

of visual signs in order more effectively to relegate it to the domain of things one has learned how to control.

This may be why the superhero and supervillain exist so comfortably in the same social space, converse on familiar terms, and wear similar style costumes when battling each other. They represent the inferred challenge to the social order (Eco's Barbarians) and the means of survival—through the exposition of virtues that might have been considered to be past their prime. The superhero by his very existence asserts American utopianism, which remains (as has been ably pointed out by Baudrillard in *America*)[9] a highly potent cultural myth. The exciting developments in superhero comics over the last decade or so have largely been the product of writers and artists who have come to understand and work around or through the superhero's cultural iconography—using the myth of the superhero to make a calculated statement about the culture which the myth attempts to comprehend.

Notes

1. *Action Comics 1,* p. 1.
2. *Action Comics, 1,* p. 5.
3. *Action Comics, 1,* p. 4.
4. *Action Comics, 1,* p. 10.
5. See, for example, *The Golden Bough,* by Sir James Frazer, Abridged Edition, Macmillan, 1957, pp. 277–279.
6. The first appearance of The Joker is in *Batman 1,* Spring 1940.
7. This long-running dispute eventually led to the cancellation of *Captain Marvel* and the whole Marvel Family line of comics in 1953. There have been several unsuccessful attempts to revive the original *Captain Marvel* since. Marvel Comics' *Captain Marvel* is a completely different character, who (paradoxically) was much closer in conception to Superman than Fawcett's character ever was.
8. By 1942, there were 143 different comic-book titles being published in the United States, with an annual industry revenue of some fifteen million dollars.
9. Several of these characters have appeared in comic-book form. Pulp hero Doc Savage appeared in his own comic in May 1940, when longtime Doc Savage publisher Street and Smith decided to enter the comic-book market. The Green Hornet and Captain Midnight—both heroes of the radio serials—entered the comic medium in 1940 and 1942 respectively.

✦ ✦ ✦

✦ *Framing the Context*

1. As a college-level reader, what relationship do you expect Reynolds to establish between you and the text published by an academic press? How does this relationship fit the occasion for this context?

2. What assumptions does Reynolds make about his readers' knowledge and interest in the subject? For example, does he believe they have read the comic book he mentions? What features of the writing indicate these assumptions?

✦ *Point of View*

3. Most scholarly writing is presented from an objective point of view. What features in Reynolds's writing indicate he uses an objective point of view?

4. How does Reynolds's objective point of view affect the readers' relationship to the subject?

✦ *Shape of Ideas*

5. Reynolds chooses to use a functional sequence as a framework. Outline those functions in the sequence in which he presents them.

6. How does the functional sequence framework complement Reynolds's objective point of view, and how does it connect the reader to Reynolds's purpose?

✦ *Choosing Voice*

7. What level of formality does Reynolds use to write academically about a popular culture subject? Cite examples where this level of formality establishes legitimacy for the subject.

8. How does Reynolds's use of colons in the first paragraph establish his voice?

✦ *Credibility*

9. The title of this excerpt, "Living in the New Middle Ages," is taken from the title of Umberto Eco's essay. Why does Reynolds wait until the end of this section (paras. 18 and 19) to acknowledge the source? In what way does delaying that reference affect Reynolds's credibility?

10. In several places Reynolds chooses to quote dialogue from the comic books. How does this use of sources contribute to his credibility?

Great Women, Bad Times

Barbara Ehrenreich

✦ ✦ ✦

What does it take for a woman to be recognized? This is the problem Barbara Ehrenreich addresses in her response to Time*'s April 13, 1998, selection of the twenty leaders and revolutionaries who most influenced the twentieth century. Ehrenreich, a regular contributor to* Time, *explores how the criteria for determining greatness managed to exclude the many women whose work has become a familiar part of history.*

Time's list of the 20 most important "leaders and revolutionaries" of the 20th century contains only three women, or 15% of the total. Expressed as a grade, this is an F-, so that if history were a classroom, women would have to take 20th century over again. Naturally, my first response was to demand a recount. Where, for example, are the feminist revolutionaries—the Betty Friedans, the Sylvia Pankhursts, the Simone de Beauvoirs? Yes, I know there are still four more categories and 80 more names to go, but it's a pretty boyish definition of revolutionary that includes only those great social upheavals that involved the storming of palaces and the execution of royal families. 1

Besides, the American civil rights movement wasn't just Martin Luther King Jr.; it was also Ella Baker, Fannie Lou Hamer, Rosa Parks. As for non-violent social activists and leaders—What about Jane Addams, Petra Kelly, Dorothy Day, Aung San Suu Kyi? And why flatter Lenin by leaving out two of his staunchest ideological opponents, the Polish-German socialist Rosa Luxemburg and the American anarchist Emma Goldman? 2

All right, this list is not a collection of the best and the brightest, much less of the good and the kindest. When you pick the "most important," you get the thugs and the monsters as well as the role models. In fact, it should be noted at once that at least five of the men on the list were opponents, in one way or another, of women's rights: Hitler, with his famed *Kinder, Küche, Kirche* policy; Khomeini, the fashion expert who brought back the chador; Reagan, with his hostility to abortion rights and the ERA; the sweet but incorrigibly patriarchal Pope John Paul II. 3

4   And then there's Lech Walesa. Those who wonder why there aren't more women on the list should consider the fate of Hanna Suchocka, the first female Prime Minister of Poland—or of any postcommunist state. It was Walesa who derailed her political career, stating, "I can't see a woman above me"—then adding, to the appreciative laughter of the press corps, "Sometimes, maybe."

5   The point being that if women aren't well represented among the movers and shakers, it isn't just because they've been too shy, too un-self-esteeming or too busy changing diapers. Part of the problem lies with the movers and shakers. For example, some of the job titles held by the males—such as Pope and Ayatullah—have never been open to women. We like to imagine, in the U.S., that guys who occupy corner offices and wear pinstripe suits are more woman-friendly than the ones whose names are stitched on their shirts. So it is depressing to realize that the Vatican and the Pentagon, Wall Street and the Senate Office Buildings, have been as tough to integrate as any coal mine or fire department.

6   But maybe, and despite all the well-publicized gains, it just wasn't our century. American women only got the vote in 1920 (and a rest room near the senate chambers only in 1992). For most of the past 98 years, much of the world's female population has been voteless, voiceless, illiterate, ground down by toil and sexist restrictions. When I griped to my daughter about the shortage of our kind among the top 20 leaders, she sighed at my paleofeminist pique: "But, Mom, it's just the 20th century. You know, the bad old days."

✦ ✦ ✦

✦ Framing the Context

1. As a regular contributor to *Time,* Ehrenreich has gained a following of readers familiar with her work, particularly on women's status. What features of the article convey this familiar relationship between writer and reader?

2. In what way does the occasion for the article influence Ehrenreich's purpose? Explain the relationship between the two.

✦ Point of View

3. As a writer who regularly contributes her opinion to *Time,* Ehrenreich writes from a subjective point of view. Cite three sentences that convey Ehrenreich's visibility without using the word *I.*

4. How does Ehrenreich's use of a subjective point of view allow readers to participate in a dialogue with her? Indicate where that interaction takes place.

✦ *Shape of Ideas*

5. Time, people, and leadership are the central focus of Ehrenreich's essay. What structural framework does she choose to develop the relationship among those three elements, and which, if any, dominates?

6. How does Ehrenreich's framework connect the readers to her purpose?

✦ *Choosing Voice*

7. A writer's attitude toward a subject influences the tone of the writer's voice. How would you describe Ehrenreich's tone of voice and what language features convey that tone?

8. The subject, purpose, and occasion of this special issue of *Time* have an inherent seriousness and formality, yet Ehrenreich uses informal language in every paragraph. Identify an example of informal language in each paragraph, and evaluate the effect it is likely to have on the intended readers.

✦ *Credibility*

9. This article included photos and a list of achievements for six women leaders (Indira Gandhi, Sirimavo Bandaranaike, Golda Meir, Corazon Aquino, Benazir Bhutto, and Violetta Barrios De Chamorro) in addition to the thirteen women Ehrenreich cites in the article. How do these sources contribute to Ehrenreich's credibility with the intended readers?

10. After analyzing the twentieth-century plight of women's leadership in six paragraphs, Ehrenreich concludes with a direct quote from her daughter. What is her strategy in using this source? What effect does that choice have on her ethos?

The Soul of a Champion
A Letter to Michael Jordan

Andrew Bernstein

✦ ✦ ✦

Extensive media coverage allows the public to follow the career of sports figures on a regular basis. For many people, the extraordinary physical feats these sports figures achieve make them worthy heroes; for others, they are merely highly paid performers who symbolize the decline in what society chooses to value. Andrew Bernstein, who identifies himself as a teacher for the past twenty years, singles out Michael Jordan as an athlete whose character makes him a hero beyond the sports arena. Bernstein wrote this opinion piece on the occasion of Michael Jordan's retirement and submitted it to the Chicago Tribune College Press Exchange *wire service.*

Dear Mr. Jordan—or if I may—Michael,

1   I would like to wish you well on your retirement and to thank you.

2   Thank you for winning six NBA titles and earning hundreds of millions of dollars. If you ask why I thank you when obviously you did it for yourself, not for me, I will respond: That is exactly why I thank you. I can see the pride you take in your achievements—in being the greatest ever in your field—but I wonder if you realize all that you have to be proud of.

3   Most people, unfortunately, do not push themselves to excel and the problem is not a lack of capacity. Over a period of 20 years as a teacher, I have observed many talented students who squander their gifts. It is hard work for a man to actualize his potential. Thomas Edison defined genius as 1 percent inspiration and 99 percent perspiration. Many of us—perhaps most—do not wish to perspire that profusely. But you, Michael, do not share such a reluctance.

4   When the teen-age boy, cut from his high school basketball team, practices hours every day before school, he displays his work ethic. When the University of North Carolina hero "busts his butt" at Bobby Knight's drill-instructor-style practice sessions in order to win the Olympic gold, he reaffirms that commitment. When the

greatest player in the history of basketball continues, at age 35, to out-hustle far younger players—on defense as well as offense—and to lead his aging team to yet another championship, he surpasses the meaning of such concepts as "dedication" and "perseverance"; he sets an example and a standard for which, perhaps, mankind has not yet developed a vocabulary.

Most of us, unlike you, are mere mortals; we cannot fly. But we can aspire. We can push ourselves to the limit of our ability and achieve the highest level possible to us. When I see you playing in a championship game with a fever that would keep most men in bed— when I see that, physically, you are almost too weak to stand but you still push yourself to score 38 points and hit the game winning shot—it moves me to ask: What can I achieve if I dedicate myself similarly to my own work and life?

It is true that basketball, like any sport, is just a game. Mankind's survival does not rest on the outcome of the World Series or the Super Bowl—not in the same way that it rests on the ability to grow food, cure diseases or invent new technologies. But in a broader sense, the world does depend on the spirit at the root of any athletic contest: the dedication to excellence. The superb athlete striving for a championship or a gold medal is a publicly visible symbol of achievement. He (or she) is a symbol of man's striving for perfection.

No athlete of our time, Michael, captures this meaning as much as you do. It isn't only, or even primarily, the dominance you exhibit on the basketball court; it is the way you conduct your life. So many of today's athletes, musicians, movie stars and politicians are guilty of drug use, infidelity, or violence; through these despicable acts, they seem determined to betray their admirers. But you stand high above them as a man of dignity and stature. I hope you realize that this is the source of your enormous popularity.

There are few heroes today. Great men are no longer revered in our society; they are derided. Our culture has, in its explicit intellectual content, become hostile to achievement. Bill Gates' great success brings him the reward of antitrust prosecution; Martha Stewart is accused of arrogance for showing people how they could lead more beautiful lives; you are attacked for allegedly endorsing "sweat shops."

The American people sense, in some visceral, non-intellectual way, that their heroes are being taken away from them. They see all around them, in books and in films, stories about losers and low-lifes. It is clear to them why ours has been called the "era of the anti-hero." They do not like it.

10   This is the reason so many people read only the sports page of the newspapers, and why sports are so popular in our country: it is the last arena of heroism tolerated and permitted by the leaders of our culture. As public figures, you—and a select few of your outstanding colleagues—are the standard-bearers of man's pursuit of excellence. Your larger-than-life stature serves as a beacon to all of us who would be the heroes of our own lives. As the only man I know of who has a statue of himself outside his place of employment—and who has earned it—you are a concrete reminder of how much is open, potentially, to us all.

11   As Ayn Rand stated in her novel, "Atlas Shrugged": "The sight of an achievement is the greatest gift a human being could offer to others." You have offered such a gift, abundantly, to us. You will continue to inspire those of us who, like you, hold a high estimate of man's proper stature and yearn to attain it. This is the full achievement for which you have a right to be proud. And this is why all Americans should say: "Thank you."

✦ ✦ ✦

✦ *Framing the Context*

1. Although Bernstein addresses his letter to Michael Jordan, he published the letter through the College Press Exchange, an organization from which college newspapers select articles for their campus newspapers. Cite examples from the letter that indicate Bernstein's attempts to form a relationship with college readers.

2. What assumptions does Bernstein make about his readers' knowledge of and interest in Michael Jordan?

✦ *Point of View*

3. Bernstein is clearly visible in paragraphs 1, 2, and 5, but not as directly in the remainder of the letter. What shift in point of view takes place, and as a result, would you identify the point of view as more subjective or merged? Explain your decision.

4. How does Bernstein's point of view define his assumed relationship to his readers?

✦ *Shape of Ideas*

5. What framework does Bernstein use to present "the soul of a champion"? Outline the flow of that structure.

6. How does Bernstein's choice of framework make his purpose apparent to the readers?

✦ *Choosing Voice*

7. Letters can be informal or formal depending on the occasion. What is Bernstein's occasion and how does it affect the formality of his writing voice?

8. Using paragraph 4, explain how his language choices—diction, punctuation, sentence structure, length, and variety—convey the formality level of his voice.

✦ *Credibility*

9. Identify four sources Bernstein includes in his letter and evaluate how the readers' respect for those sources affect Bernstein's credibility.

10. In paragraphs 4, 8, and 9, Bernstein incorporates direct quotes but does not identify the sources from which they are taken. Explain how this lack of attribution is likely to affect Bernstein's credibility and why.

Environmental Heroes

William M. Daley

✦ ✦ ✦

Since the passage of the National Environmental Protection Act in 1970, we have become more aware of our responsibilities as caretakers of the planet. We recycle, keep our roads free of litter, and use biodegradeable products on a daily basis. Some people, however, go beyond those common efforts by volunteering their time and expertise to make a difference. These are the "heroes" U.S. Secretary of Commerce William M. Daley presented awards to at the Earth Day celebration in Key Largo, Florida, on April 22, 1998. Like most public speeches, the one that follows was written before Daley delivered it, and because Daley is a government representative, a written form of the speech is published in Vital Speeches of the Day, *a government document archive that can be accessed on the Internet.*

1   Thank you Dr. Baker. What a wonderful way to spend Earth Day 1998—and what a wonderful group to spend it with! This is not only Earth Day. President Clinton has proclaimed this the Year of the Ocean. So this morning I came to Florida to see the third largest barrier reef system in the world. And I went out on the ocean with the Coral Reef Classroom students who are here—and watched them as they tested the water quality for the first time. To tell you the truth, I don't know who learned more, the kids or me. But an impression that we all shared—adults and students alike—was that this sanctuary and our oceans are truly a national treasure.

2   We face an enormous challenge. Threats to our ocean resources and even our precious coral reefs are real and growing. More than 70 percent of the Earth's surface is covered by water. And in many areas, this key source of food, recreation, energy, medicine and commerce has been badly damaged by pollution and overfishing. The Marine Sanctuary Program has been one response. There are now 12 sanctuaries. But, as successful as this program is, it is a limited solution. That is why 1998 has been designated the Year of the Ocean by President Clinton and by the United Nations.

3   The Year of the Ocean is a wake-up call: a reminder that the riches of the ocean cannot be taken for granted; that we are all stew-

ards of this strategic resource; and that the health of the ocean depends on each of us. We are hoping this message reaches every man, woman and child in this country—and beyond.

This is of special interest to those of us at the Commerce Department. Because oceans are an important part of our work. Our job is to promote our nation's economy and resources, including marine resources. One way we do this is through weather prediction. Last year, we used new technology to monitor the ocean. And, for the first time, we were able to forecast the onset of El Nino six months in advance. Over the last five years, we have more than doubled the amount of warning time to prepare for flash floods. And we've doubled the warning time for tornados.

We cannot prevent bad weather. So one of our top goals is to give communities and businesses as much warning as possible so they can prepare. This is especially important in beautiful coastal communities like this, where you welcome over 2 million visitors a year. The Florida Keys support a $275 million economy. Nationwide, one in six American jobs is marine related. Here, three out of four jobs depend on a healthy marine environment.

I remember when I was a youngster in Chicago. No oceans there, of course. But my father, who was mayor, had a dream that the Chicago River would once again be a place for fishing and recreation. A place where kids could learn how to cast a line and families could find a break from the fast-paced city. The work he started wasn't completed in his lifetime. But three years ago, we held a fishing tournament on the Chicago River. And the tournament was named in his honor.

Everywhere in this great country—the Midwest or Key West—or Key Largo—caring people can make a difference to the environment. They can help us save great places. And that is what brings us all together today. We are here to celebrate four caring people, our 1998 Florida Keys environmental heroes.

These are people who have worked closely with our Florida Keys National Marine Sanctuary. They have volunteered their time and expertise. And they have done more. They have championed projects aimed at protecting this great natural resource. So it is my honor to introduce them and present their awards and the letter from Vice President Gore.

David Holt is the director of the Center for Marine Conservation in the Florida Keys. He has been an avid supporter of the Sanctuary. And his work was instrumental in gaining support for marine zoning. He is also on the board of directors of Last Stand, a local environmental group; an adviser on policy matters ranging from channel marking and boat ramps to personal watercraft; and a member of the Sanctuary Advisory Council.

10   Captain Ed Davidson is another great friend of the Sanctuary. He is chairman of the board of the Florida Audubon Society. And he is a leader in environmental education and eco-tourism. He helped develop the Marine Sanctuary Plan and has promoted conservation issues and clean water initiatives in the region. He was one of the key supporters of the successful effort to include waters of the State of Florida in the Sanctuary.

11   Chuck Hayes is an authority on shipwreck sites and special natural resource sites. A retired Air Force pilot, Mr. Hays and his team dive nearly every day. And they record the location of any cultural site or unique resource they encounter. He has kept an on-going log of shipwreck sites and locations. These data are part of a report being released by Indiana University this spring. And they are the foundation for an historic shipwreck database. Mr. Hayes works closely with Sanctuary personnel and helps identify sensitive and important cultural resource sites.

12   While our fourth award recipient, David Whall, co-director of the Submerged Cultural Resources Assessment Program, could not be here today, I also want to take this opportunity to recognize and congratulate him. He helped develop the shipwreck trail and has been one of our most dedicated volunteers.

13   Before we conclude, I also want to take this opportunity to recognize the hundreds of volunteers, who help to promote and protect the Sanctuary. Last year, volunteers gave over 20,000 hours of their time. Independent Sector, a non-profit organization, has determined an average worth of $14.30 for each hour of volunteer time. That means that in monetary terms, the value of these volunteer service hours would exceed over $290,000. What this says to me is that this region is doubly endowed: with a bounty of caring citizens and some of the most beautiful natural resources in the world.

14   In his Year of the Ocean proclamation, President Clinton said: "Because the ocean is a treasure that all nations of the world share in common, we must work in partnership to become wise stewards of its many riches."

15   I see that happening here. I thank you. And generations to come will thank you.

16   Again, my congratulations to our award winners.

✦ ✦ ✦

✦ *Framing the Context*

1. Although Earth Day is a national event, the occasion for Daley's speech is local. How does Daley, an outsider, use the introduction to connect with his local audience?

2. Daley's immediate purpose is to present the awards, but what greater purpose does he use to frame the context?

✦ *Point of View*

3. Daley chooses to use a merged point of view. How does this point of view support his purpose and the occasion?

4. What information does Daley present to establish this shared authority with the audience?

✦ *Shape of Ideas*

5. What structure does Daley choose to make his greater purpose evident?

6. What effect does the shape of this structure have on the presentation of the awards?

✦ *Choosing Voice*

7. How does the level of formality Daley uses complement the merged point of view?

8. Identify examples of phrasing, sentence structure, and punctuation that capture the sound of oral speech.

✦ *Credibility*

9. How does Daley use his position to establish credibility?

10. What specific facts does Daley include to develop ethos with this audience?

Integrity on Trial
A Comedy Dialogue

Eric Peterson

✦ ✦ ✦

Must a musician sell his or her soul to those who control the commercial corporate world to be considered successful? Student writer and musician Eric Peterson questions the integrity of such a sacrifice. Peterson created this assignment on his homepage so his expository writing classmates and musician friends could interact with the text. Using an allegorical forum of Olympian gods, Peterson examines the role of integrity as the moral center for determining artistic heroes.

Cast of Characters

Zeus
Father of the Olympian Gods
Lord of the Sky/Rain God

Apollo
Patron of Poetry and Music/Leader of the Muses

Hermes
God of riches
Messenger and Trickster of the Gods
Escorts humans to Hades

Hades
God of the Underworld and Death

Moiré
Determine the length of life also known as the Fates

Orpheus
Greatest human musician and poet
Tamed wild beasts/nature with his music.

The Muses
Greeks prayed to the Muses for good voices
Entertained the Olympians by singing

1   Zeus wandered through the halls of his white columned temple on Mt. Olympus. The silence of this place bothered him. Some sound—anything to drown out the constant drone of his thoughts for a minute—would be welcome.

2   "APOLLO!!!! Get in here!" bellowed the sky god.

3   "Yes, Father? How can I be of assistance?" spoke Apollo from his chariot of fire.

164

"I need you to create something—some beautiful noise to compliment the ambience of my dwelling." said Zeus.   4

"I have just the thing, Father. I call it music." said the sun god.   5
"Muses! Your presence is requested." yelled Apollo at the air.

Quickly . . . silently, a cloud drifted into the room. It hovered at   6
eye level with Zeus momentarily. Ten lovely ladies clad in white togas
with white rope belts materialized around the father of the gods from
its misty insides.

"Muses! Sing for our father!"   7

The Trial of Integrity . . .

"Greetings fellow Olympians! Zeus has asked me to gather to-   8
gether my compatriots whose opinions I value most in order to
determine the value of my creation. . . .music." said Apollo in a
festive manner. His gaze drifted around the long wooden table,
studying the skin of everyone's faces. The loud slapping of his hands
together with two abrupt claps summoned his Muses who stealthily
materialized from whisper of white smoke.

"Now let us discuss this . . . music . . . while my Muses   9
tickle our ears with their voices." Apollo turned to address the
robed feminine forms behind him and beamed a proud smile at
them, **"ladies, perform something soothing, a song . . . to set the**
mood for this forum —"

"—and make sure it glorifies and praises me!" said Hades, the   10
dark lord with a snicker and a malignant grin. Clad in murky black
robes, he stood out among his with robed peers. In matters of art,
Hades knew little. He enjoyed listening to music that he could control through intimidation. The lord of the underworld often raised the
station of musicians who agreed to give their eternal souls to him.
Those who would not were regarded as mosquitoes—capable of a low
pitched, annoying buzz, yet completely harmless.

Rising from his heavy oak chair like a man who accidentally sat   11
on Hephastios forge, Orpheus questioned the death deity.

"Hades . . . distinguished lord of the underworld . . . why must   12
you twist the innocence of this art and make it serve you?" spoke Orpheus. "And you Apollo!! I never thought you would allow the
Muses, the Earth's musicians who are admired by the fair folk of this
land, to be used as mere pawns—bellows to inflate the already massive egos present here on Olympus."

13   "We are gods, you insignificant mortal. Everything created by humankind need be a monument to our greatness. If ungrateful wretches like yourself create tributes to human endeavors rather than our higher order, you raise your puny station one step closer to Olympus. Man does not belong on Olympus, he belongs below it, staring up in fear, awe, reverence!" Hades paused to study Orpheus' face. "Man and his creations are here for my entertainment. Any Human whom I see wander from that path will be sure to have their life line shortened considerably."

14   "Ahhh Hades, how quickly you forget who delivers man's soul to you. Without me to strike a deal with musicians for their souls, and reveal to them the entrance to your dark return, there would be no use for you!" came the voice of Hermes. "I am the messenger of the gods. I bring the works of those I deem worthy to the attention of man."

15   "Fools! I could prolong human life indefinitely! Both of you fools serve the Fates! Without me there would be no death and Hades, you could strike no deals for man's soul without me to cut his life strings!" spoke the strange chorus of voices that rang out as the Moiré spoke. "Following suit without me, there could be no creation because there would be no thread of life—if it glorified you or not. As I control their fates, so too, do I control yours. When I grow weary of them I snip their thread and they're gone from life's canvas."

16   "CEASE THIS BICKERING!!" bellowed Apollo. "I originally created music for MAN's pleasure. These Muses before you are here to entertain us. They do our bidding and are rewarded with a home here on Olympus. Dwelling in the presence of the gods is a great reward for any."

17   Orpheus saw his opportunity to speak again. "Yes, but can your Muses actually create anything? I create! The music I compose is about the beauty of nature. It's not to glorify Hades or Hermes. I create music because I have to. Moiré spins my thread of life and until she is no longer pleased with my work, I trust she will not cut it."

18   *"Yes Orpheus, but you are a mere mortal! We Muses are beyond the grasp of fate. We have no life threads to cut. So long as we sing hymns to the gods' liking, we will carry on!"* echoed the ever musical (yet ever irritating) voices of the Muses.

19   "Ahhh, but do you have a free spirit? The music you make is work. The music I make is recreation. Animals and trees hear my music—I

can move them with it and speak directly to their souls." remarked Orpheus with a smirk as he turned to address Hades and Hermes. "How does it feel to have hymns of praise hurled at you by whores? After all, they are incapable of expressing what they want, they only carry out your will. They only submit to you to ensure their place on Olympus! They feel no emotion for you! Their songs are empty—they're lies!"

"Orpheus, we are beloved of the Olympians— 20

"—you are whores." 21

"We have been chosen to dwell with Zeus, our father, and Apollo, 22 *your father. Why has your father not secured your place on this snowy peak?"*

"I dwell with humans. Through my music I can move mountains, turn aside stones—armed with my harp and tongue, I am invincible. Hades has tried to slay me, did he succeed? Nay! My melody turned away his beasts." Orpheus abruptly turned to address Hades once more. "My music allowed my travel into your domain— that ever dank and dreary hole. While in your domain I wrenched the soul of my wife from your very fist! Hades! You bare witness to the power I possess! These muses are whores—liars, powerless liars with no will of their own." 23

"You speak well, human, however, your logic is flawed. Unless Hades owns your soul, I do not deliver a single measure of your music to the people. If I, messenger of the gods, do not spread word of you, you are nothing." 24

"My music delivers itself. People need not hear it from the likes of you, Hermes. A single note, plucked sweetly from my harp, reverberates louder in the ears of man than any noise you deliver." 25

"My word travels faster, foolish human! My words reach more people in one hour than your silly string can reach in a lifetime!" 26

"Any word spread by you may be heard by many today, but will be long forgotten tomorrow. The message I deliver reaches further than just a person's ears. My message speaks directly to their souls and as such, is not easily forgotten." A look in Hades' eye caught Orpheus' gaze. The dark lord sat smiling—grinning evilly with eyes gleaming of his malintentions. He snickered softly to himself as if at some secret joke, turned to face Apollo and spoke. 27

"Despite the high moral ground you claim, Orpheus, the fact remains that you are mortal and we are gods. It matters not that your music is more powerful than the Muses. We might not be able to control your gift, but we can control other mortals' 28 opinions. For every person you reach with your music, I steal three souls who could be listening to you."

29   "Lord Hades, I must remain impartial on this matter, but I believe our discourse has come to a close. Music makes people happy—it matters not whether it has integrity. Integrity matters only to the people composing the music. Music is supposed to be fun to create. If there are musicians, such as my Muses, who want to make music a job—make it work and just another part of everyday life, it is their loss. You Orpheus and others like you know what the true power of music is. The fact remains that not everyone can be moved by music in the same manner as you. All music has the power to move people—it depends on the listener." spoke Apollo in a fatherly tone.

30   "Point taken, Father. I understand a bit more now. Music's power is relative to the individual. Music, and all art, is a process. It's a process that does not end when a song is finished being written or a sculpture is finished being sculpted. The process does not ever end. Once music is performed, the listeners and their interpretations of it take the reigns."

31   *"And you have proven yourself most wise, young Orpheus. Just as we control your life thread, we also spin the life thread for your and all music. Believe us when we say, your thread will be sliced long before that of your music."*

32   With that, Orpheus returned to his dwelling, on the outskirts of Athens, and all the gods returned to their godly duties. Orpheus made music, the Muses made music, and it filled the Greek peninsula. Their music traveled all around the world and mingled with other musics. Their music and the music of others raised the quality of life for everyone.

Links to Outside Resources

The Ultimate Band List   Exactly what it says. Every band in existence (almost) is here.

The Internet Underground Music Archive   A searchable archive of underground music.

The Encyclopedia Mythica   Everything you wanted to know about Mythology but were afraid to ask! Check it out, awesome site.

Hellenic Links   Hellenic information courtesy of MEDEA the Musical.

SIVA: A Smashing Pumpkin Web Site   My favorite web site.

The Official Hootie and the Blowfish Page   My least favorite web site.

✦ ✦ ✦

✦ Framing the Context

1. The cast of characters table and the links to Greek mythology sites indicate assumptions Peterson makes about his readers, his musician friends, and expository writing classmates. What are those assumptions?

2. What does Peterson's decision to present this writing on-line suggest about his relationship to his readers and their relationship to his purpose?

✦ Point of View

3. Peterson is not a visible participant in the trial he presents, but he does include subjective commentary in the links and photo gallery sections. What overall relationship does Peterson establish with his readers by combining these two points of view?

4. Using a forum of voices in dialogue rather than paragraphs of prose is likely to produce a different effect on the readers' interaction with the text. Describe that difference in interaction.

✦ Shape of Ideas

5. Peterson's use of the Greek deities creates an allegorical framework. What structure does this allegorical framework follow in presenting the trial?

6. How does the framework create a better understanding of Peterson's purpose for the readers?

✦ Choosing Voice

7. Describe the level of formality Peterson uses to create the voice of the Olympian gods, and support your description with examples from the dialogue.

8. Which voice in the dialogue represents Peterson's opinions on integrity? Identify the qualities in that voice that make it different from the other voices.

+ *Credibility*

9. How does using the mythology of the Olympian gods as the main source contribute to Peterson's credibility with his intended audience?

10. What effect do the additional links Peterson provides have on his ethos?

Georgia O'Keeffe

Joan Didion

✦ ✦ ✦

Joan Didion understands well her claim in this essay: "Style is character." As the author of four novels: Run River, Play It as It Lays, The Book of Common Prayer, *and* Democracy; *five nonfiction works:* Slouching Towards Bethlehem, The White Album, Salvador, Miami, *and* After Henry; *and numerous reviews and screenplays, Didion has faced the challenge of the blank page, the stark canvas, the empty stage that artists address alone and the voice of critics that follows creative efforts. In the essay that follows from* The White Album (1979), *Didion profiles Georgia O'Keeffe as a woman to be admired for the battle she fought to assert her individuality as an artist and a woman.*

"Where I was born and where and how I have lived is unimpor-   1
tant," Georgia O'Keeffe told us in the book of paintings and words published in her ninetieth year on earth. She seemed to be advising us to forget the beautiful face in the Stieglitz photographs. She appeared to be dismissing the rather condescending romance that had attached to her by then, the romance of extreme good looks and advanced age and deliberate isolation. "It is what I have done with where I have been that should be of interest." I recall an August afternoon in Chicago in 1973 when I took my daughter, then seven, to see what Georgia O'Keeffe had done with where she had been. One of the vast O'Keeffe "Sky Above Clouds" canvases floated over the back stairs in the Chicago Art Institute that day, dominating what seemed to be several stories of empty light, and my daughter looked at it once, ran to the landing, and kept on looking. "Who drew it," she whispered after a while. I told her. "I need to talk to her," she said finally.

My daughter was making, that day in Chicago, an entirely un-   2
conscious but quite basic assumption about people and the work they do. She was assuming that the glory she saw in the work reflected a glory in its maker, that the painting was the painter as the poem is the poet, that every choice one made alone—every word chosen or rejected, every brush stroke laid or not laid down—betrayed

one's character. *Style is character.* It seemed to me that afternoon that I had rarely seen so instinctive an application of this familiar principle, and I recall being pleased not only that my daughter responded to style as character but that it was O'Keeffe's particular style to which she responded: this was a hard woman who had imposed her 192 square feet of clouds on Chicago.

3 "Hardness" has not been in our century a quality much admired in women, nor in the past twenty years has it even been in official favor for men. When hardness surfaces in the very old we tend to transform it into "crustiness" or eccentricity, some tonic pepperiness to be indulged at a distance. On the evidence of her work and what she has said about it, Georgia O'Keeffe is neither "crusty" nor eccentric. She is simply, hard, a straight shooter, a woman clean of received wisdom and open to what she sees. This is a woman who could early on dismiss most of her contemporaries as "dreamy," and would later single out one she liked as "a very poor painter." (And then add, apparently by way of softening the judgment: "I guess he wasn't a painter at all. He had no courage and I believe that to create one's own world in any of the arts takes courage.") This is a woman who in 1939 could advise her admirers that they were missing her point, that their appreciation of her famous flowers was merely sentimental. "When I paint a red hill," she observed coolly in the catalogue for an exhibition that year, "you say it is too bad that I don't always paint flowers. A flower touches almost everyone's heart. A red hill doesn't touch everyone's heart." This is a woman who could describe the genesis of one of her most well-known paintings—the "Cow's Skull: Red, White and Blue" owned by the Metropolitan—as an act of quite deliberate and derisive orneriness. "I thought of the city men I had been seeing in the East," she wrote. "They talked so often of writing the Great American Novel—the Great American Play—the Great American Poetry. . . . So as I was painting my cow's head on blue I thought to myself, 'I'll make it an American painting. They will not think it great with the red stripes down the sides—Red, White and Blue—but they will notice it.' "

4 *The city men. The men. They.* The words crop up again and again as this astonishingly aggressive woman tells us what was on her mind when she was making her astonishingly aggressive paintings. It was those city men who stood accused of sentimentalizing her flowers: "I made you take time to look at what I saw and when you

took time to really notice my flower you hung all your associations with flowers on my flower and you write about my flower as if I think and see what you think and see—and I don't." *And I don't.* Imagine those words spoken, and the sound you hear is *don't tread on me.* "The men" believed it impossible to paint New York, so Georgia O'Keeffe painted New York. "The men" didn't think much of her bright color, so she made it brighter. The men yearned toward Europe so she went to Texas, and then New Mexico. The men talked about Cézanne, "long involved remarks about the 'plastic quality' of his form and color," and took one another's long involved remarks, in the view of this angelic rattlesnake in their midst, altogether too seriously. "I can paint one of those dismal-colored paintings like the men," the woman who regarded herself always as an outsider remembers thinking one day in 1922, and she did—a painting of a shed "all low-toned and dreary with the tree beside the door." She called this act of rancor "The Shanty" and hung it in her next show. "The men seemed to approve of it," she reported fifty-four years later, her contempt undimmed. "They seemed to think that maybe I was beginning to paint. That was my only low-toned dismal-colored painting."

Some women fight and others do not. Like so many successful guerrillas in the war between the sexes, Georgia O'Keeffe seems to have been equipped early with an immutable sense of who she was and a fairly clear understanding that she would be required to prove it. On the surface her upbringing was conventional. She was a child on the Wisconsin prairie who played with china dolls and painted watercolors with cloudy skies because sunlight was too hard to paint and, with her brother and sisters, listened every night to her mother read stories of the Wild West, of Texas, of Kit Carson and Billy the Kid. She told adults that she wanted to be an artist and was embarrassed when they asked what kind of artist she wanted to be—she had no idea "what kind." She had no idea what artists did. She had never seen a picture that interested her, other than a pen-and-ink Maid of Athens in one of her mother's books, some Mother Goose illustrations printed on cloth, a tablet cover that showed a little girl with pink roses, and the painting of Arabs on horseback that hung in her grandmother's parlor. At thirteen, in a Dominican convent, she was mortified when the sister corrected her drawing. At Chatham Episcopal Institute in Virginia she painted lilacs and sneaked time alone to walk out to where she could see the line of the Blue Ridge Mountains on the horizon. At the Art Institute in Chicago she

5

was shocked by the presence of live models and wanted to abandon anatomy lessons. At the Art Students League in New York one of her fellow students advised her that, since he would be a great painter and she would end up teaching painting in a girls' school, any work of hers was less important than modeling for him. Another painted over her work to show her how the impressionists did trees. She had not before heard how the Impressionists did trees and she did not much care.

6   At twenty-four she left all those opinions behind and went for the first time to live in Texas, where there were no trees to paint and no one to tell her how not to paint them. In Texas there was only the horizon she craved. In Texas she had her sister Claudia with her for a while, and in the late afternoons they would walk away from town and toward the horizon and watch the evening star come out. "That evening star fascinated me," she wrote. "It was in some way very exciting to me. My sister had a gun, and as we walked she would throw bottles into the air and shoot as many as she could before they hit the ground. I had nothing but to walk into nowhere and the wide sunset space with the star. Ten watercolors were made from that star." In a way one's interest is compelled as much by the sister Claudia with the gun as by the painter Georgia with the star, but only the painter left us this shining record. Ten watercolors were made from that star.

✦ ✦ ✦

✦ Framing the Context

1. In the two introductory paragraphs, Didion focuses on her seven-year-old daughter's response to O'Keeffe's art to shape her focus: *"Style is character."* How does using a child's view capture the relationship Didion wants her readers to have with O'Keeffe?

2. From the facts and details presented in the introduction, what assumptions do you think Didion makes about what readers already know about O'Keeffe? Write a paragraph profiling the audience and their assumptions.

✦ Point of View

3. After relating a personal experience in the introduction, how visible is Didion to the reader? What point of view does she adopt and why?

4. What relationship does this point of view develop between Didion and her readers?

✦ *Shape of Ideas*

5. Didion admires O'Keeffe as "a hard woman." How does her framework develop her admiration for O'Keeffe's "hardness"?

6. What definition of "hardness" are the readers likely to form from the framework Didion uses?

✦ *Choosing Voice*

7. Didion has an established reputation as a literary writer. How does the literary quality of her writing influence the formality of her voice? Cite at least one example from each paragraph.

8. In several places Didion uses italics and repetition. What effect do these devices have on the reader in each place they are used?

✦ *Credibility*

9. Didion uses O'Keeffe's own words as the primary source for her essay. Does her reliance on one source limit her credibility or enrich it? Explain using specific examples.

10. The essay begins and ends with a focus on a work of O'Keeffe's art. How does the positioning of these particular works convey the ethos Didion wants the readers to realize for both O'Keeffe and herself?

Do Heroes Exist?

Alex Hagedorn

✦ ✦ ✦

Alex Hagedorn has always believed in heroes, but he knows many people limit their belief to the superheroes of book and movie fantasies. In this essay written for his composition course, Alex analyzes why he believes that the legendary heroes of fiction would not exist unless there were heroes in real life on which to base them.

1   Hercules, King Arthur, Superman—all instantly recognizable as heroes. For centuries people have created and believed in myths and characters such as these. These heroes' adventures have immortalized our human fascination with the struggle between good and evil. However, there is more to a hero than an epic battle. While the most deserving fictional adventurers have become legends, real heroes remain unheralded and are not granted immortality through tale. A true hero is the common man who strives to overcome the weaker half of his humanity. But are there really such things as heroes? Some would deny it. However, a fictional hero could not be created if there were no real hero prototypes in our daily life.

2   If heroes do in fact exist, then how can we define them? What makes one man a hero and the next nothing more than a weak coward? I believe it is caring that is the foundation of a hero's character. Without care one will not be concerned with the welfare of himself and others. Concern ushers in a responsibility that directs a person's actions toward daily life. Care and responsibility are important basic characteristics, but more must be required to stand among others as a hero. A hero must stand unwavering when opposition glares him in the face. He must not fear difficulty and challenge, but rather learn to accept exhaustion and weariness. Fear of loneliness and self-reliance cannot consume this man. Also integral is an independence of strength and motivation so that others can depend on him. A hero must demand of himself self-sacrifice and not become frightened to shoulder the burden alone. Lastly, and perhaps most importantly, the hero must never give up. Never. Alone with a cold wall forced against his back, he must fight with or without, and through pain, fear, frus-

tration, and sorrow. With such rigorous criteria can anyone be expected to embody these attributes?

The answer is yes. Many people exemplify the characteristics of concern, responsibility, courage, independence, self-sacrifice, and dedication. A thief can be dedicated, or a lawyer courageous, but that does not make them heroes. What are they missing? What can fill a void in their character? A conscience is the overall necessity to make every quality potentially heroic. They must possess a heart and a belief in the general welfare of others through law and order. It is the heart that drives the hero and separates him from others. It gives meaning and honor to his dedication, courage, and other characteristics. So, a hero not only has a strong character but a just heart. Do real examples exist? Can anyone be expected to meet these requirements to become a true hero, or is this definition only applicable to those who inhabit the pages of legend? 3

In the unforgiving cold of the night, Batman administers justice to criminals. Law-breakers of the Wild West were checked by Wyatt Earp in *Tombstone*. But these are the characters of stories and legends; actual heroes walk among us on the street, drive past us in the same kind of cars we drive. They are the ordinary men and women who set self-imposed standards for themselves, realizing that they will never appear on the pages of the history books, newspapers, or magazines. They act as heroes because they want to, because it is the right and honorable thing to do. I am drawn to one example, the reason I write this paper. This hero is the reason for my affinity for Batman or the baseball legend, Cal Ripkin, Jr. He is the man who gave me my name, my father. Possessing the courage and responsibility of Batman and the dedication of Cal Ripkin, Jr., James Hagedorn not only wants to do the right thing, he *needs* to. 4

I remember the day that Dad called me from the fire station where he had just returned from a call. I remember the ceremony he received months later for outstanding duty. Dad had been a hero hours earlier on a rain-slicked rooftop amid thunder and lightning. A woman was on that roof with him, ready to jump off. The police were hesitant and unsure when she decided to jump. The only other man on that rooftop was James Hagedorn, and he went over that ledge with her. Grabbing her body and the ledge simultaneously, he saved both their lives. Ungrateful, she began to claw and bite him as she dangled above the ground below, but he refused to let go. He forced himself to hold on until he could pull them both up. He could 5 not surrender the woman to the wet pavement. I have always admired my father. I can see the loneliness and exhaustion in his eyes when he is in the midst of danger, and when I look in the mirror, I see his eyes in my own. He has always been a hero to me, but that day he proved to any who doubt that real heroes do exist.

6   That afternoon my father exhibited a genuine concern for another's life, and he took responsibility to save a woman from herself. He was brave to chase her over the ledge even though he knew he might be sacrificing himself. Never letting go, he would not give up. And, most importantly, his heart drove him to save her. He displayed every characteristic and requirement of a hero. A lesser man would have hidden behind such excuses as, "But there was nothing I could do."

7   Superman and Batman would not hide behind excuses, but they are not real. They could not exist if heroes did not exist in real life. We base these characters on the noble halves of our own humanity. Common men are not perfect, no one is, but their struggle to persevere over their own baseness is what makes them heroes. They surround us even if they do not have capes and six-shooters. Heroes, then, do exist. I believe in heroes and hope one day to be able to stand among them, and my father.

✦ ✦ ✦

✦ Framing the Context

1. What does Hagedorn indicate in the first paragraph that he assumes about his readers' beliefs in heroes?

2. What characteristics beyond fighting "the struggle of good versus evil" are readers likely to associate with fictional adventure heroes?

✦ Point of View

3. Hagedorn uses "I" sparingly except when recounting the story of his father's heroism. Does this limited use of "I" establish a merged point of view? Use examples from the essay to explain your decision.

4. How does Hagedorn's point of view affect his relationship with the readers?

✦ Shape of Ideas

5. How does Hagedorn's framework for the essay respond to what the readers need to know about the existence of real heroes?

6. What other framework structures would also respond to the readers' needs? Explain your choices.

✦ *Choosing Voice*

7. Describe the formality level of Hagedorn's voice and identify the features that indicate that formality.

8. How does Hagedorn's use of questions affect the readers' involvement with the essay?

✦ *Credibility*

9. In paragraphs 2 and 3, Hagedorn presents a full range of qualities a person must have to be considered a hero, yet he provides no specific examples of those qualities in action at that point in the essay. How does this decision affect his credibility? Explain your answer.

10. Hagedorn uses only the example of his father's rescue to support his claim that real heroes do exist. How does this choice contribute to his ethos?

Address to the First Annual Meeting of the American Equal Rights Association

Sojourner Truth

✦ ✦ ✦

Born Isabella Baumfree, a slave on a New York estate owned by a Dutch family, Sojourner Truth had been sold three times by the age of thirteen. Emancipated by New York State law in 1827 at the age of thirty, she worked as a domestic in New York City and gained a reputation as a gifted preacher who, in her travels throughout New England and New York in the 1840s, lectured for the end of slavery and women's rights. As a free woman, she chose the name "Sojourner" to represent her journey for freedom, and "Truth" to reflect her message.

 Although Truth neither read nor wrote English, the speeches she gave were recorded by others, notably Susan B. Anthony and her colleague editors Elizabeth Cady Stanton and Matilda Joslyn Gage who published the following selection and Truth's famous "Ain't I a Woman?" speech in their book The History of Woman Suffrage *(1886). Truth presented this address to the American Equal Rights Association on May 9, 1867, three years after she had successfully protested seating discrimination on Washington's streetcars and had won a court battle against the conductors. By her actions and her words, Sojourner Truth became a model for the twentieth-century civil rights and women's rights movements.*

1 My friends, I am rejoiced that you are glad, but I don't know how you will feel when I get through. I come from another field—the country of the slave. They have got their liberty—so much good luck to have slavery partly destroyed; not entirely. I want it root and branch destroyed. Then we will all be free indeed. I feel that if I have to answer for the deeds done in my body just as much as a man, I have a right to have just as much as a man. There is a great stir about colored men getting their rights, but not a word about the colored women; and if colored men get their rights, and not colored women

theirs, you see the colored men will be masters over the women, and it will be just as bad as it was before. So I am for keeping the thing going while things are stirring; because if we wait till it is still, it will take a great while to get it going again. White women are a great deal smarter, and know more than colored women, while colored women do not know scarcely anything. They go out washing, which is about as high as a colored woman gets, and their men go about idle, strutting up and down, and when the women come home, they ask for their money and take it all, and then scold because there is no food. I want you to consider on that, chil'n. I call you chil'n; you are somebody's chil'n, and I am old enough to be mother of all that is here. I want women to have their rights. In the courts women have no right, no voice; nobody speaks for them. I wish woman to have her voice there among the pettifoggers. If it is not a fit place for women, it is unfit for men to be there.

I am above eighty years old; it is about time for me to be going. 2 I have been forty years a slave and forty years free, and would be here forty years more to have equal rights for all. I suppose I am kept here because something remains for me to do; I suppose I am yet to help to break the chain. I have done a great deal of work; as much as a man, but did not get so much pay. I used to work in the field and bind grain, keeping up with the cradler; but men doing no more, got twice as much pay; so with the German women. They work in the field and do as much work, but do not get the pay. We do as much, we eat as much, we want as much. I suppose I am about the only colored woman that goes about to speak for the rights of the colored women. I want to keep the thing stirring, now that the ice is cracked. What we want is a little money. You men know that you get as much again as women when you write, or for what you do. When we get our rights we shall not have to come to you for money, for then we shall have money enough in our own pockets; and may be you will ask us for money. But help us now until we get it. It is a good consolation to know that when we have got this battle once fought we shall not be coming to you any more. You have been having our rights so long, that you think, like a slave-holder, that you own us. I know that it is hard for one who has held the reins for so long to give up; it cuts like a knife. It will feel all the better when it closes up again. I have been in Washington about three years, seeing about these colored people. Now colored men have the right to vote. There ought to be equal rights now more than ever, since colored people have got their freedom. I am going to talk several times while I am here; so now I will do a little singing. I have not heard any singing since I came here.

3   We are going home. There, children, in heaven we shall rest from all our labors; first do all we have to do here. There I am determined to go, not to stop short of that beautiful place, and I do not mean to stop till I get there, and meet you there, too.

✦ ✦ ✦

✦ Framing the Context

1. The laws of 1867 disallowed the participation of women in government, so the Association whom Truth addresses were all white males. Describe what their disposition toward Truth would have been. What constraints did she face in preparing her address?

2. Truth gave her address four years after Lincoln's Emancipation Proclamation. Explain what purpose the Association had for listening to her.

✦ Point of View

3. Why does Truth choose to use a subjective point of view in addressing this audience?

4. Identify those places in the speech where Truth tries to merge with her audience.

✦ Shape of Ideas

5. Truth's address is short but carefully structured. What framework does she use to make her purpose evident?

6. How does Truth's singing at the end of the address complement her structure?

✦ Choosing Voice

7. Truth repeats variations of the phrase "keep the thing stirring" several times in her address. Review where she uses the phrase and explain the effect it is likely to have on the audience.

8. On this formal occasion, Truth uses figurative language sparingly but with purpose. Make a list of the figurative language she uses and evaluate the force of its effect.

✦ Credibility

9. What personal credentials does Truth incorporate into her address to establish her credibility with the audience? Will they respect those credentials? Why or why not?

10. Truth makes many comparisons between men and women, whites and "coloreds," but she includes no specific numbers or laws to support her claims. How does the lack of specifics affect her credibility?

✦ *Suggestions for Writing about Heroes*

1. America has an infatuation with televised awards ceremonies, especially in the fields of athletics and the performing arts. Although people in other fields also receive recognition for their work, they rarely receive public attention for their achievements. Choose a field that deserves more public recognition and write a proposal directed to a national television network arguing for an annual awards ceremony in this field.

2. Sports events and the people who compete in them receive extensive media coverage. As Bernstein points out, while many of those competitors are considered celebrities, only a few can be considered heroes. Write an essay analyzing the field of sports as a worthy place to search for heroes.

3. Integrity, Peterson claims, should govern artistic creation. Write a profile of an artist or a group of performing artists who exemplify integrity in their work.

4. Ehrenreich and Didion argue that women do not receive the recognition they deserve because the criteria used to determine that recognition often excludes them. What is your position on this issue? Compose an argument supporting your position.

5. Sojourner Truth lived long enough to see some of the points in her address acted on, but some took a century to be recognized, and others still remain problems. Write an essay analyzing the status of equal rights since the first meeting of the American Equal Rights Association.

6. Did you have a favorite superhero as a child, someone whose adventures you admired for doing the right thing and helping others? Reminisce about some of those adventures and write a tribute to that hero.

7. Is there a difference between a hero and a role model? Do they share any characteristics? Examine the differences and similarities and present your decision in a position essay.

8. Edelstein argues that although "Americans perform heroic acts every day," there is no national American hero recognized by the American people in modern times. Write an essay in which you agree with Edelstein or refute his claim.

Chapter 7

✦ ✦ ✦ ✦ ✦ ✦ ✦ ✦ ✦ ✦ ✦

Finding Community

America is accredited with having a pioneering spirit, one that takes pride in individuality but seeks community. Perhaps the wide open spaces of a new frontier inculcated that spirit in us. Those of us who have moved even once in our lifetime know the isolation of being without a community, the vulnerability of evaluating who we are in order to find community with others. Location, economics, age, profession, gender, language, religion, ethnicity, marital status, politics, and myriad other factors that contribute to our image of ourselves also contribute to the identity we seek in community.

The readings in this section examine the meaning of community: how people find community; how they achieve identity; how they gain membership; how their actions are perceived by others. The writers of these selections bring a wide variety of experience and research to the views of community they share, each with a specific group of readers in mind. As readers, focus on your level of interaction with each selection, reading both *with* and *against* the writer. Let that tension lead you to discover the writer's purpose and the choices she or he made to achieve that purpose. The questions following each reading will guide you in determining what choices the writers made and how effective those choices are in connecting the reader, writer, and subject. At the end of the chapter you will find Writing Suggestions for exploring your own ideas on finding community and making writing choices to develop those ideas.

The New Community

Amitai Etzioni

✦ ✦ ✦

The evolution of American communities from predominately rural to urban has led to a decline in the spirit that bonds a community. That is sociologist Amitai Etzioni's thesis in his book, The Spirit of Community: Rights, Responsibilities, and the Communitarian Agenda *(1993), from which the following excerpt was taken. To reclaim that community spirit, Etzioni argues for building many different subcommunities that "balance both diversity and unity."*

1   It's hard to believe now, but for a long time the loss of community was considered to be liberating. Societies were believed to progress from closely knit, "primitive," or rural villages to unrestrictive, "modern," or urban societies. The former were depicted as based on kinship and loyalty in an age in which both were suspect; the latter, however, were seen as based on reason (or "rationality") in an era in which reason's power to illuminate was admired with little attention paid to the deep shadows it casts. The two types of social relations have often been labeled with the terms supplied by a German sociologist, Ferdinand Tönnies. One is gemeinschaft, the German term for community, and the other is gesellschaft, the German word for society, which he used to refer to people who have rather few bonds, like people in a crowd or a mass society [*Community and Society*].

2   Far from decrying the loss of community, this sanguine approach to the rise of modernity depicted small towns and villages as backward places that confined behavior. American writers such as Sinclair Lewis and John O'Hara satirized small towns as insular, claustrophobic places, inhabited by petty, mean-spirited people. They were depicted as the opposite of "big cities," whose atmosphere was said to set people free. Anonymity would allow each person to pursue what he or she wished rather than what the community dictated. It was further argued that relations in the gesellschaft would be based not on preexisting, "ascribed" social bonds, such as between cousins, but on contractual relations, freely negotiated among autonomous individuals.

186

Other major forms of progress were believed to accompany the   3
movement from a world of villages to one of cities. Magic, superstition, alchemy, and religion—"backward beliefs"—would be replaced
by bright, shining science and technology. There would be no more
villagers willing to sell their wares only to their own kind and not to
outsiders—a phenomenon anthropologists have often noted. Old-
fashioned values and a sense of obligation were expected to yield to
logic and calculation. Social bonds dominating all relations (you did
not charge interest on a loan to members of your community because such a charge was considered indecent usury) were pushed
aside to make room for a free market, with prices and interest rates
set according to market logic. By the same token, the network of reciprocal obligations and care that is at the heart of communities
would give way to individual rights protected by the state. The impersonal right to social services and welfare payments, for instance,
would replace any reliance on members of one's family, tribe, or ethnic benevolent association.

The sun, moon, and stars of the new universe would be individ-   4
uals, not the community. In a typical case, the U.S. Supreme Court
ruled that the Sierra Club had no legal standing to argue for the
preservation of parkland as a community resource (Glendon 112).
Rather, if the Sierra Club wished to show standing, it would have to
demonstrate that particular individuals were harmed.

Throughout twentieth-century America, as the transition to   5
gesellschaft evolved, even its champions realized that it was not the
unmitigated blessing they had expected. Although it was true that
those who moved from villages and small towns into urban centers
often shed tight social relations and strong community bonds, the
result for many was isolation, lack of caring for one another, and exposure to rowdiness and crime.

Criminologists report that young farmhands in rural America in   6
the early nineteenth-century did not always work on their parents'
land. However, when they were sent to work outside their home they
usually lived with other farmers and were integrated into their family life. In this way they were placed in a community context that sustained the moral voice, reinforced the values of their upbringing, and
promoted socially constructive behavior. It was only when these
farmhands went to work in factories in cities—and were housed
on their own in barracks without established social networks, elders, and values—that rowdy and criminal behavior, alcoholism, and

prostitution became common. Even in those early days attempts to correct these proclivities were made not by returning these young people to their families and villages, but by trying to generate Communitarian elements in the cities. Among the best analysts of these developments is James Q. Wilson, a leading political scientist. He notes that associations such as the Young Men's Christian Association (YMCA), temperance societies, and the Children's Aid Society sought to provide a socially appropriate, morality-sustaining context for young people ("Rediscovery" 13).

7   Other experiences paralleled those of the factory hands. The migration to the American West, for example, is usually thought of as a time when individuals were free to venture forth and carve out a life of their own in the Great Plains. Actually, many people traveled in caravans and settled as communities, although each family claimed its own plot of land. Mutual assistance in such rough terrain was an absolute requirement. Mining towns and trading posts, however, in which rampant individualism often did prevail, were places of much chicanery. People who had mined gold often lost their stakes to unscrupulous traders; those who owned land were driven off it with little compensation by railroad companies, among others. Fly-by-night banks frequently welshed on notes that they themselves had issued. An unfettered market, one without a community context, turned out to lack the essential moral underpinnings that trade requires, and not just by sound social relations.

8   In many ways these frontier settlements—with their washed-out social bonds, loose morals, and unbridled greed—were the forerunners of Wall Street in the 1980s. The Street became a "den of thieves," thick with knaves who held that anything went as long as you made millions more than the next guy. Moreover, the mood of self-centered "making it" of the me generation spilled over into large segments of society. It was celebrated by the White House and many in Congress, who saw in an unfettered pursuit of self-interest the social force that revitalizes economies and societies. By the end of the eighties even some of the proponents of me-ism felt that the pursuit of greed had run amok.

9   By the early nineties the waning of community, which had long concerned sociologists, became more pronounced and drew more attention. As writer Jonathan Rowe put it: "It was common to think about the community as we used to think about air and water. It is there. It takes care of itself, and it can and will absorb whatever we

unleash into it" ("Left and Right"). Now it became evident that the social environment needed fostering just as nature did. Responding to the new cues, George Bush evoked the image of a "kinder, gentler" society as a central theme for his first presidential campaign in 1988. The time was right to return to community and the moral order it harbored. Bill Clinton made the spirit of community a theme of his 1992 campaign.

The prolonged recession of 1991–1992 and the generally low and slowing growth of the American economy worked against this new concern with we-ness. Interracial and interethnic tensions rose considerably, not only between blacks and whites, but also between blacks and Hispanics and among various segments of the community and Asian-Americans. This is one more reason why the United States will have to work its way to a stronger, growing, more competitive economy: interracial and ethnic peace are much easier to maintain in a rising than in a stagnant economy. However, it does not mean that community rebuilding has to be deferred until the economy is shored up. It does indicate that enhancing we-ness will require greater commitment and effort from both the government and the people, if community rebuilding is to take place in a sluggish economy. 10

Does this mean that we all have to move back to live in small towns and villages in order to ensure the social foundations of morality, to rebuild and shore up we-ness? Can one not bring up decent young people in the city? Isn't it possible to have a modern society, which requires a high concentration of labor and a great deal of geographic mobility—and still sustain a web of social bonds, a Communitarian nexus? There is more than one sociological answer to these queries. 11

First, many cities have sustained (or reclaimed) some elements of community. Herbert Gans, a Columbia University sociologist, observed that within cities there were what he called "urban villages." He found communities where, generally speaking, "neighbors were friendly and quick to say hello to each other," where the various ethnic groups, transients, and bohemians "could live together side by side without much difficulty." Gans further noted that "for most West Enders [in Boston] . . . life in the area resembled that found in the village or small town, and even in the suburb" (*The Urban Villagers*, 14–15). Even in large metropolises, such as New York City, there are neighborhoods in which many people know their neighbors, their 12 shopkeepers, and their local leaders. They are likely to meet one another in neighborhood bars, bowling alleys, and places of worship. They watch out for each other's safety and children. They act in concert to protect their parks and bus stops. They form political clubs and are a force in local politics. (Jim Sleeper's *Closest of Strangers* provides a fine description of these New York City communities.)

13   In some instances members of one ethnic group live comfortably next to one another, as in New York City's Chinatown and Miami's Little Havana. In other cities ethnic groups are more geographically dispersed but sustain ethnic-community bonds around such institutions as churches and synagogues, social clubs, and private schools. In recent decades a measure of return to community has benefited from the revival of loyalty to ethnic groups. While the sons and daughters of immigrants, the so-called second generation, often sought to assimilate, to become Americanized to the point that their distinct backgrounds were lost in a new identity, *their* children, the third generation and onward, often seek to reestablish their ethnic identity and bonds.

14   How does one reconcile the two sociological pictures—the James Q. Wilson concept of the city as gesellschaft, with little community or moral base, and the Herbert Gans image of gemeinschaft, of urban villages? The answer, first of all, is that both exist side by side. Between the urban villages, in row houses and high rises, you find large pockets of people who do not know their next-door neighbors, with whom they may have shared a floor, corridors, and elevators for a generation. Elderly people especially, who have no social bonds at work and are largely abandoned by their families, often lead rather isolated lives. In 1950 14.4 percent of those sixty-five years of age and older lived alone (Monk 534); by 1990 the percentage stood at nearly 31 percent (U.S. Bureau of the Census, Table L, 12).

15   Also, to some extent a welcome return to small-town life of sorts has been occurring in modern America. Although not all suburbs, which attracted millions of city dwellers, make for viable communities, as a rule the movement to the suburbs has enhanced the Communitarian nexus.

16   In addition, postmodern technology helps. More people are again able to work at home or nearby, and a high concentration of labor is less and less necessary, in contrast with the industrial age. People can use their computers and modems at home to do a good part of their office work, from processing insurance claims to trad-

ing worldwide in commodities, stocks, and bonds. Architects can design buildings and engineers monitor faraway power networks from their places of residence.

It used to be widely observed that Americans, unlike Europeans, move around so much that they are hard-pressed to put down real community roots. On average, it is said, the whole country moves about once every five years. These figures, however, may be a bit obsolete. For various reasons, in recent years Americans seem to move somewhat less often (Barringer A16). One explanation is a growing desire to maintain the bonds of friendship and local social roots of their children, spouses, and themselves. In effect there is little reason to believe that the economy will suffer if this trend continues, and it may actually benefit from less shuttling around of people. Surely the Communitarian nexus will benefit.

Finally, there are new, nongeographic, communities made up of people who do not live near one another. Their foundations may not be as stable and deep-rooted as residential communities, but they fulfill many of the social and moral functions of traditional communities. Work-based and professional communities are among the most common of these. That is, people who work together in a steel mill or a high-tech firm such as Lotus or Microsoft often develop work-related friendships and community webs; groups of co-workers hang around together, help one another, play and party together, and go on joint outings. As they learn to know and care for one another, they also form and reinforce moral expectations.

Other communities are found in some law firms, on many campuses (although one community may not encompass everyone on campus), among physicians at the same hospital or with the same specialty in a town, and among some labor union members.

Some critics have attacked these communities as being artificially constructed, because they lack geographical definition or because they are merely social networks, without a residential concentration. Ray Oldenburg, author of *The Great Good Place*, decries the new definitions of community that encompass co-workers and even radio call-in show audiences. "Can we really create a satisfactory community apart from geography?" he asks (Baldwin 17). "My answer is 'no.'" But people who work every day in the same place spend more hours together and in closer proximity than people who live on the same village street. Most important, these nongeographic communities often provide at least some elements of the Communitarian nexus, and hence they tend to have the moral infrastructure we consider essential for a civil and humane society.

21   In short, our society is neither without community nor sufficiently Communitarian; it is neither gemeinschaft nor gesellschaft, but a mixture of the two sociological conditions. America does not need a simple return to gemeinschaft, to the traditional community. Modern economic prerequisites preclude such a shift, but even if it were possible, such backpedaling would be undesirable because traditional communities have been too constraining and authoritarian. Such traditional communities were usually homogeneous. What we need now are communities that balance both diversity and unity. As John W. Gardner has noted: "To prevent the wholeness from smothering diversity, there must be a philosophy of pluralism, an open climate for dissent, and an opportunity for subcommunities to retain their identity and share in the setting of larger group goals" (*Building Community* 11). Thus, we need to strengthen the communitarian elements in the urban and suburban centers, to provide the social bonds that sustain the moral voice, but at the same time avoid tight networks that suppress pluralism and dissent. James Pinkerton, who served in the Bush White House, speaks eloquently about a new paradigm focused around what he calls a "new gemeinschaft." It would be, he says, neither oppressive nor hierarchical. In short, we need new communities in which people have choices and readily accommodate divergent *sub*communities but still maintain common bonds.

Notes

Deborah Baldwin, "Creating Community," *Common Cause Magazine,* July/August 1990, 17.

Felicity Barringer, "18 percent of Households in U.S. Moved in '89," *New York Times,* December 20, 1991, A16.

Herber Gans, *The Urban Villagers: Group and Class in the Life of Italian-Americans* (New York: The Free Press, 1962, 1982), 14–15.

John W. Gardner, *Building Community* (Washington, D.C.: Independent Sector, 1991), 11.

Mary Ann Glendon, *Rights Talk* (New York: The Free Press, 1991), 112.

Abraham Monk, "Aging, Loneliness, and Communications," *American Behavioral Scientist* 31(5): 534.

Jonathan Rowe, "Left and Right: The Emergence of a New Politics in the 1990s?" sponsored by the Heritage Foundation and the Progressive Foundation, October 30, 1991, Washington, D.C.

Jim Sleeper, *Closest of Strangers: Liberalism and the Politics of Race in New York* (New York: W. W. Norton & Company, 1990).

Ferdinand Tönnies, *Community and Society,* translated and edited by Charles P. Loomis (East Lansing: Michigan State University Press, 1957).

U.S. Bureau of the Census, Current Population Reports, series P-20, no. 450, *Marital Status and Living Arrangements: March 1990* (Washington, D.C.: U.S. Government Printing Office, 1991), table L, 12.

James Q. Wilson, "The Rediscovery of Character: Private Virtue and Public Policy," *The Public Interest* 81 (Fall 1985)· 13.

✦ ✦ ✦

✦ *Framing the Context*

1. What features from this chapter indicate that Etzioni is writing to an academic audience?

2. Describe what assumptions Etzioni can make about his readers' purpose for reading this chapter.

✦ *Point of View*

3. What does Etzioni's vantage point of scholarly authority indicate about his assumed relationship to his readers?

4. Does Etzioni's relationship to his readers influence him to use a merged point of view or does he remain objectively distant?

✦ *Shape of Ideas*

5. In paragraphs 1–10, Etzioni presents a brief history of the evolution of American communities. Look carefully at the categories of information he presents and the level of detail with which he describes that evolution. From your observation of these features, determine what assumptions Etzioni makes about what his audience already knows about the subject.

6. Although Etzioni presents a brief historical overview, he does not choose a chronological structure as his main framework. What structure does he choose and how does that structure fit his purpose?

✦ *Choosing Voice*

7. Although academic writing is often quite formal, Etzioni uses a combination of both formal and informal diction. Make a list of ten

examples from the selection for each category and describe the effect Etzioni's diction choices is likely to have on the intended readers.

8. Etzioni begins paragraph 11 with a series of questions. How does this technique affect the character of his voice and what response does he expect from the readers?

✦ *Credibility*

9. Etzioni has a tendency to present words and phrases in quotations without providing any attribution (see paras. 1, 2, 3, 8). What is his purpose in using these quotes and how is the lack of attribution likely to affect his credibility?

10. Review the list of sources that appears at the end of the selection. In what way will the quality and quantity of those sources contribute to the ethos Etzioni establishes with his readers?

Intentional Communities
Lifestyles Based on Ideals

Geoph Kozeny

✦ ✦ ✦

As coordinator for the Fellowship of Intentional Communities database, Geoph Kozeny has a vested interest in publishing this article on the organization's Web site (www.ic.org), and as a "seasoned veteran of cooperative living" for 20 years and having visited over 250 intentional communities, he brings a great deal of firsthand experience to his views on the subject. To Kozeny, finding and forming a successful community requires a conscious purpose and shared values, not just geographical proximity. In this article, a version of which also appears in Claude Whitmyer's book In the Company of Others *(1993), Kozeny presents an overview of the intentional communities movement, its evolution, and its potential as a unifying social force.*

Today many people are questioning our society's values, and asking what gives meaning to life. They bemoan the "loss of community," and are looking for ways to reintroduce community values into their lives. 1

There are several options now available to the average person that satisfy at least the basic cravings: many folks get involved with various civic or social change groups; others get more deeply involved in the activities of their church; still others create friendships and support networks in their neighborhoods. Those with strong motivation to live their values "full time" often seek to join or create intentional communities. 2

An "intentional community" is a group of people who have chosen to live together with a common purpose, working cooperatively to create a lifestyle that reflects their shared core values. The people may live together on a piece of rural land, in a suburban home, or in an urban neighborhood, and they may share a single residence or live in a cluster of dwellings. 3

This definition spans a wide variety of groups, including (but not limited to) communes, student cooperatives, land co-ops, cohousing 4 groups, monasteries and ashrams, and farming collectives. Although quite diverse in philosophy and lifestyle, each of these groups places a high priority on fostering a sense of community—a feeling of belonging and mutual support that is increasingly hard to find in mainstream Western society.

5   Intentional communities are like people—you can categorize them based on certain distinguishing characteristics, but no two are ever identical. Differences among them, whether obvious or subtle, can be attributed to variations in philosophy, in mission or project emphasis, in behavioral norms, or in the personality and style of the leaders (if the group has identified leaders), and the individual members. Each group is somehow unique.

A Time-Honored Idea

6   Mainstream media typically promote the popular myth that shared living began with the "hippie crash pads" of the '60s—and died with the arrival of "yuppies" in the late '70s and early '80s.

7   The truth, however, is quite different. Today there are literally thousands of groups, with hundreds of thousands of members, that live in intentional communities and extended families based on something other than blood ties. This type of living has been around for thousands of years, not just decades.

8   It is well documented that early followers of Jesus banded together to live in a "community of goods," simplifying their lives and sharing all that they owned. That tradition continues to this day, particularly through many inner-city Christian groups that live communally. These groups often pool resources and efforts in their ministry to the homeless, the poor, orphans, single parents, battered women, and otherwise neglected and oppressed minorities.

9   Yet shared living goes back much farther than that, predating the development of agriculture many thousands of years ago. Early hunter-gatherers banded together in tribes, not just blood-related families, and depended on cooperation for their very survival.

10   The advent of the isolated nuclear family is, in fact, a fairly recent phenomenon, having evolved primarily with the rise of industrialization, particularly the development of high-speed transportation. As transportation has become cheaper and faster, we've also witnessed an increase in transience, and the demise of the traditional neighborhood.

Roots & Realities

Although many contemporary community visions emphasize the 11
creation of neighborhood and/or extended family ties, their philo-
sophic roots are amazingly diverse. The range includes Christians,
Quakers, and followers of Eastern religions, to '60s drop-outs, anar-
chists, psychologists, artists, back-to-the-land survivalists—and the
list goes on.

The scope of their primary values is equally broad, including ecol- 12
ogy, equality, appropriate technology, self-sufficiency, right livelihood,
humanist psychology, creativity, spirituality, meditation, yoga, and the
pursuit of global peace. However, even among groups that base their
philosophy on "achieving a holistic view of the world," it would be
quite surprising to discover a community that has achieved "perfection" amidst the fast-paced chaos of modern life. Communities draw
their membership from society at large, and those members bring with
them generations of social conditioning. The attitudes, behaviors, and
institutions prevalent in the broader society—including the very things
we seek alternatives to—are a significant part of our upbringing.
Merely identifying a problem and expressing a desire to overcome it
does not mean that we presently have the perspective or skills needed
to transcend it. The problems we see "out there" in the mainstream—
greed, dishonesty, excessive ego, lack of self-esteem, factionalism, inadequate resources, poor communication skills, you name it—all
manage to find a significant role in alternative cultures as well.

What is encouraging about many intentional communities is 13
their tendency to be open to new ideas, their willingness to be tolerant of other approaches, and their commitment to live in a way that
reflects their idealism. Although communities exist that are close-
minded and bigoted, they're the exception, not the rule. More often
than not, people who consciously choose to live in an intentional
community also have parallel interests in ecology, personal growth,
cooperation, and peaceful social transformation—pursuing the work
necessary to change destructive attitudes and behaviors often taken
for granted in the prevailing culture.

Some Common Threads

Spirituality or religion, regardless of the specific sect or form, is prob- 14
ably the most common inspiration for launching a new community.

Such groups bear a striking resemblance to their centuries-old predecessors—in spite of current developments in technology, education, psychology, and theology. Many of North America's leading centers for the study of meditation and yoga have been established by intentional communities based on the teachings of spiritual masters from the Far East. (Such centers include Kripalu in Massachusetts, Ananda Village in California, Satchidananda Ashram in Virginia, Ananda Marga in New York, and Maharishi University in Iowa. Each of these intentional communities serves a widely dispersed group of practitioners, including those who live in "sister" communities, and many who live "out there" in the wider society.)

15   Among secular communities, the inspiration is typically based on bold visions of creating a new social and economic order—establishing replicable models that will lead to the peaceful and ecological salvation of the planet. In some cases, however, secular groups may opt for isolation, seeking to escape the problems of the rest of the world by creating instead a life of self-sufficiency, simplicity, and serenity.

16   Most members of intentional communities share a deep-felt concern about home, family, and neighborhood. Beyond the obvious purpose of creating an extended-family environment for raising a family, communities create an environment of familiarity and trust sufficiently strong that doors can safely be left unlocked. In today's world of escalating crime, merely having that kind of security may be reason enough to join.

17   Dozens of intentional communities, alarmed by rising student/teacher ratios and falling literacy rates in public schools, have opted to establish alternative schools and to form communities as a base of support for that type of education. Intentional communities comprise a sizeable chunk of the membership of the National Coalition of Alternative Community Schools, an organization of private schools, families, and individuals who share a commitment to create a new and empowering structure for education. Coalition members publish a quarterly newsletter and organize an annual spring conference for sharing resources and skills for social change.

18   Other communities, usually smaller, have created rural homesteads where they can pursue homeschooling without fear of legal pressure from local school officials. State laws favorable to schooling at home have been promoted, and in some cases initiated, by members of intentional communities. Many communities that homeschool are active in national associations organized specifically

to support parents' rights, promote topical networking, and to increase the nation's awareness of homeschooling as a viable educational option.

Another popular issue these days is ecology. Over 90 percent of contemporary communities I've visited, including those located in urban areas, practice recycling and composting. Many serve as model environments or teaching centers for sustainable agriculture and appropriate technology, and feature such concepts as permaculture, organic gardening, grey water systems, solar and wind power, and passive solar home design. Eco-Home, a small shared household in Los Angeles, is an inspiring model of how to live ecologically in an urban environment. "The Farm," a large cooperative community in rural Tennessee, has launched a wide range of environmentally focused projects, including the development of advanced radiation detection equipment; a solar electronics company; a solar car company; the Natural Rights Center (an environmental law project); and a publishing company that specializes in books about environmental issues, vegetarian cooking, natural health care, midwifery, Native Americans, children's stories, and pesticide-free gardening.

In the late 1960s, a wave of new communities influenced by the antiwar movement, the "sexual revolution," rock music, more permissive attitudes about drugs, and the popularization of Eastern religions sprung up to create cooperative lifestyles based on sexual liberation, born-again Christianity, and everything in between. In effect, these often naively idealistic utopian experiments functioned as a pressure cooker for personal and collective growth. Although many of the '60s groups folded during the creative but turbulent decade that followed, hundreds have survived into the '90s and are now thriving—having reevaluated, restructured, and matured over the years.

B. F. Skinner's book, *Walden Two* (a futurist novel based on his theories of behavioral psychology), inspired the creation of at least a dozen communal experiments. Los Horcones, one such community near Sonora, Mexico, is today one of the world's foremost experiments in behaviorist theory.

The Franchise Approach

Some communities hit upon a combination of philosophy and lifestyle that enables them to thrive. Occasionally one will embark on a program of systematic colonization to spread its message and its influence.

23   During the Reformation, a group of German Anabaptists decided to pool their goods and unite in Christian brotherhood. Jakob Hutter emerged as a primary leader five years later, in 1533. The community prospered, and subsequently formed many new colonies. Today there are nearly 400 colonies of the Hutterian Brethren in Canada and the United States, and a few more in South America and Europe. When a Hutterian community reaches its optimum capacity (100–150 members), the group acquires a new piece of land, builds a new set of structures (homes, barns, schools, etc.) acquires more agricultural equipment, and outfits an entire new facility. Then the population divides into two groups—one group staying at the original site, and one moving on to the new one. Neighboring colonies support each other with backup labor and various resources, an approach that yields a very high ratio of success for the new colonies.

24   Each colony has common work and a common purpose, and most have an economic base of large-scale, machine-powered agriculture within an organizational structure resembling that of a producer cooperative. They have been so successful in their endeavors that in the '80s some of their neighbors on the Canadian plains initiated lawsuits to prevent Hutterites from acquiring more land, claiming that their modernized agricultural base and communal economy amounted to "unfair competition." Because the Hutterites have retained many of their original customs—including dress, family structure, a simple lifestyle, and the German language—many outsiders find the Hutterites to be quite out of place when compared to their contemporary neighbors.

25   In contrast, members of Emissaries of Divine Light, another spiritually based association, manage to fit right in with the mainstream culture. The Emissaries, founded in the early '30s, have a network of 12 major communities plus a number of urban centers that span the globe. Their overall focus is directed toward achieving a more effective and creative life experience, developing spiritual awareness without rules or a specific belief system. Their lifestyle would be described by many as "upper middle class," and business oriented. Nuclear family units, though not mandated, are the norm. Emissaries pride themselves on being on good terms with their neighbors. One long-standing resident of an Emissary community at the edge of a small Canadian town was elected mayor of the town for 15 consecutive years. The Emissary business staff is well respected—so much so that government tax officials in British Co-

lumbia regularly consult Emissary personnel before deciding on strategies for implementing new tax laws and regulations concerning nonprofit corporations.

The connections between and among the various Emissary communities worldwide are maintained in many ways: inspirational talks and special events are always recorded, and transcripts are kept on file at each Emissary center; some events are recorded on video, with copies distributed by mail; on a weekly basis, several centers link up via satellite for instantaneous transmission of related presentations originating from multiple locations. Most active members receive regular Emissary publications, some of which provide a network overview, and others which document the work of special interest subgroups. For example, many of the major Emissary centers have agricultural operations, which grow much of the food consumed by residents and guests. Known as "stewardship farms," these separate operations are managed and staffed by members who regularly share ideas and information about long-term sustainable agriculture. This special interest group publishes a regular newsletter and organizes periodic conferences, planning meetings, and exchange visits. 26

Network Alliances

The popular myth that the intentional communities movement died in the early '80s has been discouraging to many of the intentional communities that survived and thrived on their own. Many contemporary groups have suffered a lack of contact and support due to their mistaken impression that they were among the few survivors of a bygone era. Fortunately, there is growing interest shared by a growing number of independent communities who desire contact with like-minded groups, both nearby and around the world. Regional, continental, and even intercontinental networks—alliances for the sharing of ideas, resources, and social interests—are gaining support and visibility, thus enabling groups to learn from each others' failures and long-term successes. 27

One network of more than 50 Catholic Worker houses publishes a periodic newspaper and organizes occasional gatherings for the sharing of ideas, skills, rituals, friendship, and solidarity. Another values-based network is the Fellowship for Intentional Community (FIC), a North American network created to promote shared living in whatever forms it may take. The Fellowship handles thousands of inquiries yearly from seekers hoping to find a community to join, from com- 28 munities looking for new members, from academics doing research, and from media people gathering material for stories. A third organization of note is the Federation of Egalitarian Communities (FEC), established to promote and develop democratically run communities based on equality, income sharing, nonviolence, cooperation, ecology, and sustainability. FEC encourages the identification and elimination of the "isms" (racism, sexism, classism, ageism, etc.), and emphasizes the importance of ongoing contact among member groups.

29   FEC communities tax themselves $200 per year plus one percent of net revenues, using this fund to finance joint recruitment campaigns, fundraising, and travel to meetings and between communities. They have also created a voluntary joint security fund for protection against the economic strain of large medical bills. This fund has now grown to more than $100,000 and is used in part as a revolving loan fund that provides low-interest loans to projects and community businesses compatible with FEC values. Member communities also participate in a labor exchange program that allows residents of one community to visit another and receive labor credit at home for work done away. This is especially handy when one community's peak workload occurs during another's off season, and the labor flows back and forth when most appreciated. The exchange of personnel also offers an opportunity to take a mini-vacation, learn a new skill, make new friends, maintain old ones, and share insights about common experiences.

30   The Federation also aspires to document collectively acquired wisdom, making it available to the public for the cost of copying and postage. They have created a "Systems & Structures Package"—a compilation of written documents on bylaws, membership agreements, property codes, behavior norms, labor and governance systems, visitor policies, and ideas about what to do when you have too many dogs. The point of sharing this information is to help new (and even some not-so-new) communities ease through the struggles of creating appropriate structures, offering models for what to do when good will and best intentions are not enough.

A Contemporary Wave

31   Historically, participation in shared living communities has come in cycles. One major wave just ahead of the U.S. Civil War included Brook Farm, an educational experiment that attracted the likes of Henry David Thoreau, Nathaniel Hawthorne, and Ralph Waldo

Emerson. Other notable waves followed—one at the end of the last century including some still existing "Single Tax Colonies" (based on the economic philosophy of Henry George), one immediately preceding World War I, and another during the Great Depression. The last wave came out of the counter-culture in the '60s, and now a new wave is beginning. This 1994 edition of the Communities Directory documents more than 50 new communities started during the past five years, and that's merely the tip of the iceberg. Also listed are more than 160 that have survived at least a decade, and 80 others that have been in existence for more than two decades.

It is apparent that people—dissatisfied with the gap between   32
their ideals and reality—will keep trying out new approaches until they find lifestyles that solve most of the problems they see in the dominant culture. History suggests that the process is endless. To paraphrase Karl Marx: today's solutions to yesterday's problems introduce new dynamics that become tomorrow's problems. An exciting feature of today's intentional communities movement is that its members are actively seeking to identify problems, working to find solutions, and trying to implement new insights in their daily lives.

Many contemporary groups are exploring ways to achieve a true sense of community while maintaining a balance between privacy and cooperation, a concept quite compatible with values prevalent in mainstream society today. Perhaps by emphasizing common concerns rather than differences in our lifestyle choices, innovations will find their way more quickly across cultural lines.

Although shared living does not appeal to everyone, history con-   33
firms again and again that ongoing social experiments inevitably lead to a variety of new social and technical innovations—developments that will eventually find many useful applications in other segments of society. It's hard to predict just when an intentional community will come up with something new that will be assimilated by mainstream culture. However, if social experimenting results in a product, a process, or a philosophy that makes life a little easier or a bit more fulfilling, then we'd be well advised to keep an open mind as we monitor the progress.

✦ ✦ ✦

✦ Framing the Context

1. Although this article is available to anyone with access to the Internet, Kozeny uses the two opening paragraphs to define the readers for whom he writes. Describe those readers in your own words,

specifying more about their age, gender, marital status, profession, education, and community living experience.

2. In what way is Kozeny's position with the FIC likely to influence his purpose?

✦ *Point of View*

3. Despite Kozeny's personal experience with living in intentional communities, he chooses not to use a subjective, "I," point of view. What point of view does he use? What writing features indicate that choice?

4. What relationship does Kozeny establish with the readers by using that point of view? How would that relationship be different if he had used a subjective point of view?

✦ *Shape of Ideas*

5. Many people skim an article before they read it. What will Kozeny's boldfaced headings indicate about the article's organizing framework to readers?

6. How does the structure of the article connect the readers to Kozeny's purpose?

✦ *Choosing Voice*

7. Kozeny uses dashes rather liberally. Select three sentences in which he uses dashes and analyze their effect on the formality of his voice.

8. How does the formality level of Kozeny's voice complement his point of view?

✦ *Credibility*

9. Kozeny incorporates many quoted expressions with no attribution. List three quotes which indicate a special use of the word or expression and three quotes you think need attribution.

10. Kozeny does not acknowledge any sources beyond his own experience. How is this decision likely to affect his credibility with his readers? Will they view him as an expert? If so, why?

Nameless, Tennessee

William Least Heat-Moon

❖ ❖ ❖

"I took to the open road in search of places where change did not mean ruin and where time and men and deeds connected," explains William Least Heat-Moon in the opening chapter of his book Blue Highways *(1982). With a Ph.D. in English, no job, and a defunct marriage, the author, living and traveling in his 1975 van, Ghost Dancing, explored 13,000 miles of America's backroads (blue highways on the map) to discover what virtues the small towns that inhabit those roads offer. On this journey Heat-Moon discovers an unexpected sense of community that renews his spirit. "Nameless, Tennessee," the selection that follows from* Highways, *is one of those communities.*

Nameless, Tennessee, was a town of maybe ninety people if you pushed it, a dozen houses along the road, a couple of barns, same number of churches, a general merchandise store selling Fire Chief gasoline, and a community center with a lighted volleyball court. Behind the center was an open-roof, rusting metal privy with PAINT ME on the door; in the hollow of a nearby oak lay a full pint of Jack Daniel's Black Label. From the houses, the odor of coal smoke.

Next to a red tobacco barn stood the general merchandise with a poster of Senator Albert Gore, Jr., smiling from the window. I knocked. The door opened partway. A tall, thin man said, "Closed up. For good," and started to shut the door.

"Don't want to buy anything. Just a question for Mr. Thurmond Watts."

The man peered through the slight opening. He looked me over. "What question would that be?"

"If this is Nameless, Tennessee, could he tell me how it got that name?"

The man turned back into the store and called out, "Miss Ginny! Somebody here wants to know how Nameless come to be Nameless."

Miss Ginny edged to the door and looked me and my truck over. Clearly, she didn't approve. She said, "You know as well as I do, Thurmond. Don't keep him on the stoop in the damp to tell him." Miss Ginny, I found out, was Mrs. Virginia Watts, Thurmond's wife.

8   I stepped in and they both began telling the story, adding a detail here, the other correcting a fact there, both smiling at the foolishness of it all. It seems the hilltop settlement went for years without a name. Then one day the Post Office Department told the people if they wanted mail up on the mountain they would have to give the place a name you could properly address a letter to. The community met; there were only a handful, but they commenced debating. Some wanted patriotic names, some names from nature, one man recommended in all seriousness his own name. They couldn't agree, and they ran out of names to argue about. Finally, a fellow tired of the talk; he didn't like the mail he received anyway. "Forget the durn Post Office," he said. "This here's a nameless place if I ever seen one, so leave it be." And that's just what they did.

9   Watts pointed out the window. "We used to have signs on the road, but the Halloween boys keep tearin' them down."

10   "You think Nameless is a funny name," Miss Ginny said. "I see it plain in your eyes. Well, you take yourself up north a piece to Difficult or Defeated or Shake Rag. Now them are silly names."

11   The old store, lighted only by three fifty-watt bulbs, smelled of coal oil and baking bread. In the middle of the rectangular room, where the oak floor sagged a little, stood an iron stove. To the right was a wooden table with an unfinished game of checkers and a stool made from an apple-tree stump. On shelves around the walls sat earthen jugs with corncob stoppers, a few canned goods, and some of the two thousand old clocks and clock-works Thurmond Watts owned. Only one was ticking; the others he just looked at. I asked how long he'd been in the store.

12   "Thirty-five years, but we closed the first day of the year. We're hopin' to sell it to a churchly couple. Upright people. No athians."

13   "Did you build this store?"

14   "I built this one, but it's the third general store on the ground. I fear it'll be the last. I take no pleasure in that. Once you could come in here for a gallon of paint, a pickle, a pair of shoes, and a can of corn."

15   "Or horehound candy," Miss Ginny said. "Or corsets and salves. We had cough syrups and all that for the body. In season, we'd buy and sell blackberries and walnuts and chestnuts, before the blight got them. And outside, Thurmond milled corn and sharpened plows. Even shoed a horse sometimes."

16   "We could fix up a horse or a man or a baby," Watts said.

"Thurmond, tell him we had a doctor on the ridge in them days."   17

"We had a doctor on the ridge in them days. As good as any doc-   18
tor alivin'. He'd cut a crooked toenail or deliver a woman. Dead these
last years."

"I got some bad ham meat one day," Miss Ginny said, "and took   19
to vomitin'. All day, all night. Hangin' on the drop edge of yonder. I
said to Thurmond, 'Thurmond, unless you want shut of me, call the
doctor.'"

"I studied on it," Watts said.   20

"You never did. You got him right now. He come over and put   21
three drops of iodeen in half a glass of well water. I drank it down
and the vomitin' stopped with the last swallow. Would you think
iodeen could do that?"

"He put Miss Ginny on one teaspoon of spirits of ammonia in well   22
water for her nerves. Ain't nothin' works better for her to this day."

"Calms me like the hand of the Lord."   23

Hilda, the Wattses' daughter, came out of the backroom. "I re-   24
member him," she said. "I was just a baby. Y'all were talkin' to him,
and he lifted me up on the counter and gave me a stick of Juicy Fruit
and a piece of cheese."

"Knew the old medicines," Watts said. "Only drugstore he   25
needed was a good kitchen cabinet. None of them antee-beeotics
that hit you worsen your ailment. Forgotten lore now, the old medicines, because they ain't profit in iodeen."

Miss Ginny started back to the side room where she and her sis-   26
ter Marilyn were taking apart a duck-down mattress to make bol-
sters. She stopped at the window for another look at Ghost Dancing.
"How do you sleep in that thing? Ain't you all cramped and cold?"

"How does the clam sleep in his shell?" Watts said in my de-   27
fense.

"Thurmond, get the boy a piece of buttermilk pie afore he goes   28
on."

"Hilda, get him some buttermilk pie." He looked at me. "You like   29
good music?" I said I did. He cranked up an old Edison phonograph,
the kind with the big morning-glory blossom for a speaker, and put
on a wax cylinder. "This will be 'My Mother's Prayer,'" he said.

While I ate buttermilk pie, Watts served as disc jockey of Name-   30
less, Tennessee. "Here's 'Mountain Rose.'" It was one of those moments that you know at the time will stay with you to the grave: the
sweet pie, the gaunt man playing the old music, the coals in the stove

glowing orange, the scent of kerosene and hot bread. "Here's 'Evening Rhapsody.'" The music was so heavily romantic we both laughed. I thought: It is for this I have come.

31   Feathered over and giggling, Miss Ginny stepped from the side room. She knew she was a sight. "Thurmond, give him some lunch. Still looks hungry."

32   Hilda pulled food off the woodstove in the backroom: home-butchered and canned whole-hog sausage, home-canned June apples, turnip greens, cole slaw, potatoes, stuffing, hot cornbread. All delicious.

33   Watts and Hilda sat and talked while I ate. "Wish you would join me."

34   "We've ate," Watts said. "Cain't beat a woodstove for flavorful cookin'."

35   He told me he was raised in a one-hundred-fifty-year-old cabin still standing in one of the hollows. "How many's left," he said, "that grew up in a log cabin? I ain't the last surely, but I must be climbin' on the list."

36   Hilda cleared the table. "You Watts ladies know how to cook."

37   "She's in nursin' school at Tennessee Tech. I went over for one of them football games last year there at Coevul." To say *Cookeville,* you let the word collapse in upon itself so that it comes out "Coevul."

38   "Do you like football?" I asked.

39   "Don't know. I was so high up in that stadium, I never opened my eyes."

40   Watts went to the back and returned with a fat spiral notebook that he set on the table. His expression had changed. "Miss Ginny's *Deathbook.*"

41   The thing startled me. Was it something I was supposed to sign? He opened it but said nothing. There were scads of names written in a tidy hand over pages incised to crinkliness by a ballpoint. Chronologically, the names had piled up: wives, grandparents, a stillborn infant, relatives, friends close and distant. Names, names. After each, the date of *the* unknown finally known and transcribed. The last entry bore yesterday's date.

42   "She's wrote out twenty years' worth. Ever day she listens to the hospital report on the radio and puts the names in. Folks come by to check a date. Or they just turn through the books. Read them like a scrapbook."

43   Hilda said, "Like Saint Peter at the gates inscribin' the names."

Watts took my arm. "Come along." He led me to the fruit cellar under the store. As we went down, he said, "Always take a newborn baby upstairs afore you take him downstairs, otherwise you'll incline him downwards."   44

The cellar was dry and full of cobwebs and jar after jar of home-canned food, the bottles organized as a shopkeeper would: sausage, pumpkin, sweet pickles, tomatoes, corn relish, blackberries, peppers, squash, jellies. He held a hand out toward the dusty bottles. "Our tomorrows."   45

Upstairs again, he said, "Hope to sell the store to the right folk. I see now, though, it'll be somebody offen the ridge. I've studied on it, and maybe it's the end of our place." He stirred the coals. "This store could give a comfortable livin', but not likely get you rich. But just gettin' by is dice rollin' to people nowadays. I never did see my day guaranteed."   46

When it was time to go, Watts said, "If you find anyone along your way wants a good store—on the road to Cordell Hull Lake—tell them about us."   47

I said I would. Miss Ginny and Hilda and Marilyn came out to say goodbye. It was cold and drizzling again. "Weather to give a man the weary dismals," Watts grumbled. "Where you headed from here?"   48

"I don't know."   49

"Cain't get lost then."   50

Miss Ginny looked again at my rig. It had worried her from the first as it had my mother. "I hope you don't get yourself kilt in that durn thing gallivantin' around the country."   51

"Come back when the hills dry off," Watts said. "We'll go lookin' for some of them round rocks all sparkly inside."   52

I thought a moment. "Geodes?"   53

"Them's the ones. The county's properly full of them."   54

✦ ✦ ✦

✦ Framing the Context

1. The author begins the chapter with a detailed description of Nameless. What do the details he includes indicate about the assumptions he makes about his readers' familiarity with the subject?

2. Considering the author's occasion for writing, as stated in the headnote to the selection, who do you think is his primary audience and

what purpose would Heat-Moon have for presenting his travels to them?

✦ Point of View

3. Heat-Moon presents his travels from a subjective point of view. How would the merged and objective points of view change his relationship with his readers?

4. Although the author uses first person "I" to relate his experiences in Nameless, how would you describe his level of visibility?

✦ Shape of Ideas

5. The overall framework of *Blue Highways* is a sequential trip structure, but within the narrative of each chapter, the author must decide how to present the experience he had in each place. How would you describe the framework he used in presenting Nameless?

6. How does that framework connect the readers to Heat-Moon's purpose?

✦ Choosing Voice

7. The descriptive, expository paragraphs between the dialogue offer the best indication of the author's writing voice in this selection. Review those paragraphs (1, 8, 11, 30, 32, 41) and make a list of features (words, sentence structure, punctuation) that convey the formality level of Heat-Moon's voice.

8. Describe the contrast between Heat-Moon's voice and those of the Watts. How is that contrast likely to affect the readers?

✦ Credibility

9. Heat-Moon relies on direct quotes from the Watts family as his main source. Explain how that source contributes to Heat-Moon's credibility.

10. It's not likely that Heat-Moon tape-recorded his visit with the Watts. Does his re-created dialogue affect his ethos with his readers? Why or why not?

Legacy of the River Children

Amy Harvey

✦ ✦ ✦

Amy Harvey, an English Education major at the University of Central Florida, wrote the selection that follows as an assignment in her expository writing course. Harvey's family has lived on the banks of the Indian River in Central Florida for generations. By exploring the forces that shape her memory of family relationships, she discovers the defining role geography plays in finding community.

"*Quiet, girls,*" *she whispers.* "*I can hear the mullet jumping.*" *Upon hearing this, four little girls scamper up to the front of the porch. Each girl is separated by two years. Wearing denim cutoffs and hand-me-down T-shirts, the blond haired, sun-kissed children elbow each other for valuable porch screen space.* "*Shhhh,*" *they murmur. They focus their gazes past the old oak tree, past the mailbox, past the road to the river—the Indian River. With held breaths and open eyes, they hear a—plish.—*   1

"*We heard him, Grandma . . . and we saw him,*" *they squeal.*   2

"*We saw the mullet jump!*"   3

The four girls crawl back down from the screen and gather around their grandmother. The old woman begins her story . . . "*Did I ever tell you about the time when . . .*"   4

✦ ✦ ✦

The Indian River has recorded many moments like these. She is the silent observer of time and the provider of past generations. Native inhabitants hunted her shores for alligator, fished her waters, and gathered fruits from the groves that adorned her banks. In time, she saw her people change. The years brought new faces—new people for her to watch. Modern settlers found her territory exotic and chose to homestead on her coasts. My grandparents were two of her settlers. It was upon the Indian River where my grandfather built a little house with a front porch, and it was on that porch where I, along with my three younger cousins, listened for the jumping mullet with Grandma.   5

6   Wendy, Kerry, Emily, and I weren't the first blond-haired rebels to play along the river. Grandma and Grandpa produced the very first tribe of river children. My mother and her four sisters were the subjects of Grandma's "Did I ever tell you of the time . . ." stories. Many of our childhood afternoons were spent listening to the "Huckleberry Finn" experiences of our mothers.

✦ ✦ ✦

7   *Did I ever tell you that when my girls were your age the river was as clear as could be? In fact, it was just like Silver Springs. You could sail out in the middle of the river and look all the way down and see Sailor's Choice swimming at the bottom. Did you girls know that your mothers used to have an old boat? Ha, ha, that old thing had a hole in it, and those crazy children would sail out until it sunk—then they'd haul it back to shore . . .*

✦ ✦ ✦

8   Wendy, Kerry, Emily, and I couldn't share the experience of swimming in the river. In the early eighties, the river's face dimmed. Developers and road construction pollution ruined her pristine beauty. As children, we couldn't even see the river bottom in two feet of water. The sea wall was a boundary between the river and us. However, my cousins and I managed to sneak into her waters. We didn't mind the murkiness of the water. In fact, we viewed it as a mysterious excavation site, where we would explore for "priceless treasures." With old sneakers and broken branches, we probed for antique bottles, coins, driftwood, and horseshoe crabs.

9   Many summer days were spent searching for "river prizes." We thrived on the sunny salt air and relished the cool river breezes that swept by us from the east. My colleagues and I didn't mind the sunburns, the windburns, the grime of washed-up seaweed, or the river mud that ruined many pairs of shoes. We were creating memories— our own "Huckleberry Finn" experiences.

✦ ✦ ✦

10   *Did I ever tell you about the grove? You know . . . my girls loved to have adventures out behind the house. Once, all five of them decided to open a juice stand. They went out back and began picking all sorts of fruits to juice and*

sell. Your Aunt Mary used to practice her artwork by sketching the trees. Amy, your mom used to climb the trees. (Did you know that there used to be real monkeys in the trees back then?) Wendy, Kerry, and Emily's mom swore that she saw a Black Panther prowling around back there—it nearly scared her to death. Your Aunt Linda ran out of the grove screaming because she stirred up a nest of angry bees. Aunt Cathie got stuck in quick sand . . .

✦ ✦ ✦

In our time, the grove had become severely overgrown and off-limits. To deter us, our mothers' told us there were snakes behind the house. Needless to say, we obeyed and didn't sneak out back. Our mothers and aunts had spectacular adventures in the grove, but we found our own "enchanted world." Beneath our sugar-cookie exteriors raged the hearts of female warriors. The old oak tree in the front yard was our castle. We created our own battles and fought diligently to preserve our kingdom. Role-playing was one of our favorite activities. We must have been a sight for Grandma—four grubby girls complete with skinned knees, missing teeth, and red Popsicle syrup stains dripping down our chins and shirts. That tree became our own *Bridge to Terabithia*. 11

The Indian River continued to serve as the background to these events and many others. Family reunions were common every Fourth of July. Uncle Bruce taught us how to "clean a rib." My cousins and I could eat ribs by the truckload. When we finished, we would have a contest to see how far we could throw the bones in the water. There must be, at least, fifty dead cows hiding in the water. 12

Rivers can be fickle creatures. They appear to be timeless, yet an act of nature can stir and change the direction of their waters. These changes can occur swiftly. On the East Coast of Florida, the threat of hurricanes is taken very seriously. My family has endured a handful of them. They can change a river and the people that live along it. Just as the wind can stir and rile waters, a family event can surge and churn the sediment up from a river bottom. It is only when the river calms, that one can see what has surfaced. As a child, I thought the only skeletons hidden in the river were the many ribs from past barbecues . . . 13

Something strange happens as you leave childhood. I will never fully understand it, and I hope I never will. As children, my cousins and I held a sacred bond between us—closer than playmates, closer 14 than blood. Our unity [of four] became deep-rooted through family, childhood joys, and youthful ambitions. We were our mother's daughters—the next generation of river children. The river had passed her rites on to us and we were emerging as women. And yet . . . the river had one more lesson.

15   Perceptions change as you enter adulthood—that, I do know. As children, we are preoccupied with our own adventures and ourselves. Yet, as we pass through puberty, we look to our mothers and their histories. I did this with my mother, and my cousins did this with theirs. In inquiring about my mother's childhood, I found that life wasn't as wholesome as Grandma's stories made it out to be. Sure, as children they had a few memorable moments, but that was not how *my* mother perceived life by the river. Although she had four sisters, my mother felt very alone. She didn't climb the trees in the grove for fun. She climbed for escape. She craved release from my Grandmother, who had not mastered the art of unconditional love with her children. To gain acceptance, one would have to fight for it—thus the prevalence of sibling rivalry. Grandma's river children were warriors of the literal sense. Unfortunately, they are still at war today.

16   River property, inheritance, manipulation, and money are the weapons of my mother and aunts. As of late, Wendy, Kerry, Emily, and I have become their patsies. We took the emotional blows for our mothers' crimes. We were faced with the hardest choice a child could ever make: would we side with our mothers or the members of our childhood tribe?

17   The river was forcing us to decide. Were our memories worth preserving: the jumping mullet, the "river treasures," the enchanted kingdom in the oak tree, the barbecue? Ironically enough, we knew this was the decision our mothers had to make: to side with their mother's wishes or preserve their sisterly bond. My cousins and I reaped the results of their decisions.

18   We've had to live with *our* decisions. Masking your feelings is one of the hardest things an individual can do. We feel this weight every Thanksgiving, Christmas, and Easter. Our conversations are superficial and distant. We no longer confide our deepest secrets, thoughts, loves, and wishes to each other. The mask smothers us at times like these. Nevertheless, I can see the cracks in our walls during the times when we sit on the front porch watching our three younger cousins play by the river.

In Wendy's eyes, I see the far away memories of when we shared   19
our most intimate of childhood secrets. In Kerry's distant smile, I
read the joys of when we defended our castle and fought as loyal
teammates. In Emily's reserved laugh, I feel her remembering the
silly times when food became more than nourishment, rather, ammo
for mealtime games. In our quiet ways, we did not betray our devo-
tions to each another. Although the years have marched between us
and silence prevails in our presence, we love each other as much as
when we made our first steps out into the murky river.

Silently, we watch the new tribe—the next generation of river   20
children. Our three younger cousins are everything that we were: energetic, fearless, imaginative, and innocent. The river is their playmate now. And I wonder . . . how long will it take before she reveals
her secrets to them? Will they ever be forced to make the decisions
we had to make? I hope not.

Last Christmas, my cousins and I made our way to the river's   21
edge. In that instant, the river became placid and gave us our reflections. As we peered into the water we noticed that we were no longer
staring at children. Instead we were staring at women—maskless and
vulnerable. Her waters never lie—they never did —and in her depths
we saw our true selves. The river is the keeper of our secrets and the
unveiler of our futures. Her waves teach us that time moves on and
we have the power to change the course we are sailing on. Setting
sail in a new direction is a difficult thing to do. Nevertheless, it must
be done.

Wendy, Kerry, Emily, and I are quickly moving into our own   22
lives. Within the next decade we will be mothers to yet another generation of river children. One day, I will return to the Indian River
with my children and tell them of my "Huckleberry Finn" experiences with my tribe—my cousins. I will stand on the sea wall and
look out over her waters and search to find the truth of who I am. I
only pray that, by then, the silt has finally settled.

✦ ✦ ✦

✦ Framing the Context

1. The occasion of fulfilling a class assignment makes the teacher the
   primary reading audience for evaluating writing skills, but what do
   the title and first two paragraphs indicate about the audience Harvey

has in mind for the subject of this essay? Describe who those readers might be and the features that indicate their level of interest.

2. What relationship does Harvey establish with her subject in the opening paragraphs?

✦ *Point of View*

3. Harvey's frequent use of "I" clearly identifies not only her participant role but also her use of a subjective point of view. Describe the relationship this point of view allows Harvey to establish with her reader.

4. How would Harvey's relationship with the readers change if she had chosen to use a merged or objective point of view?

✦ *Shape of Ideas*

5. Harvey uses the Indian River as the focal point for structuring her framework. Identify that framework and describe its progression.

6. How does that choice of framework address the different purpose for both of Harvey's audiences: the teacher and the general reader interested in family relationships?

✦ *Choosing Voice*

7. In the first section of the essay Harvey uses italicized inserts to incorporate her grandmother's voice. In what way does this approach contribute to the character of Harvey's voice?

8. How does Harvey use literary language to create a personal yet formal relationship with her readers?

✦ *Credibility*

9. Explain and illustrate how the level of detail Harvey uses establishes her credibility with both the teacher and general reader audiences.

10. How would you describe Harvey's ethos? Identify what writing choices contribute to that ethos.

The Questionable Value
of Fraternities

George D. Kuh,
Ernest T. Pascarella,
and Henry Wechsler

✦ ✦ ✦

For many students, fraternities and sororities provide a means of find-
ing community —a way to meet people with similar interests, to forge
close friendships, to have a social life. But these relationships often
compete with academic goals and become socially destructive. This se-
lection, written collaboratively by education professors Kuh and Pas-
carella along with Weschler, the director of Harvard's College Alcohol
Studies Program, questions the role of the fraternity subcommunity
within the larger community of the university. The authors argue that
fraternities, as they now operate, are counterproductive to the univer-
sity mission and, therefore, must be reformed. The article appeared in
an April 1996 issue of the Chronicle of Higher Education, *a*
weekly newspaper for college professors and administrators.

Almost monthly, a college or university fraternity makes the na- 1
tional news because of an escapade of underage drinking or a hazing episode resulting in bodily injury or worse. In fact, so many
incidents of this sort occur that at least one law firm specializes in
fraternity-related lawsuits. Such incidents tarnish the image of fraternities as a locus of brotherhood.

The response from fraternity leaders to those events is pre- 2
dictable. With diverse memberships, they say, it is impossible for
everyone to attain the high goals set by fraternities. Moreover, it's not
just fraternity members who behave inappropriately, they note.
Abuse of alcohol is all too common among many students, whether
they belong to a fraternity or not. Besides, proponents of fraternities
assert, few other student organizations provide such an impressive
array of benefits for their members and the host institution, benefits
that far outweigh the occasional problems.

For example, fraternity leaders say, the grade-point averages of 3
fraternity members on a campus sometimes exceed those of under-

graduate men generally, evidence that fraternities contribute to academic performance. And joining a fraternity helps newcomers adjust to college; without the experience of living in a close-knit, supportive group, many students would drop out. Fraternity life also helps give students a better understanding of people from different backgrounds, supporters say, and provides opportunities for leadership within the group that cannot be matched elsewhere on campus. As a result, they add, fraternity men and sorority women are disproportionately represented among community and professional leaders.

4   Unfortunately, many of these assertions are at odds with the results of recent research.

5   While the majority of college students drink, fraternity members are much more likely than non-members to abuse alcohol, according to a recent study by the Harvard University School of Public Health. In surveying more than 17,000 students at 140 randomly selected four-year colleges, the study found that 86 per cent of those who live in fraternity houses were binge drinkers, compared with 45 per cent of nonmembers.

6   Particularly chilling but rarely mentioned is the large number of sorority women who become binge drinkers. After they enter college, 80 per cent of the residents of sorority houses reported binge drinking, although only 35 per cent said they had binged in high school. Both fraternity and sorority members reported having more problems resulting from their drinking than non-members did. One example is unwanted sexual advances, reported by 43 per cent of sorority-house residents, compared with 23 per cent of non-members.

7   Alcohol abuse is only one area in which the performance of fraternity members falls far short of the espoused values and goals of fraternity life. Even though fraternities declare that academic performance is a high priority, during the orientation period new members' grades often fall well below the campus average. Many professors are convinced that the time-consuming, often inane activities required to pledge a fraternity are the primary cause; candid fraternity members agree.

8   Fraternity membership also has a negative influence on intellectual development. Data from the National Study of Student Learning, conducted at 18 four-year colleges by the National Center on Teaching, Learning, and Assessment, show that—even after controlling for initial differences in such factors as pre-college cognitive development, academic motivation, age, and selectivity of the college

attended—fraternity men are well behind their non-member counterparts in cognitive development after the first year of college. The biggest deficit is in the area of critical thinking. The pattern is similar for sorority women, though the differences are not as pronounced as for men.

Personal development is affected, too. Although many fraternities attract people with varied academic and avocational interests, students encounter a broader spectrum of human differences in residence halls to which they are assigned randomly. In terms of race, ethnicity, and sexual orientation, fraternities tend to be more homogeneous than the student body in general. This is borne out by other data from the National Study of Student Learning. They show that, during the first year of college, fraternity and sorority members make significantly smaller gains than non-members do on measures of openness to diversity, which include valuing contact with people from different backgrounds and learning about people from different cultures. 9

The opportunity to develop leadership skills during fraternity life also may be overstated. Students gain competence in practical and interpersonal skills when they perform tasks requiring sustained effort and commitment, such as planning group and campuswide events. The majority of fraternity men do not hold positions, in their own group or elsewhere, that demand this kind of performance. Whether fraternity members are overrepresented among contemporary business and community leaders is not known. And even if this was true in the past, in the future the fraternity experience may not be considered an advantage in one's career in civic leadership, given the disappointing findings related to fraternity membership and appreciation for human differences. 10

Supporters of fraternities surely will criticize this description of their educational impact. We readily concede that some individuals are unaffected by the anti-intellectual influences common to many chapters. And in some fraternities, alcohol abuse is not the norm, and high levels of intellectual and academic achievement are common. Unfortunately, research suggests that those fraternities are in the minority. 11

Reforming fraternities clearly is difficult. Even when the national officials of fraternities work with campus administrators to carry out new programs for recruiting and initiating members—programs that do not involve alcohol and hazing—the reform efforts often fail. 12

Drinking and hazing are too deeply embedded in the cultural system of many chapters, where they are part of a complicated system of rewards and sanctions that bond the individual member to the group.

13   What is to be done? Colleges and universities need to assess how fraternities affect their educational missions, and to evaluate the political consequences of trying to change the deeply entrenched fraternity system. Generally, alumni have only fond memories of their fraternity and think it played an important part in their development and subsequent success. Campus administrators too often ignore the misdeeds of fraternity members because of the threat—direct or implied—that alumni will withhold their financial support. Therefore, before an institution undertakes any reforms, administrators must enlist the cooperation of all groups concerned and collect data related to the impact of fraternity membership on the educational development of students on that campus.

14   Most institutions would welcome assistance from the national offices of fraternities in designing reforms. But increasing the educational value of fraternities can be accomplished only campus by campus, using strategies specific to each institution. Campuses must delineate clear criteria that groups must meet for institutional recognition. Behavioral and educational standards must be set. Perhaps the best way to begin, after officials have assembled data showing the problems on their particular campus, is for the president to set up a blue-ribbon panel, headed by a top official such as the provost, to formulate strategies. The panel should include representatives of the faculty, student body, student-affairs staff, local fraternity leaders and members, and alumni. Trustee support must be solicited. Fraternities that fail to cooperate should be ineligible for any form of institutional recognition, including the use of campus space for group functions.

15   Any attempt to reform the present system without convincing all of the major players that change is necessary will surely fail. Even if reform succeeds—as seems to be happening in a few cases, such as at Colgate University—the most visible reformers can expect letters and public statements from fraternity alumni threatening to withdraw their financial support and challenging the reformers' loyalty to the institution. Such is the price of reclaiming the institution's educational integrity.

Because academic performance, intellectual development, and 16 openness to diversity seem to be negatively related to fraternity membership in the first year of college, policies barring first-year students from joining fraternities are essential. This is especially important on campuses where first-year students now can live in fraternity houses before classes begin; those institutions have little chance to socialize the newcomers to academic values. Deferring membership until the sophomore year also may make fraternity houses less rowdy, since fraternities may have strong economic incentive to make their houses more appealing to older members. Indeed, fraternity advisers report that many members now move out of the houses by their senior year, tired of the noise and drunken behavior of younger members.

Because many fraternities are indifferent to academic values and 17 seem to shortchange the education of many members, we need a careful examination of the educational benefits that fraternities provide. Colleges and universities must insure that fraternity members live up to the standards expected of all students and the standards that fraternities themselves espouse. When groups or individuals fail to meet these goals, administrators and fraternity leaders must act decisively to stem further abuse and reaffirm the institution's overarching educational mission.

✦ ✦ ✦

✦ Framing the Context

1. The authors of this selection chose to write collaboratively. How will the audience of professional peers respect this collaboration?

2. The *Chronicle of Higher Education* is a weekly publication subscribed to by institutions and professors nationally and internationally. How does the frequency and subscribership define the occasion for this article?

✦ Point of View

3. Although three people wrote this article, the information is presented from only one point of view. Identify the point of view the authors use (subjective, merged, or objective), and support your decision with features from the article.

4. Explain how using the other point of view choices would have established different relationships with the readers.

✦ *Shape of Ideas*

5. The authors devote two paragraphs to the fraternity leaders' view of their community and six paragraphs to refuting that view. In what way does this structure meet the needs of the readers?

6. In the section on reforming fraternities, paragraphs 13–17, the authors shape their proposal for a specific part of their audience, those responsible for taking action. Who are those people and what content features identify them?

✦ *Choosing Voice*

7. Academic writers writing for an academic audience generally use a formal voice. Identify six examples of that formality from the article.

8. In what way does the formal, collaborative voice used in this essay strengthen the writers' argument?

✦ *Credibility*

9. The authors cite three studies in support of their claim that fraternies have a questionable value (paras. 5, 6, 8, 9). Review how that evidence is incorporated and determine if the quality and quantity of those sources is sufficient for establishing credibility with the intended readers. Support your decision.

10. The authors decided not to use any direct quotes from sources. How is this decision likely to affect their credibility with the intended readers?

Who Am We?

Sherry Turkle

✦ ✦ ✦

Traditionally, geography has played a major role in bringing people together face-to-face to form communities. What happens when that geography shifts to a virtual environment where communication and identity are also virtual? Sherry Turkle, a professor of psychology and sociology in MIT's science, technology, and society program, explores the answer to that question in the following excerpt from her book Life on the Screen: Identity in the Age of the Internet *(1995). The excerpt also appeared in* Wired *magazine in January 1996.*

In the early 1970s, the face-to-face role-playing game *Dungeons and Dragons* swept the game culture. The term "dungeon" persisted in the high-tech culture to connote a virtual place. So when virtual spaces were created that many computer users could share and collaborate within, they were deemed Multi-User Dungeons or MUDs, a new kind of social virtual reality. (Some games use software that make them technically MUSHes or MOOs, but the term MUD has come to refer to all of the multi-user environments.) 1

MUDs are a new kind of virtual parlor game and a new form of community. In addition, text-based MUDs are a new form of collaboratively written literature. MUD players are MUD authors, the creators as well as consumers of media content. In this, participating in a MUD has much in common with scriptwriting, performance art, street theater, improvisational theater, or even commedia del l'arte. But MUDs are something else as well. 2

As players participate, they become authors not only of text but of themselves, constructing new selves through social interaction. Since one participates in MUDs by sending text to a computer that houses the MUD's program and database, MUD selves are constituted in interaction with the machine. Take it away and the MUD selves cease to exist: "Part of me, a very important part of me, only exists inside PernMUD," says one player. . . . 3

The anonymity of MUDs gives people the chance to express multiple and often unexplored aspects of the self, to play with their 4 identity and to try out new ones. MUDs make possible the creation of an identity so fluid and multiple that it strains the limits of the notion. Identity, after all, refers to the sameness between two qualities, in this case between a person and his or her persona. But in MUDS, one can be many.

5   A 21-year-old college senior defends his violent characters as "something in me; but quite frankly I'd rather rape on MUDs where no harm is done." A 26-year-old clerical worker says, "I'm not one thing, I'm many things. Each part gets to be more fully expressed in MUDs than in the real world. So even though I play more than one self on MUDS, I feel more like 'myself' when I'm MUDding." In real life, this woman sees her world as too narrow to allow her to manifest certain aspects of the person she feels herself to be. Creating screen personae is thus an opportunity for self-expression, leading to her feeling more like her true self when decked out in an array of virtual masks.

6   MUDs imply difference, multiplicity, heterogeneity, and fragmentation. Such an experience of identity contradicts the Latin root of the word, *idem,* meaning "the same." But this contradiction increasingly defines the conditions of our lives beyond the virtual world. MUDs thus become objects-to-think-with for thinking about postmodern selves. Indeed, the unfolding of all MUD action takes place in a resolutely postmodern context. There are parallel narratives in the different rooms of a MUD. The cultures of Toliden, Gibson, and Madonna coexist and interact. Since MUDS are authored by their players, thousands of people in all, often hundreds at a time, are all logged on from different places; the solitary author is displaced and distributed. Traditional ideas about identity have been tied to a notion of authenticity that such virtual experiences actively subvert. When each player can create many characters in many games, the self is not only decentered but multiplied without limit.

7   As a new social experience, MUDS pose many psychological questions: If a persona in a role-playing game drops defenses that the player in real life has been unable to abandon, what effect does this have? What if a persona enjoys success in some area (say, flirting) that the player has not been able to achieve? Slippages often occur in places where persona and self merge, where the multiple personae join to comprise what the individual thinks of as his or her authentic self.

8   Doug is a midwestern college junior. He plays four characters distributed across three different MUDS. One is a seductive woman.

One is a macho, cowboy type whose self-description stresses that he is a "Marlboros rolled in the T-shirt sleeve kind of guy." The third is a rabbit of unspecified gender who wanders its MUD introducing people to each other, a character he calls Carrot. Doug says, "Carrot is so low key that people let it be around while they are having private conversations. So I think of Carrot as my passive, voyeuristic character." Doug's fourth character is one that he plays only on a MUD in which all the characters are furry animals. "I'd rather not even talk about that character because my anonymity there is very important to me," Doug says. "Let's just say that on FurryMUDs I feel like a sexual tourist." Doug talks about playing his characters in windows and says that using windows has made it possible for him to "turn pieces of my mind on and off."

"I split my mind. . . . I can see myself as being two or three or   9 more. And I just turn on one part of my mind, and then another when I go from window to window. I'm in some kind of argument in one window and trying to come on to a girl in a MUD in another, and another window might be running a spreadsheet program or some other technical thing for school. . . . And then I'll get a real-time message that flashes on the screen as soon as it is sent from another system user, and I guess that's RL. RL is just one more window, and it's not usually my best one."

Play has always been an important aspect of our individual efforts   10 to build identity. The psychoanalyst Erik Erikson called play a "toy situation" that allows us to "reveal and commit" ourselves "in its unreality." While MUDs are not the only "places" on the Internet in which to play with identity, they provide an unparalleled opportunity for such play. On a MUD one actually gets to build character and environment and then to live within the toy situation. A MUD can become a context for discovering who one is and wishes to be. In this way, the games are laboratories for the construction of identity.

Gender-swapping on MUDs is not a small part of the game action. By some estimates, Habitat, a Japanese MUD, has 1.5 million   11 users. Habitat is a MUD operated for profit. Among the registered members of Habitat, there is a ratio of four real-life men to each real-life woman. But inside the MUD the ratio is only three male characters to one female character. In other words, a significant number of players, many tens of thousands of them, are virtually cross-dressing.

12   What is virtual gender-swapping all about? Some of those who do it claim that it is not particularly significant. "When I play a woman I don't really take it too seriously," said 20-year-old Andrei. "I do it to improve the ratio of women to men. It's just a game." On one level, virtual gender-swapping is easier than doing it in real life. For a man to present himself as female in a chat room, on an IRC channel, or in a MUD, only requires writing a description. For a man to play a woman on the streets of an American city, he would have to shave various parts of his body; wear makeup, perhaps a wig, a dress, and high heels; perhaps change his voice, walk, and mannerisms. He would have some anxiety, about passing, and there might be even more anxiety about not passing, which would pose a risk of violence and possibly arrest. So more men are willing to give virtual cross-dressing a try. But once they are online as female, they soon find that maintaining this fiction is difficult. To pass as a woman for any length of time requires understanding how gender inflects speech, manner, the interpretation of experience. Women attempting to pass as men face the same kind of challenge.

13   Virtual cross-dressing is not as simple as Andrei suggests. Not only can it be technically challenging, it can be psychologically complicated. Taking a virtual role may involve you in ongoing relationships. You may discover things about yourself that you never knew before.

14   Case, a 34-year-old industrial designer who is happily married to a co-worker, is currently MUDding as a female character. In response to my question, "Has MUDding ever caused you any emotional pain?" he says, "Yes, but also the kind of learning that comes from hard times.

15   "I'm having pain in my playing now. Mairead, the woman I'm playing in MedievalMUSH, is having an interesting relationship with a fellow. Mairead is a lawyer, and the high cost of law school has to be paid for by a corporation or a noble house. She fell in love with a nobleman who paid for her law school. [Case slips into referring to Mairead in the first person.] Now he wants to marry me although I'm a commoner. I finally said yes. I try to talk to him about the fact that I'm essentially his property. I'm a commoner . . . I've grown up with it, that's the way life is. He wants to deny the situation. He says, 'Oh no, no, no. . . . We'll pick you up, set you on your feet, the whole world is open to you.' But every time I behave like I'm now going to

be a countess some day . . . as in, 'And I never liked this wallpaper anyway,' I get pushed down. The relationship is pull up, push down. It's an incredibly psychologically damaging thing to do to a person. And the very thing that he liked about her that she was independent, strong, said what was on her mind, it is all being bled out of her."

Case looks at me with a wry smile and sighs, "A woman's life." He continues: "I see her [Mairead] heading for a major psychological problem. What we have is a dysfunctional relationship. But even though it's very painful and stressful, it's very interesting to watch myself cope with this problem. How am I going to dig my persona's self out of this mess? Because I don't want to go on like this. I want to get out of it. . . . You can see that playing this woman lets me see what I have in my psychological repertoire, what is hard and what is easy for me. And I can also see how some of the things that work when you're a man just backfire when you're a woman." [16]

Case further illustrates the complexity of gender swapping as a vehicle for self-reflection. Case describes his RL persona as a nice guy, a "Jimmy Stewart type like my father." He says that in general he likes his father and he likes himself, but he feels he pays a price for his low-key ways. In particular, he feels at a loss when it comes to confrontation, both at home and in business dealings. Case likes MUDding as a female because it makes it easier for him to be aggressive and confrontational. Case plays several online "Katharine Hepburn types," strong, dynamic, "out there" women who remind him of his mother, "who says exactly what's on her mind and is a take-no-prisoners sort." [17]

For Case, if you are assertive as a man, it is coded as "being a bastard." If you are assertive as a woman, it is coded is "modern and together." [18]

Some women who play male characters desire invisibility or permission to be more outspoken or aggressive. "I was born in the South and taught that girls didn't speak up to disagree with men," says Zoe, a 34-year-old woman who plays male and female characters on four MUDS. [19]

"We would sit at dinner and my father would talk and my mother would agree. I thought my father was a god. Once or twice I did disagree with him. I remember one time in particular when I was 10, and he looked at me and said, "Well, well, well, if this little flower grows too many more thorns, she will never catch a man." [20]

21   Zoe credits MUD with enabling her to reach a state of mind where she is better able to speak up for herself in her marriage ("to say what's on my mind before things get all blown out of proportion") and to handle her job as the financial officer for a small biotechnology firm.

22   "I played a MUD man for two years. First I did it because I wanted the feeling of an equal playing field in terms of authority, and the only way I could think of to get it was to play a man. But after a while, I got very absorbed by MUDding. I became a wizard on a pretty simple MUD. I called myself Ulysses and got involved in the system and realized that as a man I could be firm and people would think I was a great wizard. As a woman, drawing the line and standing firm has always made me feel like a bitch and, actually, I feel that people saw me as one, too. As a man I was liberated from all that. I learned from my mistakes. I got better at being firm but not rigid. I practiced, safe from criticism."

23   Zoe's perceptions of her gender trouble are almost the opposite of Case's. While Case sees aggressiveness as acceptable only for women, Zoe sees it as acceptable only for men. These stories share a notion that a virtual gender swap gave people greater emotional range in the real.

24   The culture of simulation may help us achieve a vision of a multiple but integrated identity whose flexibility, resilience, and capacity for joy comes from having access to our many selves.

✦ ✦ ✦

✦ Framing the Context

1. What do the opening three paragraphs tell you about how Turkle identifies her audience? Profile who these readers are.

2. Based on Turkle's position as a professor at MIT, explain what the occasion is for her writing the book from which this selection was taken.

✦ Point of View

3. In paragraphs 14 and 16, Turkle makes incidental references to herself ("In response to my question . . . " and "Case looks at me with a wry smile . . . "). Is this brief visibility enough to identify her point

of view as merged, or do you think hers is an objective point of view? Support your decision with examples from the essay.

4. What relationship does Turkle's point of view establish between Turkle and her readers? How does that relationship allow the readers to interact with the text?

✦ *Shape of Ideas*

5. What framework does Turkle choose to use and how does that framework connect readers to understanding how MUD players construct identity?

6. In what specific ways is that framework ordered to support the conclusion stated in paragraph 24?

✦ *Choosing Voice*

7. Review those sections that do not include quotes from the MUD participants. How formal is the diction and sentence structure Turkle uses? Support your decision with examples.

8. In what ways is Turkle's level of formality appropriate to the rhetorical context?

✦ *Credibility*

9. Turkle's main source of evidence in profiling the MUD community is a series of interviews she conducted with MUD participants. What does her extensive use of quotes from those interviews indicate about her readers' expectations for establishing credibility? How would readers respond differently if Turkle had described the participants' experiences in her own words?

10. Do you think that Turkle has participated on a MUD? Which paragraphs indicate her experience or lack of experience? How does her level of experience affect the ethos she creates with her readers?

Introduction to *The Wall*

Michael Norman

✦ ✦ ✦

The spirit that lies at the center of a community can emanate from many different sources. For Michael Norman and other Vietnam veterans, their friends, and families, the spirit that binds them together as a community emanates from the Wall, the Vietnam Veterans Memorial in Washington, D.C. Dedicated on Veterans Day in 1982, the Wall is "a mecca for the record number of Americans who flock there to commune with the dead, and the living, and who leave with a new understanding of the physical and emotional sacrifice of the Vietnam veteran." Michael Norman, a Marine combat veteran and former correspondent for the New York Times, *shares his personal reflection on visiting the Wall in this introduction to the pictorial commemoration* The Wall: Images and Offerings from the Vietnam Veterans Memorial *(1987) conceived by photojournalist Sal Lopes.*

1   They walk as if on hallowed ground. They touch the stone. They speak with the dead. They come to mourn and to remember, memory mixing with grief, making an old ritual new, creating in this time another timeless moment.

2   Seeing this, coming upon it at dawn or in the melancholy drizzle of a winter solstice, it is hard to remember that no one is buried there, that the long chevron of black granite is a memorial, not a sprawling cairn on a common grave.

3   It is a sad place—there is no denying that—especially sad for the volunteers and luckless conscripts who survived the war, men like me, trying to make sense of the senseless, trying to find a way to remember that will not mock the meaning of the dead.

4   Some men who cross the years and struggle home say they need no memorial to keep alive the memory of those cut down beside them. This is true, and yet I am pleased to see it there, stretched out under the sky a stone's throw from the Potomac River, there where Lincoln talks of the dead to "us the living."

The memorial is a way back and a way forward. A pass through 5
Constitution Gardens and a walk along "The Wall" makes us think
of the future in the language of the past and whatever message one
draws from this, it seems unlikely that anyone who makes that walk
will be able to think of war and the men who fight it in quite the
same way again.

In honor of the men and women of the Armed Forces of the United States 6
who served in the Vietnam War. The names of those who gave their lives and
of those who remain missing are inscribed in the order they were taken from us.
Fifty-eight thousand, one hundred and thirty-two names photo- 7
stenciled—etched—chronologically in the order of their deaths onto
two walls, each 246.75 feet long, that meet at an angle of 125 degrees.
The walls begin roughly at ground level and, at the vertex, rise to the
height of 10.1 feet. Each wall has 70 panels cut from black granite
mined in a quarry near Bangalore, India, and polished to form a surface that reflects the sky and the ground and those who stand before
it. Nearby is a flagpole with an American flag and an eight-foot
bronze statue of three infantrymen staring off roughly in the direction of the granite roll call.
The Wall was designed by the most unlikely of architects, Maya 8
Ying Lin, a woman of Asian descent, who knew nothing of war. In
1981, when she submitted her design to a competition held by the
Vietnam Veterans Memorial Fund, she was 21 years old, an architecture student at Yale University:
I had designed the memorial for a seminar on funerary architecture. . . . 9
We had already been questioning what a war memorial is, its purpose, its re-
sponsibility. . . . I felt a memorial should be honest about the reality of war and
be for the people who gave their lives. . . . I didn't want a static object that
people would just look at, but something they could relate to as on a journey, or
passage, that would bring each to his own conclusions. . . . I had an impulse to
cut open the earth . . . an initial violence that in time would heal. . . . It was
as if the black-brown earth were polished and made into an interface between
the sunny world and the quiet dark world beyond, that we can't enter. . . . The
names would become the memorial. There was no need to embellish.

Opinion over the design, just as it had been over the war, was 10
divided, and during the memorial's planning stages in 1981, this
political and aesthetic skirmishing threatened to kill the project.
The memorial was conceived by Jan C. Scruggs, then a 31-year-old

former infantryman who saw combat in Vietnam. He wanted a people's memorial financed entirely by contributions. In the end, he would raise some $7 million—money from unions and veterans' organizations and corporations, money from the men, women and children of the United States, 275,000 contributions in all.

11   Scruggs' memorial committee won congressional support for a bill setting aside two acres of land in Washington's Constitution Gardens in the shadow of the Lincoln Memorial. Then the committee selected a jury of architects and sculptors to hold a design competition. When entry number 1026 won, the skirmishing began.

12   Tom Carhart, a veteran who had entered the design competition, called Maya Lin's memorial "a black gash of shame," a phrase that became a rallying call for the opposition. Author Jim Webb, a Marine Corps combat veteran, thought the Wall did little to lift the spirits of the men who fought in Vietnam: "It was not supposed to be the Vietnam Dead Memorial. Art is a metaphor and the metaphorical statement of it is absolutely negative." In the end, with the bronze statue and flagpole added as a compromise, Maya Lin's design won official approval.

13   "It is a subtle design, like every great memorial capable of being given different meanings by each of us," wrote Paul Goldberger, the architecture critic of the *New York Times*. "The anguish of the Vietnam War is present here but not in a way that does any dishonor to veterans. . . . This memorial . . . honors the veterans who served in Vietnam with more poignancy, surely, than any ordinary monument ever could."

14   It was the public, of course, who made the final judgment on the people's memorial. Between 4 and 5 million came by the site in 1986, making it, perhaps, the most visited outdoor memorial in the nation's capital.

15   Gold Star Mothers look for the names of their sons, young children, the names of their fathers. Friends and family come, a second cousin from Calumet, a classmate from Iowa City. Generations pass by the Wall, one too young to have known the war, another too old to have fought it. Men and women in uniform come, some salute, some just stare. Tourists come by the busload, snapping pictures as they file by. Solitary figures come, standing silently off to one side, drifting back in memory.

16   And then there are the veterans.

Some 9 million men and women were in uniform between 1965   17
and 1975; 1.3 million are believed to have seen combat. Nearly
300,000 men were wounded in the war, 75,000 of them disabled by
their wounds. There is no final count on the number of other casu-
alties, the ones who returned with scars on their psyches or deadly
toxins in their blood.

The veterans arrive at their memorial walking and in wheel-   18
chairs, in three-piece suits and old jungle fatigues. They wear their
hats, they wear their boots, they wear their medals. Almost always
they weep. Oh, how we weep, ". . . cursing and sobbing and thinking of the dead," wrote Robert Graves.

We mourn the many, we mourn the one, perhaps the first man   19
we saw fall, perhaps the friend who took our place on patrol. I have
such a name, panel 50 east, line 52, Andrew James Payne, Jr., a member of Charlie Squad, 1st Platoon, Golf Company, 2nd Battalion, 9th
Marines, killed April 19, 1968.

Jim had grown up in the sun—red hair, freckles, a mouth full of   20
gleaming white teeth. He played baseball and football and chess. He
had a paper route and sold road flares and styrofoam snowmen at
Christmas. He studied at Hoover High, drove a vintage 1950 black
Ford jalopy, and lived at home on Thompson Street in Glendale, California, with three brothers and a sister.

He was killed on the morning of a hot day on a dusty road near   21
Khe Sanh, shot in the stomach by an enemy he could not see. He sat
in the sun against a rock, bleeding to death while his comrades tried
to finish the fight. He may have died for his country or for his God
or for nothing at all. For a long time, I thought he died for me.

It is hard to remember that no one is buried there. The memor-   22
ial is a collection point, an altar upon which the living leave tokens
of the dead and trappings for an afterlife:

Here is a can of beer or a tin of sardines—"remember how he   23
loved them so." And here is a single blood-red rose, cradled in baby's
breath, white and soft. Purple Hearts and discharge papers and uniforms are here—military trappings for a military death. A model
ship, a stuffed bear, a key chain, and a toy soldier. T-shirts, travel kits,
flight jackets, and flags.

They leave letters too, messages sent across the void: 24

"I took the solemn walk past this monument of black granite for you this   25
day. . . ."

26   *"I just wanted to come here today to tell you I love you. . . ."*

27   *"I'm so sorry Frankie—I know we left you—I hope you didn't suffer too much—give them hell—. . . ."*

28   So many letters and so many artifacts have been left—more than 4,900 at last count—that the act of leaving something behind has become a ritual at the memorial. Officials of the National Park Service, which maintains the memorial and collects and catalogs the artifacts at a climate-controlled warehouse in Lanham, Maryland, say the collection is now a memorial in itself, a remembrance of sacrifice apart from the lodestone of black polished granite on a quiet capital green.

29   Veterans Day 1987 is the fifth anniversary of the Vietnam Veterans Memorial. The controversy over the design has quieted now. Six months after the dedication, in May 1983, President Reagan made his first visit to the memorial and in so doing the commander-in-chief gave it the official sanction the fighting men of Vietnam had so long sought.

30   Looking back across the five years and all that has been said and written about that spectral place, the first description of the memorial, the words of the designer, seems most apt. Maya Lin said she wanted to create a journey, a passage, and indeed she has.

31   To follow the Wall from ground level to its vertex is to walk down into the past. As the long polished panels reflect those who move before them, the names of the past become etched on the faces of the present and, for a moment, the living and the dead are one.

32   To go to the Wall is thus to be a part of history, "to mingle," as Stephen Crane wrote, "in one of those great affairs of the earth." Perhaps this is part of the memorial's appeal: for the uninitiated, it is a way to get a sense of the experience they have only read about or have seen flickering on a small screen. But it is also more than this because the Wall has brought war home in a way television never could. Here is the mystery of death writ in stone 58,132 times. For the living, the mystery was never more palpable.

33   To touch the Wall is to touch the dead, to get close to them. And as they make this crossing—as those who never knew war come close to those taken by it—they begin to understand Vietnam and thus honor the generation of veterans who survived the war.

34   We have never asked for more than that.

✦ *Framing the Context*

1. With the exception of reproduced messages and letters left at the Wall, Norman's introduction is the only writing in this pictorial commemoration. Who is his primary audience and what features of his writing indicate this audience to you?

2. Commemorative writing, as an occasion, has a well-defined general purpose. What is that purpose related to this occasion and, more specifically, what is Norman's purpose?

✦ *Point of View*

3. Though invited to share his personal reflections, Norman seldom uses the word "I." Review Norman's use of pronouns to determine his point of view. Support your decision with quoted examples from the text.

4. What relationship does Norman establish with his readers by using that point of view?

✦ *Shape of Ideas*

5. A commemoration, by nature, includes certain components: what is being commemorated, the history of why the commemoration takes place, and who is involved. What framework does Norman use to structure these components and what additional components does he incorporate?

6. What do the beginning and end of the introduction have in common? How does this similarity connect the readers to Norman's purpose?

✦ *Choosing Voice*

7. A commemoration is a formal occasion. What features of Norman's voice indicate that formality?

8. Norman chooses to repeat one particular sentence: "It is hard to remember that no one is buried there" (paras. 2 and 22). Why do you believe he chose to repeat that sentence and what effect does he expect the repetition to have on the readers?

✦ *Credibility*

9. Make a list of the sources from which Norman quotes. How will the quality and quantity of those sources establish credibility with the intended readers?

10. What personal experiences does Norman include and how do they contribute to his ethos?

Beta Life

Matthew Peters

✦ ✦ ✦

*The social trends associated with the evolution of popular culture
have a strong influence on what social communities we join. What
we wear, the hairstyles we choose, how we present ourselves, and
where we hang out help to announce the community we want to find.
In the following essay written for his magazine writing class, creative
writing student Matthew Peters examines how his membership in
groups responding to popular music trends has given him insight to
his motivation for joining those communities.*

1   Keith and I stepped out from the alley, wingtipped and necktied.
Blanketed in blazers. Sheathed in slacks. Sharp dressed on Friday
night. Orange Avenue was already flowing with parading people
looking their best in baggy jeans, tight white T's, too-tight tube
skirts, halter tops topping tiny shorts, and zippered patterned golf-
shirts, all strutting their stuff looking for a mate. Their night just beginning, ours continuing. Michael Andrews had finished his second
set at the Atlantic Dance Hall, and we were heading for the Sapphire
Supper Club to see Rocket 88. So, Keith and I paraded too. Parting
crowds and dividing lines, floating down the sidewalk pulling heads
to laugh at us. As we approached the Sapphire, I turned to Keith, who
is already glassy eyed from vodka martinis, and asked, "It's great to
be a freak again, ain't it?" Lee, the Sapphire's super-suave ultra-large
bouncer/doorman, tipped us a nod and let us pass through the door
without paying. The brass chaos of Rocket 88 greeted us.

2   That was in July of 1997. Two years before that swanky night,
Keith and I were still ravers. We were freaks then too, driving in from
Tampa in order to attend some of Orlando's bigger raves, "Energy,"
"Passion," and the now annual "Zen." We danced all night and drove
home exhausted at noon. The decade-dominating movement that is
Rave had just broken the surface of mainstream culture in '95. Up to
that point Rave was not only feared by parents and civic leaders as it
is today, but also by most of our peers, who thought we were drugged-
out dorks. Even as late as fall of 1994, the mainstream night clubs,

always striving for the maximum amount of dollars, were still advertising on the radio that they played "absolutely no Techno." But times change and society progresses, and Techno is now the only music to be heard at these clubs, who also host their own raves. Another example of how trends can grow in popularity is from attitudes presented in television programming. In 1992 the TV series *Beverly Hills 90210* was painting Raves as an evil underground drug orgy that should be avoided (the episode where Brandon gets slipped a dose of "Euphoria" aka Ecstasy, the now-infamous "Rave Drug," which was invented in 1914 as a diet aid), but by 1995 the same group of characters were trying to put on their own rave in order to make money.

This fickle shift in Pop music trends can be tracked in four 3 stages: Alpha, Beta, Commercial, and Death. A lot of movements never make it beyond the Alpha stage; barely perceivable and never understood by mainstream culture. Fewer still gain enough momentum through mass support and club identity to leave the Beta stage: the alternative underground. Most new movements get lost in history, documented minutely, if at all, in the annals of cultural studies. The Rave and Swing movements are probably the best examples to illustrate how the Alphas and Betas, the people who begin and make up the scene, affect popular culture.

I am unfortunately a social Beta, not quite cool enough to be an 4 Alpha, but lucky enough to have Alpha friends who always let me in on what is new, the next hip cool. The cycle goes something like this: The Alphas start the new trends, riding the swell of what is cool. We Betas eventually get invited to whatever our Alpha friends are doing, adding mass and momentum to the fun; the Betas ride the crest of the new waves. But we Betas are also a bitter omen, we can open the door for commercialism. Death is the final stage and occurs several years after the beginning of the Commercial, once profits begin to die off and everyone is burned out on the movement.

In the late eighties and early nineties, Alphas responded to the 5 popularizing of subculture Grunge and Neo-punk by going further underground into House and Techno music. *Rolling Stone* did an article on Orlando Electronica for their 8/21/97 issue. *R.S.* documented that Kimbell Collins started the Orlando scene in '89 by spinning house music at the Becham Theater after hours when the club became known as Aahz. And in the early nineties Cliff Tangredi, DJ Cliff T, was spinning at private raves across Florida. By the mid-nineties, the private raves and alternative nights like Aahz became

"Rave" and moved to the full-scale corporate Commercial level, where it still is.

6   The Commercial is both a good and a bad stage for a trend to progress into. For us Betas, the Commercial stage increases the frequency of what we enjoy, more raves, more often. But Commercialism also raises the prices and overcrowds an event with people who really don't understand why it is done in the first place. For the Alphas, there is the opportunity to make money doing what they love, but the trend also grows beyond their influence, suddenly dictated by corporate whims. At the commercial stage, Alphas tend to either cash in on the movement they created or drop out and move on to the next subculture Alpha trend. The Commercial stage kills the essence of the movement, the time when the movement was still raw, friendly, and untainted by greed. By the Commercial stage, whatever essence still remains in the movement is stomped out in the race for money. Trampled beneath the soles of Doc Martens, Nikes, and Adidas, Kimbell Collins and DJ Cliff T are still prominent Rave DJs, living well, spinning at clubs, and producing records.

7   In 1995 as the Commercial stage killed off the last reminiscence of pure Raveism, I had no idea what we would be doing next. But now in '97, Swing, a retro movement from LA, has recently reached the Beta level in Orlando. There were some hints toward Swing, but my bets were on Ska or Acid Jazz, two movements still stuck in the Beta and Alpha stages respectively. I remember seeing the movie *Swing Kids* in '94 and it inspired some wonder, "Wow! To dress and dance like that!" But, like I said, I am a Beta, and in '94, I was still raving. At the time I saw the movie as a metaphor for the underground raves that were always in danger of getting raided, more than a hint of things to come.

8   Old Alphas from the Rave movement, like Stace Bass, promoter of DJs and Raves in Florida, could see and moved on to Swing. During her rave years, she operated "The Bass Line," a phone number containing information on what rave was going on where. She still operates her information hotline, but the information presented is now all about Swing, who is coming, when and where. And Stace now promotes Michael Andrews's retro swing band *Swingerhead,* instead of DJs and Raves.

9   At a Holiday party in '96, a group of people gathered in the kitchen to avoid the end of some sporting event on TV. While bitching about the evils of television, my girlfriend Kristi confessed to

getting sucked into watching the recent National Ballroom Dancing Championships, she even admitted to liking it. The strange thing was that four other people had watched and enjoyed the same broadcast. One of those people was an old rave friend named John Hynn, who like us, was getting sick of the commercial Rave scene. John called a few weeks later to invite Kristi and me to join in on a Party Bus that was heading to Disney's Atlantic Dance Hall to see a swing band called Royal Crown Revue. We went and were sucked into a new movement, Betas again.

Disney tried to jump the gun by opening the Swing club called   10
the Atlantic Dance Hall; however profits from the Beta Swing scene were not enough to fill Disney's belly, so the club soon switched its program of music from Swing to a more profitable Disco Pop. Still, the club's short Swing life, from December of '96 to September '97, was enough to cultivate a strong movement of modern Swing Kids. And Swing is now threatening to take over Rave's top spot.

In early '97, the entire Orlando Swing scene (minus four or five   11
people) fit on that party bus destined for Disney's Atlantic Dance Hall to see Royal Crown Revue. A year later, at Michael Andrews's *Swingerhead* CD-release party, which was held at Janey Lane's Sunset Strip (now a swing club called the Rat Pack), the club was so full of fedoras we couldn't even dance. My grandmother, who now insists I dance with her every time I see her, always complains that this new Swing music is impossible to dance to because it is too fast. I smile, twirl her around a few times, and remind her that Kristi and I have been dancing to two hundred-beats-per-minute Techno/Rave for the last six years.

Sometimes I long for that combat-booted, ripped-jeans, leather-   12
clad, alternative gothic-punk world that grunge killed. And I miss that strobe-lit raver underground, the raw energy and community of those private rave years that greed has killed. I nostalgically long for the fun of those past days, something my now-Swinger, ex-Raver, ex-Goth girlfriend, sees little point in.

I can not predict what will follow Swing. I am just a Beta, and do   13
not have access to such knowledge. But after watching the Commercial stage kill off the last remnants of pure Rave, we Beta-stage Swing Kids are at least aware of what will happen. Soon Rave will pass on to Death and Swing will become fully Commercial, even the kids on *90210* will be hip-cat Swing Kids. But for now we will enjoy being Swing Kids— a bunch of old punk-gothic-raver-freaks—sharp

dressed and dancing eloquently to brass chaos. Running around in our zoot suits and wingtips, our long gowns and high gloves, hiding under our fedoras from the new generation of Ravers who call us freaks.

✦ ✦ ✦

✦ *Framing the Context*

1. Peters wrote this essay as an assignment in his magazine-writing class. What type of magazine would you recommend he submit the essay to and why?

2. From the experiences Peters presents in the first two paragraphs, what assumptions does he make about his intended readers?

✦ *Point of View*

3. Peters creates a high level of visibility using a subjective point of view. How will this high visibility affect his relationship with the popular culture magazine readers?

4. If Peters had chosen an objective point of view, how would his relationship with his readers change?

✦ *Shape of Ideas*

5. What framework does Peters choose to combine his personal experiences in social communities with the evolution of the popular music culture?

6. How does that structure guide readers to discovering Peters's purpose?

✦ *Choosing Voice*

7. What diction choices does Peters make that are appropriate to writing about popular culture?

8. Describe Peters's level of formality, and using specific examples, explain how that formality matches his point of view.

✦ *Credibility*

9. Peters uses only one source in addition to his own experiences. What is that source and how does it contribute to Peters's credibility?

10. Peters bases his views on the Orlando music scene. How might this concentrated focus affect his credibility with the readers?

✦ *Suggestions for Writing about Community*

1. "Dilbert" is not the only comic strip that portrays a community. Choose a comic strip that has a well-defined view of community and analyze the strengths and weaknesses of its representation of reality. Use sample episodes to illustrate the points of your analysis.

2. Over the years you have probably been a member of several communities. Describe and analyze how being a member of one of those communities shaped your identity and continues to have an influence on who you are.

3. The cyberspace environment offers a wide range of community experiences, from MUDs and MOOs to news groups, chat rooms, and discussion groups. Write an essay that examines the level of community you have experienced in the virtual world.

4. Some communities in our society are perceived as counterproductive in the same way Kuh, Pascarella, and Wechsler judge fraternities to be counterproductive to the mission of the university. Choose a community that some consider controversial, examine its structure and purpose, and argue for or against its value to society.

5. Have you ever volunteered to work with a group on a special project to help others? Write an essay explaining how the volunteer group built a sense of community with the people receiving the help.

6. If given the opportunity to develop a utopian community, how would you design it? What would its purpose be? How would you bring members together? How would the group live and work together? What identity would you want others to perceive? Write a proposal for the development of the community.

7. Have you ever visited a monument or attended a commemoration that gave you a sense of being part of a larger community? Write an essay in which you re-create that experience.

8. If you are planning to become a member of a professional community, research the trends in the development of that profession and write an essay projecting how it will be perceived as a community in the next five years.

C*hapter* 8
◆ ✦ ✦ ✦ ✦ ✦ ✦ ✦ ✦ ✦

Exploring Cyberspace

Cyberspace, an informational-data space so vast that we're unable to measure its limits or the speed of its growth. With over forty-three million Web sites already available to visit, we may be explorers for our entire lives, and like the explorers of past frontiers, we use what we already know to experience and test this new frontier. Where do I want to go? How do I get there? What barriers will I face? How should I value what I find? How long do I want to stay?

The readings in this chapter present different directions in exploring cyberspace. And like all explorations, the ones illustrated in these readings uncover certain risks: safety, privacy, free speech, censorship, access, frustration. Some of the explorations are personal, but many raise issues that question the consequences of our infatuation with this new frontier on the future of the entire society, especially how we will relate to each other. Your own experiences in exploring cyberspace will help you to read both *with* and *against* the writers and to use that tension to discover each writer's purpose. The questions following each reading will guide you in determining what choices the writers made and how effective those choices are in connecting the intended reader to the subject and the writer's purpose. The Writing Suggestions at the end of the chapter present ways for you to explore your own ideas on cyberspace and make writing choices to develop those ideas.

Adrift on the Digital Sea

Karen Olsson

✦ ✦ ✦

Karen Olsson, who writes regularly for the Texas Observer, *is also a contributing editor of* Civilization, *where she published the following article in the April/May 1997 issue. Olsson finds herself "adrift" between two worlds of reading: the sustained reading of novels and the surfing action of the Web. "I value the World Wide Web as a research tool," she explains, "but I find its proliferation of useless information both mesmerizing and exasperating." In her article Olsson explores why she "clings to books."*

1   Back when I used to watch Saturday morning cartoons, a public-service ad ran regularly in which an animated cat, wearing a pirate's hat and squinting into a spyglass, would urge his young audience to read. His pitch was that books would take us anywhere we wanted to go—"Just read a book!" he cried, prancing about as various exotic scenes flashed in the background. That cat introduced me to the notion that reading a book—in particular a novel—transports us elsewhere, and moreover that we readers embark on a kind of voyage: We don't simply go alone to a strange place and do nothing; we accompany an orphan boy arriving in a strange city, or a woman deserting her husband.

2   Or maybe we venture out over the ocean. Perhaps we accompany a young man who, against the wishes of his father, joins up with various ship crews, is kidnapped, escapes, lives for a time in Brazil, enlists with another crew whose boat is set upon by a storm, and finally lands by himself, shipwrecked and alone, on a desert island, where he lives for many years. One of the first novels written in English, *The Life and Strange Surprizing Adventures of Robinson Crusoe,* prefigures the model of reading I learned from the cat—the ocean adventure—and also refines it, for when we read novels are we not cast away, isolated in strange territory? In writing a new kind of story, in an unusual form, the author of *Robinson Crusoe* satisfied the reader's desire to escape and to learn exotic new things. Hundreds of years later, the cartoon cat likewise lured prospective young readers with the promise of adventure.

244

But now, at the end of the 20th century, a new kind of reading is on the rise, with its own associated ocean activity: surfing. Exit Crusoe, enter all the thousands upon thousands of Web-page authors, toiling away in their electronic nooks. Catch a wave, they sing, while members of the old guard skulk around onshore—the novel readers, the authors, the booksellers and publishers. What will become of us? the traditionalists wonder as they shake the sand from their shoes. They are uncertain elitists, both proud of their noble pursuit and nervous about being left behind. They worry that books will die off. **3**

As for myself, I do not think the contest between books and other entertainments is so epic and final, but it does seem that the uses of reading will shift. While people will continue to read novels, perhaps a greater number of people will be reading Web pages, and so it becomes reasonable to ask: What happens if "reading" comes to mean not sailing but surfing, not novel reading but on-line browsing? **4**

When I refer to reading books, I mean reading fiction, and though it's common to pay tribute to books, it's not so easy to say what the merits are in something as selfish and unuseful as reading a novel on a given afternoon, when you could be doing a hundred other things. Why read? A reader might suggest any number of personal answers; she reads because she is shy, curious, antisocial, bored or just plain hooked. Reading novels hasn't always been a common pastime, however; it was only after books became available, and after authors began to write novels in some quantity, that reading books became popular and novels became the most popular kind of book to read. The question, then, is also a historical one: Why at the turn of the 18th century did people—Europeans, that is, and in particular the English—begin reading novels? **5**

The career of a man named John Dunton, who in 1674, at the age of 15, left his rural home to be apprenticed to a London bookseller, suggests the beginnings of an answer. Like Crusoe, Dunton went against the wishes of his father—who wanted him to enter the clergy—and like Crusoe he was restless. Even after he completed the apprenticeship and had his own bookshop, he would satisfy his "Humour of *Rambling*" by traveling extensively and by penning various literary rambles. His tastes ran to the miscellaneous and eccentric, and in 1691 he had a sudden insight as to how he could translate predilection into profit. Dunton began to publish a weekly newsletter, *The Athenian Mercury*, in which he offered to print answers to questions submitted by readers. The purpose of his publication, he **6** wrote, was "to satisfie all *ingenious and curious Enquirers* into *Specula-tions,* Divine, Moral and Natural, &c."

7   Dunton soon received more questions than he knew what to do with. A great number of them concerned how to act in certain sticky social situations, but others defied categorization, for example: *"Q: Whether a Badger has ev'ry Year a New Arse-Hole?"* Dunton went on to compile trivia and news into "Athenian" volumes—among them *The Athenian Catechism, The Athenian Spy,* and *Athenian News: or, Dunton's Oracle.* "Athenians" were defined as lovers of novelty, and on several of his title pages he printed the couplet:

> *We are all tainted with the Athenian Itch*
> *News, and new Things do the whole World bewitch.*

8   The success of the *Mercury* and of Dunton's subsequent ventures suggests that the Athenian Itch was in fact spreading, and this in turn hints at what sort of climate the novel was born into. While Dunton was printing his Athenian volumes, other writers and publishers were trying to satisfy the public craving for news and curiosities with es-says about science, reports of unusual weather events or other strange occurrences, travelogues, exposés, newsletters, and moralizing tracts. Novels responded to and furthered young, urban readers' desires to learn about the minutiae of daily life and conduct, about strange events, about adventures within the city and far away from it. Books became parental, supplying scattered bits of information as well as object lessons in conduct, and novel readers thus engaged in a kind of learning that set them apart from previous generations.

9   For many of *Robinson Crusoe*'s first readers the stranded Crusoe on his island, making his own clothes and growing his own food, must have been a sort of last man of a bygone era, even as he repre-sented the young readers in their rebellious, wandering ways. No longer required to know the techniques of crude survival, these read-ers followed along as Crusoe learned to fend for himself—not in order to learn themselves how to, say, farm on a lonely island but to imagine how. Books allowed readers to imagine the varieties of ex-perience, which, in the overwhelming city, were too numerous to ex-perience firsthand. Other people's lives in their great variety were perhaps even more curious, more new, more Athenian Itch–scratch-ing than accounts of odd weather events or questions about badgers' asses. Novels included the current events, the moral lessons and the

odd facts that publications like *The Athenian Mercury* featured; what's more, they hung all that around a set of characters who in the unique progress of their lives were themselves "strange" and "surprizing."

Shortly after building his island shelter, Crusoe wonders how Providence could so cruelly abandon him on this island, but then in the next paragraph he cheers up: 10

> *Reason as it were expostulated with me t'other Way, thus: Well, you are in a desolate Condition 'tis true, but pray remember, Where are the rest of you? Did not you come Eleven of you into the Boat, Where are the Ten? Why were not they sav'd and you lost? Why were you singled out? Is it better to be here or there? and then I pointed to the Sea.*

Why this life and no other? asked the novel. How many different possible lives there are! For all the various guises the novel has assumed since Defoe's time, this basic, wondering sense of the extraordinary particularity of other lives (coupled with the perception that the needs and desires and questions these lives give rise to are somehow universal) informs novel writing and novel reading. Readers yearn to navigate the enormous territory of the possible—of which only a tiny part can actually be traversed over the course of a lifetime—and novels, in their dramatic presentations of other lives, make excellent guides.

This picture of the rise of the novel is only a hasty sketch, but as such it resembles the picture of the growth of the World Wide Web commonly drawn today: In an era of considerable lifestyle change and media proliferation, a new kind of writing and reading rises up in response to new needs, establishing a new sort of commerce of information. Of course every generation will marvel at social and technological change, but the Web particularly recalls the early novel in its promise to help us negotiate the changing times by means of a simulation in which we, as readers, participate. Again there are worlds to travel to, now "virtual" rather than fictional.   11

When I first started to surf, although I was pretty dubious about the whole thing, I still felt a little shiver of discovery—as if the Web were both an absolutely new realm and a means to improve my understanding of what's going on in the world. As soon as I started poking around, however, I ran into problems. Exploring the World Wide Web is physically straining and mentally wearisome. My eyes   12 glazed over as I scanned pages and watched text scrolling up and down, my back grew sore from leaning forward to read the screen and, gradually, I became quite dizzy. Also, I spent a great deal more time waiting for text and images to arrive than I did looking at anything in particular. These problems—the strain and the waiting—are apparently no great concern for the millions of Web users, and they may diminish as the technology improves. But what's a little scary is that as I sat there, staring at the screen and waiting for yet another page to appear, I was mesmerized. I felt compelled to look up page after page even though I read very little on any one of them; the few times I came across something of interest, I skimmed the first few paragraphs, wished I had a paper copy so I could read it for real, and then went on to the next thing. Gone was the pace of reading printed matter; I could not easily pause, look away from the page, or think about anything. I pointed, I clicked, I stared as the computer forged the next connection. And when I say I wished I could read a few things "for real" I mean it: These words on-screen have a shimmery, half-baked sort of existence; they are unreliable in the sense that factual claims need not be checked and also in the sense that if you leave a site, whatever you've read may not be there when you return. Though fans of the Web celebrate the individual control afforded to its browsers, who can visit sites according to their particular interests and needs, I didn't feel in control. I felt towed along.

13   So my initial anticipation of discovery quickly gave way to exhaustion. What most struck me about the Web was the unstable, insignificant nature of each page, crushed under the weight of the many others surrounding it. Unlike reading a novel, in which the singular, specific tale is elevated, reading a Web page lacks singularity; everything is part of the network. It comes as no surprise that the Web's texts are very different from fiction books, but I hadn't realized how antifictional the entire browsing process is, inducing a mental blur of reference-upon-reference, fact-upon-uncertain-fact. It's like being trapped inside a card catalog. Even after I stopped browsing, my mind was still playing loose associations—I couldn't go from that to reading a book, which requires shutting everything out, for I was still letting everything in. Maybe the Web is just wrong for me. But maybe the Web threatens books more than I thought it did, by provoking a manic state that makes book reading difficult: the humor of rambling gone amok. Will this sort of haphazard consumption of information and images and advertisements become the dominant mode of reading?

Though the broad version of the rise of electronic texts echoes   14
the broad version of the rise of novels, the resulting reading experiences are at opposite poles; instead of adventuring someplace with a
narrator, Web browsers wander aimlessly alone. This distinction
doesn't just set novel reading apart from Web browsing. The voice of
the historian or the biographer, or even the collective voice of a print
periodical as established by its editorial range and design standards,
is traded for a thousand disjointed voices on the Web. It may seem inappropriate to compare reading something on paper with Web
browsing, since, some might argue, the latter is better compared to
visiting a newsstand or a library; of course there are a thousand voices
on the Web, just as there are on a rack full of magazines. But whereas
you go to the newsstand or library to pick something to take home
and read through, people surf the Web; they scan lots of different
things, and there's always something a little better on the horizon.

The Web is somehow appropriate, therefore, to an era that has   15
grown suspicious of the single voice. We assess politicians' strategies
rather than the contents of their speeches, and we watch talk shows
in which judging the storyteller is likewise an integral part of listening to the story. Novels themselves question the authority of the nar-
rators (and authors), telling and retelling stories from different points
of view. South African author J. M. Coetzee, for example, reenvi-
sioned the Crusoe story in his 1986 novel *Foe;* its narrator is a
woman, Susan Barton, who was shipwrecked on a desert island
where she encountered a white man named Cruso and his black
slave Friday; in the book she returns with Friday to England and approaches an eminent author, Daniel Foe, with her story. Like the
original Robinson Crusoe, Barton wonders why her life has pro-
ceeded as it has, but rather than marveling at the singularity of that
life as Crusoe did, she casts doubt upon the idea that one's life is a
unique course tracked by a single intelligence:

> *[F]or the blink of an eyelid our vigilance relaxes; we are asleep; and when we
> awake, we have lost the direction of our lives. What are these blinks of an eye-
> lid, against which the only defence is an eternal and inhuman wakefulness?
> Might they not be the cracks and chinks through which another voice, other
> voices, speak up in our lives?*

Yet even these questions are asked within a novel that holds together
as a work. The existence of other voices and other versions of a story
is entertained in contemporary novels, but these fictions still tend to

chart some kind of course; they tell some kind of tale, however fragmented and uncertain; they appeal to our sense of possibility and forward movement. In a sense, they are bested by the Web in its total
dissociation; multiple perspectives are the essence of that medium. Ask
a Web search program to look for the words "Robinson Crusoe," and
it will come up with a list of links to Crusoe-themed pages, published
by Defoe fans and literature teachers; you can find pedagogical material, historical background, reflections on the various characters, references to Coetzee's novel, to poet Derek Walcott's readaptations of
Defoe's story, to the movie starring Pierce Brosnan and to English-
department course listings at Georgetown University. It would be quite
difficult to find out just what the story is, though you could download
the entire text of Defoe's novel if you were crazy enough to want to.

16   That's the thing about these Web pages; they are always about
something else that isn't there on the page, and you try to track that
something down, and you end up going nowhere. The Web may be
useful as a reference tool, a news source or a means of exchanging
information with other users, but as I browsed I couldn't help feeling like I was feeding a bad habit, in that I have more than a little bit
of the itinerant, associationist humor already. It is precisely because
I am already a rambler—John Dunton has a place in my heart—that
I cling to books, which hold out the promise that all that movement
might get you somewhere.

✦ ✦ ✦

✦ *Framing the Context*

  1. *Civilization* is "the magazine of the Library of Congress," the national
     archive. All Library of Congress members receive the magazine, and
     it is available at newsstands. What purpose do you expect these
     readers to have for reading this publication?

  2. Olsson begins her essay with a personal childhood experience.
     What does this choice indicate about the assumptions she makes
     regarding the readers' attitude toward reading?

✦ *Point of View*

  3. Olsson establishes her point of view in the first paragraph. Identify
     that point of view.

  4. How does this point of view affect the reader's interaction with
     the writer's ideas? Identify a paragraph that illustrates that level of
     interaction.

✦ *Shape of Ideas*

5. Olsson's assumptions about what her readers already know about the two worlds of reading is reflected in the structure she chooses. What is that structure and what assumptions about the reader does it reflect?

6. Identify another arrangement strategy that Olsson could use to connect the intended audience to her subject and purpose.

✦ *Choosing Voice*

7. Explain how the last sentence in the first paragraph illustrates the formality level of Olsson's voice.

8. In what way does Olsson's level of formality complement her point of view?

✦ *Credibility*

9. Olsson refers to the novel *Robinson Crusoe* throughout the essay. How does this choice of source contribute to her credibility with the readers of *Civilization*?

10. How does Olsson's use of personal Web experiences complement her point of view and voice?

The New Technology
Is It Part of the Solution or Part of the Problem in Education?

Michael Apple

✦ ✦ ✦

Michael Apple, a professor of educational studies at the University of Wisconsin, fears that teachers and school administrators are jumping on the computer bandwagon without asking the necessary political, economic, and ethical questions about the possible consequences of technological innovations. This is a lengthy, documented academic article written for a professional audience of college education professors and school administrators directly involved in educational reform. The article first appeared in the educational journal Computers in the Schools *(1991) and is based on the research Apple conducted for his book* Teachers and Texts: A Political Economy of Class and Gender Relations in Education *(1988). This is the type of article you will consult in conducting your own research and, as college students, you are already experiencing and preparing to face many of the issues Apple analyzes.*

The Politics of Technology

1   In our society, technology is seen as an autonomous process. It is set apart and viewed as if it had a life of its own, independent of social intentions, power, and privilege. We examine technology as if it was something constantly changing and as something that is constantly changing our lives in schools and elsewhere. This is partly true, of course, and is fine as far as it goes. However, by focusing on what is changing and being changed, we may neglect to ask what relationships are remaining the same. Among the most important of these are the sets of cultural and economic inequalities that dominate even societies like our own.[1]

2   By thinking of technology in this way, by closely examining whether the changes associated with "technological progress" are really changes in certain relationships after all, we can begin to ask

political questions about their causes and especially their multitudinous effects. Whose idea of progress? Progress for what? And fundamentally, who benefits?[2] These questions may seem rather weighty ones to be asking about schools and the curricular and teaching practices that now go on in them or are being proposed. Yet, we are in the midst of one of those many educational bandwagons that governments, industry, and others so like to ride. This wagon is pulled in the direction of a technological workplace, and carries a heavy load of computers as its cargo.

The growth of the new technology in schools is definitely not what one would call a slow movement. In one recent year, there was a 56% reported increase in the use of computers in schools in the United States and even this may be a conservative estimate.[3] This is a trend that shows no sign of abating.[4] Nor is this phenomenon only limited to the United States. France, Canada, England, Australia, and many other countries have "recognized the future." At its center seems to sit a machine with a keyboard and a screen.

I say "at its center," since in both governmental agencies and in schools themselves the computer and the new technology have been seen as something of a savior economically and pedagogically. "High-tech" will save declining economies and will save our students and teachers in schools. In the latter, it is truly remarkable how wide a path the computer is now cutting.

The expansion of its use, the tendency to see all areas of education as a unified terrain for the growth in use of new technologies, can be seen in a two day workshop on integrating the microcomputer into the classroom held at my own university. Among the topics covered were computer applications in writing instruction, in music education, in secondary science and mathematics, in primary language arts, for the handicapped, for teacher record keeping and management, in business education, in health occupation training programs, in art, and in social studies. To this is added a series of sessions on the "electronic office," how technology and automation are helping industry, and how we all can "transcend the terror" of technology.[5]

Two things are evident from this list. First, vast areas of school life are now seen to be within the legitimate purview of technological restructuring. Second, there is a partly hidden but exceptionally close linkage between computers in schools and the needs of management for automated industries, electronic offices, and "skilled" personnel. Thus, recognizing both what is happening inside and outside of schools and the connections between these areas is critical to any understanding of what is likely to happen with the new technologies, especially the computer, in education.

7   As I have argued elsewhere, all too often educational debates are increasingly limited to technical issues. Questions of "how to" have replaced questions of "why."[6] In this article, I shall want to reverse this tendency. Rather than dealing with what the best way might be to establish closer ties between the technological requirements of the larger society and our formal institutions of education, I want to step back and raise a different set of questions. I want us to consider a number of rather difficult political, economic, and ethical issues about some of the tendencies in schools and the larger society that may make us want to be very cautious about the current technological bandwagon in education. In so doing, a range of areas will need to be examined: Behind the slogans of technological progress and high tech industry, what are some of the real effects of the new technology on the future labor market? What may happen to teaching and curriculum if we do not think carefully about the new technology's place in the classroom? Will the growing focus on technological expertise, particularly computer literacy, equalize or further exacerbate the lack of social opportunities for our most disadvantaged students?

8   Of course, there are many more issues that need to be raised. Given limited space, however, I shall devote the bulk of my attention to those noted above. I am certain that many of you can and will have many more that you could add to the list.

9   At root, my claim will be that the debate about the role of the new technology in society and in schools is not and must not be just about the technical correctness of what computers can and cannot do. These may be the least important kinds of questions in fact. At the very core of the debate instead are the ideological and ethical issues concerning what schools should be about and whose interests they should serve.[7] The question of interests is very important currently since, because of the severe problems currently besetting economies like our own, a restructuring of what schools are for has reached a rather advanced stage.

10   Thus, while there has always been a relatively close connection between the two, there is now an even closer relationship between the curriculum in our schools and corporate needs.[8] In a number of countries, educational officials and policy makers, legislators, curriculum workers, and others have been subject to immense pressure

to make the "needs" of business and industry the primary goals of the school system. Economic and ideological pressures have become rather intense and often very overt. The language of efficiency, production, standards, cost effectiveness, job skills, work discipline, and so on—all defined by powerful groups and always threatening to become the dominant way we think about schooling[9]—has begun to push aside concerns for a democratic curriculum, teacher autonomy, and class, gender, and race equality. Yet, we cannot fully understand the implications of the new technology in this restructuring unless we gain a more complete idea of what industry is now doing not only in the schools but in the economy as well.

Technological Myths and Economic Realities

Let us look at the larger society first. It is claimed that the technological needs of the economy are such that unless we have a technologically literate labor force we will ultimately become outmoded economically. But what will this labor force actually look like? [11]

A helpful way of thinking about this is to use the concepts of increasing *proletarianization* and *deskilling* of jobs. These concepts signify a complex historical process in which the control of labor has altered, one in which the skills workers have developed over many years are broken down and reduced to their atomistic units, automated, and redefined by management to enhance profit levels, efficiency and control. In the process, the employee's control of timing, over defining the most appropriate way to do a task, and over criteria that establish acceptable performance are slowly taken over as the prerogatives of management personnel who are usually divorced from the place where the actual labor is carried out. Loss of control by the worker is almost always the result. Pay is often lowered. And the job itself becomes routinized, boring, and alienating as conception is separated from execution and more and more aspects of jobs are rationalized to bring them into line with management's need for a tighter economic and ideological ship.[10] Finally, and very importantly, many of these jobs may simply disappear. [12]

There is no doubt that the rapid developments in, say, microelectronics, genetic engineering and associated "biological technologies," and other high-tech areas are in fact partly transforming work in a large number of sectors in the economy. This may lead to economic prosperity in certain sections of our population, but its other [13] effects may be devastating. Thus, as the authors of a recent study that examined the impact of new technologies on the future labor market demonstrate:

> *This transformation . . . may stimulate economic growth and competition in the world marketplace, but it will displace thousands of workers and could sustain high unemployment for many years. It may provide increased job opportunities for engineers, computer operators, and robot technicians, but it also promises to generate an even greater number of low level service jobs such as those of janitors, cashiers, clericals, and food service workers. And while many more workers will be using computers, automated office equipment, and other sophisticated technical devices in their jobs, the increased use of technology may actually reduce the skills and discretion required to perform many jobs.*[11]

Let us examine this scenario in greater detail.

14   Rumberger and Levin make a distinction that is very useful to this discussion. They differentiate between high-tech industries and high-tech occupations, in essence between what is made and the kinds of jobs these goods require. High-tech industries that manufacture technical devices such as computers, electronic components and the like currently employ less than 15% of the paid work force in the United States and other industrialized nations. Just as importantly, a substantial knowledge of technology is required by *less than one fourth* of all occupations within these industries. On the contrary, the largest share of jobs created by high-tech industries are in areas such as clerical and office work or in production and assembly. These actually pay below average wages.[12] Yet this is not all. High-tech occupations that do require considerable skill—such as computer specialists and engineers—may indeed expand. However, most of these occupations actually "employ relatively few workers compared to many traditional clerical and service fields."[13] Rumberger and Levin summarize a number of these points by stating that "although the percentage growth rate of occupational employment in such high technology fields as engineering and computer programming was higher than the overall growth rate of jobs, far more jobs would be created in low-skilled clerical and service occupations than in high technology ones."[14]

15   Some of these claims are supported by the following data. It is estimated that even being generous in one's projections, only 17% of new jobs that will be created between now and 1995 will be in high-

tech industries. (Less generous and more restrictive projections argue that only 3 to 8% of future jobs will be in such industries.)[15] As I noted though, such jobs will not be all equal. Clerical, secretaries, assemblers, warehouse personnel, etc., these will be the largest occupations within the industry. If we take the electronic components industry as an example here, this is made much clearer. Engineering, science, and computing occupations constituted approximately 15% of all workers in this industry. The majority of the rest of the workers were engaged in low wage assembly work. Thus, in the late 1970's, nearly two thirds of all workers in the electronic components industry took home hourly wages "that placed them in the bottom third of the national distribution."[16] If we take the archetypical high-tech industry—computer and data processing—and decompose its labor market, we get similar results. In 1980, technologically oriented and skilled jobs accounted for only 26% of the total.[17]

These figures have considerable weight, but they are made even more significant by the fact that many of that 26% may themselves experience a deskilling process in the near future. That is, the reduction of jobs down into simpler and atomistic components, the separation of conception from execution, and so on—processes that have had such a major impact on the labor process of blue, pink, and white collar workers in so many other areas—are now advancing into high technology jobs as well. Computer programming provides an excellent example. New developments in software packages and machine language and design have meant that a considerable portion of the job of programming now requires little more than performing "standard, routine, machine-like tasks that require little in-depth knowledge."[18]

What does this mean for the schooling process and the seemingly widespread belief that the future world of work will require increasing technical competence on the part of all students? Consider the occupations that will contribute the most number of jobs not just in high-tech industries but throughout the society by 1995. Economic forecasts indicate that these will include building custodians, cashiers, secretaries, office clerks, nurses, waiters and waitresses, elementary school teachers, truck drivers, and other health workers such as nurses aides and orderlies.[19] None of these are directly related to high technology. Excluding teachers and nurses, none of them require any post secondary education. (Their earnings will be approximately 30% below the current average earnings of workers, as well.)[20] If we go further than this and examine an even

16

17

larger segment of expected new jobs by including the forty job cate-gories that will probably account for about one half of all the jobs that will be created, it is estimated that only about 25% will require people with a college degree.[21]

18   In many ways, this is strongly related to the effects of the new technology on the job market and the labor process in general. Skill levels will be raised in some areas, but will decline in many others, as will jobs themselves decline. For instance, "a recent study of robotics in the United States suggests that robots will have eliminated 100,000 to 200,000 jobs as of 1990, while creating 32,000 to 64,000 jobs."[22] My point about declining skill requirements is made nicely by Rum-berger and Levin. As they suggest, while it is usually assumed that workers will need computer programming and other sophisticated skills because of the greater use of technology such as computers in their jobs, the ultimate effect of such technology may be somewhat different. "A variety of evidence suggests just the opposite: as machines become more sophisticated, with expanded memories, more compu-tational ability, and sensory capabilities, the knowledge required to use the devices declines."[23] The effect of these trends on the division of labor will be felt for decades. But it will be in the sexual division of labor where it will be even more extreme. Since historically *women's work* has been subject to these processes in very powerful ways, we shall see increased proletarianization and deskilling of women's labor and, undoubtedly, a further increase in the feminization of poverty.[24]

19   These points clearly have implications for our educational pro-grams. We need to think much more rigorously about what they mean for our transition from school to work programs, especially since many of the "skills" that schools are currently teaching are tran-sitory because the jobs themselves are being transformed (or lost) by new technological developments and new management offensives.

20   Take office work, for example. In offices, the bulk of the new tech-nology has not been designed to enhance the quality of the job for the largest portion of the employees (usually women clerical work-ers). Rather it has usually been designed and implemented in such a way that exactly the opposite will result. Instead of accommodating stimulating and satisfying work, the technology is there to make man-agers' jobs "easier," to eliminate jobs and cut costs, to divide work into routine and atomized tasks, and to make administrative control more easily accomplished.[25] The vision of the future society seen in the mi-crocosm of the office is inherently undemocratic and perhaps in-

creasingly authoritarian. Is this what we wish to prepare our students for? Surely, our task as educators is neither to accept such a future labor market and labor process uncritically nor to have our students accept such practices uncritically as well. To do so is simply to allow the values of a limited but powerful segment of the population to work through us. It may be good business but I have my doubts about whether it is ethically correct educational policy.

In summary, then, what we will witness is the creation of en-hanced jobs for a relative few and deskilled and boring work for the majority. Furthermore, even those boring and deskilled jobs will be increasingly hard to find. Take office work, again, an area that is rapidly being transformed by the new technology. It is estimated that between one and five jobs will be lost for every new computer termi-nal that is introduced.[26] Yet this situation will not be limited to office work. Even those low paying assembly positions noted earlier will not necessarily be found in the industrialized nations with their increas-ingly service oriented economies. Given the international division of labor, and what is called "capital flight," a large portion of these jobs will be moved to countries such as the Philippines and Indonesia.[27]

This is exacerbated considerably by the fact that many govern-ments now find "acceptable" those levels of unemployment that would have been considered a crisis a decade ago. "Full employ-ment" in the United States is now often seen as between 5 7% *mea-sured* unemployment. (The actual figures are much higher, of course, especially among minority groups and workers who can only get part time jobs.) This is a figure that is *double* that of previous economic periods. Even higher rates are now seen as "normal" in other coun-tries. The trend is clear. The future will see fewer jobs. Most of those that are created will not necessarily be fulfilling, nor will they pay well. Finally, the level of technical skill will continue to be lowered for a large portion of them.[28]

Because of this, we need convincing answers to some very impor-tant questions about our future society and the economy before we turn our schools into the "production plants" for creating new work-ers. *Where* will these new jobs be? *How many* will be created? Will they *equal* the number of positions lost in offices, factories, and service jobs in retailing, banks, telecommunications, and elsewhere? Are the bulk of the jobs that will be created relatively unskilled, less than meaning-ful, and themselves subject to the inexorable logics of management so that they too will be likely to be automated out of existence?[29]

24   These are not inconsequential questions. Before we give the schools over to the requirements of the new technology and the corporation, we must be very certain that it will benefit all of us, not mostly those who already possess economic and cultural power. This requires continued democratic discussion, not a quick decision based on the economic and political pressure now being placed on schools.

25   Much more could be said about the future labor market. I urge the interested reader to pursue it in greater depth since it will have a profound impact on our school policies and programs, especially in vocational areas, in working class schools, and among programs for young women. The difficulties with the high-tech vision that permeates the beliefs of the proponents of a technological solution will not remain outside the school door, however. Similar disproportionate benefits and dangers await us inside our educational institutions as well and it is to this that we shall now turn.

Inequality and the Technological Classroom

26   Once we go inside the school, a set of questions concerning "who benefits?" also arises. We shall need to ask about what may be happening to teachers and students given the emphasis now being placed on computers in schools. I shall not talk about the individual teacher or student here. Obviously, some teachers will find their jobs enriched by the new technology and some students will find hidden talents and will excel in a computer oriented classroom. What we need to ask instead (or at least before we deal with the individual) is what may happen to classrooms, teachers, and students differentially. Once again, I shall seek to raise a set of issues that may not be easy to solve, but cannot be ignored if we are to have a truly democratic educational system in more than name only.

27   While I have dealt with this in greater detail in *Ideology and Curriculum* and *Education and Power*,[30] let me briefly situate the growth of the technologized classroom into what seems to be occurring to teaching and curriculum in general. Currently, considerable pressure is building to have teaching and school curricula be totally prespecified and tightly controlled for the purposes of "efficiency," "cost effectiveness," and "accountability." In many ways, the deskilling that is affecting jobs in general is now having an impact on teachers as more and more decisions are moving out of their hands and as their jobs become even more difficult to do. This is more advanced in

some countries than others, but it is clear that the movement to rationalize and control the act of teaching and the content and evaluation of the curriculum is very real.[31] Even in those countries that have made strides away from centralized examination systems, powerful inspectorates and supervisors, and tightly controlled curricula, there is an identifiable tendency to move back toward state control. Many reforms have only a very tenuous hold currently. This is in part due to economic difficulties and partly due as well to the importing of American styles and techniques of educational management, styles and techniques that have their roots in industrial bureaucracies and have almost never had democratic aims.[32] Even though a number of teachers may support computer oriented curricula, an emphasis on the new technology needs to be seen in this context of the rationalization of teaching and curricula in general.

Given these pressures, what will happen to teachers if the new technology is accepted uncritically? One of the major effects of the current (over) emphasis on computers in the classroom may be the deskilling and depowering of a considerable number of teachers. Given the already heavy work load of planning, teaching, meetings, and paperwork for most teachers, and given the expense, it is probably wise to assume that the largest portion of teachers will not be given more than a very small amount of training in computers, their social effects, programming, and so on. This will be especially the case at the primary and elementary school level where most teachers are already teaching a wide array of subject areas. Research indicates in fact that few teachers in any district are actually given substantial information before computer curricula are implemented. Often only one or two teachers are the "resident experts."[33] Because of this, most teachers have to rely on prepackaged sets of material, existing software, and especially purchased material from any of the scores of software manufacturing firms that are springing up in a largely unregulated way.

The impact of this can be striking. What is happening is the exacerbation of trends we have begun to see in a number of nations. Rather than teachers having the time and the skill to do their own curriculum planning and deliberation, they become isolated executors of someone else's plans, procedures, and evaluative mechanisms. In industrial terms, this is very close to what I noted in my previous discussion of the labor process, the separation of conception from execution.[34]

The question of time looms larger here, especially in gender terms. Because of the large amount of time it takes to become a

28

29

30

"computer expert" and because of the patriarchal relations that still dominate many families, *men* teachers will often be able to use "computer literacy" to advance their own careers while women teachers will tend to remain the recipients of prepackaged units on computers or "canned" programs over which they have little control.

31   In her excellent ethnographic study of the effects of the introduction of a district wide computer literacy program on the lives of teachers, Susan Jungck makes exactly this point about what happened in one middle school.

> *The condition of time [needs to] be examined in terms of gender differences because it was the women teachers, not the men, in the Math Department who were unprepared to teach about computers and they were the ones most dependent on the availability of the [canned] Unit. Typically, the source of computer literacy for in-service teachers is either college or university courses, school district courses or independent study, all options that take considerable time outside of school. Both [male teachers] had taken a substantial number of university courses on computers in education. Many [of the] women, [because of] child care and household responsibilities . . . , or women who are single parents . . . , have relatively less out of school time to take additional coursework and prepare new curricula. Therefore, when a new curriculum such as computer literacy is required, women teachers may be more dependent on using the ready-made curriculum materials than most men teachers.*[35]

32   The reliance on prepackaged software can have a number of long-term effects. First, it can cause a decided loss of important skills and dispositions on the part of teachers. When the skills of local curriculum planning, individual evaluation, and so on are not used, they atrophy. The tendency to look outside of one's own or one's colleagues' historical experience about curriculum and teaching is lessened as considerably more of the curriculum, and the teaching and evaluative practices that surround it, is viewed as something one purchases. In the process—and this is very important—the school itself is transformed into a lucrative market. The industrialization of the school I talked of previously is complemented, then, by further opening up the classroom to the mass produced commodities of industry. In many ways, it will be a publisher's and saleperson's delight. Whether students' educational experiences will markedly improve is open to question.

33   The issue of the relationship of purchased software and hardware to the possible deskilling and depowering of teachers does not

end here, though. The problem is made even more difficult by the rapidity with which software developers have constructed and marketed their products. There is no guarantee that the mass of such material has any major educational value. Exactly the opposite is often the case. One of the most knowledgeable government officials has put it this way: "High quality educational software is almost nonexistent in our elementary and secondary schools."[36] While perhaps overstating his case to emphasize his points, the director of software evaluation for one of the largest school systems in the United States has concluded that of the more than 10,000 programs currently available, approximately 200 are educationally significant.[37]

To their credit, the fact that this is a serious problem is recognized by most computer enthusiasts, and reviews and journals have attempted to deal with it. However, the sheer volume of material, the massive amounts of money spent on advertising software in professional publications, at teachers' and administrators' meetings, and so on, the utter "puffery" of the claims made about much of this material, and the constant pressure by industry, government, parents, some school personnel, and others to institute computer programs in schools *immediately,* all of this makes it nearly impossible to do more than make a small dent in the problem. As one educator put it, "There's a lot of junk out there."[38] The situation is not made any easier by the fact that teachers simply do not now have the time to thoroughly evaluate the educational strengths and weaknesses of a considerable portion of the *existing* curricular material and texts before they are used. Adding one more element, and a sizable one at that, to be evaluated only increases the load. Teachers work is increasingly becoming what students of the labor process call *intensified.* More and more needs to be done; less and less time is available to do it.[39] Thus, one has little choice but to simply buy ready made material, in this way continuing a trend in which all of the important curricular elements are not locally produced but purchased from commercial sources whose major aim may be profit, not necessarily educational merit.[40]

There is a key concept found in Jungck's argument above that is essential here, that of gender. As I have demonstrated in considerable detail in *Teachers and Texts,*[41] teaching—especially at the elementary school level—has been defined as "women's work." We cannot ignore the fact that 87% of elementary teachers and 67% of teachers over all *are* women. Historically, the introduction of prepackaged or standardized curricula and teaching strategies has often been related to the rationalization and attempt to gain external control of the labor process of women workers. Hence, we cannot completely understand what is happening to teachers—the deskilling, the intensification, the separation of conception from execution, the loss of control, and so on—unless we situate these tendencies into this longer history of what has often happened to occupations that are primarily made up of women.[42] Needless to say, this is a critically important point, for only by raising the question of *who* is most often doing the teaching in many of these schools now introducing prepackaged software can we see the connections between the effects of the curricula and the gendered composition of the teaching force.

36   A significant consideration here, besides the loss of skill and control, is expense. This is at least a three-pronged issue. First, we must recognize that we may be dealing with something of a "zero-sum game." While dropping, the cost of computers is still comparatively high, though some manufacturers may keep purchase costs relatively low, knowing that a good deal of their profits may come from the purchase of software later on or through a home/school connection, something I shall discuss shortly. This money for the new technology *must come from somewhere.* This is an obvious point but one that is very consequential. In a time of fiscal crisis, where funds are already spread too thinly and necessary programs are being starved in many areas, the addition of computer curricula most often means that money must be drained from one area and given to another. What will be sacrificed? If history is any indication, it may be programs that have benefitted the least advantaged. Little serious attention has been paid to this, but it will become an increasingly serious dilemma.

37   A second issue of expense concerns staffing patterns, for it is not just the content of teachers' work and the growth of purchased materials that are at stake. Teachers' jobs themselves are on the line here. At a secondary school level in many nations, for example, layoffs of teachers have not been unusual as funding for education is cut. Declining enrollment in some regions has meant a loss of positions as well. This has caused intense competition over students within the school itself. Social studies, art, music, and other subjects must fight it out with newer, more "glamorous" subject areas. To lose the student numbers game for too long is to lose a job. The effect of the computer in this situation has been to increase competitiveness among staff, often to replace substance with both gloss and attractive packaging of courses, and to threaten many teachers with the loss of their livelihood.[43] Is it really an educationally or socially wise

decision to tacitly eliminate a good deal of the choices in these other fields so that we can support the "glamor" of a computer future? These are not only financial decisions, but are ethical decisions about teachers' lives and about what our students are to be educated in. Given the future labor market, do we really want to claim that computers will be more important than further work in humanities and social sciences or, perhaps even more significantly in working class and ethnically diverse areas, in the students' own cultural, historical, and political heritage and struggles? Such decisions must not be made by only looking at the accountant's bottom line. These too need to be arrived at by the lengthy democratic deliberation of all parties, including the teachers who will be most affected.

Third, given the expense of microcomputers and software in schools, the pressure to introduce such technology may increase the already wide social imbalances that now exist. Private schools to which the affluent send their children and publicly funded schools in more affluent areas will have more ready access to the technology itself.[44] Schools in inner city, rural, and poor areas will be largely priced out of the market, even if the cost of "hardware" continues to decline. After all, in these poorer areas and in many public school systems in general in a number of countries it is already difficult to generate enough money to purchase new textbooks and to cover the costs of teachers' salaries. Thus, the computer and literacy over it will "naturally" generate further inequalities. Since, by and large, it will be the top 20% of the population that will have computers in their homes[45] and many of the jobs and institutions of higher education their children will be applying for will either ask for or assume "computer skills" as keys of entry or advancement, the impact can be enormous in the long run.

The role of the relatively affluent parent in this situation does not go unrecognized by computer manufacturers.

Computer companies . . . gear much of their advertising to the educational possibilities of computers. The drive to link particular computers to schools is a frantic competition. Apple, for example, in a highly touted scheme proposed to "donate" an Apple to every school in America. Issues of philanthropy and intent aside, the clear market strategy is to couple particular computer usages to schools where parents —especially middle class parents with the economic wherewithal and keen motivation [to insure mobility]— purchase machines compatible with those in schools. The potentially most lucrative part of such a scheme, however, is not in the purchase of hardware (although this is also substantial) but in the sole of proprietary software.[46]

40　　This very coupling of school and home markets, then, cannot fail to further disadvantage large groups of students. Those students who already have computer backgrounds—be it because of their schools or their homes or both—will proceed more rapidly. The social stratification of life chances will increase. These students' original advantage—one *not* due to "natural ability," but to *wealth*—will be heightened.[47]

41　　We should not be surprised by this, nor should we think it odd that many parents, especially middle class parents, will pursue a computer future. Computer skills and "literacy" is partly a strategy for the maintenance of middle class mobility patterns.[48] Having such expertise, in a time of fiscal and economic crisis, is like having an insurance policy. It partly guarantees that certain doors remain open in a rapidly changing labor market. In a time of credential inflation, more credentials mean less closed doors.[49]

42　　The credential factor here is of considerable moment. In the past, as gains were made by ethnically different people, working class groups, women, and others in schooling, one of the latent effects was to raise the credentials required by entire sectors of jobs. Thus, class, race, and gender barriers were partly maintained by an ever increasing credential inflation. Though this was more of a structural than a conscious process, the effect over time has often been to again disqualify entire segments of a population from jobs, resources and power. This too may be a latent outcome of the computerization of the school curriculum. Even though, as I have shown, the bulk of new jobs will not require "computer literacy," the establishment of computer requirements and mandated programs in schools will condemn many people to even greater economic disenfranchisement. Since the requirements are in many ways artificial—computer knowledge will not be so very necessary and the number of jobs requiring high levels of expertise will be relatively small—we will simply be affixing one more label to these students. "Functional illiteracy" will simply be broadened to include computers.[50]

43　　Thus, rather than blaming an unequal economy and a situation in which meaningful and fulfilling work is not made available, rather than seeing how the new technology for all its benefits is "creating a growing underclass of displaced and marginal workers," the lack is personalized. It becomes the students' or workers' fault for not being computer literate. One significant social and ideological outcome of computer requirements in schools, then, is that they can serve as a means "to justify those lost lives by a process of mass disqualification, which throws the blame for disenfranchisement in education and employment back on the victims themselves."[51]

Of course, this process may not be visible to many parents of individual children. However, the point does not revolve around the question of individual mobility, but large scale effects. Parents may see such programs as offering important paths to advancement and some will be correct. However, in a time of severe economic problems, parents tend to overestimate what schools can do for their children.[52] As I documented earlier, there simply will not be sufficient jobs and competition will be intense. The uncritical introduction of and investment in hardware and software will by and large hide the reality of the transformation of the labor market and will support those who are already advantaged unless thought is given to these implications now.

Let us suppose, however, that it was important that everyone become computer literate and that these large investments in time, money, and personnel were indeed so necessary for our economic and educational future. Given all this, what is currently happening in schools? Is inequality in access and outcome now being produced? While many educators are continually struggling against these effects, we are already seeing signs of this disadvantagement being created.

There is evidence of class, race, and gender based differences in computer use. In middle class schools, for example, the number of computers is considerably more than in working class or inner city schools populated by children of color. The ratio of computers to children is also much higher. This in itself is an unfortunate finding. However, something else must be added here. These more economically advantaged schools not only have more contact hours and more technical and teacher support, but the very manner in which the computer is used is often different than what would be generally found in schools in less advantaged areas. Programming skills, generalizability, a sense of the multitudinous things one can do with computers both within and across academic areas, these tend to be stressed more[53] (though simply drill and practice uses are still widespread even here).[54] Compare this to the rote, mechanistic, and relatively low level uses that tend to dominate the working class school.[55] These differences are not unimportant, for they signify a ratification of class divisions.

47   Further evidence to support these claims is now becoming more readily available as researchers dig beneath the glowing claims of a computer future for all children. The differential impact is made clearer in the following figures. In the United States, while over two-thirds of the schools in affluent areas have computers, only approximately 41% of the poorer public schools have them. What one does with the machine is just as important as having one, of course, and here the differences are again very real. One study of poorer elementary schools found that white children were four times more likely than black children to use computers for programming. Another found that the children of professionals employed computers for programming and for other "creative" uses. Nonprofessional children were more apt to use them for drill and practice in mathematics and reading, and for "vocational" work. In general, in fact, "programming has been seen as the purview of the gifted and talented" and of those students who are more affluent. Less affluent students seem to find that the computer is only a tool for drill and practice sessions.[56]

48   Gender differences are also very visible. Two out of every three students currently learning about computers are boys. Even here these data are deceptive since girls "tend to be clustered in the general introductory courses," not the more advanced level ones.[57] One current analyst summarizes the situation in a very clear manner.

> While stories abound about students who will do just about anything to increase their access to computers, most youngsters working with school computers are [economically advantaged], white and male. The ever-growing number of private computer camps, after-school and weekend programs serve middle class white boys. Most minority [and poor] parents just can't afford to send their children to participate in these programs.[58]

49   This class, race, and gendered impact will also occur because of traditional school practices such as tracking or streaming. Thus, vocational and business tracks will learn operating skills for word processing and will be primarily filled with (working class) young women.[59] Academic tracks will stress more general programming abilities and uses and will be dispositionally male.[60] Since computer programs usually have their home bases in mathematics and science in most schools, gender differences can be heightened even more given the often differential treatment of girls in these classes and the

ways in which mathematics and science curricula already fulfill "the selective function of the school and contribute to the reproduction of gender differences."[61] While many teachers and curriculum workers have devoted considerable time and effort to equalize both the opportunities and outcomes of female students in mathematics and science (and such efforts are important), the problem still remains a substantive one. It can be worsened by the computerization of these subjects in much the same way as it may have a gendered impact on the teachers themselves.

Towards Social Literacy

We have seen some of the possible negative consequences of the new technology in education, including the deskilling and depowering of teachers and the creation of inequalities through expense, credential inflation, and limitations on access. Yet it is important to realize that the issues surrounding the deskilling process are not limited to teachers. They include the very ways students themselves are taught to think about their education, their future roles in society, and the place of technology in that society. Let me explain what I mean by this.

The new technology is not just an assemblage of machines and their accompanying software. It embodies a *form of thinking* that orients a person to approach the world in a particular way. Computers involve ways of thinking that under current educational conditions are primarily technical.[62] The more the new technology transforms the classroom into its own image, the more a technical logic will replace critical political and ethical understanding. The discourse of the classroom will center on technique, and less on substance. Once again "how to" will replace "why," but this time at the level of the student. This situation requires what I shall call social, not technical, literacy for all students.

Even if computers make sense technically in all curricular areas and even if all students, not mainly affluent white males, become technically proficient in their use, critical questions of politics and ethics remain to be dealt with in the curriculum. Thus, it is crucial that whenever the new technology is introduced into schools students have a serious understanding of the issues surrounding their larger social effects, many of which I raised earlier.

Unfortunately, this is not often the case. When the social and ethical impacts of computers are dealt with, they are usually addressed in a manner that is less than powerful. One example is provided by a recent proposal for a statewide computer curriculum in one of the larger states in the United States. The objectives that dealt with social questions in the curriculum centered around one particular set of issues. The curriculum states that "the student will be aware of some of the major uses of computers in modern society . . . and the student will be aware of career opportunities related to computers."[63] In most curricula the technical components of the new technology are stressed. Brief glances are given to the history of computers (occasionally mentioning the role of women in their development, which is at least one positive sign). Yet in this history, the close relationship between military use and computer development is largely absent. "Benign" uses are pointed to, coupled with a less than realistic description of the content and possibility of computer careers and what Douglas Noble has called "a gee-whiz glance at the marvels of the future." What is nearly never mentioned is job loss or social disenfranchisement. The very real destruction of the lives of unemployed autoworkers, assemblers or clerical workers is marginalized.[64] The ethical dilemmas involved when we choose between, say, "efficiency" and the quality of the work people experience, between profit and someone's job, these too are made invisible.

54 How would we counterbalance this? By making it clear from the outset that knowledge about the new technology that is necessary for students to know goes well beyond what we now too easily take for granted. A considerable portion of the curriculum would be organized around questions concerned with social literacy. "Where are computers used? What are they used to do? What do people *actually* need to know in order to use them? Does the computer enhance anyone's life? Whose? Does it hurt anyone's life? Whose? Who decides when and where computers will be used ?"[65] Unless these are *fully* integrated in a school program at *all* levels, I would hesitate advocating the use of the new technology in the curriculum. Raising questions of this type is not just important in our elementary and secondary schools. It is even more essential that they be dealt with in a serious way with teachers both in their own undergraduate teacher education programs where courses in educational computing are more and more being mandated and in the many inservice workshops now springing up throughout the country as school districts frantically seek to keep up with the "computer revolution." To do less makes it much more difficult for teachers and students to

think critically and independently about the place the new technology does and should have in the lives of the majority of people in our society. Our job as educators involves skilling, not deskilling. Unless teachers and students are able to deal honestly and critically with these complex ethical and social issues, only those now with the power to control technology's uses will have the capacity to act. We cannot afford to let this happen.

Conclusion

I realize that a number of my points may prove to be rather contentious in this essay. But stressing the negative side can serve to highlight many of the critical issues that are too easy to put off given the immense amount of work that school personnel are already responsible for. Decisions often get made too quickly, only to be regretted later on when forces are set in motion that could have been avoided if the implications of one's actions had been thought through more fully.   55

As I noted at the outset of this discussion, there is now something of a mad scramble to employ the computer in every content area. In fact, it is nearly impossible to find a subject that is not being "computerized." Though mathematics and science (and some parts of vocational education) remain the home base for a large portion of proposed computer curricula, other areas are not far behind. If it can be packaged to fit computerized instruction, it will be, even if it is inappropriate, less effective than the methods that teachers have developed after years of hard practical work, or less than sound educationally or economically. Rather than the machine fitting the educational needs and visions of the teacher, students, and community, all too often these needs and visions are made to fit the technology itself.   56

Yet, as I have shown, the new technology does not stand alone. It is linked to transformations in real groups of people's lives, jobs, hopes, and dreams. For some of these groups, those lives will be enhanced. For others, the dreams will be shattered. Wise choices about the appropriate place of the new technology in education, then, are not only educational decisions. They are fundamentally choices about the kind of society we shall have, about the social and ethical responsiveness of our institutions to the majority of our future citizens, and to the teachers who now work, in our schools.   57

58   My discussion here has not been aimed at making us all neo-Luddites, people who go out and smash the machines that threaten our jobs or our children. The new technology is here. It will not go away. Our task as educators is to make sure that when it enters the classroom it is there for politically, economically, and educationally wise reasons, not because powerful groups may be redefining our major educational goals in their own image. We should be very clear about whether or not the future it promises to our teachers and students is real, not fictitious. We need to be certain that it is a future *all* of our students can share in, not just a select few. After all, the new technology is expensive and will take up a good deal of our time and that of our teachers, administrators, and students. It is more than a little important that we question whether the wagon we have been asked to ride on is going in the right direction. It's a long walk back.

Notes

This article is based on a more extensive analysis in Michael W. Apple, *Teachers and Texts: A Political Economy of Class and Gender Relations in Education* (New York: Routledge and Kegan Paul, 1988).

1. David Noble, *Forces of Production: A Social History of Industrial Automation* (New York: Alfred A. Knopf, 1984), pp. xi–xii. For a more general argument about the relationship between technology and human progress, see Nicholas Rescher, *Unpopular Essays on Technological Progress* (Pittsburgh: University of Pittsburgh Press, 1980).
2. Ibid, p. xv.
3, Paul Olson, "Who Computes? The Politics of Literacy," unpublished paper, Ontario Institute for Studies in Education, Toronto, 1985, p. 6.
4. Patricia B. Campbell, "The Computer Revolution: Guess Who's Left Out?" *Interracial Books for Children Bulletin* 15 (no. 3 1984), p. 3.
5. "Instructional Strategies for Integrating the Microcomputer into the Classroom," The Vocational Studies Center, University of Wisconsin, Madison, 1985.
6. Michael W. Apple, *Ideology and Curriculum,* second edition (New York: Routledge and Kegan Paul, 1990).
7. Olson, "Who Computes?" p. 5.
8. See Michael W. Apple, *Education and Power* (New York: Routledge and Kegan Paul, ARK Edition, 1985).
9. For further discussion of this, see Apple, *Ideology and Curriculum,* Apple, *Education and Power,* and Ira Shor, *Culture Wars* (Boston: Routledge and Kegan Paul, 1986).
10. This is treated in greater detail in Richard Edwards, *Contested Terrain* (New York: Basic Books, 1979). See also the more extensive discussion

of the effect these tendencies are having in education in Apple, *Education and Power.*

11. Russell W. Rumberger and Henry M. Levin, "Forecasting the Impact of New Technologies on the Future Job Market," Project Report No. 84-A4, Institute for Research on Educational Finance and Government, School of Education, Stanford University, February, 1984, p. 1.

12. Ibid, p. 2.

13. Ibid, p. 3.

14. Ibid, p. 4.

15. Ibid, p. 18.

16. Ibid.

17. Ibid, p. 19.

1B. Ibid, pp. 19–20.

19. Ibid, p. 31.

20. Ibid, p. 21.

21. Ibid.

22. Ibid, p. 25.

23. Ibid.

24. The effects of proletarianization and deskilling on women's labor is analyzed in more detail in Michael W. Apple, *Teachers and Texts* (New York: Routledge, 1988). On the history of women's struggles against proletarianization, see Alice Kessler-Harris, *Out to Work* (New York: Oxford University Press, 1982).

25. Ian Reinecke, *Electronic Illusions* (New York: Penguin Books, 1984), p. 156.

26. See the further discussion of the loss of office jobs and the deskilling of many of those that remain in Ibid, pp. 136–158. The very same process could be a threat to middle and low level management positions as well. After all, if control is further automated, why does one need as many supervisory positions? The implications of this latter point need to be given much more consideration by many middle-class proponents of technology since their jobs may soon be at risk too.

27. Peter Dwyer, Bruce Wilson, and Roger Woock, *Confronting School and Work* (Boston: George Allen and Unwin, 1984), pp. 105–106.

28. The paradigm case is given by the fact that three times as many people now work in low paying positions for McDonald's as for U.S. Steel. See Martin Carnoy, Derek Shearer, and Russell Rumberger, *A New Social Contract* (New York: Harper and Row, 1983), p. 71. As I have argued at greater length elsewhere, however, it may not be important to our economy if all students and workers are made technically knowledgeable by schools. What is just as important is the production of economically useful knowledge (technical/administrative knowledge) that can be used by corporations to enhance profits, control labor, and increase efficiency. See Apple, *Education and Power,* especially Chapter 2.

29. Reinecke, *Electronic Illusions,* p. 234. For further analysis of the economic data and the effects on education, see W. Norton Grubb, "The Bandwagon Once More: Vocational Preparation for High-Tech Occupations," *Harvard Educational Review* 54 (November 1984), 429–451.

30. Apple, *Ideology and Curriculum* and Apple, *Education and Power.* See also Michael W. Apple and Lois Weis, eds., *Ideology and Practice in Schooling* (Philadelphia: Temple University Press, 1983).

31. Ibid. See also Arthur Wise, *Legislated Learning: The Bureaucratization of the American Classroom* (Berkeley: University of California Press, 1979).

32. Apple, *Ideology and Curriculum* and Apple, *Education and Power.* On the general history of the growth of management techniques, see Richard Edwards, *Contested Terrain.*

33. Douglas Noble, "The Underside of Computer Literacy," *Raritan* 3 (Spring 1984), 45. What can actually happen when computers are used in this way is detailed in Michael W. Apple and Susan Jungck, "You Don't Have to Be a Teacher to Teach This Unit," *American Educational Research Journal,* in press.

34. See the discussion of this in Apple, *Education and Power,* especially Chapter 5.

35. Susan Jungck, "Doing Computer Literacy," unpublished Ph.D. dissertation, University of Wisconsin, Madison, 1985, pp. 236–237.

36. Douglas Noble, "Jumping Off the Computer Bandwagon," *Education Week,* October 3, 1984, 24.

37. Ibid.

38. Ibid. See also, Noble, "The Underside of Computer Literacy," 45.

39. For further discussion of the intensification of teachers' work, see Apple, *Teachers and Texts.*

40. Apple, *Education and Power.* For further analysis of the textbook publishing industry, see Michael W. Apple, *Teachers and Texts.*

41. Apple, *Teachers and Texts.*

42. Ibid.

43. I am indebted to Susan Jungck for this point. See Jungck, "Doing Computer Literacy."

44. Reinecke, *Electronic Illusions,* p. 176.

45. Ibid, p. 169.

46. Olson, "Who Computes?" p. 23.

47. Ibid, p. 31. Thus, students' familiarity and comfort with computers becomes a form of what has been called the "cultural capital" of advantaged groups. For further analysis of the dynamics of cultural capital, see Apple, *Education and Power* and Pierre Bourdieu and Jean-Claude Passeron, *Reproduction in Education, Society and Culture* (Beverly Hills: Sage, 1977).

48. Ibid, p. 23. See also the discussion of interclass competition over academic qualifications in Pierre Bourdieu, *Distinction* (Cambridge: Harvard University Press, 1984), pp. 133–168.

49. Once again, I am indebted to Susan Jungck for this argument.
50. Noble, "The Underside of Computer Literacy," p. 54.
51. Douglas Noble, "Computer Literacy and Ideology," *Teachers College Record* 85 (Summer 1984), 611. This process of "blaming the victim" has a long history in education. See Apple, *Ideology and Curriculum,* especially Chapter 7.
52. R. W. Connell, *Teachers' Work* (Boston: George Allen and Unwin, 1985), p. 142.
53. Olson, "Who Computes?" p. 22.
54. For an analysis of the emphasis on and pedagogic problems with such limited uses of computers, see Michael Streibel, "A Critical Analysis of Three Approaches to the Use of Computers in Education," in Landon Beyer and Michael W. Apple, eds., *The Curriculum: Problems, Politics and Possibilities* (Albany: State University of New York Press, 1988), pp. 259–288.
55. Olson, "Who Computes?" p. 22.
56. Campbell, "The Computer Revolution: Guess Who's Left Out?" 3. Many computer experts, however, are highly critical of the fact that students are primarily taught to program in BASIC, a less than appropriate language for later advanced computer work. Michael Streibel, personal communication.
57. Ibid.
58. Ibid.
59. An interesting analysis of what happens to young women in such business programs and how they respond to both the curricula and their later work experiences can be found in Linda Valli, "Becoming Clerical Workers: Business Education and the Culture of Femininity," in Apple and Weis, eds., *Ideology and Practice in Schooling,* pp. 213–234. See also her more extensive treatment in Linda Valli, *Becoming Clerical Workers* (Boston: Routledge and Kegan Paul, 1986).
60. Jane Gaskell in Olson, "Who Computes?" p. 33.
61. Feodora Fomin, "The Best and the Brightest: The Selective Function of Mathematics in the School Curriculum," in Lesley Johnson and Deborah Tyler, eds., *Cultural Politics: Papers in Contemporary Australian Education, Culture and Politics* (Melbourne: University of Melbourne, Sociology Research Group in Cultural and Educational Studies, 1984), p. 220.
62. Michael Streibel's work on the models of thinking usually incorporated within computers in education is helpful in this regard. See Streibel, "A Critical Analysis of Three Approaches to the Use of Computers in Education." The more general issue of the relationship between technology and the control of culture is important here. A useful overview of this can be found in Kathleen Woodward, ed., *The Myths of Information: Technology and Postindustrial Culture* (Madison: Coda Press, 1980).
63. Quoted in Noble, "The Underside of Computer Literacy," p. 56.

64. Ibid, 57. An interesting, but little known fact is that the largest proportion of computer programmers actually work for the military. See Joseph Weizenbaum, "The Computer in Your Future," *The New York Review of Books,* October 27, 1983, pp. 58–62.

65. Noble, "The Underside of Computer Literacy," p. 40. For students in vocational curricula especially, these questions would be given more power if they were developed within a larger program that would seek to provide these young women and men with extensive experience in and understanding of all aspects of operating an entire industry, not simply those "skills" that reproduce workplace stratification. See Center for Law and Education, "Key Provisions in New Law Reforms Vocational Education: Focus Is on Broader Knowledge and Experience for Students/Workers," *Center for Low and Education, Inc. D.C. Report,* December 28, 1984, pp. 1–6.

✦ ✦ ✦

✦ Framing the Context

1. Professionally, Apple has a close relationship with his audience, but ideologically he knows their views on technology may differ. How does he define this difference in the introduction?

2. What is the occasion in the field of technology that motivated Apple to write this article?

✦ Point of View

3. Apple's shared authority with his professional audience makes his use of a merged point of view appropriate. If Apple had chosen to use an objective point of view, how would his relationship to his readers be changed?

4. Identify an example of how Apple's use of the merged point of view minimizes the differences they might have regarding technology.

✦ Shape of Ideas

5. Apple uses headings common to academic articles to structure the flow of his ideas. What structure do those headings indicate?

6. How do the structure headings and the length of each section guide the readers in understanding Apple's purpose?

✦ Choosing Voice

7. An academic article generally requires a formal voice. Identify two sentences which you find especially formal.

8. Throughout the article Apple poses many questions. How does his use of questions affect the formality of his voice and the relationship with his readers?

✦ Credibility

9. Identify the techniques Apple uses to incorporate sources (as outlined in Chap. 5) and explain how the quantity and quality of these techniques establish his credibility.

10. Explain how the last paragraph under the second heading contributes to Apple's ethos.

Desperately Seeking E-Mail

Lisa Dreier

✦ ✦ ✦

E-mail has grown from a form of interoffice communication to a mass communication network for conducting global business and staying in touch with family and friends. Its speed and cost-effectiveness have reduced regular postal delivery to the derogatory status of "snail mail." No wonder people have become dependent on using it. As a feature writer for the Wanderlust section of Salon, *an on-line magazine (www.salon.com), Lisa Dreier relies on e-mail for business as well as personal use. In her December 6, 1998, article, she explores the cyberspace world of e-mail beyond the reliable boundaries of the United States.*

1   Ten years ago, I stood in a dusty telegraph office in the high-altitude Bolivian city of La Paz. A man with mahogany skin and a llama-wool vest handed me a yellowed form where I was to write my message, one letter in each box. I was traveling on a rock-bottom budget and telegraphs were expensive: something like a dollar a word. But I had promised my parents that I'd let them know, at the very least, what country I was in—and I had just crossed the border from Peru. So I gripped a pockmarked pencil and scrawled the bare minimum of words to convey my message: "Lisa—fine—Bolivia."

2   Even then, things were changing fast. By the time I reached Tierra del Fuego, I was starting to find fax machines—amazing contraptions that could instantly transfer a cramped, one-page letter from the Straits of Magellan to my parents' living room. And then, a few years later, I discovered e-mail.

3   It didn't take me long to fall under the spell of this new medium: It was fast, easy and totally addictive. Working in an e-mail-crazed California workplace, I checked mine every 15 minutes. I e-mailed people more often than I spoke to them. At one point, I realized I was in closer touch with my friend in the Amazon than with my friends across town. I was never home, I was swamped at work, but you could always reach me on e-mail. By the time I left for a seven-month journey through Asia last January, I couldn't imagine living without it.

There was one major problem: I was going to India. Deep into   4
India—traveling through scrubby desert and remote villages, sput-
tering across rivers in ailing motorboats, dodging cows in the alley-
ways of 800-year-old forts. Nevertheless, I was determined to find
e-mail along the way. In India's mind-boggling clamor of life and
death and color, I would seek out both ancient mysteries and modern-day Internet access. This, at least, was the idea.

In the months before my departure, I began to ask around: Was   5
it possible to send e-mail from India? I planned to do a lot of writing on my journey; would I be crazy to bring a laptop?

Seasoned travelers reacted in horror to the whole idea. In India,   6
they said, telephone jacks were nonexistent, the phone lines were
configured wrong, the Internet was banned by the government, electricity was erratic and ungrounded and, in any case, my laptop would
surely be stolen. A few weeks before my departure, a writer friend
told me she had taken a laptop to India the year before—with disastrous results. Accessing the Internet had proved impossible. Plugging
her laptop into the wall had caused a small electrical fire in her
ashram. Finally, she abandoned the cursed thing at a friend's house
in Bombay and continued her journey with a lighter step.

Considerably chastened, I lowered my hopes but hung on to a   7
stubborn belief in the miraculous. It was, after all, a question of e-mail.

And so I stepped off a plane in Delhi as a member of a strange   8
species—a budget traveler with a laptop. I had never attempted third-
world travel with such an expensive piece of hardware before, and it
took some getting used to. First, traveling with a computer knocked
me into the pack-rat category. The lightest laptop I could find—the
slim and hardy HP Omnibook 800CT—was about the size and weight
of a small picture book about India. But try adding the required para-
phernalia—a padded case, external floppy drive and diskettes, extra
battery and charger and an array of adapters, cords and surge protectors. Suddenly, a third of my luggage was dedicated to the computer.

I wedged most of this into a beat-up, generously sized day pack.   9
From a distance, I looked like an overzealous student. But a careful
observer—say, an experienced thief—would have noticed that I was
curiously protective of the dusty old bag. Security became more of
an issue. I kept the laptop out of sight at all times, and rarely told anyone—even fellow travelers—what lay inside. When checking out
hotel rooms, I'd look for an electrical outlet and sturdy locks on the
doors. The view from the window and softness of the bed were sec-

ondary. It often seemed that the computer, like an overbearing travel companion, was calling the shots more often than I was.

10   By cobbling together a series of plugs, adapters and surge protectors, I discovered that I could tap in to the local electrical current. But I'd been warned that this could be a recipe for disaster—one developing-country electrical event, and my computer would be transformed into a sea of melted plastic and fried data. So whenever possible I used battery power, charging up the spare only when I was in the room to put out any fires that might result.

11   Problems with the phone lines, however, proved insurmountable. On my first day in India, I got down on my knees and crawled under the bed in my mid-range hotel room, following a knotted phone cord that simply disappeared into a hole in the wall. So much for phone jacks and modems. I was going to have to find public Internet access.

12   E-mail? The Internet? Nobody in my hotel had heard of it. But the five-star listings in my guidebook yielded more luck. The Hotel Imperial, one of Delhi's finest, told me I could access the Internet through the lone computer and modem in its Business Center. I put on a skirt, grabbed my address book and tried to look nonchalant as I walked through the gleaming marble entrance past liveried doormen. Mr. Jain, the Business Center manager, bowed and greeted me in a lilting voice. I asked him, almost breathlessly, if he had Internet access. "Ah yes," he said, sitting down in his three-piece suit and peering solemnly at the computer screen. With a dignified, almost ceremonial air, he dialed in over a modem that required more than 10 tries to connect, entered a special password and series of codes and then: oh joy.

13   I was connected. It was expensive in local terms, but I didn't care. I told Mr. Jain about my travel plans and asked him whether I could find Internet access in the state of Rajasthan—or anywhere outside Delhi. He shook his head gravely. I turned back to the computer and typed out a message to my friends, family and editors warning them that I didn't know when, if ever, I'd be online again.

✦ ✦ ✦

✦ Framing the Context

1. *Salon*'s Wanderlust section has the subtitle "travel with a passion" and six columns: Editor's Letter; Feature; Mondo Weirdo; Postmark; Passages; Road Warrior. Describe the assumptions Dreier can make about her readers' relationship to the subject

2. Dreier begins the article with a non-e-mail personal travel experience from ten years ago. How does this experience help her to connect with her audience?

✦ *Point of View*

3. How does Dreier's choice of a subjective point of view strengthen her relationship with the *Salon* Wanderlust readers?

4. If Dreier had chosen a merged point of view, what specific assumptions would she have to make about her readers' travel experience?

✦ *Shape of Ideas*

5. What structure does Dreier choose to shape her travel experience with e-mail?

6. Explain how a different structure would also suit Dreier's purpose.

✦ *Choosing Voice*

7. A subjective point of view can be presented in an informal voice or a formal voice. How would you characterize the level of formality Dreier uses?

8. Using paragraph 5 as an example, explain how the sentence structure, diction, and punctuation convey Dreier's level of formality.

✦ *Credibility*

9. Describe Dreier's use of sources and explain how those sources complement her point of view.

10. Explain how paragraphs 6–8 contribute to Dreier's ethos.

Surgery on the Internet

Doris Bloodsworth

✦ ✦ ✦

Where do you search for medical information? Your family doctor? Your parents? Your friends? The campus health center? The Internet? According to Orlando Sentinel *feature writer Doris Bloodsworth, an increasing number of people are going on-line to find answers to their questions, especially about surgical procedures. In her June 1, 1999, feature published in the Living section of the* Orlando Sentinel, *Bloodsworth explores several issues this new use of cyberspace has spawned.*

1   Dressed in operating-room scrubs the doctor commands the mother to "Push!" as the camera zooms in. It could be another episode of *ER,* but it's not.

2   The doctor and patient are real, and the audience is watching over the Internet. Almost a year ago, more than 1.1 million viewers logged on to America's Health Network's online companion, AHN.com (www.ahn.com), to see Baby Sean born in Orlando.

3   It was the world's first public viewing of a woman giving birth on the Web and drew the largest audience ever for any live online event, according to a spokesman of RealNetworks, which monitors Internet activity.

4   Since then, AHN has carved its niche with Webcasts of an open-heart surgery, laser eye repair and brain surgery.

5   An NFL football player and a Kissimmee woman were among those who shared their operations.

6   This upstart cable network, based at Universal Studios Florida, has an audience of about 9 million viewers, with more than 61,000 in Central Florida.

7   That audience is expected to grow when AHN relaunches in mid-July under Fox/Liberty Ventures as The Health Network, with 17 million cable and satellite subscribers.

8   AHN's Internet concept has been noticed by others in the medical community, including a Beverly Hills plastic surgeon and a Seattle cardiovascular surgeon who have broadcast surgeries.

But medical-ethics experts worry that technology could be rac-   9
ing ahead of good practice. They have questions about this new
medium:

- Are these virtual medical events done for educational purposes   10
  or commercial interests?
- Do the patients make informed choices to participate or are they   11
  unwittingly coerced into going along?
- What drives people to watch? Is it voyeurism or healthy curiosity?   12

Dr. Walt Larimore, a family physician in Kissimmee who hosts   13
Ask the Family Doctor on AHN, insists that the goal is education.

"In my office, I can teach one on one," he said. "But here, I can   14
teach one on a million."

The idea of educating others appealed to Elizabeth Oliver and   15
Nonia McQuay, two Central Florida patients whose medical stories
were Webcast on AHN.com.

Oliver, 41, of Orlando, became known as the "Internet Mom"   16
after she delivered Baby Sean at Arnold Palmer Hospital last June 16.
McQuay, a 48-year-old Kissimmee resident, had the first brain
aneurysm operation shown on the Internet Feb. 18.

Oliver said she agreed to share her delivery online only if the   17
cameras protected her modesty. She liked the idea of doctors and
families benefiting from her experience.

But the worldwide attention brought consequences that she and   18
the network never intended. Just days after she left the hospital,
Oliver said she and her husband, Gilbert, were greeted at their front
door by people posing as American Red Cross workers.

She said a photographer hiding in a tree snapped their picture.   19
The next week, a story appeared in a national tabloid alleging the
Olivers left a trail of bad checks.

Charges against Oliver and her husband for writing worthless   20
checks were dismissed.

Despite the stress and bad publicity, Oliver is adamant that she   21
would give birth online again.

"I'm sorry the media tends to judge you by the worst moment of   22
your life," she said, "and I regret it might have erased some of the
good that AHN was trying to do."

The network executives still consider the live birth a coup.   23
Launched in April 1998, AHN.com started with 72,000 Page views.

One year later, the number jumped to two million. In addition, the company sells the live birth video for $19.99.

24   As for McQuay, she agreed to cybercast her operation, in which a small bulge was removed from a brain artery, because her mother and grandmother died from untreated brain aneurysms.

25   "There is a whole world of people out there that would rather die than go and do this [operation]," she said. "As stubborn and afraid of needles as I am, if I can do it, anyone can."

26   Other potential patients might log on to the Web to watch high profile celebrities. AHN recently showed a live eye surgery involving NFL star Keith Elias.

27   But some medical professionals wonder if other forces are at work in these decisions.

28   Mark Bliton, a medical ethics expert at Vanderbilt University in Nashville, Tenn., worries that the Internet patients may be influenced by unspoken pressure, however unintentional it might be.

29   "There are these subtle forms of coercion," he said. "The patient comes to the physician because there is something wrong with them, so right off the bat someone has more power. The patient has to trust the physician."

30   Others question the educational benefits of online medical events when companies seek to profit from them.

31   "The medical professional has the duty to put the client's interests ahead of their own," said Bill Allen, professor of medical ethics and law at the University of Florida.

32   "If it's really educational and the patient understands and doesn't mind the commercial benefits the institution gets, then that might be OK," he added. "But that's what you have to watch."

33   AHN.com president J. Tod Fetherling said patients are told their participation is strictly voluntary and are warned about the publicity they might receive. Patients have the option of using their first or full name or remaining anonymous.

34   "What we're all about is helping people live a happier, healthier life," he said.

35   The potential benefits haven't gone unnoticed.

36   Dr. Richard Ellenbogen, a Beverly Hills plastic surgeon, agreed to perform the first celebrity face lift on the Internet, after Michael Sands of Sands Digital Media approached him with the idea.

37   Sands placed an ad in January's *Hollywood Reporter* offering a free face lift to any celebrity willing to have it broadcast over the Internet. Actor and comedian John Byner applied.

According to the surgeon, Byner, who was once a familiar pres-   38
ence on television, agreed to the surgery because both his face and
career were sagging.

Booking agents of a late-night talk show turned Byner away say-   39
ing they were looking for "new faces," Ellenbogen said. After the
March 8 Webcast surgery on Celebrity Doctor (www.celebritydoc-
tor.com), paparazzi swarmed the doctor's parking lot hoping to photograph Byner.

However, the Webcast had an unexpected consequence. A   40
Florida woman who scheduled a face lift with Ellenbogen changed
her mind after viewing the surgery.

In Seattle, Dr. Robert Lazzara is targeting his Virtual Operating   41
Room (www.virtual-or.com) towards health care professionals who
want to learn about the latest medical techniques in an interactive
way.

"The content we're going to put on the Internet is going to   42
change the face of medicine," he said.

But does the public log on to see new medical breakthroughs?   43
Or are browsers, who stormed the Internet in large numbers to
watch a Victoria's Secret fashion show, merely virtual voyeurs?

One adult site is betting on the latter, charging members to   44
watch a New Orleans woman give birth online without regard to
modesty.

But medical insiders make a convincing argument that other is-   45
sues are at stake.

Dr. Steven Bloch, a Chicago plastic surgeon who answers med-   46
ical questions online, said the anonymity of the Web lets consumers
with personal and even embarrassing questions get medical information in a secure, private environment.

"The public increasingly is going to get their information over   47
the Internet," Bloch said, "especially with managed care, where patients often don't get enough time with their doctors."

✦ ✦ ✦

✦ Framing the Context

1. How does Bloodsworth use the introduction to connect her local
   readers to a world event?

2. What assumptions does Bloodsworth make about her readers' use
   of the Internet and their interest in medical information?

✦ *Point of View*

3. What background do you assume Bloodsworth has that supports her writing on this subject?

4. How does Bloodsworth's point of view characterize the relationship she wants to have with her readers?

✦ *Shape of Ideas*

5. What structure does Bloodsworth use to connect her readers to the subject?

6. How does the structure Bloodsworth chooses reveal what she believes the readers need to know? In what paragraph is that need to know explicitly identified?

✦ *Choosing Voice*

7. How does the level of formality Bloodsworth uses in her writing voice complement her point of view choice?

8. Choose a paragraph that has at least two sentences and explain how the use of sentence structure, diction, and punctuation conveys Bloodsworth's level of formality.

✦ *Credibility*

9. Make a list of the "people" sources Bloodsworth includes in her article. Explain how the quantity and quality of those sources support Bloodsworth's purpose.

10. Using the list of techniques in Chapter 5, identify the techniques Bloodsworth uses to incorporate her sources and explain how each contributes to her credibility.

Looking for Love Where My Mother Never Could

Kelli Ryan

✦ ✦ ✦

The popularity of on-line dating shows no signs of decreasing. New dating services appear regularly in cyberspace for people of all ages. Kelli Ryan, a magazine-writing student and senior when she wrote the article that follows, decided to explore the enticing world of on-line dating. After her first adventure and some research into others' experiences, Ryan decided to write an article designed for the readers of Cosmopolitan, *women who look for ways to improve their relationships with the opposite sex.*

"Anyone Looking to Chat?" were the first words I read as I entered into a chat room for the first time.

I thought to myself, this could be interesting, so I replied back. This was easy. All I had to do was create a profile for myself, including what my hobbies and interests were and anything interesting going on in my life at the time.

I gave myself the screen name: *"Cyber-Virgin,"* since this was my first time. The person that originally asked to chat turned out to be a woman, not a man like I had envisioned. With her screen-name being non-gender related, *"Flame77,"* I didn't know who I was replying to.

A few minutes later, after scanning through other people's messages in the "Romance" chat room that I selected, a Personal Message box appeared on my screen.

It read: What's your a/s/loc? In computer terms, A=age, S=sex, and LOC=location. The message was from "Studmuffin," so I replied back saying I was *29, female, and in Hawaii.* Anyone smart enough to look up my profile would see that this was a lie.

Instantaneously he replied back: *30, Male, California.* I asked him what he looked like; his response came back with "Tom Cruise look-alike." Now I ask you, how can anyone compare themselves to Tom Cruise? I chatted with him for an hour, making him believe that I looked like Pamela Anderson Lee!

7   I was amazed at how easy it was to change my identity and to make someone else believe that I could look like a celebrity. This also made me wonder as to what Studmuffin really looked like.

Fairytale Romance:

8   I've had friends who have met their significant others online; some have even married those online buddies they met in chat rooms.

9   After taking a poll in a *Yahoo! Chat room,* asking why they [the chatters] were in there at the time, most replied with, "Boredom or Curiosity."

10   Most of these people did not seek true love (or even not so true love). They chatted because they could meet others from across the globe. They wanted to see just how much information they could find out about people.

11   Some online chatters were in a "dating funk" and needed a change. Those people figured that meeting a person online, hoping that they were being honest, would be easier than flirting in real life and having the fear of rejection.

12   Many people were tired after a hard day at work, or were students escaping from the reality that the final exam really was next week and they hadn't studied at all. Because it was becoming widely known that chatting was as addictive as any other drug, chat rooms became more popular and busier than ever.

13   Like all budding relationships, some chatted seeking some sort of sexual pleasure called *Cybersex.* Weird as it was, these people did not come for lovemaking like the rest of the world knew it. They came to talk about it, and talk about doing it, and got all hot and bothered by not actually doing anything at all. These were the people who were frustrated at not getting any of the real stuff.

14   But of course, with so many handsome princes and beautiful fair maidens attending these gatherings in chat rooms, it was only natural that some would fall in love (and many just as quickly out of love).

15   It was not easy for these men and women to fall in love with each other. This was a magical land of chatting, and thus by some cruel twist of fate, they could not see or hear each other. They could only write messages back and forth.

16   It was not an ideal form of romance, but like all true romance stories, these obstacles were overcome, and love blossomed.

Fact or Fiction:

A close girlfriend of mine, who wants to remain anonymous, but I'll   17
call her Ginny, has had several "dates" with her online buddies. She
has met them online, chatted with them and, eventually, after actually talking on the phone, met them in person. For her, this was a recurring disaster—date after date—but she chose to keep "looking for
her Mr. Right" online.

"I met a Tom Cruise look alike in a Christian chat room," Ginny   18
says. "His aunt set us up in the chat room because he was new to the
area." Day after day, Ginny came home to find e-mails on her computer from Mr. Tom Cruise look alike. She was happy as her relationship progressed.

After two months of online chatting and a few weeks of talking on   19
the phone, getting to know each other, they decided to meet in person.

On their first date, Ginny and her Internet beau met outside of   20
her dorm, because she was only 19 years old and a college freshman
at the time. "A guy friend of mine gave me a sign to tell me how he
looked," she laughed as she recreated a puking face. "I should have
never even gone out with the guy, but he had driven two hours to go
out with me."

They had made plans to dine at the local Applebee's Restaurant.   21
After the initial meeting and viewing his acid washed blue jeans, boat
shoes with no socks on and a very receding hair line, Ginny was not
as excited to spend an evening with him.

She was mortified when the date ordered a beer and asked if she   22
wanted one. "I'm only 19," she said to him, and ordered a cookies-
n-cream shake.

Ginny's ex-boyfriend happened to be in the restaurant and while   23
he was enjoying a few pilsners of ice cold beer, he was also getting a
very jealous streak through him. Ginny recalled, "The night ended
with me and my date getting kicked out of Applebee's, because he and
my ex got into a huge fight. Ugh! I told him that I don't like violent
people and that I didn't want to be around him anymore—and left."

She laughs now, thinking back on the whole situation, but is also   24
a lot more cautious when she meets people online.

To say they were blind dates would be wrong on my part because   25
Ginny knew the basics of the online Don Juan's (except for his real
facial features). "I met his aunt on a Christian chat room. How would
I know that he would be a freak," Ginny restated.

26   Even though she still chats with people online, Ginny doesn't get involved as deeply as she did the first time.

Virtual Addicts:

27   Some would say that it is harmless to flirt online. Some would also say that cybersex and online flirting are always harmful. Regardless of what your opinion is, there are unique factors that make cyberflirting different than real-time flirting and therefore are worth noting.

28   In normal real-life flirtation, there is typically an implicit, and sometimes explicit, boundary. The boundary states that this flirtatious behavior is pleasant, but that it has a clear limit.

29   There is an absolute distinction made that we may engage in casual flirtatious language, share a glance, make a sexual joke, or tease each other in a provocative manner, but that this is as far as it will go.

30   Most of these cues are a complex combination of verbal and non-verbal communications, many of which are not available on the Internet.

31   Innuendo, exclamations, verbal punctuation, facial gestures, intonations are all absent on the Net (with the exclusion of smileys and other computer generated emoticons). Combine these factors with the ease of availability, anonymity and the disinhibition that occurs on the Net, and you have fertile ground for an intensely flirtatious experience without the healthy boundaries found in real-life interaction.

32   One would have to wonder how can everyday life compete with the intense, uninhibited excitement of relationships online?

33   Another consideration to remember is the effect that the online relationship has on the user's spouse or significant other.

34   Maybe the online chatting starts out as innocent cyberflirting. It may proceed to more cyberflirting. After a while, the spouse is going to feel neglected and feel like they are being cheated on.

35   Would you consider having an online affair as cheating? If you are spending many hours of a day or night having cybersex, or flirting, you cannot be engaging in those same behaviors within your primary relationship.

36   About 22% of regular Net users report cyberflirting. These are the people who are not addicted to cybersex and who, occasionally, flirt while online. On the flip side, about 31% of the time, cyber-relationships become real-time sexual one's!

37   Although Netheads are involved in other areas of the Internet, there is clearly a significant sexual component for Internet addicts,

as evidenced by very high percentages of chat room, e-mail, viewing pornography, and having both online and real-time affairs!

What to Do Now?

There is significant and great potential in this new communications medium, but this power needs to be recognized and understood before we can dismiss it as harmless. 38

So, the next time you are casualty cyberflirting, think of the person on the other end of the chat, and how he/she might take this as a real relationship in the making. 39

Consider your alternatives to dating, whether it's going back to the old fashioned Singles Bar Scene or using the Personal Ads from your local paper. 40

Maybe you'll be on "Love Connection" or test out the video dating store. Whether you plan your own *Dating Game Show* or continue to chat online, be careful who you choose to flirt with, it's a multimedia jungle out there! 41

The Unofficial Smiley Directory

These unique and addictive "faces" can be made with the simplest of tools: your very own keyboard. The basic features used are numbers, letters, and punctuation keys. 42

:-)	Basic Smiley
:-(	Frowning
>:->	Devilish
:->	Sarcastic
8-)	wearing sunglasses
:-@	Screaming
:-X	"Lips are Sealed"
:-o	Uh-oh!
[]	hugs
:-*	and Kisses

Common Courtesies:

Before entering chat rooms, one must learn about some "nettiquette" that is useful to know. 43

- When entering a chat room, always start with a "Hello."
- Don't barge in on other people's chats if you haven't let them know you are online also.

- All caps is YELLING.
- Anytime it looks fun to pretend to be someone you aren't, remember the other people may be doing the same.
- Foul language is the final refuge on the intelligent man.
- If you have nothing to add to the conversation, don't try to be cute and add, "Me too!!" Bandwidth (speed/time) on the net is expensive.
- Last of all: Try. The saddest thing in the world is "I shoulda . . . "

Abbreviations:

LOL	Laugh Out Loud
AFAIK	As Far As I Know
CYA	See Ya
QT	Cutie
TOY	Thinking of You
L8RG8R	Later Gator
GMTA	Great Minds Think Alike
PMFJI	Pardon Me For Jumping In

✦ ✦ ✦

✦ *Framing the Context*

1. The readers of *Cosmo* already have a well-defined relationship to the subject of "finding love." What assumptions does Ryan make about the readers' experience with on-line dating? What features indicate those assumptions?

2. How does Ryan's use of a personal experience at the beginning of the article reveal her relationship to the readers?

✦ *Point of View*

3. Ryan chooses to use a subjective point of view, but her actual visibility is more concentrated in some sections than in others. For each heading, including the introduction, describe Ryan's level of visibility.

4. If Ryan had used an objective point of view, how would it change her relationship with the readers?

✦ *Shape of Ideas*

5. The use of headings is common to magazine articles. What do Ryan's headings indicate about the structure of her article?

6. What does Ryan's structure of ideas indicate about the purpose she hopes to achieve?

✦ *Choosing Voice*

7. Identify the level of formality Ryan uses and list five diction choices (words and phrases) that indicate that level.

8. In several places Ryan uses parenthetical expressions. How do these expressions contribute to the point of view she uses?

✦ *Credibility*

9. At the end of the article Ryan includes a directory of items to use in on-line communication. How do these sources add to Ryan's ethos?

10. Considering their purpose for reading *Cosmopolitan*, what kind of sources are the readers likely to expect? How does Ryan's choice of sources meet those expectations?

Cyberstalking:
Don't Gamble Your Safety Online

Bonnie Bucqueroux

✦ ✦ ✦

Bonnie Bucqueroux, Executive Director of the Michigan Victim Alliance, uses the Michigan Crime Victims Web site (www.mivictims.org) the Alliance maintains both to help victims and to prevent more crime from occurring. Although the Web site was designed for Michigan residents with a grant from the U.S. Department of Justice, the site is linked to others concerned with on-line safety. In the same way that large metropolitan areas experience a higher rate of crime than small and medium-size towns do, as the number of on-line users increases and diversifies, so does the possibility for crime. Bucqueroux's article, accessed June 9, 1999, explains how these crimes occur and how to protect yourself from becoming a victim in cyberspace.

1   Cyberstalking is a term used to cover three distinctly different kinds of problems. The most frequent form is simple harassment, where you find yourself "flamed" (criticized or attacked) by people who take issue with what you said (or how you said it). A typical scenario is that you post something in a newsgroup that sparks others to post nasty messages in response, or they fill your e-mailbox with notes warning you not to sin again. Cyberstalking also refers to a situation where individuals—often women or children—receive unwanted advances or hate-filled threats in chat rooms, through instant messages, or in their e-mail. Most dangerous of all, of course, is when the cyberstalker makes the leap to stalking the person in real life.

2   In all three situations, an ounce of prevention is far preferable to attempting to devise a cure, since nothing short of incarceration can stop a relentless and determined harasser or stalker. As Michael Banks, author of *Web Psychos, Stalkers and Pranksters,* writes: "It's easier to stay out of trouble than to get out of trouble."

3   Fortunately for Michiganders (or Michiganians, if you prefer), ours is one of only seven states that has passed legislation that specifically addresses harassment and stalking in electronic correspondence, and that can make prosecution easier. Unfortunately,

294

Michigan needed new laws because of an internationally infamous case where University of Michigan student Jake Baker published an erotic fantasy online, detailing how he raped and tortured a female classmate—using her real name.

Baker was originally charged with "transmitting threats across 4 states lines," which was revised to making a "threat to injure another person." He was ultimately acquitted because the story was deemed "self-expression" and not as a real "threat."

Preventing the problem not only helps to ensure your safety, but 5 it spares you from experiencing the fear and turmoil that stalking victims endure. And prosecuting these crimes is often complicated by the fact that your stalker could live in another state—or another country.

Prevent Flames: Learn Netiquette

The culture of the World Wide Web continues to evolve, and standards 6 for online behavior are changing. Yet newbies (newcomers) would be well advised to remember the Internet's relatively short history.

The Internet began as the Aarpanet, a network of computers 7 used primarily to share military information. University researchers soon found that this emerging network was a great way to exchange data and ideas. But then, particularly with the advent of commercial services such as America Online, Prodigy, and Compuserve, the Internet and its World Wide Web became a lively new cyber-environment with a broad range of new cyber-citizens.

As this suggests, the Internet's originators tended to be highly 8 educated and courteous—the online equivalent of soft-spoken and thoughtful communicators. USING ALL CAPS was quickly deemed akin to shouting. Personal critiques were beyond the pale. Ignore the conventions and you would soon find yourself flamed, if only to ensure that you took the time to learn the online rules quickly. But what are the rules?

Netiquette refers to the body of rules that were originally devel- 9 oped as a foundation for proper online behavior. While the range of acceptable communication has broadened, as millions of new users have come on board, it still pays to know the rules, so that you do not break them out of ignorance.

As any writer will tell you, communicating through the written 10 word requires care. Humor is especially tricky to express, which led to the invention of emoticons such as or :), which signal others that you meant what you wrote as a joke.

11　　Flaming is also a common response to spamming—the funny name given to the not-so-funny practice where companies buy lists of e-mail addresses to hawk their wares and thereby clog your e-mailbox. The way to avoid this kind of flame is to make sure that you do not succumb to the lure of marketers eager to persuade you that spamming is a great way to sell your goods or services over the Internet. Again, prevention is the key.

12　　There are, however, rare cases where you could find yourself erroneously fingered as a spammer, when you are not. Spammers often go to great lengths to hide their identities, which can mean that the innocent are accused. If it gets bad enough, the only solution may be to log off, and then sign on again with a new online identity.

Basic Precautions: Protect Your Privacy

13　　One of the best ways to protect yourself from all forms of cyber-stalking is to remember that the Internet is a very public global forum. Anything you post to a BBS, newsgroup, message board, guest book, or in a chat room is being broadcast to people whose motives may be sinister. You should even think of your e-mail as more like a postcard than a letter.

14　　• **Screen name and password:** Start with thinking safety when choosing your **screen name** (or one for your child). Don't use your real name or even your nickname—and pick something gender, age, and geography neutral. Log on as SexiSadi, and you will soon wish you hadn't. Change your password often as part of basic security precautions.

15　　• **Personal profiles:** Particularly if you are female or young, you should think twice before posting personal information as part of a user profile. Commercial services offer opportunities for members to list personal data, along with interests and hobbies, so that other members can search for like-minded friends. Yet the benefits may be clearly outweighed by the dangers that cyberstalkers will use that profile to target you.

16　　• **Sig files:** Another potential problem area are **sigs** (signatures) that you set up to appear automatically at the end of your messages. Read that file as if you were a cyberstalker—is there something that you should change? Maybe it would be best to write a specific signature each time?

- **Check your headers:** An e-mail program such as Netscape 17 Communicator 4.0 does not routinely display all of the routing information that tells me where the e-mail I received comes from. (You can, however, click on View-Headers and then click All to see this information.) A service such as American Online, on the other hand, does provide routing information on its e-mails. To find out what your e-mail messages tell others about you, send yourself an e-mail (after making sure that you set your program to view all of the routing information). Some e-mail software includes what's called an "x-header" that tells others your real account name and ISP (Internet Service Provider), even if you have chosen the option of changing the screen name you used in that specific e-mail.

- **Anonymity:** If you are truly concerned, you could consider 18 using an anonymous remailer for your e-mail or an anonymous web browser such as the Anonymizer which shields your identity from others.

- **Cookies:** These are controversial bits of code that website can 19 actually insert into your browser. Usually, these are benign—a cookie is what allows the *New York Times* website to recognize members and usher them into the site without asking for their password. Yet there is the opportunity for unscrupulous individuals to use them to track your visits. Most browsers allow you the option of refusing all cookies, and Anonymizer can help here as well.

- **Watch what you say:** Do not be quick to share personal infor- 20 mation anywhere online, including in e-mail. Think twice before revealing your name, address, telephone, where you live or work, and names of parents, spouse, children, and even friends.

You may be surprised to learn that a post made to a message 21 board made months ago will still show up in a search engine today. So you can face unwelcome advances or threats months later without any idea where they came from.

It also pays to use care in choosing chat options—consider stick- 22 ing with moderated groups. And one way to avoid being harassed by instant messages is simply to turn off that option.

23   • **Use care in all contacts:** You're a single woman in a new job in Detroit, and you meet a kindred soul in an online chat room. Sally has lived here for six months, and after you run into each other in a chat room, she asks you for your phone number. What could be wrong with that?

24   Remember that Sally could instead be Sam, and he may use your telephone number to learn where you live.

25   Even when you are sure that the person asking for your telephone number is trustworthy, ask for theirs instead and give them a call. (And before you dial, check that number through a service such as AnyWho, a free online reverse telephone directory.)

26   Even more risky, of course, is a personal meeting. You should always talk by telephone at least once and preferably many times before agreeing to meet any online friend in person. Also make sure to make your initial few meetings public—and let the person know that you are telling others when and where you will meet. (There is now a commercial service called Smartdate.com that will allow you to file a "preflight plan." It is named for Kristin Smart who went on a date and disappeared, and no one knows with whom she had the date.)

27   • **Encryption:** The Massachusetts Institute of Technology offers free PGP (Pretty Good Privacy) software that allows you to send e-mail without fear that prying eyes can read what you say. You send your encrypted messages and your personal PGP key to the person you authorize to read the e-mail, and they use that key to de-code what you said. It requires extra effort, but it can be better to be safe than sorry.

If You Are Being Stalked

28   **If you have any reason to think that you may be in any physical danger, dial 911 immediately.**

29   Don't worry about looking foolish—better to be embarrassed than dead.

30   If you are instead receiving unwanted online advances or messages that seem threatening or hateful, the best first line of defense is to ignore your stalker. Don't succumb to the desire to tell them off by return e-mail or instant message—often that encourages escalation. If you are lucky, you have merely run into teenagers with a short attention span who think of this as a prank. (Which should serve as

a reminder to us all to make sure that our own youngsters do not see such behavior as a joke.)

If the person is instead a real and persistent cyberstalker, they 31 will not easily get bored and give up. So do not delete even that one upsetting message you receive—it may be the first of a series of communications that you must document to prosecute your online attacker successfully.

Keep in mind that many police agencies do not know how to 32 deal with this new kind of crime. Cyberlawyer Mark D. Grossman says, "Remember, you're likely to be the first cyberstalking case that your particular police person has ever seen. You're likely to be greeted with skepticism and the same blank look that you might get reporting that ET is in your house. So at least come in with some printouts demonstrating the problem."

There are also numerous online sources of support. One of the 33 most complete and most useful is CyberAngels. Curtis Sliwa, founder of the Guardian Angels, and Colin Gabriel Hatcher, an Internet expert from England who has moved to Los Angeles, launched this site as a place where victims of cyberstalking can find practical information, advice, and support.

Other sites worth visiting include: 34

- Online and Real Life Stalking Resources
- Women Halting Online Abuse (WHOA)
- Stalking Victims Sanctuary
- Stalked—Tips and Stories
- Sexual Assault Information Page

1. CYBERSTALKING: Don't Gamble Your Safety Online
2. PREVENT FLAMES: Use Netiquette
3. PRECAUTIONS: Protect Your Privacy
4. If You Are Being Stalked

✦ ✦ ✦

✦ Framing the Context

1. Although the Web site was designed for Michigan residents, what other kinds of on-line users would you expect to visit this site?
2. From her opening definition of cyberstalking and the occasion she identifies, what does Bucqueroux assume her readers need to know?

✦ Point of View

3. Although Bucqueroux has the expertise to write from a subjective point of view, she chooses not to. What point of view does she choose?

4. What kind of relationship does this point of view allow her readers to form with the subject?

✦ Shape of Ideas

5. Web articles are often separated into sections so readers can click onto the section that suits their purposes. What do Bucqueroux's sections and their sequence indicate about the readers' relationship to the subject of cyberstalking?

6. How does the structure indicated by the sections convey Bucqueroux's purpose?

✦ Choosing Voice

7. How does Bucqueroux's writing voice—the level of formality—fit her position as a victims' advocate?

8. Explain how Bucqueroux's use of "you" affects her relationship with the audience?

✦ Credibility

9. What kinds of sources does Bucqueroux choose to construct her credibility?

10. How does Bucqueroux's use of sources in section 4, "If You Are Being Stalked," establish her ethos?

✦ *Suggestions for Writing about Cyberspace*

1. Do you find yourself surfing the Web just for entertainment? Were you ever surprised by the Web sites you found and the links you followed? Write an essay in which you re-create one of those experiences, or go on a new adventure and write about what you discover and the paths of your discovery.

2. Exploring cyberspace can be frustrating for people when they feel intimidated by technology and the range of choices available on various tool and navigation bars. If you have the experience to guide others, write an essay explaining the basic skills needed to explore cyberspace in a way that instills confidence in those who feel inept.

3. Olsson explains that the way she reads material on the Internet differs from the way she reads a novel. Do you experience the same difference? How would you describe your process of reading on the Internet? Do you enjoy drilling down through a link? Are you a skimmer? What features invite you to pay close attention to text? Write an essay in which you define and analyze that reading process.

4. Who can you trust on-line? When is it safe to use a credit card? Give your phone number? Do devious people hide behind nice "nettiquette"? Is the action or procedure you view authentic? Research the amount and types of crime occurring on the Internet, and write a status report for the purpose of persuading your readers to be more cautious in using the Internet.

5. If someone presented you with a log of the Web sites you most frequently visit, what kind of profile would that log create? Take an inventory of your explorations and develop a profile of yourself as a cyberspace explorer.

6. Two kinds of literacy serve the educational goals of the technology-enhanced classroom: computer literacy and information literacy. How would you define information literacy? Do you consider yourself information literate? How do people use their information literacy? If the Internet is constantly changing and expanding, how does a person maintain that literacy? Write an essay that defines information literacy, its development, and uses.

7. How dependent is society on the use of e-mail? What does that level of dependency indicate about society's trust in virtual connections? Conduct research using both primary and secondary sources to

explore the answers to these questions, and present a position paper advocating an increase, a decrease, or a change in the use of e-mail.

8. First amendment rights will continue to be an issue as the Internet continues to grow globally. Do we need new laws to protect those rights on the Internet? Who would make those laws? How could those laws be enforced on a network so vast? Explore the possible answers to those questions, and write a research essay that projects those needs.

Chapter 9

◆ ✦ ✦ ✦ ✦ ✦ ✦ ✦ ✦ ✦ ✦

Making Health Decisions

As we begin a new century, people are living longer than ever before. Celebrating a hundredth birthday rarely gets front-page coverage. Are we actually living healthier lives or are medical and technological advances just keeping us alive longer? The promise of living longer encourages some people to make healthy living a priority while others are willing to rely on science to have the cures available when and if they need them. Making health decisions today is considerably more complex because so much information is available from which to choose. How do you determine when you need information and what sources to use?

The readings in this chapter offer advice and raise concerns about a variety of health issues, but regardless of the issue, a common thread is apparent: making health decisions is an individual responsibility. As you read, keep in mind the context for each reading and how the writer made choices to achieve a specific purpose with a specific audience of readers. Look for those moments when you interact most closely with the text—when you connect with the language, a quote, a statement of fact, a well-drawn conclusion. The questions following each reading will help you to determine those choices and connections. At the end of the chapter you will find Writing Suggestions for exploring your own ideas on making health decisions and for making writing choices to develop those ideas.

Steak in the Heart
Chewing the Fat
with a Cardiac Surgeon
Bill Tonelli

✦ ✦ ✦

*For many of us the philosophy "You are what you eat" translates to
an attempt to include all the right food groups—dairy, vegetables,
fruits, fibers, proteins—into our daily diet. It's not until we experience a noticeable change in weight, energy, or complextion that we
know our choices are out of balance. In the following article from*
Men's Journal, *November 1999, Bill Tonelli, assistant managing
editor for* Rolling Stone *and author of* The Amazing Tonelli
Family in America *(1994), uses his dinner conversation with a
cardiologist to take the reader literally "inside" the you-are-what-
you-eat process of ingesting steak. From the play on words in the title
"Steak in the Heart," the readers know they are in for a humorous,
though painful, experience.*

1   "I'm very happy they have these places," says Dr. Mehmet Oz,
gazing around at the jolly, well-fed burghers crowding into Sparks
Steak House, on the east side of Manhattan. "This and cigarettes,"
he adds, grinning at the thought. "It's like an annuity."

2   Well, what do you expect from a cardiovascular surgeon whose job
it is to replace 75 or so hearts a year, either with real ones or with artificial ones, and to perform a great many coronary bypasses, too; a
heart specialist at Columbia-Presbyterian Medical Center in New York
City who pioneered the use of the left ventricular assist device, a gad-
get that sustains patients with deadbeat hearts until compatible human
donors can be found. When he looks around the room, Oz sees, in his
mind's eye, a bunch of expense account Charlies not seated at, but
lying atop, tables—naked, sedated, chests cracked open like lobsters.

3   We're here to eat as we discuss the effects of red meat on heart
health. He gets off to a thrilling start.

4   "Most people think arteries are blocked by the slow buildup of
plaque—by a lifetime of steak after steak after steak," he says. "But

304

that's not the case at all. Don't be scared by the long-term, incremental buildup of plaque, I tell my patients. Plaque is important, but only as a starting point. Heart attacks are caused by the sudden closure of arteries. This is a much more acute process than people realize, and it has to do with what we've done, or eaten, today."

"You mean the next steak could kill me?" I ask. 5

"After we eat this fatty meal," Oz continues, "our arteries will 6 close down by 20 percent or so. Now, most people think of the coronary artery as a pipe—a piece of plumbing. But it's not rigid. It's made of tissue, and it reacts to any stress placed upon it. Fat is a major stress to the lining of your blood vessels. It irritates them and then causes what we call spasming, which means 'closing up.' The fat also produces an immediate change in your blood chemistry: It makes your blood more viscous. It becomes sludgy, and the platelets get sticky. After you have eaten your steak, I could take a blood sample and show you the globules of fat in it."

"Would they be visible to the naked eye?" 7

"Yes," he says. "Sometimes the blood actually looks like cream, 8 there are big blobs of fat floating in it."

Wow! Let's eat! 9

I suggest we order fast, before I learn any more. He takes a mo- 10 ment or two to settle on the wine, a cabernet, but he's swift in choosing his meal: an appetizer of scallops, followed by Chilean sea bass with spinach.

"Fish and fish!" I say. 11

"I eat it five times a week," he replies. 12

Screw it, I figure, and go right up the middle—lettuce-and- 13 tomato salad and a rare sirloin steak, somewhere between 16 and 18 ounces of murderous cow muscle. Spinach on the side.

"Now that I've ordered," I say, "tell me how I'm about to die. Step 14 by step."

"Okay," says Oz. "You pick up a half-ounce piece of steak on 15 your fork. As you do, you smell the incredible aroma, and you see the beautiful, glistening fat. It's very appetizing. You start to salivate. And in that saliva are enzymes that will begin to break down the meat as soon as it enters your mouth. As you chew, the enzymes start your body's work of separating the elements in the food—the proteins, carbohydrates, and fats.

"And then you swallow, which takes a few seconds, and the meat 16 hits the acid in your stomach, which has been at a high level ever since you saw and smelled the food. The meat will sit in the stomach acid for a few minutes and then pass down into the small intestine. At this point, it's pretty chewed up, like a thick brown sludge.

17   "Next, your small intestine works on the steak like a python, mechanically breaking it down even further. The intestines are lined with little fronds, like fingers, that trap the various elements. The fat gets taken up through special channels into the intestinal wall. There, the blood supply is very rich. The fat globules enter the bloodstream and off they go to your liver for the most part. It's your liver's job to metabolize that fat."

18   The waiter arrives with our appetizers.

19   "How often do you eat steak?" I ask him.

20   "Maybe once every two weeks," he says as he sets the scallops before Oz.

21   "That's all?"

22   "My cholesterol was high," he says.

23   "How high?" asks Oz.

24   "Four hundred," the man says.

25   Anything over 200 for a total cholesterol count is considered borderline problematic by most doctors. At 400, your veins run with sweet butter.

26   "What's it now?"

27   "About 180."

28   "How often did you eat steak before that?" asks Oz, slipping a scallop onto my plate.

29   *"Ohhh!"* he says, his eyes going a little dreamy. "Twice a day. I'm from Argentina. There, steak is the first food a baby gets."

30   So, we were discussing the fat in my liver. "Metabolizing that fat takes time," says Oz. "In fact, four hours or so after you've eaten your steak, the fat content of your blood will be at its highest. Now your blood vessels are lined with epithelial cells—similar to the stuff that makes up skin. We think those cells are damaged by things like high blood pressure, nicotine, and diabetes, all of which are also risk factors for heart disease. Your body sends cholesterol to repair the damaged artery lining. That's cholesterol's job—it's like plaster for your blood vessels. That's why we need it. No cholesterol, no cells."

31   At this point, the scientific explanation becomes too complex for any lay carnivore to safely digest. In essence, as all amateur doctors know by now, there are two kinds of cholesterol, commonly called

the "good" (HDL, or high-density lipoproteins) and the "bad" (LDL, or low-density lipoproteins). Good cholesterol is deployed neatly and efficiently. Bad cholesterol is slopped onto the artery walls in excessive, uneven deposits. LDL does a poor repair job. It creates plaque. The plaque builds up, and before long it begins to block the artery, triggering turbulence in the flow of blood, which then does even more damage to the artery.

"And then one day," says Oz, "you go to McDonald's . . ." 32

"Or Sparks." 33

". . . you go to Sparks and eat a big fatty meal. And you smoke a 34
cigarette or two. And later you get into a fight with your wife . . ."

"Or you get into a fight with your wife at Sparks." 35

"Yes. Don't fight in steakhouses. Anyway, all these factors—a 36
fatty meal, nicotine, emotional stress—cause your arteries to narrow even further. Plus, the saturated fats in the meat inhibit the normal metabolization of prostaglandins—hormonelike fatty acids—leading to inflammation of the artery lining. And the fat in the steak has made your blood thicker and more sluggish. Suddenly, you get a thrombosis—in other words, a blood clot. It would feel just like a scab if you were to touch it. It can't get through that narrow space. Once that scab stops moving, you are done. The artery can't open on its own again. That is a heart attack."

Boom. I'm dead. 37

And that's pretty much the worst of it. Oh, there's also the fact 38
that our bodies take twice as long to digest meat as they do to digest anything else. As a result, a steak can sit in our guts for as long as two days "rotting as it would at the bottom of a garbage can," as Oz puts it so poetically—a fitting comment from the author of *Healing from the Heart: A Leading Heart Surgeon Explores the Power of Complementary Medicine.*

As a rule, therefore, Oz advises patients to avoid beef completely. 39
Which is not to say that eating a steak is the most terrible thing you can do.

"The case against meat is a lot softer than the zealots think," he 40
says. "Fried fish is worse for you than good, lean red meat, for instance. Margarine, which contains transfats—substances that our bodies don't know how to metabolize—is in many ways worse for you than meat. Eggs and organs contain much higher levels of cholesterol, if that's your main concern. I would rather eat a steak than a doughnut, French fries, or anything from [fast-food places like]

McDonald's. You can metabolize everything in meat, but you can't metabolize synthetic food, such as margarine. Or partially hydrogenated vegetable oils used for making French fries, baked goods, and snack foods. Your body doesn't know what to do with that junk, which blocks your ability to metabolize other fats.

41   "Even chicken and fish are misunderstood by most people. We have strong evidence that poultry is no better for you than red meat when it comes to cholesterol. So this fallacy should be exposed. If you eat the same amount of lean T-bone steak or skinless white-meat chicken, you are getting virtually identical amounts of cholesterol."

42   "Which is one of the benefits of beef," he winds up. "You know what's coming at you. So if you're going to eat it, eat it rare or medium-rare so you can taste it. Do it right. Don't be a wimp."

43   At that moment, our entrees arrive. His bass. My beef. The first thing I do is cut off maybe three ounces of steak and slide it onto his plate.

44   He digs in.

45   "This is wonderful," he says, the poor guy.

✦ ✦ ✦

✦ Framing the Context

1. Identify what assumptions Tonelli can make about the reader's purpose for reading *Men's Journal*.

2. Describe the attitude this audience is likely to have toward the subject.

✦ Point of View

3. How does Tonelli's choice of point of view affect the distance between the reader and the subject?

4. Had Tonelli used an objective point of view, how would his relationship to his readers differ?

✦ Shape of Ideas

5. Tonelli uses two complementary structures to present his information: an overall framework to establish his relationship with the cardiologist and an internal structure to present the ideas they discuss. Identify these two shapes and explain how they complement one another.

6. How does the structure connect the readers to Tonelli's purpose?

◆ *Choosing Voice*

7. How does Tonelli's use of dialogue influence the formality level of his writing voice?

8. Identify three diction choices Tonelli makes that help the readers feel comfortable with this technical subject.

◆ *Credibility*

9. Tonelli relies on only one expert. Explain how the use of one source is likely to affect Tonelli's credibility with his intended readers.

10. What techniques does Tonelli use to establish the credibility of the source he uses?

The Brain's Balancing Act

Kari Watson

✦ ✦ ✦

After a grueling midterm exam schedule, you might find yourself saying, "Help, my brain hurts!" Is this an indication that your brain is not in balance? If so, what can you do to balance your brain? In this article, which appeared in the September/October 1998 issue of Natural Health, *Kari Watson, a freelance writer from New York City, explores the concept of brain balance and how working either the left or right side of your brain too hard can wreak havoc with your whole body.*

1   Your brain is like a committee. Committees don't work well if they rely on just one member to do all the work; likewise, your brain can't rely on just its right or left side. Nevertheless, many people fall into the habit of relying on one method of problem solving that is either right- or left-brain oriented. It's as if one member of the committee ran the meetings and refused to listen to anyone else. In your brain, this tendency is called hemisphericity.

2   The left and right hemispheres of your brain, although connected by a bundle of nerve fibers called the *corpus callosum,* have entirely separate functions. The left side of the brain sees individual parts that make up a whole. It organizes, analyzes, and rationalizes information. It is also the verbal side of your brain, responding to speech and using words to name and describe things. The left side keeps track of time and thinks in terms of consequences. The right side of the brain, on the other hand, is holistic, seeing the whole all at once and then breaking it down into parts. It is the visual side, responding to pictures, colors, and shapes. The right brain addresses emotions, is affected by music, touch, and body language, and follows hunches and feelings rather than logic.

3   Over-reliance on one hemisphere can create the same kind of bad situation that a pushy, overworked committee member does: No new ideas are expressed, frustration ensues, and the overworked side of your brain burns out. But the effects don't end with your mind. Hemisphericity can lead to physical problems, such as headaches, fa-

tigue, and insomnia. This is because a healthy body cannot maintain homeostasis, or an internal equilibrium, if the brain is not in balance.

"When your brain is in a state of balance, your well-being increases. Your health and immune system receive immediate benefit," says Robin Carter, a psychotherapist in Gig Harbor, Wash. "You simply feel better." 4

The concept of hemisphericity, especially the toll it takes on the mind and body, has stimulated the curiosity of many members of the natural health community. Still in its infancy, brain balance is rapidly gaining respect in the holistic medical world. As a result, some osteopathic doctors, traditional Chinese medical doctors, and scientific researchers are finding ways to alleviate the strain of hemisphericity. 5

Here are the approaches of two pioneers in the field of brain balance. 6

Healing Hobbies

Holistic physician Ann McCombs, D.O., prescribes hobbies for her patients who suffer from hemisphericity. "You have to get creative when it comes to dealing with brain strain," says McCombs. "That's why I think hobbies are really important. They help bring your brain back into balance by stimulating the underused side." 7

One of McCombs' regular patients, a woman in her early 30s, is an accountant whose left brain is often fatigued from overuse. During tax time the stress and strain manifest themselves in symptoms that include a painful jaw, headaches, colds, and flu. During one of her visits with McCombs, the patient mentioned that she'd once studied to be a singer. Instantly, McCombs thought of a way to help her patient restore balance: through music. With McCombs' encouragement, the young woman began singing again, which stimulated her right brain. She also took up the guitar and the piano, and gradually her stress symptoms decreased. Even at tax time, she is more relaxed and fares much better. 8

Another patient who came to see McCombs for help was a full-time housewife and mother of three. This woman relied heavily on her right brain as she raised and nurtured her children. As a result, she experienced extreme physical and emotional fatigue. McCombs suggested that she enlist her underused left brain by verbalizing her feelings and putting her problems in words; she advised her to read the newspaper. In the end, the patient found her ultimate cure doing analytical work on a computer. 9

10   "Most people see the brain as a whole, not thinking of it as two separate pieces, which is why brain imbalance often goes untreated," says McCombs. "But in holistic medicine, brain balance is often a key to people getting well."

Take This Job

11   Research shows that most of us use one or more parts of the brain rather than the whole when doing our jobs. Once that rut is established at work, it often extends to other parts of our lives.

12   "Occupationally, there are relatively few people who achieve brain balance," says Ned Herrmann, founder of the Herrmann Brain Dominance Instrument (HBDI), a tool for identifying thinking style preferences. "This is because most professions require a particular distribution of brain dominance."

13   Herrmann and his research colleagues have spent the past 20 years examining how the brain functions at work. They've profiled tens of thousands of people, and asked questions like what work activities "most turn you on" to learn which part of their brains workers use the most. And they've suggested ways that their clients could exercise the underused portions of their brains. Sometimes they urge them to find new jobs.

14   "People need to find work in areas that they are good at," says Herrmann. "Many people are in work that they can do, but don't enjoy, and they often feel trapped there for economic reasons."

15   Not surprisingly, Herrmann has found that most jobs use only half the brain. "After researching over 300 occupations, we've found that each profession has its own particular flavor, each one using more of one area," he says. For example, engineers, finance managers, lawyers, scientists, and surgeons rely heavily on the left half of the brain, while human resources managers, kindergarten teachers, artists, social workers, entrepreneurs, and salespeople place the burden on the right.

16   "The idea," Herrmann says, "is to learn how to use your whole brain."

Detecting and Correcting a Brain Drain

In her work with hemisphericity, Ann McCombs, D.O., has found that certain symptoms indicate a brain imbalance. Although some signs (lack of energy, recurring headaches, and flu-like symptoms) could indicate a strain of either the left or the right brain, some symptoms are side-specific.

Signs That the Right Brain Is Overtaxed:
- staring off into space
- feeling overly emotional and sensitive
- feelings of panic
- difficulty paying attention

Signs That the Left Brain Is Overtaxed:
- difficulty communicating
- feelings of worry
- difficulty problem solving
- inability to follow a schedule

These simple activities can give an overworked hemisphere of your brain a needed break.

For Right-Brain Relief:
- Play a game of logic (such as chess).
- Write a critical review of your favorite movie.
- Learn new software.
- Work on a crossword puzzle.
- Develop a personal budget.
- Organize your closet.

For Left-Brain Relief:
- Make a gourmet dish that you create yourself.
- Dance.
- Go for a scenic drive.
- Take a walk outdoors.
- Listen to music.
- Play with your children.

✦ ✦ ✦

✦ *Framing the Context*

1. Watson uses a simile to introduce the subject. How does this choice reveal the assumptions Watson makes about her readers' relationship to the subject?

2. Identify what specific purposes readers are likely to have for reading *Natural Health*?

✦ *Point of View*

3. How does Watson's point of view convey her relationship to the subject?

4. Describe the relationship Watson forms with her readers using that point of view?

✦ *Shape of Ideas*

5. What is Watson's purpose for presenting the information to the readers of *Natural Health*?

6. How does the structure Watson uses connect her readers to her purpose?

✦ *Choosing Voice*

7. Explain how the language features (sentence length and structure; diction; punctuation) in paragraph 3 indicate the formality level Watson chooses for her writing voice.

8. How does Watson's voice complement her point of view?

✦ *Credibility*

9. Watson uses three sources to inform her readers. Explain how these sources contribute to her credibility with the readers of *Natural Health*.

10. Explain how Watson's incorporation of her sources affects how she achieves her purpose.

Filtering the Flood

Jim Thornton

✦ ✦ ✦

*As students you might find yourselves too busy to feel bombarded by
the deluge of medical news that worries writer Jim Thornton in this
article that appeared in the "Better Health" section of* Cooking
Light *(1999). Still, as Thornton, who won a 1998 National Magazine Award for first-person health articles and who is a contributing writer to* Cooking Light *and the* Men's Journal, *points out,
when you do need to rely on medical reports, you need a strategy for
selecting the information you use.*

One recent morning, while scanning the newspaper, I came   1
across one of those "Ask the Doctor" columns that have popped up
like mushrooms nationwide. A reader wondered if it was true that a
crease on the earlobe portended heart disease due to too much dietary fat and cholesterol. Indeed, said the doctor, "Some studies" indicated this might be the case.

I sprinted to the nearest mirror, where I noticed, for the first time   2
in my life, the ever-so-subtle line grazing my bulbous left lobe. The
crease smirked back at me like the pitiless grin of the Grim Reaper.
Thus began several months of medical agonizing, doctor visits, and
expensive diagnostic testing. Eventually, I received a completely
clean bill of health—but not without some "intimations of mortality" misery and equally profound wallet-draining.

Granted, most Americans are probably less vulnerable than I am   3
to hypochondriacal panic attacks. Still, who among us hasn't felt the
occasional stab of worry spawned by some "latest finding" in medical research? Nutritional studies seem particularly prone to augur
ill—after all, so many of the world's most seductive foods seem
linked to heart disease, cancer, stroke, and the like.

It's probably impossible to quantify the toll taken by constant sci-   4
entific doomsaying, though for suggestible types like me, it can be
considerable. "After a while, many people do come to feel that life is
a minefield, that at any moment you could slip, eat a chocolate bar,
and end up in the hospital with a heart attack," comments Arthur

Barsky, M.D., professor of psychiatry at Harvard Medical School and the author of an influential article, "The Paradox of Health," in *The New England Journal of Medicine.* Barsky notes that there has never been a healthier population than the middle-class Americans of today. Ironically, however, their sense of well-being has declined. Case in point: 61% of Americans reported being satisfied with their health during the 1970s; a decade later, the number had dropped to 55%.

5   Why this growing discontent? As more medical conditions have become treatable, Barsky suggests, people have come to believe that good health means they shouldn't have to endure *any* discomforts, even minor ones. Capitalizing on this unrealistic expectation, he says, are fiercely competitive health-care providers bent on convincing prospective patients that "something is dangerously wrong or about to go wrong, and that immediate steps must be taken to remedy the situation."

6   The media also plays a role—largely because health stories have proven so popular. But not all those stories are accurate. When a recent finding from the Framingham Heart Study showed that higher fat intake in men was associated with a lower risk of a certain type of stroke, many media took pains to put the news in context, explaining that it didn't negate strong evidence linking excess dietary fat to other debilitating and fatal diseases. But the sensationalizers chose headlines such as "Fat Is Good for You!"

7   Examples like that may tempt you to ignore medical news altogether, but the head-in-the-sand strategy isn't the answer. "It is important that you educate yourself and take some responsibility for your own health," Barsky says. "On the other hand, there is a point where the quest for information becomes burdensome."

8   How can you know when enough is enough? The key, experts say, is learning to evaluate new findings rationally—and not let your emotions run as amok as the hype. To that end, ask questions like these when assessing medical news.

9   • *Where did the study appear?* Was it published in any of the top-ranked "big four" (*The New England Journal of Medicine, The Journal of the American Medical Association, Nature,* or *Science*)?

10   • *If not, was the journal at least "peer-reviewed,"* i.e., did impartial experts evaluate the study before recommending it be published? Some journals with impressive names are actually little more than shills for advertisers.

- *How big was the population being studied?* A rule of thumb: Studies involving a small number of subjects—a dozen or so—are close to worthless.   11
- *Was it a human or animal study?* Research involving animals is very preliminary; as tempting as it may sometimes be to draw analogies, rats are different from you and me.   12
- *Was the research the first of its kind?* Until a study has been replicated by other scientists, its conclusions are at best only indicators. Indeed, any single study needs to be viewed as just one piece in a complicated puzzle.   13
- *Finally, who was the sponsor?* Though funding bias doesn't always occur, readers should know if, say, the cereal industry underwrote a study on the health benefits of dietary fiber.   14

If the news report doesn't answer those questions, you can go directly to the original study. Ask your local reference librarian either to access the information for you directly via the Internet or to help you find it. Just don't go overboard in your quest. If you're truly concerned, you're better off talking with your physician—especially if you're considering a major life-style change.   15

Approaching medical news with a cool head can help you decide when taking action really does make sense—and spare you from having the daylights needlessly scared out of you in the process. Despite sodium's much maligned reputation, the ingestion of health information clearly remains one area where you owe it to yourself to take things with a grain of salt.   16

✦ Framing the Context

1. How does Thornton's introduction establish his relationship to the subject?
2. What assumptions does Thornton make about his readers' relationship to the subject?

✦ Point of View

3. What point of view does Thornton choose to use?
4. How does Thornton's level of visibility affect the relationship he establishes with his readers?

✦ *Shape of Ideas*

5. How does Thornton's choice of structure reveal his purpose?

6. What effect does Thornton's use of questions throughout the article have on connecting his readers to his purpose?

✦ *Choosing Voice*

7. Identify five diction choices that convey the level of formality Thornton wants to establish in his writing voice.

8. Explain how Thornton's use of dashes affects his voice and complements his point of view.

✦ *Credibility*

9. Make a list of the types of sources Thornton uses. How is the range of those sources likely to affect his credibility with the readers of *Cooking Light*?

10. How does Thornton establish credibility for the one source from whom he quotes?

Designer Babies

Michael D. Lemonick

✦ ✦ ✦

In a country respected for its ingenuity, inventions, and pioneering
spirit, Michael D. Lemonick, a senior writer for Time, *questions just*
how far we will go in using gene theory to design our future popu-
lation. In this article published in the special January 1999 issue on
"The Future of Medicine," Lemonick speculates on the consequences
of the decisions we may face in the near future.

Until just a few years ago, making a baby boy or a baby girl was   1
pretty much a hit-or-miss affair. Not anymore. Parents who have access to the latest genetic testing techniques can now predetermine
their baby's sex with great accuracy—as Monique and Scott Collins
learned to their delight two years ago, when their long-wished-for
daughter Jessica was born after genetic prescreening at a fertility
clinic in Fairfax, Va.

And baby Jessica is just the beginning. Within a decade or two,   2
it may be possible to screen kids almost before conception for an
enormous range of attributes, such as how tall they're likely to be,
what body type they will have, their hair and eye color, what sorts of
illnesses they will be naturally resistant to, and even, conceivably,
their IQ and personality type.

In fact if gene therapy lives up to its promise, parents may some-   3
day be able to go beyond weeding out undesirable traits and start actually inserting the genes they want—perhaps even genes that have
been crafted in a lab. Before the new millennium is many years old,
parents may be going to fertility clinics and picking from a list of options the way car buyers order air conditioning and chrome-alloy
wheels. "It's the ultimate shopping experience: designing your baby,"
says biotechnology critic Jeremy Rifkin, who is appalled by the
prospect. "In a society used to cosmetic surgery and psychopharma-
cology, this is not a big step."

The prospect of designer babies, like many of the ethical co-   4
nundrums posed by the genetic revolution, is confronting the world
so rapidly that doctors, ethicists, religious leaders and politicians are

319

just starting to grapple with the implications—and trying to decide how they feel about it all.

5   They still have a bit of time. Aside from gender, the only traits that can now be identified at the earliest stages of development are about a dozen of the most serious genetic diseases. Gene therapy in embryos is at least a few years away. And the gene or combination of genes responsible for most of our physical and mental attributes hasn't even been identified yet, making moot the idea of engineering genes in or out of a fetus. Besides, say clinicians, even if the techniques for making designer babies are perfected within the next decade, they should be applied in the service of disease prevention, not improving on nature.

WHAT PEOPLE THINK

If you could choose traits for your baby, would you choose to:

	Yes
Rule out a fatal disease	60%
Ensure greater intelligence	33%
Influence height or weight	12%
Determine sex	11%

Should parents with genetically linked diseases be required to test their children for them?

Yes 39%   No 55%

6   But what doctors intend is not necessarily what's going to happen. Indeed, the technology that permitted the Collinses family to pick the sex of their child was first used to select for health, not gender per se. Adapting a technique used on livestock, researchers at the Genetics & IVF Institute in Fairfax took advantage of a simple rule of biology: girls have two X chromosomes, while boys have one X and one Y. The mother has only Xs to offer, so the balance of power lies with the father—specifically with his sperm, which brings either an X or a Y to the fertilization party.

7   As it happens, Y chromosomes have slightly less DNA than Xs. So by staining the sperm's DNA with a nontoxic light-sensitive dye, the Virginia scientists were able to sort sperm by gender—with a high rate of success—before using them in artificial insemination. The first couple to use the technique was looking to escape a deadly disease known as X-linked hydrocephalus, or water on the brain, which almost always affects boys.

8   But while the technique is ideal for weeding out this and other X-linked disorders, including hemophilia, Duchenne muscular dystrophy and Fragile X syndrome, most patients treated at Genetics & IVF want to even out their families—a life-style rather than a medical decision. The Fairfax clinic has been willing to help, but such a trend doesn't sit well with some other practitioners. "Our view at the moment," says Dr. Zev Rosenwaks, director of the Center for Re-

productive Medicine and Infertility at Cornell Medical Center in New York City, "is that these techniques should be used for medical indications, not family balancing."

But now that parents know that the technology is available, and   9 that at least some clinics will let them choose a child's gender for nonmedical reasons, it may be too late to go back. In a relatively short time, suggests Princeton University biologist Lee Silver, whose book *Remaking Eden* addresses precisely these sorts of issues, sex selection may cease to be much of an issue. His model is in vitro fertilization, the technique used to make "test-tube" babies. "When the world first learned about IVF two decades ago," he says, "it was horrifying to most people, and most said that they wouldn't use it even if they were infertile. But growing demand makes it socially acceptable, and now anybody who's infertile demands IVF."

That's not to say in vitro fertilization hasn't created its own set of ethical problems, including custody battles over fertilized embryos that were frozen but never used, questions about what to do with the embryos left over after a successful pregnancy, and the increased health risks posed by multiple births. Yet no one is suggesting the practice be stopped. Infertile couples would never stand for it.

Sex selection will undoubtedly raise knotty issues as well. Societies that value boys more highly than girls, including China and India, are already out of balance; this could tip the scales even further. Such an outcome is unlikely in the U.S., where surveys show that equal numbers of parents want girls as boys. But the same polls report that Americans believe an ideal family has a boy as the oldest child. Boys often end up being more assertive and more dominant than girls, as do firstborn children; skewing the population toward doubly dominant firstborns could make it even harder to rid society of gender-role stereotypes.

> **WHAT PEOPLE THINK**   10
>
> If you had the gene for an incurable life-threatening disease, would you have your unborn child tested for the disease?
> **Yes 70%**   **No 26%**
>
> If the test showed that the baby would have the disease, would you consider ending the pregnancy through abortion*
> **Yes 39%**   **No 48%**   11
>
> *Asked of those who would have the child tested

The ethical issues raised by techniques emerging from the genet-   12 ics labs are likely to be even more complex. What if parents can use preimplantation genetic diagnosis to avoid having kids with attention-deficit disorder, say, or those predestined to be short or dullwitted or predisposed to homosexuality? Will they feel pressure from friends and relations to do so? And will kids who are allowed to be born with these characteristics be made to feel even more like second-class citizens than they do now?

13   Even thornier is the question of what kinds of genetic tinkering parents might be willing to elect to enhance already healthy children. What about using gene therapy to add genes for HIV resistance or longevity or a high IQ? What about enhancements that simply stave off psychological pain—giving a child an attractive face or a pleasing personality? No one is certain when these techniques will be available—and many professionals protest that they're not interested in perfecting them. "Yes, theoretically you could do such things," says Baylor University human-reproduction specialist Larry Lipshultz. "It's doable, but I don't know of anyone doing it."

14   Sooner or later, however, someone will do it. In countries with national health services, such as Canada and Britain, it tends to be easier to dictate what sorts of genetic enhancement will be permitted and what will be forbidden. But in the U.S., despite the growth of managed care, there will always be people with enough money—or a high enough limit on their credit cards—to pay for what they want. "Typically," says Princeton's Silver, "medical researchers are moved by a desire to cure disease more effectively. Reprogenetics [a term Silver coined] is going to be driven by parents, or prospective parents, who want something for their children. It's the sort of demand that could explode."

15   Silver even contemplates a scenario in which society splits into two camps, the "gen-rich" and the "gen-poor," those with and those without a designer genome. The prospect is disturbing, but trying to stop it might entail even more disturbing choices. "There may be problems," admits James Watson, whose co-discovery of the structure of DNA in 1953 made all this possible. "But I don't believe we can let the government start dictating the decisions people make about what sorts of families they'll have."

✦ ✦ ✦

✦ Framing the Context

1. How does the *Time* readers' general purpose for reading affect their relationship to this particular subject in this "Future of Medicine" issue?

2. What occasion does Lemonick use to establish a relationship between the readers and the subject?

✦ *Point of View*

3. How does Lemonick's point of view complement the readers' purpose for reading?

4. What relationship does that point of view establish between Lemonick and his readers?

✦ *Shape of Ideas*

5. What is Lemonick's purpose for presenting this information?

6. How does the structure Lemonick uses reveal his purpose to the readers?

✦ *Choosing Voice*

7. Describe the level of formality Lemonick uses in his writing voice and identify three examples using diction and sentence structure.

8. How does this level of formality complement Lemonick's point of view and purpose?

✦ *Credibility*

9. How do the sources Lemonick uses convey the fairness and goodwill that construct ethos?

10. In what way do the poll charts complement Lemonick's purpose?

Drugs, Sports, Body Image and G.I. Joe

Natalie Angier

✦ ✦ ✦

Pulitzer prize–winning author Natalie Angier, who writes about biology for the New York Times, *has earned wide acclaim for her insight and stylistic expression in such works as* The Beauty of the Beastly, Natural Obsessions, *and most recently* Woman: An Intimate Geography. *In this December 22, 1998,* New York Times *article, accessed on-line (www.nytimes.com), Angier probes the influence of the G.I. Joe toy, which has become an icon in our society over the last thirty-five years.*

1   Which classic American doll has been a staple of childhood from the boomer babies onward, has won iconic, if politically freighted, status in our culture, and possesses a waist so small and hemispheric projections so pronounced that no real adult could approach them without the help of potentially dangerous body enhancement therapies? Barbie? Well, yes.

2   But Barbie has a male companion in the land of the outlandish physique, and his name is not Ken. Instead, we must look to a recent model of that old trooper, G.I. Joe, to see a match for Barbie's cartoon anatomy, and to find a doll that may be as insidious a role model for boys as Ms. Triple-D top, Size-2 bottom is for girls.

3   Some researchers worry that Joe and other action-hero figures may, in minor fashion, help fan the use of muscle-building drugs among young athletes, even as doctors and sports officials struggle to emphasize that such drugs are not only risky, illegal and unsporting, but, in many cases, worthless in enhancing performance.

4   Dr. Harrison G. Pope Jr., a psychiatrist at McLean Hospital in Belmont, Mass., has studied how the morphology of G.I. Joe has evolved since the doll was introduced in 1964.

5   Just as Barbie has become gradually thinner and bustier, Dr. Pope said, so each new vintage of G.I. Joe has been more muscular and sharply defined, or "cut," than the model before.

The most extraordinary G.I. Joe on the market, "G.I. Joe Extreme," wears a red bandanna and an expression of rage.   6

His biceps bulge so much that they are larger around than his   7
waist, and, if ratcheted up to human size, they would be larger than
even the arms of the grotesquely muscular Mr. Olympias of today,
said Dr. Pope.

Hasbro Industries, maker of the G.I. Joe dolls, disagrees with Dr.   8
Pope's contention that the body type of the standard Joe doll has
changed much over the years.

The company adds that it has stopped manufacturing the "Extreme" model, although a recent shopping expedition showed that   9
the doll was still available in toy stores.

G.I. Joe is the only action figure that has been around long   10
enough for Dr. Pope to be able to make comparisons between old
and new models. But he said that a survey of other popular action
figures, including the Power Rangers, Batman and Cyberforce
Stryker showed the same excessive muscularity.

Dr. Pope said the dolls might be planting in boys' minds a template for a he-man's body that cannot be attained without engaging   11
in obsessive behaviors to build muscle and strip off fat, and then
augmenting those efforts through the consumption of drugs like
human growth hormone and anabolic steroids, which are synthetic
versions of the male hormone, testosterone.

His study of the evolution of action dolls will be published early   12
next year in *The International Journal of Eating Disorders.*

"Prior to 1960, and the introduction of anabolic steroids, even   13
the most dedicated bodybuilders couldn't get larger than a certain
maximum size," Dr. Pope said.

"Steroids made it possible for men to look as big as supermen, and   14
now we see that standard reflected in our toys for the very young."

Given the ubiquitous images of muscularity, as well as the   15
mounting demands on young athletes to sprint faster, vault higher,
lift heavier and otherwise impress cadres or easily disgruntled sports
fans, experts say it is not surprising that the use of muscle-enhancing
drugs has reached pandemic proportions, even among barely pubescent boys.

Some 18 percent of high school athletes in the United States are   16
thought to use anabolic steroids, about twice the figure of 10 years
ago, according to some estimates.

17   Although performance-enhancing drugs are generally banned by athletic organizations, it is considered laughably easy to cheat and escape detection in drug screens.

18   In addition, health food stores now offer a variety of "nutritional supplements" reputed to have anabolic properties. The supplements include creatine, DHEA, beta agonists and androstenedione, a precursor of testosterone recently made famous by the baseball slugger Mark McGwire, who admitted with pride that he ate it. Such supplements are not strictly regulated, like drugs, their side effects are uncharted and their effectiveness is unproved.

19   Doctors have long emphasized the dangers of muscle-building drugs. The use of anabolic steroids lowers the levels of protective high-density lipoproteins, suppresses sperm production and raises the risk of heart attacks, strokes and liver disease.

20   The chronic use of human growth hormone in ultra-high doses has its own hazards, among them an increased risk of arthritic-type disorders, diabetes and some cancers.

21   Yet experts acknowledge that it is not enough to harangue athletes about the risks to their health.

22   Surveys have shown that competitive athletes—who are, after all, quite young and still unconvinced of their mortality—say they would gladly trade years of their life for the chance at winning a gold medal or breaking a world record.

23   Arnold Schwarzenegger has pointed out that top-tier athletes are not in it for the sake of "fitness," and that they often go to grueling, distinctly unhealthy extremes in their training regimens; he has said that, when he was a competitive bodybuilder, he often worked out so intensively that he vomited afterward.

24   The great Alberto Salazar twice was given last rites at the end of a marathon after pushing himself so hard in the race that he nearly died at the finish line.

25   What is the difference between overtraining and overcompeting yourself to death, and killing yourself slowly with steroids?

26   "We can be so hypocritical," said George Annas, chairman of the health law department in the Boston University School of Public Health. "We say, it's O.K. to spend 18 hours a day training, and we put our kids through all kinds of inhumane regimens that can border on child abuse, but take one drug and that's the end of it.

27   "We're really crazy about drugs."

28   According to many researchers, the paradoxical element in the seemingly unstoppable epidemic of doping, or using performance

enhancing drugs, is that most of the drugs do not work nearly as well as billed.

Human growth hormone may increase muscle mass, but bigger does not necessarily mean stronger, said Shalender Bhasin, a professor of medicine and chief of the division of endocrinology metabolism and molecular medicine at Charles Drew University in Los Angeles.   29

"Patients with acromegaly, who naturally overproduce growth hormone, often have muscle hypertrophy," he said. "But their muscles are weak."   30

As for the effectiveness of anabolic steroids and other types of testosterone supplements, scientists for years debated whether the drugs truly increased muscle mass and strength, or merely bloated muscle cells with water and encouraged athletes to train harder through a placebo effect.   31

Two years ago, Dr. Bhasin and his colleagues showed in a comprehensive report in *The New England Journal of Medicine* that super-high doses of testosterone given to healthy young men could increase muscle size and muscle strength, as measured by the ability to do exercises like bench-pressing and leg-squatting.   32

But the results were far from spectacular, and high-intensity, drug-free workouts proved nearly as good at building muscle strength as did exercise and testosterone combined. For reasons that remain unclear, said Dr. Bhasin, a pound of muscle gained through exercise is stronger than a pound of muscle gained through the grace of testosterone. He also emphasized that neither his study, nor any other that he knew of, had shown testosteronelike drugs capable of improving muscle performance—that is, the capacity of a muscle to do the sports maneuver an athlete wants it to do.   33

The extra muscle bulk that comes from steroid use may drag an athlete down without compensating for the added weight through better performance. For any event that requires moving against friction or gravity, Dr. Bhasin said, including sprinting, pole-vaulting or swimming, and for endurance activities like marathon running, taking testosterone may be counterproductive.   34

Some athletes know as much, and sneer at their doping friends.   35

Whether performance drugs will ever be eliminated from sports, though, nobody can say. "I'm afraid I'm very cynical," Dr. Pope said.   36 37

"From my research, I've seen that the use of steroids and other drugs has infiltrated deeper into sports than the vast majority of the public realizes. It's like asking, how can we turn back from nuclear weapons? The technology is there.

38   "The genie is out of the bottle."

39   It might help to begin by tinkering at Santa's workshop.

40   Mattel has talked about releasing a more realistic Barbie doll with a thicker waist and smaller bust.

41   How about a G.I. "Love Handles" Joe?

✦ ✦ ✦

✦ *Framing the Context*

1. The *New York Times* is one of only a few newspapers that is nationally archived. What assumptions can Angier make about the readers' expectations for her writing?

2. How does Angier use the date of publication as an occasion for writing on this subject? How does that occasion affect the readers' relationship to the subject?

✦ *Point of View*

3. How does Angier's point of view meet the *New York Times* readers' purpose for reading?

4. Describe how the level of writer visibility in that point of view affects Angier's relationship with her readers.

✦ *Shape of Ideas*

5. What purpose underlies Angier's presentation of information on this subject? What does she believe her readers need to know and why?

6. How does the structure Angier uses to present the information reveal that purpose?

✦ *Choosing Voice*

7. Identify three places in the article where Angier's writing voice stimulates the readers' interaction with the text.

8. Make a list of five diction choices which reveal indirectly Angier's personal attitude toward the subject.

✦ *Credibility*

9. Explain how Angier establishes credibility for her two main sources.

10. In what ways is Angier's reputation as a writer for the *New York Times* likely to affect her credibility with the readers?

Journey of a Latent Vegetarian

Kathy Gay

✦ ✦ ✦

For two years, Kathy Gay, a San Francisco Bay Area resident and business analyst for a leading California bank, wrote a regular column, "To All Living Things," for VegSource On-Line Magazine *(www.vegsource.com). Gay's ten-year history as a member of Amnesty International and her vegan lifestyle served as the background for her column. In the following article, which appeared in the March 1997 column, Gay reflects on the events that led to her becoming a vegetarian.*

Have you ever done something in your life and, looking back on it, wondered why you did it? Or perhaps it was something you didn't do? Let me guess—you're nodding your head in agreement, right? After all, that's part of what it means to be human. We live and learn, and sometimes, some of us, for reasons we can't totally comprehend, we take the long way around.   1

I always find myself thinking about such things whenever I contemplate the long and winding road I took becoming a vegetarian. I should probably qualify that statement. The change was a long time coming, but when it happened, it happened fast. I started to eliminate meat completely from my diet just over a year ago, initially intending to stop there. But as it turned out, it didn't stop there. Before I knew it, I had said adios to eggs and dairy as well. It all seemed very natural, and it continues to feel so right that I can't help wondering what took me so doggone long. Then I call to mind certain incidents in my life, and I realize I should have paid closer attention then to my reactions to those events, for if I had, I would have made the change a long time ago. Here's the kind of thing I'm talking about . . .   2

I'll begin with the story of the time Mom fixed something different for Sunday dinner. Have you ever found yourself looking down at a plate in front of you and wondering just what it is you're looking at? It happened to me. Mom had called us all to dinner —my dad, my sister and me. I had been studying while she was preparing the meal, so I had no idea what was in store. For that matter, neither   3 did anyone else. Even before sitting down, I noticed that *something* was different. Ah-h-h, yes, she had already placed the meat on each of our plates. Our normal way of doing things was to pass the plates or dishes of food around.

4   So, here was this piece of meat already sitting on my plate, and, to tell you the truth, it looked a bit odd. I asked Mom what it was, and she said it was chicken. I said there was no way this could be chicken unless it was a very deformed chicken. It certainly didn't look like any chicken I had ever seen, and I wanted to know what it was before I would eat it. Finally, she admitted that it wasn't chicken after all—it was rabbit!!! A-a-a-ek!! Without even thinking, I said, "Thumper? Thumper? You're feeding us Thumper? There's no way I'm gonna eat Thumper!" (This is what happens when one is raised on Disney. Obviously, there's no way I could ever eat Bambi either.)

5   Needless to say, I didn't touch that meat, and I pretty much ruined this momentous occasion for everyone else. Even Mom couldn't eat it after that. Thumper's relative was fed to our dog Josie, and Mom never tried springing that kind of surprise again. At least, not that I know of.

6   So now I knew I couldn't eat a cute animal that starred in a Disney film. It would have been nice if I had reflected a bit at the time on why I could eat some animals and not others, but I didn't do that. As a result, I had to endure a few more such incidents . . .

7   It's now 1976, and I'm spending the summer in England. For eight weeks I was studying at New College at Oxford University as part of an exchange program the university had with Ohio State, and for another four weeks I was traveling around the country. That time was probably the best three months of my life. I was in a state of awe most of the time, pinching myself and hardly believing I was really there, surrounded by all that history. And all that stunning architecture—they're not called the "dreaming spires" of Oxford for nothing. The garden wall at New College dated back to the Middle Ages and our "dorms" were 500 years old. Meals were served in a huge hall with high ceilings and wood-paneled walls hung with paintings of men I'd never heard of, and several long rows of oak tables ran the full length of the room. It really was grand.

8   It was sometime during the first week of the program that lamb was served for dinner. I had never eaten a cute little lamb before. Not only had I never eaten a cute little lamb, but just two years before, in the spring of 1974, I had fed some lambs born on my grandparent's

farm, fed them special formula out of baby bottles. That spring three lambs were born whose mothers disowned them—two male lambs that Grandma named George and Blackie, and one very fragile little girl she called Annie. One of my very favorite photographs of my grandmother, which I keep in a frame on the table next to my bed, comes from that time. She's feeding George and Blackie their formula through the pasture fence, their little rear ends facing the camera.

Just in case you don't know, I'll tell you now—little lambs are terribly cute. They've got beautiful, sweet faces with gorgeous eyes, and they are fun to watch when they play. Once they learn to trust you, they might even follow you around, and they're sure to come running over when they see you've got a baby bottle in your hand.   9

So, two years later, I'm supposed to eat lamb for dinner? I think not. All I could see were George and Blackie and Annie. I couldn't even stand to watch anyone else eat it. For the rest of the term, whenever lamb was being served for dinner, I rounded up at least one other student and we went OUT.   10

Another similar memorable moment occurred during that summer in England, this time at Stratford-upon-Avon. The Oxford Program was over, and I was now doing some traveling around the country. For the final two weeks, I was joined by my mother and sister and one of Mom's friends. We had spent the day looking around the town, visiting William Shakespeare's birthplace and Anne Hathaway's Cottage, all the things that tourists do. That evening we were going to the theater, and we decided to eat dinner at a restaurant nearby. After looking over the menu, I ordered the trout. I had never had it before and thought I'd "give it a go."   11

Well, when the waiter brought us our dinners, there was the trout lying on the plate set down in front of me. It wasn't moving, of course, but it looked like it could have. Its tail was there, and so was its head. And let's not forget the eyes. Here was a fish that truly looked like a fish, and that didn't sit well with me. No way I wanted to look at that fish-on-a-plate staring up at me.   12

When the waiter came back to our table to see if everything was all right, I politely asked him if he could please take the fish-on-a-plate back to the kitchen, and either he or someone else—anyone else—could someone please cut off the head and the tail of the fish? He looked at me, not totally comprehending the gravity of the situation, and said, "It's really very easy to do . . ." And I said, "It doesn't matter how easy it is to do, I just can't look at it."   13

14   So, the waiter took the fish-on-a-plate back to the kitchen and emerged shortly thereafter with a decapitated and tail-less fish-on-a-plate, and set it back down on the table in front of me. You've probably guessed how the rest of this story goes. By this time, the damage was done. I not only couldn't eat the fish-on-a-plate, I couldn't eat anything else on the plate, not even the peas (yes, there were peas— there were *always* peas). I never had trout again.

15   So, now let's fast-forward to around 1982. I had moved to California by then, and one of the men I worked for was hosting a huge dinner party at his home. So what was for dinner, you ask? Lobster. I had never eaten lobster and by now fully understood it was too late for me to learn to eat some new kind of animal, particularly one that looked like what it really was. And one that was going to be boiled alive at that. So I told him, "Thanks anyway, but I think I'll pass on the party, I just don't care for lobster," and he said, "No-no-no, not a problem, I'll barbecue a steak for you, you're coming to the party." So I went to the party.

16   I'm not going to discuss how much I enjoyed hearing the scraping sounds of those poor lobsters' claws as they struggled with all their might to escape the big tubs on the kitchen floor. And I'm not going to tell you how much fun it was to be surrounded on all sides by people cracking and mangling and picking at the bodies of those same poor lobsters. It's fifteen years down the road, and I'm still amazed at how much I remember about that party, particularly considering the amount of champagne I consumed. I even remember the horrendous headache that followed.

17   There you have it—just a few of the incidents in my life that could have been turning points at the time, if I'd have let them. If I had paid better attention then, I think I would have recognized that maybe, just maybe I had a veggie heart, and maybe, just maybe I'd be a whole lot happier not eating animals of any kind. I guess some of us have thicker skulls than others, and it takes a bit longer for the truth to hit us, and finally and absolutely sink in.

18   So, if by chance you're reading this and thinking, "This sounds so much like me" or "That reminds me of the time that . . . ," please take the advice of one who's been there. Close your ears to the din of the meat-eating world and listen to your heart. Follow where it leads, and do it sooner rather than later. You'll be glad you did.

✦ ✦ ✦

✦ *Framing the Context*

1. How does the title of Gay's article convey to the reader her relationship to the subject?

2. Explain how the first two paragraphs convey the assumptions Gay makes about her readers' relationship to the subject.

✦ *Point of View*

3. How does Gay's use of a subjective point of view affect her relationship with the range of readers who may be accessing the on-line magazine?

4. How is this point of view likely to affect the readers' relationship to the subject?

✦ *Shape of Ideas*

5. Gay identifies a basic shape in her title. Outline the timeline of episodes she presents.

6. Explain how the structure of Gay's article conveys her purpose to the readers.

✦ *Choosing Voice*

7. How does Gay use diction and punctuation to convey the tone of her voice? Identify her tone and select four examples to illustrate how she conveys tone to her readers.

8. Which sections of the article are the most interactive for you as a reader? Choose two of those sections and explain how Gay uses her writing voice to create that dialogue.

✦ *Credibility*

9. Explain how Gay creates a sense of authenticity in the episodes she presents.

10. What do each of the episodes have in common that helps Gay achieve her purpose?

Eating Disorders

Harvard Health Publications

✦ ✦ ✦

Using the Internet as a source for health information can be over-whelming with so many sites available. Some sites contain articles written in complex, scientific language; others identify only a name, but not the credentials, of a person who appears to be a member of the medical field. The Harvard Mental Health Letter (HMHL), *in which the following article (October/November 1997) appeared, is one of four newsletters published by Harvard Health Publications (www.health.harvard.edu), which began publishing newsletters for the general public a quarter of a century ago. Harvard Health Pub-lications, a division of Harvard Medical School, uses the expertise of its faculty physicians at the Harvard Medical School and eighteen affiliated hospitals and health-care institutions to author its reports. The article that follows was accessed on the Internet Mental Health site (www.mentalhealth.com).*

Part I

1   The conflicting feelings about food and eating that trouble so many young women take an especially demoralizing and debilitating form in the eating disorders, anorexia and bulimia. *Anorexia nervosa* (its Greek and Latin roots mean "lack of appetite of nervous origin") usu-ally appears in early or middle adolescence. A girl or young woman begins to starve herself and sometimes exercise compulsively as well. Her weight falls and her health deteriorates, but she persists in deny-ing that her behavior is abnormal or dangerous. She may say she feels or looks fat, although everyone else can see that she is gaunt. To con-ceal her weight loss from parents and others, she may wear baggy clothes or secretly pocket and discard food instead of eating it. De-spite her refusal to eat (and despite the misleading term "anorexia"), her appetite is usually normal, at least at first. Her reasons for reject-ing food are a mystery that researchers are still trying to solve.

2   According to the current diagnostic manual of the American Psychiatric Association (*DSM-IV*), a woman is suffering from clini-

cal anorexia, not just dieting or fasting, when her weight has fallen
to 15% below the normal range and she has not menstruated for at
least three months. Sometimes the diagnosis is made because of
drowsiness and lethargy that are affecting her schoolwork. Other
symptoms are dry skin, brittle nails and hair, lanugo (fine downy hair
on the limbs), constipation, anemia, and swollen joints. The level of
female hormones in the blood of an anorectic woman falls drastically, and her sexual development may be delayed. Her heart rate and
blood pressure can become dangerously low, and loss of potassium
in the blood may cause irregular heart rhythms. Over a 10-year period, about 5% of women diagnosed as anorectic die, mainly from
infections or cardiac failure. Other serious long-term dangers are os-
teoporosis and kidney damage.

Bulimia

Bulimia nervosa ("oxlike hunger of nervous origin") is defined as two   3
or more episodes of binge eating (rapid consumption of a large
amount of food, up to 5,000 calories) every week for at least three
months. The binges are sometimes followed by vomiting or purging
(use of laxatives or diuretics) and may alternate with compulsive exercise and fasting. The symptoms can develop at any age from early
adolescence to 40, but usually become clinically serious in late adolescence.

Bulimia is not as dangerous to health as anorexia, but it has   4
many unpleasant physical effects, including fatigue, weakness, constipation, fluid retention (bloating), swollen salivary glands, erosion
of dental enamel, sore throat from vomiting, and scars on the hand
from inducing vomiting. Overuse of laxatives can cause stomach
upset and other digestive troubles. Other dangers are dehydration,
loss of potassium, and tearing of the esophagus. Women with diabetes, who have a high rate of bulimia, often lose weight after an eating binge by reducing their dose of insulin. According to recent
research, this practice damages eye tissue and raises the risk of dia-
betic retinopathy, which can lead to blindness.

Many anorectic women also indulge in occasional eating binges,   5
and half of them make the transition to bulimia. About 40% of the
most severely bulimic patients have a history of anorexia. It is not
clear whether the combination of anorexia with bingeing and purging is more debilitating, physically or emotionally, than anorexia
alone (which is also called restricting anorexia). According to some

research, anorectic women who binge and purge are less stable emotionally and more likely to commit suicide. But one recent study suggests that, on the contrary, they are more likely to recover.

The Prevalence of Eating Disorders

6   Anorexia is rare compared to most other serious psychiatric disorders. Its prevalence in the United States is 0.1% to 0.6% in the general population and several times higher in adolescent girls. Ninety percent of the sufferers are women (there is some evidence that homosexuality and concerns about sexual identity are common among the few boys and men with anorexia). Bulimia is at least two or three times as common. A survey based on interviews with more than 2,000 people in the early 1990s found a prevalence of 1% in the general population and 4% among women aged 18 to 30. As many as 10% of women may suffer from bulimia at some time in their lives. In a questionnaire answered by 2,000 college women in 1986, nearly 5% reported a current eating disorder and 4% admitted symptoms of bulimia.

7   Some believe that eating disorders are becoming more common, but the evidence from systematic surveys is inconclusive. What is clear is that fewer cases are going undiagnosed. One reason is that the average age of puberty in American women has retreated three or four years during this century, probably because of better nutrition and less infectious disease. That means a girl is more likely to develop anorexia while she is still living with her parents, and the disorder is more likely to be noticed and acknowledged as the serious problem it is. Bulimia was not even recognized as a distinct psychiatric disorder until the 1970s, and it did not appear in the diagnostic manual of the American Psychiatric Association until 1980.

8   As social critics like to point out, drawing a line between eating disorders and the consequences of "normal," socially approved dieting is not easy. Many women have symptoms that resemble anorexia or bulimia in milder forms—they may be losing too much weight but still menstruating, or binge eating without vomiting or using laxatives, or bingeing less often than twice a week. According to one estimate, more than two-thirds of college women indulge in an eating binge once a year, 40% at least once a month, and 20% once a week. As many as 4% of all adults (60% of them women) and 30% of the seriously overweight are thought to be binge eaters. Binge eating without attempts to compensate by vomiting or using laxatives is

one of the conditions included in the current APA diagnostic manual under the label "eating disorders not otherwise specified."

Genetic Influence

Like most psychiatric disorders, anorexia and bulimia run in families. The rate of anorexia among mothers and sisters of anorectic women is 2% to 10%. In one study, researchers found that 20% of anorectic patients but only 6% of people with other psychiatric disorders had a family member with an eating disorder. Several twin studies suggest that this family susceptibility is largely hereditary. In one comparison, anorexia was found in 9 of 16 identical twins of anorectic patients but only 1 of 14 fraternal twins. In another study, researchers found that when one of a pair of identical twins had bulimia, the chance that the other would also have it was 23%—eight times higher than the rate in the general population. For fraternal twins, the rate was 9%, or three times higher than average. The authors calculate a heritability (the genetically determined proportion of individual differences in susceptibility) of 55%. [9]

One cause of eating disorders could be abnormalities in the activity of hormones and neurotransmitters that preserve the balance between energy output and food intake. This regulation is a complex process involving several regions of the brain and several body systems. Nerve pathways descending from the hypothalamus, at the base of the brain, control levels of sex hormones, thyroid hormones, and the adrenal hormone cortisol, all of which influence appetite, body weight, mood, and responses to stress. The neurotransmitters serotonin and norepinephrine are found in these hypothalamic pathways. Serotonin activity is low in starving anorectic patients but higher than average when their weight returns to normal. According to some reports, bulimic patients respond weakly to serotonin and to cholecystokinin, a hormone that induces fullness. Their response improves when they take antidepressant drugs that enhance the effects of serotonin. [10]

Another speculation is that eating disorders are influenced by enkephalins and endorphins, the opiate-like substances produced in the body. Some studies have found that the spinal fluid of anorectic patients contains high levels of these endogenous opioids, and some of the patients gain weight when given naloxone, which inhibits opioid activity. It is interesting that the German word for anorexia is *Pubertätsmagersucht,* pubertal addiction to thinness. [11]

12   An unusual, not widely accepted but interesting theory is that in some cases anorexia results from excessive physical activity. Evidence for this theory comes from experiments in which rats are allowed to exercise on a wheel at will but fed only a single daily meal (adequate for survival) and given only a brief time to eat it. When put on this regime, they start to run more and more and eat less and less. Eventually they may die of starvation. According to the theory, these conditions are equivalent to self-imposed diet and exercise regimens. Normal people eat more when physical activity rises. But if food intake is restricted at the same time, a self-perpetuating cycle may develop in which restricted food intake heightens the urge to move, and constantly increasing exercise depresses interest in eating.

Psychology of Eating Disorders

13   In the vast psychological and sociological literature on eating disorders, a wide variety of influences has been suggested, from peer pressure to sexual anxieties. One common theme is starvation as a form of self-punishment with the unacknowledged purpose of pleasing an introjected (internalized) parent who is seen as needing to impose harsh restrictions. Most anorectic women—before, during, and after the illness—are serious, well behaved, orderly, perfectionist, hypersensitive to rejection, and inclined to irrational guilt and obsessive worry. Anorexia has been described as one way a girl with this kind of personality may respond to the prospect of adult sexuality and independence. She wants to be strong and successful, but is afraid of asserting herself and separating from her family. Being a good girl and pleasing her parents and teachers no longer sustain her. She is unable to acknowledge her sexual desires and may regard her developing woman's body as an alien invasion. Her fear of adult femininity may also be a fear of becoming like her mother. According to this theory, fasting restores a sense of order to her life by allowing her to exert control over herself and others. She is proud of her ability to lose weight, and self-imposed rules about food are a substitute for genuine independence.

14   Some students of anorexia believe that these girls starve themselves to suppress or control feelings of emotional emptiness. They struggle for perfection to prove that they need not depend on others to tell them who they are and what they are worth. According to some psychodynamic theories, a young woman has come to this desperate pass because her parents have never responded adequately to

her initiatives or recognized her individuality. Now that she is an adolescent, they are implicitly making conflicting demands: show your capacity for adult independence, but do not separate yourself from the family.

According to this theory, the anorectic girl has trouble distinguishing her own wants from those of other people, and she fears abandonment if she takes any action on her own. Denying her needs is the only way she knows how to show that she will not permit anyone else to control her. She will not allow outside influences, including food, to invade her. 15

Since women with anorexia are usually living with their parents when the symptoms develop, psychotherapists have often found it helpful to work with the whole family. The resulting discoveries and speculations are an important source of family systems theory, in which the family is conceived as a social unit with internal structures and processes that have a life of their own. Psychiatric disorders are regarded as defenses that compensate for disturbances and preserve family stability in a way analogous to the preservation of individual stability by neurotic symptoms in psychodynamic theory. Family systems theorists speak of family rules, roles, rituals, and myths; they analyze the distribution of power within a family and the workings of subsystems of various combinations of parents and children. According to the theory, families with inflexible self-regulating mechanisms often produce psychopathology in one member, the person with obvious psychiatric symptoms, who is sometimes called the "identified patient." 16

A daughter who refuses to eat may be seen as trying to keep the family together by providing an object of common concern for parents who would otherwise be drifting apart. Or she may be trying to restore the balance of the family by siding with one parent in a conflict with the other. Families with anorectic daughters are often said to be smothering or "enmeshed." The responsibilities of each person and the boundaries between them are indistinct. Everyone in the household is said to be overresponsive to and overprotective of everyone else. Conventional social roles are maintained, but individual needs are not met, feelings are not honestly acknowledged, and conflicts are not openly resolved. When the daughter reaches puberty, her parents are reluctant to make necessary changes in the family rules and roles. In this view, anorexia is a symptom of a rigid family system's need and inability to adapt to a new stage of development. 17

18   Bulimia has been recognized for a much shorter time than anorexia, and there is less research on its origins. One theory is that bulimic women lack all the parental affection and involvement they need and soothe themselves with food as compensation. The overeating subdues feelings of which they are barely conscious, at the price of later shame and self-hatred. One recent study found that bulimic women differed from depressed and anxious women in several ways. They were more likely to be overweight, to have overweight parents, and to have begun menstruating early. They were also more likely to say that their parents had high expectations for them but limited contact with them. The parents themselves were not interviewed.

19   In some families of women with anorexia and bulimia, the problem may be more serious than rigidity, overprotectiveness, or inadequate nurturing. Child sexual abuse, an increasingly common explanation for psychiatric symptoms in women, has naturally been proposed as a cause of eating disorders. The connection has not been confirmed, and some recent studies raise serious doubts about it. Women with anorexia and bulimia do not report more sexual abuse than anxious and depressed women in general.

Related Physical Disorders

20   Like most psychiatric patients, women with eating disorders often have more than one diagnosis. The rate of alcoholism in bulimic women and their parents may be somewhat higher than average, although the evidence is disputed. Bulimia has also been associated with personality disorders, especially borderline personality. In a recent Swedish study, researchers found that one-third of anorectic women had what the researchers interpreted as mild autistic symptoms as well as personality disorders of the avoidant, naturally attracted the attention of feminists. Anorexia nervosa may illuminate the influence of culture on psychopathology better than any other disorder. In this country women are becoming heavier with each generation, while the body presented as ideal for health or beauty becomes slimmer. Possibly as a result, more than half of American women say they are on a diet. In a recent survey of fifth- to eighth-grade girls, 31% said they were dieting, 9% said they sometimes fasted, and 5% had deliberately induced vomiting. In a 1950 survey, 7% of men and 14% of women said they were trying to lose weight. By the early 1990s, 37% of men and 52% of women thought they were overweight; 24% of men and 40% of women said they were dieting.

The more intense the social pressure for slenderness, the more 21
likely it seems that a troubled young woman will develop an eating
disorder rather than (or in addition to) other psychiatric symptoms—
especially if she believes that control over one's appetite is the way
to win admiration and attain social success. A wish to mold one's
body is also consistent with cultural ideals of achievement and self-
sufficiency. Anorexia and bulimia are especially common among
girls committed to the demanding disciplines of ballet, competitive
swimming, and gymnastics. According to one survey, 15% of female
medical students have had an eating disorder at some time. But
the common belief that high social status raises the risk for eating
disorders may no longer be correct, at least for American women.
In a 1996 review of 13 surveys, researchers found that eating disorders were equally common among whites and blacks and in all
social classes.

Wealth and social status may be more important in underdevel- 22
oped countries, where eating disorders are generally thought to be
rare. Certainly self-starvation cannot be a form of self-discipline unless the supply of food is abundant and reliable, as it usually is for
the vast majority in Western industrial societies. For most women at
most places and times, food has not been so easy to come by. But
that does not mean eating disorders are uniquely a product of modern social conditions and the ideal of body shape promoted by contemporary Western culture. Rules about food have carried many
other meanings as well.

Fasting and a Denial of Womanhood

Prolonged fasting, a recognized religious discipline, is usually prac- 23
ticed by men but was also used by certain noblewomen of medieval
Europe to demonstrate their moral strength and spiritual purity. The
most famous of these women was Catherine of Siena, born in 1347.
At age 15, after seeing visions of Christ, she decided to preserve her
virginity and devote her life to helping the poor. She died at 33, presumably from the effects of starvation, and was later beatified by the
Catholic Church. Saint Catherine wrote: "Make a supreme effort to
root out that self-love from your heart and to plant in its place this
holy self-hatred. This is the royal road by which we turn our back on
mediocrity and which leads us without fail to the summit of perfection." The choice of words may seem peculiar to most anorectic
patients, but the sentiment is not alien.

24   Historians have suggested that female saints of the Middle Ages wanted to liberate themselves from subordinate social roles, including marriage and childbearing, to which they considered themselves unsuited. Catherine of Siena is said to have begun fasting soon after a customary aristocratic marriage had been arranged for her. What Saint Catherine had in common with the fasting male ascetics of India or early Christianity was a socially accepted way to satisfy her unusual needs and ambitions. In more completely male-dominated cultures, like parts of the Moslem world today, eating disorders among women are practically unknown. In these societies women have no alternatives to subordination and no opportunities to gain recognition as exceptional. The prestige of female religious fasting eventually declined in Europe, and by the 17th century the attitude of the Church had changed. Women like Catherine of Siena were no longer considered candidates for sainthood. It is probably no coincidence that at this time physicians made the first known clinical observations of anorexia as a disorder of the mind.

25   Presumably neither Saint Catherine nor male religious ascetics were worried about being slim or beautiful. In a recent study of anorectic Chinese women in Hong Kong, researchers found that they too deny concern about their weight and their looks. They say only that they have family problems, lack appetite, or cannot explain their behavior. Whether they seek slenderness or saintliness or simply "don't know" why they act as they do, women who starve themselves may be rejecting unacceptable biological and social demands—a woman's body and a woman's place. If this idea is right, some women with eating disorders are making an inarticulate social protest—a hunger strike (as it has been called) without a conscious political purpose. Fear of gaining weight may be just one cultural expression of the illness rather than its central feature. As if acknowledging this, the American Psychiatric Association now includes in its diagnostic manual, among eating disorders not otherwise specified, a condition with all the symptoms of anorexia nervosa except an obsession with body shape.

26   Cultural comparisons and historical studies confirm evidence from our own society that eating habits and preoccupations with similar effects may have different causes in different circumstances. For example, a woman is temperamentally predisposed to depression or anxiety, or suffers from family troubles or a neurochemical imbalance. The value her culture places on slenderness (or holy self-abnegation) encourages her to diet (or fast). The weight loss causes physical and emotional changes that make it still more difficult to eat normally.

The resulting hunger may lead to eating binges followed by vomiting and purging with laxatives. These episodes cause anxiety and depression that lead to further bingeing and further dieting.

Weight Gain: The First Therapeutic Step

In the treatment of eating disorders, several therapeutic techniques are used in different combinations, with different patients. The services of psychiatrists, physicians, and dietitians may be needed. An anorectic woman must first eat until her weight is normal. She is hospitalized in the most severe cases—when her weight has been more than 20% below normal for several months, serious physical symptoms are developing, or she is in mortal danger. Occasionally tube feeding may be needed at first just to keep the patient alive. Simple forms of operant conditioning (behavior therapy) are used to encourage her to eat. She may be started on a liquid diet or frequent small meals and told every day how much she has eaten and how much she weighs. Nurses may have to sit with her during meals to provide moral support, make sure she eats, and prevent vomiting. The reward for gaining weight is greater freedom of movement and more visitors; if she does not eat, she may be confined to bed until she does. Laxatives are forbidden, and she must clean up if she vomits. Recent research suggests that strict regimes with detailed schedules, graduated privileges, and careful recording of food consumption may be less effective than more limited programs that use only the threat of bedrest for not eating. In the looser arrangements, the patient is more likely to cooperate and hospital staff members have less need to compromise their therapeutic function by acting as a police force. 27

Gaining weight while hospitalized is no guarantee of long-term success; anorectic patients are sometimes said to "eat their way out of the hospital" and then stop. Their emotional condition may improve when their weight is closer to normal, but preventing relapse is difficult, partly because of the tendency to deny the illness. Drugs, even those that tend to cause weight gain, are not especially useful. Anorectic patients are predictably reluctant to take them, and the side effects can be uncomfortable or dangerous to their enfeebled bodies. 28

Behavior and Cognitive Therapies

When the patient's health is no longer (if it ever was) in immediate danger, various behavioral and cognitive techniques can be used to preserve and promote weight gain. One of these is systematic 29

desensitization—muscle relaxation with visual imagery or direct exposure to a graded series of situations that involve food and eating.
Cognitive techniques are used to correct the patient's false beliefs
about food and about herself, including harsh self-criticism, perfec-
tionism, and exaggerated fears of separation from her parents. Questioning is a common device. The therapist and patient explore the
patient's tendency to all-or-nothing thinking, her superstitions
about food and exercise, and her unjustified interpretations of other
people's behavior (for example, the belief that strangers will notice if
she gains a few pounds). The therapist asks the patient to articulate
half-conscious automatic thoughts that may be ruling her life. She
may be told to look at herself from another point of view (for example, she feels fat but says that others of the same height and weight
are too thin), make vague fears explicit ("What would be the worst
thing that could happen if you ate more?"), test hypotheses ("Will
other people think you are gluttonous if you eat dessert?"), and
achieve a more accurate impression of the size of her body and the
amount of food she is consuming.

30   Some therapists move on to an insight-oriented approach at a
later stage, when the patient must learn to do without the comforting discipline that has given life a meaning and goal. Interpersonal
therapists examine the patient's present situation and her recent and
future relations with others. Psychodynamic therapists also try to explore and resolve emotional problems that may have created the
need for self-starvation. Some speak of providing an experience that
serves as a symbolic equivalent of the relationship between a mother
and a child. If child sexual abuse is part of the story, treatment for
post-traumatic stress may be needed.

31   Most families of anorectic patients can use some help, if only education and counseling. Parents may also be asked to record family
conversations and listen to them. They may be told to answer the
anorectic daughter's requests and provocations in new ways, spend
time with her in unfamiliar settings, or communicate with her in
writing to make it clear what everyone in the family wants. Parents
are usually instructed not to beg, plead, or scold, and told to avoid
discussing food while eating with their daughter. She should not be
told that she looks better if she gains weight, since she may already
be convinced that people care only about her appearance. Food and
eating should be discussed only in connection with health. Therapists influenced by family systems theory also try to change what

they see as the family's overprotectiveness, inability to admit conflicts, and uncertainty about the roles of parents and children.

Bulimia and Obesity

Bulimia is often treated more successfully than anorexia, partly because bulimic patients usually want to be treated. Most antidepressant drugs relieve the symptoms, usually more quickly than they relieve depression. Selective serotonin reuptake inhibitors (SSRIs) are probably most useful, because they have relatively few side effects and tend to cause weight loss rather than weight gain. In 1997 *fluoxetine (Prozac)* became the first drug specifically approved by the Food and Drug Administration (FDA) as a treatment for bulimia.

The problem with bulimia is closely related to the problem of obesity, since almost all bulimic women either are or think they are overweight. According to a widely accepted theory, each person's body weight has a biological setpoint that is strongly influenced by heredity and difficult to change. Studies in several countries have found that mothers and their biological daughters have a similar weight-height ratio, while the correlation between adoptive parents and adoptive children is low. According to the setpoint theory, metabolism during a diet slows to counteract the effect of reduced intake until it settles at a lower level consistent with the new weight. A person who continues the same diet will eventually regain weight until the setpoint is reached.

The setpoint may be determined by a brain center in the hypothalamus that regulates the amount of fatty tissue stored by the body. A substance called leptin is produced by fat cells and circulates in the blood until it reaches the brain. When this hypothalamic region detects sufficient leptin, it tells the body to stop storing fat. An animal in which the region has been cut out cannot "know" it is already fat enough and will continue to gain weight even on a restricted diet. Neurons in this region use serotonin, and enhancement of serotonin activity is the main effect of the only diet drug approved by the FDA, dexienfluramine (Redux). Some bulimic patients seem to be otherwise emotionally stable women whose concern about weight is more or less realistic given their social circumstances and cultural expectations. If a woman is bingeing and purging merely to circumvent her fat storage mechanism in order to pursue a body shape incompatible with her biological setpoint, a weight-reducing drug might be useful, but only as long as she continues to take it—probably for a lifetime, with all the attendant risks, which include possible heart valve damage and pulmonary hypertension (dangerously high blood pressure in the arteries carrying blood to the lungs) in the case of fenfluramine. Exercise may be a better way, since, apart from the expenditure of energy involved, it seems to reduce fat storage by altering the leptin mechanism.

Behavioral and Group Therapies

35   More often bulimic patients are given behavior therapy. One behavioral treatment for self-induced vomiting is exposure and response prevention. The patient is allowed to eat until she is nauseated and then asked to concentrate on her discomfort and write down her thoughts and feelings. Bathrooms are locked so that she will be ashamed to vomit and has to tolerate her anxiety. The effectiveness of this method is disputed. Bulimic patients are also asked to examine self-defeating beliefs, such as the fear that any momentary lapse must precipitate a binge, the conviction that a slight weight gain is obvious to every one, or the illusion that their worth depends on their looks. Insight-oriented or exploratory psychotherapy may be especially useful for the many bulimic women who have other emotional problems or psychiatric disorders. If they are living with their families, family therapy may also help.

36   Group therapy is popular with both bulimic and anorectic patients. Groups are an efficient setting in which to present information and advice on eating habits. They are also used to apply a variety of therapeutic techniques, with cognitive and behavioral methods dominant. Apart from any specific therapeutic procedures, groups provide a sense of belonging and a source of friendship. The members learn from one another, teach, comfort, and are comforted. They watch one another for signs of relapse. They feel less ashamed when they realize that they are not alone, and they can correct distorted notions about themselves by watching and imitating others. Self-help groups are available as well as professional group therapy; Overeaters Anonymous, an organization modeled on Alcoholics Anonymous, provides support and advice for these groups.

Prospects for Recovery

37   Treatment of anorexia can be frustrating, and recovery is usually prolonged and difficult. Even women whose most serious symptoms are relieved often relapse or suffer from various residual effects and

chronic troubles. In long-term studies covering periods from 4 to 30 years, 50% to 70% are found to be no longer clinically anorectic: they are menstruating and maintaining a weight in the normal range. About 25% show some menstrual irregularities, and their weight is sometimes low. The outcome is poor for another 25%; they are not menstruating and their weight is far below normal. Whether they recover or not, many of these women are still preoccupied with weight and dieting. Bulimia is the most frequent diagnosis, and depression and anxiety disorders are also common. Women with personality disorders and those who have symptoms for a long time before seeking treatment are least likely to recover.

Full recovery from bulimia is more common. In a 1997 meta-analysis (combined statistical analysis) of studies on the outcome of treatment, researchers found an average recovery rate of 50% after periods of 6 months to 5 years. Relapse was common (about 30% in 6 years), but so was a second recovery. In a recent meta-analysis examining the effectiveness of various treatments, researchers found no differences between group and individual therapy. The best treatments concentrated on emotional problems and family relations, without reference to therapeutic theory or persuasion. In one recent study with a 6-year follow-up, both cognitive-behavioral and interpersonal therapies were effective even when eating habits and weight were not made the center of interest. Simple behavior therapy was less successful, with a high dropout rate. In another study, bulimic patients improved more with a combination of cognitive-behavioral therapy and a drug than with either treatment alone. Patients are least likely to recover if they have other disorders, especially alcoholism and borderline personality. In one recent study, the lowest recovery rate was found among women who were seriously overweight or whose fathers (not mothers) were overweight. In the long run, symptoms of bulimia often fade even without treatment, and the disorder is uncommon (although not unknown) in women over 40.

Evidence on the effectiveness of treatment is limited. Many women with anorexia or bulimia are never treated, and in long-term studies many drop out—possibly those who are doing worst. Researchers are calling for further cross-cultural research and more studies in which women are interviewed for the first time before developing symptoms. More information about self-help groups is needed. Researchers must examine more closely the relationship between eating problems and other psychiatric disorders, including addictions and compulsive behavior, partly so that treatments can be modified for different combinations of symptoms. An especially important goal of research is finding ways to prevent eating disorders or recognize and treat them at an early stage.

40   The following groups offer advice and help for people with eating disorders and their families:

> *The American Anorexia/Bulimia Association*
> *293 Central Park West, Suite 1R*
> *New York, NY 10024*
> *tel. 212–501–8351*
> *Internet: http://members.aol.com/amanbu/index.html*

> *Overeaters Anonymous*
> *World Service Office*
> *6075 Zenith Court, NE*
> *Rio Rancho, NM 87124*
> *tel. 505–891–2664*
> *Internet: http://www.overeatersanonymous.org*

For Further Reading

American Psychiatric Association Practice Guideline for Eating Disorders. Washington, DC: American Psychiatric Press, 1993.

Jules R. Bemporad. *Self-starvation through the ages: Reflections on the pre-history of anorexia nervosa.* International Journal of Eating Disorders 19:3: 217–237 (1996).

Kelly Brownell and Christopher G. Fairburn, eds. *Eating Disorders and Obesity: A Comprehensive Handbook.* Guilford Press, 1995.

Joel Yager, ed. *Eating Disorders.* Psychiatric Clinics of North America. Vol. 19, No. 4, 1996.

Kathryn J. Zerbe. *The Body Betrayed: Women, Eating Disorders, and Treatment.* Washington, DC: American Psychiatric Press, 1993.

✦ ✦ ✦

✦ *Framing the Context*

1. Harvard Health Publications prepares materials for use by the general public. Describe the range of purposes readers might have for consulting this material.

2. How do the readers' purposes for consulting the *Harvard Mental Health Letter (HMHL)* guide the editorial board (the writer) in making assumptions about the readers' relationship to the subject?

✦ *Point of View*

3. How is the point of view used appropriate to the readers' relationship to the subject?

4. What relationship does the point of view establish between the reader and the *HMHL* editorial board?

✦ *Shape of Ideas*

5. How does dividing the article into parts and headings complement the readers' purposes for reading?

6. How does the structure convey the writer's (editorial board) purpose?

✦ *Choosing Voice*

7. How does the level of formality in the writing voice complement the needs of the readers?

8. Review the use of parenthetical statements in the article. How do these statements affect the writing voice in relating to the readers?

✦ *Credibility*

9. Harvard Health Publications is a division of the Harvard Medical School. How does the reputation of the institution contribute to the credibility of the article?

10. Explain how the supplementary sources included with the article help to establish the ethos of the publication.

Dialing Up Angels

Jill Kramer

✦ ✦ ✦

What is the connection between body and mind in maintaining health? Jill Kramer, the editorial director of Hay House, a self-help and transformational publishing company in Carlsbad, California, explores the answer to that question by reflecting on a personal health-related experience. Kramer's article appeared in the "My Story" column of the September/October 1998 issue of Natural Health.

1   About four years ago I let anger consume me. It was a seething, festering anger directed toward a woman who had done me wrong. The situation was complex, laced with gossip, lying, and betrayal. Looking back, I realize the events weren't that deserving of rage, but resentful thoughts swirled through my head all day long. I couldn't stand how I felt, but neither could I shake the negativity.

2   One morning about two weeks after my anger first surfaced, I was in my car leaving for work, silently cursing the woman I was angry with. I pulled out of my parking space and smashed my side-view mirror on a pole. It cost me $280 to replace.

3   During the same week, I developed a hard, round lump on left eyelid. It was whitish-red and about the size of a pea—a real eyesore. Having a healthy amount of vanity, I was appalled by it, but I'm sure that even if I saw this lump on someone else's eyelid, I would have thought it disturbing.

4   Although the lump didn't affect my vision, I started wearing glasses all the time instead of contact lenses. I stopped wearing eye makeup because I thought that would attract attention. When people talked to me and looked me in the eye (as people do when they talk to you), I was certain they were really staring at my lump. Sleep offered little escape; I started having dreams in which children would point and laugh at my eye. I couldn't stop these feelings because my growth had become an obsession of sorts. Even my female friends who sympathized with my anguish failed to comfort me.

I pored over medical books and diagnosed my bump as a cha- 5
lazion, a painless swelling on the edge of the eyelid caused by a
blocked lubrication gland. I read that small chalazions often disappear on their own within several weeks; larger ones do not. Then I
turned to alternative healing books, a couple of which pointed to a
possible cause for my growth: unresolved, unreleased anger. I decided to ignore the possibility that my emotions had triggered my
condition, even though I work for a publisher whose many books on
mind-body healing offer impressive evidence that the mind has a
role in causing sickness and healing it. Instead, I chose the easy solution and made an appointment with my eye doctor.

A busy, impatient man, he confirmed my layman's diagnosis and 6
brusquely told me he could easily remove the lump by injecting
anesthetic, flipping my eyelid back, and puncturing the chalazion.
Being someone known to faint during a blood test, I almost blacked
out as he described the procedure. I said, "That's unacceptable." He
then said I could apply warm compresses, which would offer a 40
percent chance of making it go away.

Perhaps if my doctor had said 60 percent instead of 40 percent, 7
my body and mind would have cooperated with the treatment. But
40 percent told me this was a losing battle. Nevertheless, I applied
the compresses morning and night for weeks. But not only did the
chalazion not diminish in size, it actually looked like it was getting
bigger. I found myself staring at people's eyes, envying their un-
blemished lids. I thought about getting one of those big black eye
patches. I finally stopped applying the compresses, but I never
stopped hoping it would go away by itself.

Ten months later, the chalazion was still firmly in place. A co- 8
worker suggested I contact Renée Swisko, a spiritual healer from
Marina Del Rey, Calif. Swisko has helped people with what she calls
her clairvoyant, direct link with "spirit," a powerful life-giving force.
Using a hands-off technique and calling on spiritual forces such as
angels, she works to clear blocks from the body's energy field and to
release harmful memories, including those from prenatal and past-
life experiences. Once these are removed, Swisko says, emotional and
physical well-being are possible. I was fascinated by her work but
also suspicious of it—especially since she worked over the phone for
long-distance clients. Nonetheless, I made an appointment; she told
me our session would last about two hours.

9   With my cordless phone in hand on a Wednesday evening, I followed Swisko's directions to lie down on my sofa and make myself comfortable. She asked for the name, ages, and personality traits of anyone toward whom I felt a lingering anger—whether a grade-school classmate or old boyfriend. I could instantly pinpoint about five people, most notably the woman who had inspired my recent fury. Then Swisko had me rate the degree of anger felt toward each person—zero being a feeling of peace and 10 being the strongest negative feelings. I gave the woman in question an eight. In each case Swisko asked for details of the incidents that had inspired my acrimony.

10   When I finished my recounting, which took about 30 minutes, Swisko invoked spiritual forces—including Emmanuel (considered an ascended teacher) and my own spirit guides and angels—asking them to lift me to a state of pure, positive energy. At this point, when I was feeling very mellow, she had me focus my attention on areas of stress in my life—anything from a relationship challenge to money problems—and on the people on my "anger list." Using her notes, she led me to examine each issue and person, one at a time. For each, she asked my guides and angels to help me "be willing to release into the light all negative energy attachments"; this was followed by a few minutes of silence while the work was being done. At certain points, Swisko asked if I felt energy moving through me. To be honest, I didn't feel much on a physical level—only an occasional tremble—but I did notice a growing sense of lightness and peace.

11   After about an hour and a half, she had me compare my initial ratings toward each person on my list to how I now felt. I had to admit I felt completely neutral toward all of them, including the woman I had been so angry at. After some beautifully uplifting closing statements—thanking my angels and so on—Swisko ended the session. Telling me she had seen a lot of anger and resentment being pulled out of me, she wished me well and said goodbye.

12   I immediately, called my friend Christy and told her what had happened. We were both skeptical, wondering if the session had simply been an exercise in relaxation. I went to bed shortly afterward.

13   The next morning I awoke unusually early, walked into the bathroom, and took a look at myself in the mirror. I gaped in disbelief. The chalazion was less than half its original size. I screamed with delight. When I got to work, my co-workers were astonished that it had shrunk. The following day, the lump was completely gone.

Quite a number of my friends downplayed the whole incident, insisting it had been only a coincidence. I resisted my own temptation to agree with them, partly because I thought my skepticism would tell my body that the healing hadn't really happened, which would encourage the lump to reappear. I also didn't really believe it had been a coincidence; in fact, it seemed clear to me that if my doctor had excised the lump it could have returned because we would've neglected the root cause.   14

That was three years ago. The chalazion has not returned, nor have any angry thoughts about the woman I was mad at. What has arrived is a firmer belief that my thoughts and feelings—and the words of others (such as my eye doctor's unhopeful "40 percent chance")—do affect my mind and body. Deep inside, I have always believed in our power to heal ourselves. But it sure didn't hurt to get some visible corroboration of that power.   15

✦ ✦ ✦

✦ Framing the Context

1. Kramer's article appeared in the "My Story" column of *Natural Health*. What would the readers' purposes be for reading that column?

2. What assumptions does Kramer make about her readers' relationship to the subject?

✦ Point of View

3. The "My Story" column allows Kramer to write from a subjective point of view. What relationship does this point view establish between Kramer and her readers?

4. How does this point of view affect the readers' relationship to the subject?

✦ Shape of Ideas

5. What structure does Kramer use to present her personal experience?

6. How does that structure convey Kramer's purpose?

✦ Choosing Voice

7. How does the level of formality Kramer uses in her writing voice complement her point of view?

8. How does that level of formality affect Kramer's relationship to her readers?

✦ *Credibility*

9. Identify two examples that illustrate how Kramer's use of detail establishes credibility.

10. Kramer informally incorporates sources to document her experience and give it more dimension. What are those sources and how are they likely to affect the readers' view of Kramer's credibility?

Hospitals Were Made
for Recovery

Stacey Mihm

✦ ✦ ✦

*As a first-semester composition student, Stacey Mihm was assigned
to write a short, documented position statement as a means of identifying a subject for a full research project. In the essay that follows,
Mihm draws on her experiences in hospitals to launch her ideas for
further research.*

I've seen it all. An elderly man, confused, sure gall bladder surgery   1
required more time in the hospital than he had had. But the doctor
had signed the discharge papers. And once that's done, you're no
longer the hospital's responsibility. A woman, going home the day
after she'd had a cesarian section. Reason? Insurance only covered a
certain amount of hours in the hospital, even for new mothers. Now,
with only a handful of staples holding her stomach together, she must
leave the day after major surgery when every movement is painful.
Even my own grandmother was recently transferred from a therapy
floor where she'd been making significant progress after a stroke, to
a nonaffiliated part of the hospital where we had to fight to get therapy for her once again. To blame? Insurance only covered twenty-one
days in the rehab unit. These are only a few of the examples I've witnessed both as a teen volunteer at a local hospital and in personal experiences with family members. For whatever reason, hospitals across
the country are sending home patients to an environment that does
not promote recovery the way a hospital was designed to do.

Some would say hospitals are too expensive to stay in nowadays.   2
True, patients and their insurers get footed a large bill at the end of the
hospital stay. And some hospitals are dealing with understaffed positions and budget-cuts. Creativity is important in these situations. St.
Martha's Regional Hospital in Nova Scotia has dealt with a $6 million
budget reduction by resorting to using a nearby motel to house same-
day surgery patients. A good idea considering motel rates are much
cheaper than hospital rates—thirty-eight dollars a night is 75 percent
less than an equal amount of time charged by a hospital (Wickens 14).

355

3   In 1988, four million people chose to be cared for at home. This is another method people are using to combat hospital costs. *U.S. News & World Report* published that "rising medical costs are compelling doctors, hospitals and insurers to get patients out of expensive hospital beds quickly, or keep them out to begin with" (Findlay 68). But when people choose home care, they are essentially taking their health in their own hands. Being a new field, many home care places are not governed by the state and can avoid necessary red tape brought on by licensing. A person has to be picky and conduct investigation into various home care agencies, and that is not such an easy task when illness hits suddenly. And let it be noted that home care is the latest trend. Look closely at the word "trend" (68). Will home care be around in a few years?

4   Ask yourself, "Can a value be placed on my health?" There should be no consideration of money when one's health or, especially, the health of a loved one is on the line. The hospital was designed to recuperate people. Everything is accessible to the patient. If medication is needed, one doesn't have to run to the corner drugstore. You ask the nurse and you'll have the prescription you need in minutes. And, God forbid, if a patient goes into cardiac arrest, each room is equipped with oxygen and crash carts are stored on every unit. You don't find these contrivances at home.

5   To further justify hospital stays, the esteemed *Journal of the American Medical Association* recently reprinted an article on the subject that was originally published in an 1896 edition of the journal. The article concerned the advantages to be gained from having surgery performed and convalescence undertaken in a hospital setting versus home care where the doctor made house calls. Not only did technological improvements aid hospitals' reputations and draw physicians to work there, but, naturally, surgeries performed in the hospital had both much greater success and more favorable outcomes than did surgeries done at home (Martensen 325). And most importantly, the journal suggests:

> *the perfect quiet and routine of the hospital regime are more desirable than being surrounded by home and friends . . . in being removed from the everyday, familiar scenes, where every object is apt to remind the invalid of some duty undone or some mountain ahead. (Pace 324)*

In the hospital, you're temporarily disconnected from outside pressures.

The existence today of millions of hospitals proves that what was   6
written about in 1896 as a new venture for the populace of the Americas was not just a short-lived "trend" as home care may well be.
Hospitals are a force to be reckoned with. They've been around more
than one hundred years, and they are the place where healing happens, a place where worries are put on hold. Patients should not have
to concern themselves with trivial aspects of having their visit cut
short at the hospital or finding alternatives for recuperation. They
should be able to concentrate on what they need to do: heal. And
they should be able to do this in the most beneficial environment:
the hospital.

Works Cited

Findlay, Steven. "There's No Place Like Home." *U.S. News & World Report* 25
    January 1988: 68–70.
Martensen, Robert L. "Hospital Hotels and the Care of the 'Worthy Rich.' "
    Journal of the American Medical Association 275.4(1996): 325.
Pace, Brian P. "The Hospital Hotel." *Journal of the American Medical Association*
    275.4(1996): 324.
Wickens, Barbara. "Welcome to the Motel Convalescence." *Maclean's* 18
    March 1996: 14.

✦ Framing the Context

1. Mihm writes her position statement to a general, educated audience. What does she assume about their relationship to the subject?

2. What is Mihm's relationship to the subject?

✦ Point of View

3. How does Mihm use point of view to establish a relationship with
   her readers?

4. How does that level of visibility affect the readers' relationship to the
   subject?

✦ Shape of Ideas

5. Outline the function of each paragraph in this position statement.
   Identify the shape of the structure it forms.

6. In what way does this structure develop Mihm's claim?

✦ *Choosing Voice*

7. Identify two diction choices and two sentence structure choices to illustrate the level of formality Mihm uses in her writing voice.

8. How does Mihm's level of formality affect the readers' relationship to the subject?

✦ *Credibility*

9. What techniques presented in Chapter 5 does Mihm use for incorporating her sources?

10. How does the range of sources Mihm uses contribute to her credibility?

✦ *Suggestions for Writing about Health Decisions*

1. As we age, our health issues become more pronounced, but being aware of potential health risks when we are younger could prevent later problems from occurring. What are the major health risks for people aged eighteen to twenty-two? After conducting research on this subject, present a documented paper on making decisions earlier in life to ensure better health as you age.

2. What role does gender play in making health decisions? Does your gender place you at risk for particular health problems? Research the relationship between gender and health and present your findings to an audience of your same gender and age.

3. How balanced is your brain? Analyze how the activities in your present lifestyle rely on the hemispheres of your brain and the effects that result. Then present that analysis with action steps you can take to balance your brain activity.

4. Some professions make greater demands on a person's physical and mental health than others. Choose a profession of interest to you and research the effects of that profession on a person's health. Present your findings in an informative, documented essay directed to readers who are considering entering that profession.

5. In the early years of life our eating habits are usually established by our families, but as we become more independent, those habits sometimes begin to change. Trace the cause and effects of the evolution of your eating habits and present your findings in a personal essay.

6. Advances in genetics have already raised ethical issues regarding the legal protection of our privacy and the designing of future populations. What is your position on how these advances should be applied? Who should control the applications? What new laws will be needed? What will the impact be on society? Choose a genetics issue that interests you, and after researching it, present an argument to support your projections.

7. Natural health practices—from yoga to macrobiotics to aromatherapy—have increased in popularity over the past decade in this country. What is the philosophy underlying the practice of "natural health," what is its origin, who are its proponents, and what proven advantages can these practices have on a person's health? Research this growing field and present a well-documented paper on adopting the principles and practices of natural health.

8. With so much health information available, it's difficult to determine which sources to use. Do you consult a doctor first, or do you scan books and Web sites for basic information before you speak to the doctor? Is it safe to follow the lastest diet or vitamin supplement trend advertised in every form of media? Just who do you believe and why? Take an inventory of conscious health decisions you have made over the past year—eating more fruit, taking vitamin E, joining a gym, stopping smoking, scheduling an annual blood test, having safe sex, flossing regularly. Next to each decision, identify the source and facts that convinced you to make the decision—doctor, book, roommate, parents, advertisement, report. Select the decision you made based on the *least* credibility, research sources available in that health topic, and present you findings in a report to guide yourself and others in making informed decisions.

C *h a p t e r 1 0*

✦ ✦ ✦ ✦ ✦ ✦ ✦ ✦ ✦ ✦

Re-Viewing Media

Over the past century society has witnessed the evolution of media from the Industrial Age at the turn of the century to the Information Age we are currently experiencing. When Intel cofounder Gordon Moore predicted that microchips would double in power and halve in price every eighteen months, he was right, but his prediction did not include the extraordinary effects that rate of change would have on us. The readings in this chapter re-view the changes in media that affect our daily lives. How have we responded to those changes? What does our skepticism or acceptance reflect about our culture? How do we evaluate new forms of media? These are the issues the writers of these articles address, some more positively than others.

No doubt you will find that your experiences with the different media covered in these articles will produce different levels of tension in reading *with* and *against* the writers, but that tension will help you to discover what assumptions the writers make about their readers and what purpose they have for re-viewing changes that are taking place. The questions following the readings will guide you in identifying the choices the writers make to connect the intended readers to the subject and purpose, and the Writing Suggestions at the end of the chapter give you the opportunity to make your own writing choices in reflecting on what effect those changes have had on you and others.

The Argument against TV

Corbett Trubey

✦ ✦ ✦

*On the occasion of "TV Turnoff Week," Corbett Trubey, an English
major at the time, wrote the article that follows for* Lotus, *an on-
line magazine (www.lotusmag.com) for those interested in the rave
scene and underground music. Few people extol the virtues of television these days, but Trubey knows that everyone watches it. What
concerns him is the accumulation of hours spent being passive. After
calculating the average number of hours a person his readers' age has
watched television he asks, what would you do with nine years?*

1   From April 22–28, various anti-media groups will be sponsoring
"TV Turnoff Week," a challenge to the 98 percent of Americans who
own at least one television to switch it off and find something better
to do. For those of us who prefer our entertainment live, interactive
and complete with Djs, vinyl and 30-foot speaker stacks, this might
seem like a breeze. In all reality though, the omnipresent box sitting
somewhere in our homes, workplaces, and just about everywhere
else has a much greater hold on our lives than we think. Do we really
know what we're up against?

2   Television has grown over the past 60 years from an experimen-
tal form of image transmission available only to the middle and
upper classes, to the ultimate in low-end entertainment. People like
to think that television is one of the best inventions of the 20th century, and it just might have been. Unfortunately, our old friends
greed and sloth entered the picture and transformed it into a 24-
hour ad-plastered, brainwashing, individuality bleaching, stereotyp-
ing, couch-potato-making tool of society. Never in the history of
civilization has one manufactured product (along with an industry
consisting of millions of people and billions of dollars) been able to
induce such widespread passivity for hours on end.

3   The hours add up. The average American spends nine years of
their life glued to the box. Imagine for a moment that you're one of
these average Americans (it might be a stretch, but just do it anyway).
In the span of your nine-year affair with television, what do you

362

think you've accomplished? Imagine spending nine years pursuing other activities . . . you could have earned a PhD, achieved master DJ status, or cultivated a garden that amazes you every spring.

The television audience is divided into two categories: passive and interpretive. If you're the passive type, you're simply picking up the remote and foregoing the role of participant in the real world. Passive viewers are prone to resembling zombies after a good while and will exit their experience getting nothing more than wasted time. If you're an active viewer, you have an advantage. Unlike passive viewers, you're actually taking in what you see and forming an opinion on it. It might not be anything more than a little emotional stimulation, but at least there is meaning given to what an active viewer has watched.

Regardless of these two categories, everyone watching is a television viewer, a role defined by its passivity. You sit, you face forward, you are entertained. Many of us have grown up around television and can't imagine life without it. It's one of our favorite escapes from reality. From soap operas to crime dramas, stepping into a fantasy world takes our mind off whatever we choose not to deal with.

One question still remains: *What are we getting done?* The stream of images that flow into our brain when we watch television is doing nothing more than keeping us indoors and preoccupied with an alternate reality, lulled into physical and mental inactivity. It's no wonder then that a study done on teenagers ages 13 to 17 showed that only 25 percent could name the city where the U.S. Constitution was written, while 75 percent knew where you would find the zip code 90210. Is this how we're supposed to be enlightening ourselves?

What's even scarier about this waste of time is that it influences what we say, think, feel, wear and do. By the time we reach the age of 65, we will have seen over two million commercials. It would be completely irrational to think that not one of those ads affects us. Liberal consumerism is a dominant theme in modern society. The freedom to spend, spend, spend, and accumulate as much crap as possible is brought to you by . . . you get the picture.

So is this what we've turned into? A bunch of MTV-addicted, Jerry Springer–loving mall rats? Hell no! We are all unique individuals capable of free and creative thought, and while television can make us laugh and think, we all know that there are much better forms of entertainment to indulge in. We can all go out and shake our asses all night. We can all engage in deep illuminating conversations

9 with our closest buds. And one thing's for damn sure, we can all read a book.

In a society that increasingly values work over pleasure, our leisure time has become a precious commodity. Making the most of the hours that we have to ourselves is essential. There's a big, beautiful world out there, and not even the widest TV screen or the sweetest *Animal Planet* documentary can compare to the real view. Television is just an infinitesimal speck compared to all the things you can do in your free time, and the longer you take to get off your

10 butt and do it, the more time you waste watching other people have all the fun. This might explain why everybody wants to be on TV.

The next step is to face the challenge and turn off the television. Considering what you might be able to do with a little less programming in your diet, does taking part in TV Turnoff Week sound all that bad? Get together with some friends and unplug it together if it makes it easier. Then, when you're all in the same room together, you can discuss what you'd like to see with the nine years of your life you've just gained. What's most important is that we all need to elevate above the blatant commercialism and mindlessness of television, and to sit pretty on a plane where we can enjoy a richer and more fulfilling existence.

Facts about Television Viewing:
- Number of videos rented daily in the US: 6 million
- Number of public library items checked out daily: 3 million
- Hour per year the average American youth watches television: 1,500
- Hours per year the average American youth spends in school: 900
- Number of violent acts the average American child sees on TV by age 18: 200,000
- Percent increase in network news coverage of homicide between 1990 and 1995: 336
- Percentage of local TV news broadcast time devoted to advertising: 30
- Percentage devoted to public service announcements: 0.7
- Number of medical studies since 1985 linking excessive television watching to increasing rates of obesity: 12
- Chance that an American falls asleep with the TV on at least three nights a week: 1 in 4

Resources on Television Viewing:

- TV Free America: www.tvfa.org
  A major organization with a very thorough and informative website
- Center for a New American Dream: www.newdream.org
  Another informative site dedicated to reducing consumption with lots of fun interactive stuff
- Adbusters: www.adbusters.org
  Slick, hilarious ad spoofs and information on other anti-media campaigns (they also publish an excellent magazine)
- Whitedot: www.whitedot.org
  The UK version of TV Free America; also big supporters of TV Turnoff Week
- The Kill Your TV Website: www.Othello.localaccess.com/hardebeck
  Links, cartoons, and plenty of thoughtful comments
- The "un-TV" Guide: www.com/GMWS/unTV
  Practical tips on reducing television consumption from a school in Vermont

✦ ✦ ✦

✦ *Framing the Context*

1. Trubey writes to the readers of *Lotus,* a group into the rave scene and underground music. How does his introduction convey the assumptions he makes about the readers' relationship to the subject?

2. What is the occasion for Trubey writing the article, and how does that occasion affect the readers' relationship to the subject?

✦ *Point of View*

3. What relationship with his readers does Trubey form with his point of view?

4. How does the vantage point allow the reader to interact with the writing?

✦ *Shape of Ideas*

5. How does the question Trubey poses in the introduction forecast the structure to the readers?

6. Describe the structure Trubey uses and how it connects the readers to his purpose.

✦ *Choosing Voice*

7. What level of formality does Trubey use to complement his point of view?

8. Make a list of phrases and sentences Trubey uses to speak directly to the readers. How do these direct comments affect his tone of voice?

✦ *Credibility*

9. In paragraph six Trubey cites figures from a study but does not document the source. How is this likely to affect his credibility with these readers?

10. How do the lists of information at the end of the article support Trubey's purpose?

Millenial McLuhan
Clues for Deciphering the Digital Age

Paul Levinson

✦ ✦ ✦

McLuhan's words "the medium is the message" have just as much meaning today as they did in 1960, Paul Levinson reminds us in this article that appeared in the October 19, 1999, issue of the Chronicle of Higher Education. *Addressing an audience of university professors and administrators, Levinson, a visiting professor of communications at Fordham University at that time, explains how McLuhan's theory helps us to understand how "new media make waves all across our culture." Paul Levinson is also the president of the distance-learning company Connected Education; his most recent book is* Digital McLuhan: A Guide to the Information Millenium *(Routledge, 1999).*

Marshall McLuhan died on the last day of 1980, just as the personal-computer revolution was beginning. But his previous 30 years' study of television, radio, newspapers, and other media—and the resulting collections of his metaphorically written assertions—provide a surprisingly current guide to today's communication technologies and their effects on society. A quick look back at some of McLuhan's ideas provides an opportunity to correct some common misconceptions about his work, as well as to appreciate his relevance as we travel deeper into the digital age. 1

McLuhan, of course, knew about mainframe computers. They had figured prominently as number crunchers and record keepers in government, academe, and popular culture since the 1950s. He and I discussed the role of mainframes after I provided a preface to an article he wrote in the late '70s on his laws of media. He believed that computers, with their deep memories, increasingly enabled authorities to keep track of huge amounts of personal information and, therefore, to exert ever-more control over society. But neither of us foresaw the liberating digital transformation of all aspects of society that lay just ahead. 2

3   McLuhan was, nonetheless, almost presently ahead of his time, not only in his ideas, but in how he conveyed them. His very style of writing was digital, electronic, holographic—numerous little pieces of keen insight, each of which provided an entree to all of the others.

4   This was not your professor's scholarly writing—no long paragraphs of logically developed argument. Reading the first chapter was no guarantee that you'd understand the second, and often you'd do just as well to start with the third. But the resemblance between the way McLuhan thought and wrote, and the way people communicate via computer today, is striking. I realized that the first time I logged on to an on-line system in 1984. The shorthand wording and aphorisms were uncannily familiar to me, because I'd long ago learned to follow McLuhan's mental hot links and to decode his incisive missives.

5   The most famous of McLuhan's missives, characteristically both straightforward and enigmatic, was "the medium is the message," one of his best-known and least understood insights. It meant that the mere use of a medium has a greater impact on society than does any particular way in which that medium is used. The world changed drastically when people started watching television, for example, regardless of what they were watching.

6   However, the statement—first presented in McLuhan's "Report on Project in Understanding New Media," prepared for the U.S. Department of Health, Education, and Welfare in 1960—was often misconstrued to mean that content is totally unimportant. A moment's reflection shows why that cannot be. There is no such thing as a medium without content, for if it had no content, what would it be a medium of? A television with no programs could have no influence on us as a medium, any more than a computer, devoid of its very different kind of programs, would be anything other than an interesting piece of junk. The earliest personal computers revolutionized our lives, despite the fact that they were rendered obsolete by— among other things—their inability to link to the World-Wide Web. Now, they are anachronisms, souped-up typewriters and calculators that perform just a tiny fraction of what computers do for us today.

7   McLuhan also observed that one medium suddenly becomes more noticeable and comprehensible when it is superseded by a newer medium. In his early writing on literary theory, McLuhan argued that awareness of the narrative structure of the novel was

heightened when novels were adapted for the movie screen. By the 1960s, television was beginning to have the same effect on film—increasing our appreciation of film's art and artifice, and making us long for the visceral impact of the big screen that was missing on TV.

In the decade after McLuhan's death, VCR's and cable, in turn, boosted our awareness of network television's content—highlighting, for instance, the fact that, because of advertising time, half-hour programs are really only about 20 minutes long. McLuhan pointed out that the subsuming of prior media (or, I would add, of the same medium in an earlier stage of development) carries with it a celebration of prior content. Take, for example, the nostalgic airing on Nick at Nite and the TV Land network of pre–cable-era sitcoms.

Ads also became pop-cultural artifacts with the advent of cable and VCR's, with old advertising idioms even being incorporated—for their camp value—into new commercials. Ironic "promos" on Nick at Nite—pointing out inconsistencies in sets, costumes, and props—turned us all, to some extent, into pop-culture–savvy critics and connoisseurs.

The Internet today is poised to trump each and every one of the prior "liberations," as I call them, of media into content, because the Internet is making content of all previous media. The Internet, in fact, is fast becoming the medium of media. The Net began as a conveyer solely of text, but meets the turn of the century as a horn of plenty, offering telephone, radio, and television. *Star Wars* trailers and the latest MP3 files of top-40 songs are just a click away.

When we're on the Net, we become illustrative of another of McLuhan's concepts. We become virtual—or, in McLuhan's vocabulary, "discarnate"—meaning that, in cyberspace, our physical bodies play no role in our relationships. We might say that, on line, everybody is nobody. McLuhan noted the discarnate effect of, for instance, talking on the phone, and he wondered what impact the effect has on our morality. The on-line participant is incorporeal in the same interactive way as the person on the phone. Cyber sex, like phone sex, entails no physical risks, but on line we can be angels or devils, Romeos or Mata Haris. No wonder pornography is the best-selling business on the Internet. The Internet liberates not only prior media, but also our libidos.

The Internet also has geopolitical effects. McLuhan suggested that electronic media, television in particular, were turning the world into a "global village." The world watches spectacles on television in the same way that villagers see local events on Main Street. But the Internet more truly exemplifies that oft-cited concept even better than does television, because it gives all villagers the opportunity to be active explorers, not just passive spectators. The on-line villager—who can live anywhere in the world with a personal computer, a telephone line, and a Web browser can seek out rather than merely receive news, and can exchange information with other villagers around the globe, much like the inhabitants of any physical village.

13   Personal computers also illustrate an aesthetic phenomenon that McLuhan noted. He saw a common perceptual denominator in television and stained-glass windows, and speculated that both command our attention to a hypnotic, almost religious, degree. Such "light-through" media, as he called them, tap some primordial notion of heaven. I know, that may sound a little bizarre; but consider it next time you read, or watch, one of those news reports about how we look at seven hours a day of television, or about how people surf the Net to the exclusion of many other activities. Are the shows on TV, are the Web sites we visit, really that good?

14   References to the past—such as stained-glass windows—are an inevitable part of our attempts to understand the media of the present; we first make sense of the new by seeing how it relates to what we already know. But McLuhan warned against looking too long into what he termed the "rear-view mirror." Its linguistic reflections are everywhere. The telephone was first called the talking telegraph, the automobile the horseless carriage, the radio the wireless. But each of those technologies was much more. The telephone breached the privacy of our home; the automobile empowered countries that had oil; radio became the first nationwide, simultaneous mass medium; and since none of those consequences were highlighted in the initial retro-labels, those rear-view mirrors distracted us from crucial developments and implications.

15   The Web is a veritable hall of rear-view mirrors. Its critics are prone to see it as a television screen; its devotees, including me, are inclined to see it as an improved kind of book. But the truth is that the Internet is, or at least is becoming, a combination and transformation of both books *and* TV, as well as telephones, stereo systems, and movie theaters.

16   The driver who looks too often at the rear-view mirror, and pays too little attention to the road ahead, is in peril. And in seeing the

Web simply as a futuristic phenomenon entwining technological strands of the past, we could be missing what lies right in front of us.

McLuhan's "tetrad"—or "four laws of media"—might help give us a better view of the road we've traveled, and where we're going. Four questions, he explained, can help us size up any medium and its impact. (1) What does it enhance or amplify in the culture? (2) What does it make obsolete, or push out of a position of prominence? (3) What does it retrieve from the past? (4) And what does the medium "reverse into" or "flip into" when it reaches the limits of its potential?

Radio, for example, enhanced oral/audio communication across great distances; pushed out of prominence the newspaper as the leading source of breaking news; retrieved some of the prominence that oral communication had had in pre-literate times; and flipped into broadcasts of both sounds and images—i.e., television. In turn, television enhanced instant, visual, long-distance communication; pushed out of prominence aspects of radio, whose serials and soap operas were co-opted by TV; retrieved visual idioms that radio had somewhat overshadowed, such as costume, lighting, and fashion, and reversed into . . . Well, we aren't there yet, but certainly oligarchic network television has flipped into such diverse but overlapping media as cable, videotape, and the Web.

New media make waves all across our culture. If the advent of new technologies simply brought about, say, reading your local newspaper on line instead of in print, applying the four laws of media would be little more than an intriguing parlor game. But, in reality, each new major technology brings about a cascade of social, political, personal, and aesthetic changes. For instance, the easy, interactive communication facilitated by the Internet seems to undermine aspects of central authority (consider its use by political dissidents in China, or by various factions during the recent Balkan conflicts). Authors can put books directly on line without the imprimatur of publishers. Investors skip the middleman and buy and sell stock shares electronically.

But then, might not the Internet reverse into a Web where choice is a sham, where every hot link leads to the same few destinations, controlled by government or an ever-merging entertainment-media industrial complex? Or are the centrifugal forces that the digital age has already unleashed so powerful that they will undermine all future authoritarian trends?

The conjectures depend on your frame of mind, on how Orwellian you're feeling today. McLuhan didn't have the answers. But

17

18

19

20

21

when we do, McLuhan—never mind that he left us a media liberation or two ago—will help us better understand what happened.

✦ ✦ ✦

✦ *Framing the Context*

1. Consider the role that media—books, television, video, radio, film,
   computers—play in education. How are the university professors
   and administrators who read the *Chronicle* likely to relate to Levinson's subject?
2. What can Levinson assume about the way these readers will relate
   to him as the writer?

✦ *Point of View*

3. How does Levinson's point of view convey his professional relationship to the readers?
4. In what way does that point of view also capture Levinson's relationship to the subject?

✦ *Shape of Ideas*

5. What structure might the readers expect from the title of the article?
6. Describe how the structure Levinson uses connects the readers to
   his purpose.

✦ *Choosing Voice*

7. Levinson's article appears in the "Opinion" section of the *Chronicle,*
   so his readers will expect him to write with authority on the subject.
   Identify three examples where Levinson's writing voice conveys that
   authority.
8. Levinson frequently uses dashes in this article. Find three examples
   and explain how each contributes to Levinson's voice.

✦ *Credibility*

9. Levinson's main source for this article is McLuhan. How does that
   choice affect his credibility?
10. How does Levinson's use of sources complement his point of view
    and voice?

Will RealAudio Kill
the Radio Star?

James Poniewozik

✦ ✦ ✦

"Commercial radio will have only itself to blame if the Internet ends up eating its pablum lunch." James Poniewozik, the "Media" column editor for Salon *(www.salon.com), addresses the conditions on commercial radio that have led to the development of on-line audio in his May 24, 1999, article.*

Like not a few people I know, I pretty much stopped listening to radio after I moved to New York. (Hereinafter "radio" excludes public radio, a genre which, in New York anyway, is largely a magazine for people with busy hands and eyeballs.) With a few exceptions, the 10-hits-all-the-time sameness of what this bumpkin had naively assumed would be a cooler radio market left me nostalgic even for the Detroit area's mediocre offerings.

I'm not saying there's no decent radio in New York, though its quality is inversely proportional to its receivability in my apartment (like free-form WFMU, which I have to catch online). And I freely admit I'm making gross generalizations. But gross generalization is what makes or breaks radio, by its passive nature: You turn on the radio to *leave* it on, so if you find a station—or the entire radio palette—disappointing in general, you're not going to turn it on at all.

And gross generalization, especially in a big market like New York's, is what radio programming is all about: With a high listener-to-bandwidth ratio, the market has a hard time sustaining anything not aimed at the broadest swaths of listeners. It may be doing right by those swaths, but my misanthropic little demographic of one is now getting its highly narrow-cast broadcasts online, trading solidarity with the Radioland masses for the chance to hear Marc Ribot y Los Cubanos Postizos instead of Backstreet Boys.

In addition to thousands of Netcasts of offline radio stations and numerous DIY amateurs, a number of new-media companies are jumping into online audio. Recently Lycos and Yahoo have claimed a piece of a field that includes Viacom's Imagine Radio, Spinner.com and Rolling Stone Radio, among others. (The latter just hooked David Bowie, the recidivist Net opportunist, to DJ an online channel.)

5   Commercial broadcasters discount their online competition, and if it principally appeals to already-lost causes like me, they may have a point. Compared with the single-application appliance for receiving broadcast radio—a "radio"—sound quality is still a problem over low-bandwidth connections. And although Internet audio can allow listeners to customize their own "stations" and can offer theoretically endless micro-categories—drum 'n' bass, a zillion variations of "alternative" (ironically, probably the most common category)—content is still a problem for some. Lycos, with its whopping five channels— Adult Contemporary! Smooth Jazz!—has yet to catch up with the daring programming offered by an airplane-seat armrest. And sites are still struggling for viable advertising; many use banner ads, which I suppose are effective on listeners used to staring blankly at their radios. (There's also the potential for channel branding, hinted at by Spinner's "Doritos Radio," a mild ranch-flavored blend of alt-rock staples. The first broadcaster to offer channels of Gap and Banana Republic commercial music will be sitting on a gold mine.)

6   But if online music servers do someday cut into traditional radio's audience, the irony is that they'll do so by employing every strategy broadcast companies have used to ruin radio—only better and more efficiently.

7   Is having your music picked by algorithm and spun by computer heartless and sad? Given that that's more or less standard operating procedure in commercial radio—as a fine "Marketplace" radio series just detailed—it might as well be *your* algorithm and machine. Will millions mourn the companionable DJ's voice? They'll dance in the freaking streets! The great delight of most Internet radio, not including simulcasts of broadcast stations, is the near absence of speech. (This ignores some loquacious amateur Net-casters, but they're really competition for, if anyone, public radio—they're far more public than it is.) Radio stations have for years acknowledged they've turned jocks into liabilities: hence "More Rock, Less Talk!"

8   Likewise, broadcasters might counter that they provide local flavor you can't get by surfing MacroRadio or choosing an out-of-town station. Except that the radio business long ago made locality irrelevant—you can go to any city and hear your K-Rock or Z-Rock or Q-Rock, something called "The Edge" that still has the MTV Unplugged version of "About a Girl" in heavy rotation, a Hot 100 or 95

or 104, a classical station that plays a lot of Pachelbel. DJs, weather-casters, even traffic reporters are piped in. Even the commercials are site-generic: I recently heard an ad saying a "local doctor" was look-ing for subjects for a heartburn study and giving a toll-free number. Act now, citizen of Your City Here!

In other words, if radio stations can be easily improved on by button-pushing online, they have no one to bitch to: That's what they've turned themselves into. If I'm going to listen to a piped-in newscaster sitting in some bunker in Pennsylvania, I might as well hire my own. Radio sites already collect ZIP codes, the better to tar-get ads; use that info to plug in local headlines here, weather, traffic and Lotto numbers there, and you've already got a station as local as most of what "local radio" offers.

A larger question is whether the resulting audience atomization— All You, All the Time—is antisocial, misanthropic, even. On the one hand, customized broadcasting allows for community building: Imag-ine Radio allows listeners to post their customized channels for pub-lic listening, as can the much more active DJs at Shoutcast, who create and share programming online. On the other hand, these are ever smaller communities. One of Imagine's slogans is: "It's what *you* want to hear!" It's an empowering declaration; it's a 3-year-old's tantrum. Could narrow-cast, interactive music be another ATM, another online catalog—another friction-free convenience that spares wired individ-ualists the messy, frustrating contact with the masses? Another elec-tronic 10-foot pole that exacerbates our sense of entitlement, of impatience, of dissatisfaction with the ability of biological humans to service our desires perfectly?

Maybe. Maybe that's what I like about it, whatever that says about me. Lately I've been listening to Imagine, which boasts a listener-feed-back feature. You can give any artist a frequency ranking on your cus-tomized station, from 0 (never again) to 5. Having this power animated a silent, constant critic in my head, a really harsh little son-of-a-bitch who judges immoderately and grows harder to please with every cen-sorial ruling. I just offed Dishwalla, for instance. Pow! Over! Hoover-phonic? Screw that! Soul Coughing? See you in hell!

I have begun employing this Godlike power liberally, and lately I have come to believe that—unless laws forbidding the Net-casting of too many consecutive songs by the same artist intervene—through various dyspeptic fiats I will ultimately arrive at my perfect radio station, which will play absolutely no artists at all. Leaving me,

₉

₁₀

₁₁

₁₂

in the end, no worse off than I was with all of New York City radio at my disposal.

✦ ✦ ✦

✦ *Framing the Context*

1. Poniewozik writes to an on-line reader, one willing to scroll down several pages of text for information. What assumptions can he probably make about their attitude toward his subject?

2. What relationship does Poniewozik establish with his readers in the first two paragraphs?

✦ *Point of View*

3. As the "Media" column editor for *Salon,* Poniewozik chooses to use a subjective point of view. Identify the paragraphs in which he is most visible.

4. How does Poniewozik's point of view complement the relationship his on-line readers want?

✦ *Shape of Ideas*

5. What structure does Poniewozik use to connect his readers to the subject?

6. How does that structure help the reader to answer the question Poniewozik poses in the title?

✦ *Choosing Voice*

7. Poniewozik's voice is sometimes conversational, even colloquial, but some of his vocabulary is also elevated. Find five words that illustrate that elevated diction and describe what effect they have on Poniewozik's voice.

8. How does Poniewozik's use of "you" affect his readers' relationship to the subject?

✦ *Credibility*

9. Poniewozik uses his own experiences with commercial radio and on-line RealAudio as his main source. How will this choice affect his credibility with his readers?

10. Poniewozik incorporates several links into his article. Review the diversity of those sources and explain how they contribute to Poniewozik's credibility.

Culture of Thin Bites Fiji Teens

Ellen Goodman

✦ ✦ ✦

The effects of media images on different groups in our culture are regularly studied and reported. Those reports are rarely favorable, and often numbing. But the research Pulitzer prize–winning writer Ellen Goodman uses as the occasion for her syndicated column on May 28, 1999, raises a new alarm. Goodman, an associate editor for the Boston Globe, *sheds new light on a familiar problem.*

BOSTON—First of all, imagine a place women greet each other at the market with open arms, loving smiles and a cheerful exchange of ritual compliments:

"You look wonderful! You've put on weight!"

Does that seem like dialogue from Fat Fantasyland? Or a skit from fat-is-a-feminist-issue satire?

Well, this Western fantasy was a South Pacific fact of life. In Fiji, before 1995, big was beautiful and bigger was more beautiful—and people really did flatter each other with exclamations about weight gain.

In this island paradise, food was not only love, it was a cultural imperative. Eating and overeating were rites of mutual hospitality. Everyone worried about losing weight—but not the way we do. "Going thin" was considered to be a sign of some social problem, a worrisome indication the person wasn't getting enough to eat.

The Fijians were, to be sure, a bit obsessed with food; they prescribed herbs to stimulate the appetite. They were a reverse image of our culture. And that turns out to be the point.

Something happened in 1995. A Western mirror was shoved into the face of the Fijians. Television came to the island. Suddenly the girls of rural, coastal villages were watching the girls of *Melrose Place* and *Beverly Hills 90210,* not to mention *Seinfeld* and *ER.*

Within 38 months, the number of teens at risk for eating disorders more than doubled to 29 percent. The number of high-school girls who vomited for weight control went up five times to 15 percent. Worse yet, 74 percent of the Fiji teens in the study said they felt

1

2

3

4

5

6

7

8

"too big or fat" at least some of the time and 62 percent said they had dieted in the past month.

9   This before-and-after television portrait of a body image takeover was drawn by Anne Becker, an anthropologist and psychiatrist who directs research at the Harvard Eating Disorders Center. She presented her research at the American Psychiatric Association last week with all the usual caveats. No, you cannot prove a direct causal link between television and eating disorders. Heather Locklear doesn't cause anorexia. Nor does Tori Spelling cause bulimia.

10   Fiji is not just a Fat Paradise Lost. It's an economy in transition from subsistence agriculture to tourism, and its entry into the global economy has threatened many old values.

11   Nevertheless, you don't get a much better lab experiment than this. In just 38 months, and with only one channel, a television-free culture that defined a fat person as robust has become a television culture that sees robust as, well, repulsive.

12   All that and these islanders didn't even get Calista Flockhart in *Ally McBeal*.

13   "Going thin" is no longer a social disease but the perceived requirement for getting a good job, nice clothes and fancy cars. As Becker said carefully, "The acute and constant bombardment of certain images in the media are apparently quite influential in how teens experience their bodies."

14   Speaking of Fiji teens in a way that seems all-too familiar, she added, "We have a set of vulnerable teens consuming television. There's a huge disparity between what they see on television and what they look like themselves—that goes not only to clothing, hairstyles and skin color but size of bodies."

15   In short, the sum of Western culture, the big success story of our entertainment industry, is our ability to export insecurity: We can make any woman anywhere feel perfectly rotten about her shape. At this rate, we owe the islanders at least one year of the ample lawyer Camryn Manheim in *The Practice* for free.

16   I'm not surprised by research showing that eating disorders are a cultural byproduct. We've watched the female image shrink down to Calista Flockhart at the same time we've seen eating problems grow. But Hollywood hasn't been exactly eager to acknowledge the connection between image and illness.

17   During the past few weeks since the Columbine High School massacre, we've broken through some denial about violence as a

teaching tool. It's pretty clear that boys are literally learning how to hate and harm others.

Maybe we ought to worry a little more about what girls learn: To   18
hate and harm themselves.

✦ Framing the Context

1. How does Goodman's introduction convey the assumptions she makes about her readers' relationship to the subject?

2. As a syndicated columnist, what can Goodman assume about how her readers relate to her?

✦ Point of View

3. How does Goodman's choice of point of view reflect the relationship she has with her readers as a syndicated columnist?

4. How does Goodman's level of visibility affect the readers' relationship to the subject?

✦ Shape of Ideas

5. Describe how Goodman structures her article.

6. How does this structure allow Goodman's purpose to unfold?

✦ Choosing Voice

7. What level of formality does Goodman choose to complement her point of view?

8. Identify those places where Goodman uses colons. How does her use of that punctuation affect her voice?

✦ Credibility

9. Goodman makes several references to television shows. How do the references she chooses contribute to her ethos with her readers?

10. Goodman uses one research study as her main source. Describe the ways in which she incorporates that source to construct her credibility.

How Newspapers Don't Get It about Cyberspace

Hoag Levins

✦ ✦ ✦

How can newspapers make the transition to the Internet? This is one of the questions Hoag Levins, editor of the Editor & Publisher mediainfo.com Web site, addresses in his March 28, 1998, on-line article. As consumer expectations for instant news updates increase, he explains, the structure of the on-line news industry needs to respond. Hoag Levins is now the executive editor of APBnews.com, a national news Web site focused on crime, justice, and safety issues.

1   The keynote speech by MSNBC-on-the-Internet editor-in-chief Merrill Brown was one of the most eagerly anticipated and heavily attended events of Editor & Publisher's recent Interactive Newspapers '98 conference in Seattle. Brown, who spent many years in newspapers, gave a one-hour presentation rich in data about dramatic audience shifts now occurring across the country.

2   Perhaps one of the most stunning statistics he noted was this one: At the Web sites of MSNBC, USA Today, CNN, and ABC, on-line readers are now accessing a total of more than 700 million pages of news and features each month. This is an audience that did not exist two years ago—a fact that Brown used to illustrate his case that the Internet is "the fastest growing major new media in the history of the news and information industry."

Fundamental Change

3   In fact, evidence visible everywhere suggests that what is happening in cyberspace is no longer about the wiring of growing numbers of desktop computers, but rather about the wiring of the collective North American psyche.

4   This is all so new that many in the print newspaper industry have yet to come to grips with the true enormity of such change. It's not just that millions of people are using computers and phone wires every day to obtain news of a sort they used to get exclusively from newspa-

pers, television, and radio. It's that these growing millions of North Americans now expect to find nearly instant news updates about the major events of the day whenever they log onto the Internet.

This consumer expectation—which is not being met by most 5 newspaper Web sites currently operating in the U.S. and Canada—is the new force shaping the emerging structure of the online news industry. It is the force determining which news Web sites are building broad and dynamic brand presence throughout markets where a majority of households will have Internet access within the next five years. It is the force turning some online news entities—like MSNBC, USA Today, CNN, and ABC—into giants with the reach and potential to dominate the Internet news business in the coming years in a manner difficult for online newspapers to match.

Nor is this issue simply about national news. Next time you visit 6 MSNBC.com, click on the "Local News" button to see the surprising number of metro markets whose residents need click no further than that one URL to obtain local as well as national breaking news online.

Are Newspapers Moving Fast Enough?

Meanwhile, back in newspaper land, New Century Network (NCN)— 7 the collaborative effort that was supposed to create a highly promotable Web gateway or "portal" to drive readers to online newspaper sites for national and local news—imploded and announced its closing several weeks ago.

All of which seems to beg the increasingly troubling question: 8 Are newspapers really doing enough to meet the new threats coming at them from cyberspace? Are enough newspaper publishers even contemplating the concept and implications of a society that isn't just *using* the Internet, but is *becoming* the Internet? And by the time these publishers finally do wake up to this new reality, will it be too late?

✦ ✦ ✦

✦ *Framing the Context*

1. The online readers of *Editor & Publisher* read to stay informed on the activities of newspaper companies. How does Levins's opening sentence convey that he assumes that purpose?

2. What similarities in attitude toward the subject can Levins assume he and his readers share?

✦ *Point of View*

3. How does the point of view Levins uses complement his readers' purpose for reading?

4. How does Levins's level of visibility affect his relationship to his readers?

✦ *Shape of Ideas*

5. Levins uses headings to structure his article. How do those headings connect his readers to his purpose?

6. Explain how a different structure would also connect the readers to his purpose.

✦ *Choosing Voice*

7. Levins writes to other professionals in his field. How does the formality level of his voice indicate that relationship?

8. Review the places where Levins uses dashes. Explain how his use of this punctuation affects the tone of his voice.

✦ *Credibility*

9. How does Levins use his authority as an online editor as a source to establish credibility?

10. How does Levins's incorporation of sources complement his point of view and voice?

Your Wireless Future

Michael Mattis

✦ ✦ ✦

"A market in flux is a market rife with opportunity." This is the attitude Michael Mattis, associate editor of Business 2.0, *would like his readers to adopt. In his August 1999 article, which appears in print and on-line, Mattis invites his audience to join the "revolution" of the quickly evolving wireless future—a world in which phone, fax, e-mail, voice data, and Web page browsers merge into one hand-held "information appliance."*

Revolutions have a tendency to sneak up on people, the way 1
communism crept up on the Romanovs, the PC on Hewlett-Packard, and the Internet on just about everybody. The wireless revolution has been happening all around us for more than a decade, but we only notice it when the person next to us in a crowded movie theater suddenly starts yakking into a cell phone. Now, cell phones and PDAs are evolving into information appliances that combine voice with data, send and receive faxes and email, browse Webpages, and serve as personal organizers. Taking network access, and ecommerce—heretofore confined to the home and office—out into the world at large may be as revolutionary a development as the Web itself.

Until now, wireless data exchange has been largely a blue-collar 2
affair. Companies such as Otis Elevator, J. B. Hunt Transport, and Federal Express have utilized wireless data swapping for years to keep their legions of mobile workers in touch with corporate HQ and keep track of far-flung inventories. Today, on-the-go professionals—"mobile knowledge workers"—and executives want the same access to enterprise data and applications, with access to the Web thrown in. And they want it anytime, anywhere, from the London Underground to the beach in Saint-Tropez.

Consumers, too, will realize the benefits of staying wired with- 3
out wires, just as businesses will benefit from wireless ecommerce. Knowing that opening night tickets to *Titanic II: The Bottom of the Deep Blue Sea* next week are going to run scarce, you pull your Nokia smart phone and tap into your customized My Yahoo! page, check

availability, locations, and curtain times on MovieFone.com, and place your order. A week later you receive a call. It's your calendar, ringing up with a reminder that the show begins in an hour—which you had completely forgotten. Also forgotten was your date. And the flowers. Again you consult the phone. MapQuest.com shows you the quickest way to the nearest 1–800-Flowers florist. On the way you place your order, which is waiting for you on the counter when you walk through the door.

4   All this may seem a little far-fetched today. But five years ago the Web seemed a little far-fetched, too. Now try working without it. Once the novelty of ubiquitous access to the network and anytime, anywhere communications and transactions wears off, we'll wonder how we ever got along without it.

5   And, analysts predict, we'll be willing to pay for it. In 1998, Americans spent almost $30 billion on wireless voice services and almost none on data, according to Forrester Research. In 2005, Forrester predicts, Americans will spend nearly $60 billion for wireless services, $8.4 billion of it on data. Overall revenues from wireless intelligent terminals—which include everything from email—enabled cell phones to Web-browsing PDAs—will reach nearly $600 million in 1999, and are forecast to rise to more than $4 billion in 2003, according to The Yankee Group.

6   Software providers, equipment manufacturers, carriers, and dot-coms are engaged in a frenzy of mergers and partnerships, gearing up for the shift to wireless. Microsoft, eager to shed its fast-follower reputation for the mantle of early adopter, announced in June the launch of its MSN Mobile portal site after having acquired Internet/ wireless convergence startup OmniBrowse. The Redmond giant also has hopped into bed with carrier Nextel, and has a joint venture with Qualcomm called Wirelessknowledge to create applications and services for wireless carriers. Meanwhile, Netscape is working with Lucent Technologies to develop a portal for wireless applications. Not to be outdone, Yahoo! has acquired Online Anywhere to provide wireless delivery of Web content to handhelds. America Online recently invested $1.5 billion in Hughes Electronics to deliver Internet access via satellite. Excite@Home is working with Japan's NTT Do-CoMo. And these are just a few examples.

7   There's a lot of work to be done. Over the next few years, standards will be hammered out. Coverage, uneven at best, is moving slowly but inexorably toward ubiquity. Critical questions, such as

how this will be paid for, remain. But a market in flux is a market rife with opportunity. Content, services, and applications must be re-imagined—and new ones invented—to fit the new breed of small, mobile information appliances. The wireless future is a revolution you can't afford to miss.

✦ ✦ ✦

✦ *Framing the Context*

1. Mattis's article, available on-line and in print, is written to the *Business 2.0* readers. What can Mattis assume about their attitude toward a wireless future?

2. What can Mattis assume about how his readers perceive him?

✦ *Point of View*

3. What point of view does Mattis use to relate to his readers?

4. Describe how this point of view affects his relationship with both print and on-line readers.

✦ *Shape of Ideas*

5. As the associate editor, Mattis writes this article as an introduction to the issue's cover story. What do you assume his purpose is?

6. How does the structure Mattis uses connect his readers to his purpose?

✦ *Choosing Voice*

7. How does the formality level of Mattis's voice complement his point of view?

8. What effect does shifting to the pronoun "you" have on Mattis's voice?

✦ *Credibility*

9. Describe how the methods Mattis uses to incorporate sources constructs his credibility.

10. What effect does Mattis's use of sources have on preparing the readers to read the cover story?

Hey Kids, Let's Put on a Show

Greg Lindsay

✦ ✦ ✦

Going to the movies has always been one of the great American pastimes, but making movies was usually left to the expertise of Hollywood and a few independents. Now, Greg Lindsay, an assistant producer at Fortune Online *(www.fortune.com), informs us that opportunity is knocking if we want to make our own films. In the following article, which appeared in the issue of* Time Digital, *Lindsay introduces readers to the world of low-budget, digital filmmaking.*

1   I first did it for the fun of it. In the fall of 1998, when I was still in college, a friend and I collaborated on a short story. When we finished, we weren't content just to throw the text online, so we rounded up a photographer, a film student and a music-composition student and cast ourselves as actors. Over the next 10 months, we shot video on location at Chicago's O'Hare Airport, turned our apartments into sets and dubbed voiceovers and a score. I scanned and recorded everything into Macintosh computers at a school computer lab to give it some semblance of design. This month our CD-ROM story, titled *coffee,* will be sent out to industry people. We made it all on a budget of less than $1,000.

2   These days, every new PC has more than enough power to make movies or animations for CD-ROMS or the Web. The computers are affordable, and aggressive pricing of software has put suites of photo- and video-editing tools on the desktop for just hundreds of dollars. Even better, the Internet has emerged as the perfect distribution model for do-it-yourself projects. It's cheap to get on, it's free for your viewers, and it's a truly global theater.

3   Fans of last summer's sleeper megahit, *The Blair Witch Project,* have already tasted this latest DIY aesthetic—most of the film was shot on a $500 camcorder from Circuit City and edited on a high-end digital system. The digital feature *The Last Broadcast* was shot on a single digital camcorder, then run through Adobe Premiere, a sophisticated video-editing program made for Standard desktop PCs. The plot of the 90-minute film eerily resembles that of *Blair Witch:* a

cable crew goes into the woods to search for the New Jersey Devil. Its total budget? $900. Two New York filmmakers not only made an award-winning independent film called *The Definite Maybe* for under $100,000; they're also distributing it themselves, via Amazon.com, on VHS tape. And thousands of Web surfers have laughed at the on-line sensation *Troops,* a *Star Wars/Cops (www.theforce.net/froops)* parody made by one Kevin Rubio. His project landed him work producing promotional cartoons at Kids' WB. While garage bands aspire to rock-'n'-roll stardom, these garage directors are seizing their family PCs and starting to work on their dream projects right now.

"If you were a 16-year-old and you wanted to make music, you picked up a guitar and made music," says Mika Salmi, founder of Atom Films and former talent scout who discovered Nine Inch Nails. "If you had a desire to make visuals, you needed equipment and distribution. Now, with a Sony VX 1000 camera and some editing equipment on your $1,500 PC, you can express that desire."

Atom is an online showcase for the short films and animations of aspiring artists. Staff members screen hundreds of clips each month, and Atom buys the rights to those it deems worthiest. But Atom and other companies traveling the same digital road are not satisfied with the role of helping young wannabes break into celluloid Hollywood. A page on *www.dfilm.com,* a traveling and online festival of digital films, boasts an inspiring quote from Francis Ford Coppola (mix his media though he does): "One day a fat little girl in Ohio is going be the new Mozart and make a beautiful film with her father's camcorder. For once the so-called professionalism about movies will be destroyed and it will really become an art form."

Bart Cheever, Dfilm's executive producer, says, "If you look at how many people out there have camcorders, they're going to want to learn to edit." In fact, the current stumbling block is the editing software that is required. While working on my project, I needed access to a dozen software packages to produce something resembling professional work. Most of them, while somewhat intuitive, still ship with much needed thick manuals. (A stripped-down consumer package like Avid Cinema lacks features you may find indispensable.)

Unfortunately, software manufacturers show little inclination to make their products easier to manipulate. Macromedia, which produces such leading digital multimedia programs as Director and Flash, designs its software for sophisticated users. "'There's a real gap between the two [markets]," agrees Norm Meyrowitz, president of

Macromedia Products, who adds that the company plans to keep it that way. Yet the barriers to DIY multimedia are dropping further every day. As high-end programs trickle down to consumers, most big bookstores are stocking more readable, in-depth manuals with CD-ROM tutorials. And if you're wily, there are work-arounds. Cheever tells an amateur-to-auteur tale: "Rodney Ascher had done some traditional film stuff but had no idea about digital editing. He bought the *Classroom in a Book* for After Effects by Adobe. Instead of using the tutorial footage, he substituted his project. Before he even finished the book, he sent in a rough cut to some recruiters, and a *Saturday Night Live* producer offered him a job."

8   Luckily, on the hardware side, the blooming of the Digital Video (DV) standard has greatly simplified getting the video from your camera to your PC. Sony's new line of Digital8 cameras combines traditional 8-mm videocassettes and DV into one camera. Transferring the digital footage is as simple as attaching Sony's i.Link (a.k.a. FireWire, or IEEE 1394) cable to the camera and PC and using your video editor to pull the footage across.

9   The hardest part, of course, may be selling your masterpiece. An executive at a company where I applied for work saw a demo of *coffee,* and now his company is considering buying it. Not bad for a group of frustrated college students looking to let off a little creative steam. Of course, a friend still thinks we should have followed an idea she had—you know, three film students who go into the woods to make a documentary about a witch . . .

✦ ✦ ✦

✦ *Framing the Context*

　　1. From reading the title, how would you describe Lindsay's relationship to the subject?

　　2. How are the readers of *Time Digital* likely to relate to the subject?

✦ *Point of View*

　　3. How does Lindsay's use of a subjective point of view complement his readers' relationship to the subject?

　　4. How would an objective point of view change Lindsay's relationship to his readers?

✦ *Shape of Ideas*

5. What does Lindsay want to achieve with his readers?

6. Explain how the structure Lindsay uses achieves that purpose.

✦ *Choosing Voice*

7. How does Lindsay's level of formality contribute to achieving his purpose?

8. Identify six diction choices (words or phrases) that illustrate Lindsay's level of formality.

✦ *Credibility*

9. What value do Lindsay's personal experiences have in constructing his credibility?

10. Make a list of the people Lindsay quotes and their positions. Explain how these sources affect Lindsay's credibility.

World Wide Web Helps
War on Poverty

Netaid.org

✦ ✦ ✦

*On October 9, 1999, the Netaid.org organization was promoted
through a well-advertised Webcast concert: three live overlapping
concerts in New York, London, and Geneva were broadcast simultaneously on television, radio, and the Internet. Like Farm Aid and
other cause-related concerts, Netaid.org sought to gather together a
large community to inform them of its cause—extreme poverty. The
Netaid.org also sought to create an unprecedented global partnership
against extreme poverty. The Netaid.org Web site is "designed to use
the powers of the Internet to highlight successful initiatives to fight
poverty and create long-term community for change." The following
article, excerpted from www.netaid.org, argues for using the Internet
to fight poverty.*

1   "Wealth is the blanket we wear. Poverty is to have that blanket
taken away." These simple yet powerful words come from an African
activist in Botswana. But what's that blanket made of? Before 1990,
it was woven with food, shelter, clinics, and schools. Now, if you're
not on the Net, you're out in the cold.

2   The Net's the new frontier: the Wild West has become the World
Wide Web. Research shows that if you're logged on, you're likely to
be young, white, male, and making good money. Women, poor
people, ethnic groups are likely to be excluded.

3   But UNDP's Sustainable Development Networking Programme
[SDNP] is "helping to level the playing field in over 40 developing
countries world-wide by assisting in connectivity and access to sustainable development information."

4   Why is access to the Net so important? Will it put food in the
mouths of starving children or raise a roof over a homeless family?
When you have no clean water to drink or can't read and write, why
do computers matter? Here are just a few examples of how the Internet works for poor people.

Saving Lives   When the Internet was used, it took hours instead of   5
weeks to link groups managing relief supplies in Washington, D.C.
to needy communities in remote Honduras after Hurricane Mitch
hit in 1998. In Gambia the grandparents of AIDS orphans can visit
electronic workshops to find out how to organize their neighborhood to care for the sick. Global networks are as important as national ones: when former Zaire suffered a deadly outbreak of Ebola
in 1995, local doctors used HealthNet to both alert neighbors and
communicate with the outside world.

Creating Jobs   In just one Egyptian town (Zagazig), 119,000 grad-   6
uates are unemployed; young men and women are now getting
trained at technology access community centers on new skills that
will help find jobs. In Asia, students can start young, thanks to a program (APDIP) that's bringing the Net to schools in mobile units. All
over the world, PEOPLink helps bridge the gap between traditional
artisans and their ultimate consumers by training and equipping
them to use digital cameras and the Internet to market their crafts
and showcase their rich cultural heritage.

   Through an innovative partnership with educational institutions   7
across the world, Cisco Systems is preparing students for the demands and enormous opportunities of the information economy
while creating a qualified talent pool for building and maintaining
networks.

Assisting Farmers   The arrival of Internet to the remote Himalayan   8
kingdom of Bhutan is expected to transform the lives of its people
dramatically. With links to the Internet, extension workers now have
access to the rapidly expanding knowledge that could help farmers
raise their production immensely. Believing that food security is as
fundamental as the right to vote, FAO has developed the Virtual extension and research Communication Network (VERCON) to link
agricultural institutions to extension stations in the field through the
Internet.

Saving the Environment   In Jamaica, farmers and students can now   9
go to community cyber-centers to access information about new
environment-friendly technologies, as can women's' groups in
Cameroon and in Gambia—all for the cost of a local call. In rural Sri

Lanka, a community radio team browses the Net for information re-quested by the audience, translates it into local languages and then broadcasts it in a daily program. In fact, the Net is so valued in new countries that in Estonia, where one in 10 people is already on line, there is talk of making Internet access itself a human right; and walk-in Internet posts are mushrooming in one of the newest on-line countries, Mongolia.

10   This is the aim of the NetAid partnership—backed by the United Nations Development Programme (UNDP), Cisco, and others—to make access to information a *right* rather than a privilege, and help win the war on poverty.

✦ ✦ ✦

✦ Framing the Context

1. How does the occasion of the Netaid concert Webcast define the readers likely to view this Web site article?

2. What attitudes toward the subject of poverty can Netaid assume these readers have?

✦ Point of View

3. What point of view does the organization choose in order to estab-lish a relationship with the readers?

4. How does that vantage point affect the readers' relationship to the subject?

✦ Shape of Ideas

5. Netaid.org is a new initiative. What does the organization assume the readers need to know?

6. How does the use of italicized headings in the article contribute to the structure and purpose of the article?

✦ Choosing Voice

7. What level of formality does the Web site use to create a dialogue with the readers?

8. How does the series of questions used in paragraph 4 affect the voice of the Web site? What effect will posing those questions have on the readers?

✦ *Credibility*

9. Netaid.org chooses to incorporate several (underscored) links in this article. How will the range and number of links affect the Web site's credibility with readers?

10. How do the links incorporated in this article contribute to the article's credibility as a potential research source?

Future Schlock

Neil Postman

✦ ✦ ✦

Neil Postman first established himself as a committed advocate of educational reform with his books Teaching as a Subversive Activity *(1969) and* The Soft Revolution *(1971). As education has become more media-centered, Postman, Chair of the Department of Culture and Communication at New York University, has become more critical of the effects of mass media on U.S. culture. His critical views on the subject have appeared in* The Atlantic Monthly, The Nation, *and several of his other books, such as* Technopoly: The Surrender of Culture to Technology *(1992),* How to Watch the TV News *(1992), and* The End of Education: Redefining the Value of School *(1995). The following essay from his book* Conscientious Objections: Stirring Up Trouble about Language, Technology, and Education *(1988) warns readers of the cultural risk that results from the perpetual entertainment of our media.*

1   Human intelligence is among the most fragile things in nature. It doesn't take much to distract it, suppress it, or even annihilate it. In this century, we have had some lethal examples of how easily and quickly intelligence can be defeated by any one of its several nemeses: ignorance, superstition, moral fervor, cruelty, cowardice, neglect. In the late 1920s, for example, Germany was, by any measure, the most literate, cultured nation in the world. Its legendary seats of learning attracted scholars from every corner. Its philosophers, social critics, and scientists were of the first rank; its humane traditions an inspiration to less favored nations. But by the mid-1930s—that is, in less than ten years—this cathedral of human reason had been transformed into a cesspool of barbaric irrationality. Many of the most intelligent products of German culture were forced to flee—for example, Einstein, Freud, Karl Jaspers, Thomas Mann, and Stefan Zweig. Even worse, those who remained were either forced to submit their minds to the sovereignty of primitive superstition, or—worse still—willingly did so: Konrad Lorenz, Werner Heisenberg, Martin Heidegger, Gerhardt Hauptmann. On May 10, 1933, a huge

bonfire was kindled in Berlin and the books of Marcel Proust, André Gide, Emile Zola, Jack London, Upton Sinclair, and a hundred others were committed to the flames, amid shouts of idiot delight. By 1936, Joseph Paul Goebbels, Germany's Minister of Propaganda, was issuing a proclamation which began with the following words: "Because this year has not brought an improvement in art criticism, I forbid once and for all the continuance of art criticism in its past form, effective as of today." By 1936, there was no one left in Germany who had the brains or courage to object.

Exactly why the Germans banished intelligence is a vast and largely unanswered question. I have never been persuaded that the desperate economic depression that afflicted Germany in the 1920s adequately explains what happened. To quote Aristotle: Men do not become tyrants in order to keep warm. Neither do they become stupid—at least not *that* stupid. But the matter need not trouble us here. I offer the German case only as the most striking example of the fragility of human intelligence. My focus here is the United States in our own time, and I wish to worry you about the rapid erosion of our own intelligence. If you are confident that such a thing cannot happen, your confidence is misplaced, I believe, but it is understandable. 2

After all, the United States is one of the few countries in the world founded by intellectuals—men of wide learning, of extraordinary rhetorical powers, of deep faith in reason. And although we have had our moods of anti-intellectualism, few people have been more generous in support of intelligence and learning than Americans. It was the United States that initiated the experiment in mass education that is, even today, the envy of the world. It was America's churches that laid the foundation of our admirable system of higher education; it was the Land-Grant Act of 1862 that made possible our great state universities; and it is to America that scholars and writers have fled when freedom of the intellect became impossible in their own nations. This is why the great historian of American civilization Henry Steele Commager called America "the Empire of Reason." But Commager was referring to the United States of the eighteenth and nineteenth centuries. What term he would use for America today, I cannot say. Yet he has observed, as others have, a change, a precipitous decline in our valuation of intelligence, in our uses of language, in the disciplines of logic and reason, in our capacity to attend to complexity. Perhaps he would agree with me that the Empire of Reason is, in fact, gone, and that the most apt term for America today is the Empire of Schlock. 3

4   In any case, this is what I wish to call to your notice: the frightening displacement of serious, intelligent public discourse in American culture by the imagery and triviality of what may be called show
business. I do not see the decline of intelligent discourse in America
leading to the barbarisms that flourished in Germany, of course. No
scholars, I believe, will ever need to flee America. There will be no
bonfires to burn books. And I cannot imagine any proclamations
forbidding once and for all art criticism, or any other kind of criticism. But this is not a cause for complacency, let alone celebration.
A culture does not have to force scholars to flee to render them impotent. A culture does not have to burn books to assure that they
will not be read. And a culture does not need a Minister of Propaganda issuing proclamations to silence criticism. There are other
ways to achieve stupidity, and it appears that, as in so many other
things, there is a distinctly American way.

5   To explain what I am getting at, I find it helpful to refer to two
films, which taken together embody the main lines of my argument.
The first film is of recent vintage and is called *The Gods Must Be Crazy*.
It is about a tribal people who live in the Kalahari Desert plains of
southern Africa, and what happens to their culture when it is in-
vaded by an empty Coca-Cola bottle tossed from the window of a
small plane passing overhead. The bottle lands in the middle of the
village and is construed by these gentle people to be a gift from the
gods, for they not only have never seen a bottle before but have never
seen glass either. The people are almost immediately charmed by the
gift, and not only because of its novelty. The bottle, it turns out, has
multiple uses, chief among them the intriguing music it makes when
one blows into it.

6   But gradually a change takes place in the tribe. The bottle becomes an irresistible preoccupation. Looking at it, holding it, thinking of things to do with it displace other activities once thought
essential. But more than this, the Coke bottle is the only thing these
people have ever seen of which there is only one of its kind. And so
those who do not have it try to get it from the one who does. And
the one who does refuses to give it up. Jealousy, greed, and even violence enter the scene, and come very close to destroying the harmony that has characterized their culture for a thousand years. The
people begin to love their bottle more than they love themselves, and
are saved only when the leader of the tribe, convinced that the gods
must be crazy, returns the bottle to the gods by throwing it off the
top of a mountain.

The film is great fun and it is also wise, mainly because it is about   7
a subject as relevant to people in Chicago or Los Angeles or New
York as it is to those of the Kalahari Desert. It raises two questions
of extreme importance to our situation: How does a culture change
when new technologies are introduced to it? And is it always desirable for a culture to accommodate itself to the demands of new technologies? The leader of the Kalahari tribe is forced to confront these
questions in a way that Americans have refused to do. And because
his vision is not obstructed by a belief in what Americans call "technological progress," he is able with minimal discomfort to decide that
the songs of the Coke bottle are not so alluring that they are worth
admitting envy, egotism, and greed to a serene culture.

The second film relevant to my argument was made in 1967. It is   8
Mel Brooks's first film, *The Producers*. *The Producers* is a rather raucous
comedy that has at its center a painful joke: An unscrupulous the-
atrical producer has figured out that it is relatively easy to turn a buck
by producing a play that fails. All one has to do is induce dozens of
backers to invest in the play by promising them exorbitant percentages of its profits. When the play fails, there being no profits to disperse, the producer walks away with thousands of dollars that can
never be claimed. Of course, the central problem he must solve is to
make sure that his play is a disastrous failure. And so he hits upon an
excellent idea: he will take the most tragic and grotesque story of the
century—the rise of Adolf Hitler—and make it into a musical.

Because the producer is only a crook and not a fool, he assumes   9
that the stupidity of making a musical on this theme will be immediately grasped by audiences and that they will leave the theater in
dumbfounded rage. So he calls his play *Springtime for Hitler,* which is
also the name of its most important song. The song begins with the
words:

Springtime for Hitler and Germany;
Winter for Poland and France.

The melody is catchy, and when the song is sung it is accompa-   10
nied by a happy chorus line. (One must understand, of course, that
Springtime for Hitler is no spoof of Hitler, as was, for example, Charlie
Chaplin's *The Great Dictator.* The play is instead a kind of denial of
Hitler in song and dance; as if to say, it was all in fun.)

The ending of the movie is predictable. The audience loves the   11
play and leaves the theater humming *Springtime for Hitler.* The musi-

cal becomes a great hit. The producer ends up in jail, his joke having turned back on him. But Brooks's point is that the joke is on us. Although the film was made years before a movie actor became President of the United States, Brooks was making a kind of prophecy about that—namely, that the producers of American culture will increasingly turn our history, politics, religion, commerce, and education into forms of entertainment, and that we will become as a result a trivial people, incapable of coping with complexity, ambiguity, uncertainty, perhaps even reality. We will become, in a phrase, a people amused into stupidity.

12   For those readers who are not inclined to take Mel Brooks as seriously as I do, let me remind you that the prophecy I attribute here to Brooks was, in fact, made many years before by a more formidable social critic than he. I refer to Aldous Huxley, who wrote *Brave New World* at the time that the modern monuments to intellectual stupidity were taking shape: Nazism in Germany, fascism in Italy, communism in Russia. But Huxley was not concerned in his book with such naked and crude forms of intellectual suicide. He saw beyond them, and mostly, I must add, he saw America. To be more specific, he foresaw that the greatest threat to the intelligence and humane creativity of our culture would not come from Big Brother and Ministries of Propaganda, or gulags and concentration camps. He prophesied, if I may put it this way, that there is tyranny lurking in a Coca-Cola bottle; that we could be ruined not by what we fear and hate but by what we welcome and love, by what we construe to be a gift from the gods.

13   And in case anyone missed his point in 1932, Huxley wrote *Brave New World Revisited* twenty years later. By then, George Orwell's *1984* had been published, and it was inevitable that Huxley would compare Orwell's book with his own. The difference, he said, is that in Orwell's book people are controlled by inflicting pain. In *Brave New World,* they are controlled by inflicting pleasure.

14   The Coke bottle that has fallen in our midst is a corporation of dazzling technologies whose forms turn all serious public business into a kind of *Springtime for Hitler* musical. Television is the principal instrument of this disaster, in part because it is the medium Americans most dearly love, and in part because it has become the command center of our culture. Americans turn to television not only for their light entertainment but for their news, their weather, their politics, their religion, their history—all of which may be said to be their serious entertainment. The light entertainment is not the problem.

The least dangerous things on television are its junk. What I am talking about is television's preemption of our culture's most serious business. It would be merely banal to say that television presents us with entertaining subject matter. It is quite another thing to say that on television all subject matter is presented as entertaining. And that is how television brings ruin to any intelligent understanding of public affairs.

Political campaigns, for example, are now conducted largely in   15
the form of television commercials. Candidates forgo precision, complexity, substance—in some cases, language itself—for the arts of show business: music, imagery, celebrities, theatrics. Indeed, political figures have become so good at this, and so accustomed to it, that they do television commercials even when they are not campaigning, as, for example, Geraldine Ferraro for Diet Pepsi and former Vice-Presidential candidate William Miller and the late Senator Sam Ervin for American Express. Even worse, political figures appear on variety shows, soap operas, and sitcoms. George McGovern, Ralph Nader, Ed Koch, and Jesse Jackson have all hosted "Saturday Night Live." Henry Kissinger and former President Gerald Ford have done cameo roles on "Dynasty." Tip O'Neill and Governor Michael Dukakis have appeared on "Cheers." Richard Nixon did a short stint on "Laugh-In." The late Senator from Illinois, Everett Dirksen, was on "What's My Line?" a prophetic question if ever there was one. What is the line of these people? Or, more precisely, *where* is the line that one ought to be able to draw between politics and entertainment? I would suggest that television has annihilated it.

It is significant, I think, that although our current President, a for-   16
mer Hollywood movie actor, rarely speaks accurately and never precisely, he is known as the Great Communicator; his telegenic charm appears to be his major asset, and that seems to be quite good enough in an entertainment-oriented politics. But lest you think his election to two terms is a mere aberration, I must remind you that, as I write [1988], Charlton Heston is being mentioned as a possible candidate for the Republican nomination in 1988. Should this happen, what alternative would the Democrats have but to nominate Gregory Peck? Two idols of the silver screen going one on one. Could even the fertile imagination of Mel Brooks have foreseen this? Heston giving us intimations of Moses as he accepts the nomination; Peck re-creating the courage of his biblical David as he accepts the challenge of running against a modern Goliath. Heston going on the stump as Michelangelo; Peck countering with Douglas MacArthur. Heston

accusing Peck of insanity because of *The Boys from Brazil*. Peck replying with the charge that Heston blew the world up in *Return to Planet of the Apes*. *Springtime for Hitler* could be closer than you think.

17   But politics is only one arena in which serious language has been displaced by the arts of show business. We have all seen how religion is packaged on television, as a kind of Las Vegas stage show, devoid of ritual, sacrality, and tradition. Today's electronic preachers are in no way like America's evangelicals of the past. Men like Jonathan Edwards, Charles Finney, and George Whitefield were preachers of theological depth, authentic learning, and great expository power. Electronic preachers such as Jimmy Swaggart, Jim Bakker, and Jerry Falwell are merely performers who exploit television's visual power and their own charisma for the greater glory of themselves.

18   We have also seen "Sesame Street" and other educational shows in which the demands of entertainment take precedence over the rigors of learning. And we well know how American businessmen, working under the assumption that potential customers require amusement rather than facts, use music, dance, comedy, cartoons, and celebrities to sell their products.

19   Even our daily news, which for most Americans means television news, is packaged as a kind of show, featuring handsome news readers, exciting music, and dynamic film footage. Most especially, film footage. When there is no film footage, there is no story. Stranger still, commercials may appear anywhere in a news story—before, after, or in the middle. This reduces all events to trivialities, sources of public entertainment and little more. After all, how serious can a bombing in Lebanon be if it is shown to us prefaced by a happy United Airlines commercial and summarized by a Calvin Klein jeans commercial? Indeed, television newscasters have added to our grammar a new part of speech—what may be called the "Now . . . this" conjunction, a conjunction that does not connect two things, but disconnects them. When newscasters say, "Now . . . this," they mean to indicate that what you have just heard or seen has no relevance to what you are about to hear or see. There is no murder so brutal, no political blunder so costly, no bombing so devastating that it cannot be erased from our minds by a newscaster saying, "Now . . . this." He means that you have thought long enough on the matter (let us say, for forty seconds) and you must now give your attention to a commercial. Such a situation is not "the news." It is merely a daily version of *Springtime for Hitler*, and in my opinion accounts for the fact

that Americans are among the most ill-informed people in the world. To be sure, we know of many things; but we know *about* very little.

To provide some verification of this, I conducted a survey a few years back on the subject of the Iranian hostage crisis. I chose this subject because it was alluded to on television *every day for more than a year.* I did not ask my subjects for their opinions about the hostage situation. I am not interested in opinion polls; I am interested in knowledge polls. The questions I asked were simple and did not require deep knowledge. For example, Where is Iran? What language do the Iranians speak? Where did the Shah come from? What religion do the Iranians practice, and what are its basic tenets? What does "Ayatollah" mean? I found that almost everybody knew nothing about Iran. And those who did know something said they had learned it from *Newsweek* or *Time* or the *New York Times.* Television, in other words, is not the great information machine. It is the great disinformation machine. A most nerve-wracking confirmation of this came some time ago during an interview with the producer and the writer of the TV mini-series *Peter the Great.* Defending the historical inaccuracies in the drama—which included a fabricated meeting between Peter and Sir Isaac Newton—the producer said that no one would watch a dry, historically faithful biography. The writer added that it is better for audiences to learn something that is untrue, if it is entertaining, than not to learn anything at all. And just to put some icing on the cake, the actor who played Peter, Maximilian Schell, remarked that he does not believe in historical truth and therefore sees no reason to pursue it.

I do not mean to say that the trivialization of American public discourse is all accomplished on television. Rather, television is the paradigm for all our attempts at public communication. It conditions our minds to apprehend the world through fragmented pictures and forces other media to orient themselves in that direction. You know the standard question we put to people who have difficulty understanding even simple language: we ask them impatiently, "Do I have to draw a picture for you?" Well, it appears that, like it or not, our culture will draw pictures for us, will explain the world to us in pictures. As a medium for conducting public business, language has receded in importance; it has been moved to the periphery of culture and has been replaced at the center by the entertaining visual image.

Please understand that I am making no criticism of the visual arts in general. That criticism is made by God, not by me. You will remember that in His Second Commandment, God explicitly states

20

21

22

that "Thou shalt not make unto thee any graven image, nor any likeness of anything that is in Heaven above, or that is in the earth beneath, or the waters beneath the earth." I have always felt that God was taking a rather extreme position on this, as is His way. As for myself, I am arguing from the standpoint of a symbolic relativist. Forms of communication are neither good nor bad in themselves. They become good or bad depending on their relationship to other symbols and on the functions they are made to serve within a social order. When a culture becomes overloaded with pictures; when logic and rhetoric lose their binding authority; when historical truth becomes irrelevant; when the spoken or written word is distrusted or makes demands on our attention that we are incapable of giving; when our politics, history, education, religion public information, and commerce are expressed largely in visual imagery rather than words, then a culture is in serious jeopardy.

23   Neither do I make a complaint against entertainment. As an old song has it, life is not a highway strewn with flowers. The sight of a few blossoms here and there may make our journey a trifle more endurable. But in America, the least amusing people are our professional entertainers. In our present situation, our preachers, entrepreneurs, politicians, teachers, and journalists are committed to entertaining us through media that do not lend themselves to serious, complex discourse. But these producers of our culture are not to be blamed. They, like the rest of us, believe in the supremacy of technological progress. It has never occurred to us that the gods might be crazy. And even if it did, there is no mountaintop from which we can return what is dangerous to us.

24   We would do well to keep in mind that there are two ways in which the spirit of a culture may be degraded. In the first—the Orwellian—culture becomes a prison. This was the way of the Nazis, and it appears to be the way of the Russians. In the second—the Huxleyan—culture becomes a burlesque. This appears to be the way of the Americans. What Huxley teaches is that in the Age of Advanced Technology, spiritual devastation is more likely to come from an enemy with a smiling countenance than from one whose face exudes suspicion and hate. In the Huxleyan prophecy, Big Brother does not watch us, by his choice; we watch him, by ours. When a culture becomes distracted by trivia; when political and social life are redefined as a perpetual round of entertainments; when public conversation becomes a form of baby talk; when a people become, in short,

an audience and their public business a vaudeville act, then—Huxley argued—a nation finds itself at risk and culture-death is a clear possibility. I agree.

✦ ✦ ✦

✦ *Framing the Context*

1. What does the title of Postman's book convey about his attitude toward his subject?

2. What type of readers will the title of Postman's book attract? Describe those readers and the relationship Postman can assume they have to the subject.

✦ *Point of View*

3. How does Postman's choice of point of view reflect what expectations readers will have from the title?

4. What relationship does Postman establish with his readers using that point of view?

✦ *Shape of Ideas*

5. What is Postman's purpose in this essay?

6. Describe the structure he uses and how it connects the readers to that purpose.

✦ *Choosing Voice*

7. What level of formality does Postman use in his writing voice to raise his objections?

8. Identify six diction choices (words or phrases) that illustrate Postman's level of formality. Explain how Postman's intended audience is likely to be affected by those choices.

✦ *Credibility*

9. Make a list of the categories of sources Postman incorporates. How will that range of sources contribute to establishing Postman's credibility with his readers?

10. Postman is a professor of culture and communication at New York University and a recognized authority in the fields of language, technology, and education. How does he use these credentials to convey his ethos in the essay?

✦ *Suggestions for Writing about Re-Viewing Media*

1. Television, a medium that has existed during your entire lifetime, has probably played a changing role in your life as you have aged. Make an inventory of those changing roles, and write an essay defining the influence television has had on shaping you as a person.

2. In comparison to other media, the Internet is often praised for its interactivity. How influential is interactivity to people's choice of media? Conduct both field research and secondary source research to answer this question. Present your findings in a documented position essay.

3. How likely is it that on-line audio will eventually have a larger audience than commercial radio? Analyze your own use of commercial radio and explore the alternatives on the Internet. Then write an essay that supports one possible answer to the question above.

4. A wireless future may have far-reaching effects on our society. After re-viewing how the separate mediums—pager, fax, cell phone, e-mail, Web browser, voice mail—have individually affected our lives, write an essay speculating on how the merged, wireless form will effect the way we live.

5. What will be the eventual fate of newspapers in our society? Research the current status of newspapers in both print and on-line versions, and write an essay predicting which form society will prefer.

6. Although viewing movies in theaters remains popular, many people have replaced the experience by renting videos and using pay-for-view cable options. Is the new world of digital films on-line likely to become a preferred alternative? Using McLuhan's four laws of media outlined in Levinson's article, analyze the possibilities for the acceptance of this alternative and present your analysis in support of your decision.

7. If you had to choose between a television with interactive Internet capacity and a computer with a digital television receiver, which would you choose? Present and defend your choice in an argument essay.

8. As the Internet grows in the services it offers, people seem to be relying on it more as a source for information. Is the Internet subject to the same criticism Postman argues against television: that "all subject matter is presented as entertaining"? Visit three Web sites designed for different purposes and analyze each with respect to Postman's criticism. Present your findings in a critical essay.

C h a p t e r *11*

◆ ◆ ◆ ◆ ◆ ◆ ◆ ◆ ◆ ◆ ◆ ◆

Defining Environmental Ethics

Everyday we face ethical decisions. Our families, friends, and experiences have helped us to develop a sense of what is right and wrong, of what to value. But in a country that did not develop any environmental protection policies until 1964, the tradition of valuing the environment is still relatively young. The writers of the readings in this chapter do value the environment, and they demonstrate those values in a variety of ways. From the survival of an individual species, the struggle over water rights, and the planting of trees to ensure human survival to researching solutions to inequities or becoming an eco-warrior, these writers define how to make an ethical commitment to the environment.

These readings also focus on a variety of contexts, including urban environments impacting race, geographies affecting culture and gender, and endangered areas threatened by extinction, but at the center of the various conflicts is the understanding that each individual problem is a part of the earth we all share. Can we make a decision about one part of the environment without affecting another part? The questions following the readings will help you to discover how the writers make choices to create interaction with the intended readers and how those writing choices lead the readers to a better understanding of environmental ethics. Use the Writing Suggestions at the end of the chapter to express your own views about environmental ethics and to demonstrate your understanding of how to make effective writing choices.

Out of the Garden
The Land

Jocelyn Bartkevicius

✦ ✦ ✦

How do we make our first connections to the environment? What sparks the realization that we are related in some mysterious, respectful way? Jocelyn Bartkevicius, a professor of creative writing at the University of Central Florida, discovers her own answers to these questions in the selection that follows. "The Land" is a section from her memoir Out of the Garden, *which won the* Missouri Review's *essay prize in 1998. Her essays have also appeared in the* Hudson Review, *the* Iowa Review, *and the textbook* The Fourth Genre. *Currently she is working on an eco-theoretical study of Virginia Woolf's writing.*

1   In the deepening dusk, in the forest, my father drives too fast down narrow Transylvania Road, winding along the edge of a cliff. It's 1967 and he's going back to the land and taking me with him. We're speeding toward some farm up for sale, and he's talking about living far away from the factory, about putting money to work. I am eleven, and strain to understand.

2   We're nearly an hour north of industrial southern Connecticut where I've always lived, far from the river we followed to get here, a river the color of his marine fatigues, a river whose wretched smell permeated the closed-up car. "Tire factories," my father said when I covered my nose and mouth. We're just off the narrow road that heads west from the river, where factories and strip malls taper off, where farmhouses, barns, stone walls, and open fields are all you see.

3   Now, I look down on treetops and grip the Mustang's vinyl bucket seat. I rub my Keds together, streaking dirt into white canvas. At the bottom of a long hill, surrounded by tall grass and bushes, he slows down. "The pond must be in there," he says, consulting a map. At the hairpin curve he realizes we've passed the overgrown driveway and backs up fast, transmission whining. He turns in; plants and rocks scrape the floorboards.

We wade through waist-high grass between a bramble of berries 4
and a tumbling stone foundation. "The house burned down," he
says. I think of the Hardy Boy mysteries my mother reads to me at
night, the danger such a sight forebodes. We walk between a dull
brown barn and sheds barely visible in the fading light. Bats and
swallows swoop in and out of a gaping hole in the barn's roof. I reach
for my father's hand. It's spring and crickets chirp, much louder than
in Milford. A higher chorusing joins them as we walk, a sound I
don't recognize, for the frogs that should inhabit the marsh behind
my mother's house have been gone for as long as I can remember.
My father lets go of my hand to open the barn door. He struggles
against the rusty horseshoe and wheel contraption until the door
slides open. Musty damp smell, the sweet redolence of decay. He
steps tentatively into complete darkness then immediately with-
draws. A noise down the hill near where the pond should be. Something walking, parting grass. My father walks toward it, hushing me.
The remaining sunlight fades to nothing. He holds a flashlight but
won't turn it on.

I take his hand again. Tall grass clings to my pants, scratches my 5
naked arms. Stars become visible in a sky I've never seen before. At
home, lights come on at dusk—street lights, house lights, headlights,
factory lights, landing lights on planes descending to the airport
across the marsh. But here, as we walk toward the pond, in the deep
dark of the country, I can't see my father even though our hands are
touching. I can't tell if my eyes are open or shut, so I shut them,
open, shut, open, to test for difference. Closed lids warm my eyes. I
shiver in the breeze. What if he lets go of my hand and disappears, I
wonder. What if I am suddenly alone in such darkness.

Never was a place so wild, so dark. Never for me. But my father 6
buys that hundred acre farm and moves into the small log cabin built
from hand-hewn logs. He trades in his gold Mustang for a sky blue
Chevy pickup and makes a red-and-white label for the dashboard:
Transylvania Farm. " 'Transylvania' means 'through the forest,' " he
tells me, " 'trans' is through, 'sylvania' is like 'sylvan'—forest." But to
me, Transylvania means Bela Lugosi, blood sucking bats, the dark
mysteries of Eastern Europe.

At the farm, my father builds a dream collage: He becomes the 7
Marlboro cowboy with an Eastern European twist; he follows a
sixties hippie impulse with the flourish of an ex-Marine. He buys

cowboy hats and boots for both of us at Dan's Western Supply Company. He scares off copperheads to draw water from a stone well, and when I ask for the bathroom—until he gets the electricity connected and the water pump going—he points to the old oak behind the cabin. He buys two hard-mouthed, half-wild, former rental horses from a Connecticut cowboy with a Western drawl. He buys material for split rail fences, and spends a weekend wearing dirty Marine pants and a sweat-drenched undershirt, slamming the post hole digger into the earth. Over and over, around the barns, down the hill to the stone wall at the pond, he measures then digs, measures then digs, before setting pine posts into the holes. I watch from the shade of the oak tree, joining him to guide the long rails into post notches. At the end of each day, our blistered hands smell of pine.

8 He gets a cattle farmer with a real tractor to cut and bale hay and takes a quarter of the yield. Prickly hay pierces my skin and sweat stings the tiny punctures as we stack forty-pound bales into the back of the truck. I ride on top, higher than the pickup's cab, swaying over uneven ground as my father drives to the barn. Afterwards, we jump into a river a few miles down the road, climb out, soap around our bathing suits, and jump back in again. He buys a miniature John Deere tractor with a sickle bar and cuts wild grass around the barns and cabin. He buys a machete and I walk behind him picking up as he hacks down young trees, weeds, tall grass, and bushes to clear trails to the pond and through his woods.

9 We pick blackberries for breakfast and eat them on the cabin's back porch, horses sniffing us through the screen. I run around barefooted with country neighbors who teach me to climb a rope swing and tell ghost stories in their dark shed. I learn to ride horses and to race them, letting them run wild while I cling to their backs. We tend the horses, filling buckets with grain, and coating their bodies with insecticide sprayed through long, slender pneumatic pumps. Horseflies subside, but botflies fat as hummingbirds persist, laying yellow eggs in the horses' fetlocks. I swat the flies and comb and pick at the tiny eggs. From the tall roan's back, I nearly swat a hummingbird as we ride through tall lilies. To protect the horses' legs from holes, my father shoots woodchucks, and to protect the hay from droppings, teaches me to shoot bats with a BB gun. I learn to love animals and to kill them. I learn to love the wild woods and to hack it down.

✦ ✦ ✦

✦ *Framing the Context*

1. In this section of the memoir Bartkevicius relates to the environment as a young girl. Describe what that relationship is at the beginning of this section.

2. How is that relationship likely to affect the adult reader's relationship to the subject?

✦ *Point of View*

3. Bartkevicius uses the subjective point of view not as an authority stating opinions but as a participant. How does the participant vantage point develop her relationship to the reader?

4. As a reader, at what point do you feel closest to the writer's experience?

✦ *Shape of Ideas*

5. Describe the structure Bartkevicius uses to shape this section of her memoir.

6. How does this structure allow her purpose to unfold?

✦ *Choosing Voice*

7. What level of formality does Bartkevicius use in her voice to complement her subjective point of view?

8. Using paragraph 3, explain how the sentence structure, length, and variety; the diction; and the punctuation characterize the level of formality Bartkevicius uses.

✦ *Credibility*

9. Bartkevicius limits her use of sources to her own personal experience. How does she use that experience to establish credibility with her literary readers?

10. Describe the ethos Bartkevicius establishes with respect to the subject and the reader?

The Obligation to Endure

Rachel Carson

❖ ❖ ❖

When did we as a society become conscious of the need to protect the environment? Many would claim that Rachel Carson's book Silent Spring *marks the beginning of that awareness. Carson, a biologist, won many awards for her science writing, including the National Book Award for* The Sea Around Us *(1951), but it was* Silent Spring *(1962) that captured the attention of president John F. Kennedy, who appointed a Science Advisory Committee to explore her claims. Once the committee confirmed those claims, government agencies were mandated to revise the pesticide program and to inform the public of the decisions they make regarding pesticide use. The excerpt from* Silent Spring *that follows presents a defining moment in the struggle for environmental ethics.*

1   The history of life on earth has been a history of interaction between living things and their surroundings. To a large extent, the physical form and the habits of the earth's vegetation and its animal life have been molded by the environment. Considering the whole span of earthly time, the opposite effect, in which life actually modifies its surroundings, has been relatively slight. Only within the moment of time represented by the present century has one species—man—acquired significant power to alter the nature of his world.

2   During the past quarter century this power has not only increased to one of disturbing magnitude but it has changed in character. The most alarming of all man's assaults upon the environment is the contamination of air, earth, rivers, and sea with dangerous and even lethal materials. This pollution is for the most part irrecoverable; the chain of evil it initiates not only in the world that must support life but in living tissues is for the most part irreversible. In this now universal contamination of the environment, chemicals are the sinister and little-recognized partners of radiation in changing the very nature of the world—the very nature of its life. Strontium 90, released through nuclear explosions into the air, comes to earth in rain or drifts down as fallout, lodges in soil, enters into the grass or

410

corn or wheat grown there, and in time takes up its abode in the bones of a human being, there to remain until his death. Similarly, chemicals sprayed on croplands or forests or gardens lie long in soil, entering into living organisms, passing from one to another in a chain of poisoning and death. Or they pass mysteriously by underground streams until they emerge and, through the alchemy of air and sunlight, combine into new forms that kill vegetation, sicken cattle, and work unknown harm on those who drink from once pure wells. As Albert Schweitzer has said, "Man can hardly even recognize the devils of his own creation."

It took hundreds of millions of years to produce the life that now   3
inhabits the earth—eons of time in which that developing and evolving and diversifying life reached a state of adjustment and balance with its surroundings. The environment, rigorously shaping and directing the life it supported, contained elements that were hostile as well as supporting. Certain rocks gave out dangerous radiation; even within the light of the sun, from which all life draws its energy, there were short-wave radiations with power to injure. Given time—time not in years but in millennia—life adjusts, and a balance has been reached. For time is the essential ingredient; but in the modern world there is no time.

The rapidity of change and the speed with which new situations   4
are created follow the impetuous and heedless pace of man rather than the deliberate pace of nature. Radiation is no longer merely the background radiation of rocks, the bombardment of cosmic rays, the ultraviolet of the sun that have existed before there was any life on earth; radiation is now the unnatural creation of man's tampering with the atom. The chemicals to which life is asked to make its adjustment are no longer merely the calcium and silica and copper and all the rest of the minerals washed out of the rocks and carried in rivers to the sea; they are the synthetic creations of man's inventive mind, brewed in his laboratories, and having no counterparts in nature.

To adjust to these chemicals would require time on the scale that   5
is nature's; it would require not merely the years of a man's life but the life of generations. And even this, were it by some miracle possible, would be futile, for the new chemicals come from our laboratories in an endless stream; almost five hundred annually find their way into actual use in the United States alone. The figure is staggering and its implications are not easily grasped—500 new chemicals to

which the bodies of men and animals are required somehow to adapt each year, chemicals totally outside the limits of biologic experience.[1]

6   Among them are many that are used in man's war against nature. Since the mid-1940's over 200 basic chemicals have been created for use in killing weeds, rodents, and other organisms described in the modern vernacular as "pests"; and they are sold under several thousand different brand names.

7   These sprays, dusts, and aerosols are now applied almost universally to farms, gardens, forests, and homes—nonselective chemicals that have the power to kill every insect, the "good" and the "bad," to still the song of birds and the leaping of fish in the streams, to coat the leaves with a deadly film, and to linger on in soil—all this though the intended target may be only a few weeds or insects. Can anyone believe it is possible to lay down such a barrage of poisons on the surface of the earth without making it unfit for all life? They should not be called "insecticides," but "biocides."

8   The whole process of spraying seems caught up in an endless spiral. Since DDT was released for civilian use, a process of escalation has been going on in which ever more toxic materials must be found. This has happened because insects, in a triumphant vindication of Darwin's principle of the survival of the fittest, have evolved super races immune to the particular insecticide used, hence a deadlier one has always to be developed—and then a deadlier one than that. It has happened also because, for reasons to be described later, destructive insects often undergo a "flareback," or resurgence, after spraying, in numbers greater than before. Thus the chemical war is never won, and all life is caught in its violent crossfire.

9   Along with the possibility of the extinction of mankind by nuclear war, the central problem of our age has therefore become the contamination of man's total environment with such substances of incredible potential for harm—substances that accumulate in the tissues of plants and animals and even penetrate the germ cells to shatter or alter the very material of heredity upon which the shape of the future depends.

10   Some would-be architects of our future look toward a time when it will be possible to alter the human germ plasm by design. But we may easily be doing so now by inadvertence, for many chemicals, like radiation, bring about gene mutations. It is ironic to think that man might determine his own future by something so seemingly trivial as the choice of an insect spray.

All this has been risked—for what? Future historians may well 　11
be amazed by our distorted sense of proportion. How could intelligent beings seek to control a few unwanted species by a method that
contaminated the entire environment and brought the threat of disease and death even to their own land? Yet this is precisely what we
have done. We have done it, moreover, for reasons that collapse the
moment we examine them. We are told that the enormous and expanding use of pesticides is necessary to maintain farm production.
Yet is our real problem not one of *overproduction?* Our farms, despite
measures to remove acreages from production and to pay farmers
not to produce, have yielded such a staggering excess of crops that
the American taxpayer in 1962 is paying out more than one billion
dollars a year as the total carrying cost of the surplus-food storage
program. And is the situation helped when one branch of the Agriculture Department tries to reduce production while another states,
as it did in 1958, "It is believed generally that reduction of crop
acreages under provisions of the Soil Bank will stimulate interest in
use of chemicals to obtain maximum production on the land retained in crops."[2]

All this is not to say there is no insect problem and no need of 　12
control. I am saying, rather, that control must be geared to realities,
not to mythical situations, and that the methods employed must be
such that they do not destroy us along with the insects.

The problem whose attempted solution has brought such a train 　13
of disaster in its wake is an accompaniment of our modern way of
life. Long before the age of man, insects inhabited the earth—a
group of extraordinarily varied and adaptable beings. Over the
course of time since man's advent, a small percentage of the more
than half a million species of insects have come into conflict with
human welfare in two principal ways: as competitors for the food
supply and as carriers of human disease.

Disease-carrying insects become important where human be- 　14
ings are crowded together, especially under conditions where sani-
tation is poor, as in time of natural disaster or war, in situations of
extreme poverty and deprivation. Then control of some sort becomes necessary. It is a sobering fact, however, as we shall presently
see, that the method of massive chemical control has had only limited success, and also threatens to worsen the very conditions it is
intended to curb.

15   Under primitive agricultural conditions the farmer had few insect problems. These arose with the intensification of agriculture—the devotion of immense acreages to a single crop. Such a system set the stage for explosive increases in specific insect populations. Single-crop farming does not take advantage of the principles by which nature works; it is agriculture as an engineer might conceive it to be. Nature has introduced great variety into the landscape, but man has displayed a passion for simplifying it. Thus he undoes the built-in checks and balances by which nature holds the species within bounds. One important natural check is a limit on the amount of suitable habitat for each species. Obviously then, an insect that lives on wheat can build up its population to much higher levels on a farm devoted to wheat than on one in which wheat is intermingled with other crops to which the insect is not adapted.

16   The same thing happens in other situations. A generation or more ago, the towns of large areas of the United States lined their streets with the noble elm tree. Now the beauty they hopefully created is threatened with complete destruction as disease sweeps through the elms, carried by a beetle that would have only limited chance to build up large populations and to spread from tree to tree if the elms were only occasional trees in a richly diversified planting.

17   Another factor in the modern insect problem is one that must be viewed against a background of geologic and human history: the spreading of thousands of different kinds of organisms from their native homes to invade new territories. This worldwide migration has been studied and graphically described by the British ecologist Charles Elton in his recent book *The Ecology of Invasions*. During the Cretaceous Period, some hundred million years ago, flooding seas cut many land bridges between continents and living things found themselves confined in what Elton calls "colossal separate nature reserves." There, isolated from others of their kind, they developed many new species. When some of the land masses were joined again, about 15 million years ago, these species began to move out into new territories—a movement that is not only still in progress but is now receiving considerable assistance from man.[3]

18   The importation of plants is the primary agent in the modern spread of species, for animals have almost invariably gone along with the plants, quarantine being a comparatively recent and not completely effective innovation. The United States Office of Plant Introduction alone has introduced almost 200,000 species and varieties of plants from all over the world. Nearly half of the 180 or so major

insect enemies of plants in the United States are accidental imports from abroad, and most of them have come as hitchhikers on plants.

In new territory, out of reach of the restraining hand of the natural enemies that kept down its numbers in its native land, an invading plant or animal is able to become enormously abundant. Thus it is no accident that our most troublesome insects are introduced species.

These invasions, both the naturally occurring and those dependent on human assistance, are likely to continue indefinitely. Quarantine and massive chemical campaigns are only extremely expensive ways of buying time. We are faced, according to Dr. Elton, "with a life-and-death need not just to find new technological means of suppressing this plant or that animal"; instead we need the basic knowledge of animal populations and their relations to their surroundings that will "promote an even balance and damp down the explosive power of outbreaks and new invasions."

Much of the necessary knowledge is now available but we do not use it. We train ecologists in our universities and even employ them in our governmental agencies but we seldom take their advice. We allow the chemical death rain to fall as though there were no alternative, whereas in fact there are many, and our ingenuity could soon discover many more if given opportunity.

Have we fallen into a mesmerized state that makes us accept as inevitable that which is inferior or detrimental, as though having lost the will or the vision to demand that which is good? Such thinking, in the words of the ecologist Paul Shepard, "idealizes life with only its head out of water, inches above the limits of toleration of the corruption of its own environment . . . Why should we tolerate a diet of weak poisons, a home in insipid surroundings, a circle of acquaintances who are not quite our enemies, the noise of motors with just enough relief to prevent insanity? Who would want to live in a world which is just not quite fatal?"[4]

Yet such a world is pressed upon us. The crusade to create a chemically sterile, insect-free world seems to have engendered a fanatic zeal on the part of many specialists and most of the so-called control agencies. On every hand there is evidence that those engaged in spraying operations exercise a ruthless power. "The regulatory entomologists . . . function as prosecutor, judge and jury, tax assessor and collector and sheriff to enforce their own orders," said Connecticut entomologist Neely Turner. The most flagrant abuses go unchecked in both state and federal agencies.

24   It is not my contention that chemical insecticides must never be used. I do contend that we have put poisonous and biologically potent chemicals indiscriminately into the hands of persons largely or wholly ignorant of their potentials for harm. We have subjected enormous numbers of people to contact with these poisons, without their consent and often without their knowledge. If the Bill of Rights contains no guarantee that a citizen shall be secure against lethal poisons distributed either by private individuals or by public officials, it is surely only because our forefathers, despite their considerable wisdom and foresight, could conceive of no such problem.

25   I contend, furthermore, that we have allowed these chemicals to be used with little or no advance investigation of their effect on soil, water, wildlife, and man himself. Future generations are unlikely to condone our lack of prudent concern for the integrity of the natural world that supports all life.

26   There is still very limited awareness of the nature of the threat. This is an era of specialists, each of whom sees his own problem and is unaware of or intolerant of the larger frame into which it fits. It is also an era dominated by industry, in which the right to make a dollar at whatever cost is seldom challenged. When the public protests, confronted with some obvious evidence of damaging results of pesticide applications, it is fed little tranquilizing pills of half truth. We urgently need an end to these false assurances, to the sugar coating of unpalatable facts. It is the public that is being asked to assume the risks that the insect controllers calculate. The public must decide whether it wishes to continue on the present road, and it can do so only when in full possession of the facts. In the words of Jean Rostand, "The obligation to endure gives us the right to know."

Notes

1. "Report on Environmental Health Problems," *Hearings,* 86th Congress, Subcom. of Com. on Appropriations, March 1960, p. 170.
2. *The Pesticide Situation for 1957–58,* U.S. Dept of Agric., Commodity Stabilization Service, April 1958, p. 10.
3. Elton, Charles S., *The Ecology of Invasions by Animals and Plants,* New York: Wiley, 1958.
4. Shepard, Paul, "The Place of Nature in Man's World," *Atlantic Naturalist,* Vol. 13 (April–June 1958), pp. 85–89.

✦ ✦ ✦

✦ *Framing the Context*

1. *Silent Spring,* the book from which the excerpt was taken, would be classified as nonfiction, science written for the general public. What assumptions could Carson make about the portion of the general public who would read this book published in 1962?

2. What is the occasion that prompted Carson to write this book?

✦ *Point of View*

3. What relationship to the reader does Carson define through her choice of point of view?

4. As a well-respected biologist, Carson has the authority to write from a subjective point of view. How would that choice have affected her relationship to the reader?

✦ *Shape of Ideas*

5. What structure does Carson use to connect her readers to the subject?

6. What does this structure reveal to the readers about what they need to know?

✦ *Choosing Voice*

7. Carson chooses to use a more formal voice to write about this serious subject. Explain how the language features (sentence structure, length; diction; punctuation) in paragraph 4 illustrate that level of formality.

8. Carson frequently uses dashes in her writing. Review where she uses dashes, and explain the effect on her voice.

✦ *Credibility*

9. Review the quotes Carson incorporates and the list of sources cited in her end notes. How does the range of those sources contribute to her credibility with the general public science readers?

10. Carson is a recognized authority, yet she inserts her opinion directly in only three places (paras. 12, 24, 25). How does this decision characterize her ethos?

Toward Environmental Equity
Colleges and Universities Can Help Find Solutions

Bailus Walker, Jr.

✦ ✦ ✦

Bailus Walker, Jr., associate director of the Cancer Center at Howard University Medical Center and a professor of environmental and occupational medicine, seeks the support of his professional colleagues in finding solutions to the problems of environmental inequity. His article, published in the "Opinion" section of The Chronicle of Higher Education *(May 30, 1997), a weekly newspaper read by university professors and administrators, exposes the problems of environmental inequity and proposes directions for solutions that can make a difference.*

1   Environmental policies have improved steadily and substantially in the United States since Americans celebrated the first Earth Day in 1970 to demonstrate their growing concerns about the environment. But geographic areas inhabited chiefly by racial minority groups still are more likely than mostly white areas to experience serious air, water, and soil pollution from industries such as oil refineries and chemical plants. Low-income and minority communities also are more likely to house waste-treatment facilities, incinerators, and toxic-waste dumps. And children in minority communities face a higher-than-average risk of lead poisoning because of lead-based paint in their homes.

2   The realization that people of color, as well as other low-income groups, are exposed to more environmental pollution than are whites has added the concept of "environmental equity" to the modern environmental movement. Yet most colleges and universities, especially those in urban areas and near communities suffering the effects of pollutants, can do more than they have to help combat environmental inequities, through intensified research and greater involvement in regional development that promotes environmental equity. Indeed, academic institutions can be particularly useful in

418

finding new solutions to environmental inequities, because the most likely soldiers in this war—the federal government and many environmental groups—are viewed with suspicion by many blacks and Hispanics.

Some critics believe that the federal government enforces environmental laws less stringently in black communities than in predominantly white neighborhoods. A *National Law Journal* report a few years ago, which pulled together census data, dockets of court cases involving the Environmental Protection Agency, and the E.P.A.'s record of cleaning up hazardous waste sites, supported this view. And many black and Hispanic leaders long have felt that mainstream environmental organizations appear more concerned with plant and animal habitats than with conditions in urban centers, where economic problems and demographic changes have led to deterioration in the quality of life in heavily minority neighborhoods.

In fact, as Jonathan Adler, director of environmental studies at the Competitive Enterprise Institute, a Washington-based public-interest group, pointed out in his book *Environmentalism at the Crossroads* (Capital Research Center, 1995), some leaders of the environmental-equity movement argue that "the environmental movement itself is responsible for much of the inequity."

These critics charge that environmentalists have devoted their energies to making life in the mostly white suburbs better by concentrating on issues such as reducing noise from airliners, protecting bird populations, preserving grasslands and forests in the suburbs, and improving public transportation to reduce pollution from cars. Where they have succeeded, the result has been to draw investments, jobs, and residents away from inner cities, making life there even bleaker.

To be fair, environmentalists now are paying more attention to the problems of minority communities that are exposed to high concentrations of toxic pollutants, following two decades of complaints from residents in areas such as Louisiana's "Cancer Alley," an area between Baton Rouge and New Orleans that is home to a huge cluster of chemical plants and oil refineries. Residents there contend that cancer and many other diseases affect disproportionate numbers of low-income, minority residents in the area.

Although members of minority groups believe that environmental activists are paying more attention to their concerns now, they do not think that the environmentalists' usual response—to push federal agencies such as the E.P.A. and the Department of

Energy to do more—is enough. Critics do not trust the government to give them accurate information about, or to protect them from, environmental dangers. In the face of this alienation, federal and state environmental-equity programs must leap a substantial credibility gap before they can begin to operate effectively.

8   Blacks' suspicions of federal- and local-government programs seem understandable in the face of many documented instances of such practices as the "targeting" of black communities as sites for new hazardous-waste facilities. In 1990, for example, Robert Bullard, a professor of sociology and head of the Environmental Justice Resource Center at Clark Atlanta University, found that six of the eight waste-disposal incinerators in the city of Houston were located in black neighborhoods.

9   And last September, Brent Staples, a member of the editorial board of *The New York Times,* reported on environmental conditions in Chester, Pa., a mainly black city of approximately 30,000 south of Philadelphia. He found that Chester contained five hazardous-waste facilities, compared with two in the rest of Delaware County, which is overwhelmingly white. The Chester plants process more than two million tons of waste per year; the other two plants handle less than 1 per cent of that amount. Facilities in Chester also treat most of the county's raw sewage. Because of the concentration of such facilities, Chester accounts for 75 per cent of the county's air pollution complaints.

10   The effects of environmental inequity have been magnified by the increase in income inequality that has made it difficult for many black Americans to move to less-polluted areas. Beginning in the 1980s, the income gap widened between low-wage workers—many of whom were black—and high-wage workers. And studies show that racial discrimination, a feature of the American housing market since colonial times, continued in the 1980s and 1990s despite state and federal fair-lending laws.

11   Clearly, issues of environmental inequity are not solely ecological, environmental, or health-related. They are also social, economic, and political. We cannot address one facet of the problem at a time. A key need in finding remedies, however, is more medical research on the epidemiology of environmentally provoked disease and dysfunction, such as learning difficulties related to lead poisoning, among racial minorities. We also need to devote more money to programs that increase the number of minority-group students pursuing ca-

reers in environmental science, as well as to such efforts as the National Library of Medicine's program to strengthen environmental teaching and research at historically black colleges and universities.

Florida A&M University provides an example of what can be done. It has worked with the National Library of Medicine to develop a multidisciplinary program in environmental health that emphasizes preventing pollution and enhancing equity. The program's goal is to make environmental awareness an integral part of the uni versity's curricula in the physical and biological sciences. Meharry Medical College is another example; experts there are studying environmental conditions in black communities in the Mississippi delta, which has a high concentration of transportation routes, petrochemical industries, waste sites, and other polluting facilities.

Since 1990, the Energy Department has assisted a consortium of historically black colleges to expand environmental courses, set up outreach programs in communities, and develop technologies to manage and dispose of hazardous and radioactive wastes safely. Federal grants from the E.P.A. also have helped some universities in the consortium to develop research centers to work with affected communities.

Experts at these institutions have learned that environmental inequity may result from haphazard land-use decisions and zoning that designate parcels of land for industry without providing adequate buffer zones for nearby working-class residences. In such cases, different members of the community may have radically different goals for and perspectives on environmental planning. University researchers frequently can help by posing questions for local debate and by helping negotiate resolutions to disputes over land use and the location of pollution-producing facilities.

In urban centers, the poor frequently have little political clout, so broad coalitions of concerned individuals and groups must be fashioned—including economists, public-health specialists, and experts in conflict resolution. Universities not only can supply faculty experts but also can convene local groups for in-depth discussion and analysis of particular problems.

Even universities not located in urban centers or polluted environments can play a valuable role. For example, we need more scholars investigating the effectiveness of state environmental-equity projects as well as the Clinton Administration's executive order on environmental justice. The latter directed federal agencies to identify and correct policies that have disproportionately adverse affects on minority or low-income populations. It is important to assess the *impact* of policies, however, rather than their stated goals. We must insure, for example, that hazardous-waste sites are not disproportionately located in minority communities, even if the equipment used is engineered to be less polluting than older equipment, and even if new processes for detoxifying waste are mandated.

17   Scholars need to go beyond evaluation, though, to communication—talking with neighborhood groups, issuing reports and press releases, condensing research findings into easy-to-understand fact sheets, and testifying before legislative bodies. And we can all do a better job of teaching students about the close links between environmental questions and social and economic questions. The engineers, scientists, and doctors whom we train will be more effective in addressing environmental issues if they understand how the social and behavioral sciences can contribute to equitable plans for protecting and managing the environment—for instance, suggesting whether bans, incentives, or persuasion will be most effective in changing the behavior of polluters.

18   Those of us with expertise in the medical, social, and economic dimensions of environmental problems owe it to our fellow citizens to use that knowledge to halt environmental inequities. Colleges and universities can offer both moral and intellectual leadership in eradicating environmental injustice.

✦ ✦ ✦

✦ *Framing the Context*

1. The readers of the *Chronicle* represent many disciplines of study. What assumptions can Walker make about their relationship to the subject of environmental inequity?

2. As a university professor, what can Walker assume about his readers' relationship to him?

✦ *Point of View*

3. As a professor of environmental and occupational medicine at a leading historically black university Walker has the authority to write from a subjective point of view. How does using an objective point of view affect his relationship with his readers?

4. How would using a subjective point of view alter that relationship with his readers?

✦ *Shape of Ideas*

5. What structure does the title of Walker's article project to the reader?

6. Explain how the structure Walker uses meets the expectations conveyed by the title and connects readers to his purpose.

✦ *Choosing Voice*

7. Walker's article, written to an academic audience, appeared in the "Opinion" section of the *Chronicle*. How does that context affect the formality level of Walker's writing voice?

8. Using paragraph 6, explain how the sentence structure and diction convey Walker's level of formality.

✦ *Credibility*

9. Walker constructs his credibility using many of the techniques outlined in Chapter 5. Make a list of the techniques Walker uses and identify the paragraphs in which they appear.

10. How does Walker's authority in the field contribute to his ethos?

Foresters without Diplomas

Wangari Maathai

◆ ◆ ◆

*Can one person really make a difference in solving an environmen-
tal problem? This is the question Wangari Maathai asked herself
when she returned to Kenya after earning a biology degree in America. In the following article from the March/April 1991 issue of Ms.,
Maathai, who has received many awards for her environmental ac-
tivism, including the Woman of the World Award and the Africa
Peace Prize for Leadership, describes the Green Belt movement she
began in Kenya.*

1   The Green Belt movement started in my backyard. I was involved in a political campaign with a man I was married to; I was trying to see what I could do for the people who were helping us during
our campaign, people who came from the poor communities. I decided to create jobs for them—cleaning their constituency, planting
trees and shrubs, cleaning homes of the richer people in the communities, and getting paid for those services. That never worked, because poor people wanted support right away, and I didn't have
money to pay them before the people we were working for had paid
me. So I dropped the project but stayed with the idea. Then, in
1976—two years after the first backyard idea—I was invited to join
the National Council of Women of Kenya.

2   We were into the U.N.'s "women's decade," and I got exposed to
many of the problems women were facing—problems of firewood,
malnutrition, lack of food and adequate water, unemployment, soil
erosion. Quite often what we see in the streets of our cities, in the
rural areas, in the slums, are manifestations of mistakes we make as
we pretend we are "developing," as we pursue what we are now calling *mal*development.

3   And so we decided to go to the women. Why? Well, I am a
woman. I was in a women's organization. Women are the ones most
affected by these problems. Women are concerned about children,
about the future.

So we went to the women and talked about planting trees and   4
overcoming, for example, such problems as the lack of firewood and
building and fencing materials, stopping soil erosion, protecting
water systems. The women agreed, although they didn't know how
to do it.

The next few months we spent teaching them how to do it. We   5
first called the foresters to come and show the women how you plant
trees. The foresters proved to be very complicated because they have
diplomas, they have complicated ways of dealing with a very simple
thing like looking for seeds and planting trees. So eventually we
taught the women to just do it using common sense. And they did.
They were able to look for seeds in the neighborhood, and learn to
recognize seedlings as they germinate when seeds fall on the ground.
Women do not have to wait for anybody to grow trees. They are
really foresters without a diploma.

We started on World Environment Day, June 5, 1977; that's   6
when we planted the first seven trees. Now, only two are still standing. They are beautiful *nandi* flame trees. The rest died. But by 1988,
when we counted according to the records women sent back to us,
we had *10 million trees surviving*. Many had already matured to be
used by the women. But the most important thing is that the women
were now independent; had acquired knowledge, techniques; had
become empowered. They have been teaching each other. We started
with one tree nursery in the backyard of the office of the National
Council of Women. Today we have over 1,500 tree nurseries, 99 percent run by women.

The women get a very small payment for every seedling that sur-   7
vives. The few men who come are extremely poor, so poor that they
don't mind working with women. Women do a lot of work that requires caring. And I don't believe that it is solely indoctrination.
Women started the environmental movement, and now it has become a movement that even financial donors see they should put
money in, because the efforts are providing results. But the minute
money is in, the men come in. I would not be surprised that eventually the more successful the Green Belt movement becomes, the
more infiltrated it will be by men, who will be there more for the economic benefit than the commitment.

Although men are not involved in the planting at the nursery, they   8
are involved in the planting of trees on farms. These are small-scale

farmers. In our part of Africa, men own land; in some communities they own separate titles to the land; in others there is still communal ownership, which is the tradition in Africa. We are most successful in communities where women are involved in land farming.

9   In Kenya, as in so much of the African continent, 80 percent of the farmers—and the fuel gatherers—are women. Women also keep animals. A large population of Kenyans are nomadic communities: the Maasai, the Samburu, the Somalis, most of the northern communities. We have been unsuccessful there. Yet this is where trees are much needed. Areas that are green now will soon be a desert if not cared for.

10   We have been approached by other countries, and in 1987–88 we launched what we hoped would become an effort to initiate Green Belt—like activities in other African countries. Unfortunately, we have not been able to follow up. We started having our own problems in Kenya because of our having criticized the government for wanting to put up a big building in a Nairobi public park. But we are encouraging an establishment of a Green Belt Center in Nairobi, where people can come and experience development that is community oriented, with community decision-making, and with development appropriate to the region.

11   Funding is always a problem. We never received any financial support from the Kenyan government. They gave us an office— which they took away as soon as we criticized them. (In a way, it is good they didn't give us money because they would have withdrawn that.) We receive much of our support from abroad, mostly from women all over this world, who send us small checks. And the United Nations Development Fund for Women gave us a big boost, $100,000 in 1981. We also received support from the Danish Voluntary Fund and the Norwegian Agency for International Development. In the U.S. we are supported by the African Development Foundation, which helped us make a film about the Green Belt movement in 1985. Information on the film can be obtained from the Public Affairs Officer of the African Development Foundation, 1400 I Street, N.W., Washington, D.C. 20005.

12   In the field, we now have about 750 people who teach new groups and help with the compilation of the reports, which we monitor to have an idea of what is happening in the field. At the headquarters we now have about 40 people. When we were kicked out of

our office, the headquarters moved back to my house; a full-circle return to where we started.

But it's 10 million trees later—not quite where we started. For myself, now that my two boys and a girl are big—the last boy is still in high school—when we have trained enough women in leadership and fund-raising, I would love to go back into an academic institution. I do miss it. My field is biology. But I was into microanatomy and developmental anatomy. I would love to be able to read more about community development and motivation and write about the experience that I have had in the field. And perhaps train people on grass-roots projects. But that will have to wait. I earn maybe a tenth of what I could earn on the international market if I sold my expertise and energy, and I'm sure many people would probably consider me a fool. At home the men don't believe that I don't make a fortune out of the Green Belt movement. But all over the world we women do this sort of thing. 13

My greatest satisfaction is to look back and see how far we have come. Something so simple but meaning so much, something nobody can take away from the people, something that is changing the face of the landscape. 14

But my greatest disappointment has been since I returned to Kenya in 1966 after my education in the United States. When I was growing up and going through school, I believed that the sky is the limit. I realized when I went home that the sky is not the limit, that human beings can make the limit for you, stop you from pursuing your full potential. I have had to fight to make a contribution. We lose so much from people because we don't allow them to think freely and do what they can. So they lose their interest; their energy; the opportunity to be creative and positive. And developing countries need all the energy they can get. 15

I tell people that if they know how to read and write it is an advantage. But that all we really need is a desire to work and common sense. These are usually the last two things people are asked for. They are usually asked to use imposed knowledge they do not relate to, so they become followers rather than leaders. 16

For example, because I criticized the political leadership, I have been portrayed as subversive, so it's very difficult for me to not feel constrained. I have the energy; I want to do exactly what they spend hours in the U.N. talking about. But when you really want to *do* it 17

18   you are not allowed, because the political system is not tolerant or encouraging enough.

But we must never lose hope. When any of us feels she has an idea or an opportunity, she should go ahead and do it. I never knew when I was working in my backyard that what I was playing around with would one day become a whole movement. One person *can* make the difference.

✦ ✦ ✦

✦ Framing the Context

1. How would you define the reader's purpose for reading *Ms.*?

2. What assumptions can Maathai make about the *Ms.* readers' relationship to the subject?

✦ Point of View

3. How does Maathai's choice of a subjective point of view develop her relationship to the *Ms.* reader?

4. How would using an objective point of view change that relationship?

✦ Shape of Ideas

5. What is Maathai's purpose for writing to the *Ms.* readers about the Green Belt movement?

6. How does the structure she chooses to use connect the readers to her purpose?

✦ Choosing Voice

7. Maathai includes several conversational passages in her essay. Make a list of four examples of those passages.

8. How do the conversational elements in Maathai's writing voice affect the readers' connection to the writer and the subject?

✦ Credibility

9. How do the numbers and statistics Maathai incorporates contribute to her credibility?

10. Maathai makes several comments about the African men's relationship to the Green Belt movement. How are those comments likely to affect her ethos with the *Ms.* readers?

Recycling Yourself

Martin Kaufman

❖ ❖ ❖

Defining environmental ethics rarely gives rise to humor, but envi-
ronmental writer and humorist Martin Kaufman finds an ironic twist
in our recycling efforts. What ethical ecological considerations govern
our burial decisions? Kaufman, who has published in Sierra, E, The
Environmental Magazine, Animals' Agenda, Progressive Pop-
ulist, Earth First, *and* Steamshovel Press, *published the follow-*
ing article online in Earth Island Journal *(Summer 1999), the*
publication of the Earth Island Institute (www.earthisland.org).

They gingerly place the material into a massive, virtually impen-   1
etrable, hermetically sealed container, then place the container into
a second fortress-like enclosure of concrete and steel that weighs
more than a ton. The whole works is entombed underground.

Are they burying nuclear waste? No, dear reader, they are bury-   2
ing you.

Not very ecological, is it? How are we to return to the earth   3
whence we sprung when we are literally isolated from it by thick, enduring barriers? How are we to know the comfort of "dust to dust"
when sequestered—by caskets and steel-reinforced concrete burial
vaults—from the natural processes that bring this transformation
about?

As most U.S. cemeteries require us to be buried today, earth   4
never comes in contact with our bodies for many decades or even
centuries. Indeed, there's little earth to come in contact with—the
adjacent space consists mainly of our neighbors' vaults, all crammed
in tightly like safe deposit boxes to maximize the cemetery owners'
return on their land. To put the problem in perspective: wood coffins
buried without a vault have in some cases remained intact for over
300 years. How long will today's coffins, often made of fiberglass,
stainless steel, or other non-biodegradable material, endure when
placed not in soil, but in concrete? One can only speculate.

The result of this unnatural isolation from the soil is that peo-   5
ple decompose in a thoroughly unnatural way. Instead of a quick

transformation into sweet earth, they undergo an extended putre-
faction that can last centuries. They don't become part of nature
again, taken up into roots and becoming a flower, or a tree, perhaps
a berry, perhaps the bird that eats the berry. They just lie there and
putrefy.

6   They also turn into monsters. Corpses kept from decomposing
swiftly are things of horror, well-suited to the most ghastly monster
movie you can imagine. Do you want to look like Norman Bates's
mother in Psycho or one of those nightmarish corpses rising out of
the grave in *Poltergeist?* Well, with coffin or vault burial, you will. (And
don't get your hopes up that this will mean a lucrative new career in
film. Horror directors generally use wax corpses.)

7   Environmentalists rightly protest excess packaging of everything
from fast food to household gadgets. What bitter irony to be over-
packaged ourselves.

Modern Mouldering

8   The British have other ideas. Over 80 Nature Reserve Burial
Grounds are already open in Britain, or have received permits, and
many more are planned.

9   In these cemeteries, people are buried ecologically, in a shroud
or biodegradable coffin. Instead of a headstone, a tree is planted over
the grave. Many of Britain's green cemeteries double as habitats for
endangered owls, ducks, herons, butterflies, red squirrels, and other
creatures.

10   Outside the U.S., enlightened attitudes are common even among
businesses. An English company makes "eco-coffins," designed to
decompose quickly. Other European firms make biodegradable flax
coffins, cork urns—even urns of chicken excrement for those who
want to rest in their gardens. Coffins made from cardboard or recy-
cled newspapers are readily available overseas. A British store called
Green Undertakings sells biodegradable body bags for as little as £14
($23) and wicker burial stretchers from £22 ($36). In the US, where
death is a 25-billion-dollar industry and coffins commonly cost be-
reaved families many thousands of dollars, such sensible, inexpen-
sive solutions are virtually unheard-of.

11   Posters to the Natural Death Centre's web site have even proposed such good ideas as composting the corpse, then incorporating the compost into a memorial garden. In India, the dead are often

tied to tree limbs so that vultures can quickly reduce them to skeletons, then the bones buried. This seems a reasonable way to become part of the chain of life, yet one can imagine the neighbors complaining if you tried to do it in the States.

What can North Americans do? Well, there's cremation, but that produces carcinogenic dioxins, trace metals, hydrochloric and hydrofluoric acids, sulfur dioxide and carbon dioxide. Not very green. Only your bone chips get to return to earth, assuming they're scattered. The rest of you just becomes air pollution.   12

Lisa Carlson, author of *Caring for the Dead: Your Final Act of Love,* says it's legal in most states to bury your loved one on your own rural land. So why not buy some? For less than the cost of a single cemetery plot (commonly five to ten thousand dollars), you could buy several acres of beautiful land you can enjoy now and be buried on later. And nobody will dictate that you use a coffin and vault.   13

Corpses need soil as fish need water. To isolate them from their natural habitat is to impose a kind of death sentence on the dead, because it keeps the earth from resurrecting them as new forms of life. Dead bodies lying separated from the earth in coffins and vaults highlight the lunacy, and vanity, of a human race that insists it's not a part of nature, but somehow above it.   14

What's at stake? Nothing less than our right to life after death.   15

For more information on green burial, see <www.worldtrans.org/naturaldeath.html>.

✦ ✦ ✦

✦ *Framing the Context*

1. The readers of the *Earth Island Journal* are either members of the Earth Island Institute who support "innovative action for the environment" or people interested in visiting environmental-related Web sites. What assumptions can Kaufman make about these readers interest in recycling?

2. What relationship does Kaufman establish with his readers in the article's introduction?

✦ *Point of View*

3. How does Kaufman's use of an objective point of view affect his relationship with the readers?

4. If Kaufman had chosen a subjective point of view, how would that relationship be altered?

✦ *Shape of Ideas*

5. Describe the structure Kaufman uses to present his ideas.

6. How does this structure reveal Kaufman's purpose to his readers?

✦ *Choosing Voice*

7. Kaufman addresses the readers directly as "you." What effect does this decision have on his writing voice and point of view?

8. Kaufman frequently incorporates questions. What quality does this technique contribute to his voice?

✦ *Credibility*

9. Kaufman informally incorporates his sources. How will this approach affect his credibility with his readers?

10. At the end of the article Kaufman includes a Web site address reference. Read the address carefully and explain how this reference contributes to Kaufman's ethos with this particular group of readers.

Navajo vs. Navajo

Dan Cray

✦ ✦ ✦

*As a country America extols the value of its natural resources through
its vast system of state and national parks. Many of those same natural resources, however, also provide the ingredients for both our
basic survival and new products. In his July 27, 1998, article for
Time, contributing writer Dan Cray presents the ethical dilemma
this conflict over natural resources raises for the Navajo residents of
Crownpoint, New Mexico. In this small town Cray reveals that the
battle over whether to preserve natural resources or develop them is
heightened by ethics of the Native American culture.*

In the desiccated climate of New Mexico's San Juan Basin, a land   1
of red sandstone mesas peppered with piñon trees, water is so precious that Navajo tradition regards it as a living entity. Survival here
has long depended on the health of underground pools and streams
that feed wells and the occasional surface spring. That's why Billy
Martin is worried. The water supply to his tiny town of Crownpoint
(pop. 2,500) is threatened, he says, by moneygrubbers who don't understand water's importance to Native American culture. It sounds
like a familiar story . . . until you realize that Martin, 69, isn't upset
with white businessmen. He's talking about his Navajo brethren.

Challenging the stereotype of Indians as uncompromising con-   2
servationists, more than 200 individual Navajo landowners have quietly leased 1,440 acres to Hydro Resources Inc., an Albuquerque
company that plans to mine uranium ore from a local aquifer (a layer
of water-bearing rock). The company has promised a lucrative pay-
off: more than $40,000 for each property it leases, plus royalties as
high as 25% on the sale of the uranium ore. For some Navajo
landowners that could translate into more than $1 million a year—
a nice paycheck anywhere, but especially in a region with double-
digit unemployment and an average annual income of less than
$10,000. Hydro Resources president Richard Clement Jr. says his
company will eventually employ about 150 local workers to develop
the site, one of the two largest beds of untapped uranium in the U.S.

3   But the aquifer containing the ore also supplies water to an estimated 10,000 people in and around Crownpoint, a town in which
dusty yards are decorated with stripped-down car frames and visiting neighbors honk their horn rather than ring the doorbell. Less
than 10% of the local Navajo stand to benefit directly from the mining leases, and many of the rest, conditioned by a history of false
promises from outsiders, aren't buying Hydro Resources' assurances
that their water will remain unpolluted by the mine.

4   The town's primary well is situated only 2,000 ft. from the nearest proposed mining site. A similar uranium-mining effort in the
1980s failed to preserve the water's purity, says Mitchell Capitan, the
soft-spoken leader of a grass-roots organization opposed to the
mine. "We can't afford to risk our children and our future," says Capitan. Martin agrees, "It's a disruption to Mother Earth, and it's not
the Indian way."

5   Or is it? Hydro Resources contends that its extraction process
poses no threat to the groundwater. The U.S. Nuclear Regulatory
Commission concurs, and the company has been granted a license
to mine. "If there's a resource there, why shouldn't our people be
able to enjoy the proceeds of it?" argues Ruth Bridgeman, 79, who
leased her property to Hydro Resources several years ago. Leonard
Arviso, a Navajo who acts as the company's liaison to his tribe, talks
not of land or money but of children who are forced to leave the
community for lack of jobs. "We can respect Mother Earth," he says,
"without wasting it."

6   Today the Navajo Nation is but one of many tribes in which
some members believe they can exploit their natural resources with
minimal risk while others don't want to take any chances. In Alaska
spruce forests that served as traditional hunting grounds have been
clear-cut by Tlingit loggers. Florida's Miccosukee Indians are attempting to build housing within Everglades National Park, while
Utah's Goshute are actively seeking a nuclear-waste dump. And last
year Arizona's White Mountain Apaches, protecting their logging
and cattle interests, declared that federal agents would be forbidden
to enforce the Endangered Species Act on tribal land. Says Rosita
Worl, a Tlingit anthropologist: "There has never been more tension
between the need for resources and our reverence for nature."

7   In Crownpoint the uranium issue has sharply divided the
Navajo. At the tribe's chapter house (where the local governing body
sits), a recent motion to oppose the mine sparked such furious de-

bate that the issue was permanently tabled. "Anyone who wants to get re-elected can't touch this," says Rosemary Silversmith, the chapter-house treasurer.

The issue has split not only the tribe but also individual families.   8
For example, Capitan, the grass-roots opposition leader, is the nephew of Arviso, the employee of Hydro Resources. And there is a generational clash as well: some younger Navajo accuse the landowners, many of them tribal elders, of selling out. "The older people always say human life is more important than material things," says LaJuanna Daye, a health-care worker, "but here they have the chance to prove it, and all we see is greed."

With the land in question a checkerboard ownership of Navajo,   9
other private landholders and the U.S. government, the ultimate fate of the mine may depend on who wins jurisdiction in court. Regardless, the Navajo syllables *Tó eii be' iiná át é* (Water is life) have become fighting words in Crownpoint.

✦ ✦ ✦

✦ Framing the Context

1. The title of the article projects the court-battle intensity of the subject. How does this announcement fit the *Time* readers' purpose for reading the publication?

2. What assumptions can Cray make about the readers' knowledge on this subject? What information does Cray include in the opening paragraph that reveals some of those assumptions?

✦ Point of View

3. Explain what relationship Cray establishes with the readers by using an objective point of view.

4. The numerous quotes and specific descriptions Cray includes suggest that he visited the site of the controversy. Why, then, didn't he choose to use a subjective point of view?

✦ Shape of Ideas

5. From the title of the article, what arrangement of ideas will the readers expect?

6. How does Cray's choice of structure convey what he believes his readers need to know?

✦ *Choosing Voice*

7. How does the formality level of Cray's writing voice match the readers' relationship to the subject?

8. Although Cray writes from an objective point of view, his voice, at times, is personal and distinctly audible. Identify two examples of this use of voice.

✦ *Credibility*

9. Make a list of the sources Cray uses for each side of the conflict. How balanced is his support and how does that balance contribute to his credibility?

10. How does Cray's use of parenthetical information help to shape his ethos with the readers?

from *Confessions of an Eco-Warrior*

Dave Foreman

✦ ✦ ✦

The ethics of protecting the environment, Dave Foreman tells us, depend on our own sense of personal ethics. When people's personal ethics conflict, more extreme measures are needed to fight environmental protection battles. In the following excerpt from Confessions of an Eco-Warrior *(1992), a follow-up to his* Ecodefense: A Field Guide to Monkeywrenching, *written with Bill Haywood, Foreman reflects on his roles in the environmental movement since its inception, the founding of Earth First!, and the direction the movement needs to take.*

If opposition is not enough, we must resist. And if resistance is not enough, then subvert.

—Edward Abbey

The early conservation movement in the United States was a child—and no bastard child—of the Establishment. The founders of the Sierra Club, the National Audubon Society, The Wilderness Society, and the wildlife conservation groups were, as a rule, pillars of American society. They were an elite band—sportsmen of the Teddy Roosevelt variety, naturalists like John Burroughs, outdoorsmen in the mold of John Muir, pioneer foresters and ecologists on the order of Aldo Leopold, and wealthy social reformers like Gifford Pinchot and Robert Marshall. No anarchistic Luddites, these.

When the Sierra Club grew into the politically effective force that blocked Echo Park Dam in 1956 and got the Wilderness Act passed in 1964, its members (and members of like-minded organizations) were likely to be physicians, mathematicians, and nuclear physicists. To be sure, refugees from the mainstream joined the conservation outfits in the 1950s and 1960s, and David Brower, executive director of the Sierra Club during that period, and the man most responsible for the creation of the modern environmental movement, was

1

2

437

beginning to ask serious questions about the assumptions and direction of industrial society by the time the Club's board of directors fired him in 1969. But it was not until Earth Day in 1970 that the environmental movement received its first real influx of antiestablishment radicals, as Vietnam War protesters found a new cause—the environment. Suddenly, beards appeared alongside crewcuts in conservation group meetings—and the rhetoric quickened.

3   The militancy was short-lived. Eco-anarchist groups like Black Mesa Defense, which provided a cutting edge for the movement, peaked at the United Nations' 1972 Stockholm Conference on the Human Environment, but then faded from the scene. Along with dozens of other products of the 1960s who went to work for conservation organizations in the early 1970s, I discovered that compromise seemed to work best. A suit and a tie gained access to regional heads of the U.S. Forest Service and to members of Congress. We learned to moderate our opinions along with our dress. We learned that extremists were ignored in the councils of government, that the way to get a senator to put his arm around your shoulders and drop a Wilderness bill in the hopper was to consider the conflicts—mining, timber, grazing—and pare back the proposal accordingly. *Of course* we were good, patriotic Americans. *Of course* we were concerned with the production of red meat, timber, and minerals. We tried to demonstrate that preserving wilderness did not conflict all that much with the gross national product, and that clean air actually helped the economy. We argued that we could have our booming industry and still not sink oil wells in pristine areas.

4   This moderate stance appeared to pay off when Jimmy Carter, the first President who was an avowed conservationist since Teddy Roosevelt, took the helm at the White House in 1977. Self-professed conservationists were given decisive positions in Carter's administration. Editorials proclaimed that environmentalism had been enshrined in the Establishment, that conservation was here to stay. A new ethic was at hand: Environmental Quality and Continued Economic Progress.

5   Yet, although we had access to and influence in high places, something seemed amiss. When the chips were down, conservation still lost out to industry. But these were our friends turning us down. We tried to understand the problems they faced in the real political world. We gave them the benefit of the doubt. We failed to sue when we should have. . . .

I wondered about all this on a gray day in January 1979 as I sat   6
in my office in the headquarters of The Wilderness Society, only
three blocks from the White House. I had just returned from a news
conference at the South Agriculture Building, where the Forest Service had announced a disappointing decision on the second Roadless Area Review and Evaluation, a twenty-month exercise by the
Forest Service to determine which National Forest lands should be
protected in their natural condition. As I loosened my tie, propped
my cowboy boots up on my desk, and popped the top on another
Stroh's, I thought about RARE II and why it had gone so wrong.
Jimmy Carter was supposedly a great friend of wilderness. Dr. M. Ru-
pert Cutler, a former assistant executive director of The Wilderness
Society, was Assistant Secretary of Agriculture over the Forest Service and had conceived the RARE II program. But we had lost to the
timber, mining, and cattle interests on every point. Of 80 million
acres still roadless and undeveloped in the 190 million acres of National Forests, the Department of Agriculture recommended that
only 15 million receive protection from road building and timber
cutting.* Moreover, damn it, we—the conservationists—had been
moderate. The antienvironmental side had been extreme, radical,
emotional, their arguments full of holes. We had been factual, rational. We had provided more—and better—serious public comment.
But we had lost, and now we were worried that some local wilderness group might go off the reservation and sue the Forest Service
over the clearly inadequate environmental impact statement for
RARE II. We didn't want a lawsuit because we knew we could win
and were afraid of the political consequences of such a victory. We
might make some powerful senators and representatives angry. So
those of us in Washington were plotting how to keep the grassroots
in line. Something about all this seemed wrong to me.

After RARE II, I left my position as issues coordinator for The   7
Wilderness Society in Washington to return to New Mexico and my
old job as the Society's Southwest representative. I was particularly
concerned with overgrazing on the 180 million acres of public lands

---

*Only 62 million acres were actually considered by the Forest Service in RARE
II. Another 18 million acres that were also roadless and undeveloped were not
considered because of sloppy inventory procedures, political pressure, or because
areas had already gone through land-use plans that had supposedly considered
their wilderness potential.

in the West managed by the Department of the Interior's Bureau of Land Management. For years, these lands—rich in wildlife, scenery, recreation, and wilderness—had been the private preserve of stock growers in the West. BLM had done little to manage the public lands or to control the serious overgrazing that was sending millions of tons of topsoil down the Colorado, the Rio Grande, and other rivers, wiping out wildlife habitat, and generally beating the land to hell.

8   Prodded by a Natural Resources Defense Council lawsuit, BLM began to address the overgrazing problem through a series of environmental impact statements. These confirmed that most BLM lands were seriously overgrazed, and recommended cuts in livestock numbers. But after the expected outcry from ranchers and their political cronies in Congress and in state capitals, BLM backtracked so quickly that the Department of the Interior building suffered structural damage. Why were BLM and the Department of the Interior so gutless?

9   While that question gnawed at my innards, I was growing increasingly disturbed about trends in the conservation organizations themselves. When I originally went to work for The Wilderness Society in 1973, the way to get a job with a conservation group was to prove yourself first as a volunteer. It helped to have the right academic background, but experience as a capable grassroots conservation activist was more important.

10   We realized that we would not receive the salaries we could earn in government or private industry, but we didn't expect them. We were working for nonprofit groups funded by the contributions of concerned people. Give us enough to keep food on the table, pay rent, buy a six-pack—we didn't want to get rich. But a change occurred after the mid-1970s: people seeking to work for conservation groups were career-oriented; they had relevant degrees (science or law, not history or English); they saw jobs in environmental organizations in the same light as jobs in government or industry. One was a steppingstone to another, more powerful position later on. They were less part of a cause than members of a profession.

11   A gulf began to grow between staff and volunteers. We also began to squabble over salaries. We were no longer content with subsistence wages, and the figures on our paychecks came to mark our status in the movement. Perrier and Brie replaced Bud and beans at gatherings.

12   Within The Wilderness Society, executive director Celia Hunter, a prominent Alaskan conservationist and outfitter, World War II pilot, and feminist, was replaced in 1978 by Bill Turnage, an eager

young businessman who had made his mark by marketing Ansel
Adams. Within two years Turnage had replaced virtually all those on
the staff under Celia with professional organization people. The governing council also worked to bring millionaires with a vague environmental interest on board. We were, it seemed to some of us,
becoming indistinguishable from those we were ostensibly fighting.

What have we really accomplished? I thought. *Are we any better off as*   13
far as saving the Earth now than we were ten years ago? I ticked off the
real problems. world population growth, destruction of tropical
forests, expanding slaughter of African wildlife, oil pollution of the
oceans, acid rain, carbon dioxide buildup in the atmosphere, spreading deserts on every continent, destruction of native peoples and the
imposition of a single culture (European) on the entire word, plans
to carve up Antarctica, planned deep seabed mining, nuclear proliferation, recombinant DNA research, toxic wastes. . . . It was staggering. And I feared we had done nothing to reverse the tide. Indeed,
it had accelerated.

And then: Ronald Reagan. James "Rape 'n' Ruin" Watt became   14
Secretary of the Interior. The Forest Service was Louisiana Pacific's. Interior was Exxon's. The Environmental Protection Agency was Dow's.
Quickly, the Reagan administration and the Republican Senate spoke
of gutting the already gutless Alaska Lands bill. The Clean Air Act, up
for renewal, faced a government more interested in corporate black ink
than human black lungs. The lands of the Bureau of Land Management appeared to the Interior Department obscenely naked without
the garb of oil wells. Concurrently, the Agriculture Department directed the Forest Service to rid the National Forests of decadent and
diseased old-growth trees. The cowboys had the grazing lands, and
God help the hiker, Coyote, or blade of grass that got in their way.

Maybe, some of us began to feel, even before Reagan's election,   15
it was time for a new joker in the deck: a militant, uncompromising
group unafraid to say what needed to be said or to back it up with
stronger actions than the established organizations were willing to
take. This idea had been kicking around for a couple of years. Finally,
in 1980, several disgruntled conservationists—including Susan Morgan, formerly educational director for The Wilderness Society;
Howie Wolke, former Wyoming representative for Friends of the
Earth; Bart Koehler, former Wyoming representative for The Wilderness Society; Ron Kezar, a longtime Sierra Club activist; and I—
decided that the time for talk was past. We formed a new national

group, which we called Earth First! We set out to be radical in style, positions, philosophy, and organization in order to be effective and to avoid the pitfalls of co-option and moderation that we had already experienced.

16   What, we asked ourselves as we sat around a campfire in the Wyoming mountains, were the reasons and purposes for environmental radicalism?

- To state honestly the views held by many conservationists.
- To demonstrate that the Sierra Club and its allies were raging moderates, believers in the system, and to refute the Reagan/Watt contention that they were "environmental extremists."
- To balance such antienvironmental radicals as the Grand County commission and provide a broader spectrum of viewpoints.
- To return vigor, joy, and enthusiasm to the tired, unimaginative environmental movement.
- To keep the established groups honest. By stating a pure, no-compromise, pro-Earth position, we felt that Earth First! could help keep the other groups from straying too far from their original philosophical base.
- To give an outlet to many hard-line conservationists who were no longer active because of disenchantment with compromise politics and the cooption of environmental organizations.
- To provide a productive fringe, since ideas, creativity, and energy tend to spring up on the edge and later spread into the center.
- To inspire others to carry out activities straight from the pages of *The Monkey Wrench Gang* (a novel of environmental sabotage by Edward Abbey), even though Earth First!, we agreed, would itself be ostensibly law-abiding.
- To help develop a new worldview, a biocentric paradigm, an Earth philosophy. To fight, with uncompromising passion, for Earth.

17   The name Earth First! was chosen because it succinctly summed up the one thing on which we could all agree: That in *any* decision, consideration for the health of the Earth must come first.

18   In a true Earth-radical group, concern for wilderness preservation must be the keystone. The idea of wilderness, after all, is the most radical in human thought—more radical than Paine, than Marx, than Mao. Wilderness says: Human beings are not paramount, Earth is not for *Homo sapiens* alone, human life is but one life form on the planet

and has no right to take exclusive possession. Yes, wilderness for its own sake, without any need to justify it for human benefit. Wilderness for wilderness. For bears and whales and titmice and rattlesnakes and stink bugs. And . . . wilderness for human beings. Because it is the laboratory of human evolution, and because it is home.

It is not enough to protect our few remaining bits of wilderness. The only hope for Earth (including humanity) is to withdraw huge areas as inviolate natural sanctuaries from the depredations of modern industry and technology. Keep Cleveland, Los Angeles. Contain them. Try to make them habitable. But identify big areas that can be restored to a semblance of natural conditions, reintroduce the Grizzly Bear and wolf and prairie grasses, and declare them off limits to modern civilization.

In the United States, pick an area for each of our major ecosystems and recreate the American wilderness—not in little pieces of a thousand acres, but in chunks of a million or ten million. Move out the people and cars. Reclaim the roads and plowed land. It is not enough any longer to say no more dams on our wild rivers. We must begin tearing down some dams already built—beginning with Glen Canyon on the Colorado River in Arizona, Tellico in Tennessee, Hetch Hetchy and New Melones in California—and freeing shackled rivers.

This emphasis on wilderness does not require ignoring other environmental issues or abandoning social issues. In the United States, blacks and Chicanos of the inner cities are the ones most affected by air and water pollution, the ones most trapped by the unnatural confines of urbanity. So we decided that not only should eco-militants be concerned with these human environmental problems, we should also make common ground with other progressive elements of society whenever possible.

Obviously, for a group more committed to Gila Monsters and Mountain Lions than to people, there will not be a total alliance with other social movements. But there are issues in which Earth radicals can cooperate with feminist, Native American, anti-nuke, peace, civil-rights, and civil-liberties groups. The inherent conservatism of the conservation community has made it wary of snuggling too close to these leftist organizations. We hoped to pave the way for better cooperation from the entire conservation movement.

We believed that new tactics were needed—something more than commenting on dreary environmental-impact statements and

19

20

21

22

23

writing letters to members of Congress. Politics in the streets. Civil disobedience. Media stunts. Holding the villains up to ridicule. Using music to charge the cause.

24   Action is the key. Action is more important than philosophical hairsplitting or endless refining of dogma (for which radicals are so well known). Let our actions set the finer points of our philosophy. And let us recognize that diversity is not only the spice of life, but also the strength. All that would be required to join Earth First!, we decided, was a belief in Earth first. Apart from that, Earth First! would be big enough to contain street poets and cowboy bar bouncers, agnostics and pagans, vegetarians and raw-steak eaters, pacifists and those who think that turning the other cheek is a good way to get a sore face.

25   Radicals frequently verge on a righteous seriousness. But we felt that if we couldn't laugh at ourselves we would be merely another bunch of dangerous fanatics who should be locked up—like oil company executives. Not only does humor preserve individual and group sanity; it retards hubris, a major cause of environmental rape, and it is also an effective weapon. Fire, passion, courage, and emotionalism are also needed. We have been too reasonable, too calm, too understanding. It's time to get angry, to cry, to let rage flow at what the human cancer is doing to Earth, to be uncompromising. For Earth First! there is no truce or cease-fire. No surrender. No partitioning of the territory.

26   Ever since the Earth goddesses of ancient Greece were supplanted by the macho Olympians, repression of women and Earth has gone hand in hand with imperial organization. Earth First! decided to be nonorganizational: no officers, no bylaws or constitution, no incorporation, no tax status, just a collection of women and men committed to the Earth. At the turn of the century, William Graham Sumner wrote a famous essay titled "The Conquest of the United States by Spain." His thesis was that Spain had ultimately won the Spanish-American War because the United States took on the imperialism and totalitarianism of Spain. We felt that if we took on the organization of the industrial state, we would soon accept their anthropocentric paradigm, much as Audubon and the Sierra Club already had.

27   And when we are inspired, we *act*.

28   Massive, powerful, like some creation of Darth Vader, Glen Canyon Dam squats in the canyon of the Colorado River on the Ari-

zona-Utah border and backs the cold, dead waters of "Lake" Powell some 180 miles upstream, drowning the most awesome and magical canyon on Earth. More than any other single entity, Glen Canyon Dam is the symbol of the destruction of wilderness, of the technological ravishment of the West. The finest fantasy of eco-warriors in the West is the destruction of the dam and the liberation of the Colorado. So it was only proper that on March 21, 1981—at the spring equinox, the traditional time of rebirth—Earth First! held its first national gathering at Glen Canyon Dam.

On that morning, seventy-five members of Earth First! lined the walk-way of the Colorado River Bridge, seven hundred feet above the once-free river, and watched five compatriots busy at work with an awkward black bundle on the massive dam just upstream. Those on the bridge carried placards reading "Damn Watt, Not Rivers," "Free the Colorado," and "Let it Flow." The five of us on the dam attached ropes to a grille, shouted out "Earth First!" and let three hundred feet of black plastic unfurl down the side of the dam, creating the impression of a growing crack. Those on the bridge returned the cheer.

Then Edward Abbey, author of *The Monkey Wrench Gang,* told the protesters of the "green and living wilderness" that was Glen Canyon only nineteen years ago:

> *And they took it away from us. The politicians of Arizona, Utah, New Mexico, and Colorado, in cahoots with the land developers, city developers, industrial developers of the Southwest, stole this treasure from us in order to pursue and promote their crackpot ideology of growth, profit, and power—growth for the sake of power, power for the sake of growth.*

Speaking toward the future, Abbey offered this advice: "Oppose. Oppose the destruction of our homeland by these alien forces from Houston, Tokyo, Manhattan, Washington, D.C., and the Pentagon. And if opposition is not enough, we must resist. And if resistance is not enough, then subvert."

Hardly had he finished speaking when Park Service police and Coconino County sheriff's deputies arrived on the scene. While they questioned Howie Wolke and me, and tried to disperse the illegal assembly, outlaw country singer Johnny Sagebrush led the demonstrators in song for another twenty minutes.

The Glen Canyon Dam caper brought Earth First! an unexpected amount of media attention. Membership quickly spiraled to more than a thousand, with members from Maine to Hawaii. Even the government became interested. According to reports from friendly park rangers, the FBI dusted the entire Glen Canyon Dam crack for fingerprints!

34   When a few of us kicked off Earth First!, we sensed a growing environmental radicalism in the country, but we did not expect the response we received. Maybe Earth First! is in the right place at the right time.

35   The cynical may smirk. "But what can you really accomplish? How can you fight Exxon, Coors, the World Bank, Japan, and the other great corporate giants of the Earth? How, indeed, can you fight the dominant dogmas of Western civilization?"

36   Perhaps it *is* a hopeless quest. But one who loves Earth can do no less. Maybe a species will be saved or a forest will go uncut or a dam will be torn down. Maybe not. A monkeywrench thrown into the gears of the machine may not stop it. But it might delay it, make it cost more. And it feels good to put it there.

✦ ✦ ✦

✦ Framing the Context

1. When Foreman published *Confessions* in 1992, he had been deeply involved as an environmentalist for over twenty years. How does that experience shape his relationship to his readers?

2. What assumptions does Foreman make about his readers that are indicated by the information he presents in the first four paragraphs?

✦ Point of View

3. The title of Foreman's book forecasts his use of a subjective point of view. Foreman chooses to use both the singular, "I," and plural, "We," to express that point of view. How will his use of both pronoun forms affect his relationship to the readers?

4. During the course of his confession, Foreman changes his group affiliation several times. How does this change in membership affect his use of the pronoun "we"?

✦ Shape of Ideas

5. How does the title of Foreman's book project the structure his readers might expect?

6. How does the structure Foreman chooses to use connect his readers to his purpose?

✦ *Choosing Voice*

7. In what way does the formality level of Foreman's writing voice complement his subjective point of view?

8. Foreman is a self-proclaimed militant environmentalist. Identify how the language features he uses convey that tone of voice. Diversify your examples using the following features: diction, italics, punctuation, sentence structure, figurative language.

✦ *Credibility*

9. How does Foreman establish the credibility needed to write from a subjective point of view?

10. Foreman uses quotes from author and environmental activist Edward Abbey. How do those quotes contribute to Foreman's ethos?

Life in a Tree

Kate Santich

✦ ✦ ✦

Is there a particular stage in a person's life when he or she develops a sense of environmental ethics? For Julia Hill this development began recently at the age of twenty-three. Now, after two years of protesting, the young eco-warrior finds herself literally up a tree. Kate Santich, writer for Florida *magazine, a Sunday supplement of the* Orlando Sentinel, *presents Julia Hill's quest for environmental protection in her article published April 18, 1999.*

1   The tree is owned by a logging company, which has painted a slash across the trunk, marking it for "harvest."

2   The woman is cold and damp and worries that her leg muscles may be shriveling after 15 months without walking. Her only exercise is to clamber barefoot about the limbs, 100 feet or more above terra firma.

3   Julia "Butterfly" Hill was 23 years old when she first scaled the redwood, in December 1997, in an effort to save it from being cut down. Now she is 25.

4   "The [logging] company posted an eviction notice a few months ago on the trunk," she says, laughing at the absurdity of the move. "[But] I gave my word to this tree, the forest, and to all the people that my feet would not touch the ground until I had done everything in my power to make the world aware of this problem and to stop the destruction."

5   The destruction, in this case, is the logging of old-growth forests, an international problem that threatens trees from the Amazon to Siberia. The United States, by one estimate, has already lost 96 percent of such forests, victims of man's voracious appetite for lumber, paper and profit.

6   Hill's specimen, a tree she calls "Luna" because activists spotted it during a full moon, is a 200-foot-tall vestige of the virgin forests that once blanketed much of the northern Pacific coast.

7   It is also the current staging ground for interviews with *Time, Mother Jones,* CNN, German television and newspapers from Los An-

geles to New York. From her loft, Hill, who makes an eloquent spokeswoman, spends her days conducting interviews, lobbying by phone, writing poetry and letters and reading by candlelight. In addition to a solar-powered cell phone, she has a pager, sleeping bag, hand-cranked radio and single-burner camp stove for cooking her vegan meals and heating water for sponge baths. She has a bucket for her toilet.

Every couple of days, her support crew hikes in supplies, which   8
Hill pulls up through the branches with a haul line.

She has endured heavy El Nino rains, 40-mph winds, several   9
snowstorms and near-freezing temperatures. And in the early days, she says, Pacific Lumber Company tried to get her down by sounding air horns, shining floodlights, even buzzing the tree with a logging helicopter.

The company denies the harassment but does say it posted guards   10
at the base of the tree for a week, trying to cut off supplies. Guards gave up, spokeswoman Mary Bullwinkel says, when they were outnumbered by activists.

Now, the two sides are at a standoff. Hill wants a promise that   11
Luna will be spared; Pacific Lumber won't make one.

The company, which cut down many of the redwoods sur-   12
rounding Luna, says it has finished its logging in the area and may not go back in. But it won't negotiate because Hill, like other tree-sitting eco-warriors before her, is trespassing, Bullwinkel says.

"It's unfortunate that she has broken the law to get her message   13
across," the company spokeswoman says. "I don't think it sets a good example for young people."

Hill finds the comment ironic. Shortly after she set up residence   14
in Luna, the California Department of Forestry revoked Pacific Lumber Company's logging license, citing 100 violations of state rules. The company, owned by Texas junkbond wizard Charles Hurwitz, continues to operate under a conditional permit.

It is also being sued by the residents of tiny Stafford, Calif., who   15
say clear-cutting on a nearby slope prompted a mudslide that damaged or destroyed 10 homes in late 1996. The company blames El Nino.

"Climbing a tree," Hill says, "pales in comparison."   16

The daughter of an evangelist, Hill used to work tending bar in   17
Arkansas. One night, the compact car she was driving was rear-ended by a drunk driver. Her head slammed into the steering wheel,

and she spent months afterward in therapy to recapture short-term memory, speech and motor skills. It made her reevaluate her life.

18　　　She took off on what she intended to be a trip around the world. But on her first stop, among a grove of ancient redwoods, she fell to her knees in tears, humbled by the majesty of the cathedral around her.

19　　　"I had no notion that it would go on this long," she says on this bitterly cold March afternoon. "It began simply as a drive in the depth of my being to protect the trees."

20　　　Of course, she knows that one tree is not enough, that her gesture is largely symbolic. She knows that the nature of corporations is to turn a profit and that, for change to come, consumers must educate themselves. We must stop buying lumber that comes from old-growth forests and look for labels that certify sustainable-forestry practices. There are alternatives.

21　　　"Yes, this is only one tree in the forest," she says. "One, 1,000-year-old, 200-foot-tall, 15-foot-wide tree that is marked to become somebody's deck and siding."

✦ ✦ ✦

✦ Framing the Context

1. Santich writes about a Northern California environmental issue to a Central Florida audience. What must she assume about her readers' relationship to the subject to select it for her article?

2. Santich writes regularly for the local audience who read the *Orlando Sentinel* and the Sunday *Florida Magazine*. How would you characterize the relationship she has with her readers?

✦ Point of View

3. What point of view does Santich use and what angle does it give the readers on the subject?

4. How does that point of view affect the relationship between the writer and the reader?

✦ Shape of Ideas

5. Santich's article appears under the column heading "That's News to Us." How does this column heading factor into Santich's purpose for the article?

6. Describe how Santich structures her ideas to achieve her purpose.

+ *Choosing Voice*

   7. How does the level of formality Santich uses in her writing voice complement the Sunday magazine reader's purpose for reading?

   8. Identify four diction choices Santich uses to convey her attitude toward Julia Hill's protest.

+ *Credibility*

   9. Santich includes both direct and indirect quotes in her article. What are the sources of these quotes and how do they help to construct Santich's credibility?

   10. Santich begins her article with an on-site scene. How does that scene contribute to defining her ethos for the readers?

Gone Back into the Earth

Barry Lopez

✦ ✦ ✦

How do we make enduring connections to the environment? How do those connections inform our lives and how we live them? Barry Lopez, whose nature writing has earned him the John Burroughs Medal for Of Wolves and Men *(1978) and the American Book Award for* Arctic Dreams *(1986), travels down the Colorado River to Inner Gorge to answer those questions in this essay from* Crossing Open Ground *(1988).*

1   I am up to my waist in a basin of cool, acid-clear water, at the head of a box canyon some 600 feet above the Colorado River. I place my outstretched hands flat against a terminal wall of dark limestone which rises more than a hundred feet above me, and down which a sheet of water falls—the thin creek in whose pooled waters I now stand. The water splits at my fingertips into wild threads; higher up, a warm canyon wind lifts water off the limestone in a fine spray; these droplets intercept and shatter sunlight. Down, down another four waterfalls and fern-shrouded pools below, the water spills into an eddy of the Colorado River, in the shadow of a huge boulder. Our boat is tied there.

2   This lush crease in the surface of the earth is a cleft in the precipitous desert walls of Arizona's Grand Canyon. Its smooth outcrops of purple-tinged travertine stone, its heavy air rolled in the languid perfume of columbine, struck by the sharp notes of a water ouzel, the trill of a disturbed black phoebe—all this has a name: Elves Chasm.

3   A few feet to my right, a preacher from Maryland is staring straight up at a blue sky, straining to see what flowers those are that nod at the top of the falls. To my left a freelance automobile mechanic from Colorado sits with an impish smile by helleborine orchids. Behind, another man, a builder and sometime record producer from New York, who comes as often as he can to camp and hike in the Southwest, stands immobile at the pool's edge.

4   Sprawled shirtless on a rock is our boatman. He has led twelve or fifteen of us on the climb up from the river. The Colorado en-

trances him. He has a well-honed sense of the ridiculous, brought on, one believes, by so much time in the extreme remove of this canyon.

In our descent we meet others in our group who stopped climbing at one of the lower pools. At the second to the last waterfall, a young woman with short hair and dazzling blue eyes walks with me back into the canyon's narrowing V. We wade into a still pool, swim a few strokes to its head, climb over a boulder, swim across a second pool and then stand together, giddy, in the press of limestone, beneath the deafening cascade—filled with euphoria.

One at a time we bolt and glide, fishlike, back across the pool, grounding in fine white gravel. We wade the second pool and continue our descent, stopping to marvel at the strategy of a barrel cactus and at the pale shading of color in the ledges to which we cling. We share few words. We know hardly anything of each other. We share the country.

The group of us who have made this morning climb are in the middle of a ten-day trip down the Colorado River. Each day we are upended, if not by some element of the landscape itself then by what the landscape does, visibly, to each of us. It has snapped us like fresh-laundered sheets.

After lunch, we reboard three large rubber rafts and enter the Colorado's quick, high flow. The river has not been this high or fast since Glen Canyon Dam—135 miles above Elves Chasm, 17 miles above our starting point at Lee's Ferry—was closed in 1963. Jumping out ahead of us, with its single oarsman and three passengers, is our fourth craft, a twelve-foot rubber boat, like a water strider with a steel frame. In Sockdolager Rapid the day before, one of its welds burst and the steel pieces were bent apart. (Sockdolager: a nineteenth-century colloquialism for knockout punch.)

Such groups as ours, the members all but unknown to each other on the first day, almost always grow close, solicitous of each other, during their time together. They develop a humor that informs similar journeys everywhere, a humor founded in tomfoolery, in punning, in a continuous parody of the life-in-civilization all have so recently (and gleefully) left. Such humor depends on context, on an accretion of small, shared events; it seems silly to those who are not there. It is not, of course. Any more than that moment of fumbling awe one feels on seeing the Brahma schist at the dead bottom of the canyon's Inner Gorge. Your fingertips graze the 1.9-billion-year-old stone as the boat drifts slowly past.

10   With the loss of self-consciousness, the landscape opens.

11   There are forty-one of us, counting a crew of six. An actor from Florida, now living in Los Angeles. A medical student and his wife. A supervisor from Virginia's Department of Motor Vehicles. A health-store owner from Chicago. An editor from New York and his young son.

12   That kind of diversity seems normal in groups that seek such vacations—to trek in the Himalaya, to dive in the Sea of Cortez, to go birding in the Arctic. We are together for two reasons: to run the Colorado River, and to participate with jazz musician Paul Winter, who initiated the trip, in a music workshop.

13   Winter is an innovator and a listener. He had thought for years about coming to the Grand Canyon, about creating music here in response to this particular landscape—collared lizards and prickly pear cactus, Anasazi Indian ruins and stifling heat. But most especially he wanted music evoked by the river and the walls that flew up from its banks—Coconino sandstone on top of Hermit shale on top of the Supai formations, stone exposed to sunlight, a bloom of photons that lifted colors—saffron and ochre, apricot, madder orange, pearl and gray green, copper reds, umber and terra-cotta browns—and left them floating in the air.

14   Winter was searching for a reintegration of music, landscape and people. For resonance. Three or four times during the trip he would find it for sustained periods: drifting on a quiet stretch of water below Bass Rapids with oboist Nancy Rumbel and cellist David Darling; in a natural amphitheater high in the Muav limestone of Matkatameba Canyon; on the night of a full June moon with euphonium player Larry Roark in Blacktail Canyon.

15   Winter's energy and passion, and the strains of solo and ensemble music, were sewn into the trip like prevailing winds, like the canyon wren's clear, whistled, descending notes, his glissando—seemingly present, close by or at a distance, whenever someone stopped to listen.

16   But we came and went, too, like the swallows and swifts that flicked over the water ahead of the boats, intent on private thoughts.

17   On the second day of the trip we stopped at Redwall Cavern, an undercut recess that spans a beach of fine sand, perhaps 500 feet wide by 150 feet deep. Winter intends to record here, but the sand

absorbs too much sound. Unfazed, the others toss a Frisbee, practice Tai-chi, jog, meditate, play recorders, and read novels.

No other animal but the human would bring to bear so many activities, from so many different cultures and levels of society, with so much energy, so suddenly in a new place. And no other animal, the individuals so entirely unknown to each other, would chance together something so unknown as this river journey. In this frenetic activity and difference seems a suggestion of human evolution and genuine adventure. We are not the first down this river, but in the slooshing of human hands at the water's edge, the swanlike notes of an oboe, the occasional hugs among those most afraid of the rapids, there *is* exploration. 18

Each day we see or hear something that astounds us. The thousand-year-old remains of an Anasazi footbridge, hanging in twilight shadow high in the canyon wall above Harding Rapid. Deer Creek Falls, where we stand knee-deep in turquoise water encircled by a rainbow. Havasu Canyon, wild with grapevines, cottonwoods and velvet ash, speckled dace and mule deer, wild grasses and crimson monkey flowers. Each evening we enjoy a vespers: cicadas and crickets, mourning doves, vermilion flycatchers. And the wind, for which chimes are hung in a salt cedar. These notes leap above the splash and rattle, the grinding of water and the roar of rapids. 19

The narrow, damp, hidden worlds of the side canyons, with their scattered shards of Indian pottery and ghost imprints of 400-million-year-old nautiloids, open onto the larger world of the Colorado River itself, but nothing conveys to us how far into the earth's surface we have come. Occasionally we glimpse the South Rim, four or five thousand feet above. From the rims the canyon seems oceanic; at the surface of the river the feeling is intimate. To someone up there with binoculars we seem utterly remote down here. It is this known dimension of distance and time and the perplexing question posed by the canyon itself—What is consequential? (in one's life, in the life of human beings, in the life of a planet)—that reverberate constantly, and make the human inclination to judge (another person, another kind of thought) seem so eerie. 20

Two kinds of time pass here: sitting at the edge of a sun-warmed pool watching blue dragonflies and black tadpoles. And the rapids: down the glassy-smooth tongue into a yawing trench, climb a ten-foot wall of standing water and fall into boiling, ferocious hydraulics, sucking whirlpools, drowned voices, stopped hearts. Rapids can fold 21 and shatter boats and take lives if the boatman enters at the wrong point or at the wrong angle.

22   Some rapids, like one called Hermit, seem more dangerous than they are and give us great roller-coaster rides. Others—Hance, Crystal, Upset—seem less spectacular, but are technically difficult. At Crystal, our boat screeches and twists against its frame. Its nose crumples like cardboard in the trough; our boatman makes the critical move to the right with split-second timing and we are over a standing wave and into the haystacks of white water, safely into the tail waves. The boatman's eyes cease to blaze.

23   The first few rapids—Badger Creek and Soap Creek—do not overwhelm us. When we hit the Inner Gorge—Granite Falls, Unkar Rapid, Horn Creek Rapid—some grip the boat, rigid and silent. (On the ninth day, when we are about to run perhaps the most formidable rapid, Lava Falls, the one among us who has had the greatest fear is calm, almost serene. In the last days, it is hard to overestimate what the river and the music and the unvoiced concern for each other have washed out.)

24   There are threats to this separate world of the Inner Gorge. Down inside it one struggles to maintain a sense of what they are, how they impinge.

25   In 1963, Glen Canyon Dam cut off the canyon's natural flow of water. Spring runoffs of more than two hundred thousand cubic feet per second ceased to roar through the gorge, clearing the main channel of rock and stones washed down from the side canyons. Fed now from the bottom of Lake Powell backed up behind the dam, the river is no longer a warm, silt-laden habitat for Colorado squawfish, razorback sucker and several kinds of chub, but a cold, clear habitat for trout. With no annual scouring and a subsequent deposition of fresh sand, the beaches show the evidence of continuous human use: they are eroding. The postflood eddies where squawfish bred have disappeared. Tamarisk (salt cedar) and camel thorn, both exotic plants formerly washed out with the spring floods, have gained an apparently permanent foothold. At the old high-water mark, catclaw acacia, mesquite and Apache plume are no longer watered and are dying out.

26   On the rim, far removed above, such evidence of human tampering seems, and perhaps is, pernicious. From the river, another change is more wrenching. It floods the system with a kind of panic

that in other animals induces nausea and the sudden evacuation of the bowels: it is the descent of helicopters. Their sudden arrival in the canyon evokes not jeers but staring. The violence is brutal, an intrusion as criminal and as random as rape. When the helicopter departs, its rotor-wind walloping against the stone walls, I want to wash the sound off my skin.

The canyon finally absorbs the intrusion. I focus quietly each day on the stone, the breathing of time locked up here, back to the Proterozoic, before there were seashells. Look up to wisps of high cirrus overhead, the hint of a mare's tail sky. Close my eyes: tappet of water against the boat, sound of an Anasazi's six-hole flute. And I watch the bank for beaver tracks, for any movement.   27

The canyon seems like a grandfather.   28

One evening, Winter and perhaps half the group carry instruments and recording gear back into Blacktail Canyon to a spot sound engineer Mickey Houlihan says is good for recording.   29

Winter likes to quote from Thoreau: "The woods would be very silent if no birds sang except those that sing best." The remark seems not only to underscore the ephemeral nature of human evolution but the necessity in evaluating any phenomenon—a canyon, a life, a song—of providing for change.   30

After several improvisations dominated by a cappella voice and percussion, Winter asks Larry Roark to try something on the euphonium; he and Rumbel and Darling will then come up around him. Roark is silent. Moonlight glows on the canyon's lips. There is the sound of gurgling water. After a word of encouragement, feeling shrouded in anonymous darkness like the rest of us, Larry puts his mouth to the horn.   31

For a while he is alone. God knows what visions of waterfalls or wrens, of boats in the rapids, of Bach or Mozart, are in his head, in his fingers, to send forth notes. The whine of the soprano sax finds him. And the flutter of the oboe. And the rumbling of the choral cello. The exchange lasts perhaps twenty minutes. Furious and sweet, anxious, rolling, delicate and raw. The last six or eight hanging notes are Larry's. Then there is a long silence. Winter finally says, "My God."   32

I feel, sitting in the wet dark in bathing suit and sneakers and T-shirt, that my fingers have brushed one of life's deep, coursing threads. Like so much else in the canyon, it is left alone. Speak, even notice it, and it would disappear.   33

34   I had come to the canyon with expectations. I had wanted to see snowy egrets flying against the black schist at dusk; I saw blue-winged teal against the deep green waters at dawn. I had wanted to hear thunder rolling in the thousand-foot depths; I heard Winter's soprano sax resonating in Matkatameba Canyon, with the guttural caws of four ravens which circled above him. I had wanted to watch rattlesnakes; I saw in an abandoned copper mine, in the beam of my flashlight, a wall of copper sulphate that looked like a wall of turquoise. I rose each morning at dawn and washed in the cold river. I went to sleep each night listening to the cicadas, the pencil-ticking sound of some other insect, the soughing of river waves in tamarisk roots, and watching bats plunge and turn, looking like leaves blown around against the sky. What any of us had come to see or do fell away. We found ourselves at each turn with what we had not imagined.

35   The last evening it rained. We had left the canyon and been carried far out onto Lake Mead by the river's current. But we stood staring backward, at the point where the canyon had so obviously and abruptly ended.

36   A thought that stayed with me was that I had entered a private place in the earth. I had seen exposed nearly its oldest part. I had lost my sense of urgency, rekindled a sense of what people were, clambering to gain access to high waterfalls where we washed our hair together; and a sense of our endless struggle as a species to understand time and to estimate the consequences of our acts.

37   It rained the last evening. But before it did, Nancy Rumbel moved to the highest point on Scorpion Island in Lake Mead and played her oboe before a storm we could see hanging over Nevada. Sterling Smyth, who would return to programming computers in twenty-four hours, created a twelve-string imitation of the canyon wren, a long guitar solo. David Darling, revealed suddenly stark, again and then again, against a white-lightning sky, bowed furious homage to the now overhanging cumulonimbus.

38   In the morning we touched the far shore of Lake Mead, boarded a bus and headed for the Las Vegas airport. We were still wrapped in the journey, as though it were a Navajo blanket. We departed on various planes and arrived home in various cities and towns and at some point the world entered again and the hardest thing, the translation of what we had touched, began.

I sat in the airport in San Francisco, waiting for a connecting [39] flight to Oregon, dwelling on one image. At the mouth of Nankoweap Canyon, the river makes a broad turn, and it is possible to see high in the orange rock what seem to be four small windows. They are entrances to granaries, built by the Anasazi who dwelled in the canyon a thousand years ago. This was provision against famine, to ensure the people would survive.

I do not know, really, how we will survive without places like the [40] Inner Gorge of the Grand Canyon to visit. Once in a lifetime, even, is enough. To feel the stripping down, an ebb of the press of conventional time, a radical change of proportion, an unspoken respect for others that elicits keen emotional pleasure, a quick, intimate pounding of the heart.

Some parts of the trip will emerge one day on an album. Others [41] will be found in a gesture of friendship to some stranger in an airport, in a letter of outrage to a planner of dams, in a note of gratitude to nameless faces in the Park Service, in wondering at the relatives of the ubiquitous wren, in the belief, passed on in whatever fashion—a photograph, a chord, a sketch—that nature can heal.

The living of life, any life, involves great and private pain, much [42] of which we share with no one. In such places as the Inner Gorge the pain trails away from us. It is not so quiet there or so removed that you can hear yourself think, that you would even wish to; that comes later. You can hear your heart beat. That comes first.

✦ ✦ ✦

✦ Framing the Context

1. Lopez has earned a reputation for his literary writing about the environment. What can he assume his readers' relationship to the subject is?

2. How does Lopez establish his relationship to the subject in the opening paragraphs?

✦ Point of View

3. Readers expect writers to use a subjective point of view when they present a personal experience, but the writer chooses just how often he or she will be visible. What decision does Lopez make about his visibility?

4. How does Lopez's level of visibility affect his relationship with his readers?

✦ *Shape of Ideas*

5. There are several features involved in Lopez's trip on the Colorado River that he can use to structure his narrative: locations, days, episodes, people—just to name a few. What focus and strategy does Lopez use for structuring his narrative?

6. How does that structure bring the readers closer to his purpose?

✦ *Choosing Voice*

7. Identify six examples of figurative language that establish Lopez's literary voice.

8. Explain how Lopez's use of parallel structure in paragraph 34 affects his writing voice and the dialogue with his readers.

✦ *Credibility*

9. Lopez relies on his own observations and personal knowledge as his sources for this narrative. Explain how those sources establish credibility with his intended readers?

10. Select three comments Lopez makes about human nature that convey his ethos.

The Dusky Seaside Sparrow

Brian Burke

✦ ✦ ✦

The consequence of ethical environmental dilemmas is often extinction. Brian Burke, a surfing enthusiast and liberal arts major at the University of Central Florida, discovered that sad result during his canoeing experiences at the Merritt Island National Wildlife Refuge. In the following article he wrote for River *magazine, a publication devoted to river environments and exploration, Burke re-creates that discovery.*

Paddling the Canaveral National Seashore proves to be an en- 1
riching experience when looking for manatees, dolphins, and especially birds. But there is one species of bird you won't find in this area
that once was very abundant. In 1990, the Dusky Seaside Sparrow
was declared extinct from trial-and-error methods of mosquito control. It couldn't eat, it couldn't breed, therefore it couldn't exist.

Haulover Canal is what first brought me out to the Merritt Is- 2
land National Wildlife Refuge on the east coast of Florida. I heard
from acquaintances about the good fishing there, and during man-
atee season, that was the place to go in a canoe. There were a few
places to do some backcountry camping in the Refuge as well, so
after a day of paddling the Indian River and Mosquito Lagoon
(joined by Haulover), I headed to the Information Center. Instead of
uncovering some of the ranger's secret spots, I discovered the striking fact of the Dusky (*Ammospiza nigrescens*).

The people of Titusville, Florida, used to wake up to the chirp of 3
a songbird, the Dusky Seaside Sparrow. A high-pitched buzz follows
two or three faint notes; the song is especially heard during their
nesting season. In the early mornings as well as at dusk, the Dusky
Seaside Sparrow would sing its song every six or seven seconds.

Resembling the many other subspecies of seaside sparrow, the 4
Dusky is a small, stout, little bird, keeping low to the ground,
whizzing here and there, stopping to perch on tall blades of grass to
let out a song. The Dusky, by its markings, was easy to recognize and
distinguish from other sparrows by its dark-brown-to-black stripes

and shades along its back and wings. Taxonomists reported an astounding difference in genetic structure putting the Dusky Seaside Sparrow into a debatable species of its own.

5   Very picky about its surroundings, this nonmigratory bird chose to live in the strongly salted marshes that encompass the area. It was so picky, in fact, that it only lived within an area a couple of hundred square miles, Titusville almost marking the center of its habitat. SR 46, SR 520, the St. Johns River, and the coastline draw the boundary at its entirety; the marshes bordering the St. Johns River provided the nesting ground where they built their nests a couple of inches from the water. The rest of its range provided front-row seats to witness the completion of NASA's Cape Kennedy.

6   In 1945, Central Florida was the first area to use DDT to control various insects on farms. Before air conditioning and Skin So Soft were popular methods in warding off mosquitoes, use of DDT was put into action by the newly formed Titusville Mosquito Control District. As a result, the Dusky lost its food source, mainly insects and grubs, to the poison. Egg shells were weakened by this chemical as well. During the forties, the population plummeted from two thousand breeding pairs to six hundred, which was only the beginning of its decline.

7   In the late fifties, the race for space was on. Not only were the residents of Titusville encouraging and contributing to our reaching for the stars, they were still swatting mosquitoes by the handfuls. Freshwater flooding was another method that the Mosquito Control District used in preventing mosquito breeding but in doing so, deprived the Dusky of its cherished salt marsh. Fresh water brought more trouble as well. The pig frog and the boat-tailed grackle that inhabit freshwater areas take Dusky hatchlings. Adding to the habitat destruction, pastureland spread along the St. Johns during this time, leaving the Dusky nowhere to nest, nothing to eat, and no possibility of survival.

8   The window is closing in Florida for comfortable paddling. The U.S. Fish and Wildlife Service use mosquito netting to cover every part of their body except their hands. You might catch me out there dressed in the same garb. I just can't get enough of the area: the uninhabited islands, the many stingrays, enough oysters and clams to feed a tribe, many different species of birds. This May I look forward to sitting on the seawall, swatting mosquitoes, watching the space

shuttle launch, wishing the whole time I had the company of one creature in particular, the Dusky Seaside Sparrow.

✦ ✦ ✦

✦ Framing the Context

1. Burke uses the opening paragraph to establish his relationship to the subject. Describe that relationship.

2. Burke designed his article for the readers of *River* magazine, a publication devoted to river environments and exploration. In what ways is Burke's relationship to the subject likely to complement his readers' attitude toward the subject?

✦ Point of View

3. What point of view does Burke choose to use to establish a relationship with his readers?

4. How does the angle that point of view creates complement the readers' purpose for reading?

✦ Shape of Ideas

5. *River* magazine articles include a photo montage and a fact sheet on each featured river area. How does the structure Burke uses complement this publication design?

6. How does that structure lead the reader to Burke's purpose?

✦ Choosing Voice

7. How does the formality level of Burke's writing voice complement his point of view?

8. At the end of paragraphs 1 and 7, Burke uses similar sentence structure techniques. Describe the technique he uses and explain the effect it has on his voice.

✦ Credibility

9. How does Burke establish credibility through his personal experience?

10. Identify three sentences that convey Burke's ethos.

✦ Suggestions for Writing about Environmental Ethics

1. Both Bartkevicius and Lopez write about defining experiences with the environment, a time when the connection was so strong that they understood "place" as a living organism that needs care and protection. Reflect on your connections to different places, and write an essay on the connection you most value.

2. The media often enlist our help to save an endangered species. Research one of those species and what needs to be done to protect it. Then write a proposal persuading others to join you in efforts to save that species.

3. Does environmental inequity exist in your city or one nearby? Research what impact industry has on the various neighborhoods in the location you choose. Determine what ethics are in practice and write an editorial on the status of environmental equity in that location.

4. Can one person make a difference? Who do you know whose work for the environment you admire—some local, someone famous? Search for a person whose environmental ethics you deem worthy of emulating, and write a profile of that person to inspire others.

5. Where do we learn environmental ethics? Should it be a required course of study? Write a documented argument advocating the inclusion of environmental ethics in the school curriculum.

6. Recycling appears to be a success in this country: recycling centers are plentiful; separate receptacles in public areas are widespread; most cities provide separate trash containers for glass, cans, plastic jugs, and newspapers or schedule separate pick-up days. Is that effort sufficient or do we need to go further, as Kaufman suggests? Write a status report on this country's recycling program and propose in what direction we need to focus our efforts.

7. How would you define your environmental ethics? Make an inventory of your involvement in activities, projects, readings, and organization memberships related to working for the environment. From that list construct a definition of your environmental ethics.

8. Can environmental ethics be legislated by the government? Several of the writers in this chapter would answer "No." The government can pass laws, but how well are those laws enforced? Choose a particular environmental problem that concerns you, and research the laws and enforcement of the laws related to that problem. Write a documented research essay on your findings.

Chapter 12

✦ ✦ ✦ ✦ ✦ ✦ ✦ ✦ ✦ ✦ ✦

Speculating on
the New Century

The push and pull of change has a way of dividing people: some embrace it with great enthusiasm, waking each day with their glass half-full wanting to add more to it; others shake their heads, watching the contents of their half-empty glass evaporate a little more with each changing movement. Gains and losses are characteristic of all change, but the speed at which change takes place is a major factor in adjusting to the impact. The ability to consult with a physician without making an appointment can save a life, but if communicating virtually becomes the dominant form of our relationships, what happens to us as a society?

The readings in this chapter conjure both fears and promises in their crystal balls. Can everyone become a millionaire via the Internet? Will my education prepare me to adapt to change professionally? Will my children ever read a book? How will I use this individual power to control information? Will we finally dissolve the boundaries of geography, race, language, and gender? The writers of the selections that follow speculate on these possibilities, and the suggestions for writing at the end of the chapter give you an opportunity to develop your own ideas about the new century.

As you read these speculations, think carefully about the assumptions the writers make and how they use language, point of view, structure, and sources to convince readers. The questions following the readings will guide you in analyzing the writers' choices.

Will We Be One Nation, Indivisible?

Bruce Agnew

✦ ✦ ✦

Racial tensions have made a profound mark on the twentieth century. Are those tensions likely to ease in the next century? In this article from the Fall 1999 Scientific American *special issue, "Your Bionic Future," author Bruce Agnew, a freelance journalist based in Bethesda, MD, who writes about science, politics, and economics, explores how changing demographics and attitudes will influence the answer to that question. Agnew has written for UPI in various metropolitan areas, including Washington, D.C., where he covered the 1963 civil rights March on Washington for the* New York Post, Business Week, *and served as news editor of* The Journal of NIH Research, *covering biomedical research.*

1　　Nearly 100 years ago the African-American scholar W. E. B. Du Bois predicted that the challenge of the 20th century would be "the problem of the color line." Echoing Du Bois, historian John Hope Franklin, who headed the advisory board of President Bill Clinton's 1997–98 Initiative on Race, wrote recently, "I venture to state categorically that the problem of the 21st century will be the problem of the color line."

2　　Will we solve it this time around?

3　　No, say many who have studied, worked against and lived with racism. "I would think people sitting down in 2099 will say, 'Well, how much progress have we made? And how much longer do we have to go?'" says Roger W. Wilkins, who headed the justice Department's Community Relations Service during the Lyndon B. Johnson administration and now teaches history at George Mason University. "I do not believe that we will have a racially equal society 100 years from now. Antiblack racism is too deep, and it's too entrenched."

4　　Others are more optimistic. Abigail Thernstrom, a senior fellow at the Manhattan Institute and co-author of *America in Black and White: One Nation, Indivisible,* points to growing rates of intermarriage among whites, blacks and other minority groups and predicts, "As we move toward a country increasingly made up of Tiger Woodses, I think this whole mind-set [of racial classifications] is going to crumble over time, and it's going to change public policy."

The Numbers Game

The difference between the experts is one of perspective—and emphasis—not a quarrel over facts. The facts themselves, the statistical measurements of where U.S. race relations have been and where they are headed, are both heartening and dismaying.

Since the passage of the Civil Rights Act of 1964 and the Voting Rights Act of 1965, African-American and other minority groups have made enormous strides toward equality with whites. More than 40 percent of African-Americans described themselves as "middle class" in 1996, compared with just 12 percent in 1949. About 42 percent of black householders own their own homes; more than 30 percent are suburbanites. About the same proportion of blacks and whites finish high school—nearly 90 percent—and more than 13 percent of blacks older than 25 years of age have completed college, compared with 3 percent in 1960. Nearly a quarter of black families had incomes above $50,000 a year in 1996, compared with 44 percent of white families and about 22 percent of Hispanics. Asian-American incomes exceed those of all other groups.

Harvard University historical sociologist Orlando Patterson was surely right when he wrote in *The Ordeal of Integration* that "the changes that have taken place in the United States over the past 50 years are unparalleled in the history of minority-majority relations."

But a significant proportion of African-Americans have been left behind. More than a quarter of black families live below the poverty line. Blacks are arrested at a rate more than twice their proportion in the population. And about 70 percent of African-American babies were born out of wedlock in 1996 (23 percent to teenage mothers), compared with 26 percent of white babies born out of wedlock. "A social pattern with devastating economic consequences has become the norm in the black community, while it is still the deviant pattern among whites," write Thernstrom and her co-author (and husband), Harvard history professor Stephan Thernstrom, in *America in Black and White*.

So Harvard law professor Lani Guinier—whose 1993 nomination as assistant attorney general for civil rights was blocked by conservative opposition—is right when she calls the landmark civil-

5

6

7

8

9

rights laws of the 1960s "a significant step, [but] a baby step." Guinier was branded a "quota queen" in 1993 because of law review publications advocating novel voting procedures, such as so-called cumulative voting, to enhance minorities' electoral clout. Today she says the structures of segregation and voting-rights denial that were torn down in the 1960s "both camouflaged and reinforced tremendous inequities in the distribution of resources, and if we're going to talk about a just society, I think we have a lot of work to do."

10   Guinier and Patterson both consider themselves optimists, however. "If the American people were aware that there are other policy choices, I think that we could create a national will to change," Guinier says.

11   At least one dramatic change already seems inevitable: sometime in the late 21st century, white Americans will no longer be a majority. Currently about 72 percent of the population is white, 12 percent non-Hispanic black, 11 percent Hispanic, 4 percent Asian/Pacific Islander and 0.7 percent American Indian, Eskimo and Aleut. But by the year 2050, the U.S. Census Bureau projects that whites will account for only 52.8 percent of the population, non-Hispanic blacks 13.6 percent, Hispanics 24.5 percent, Asian/Pacific Islanders 8.2 percent and American Indian, Eskimo and Aleut 0.9 percent. "I think that means that an awful lot of white people will have to make very serious identity adjustments," Wilkins says.

12   In fact, many Americans are already making surprisingly serious identity and attitude adjustments. Interracial marriage, outlawed in some states as recently as the 1960s, is growing. "We already have half of all Asians marrying non-Asians and half of all Hispanics [marrying outside their ethnic group] by the third generation," Abigail Thernstrom notes. "The black-white intermarriage rate is higher than the Jewish-gentile rate was in 1940. It won't go up at the same rate, but nevertheless, it's going up."

13   The numbers are still tiny, but the trend is clear. In 1980 there were just 167,000 married couples in the U.S. in which one partner was white and the other was black. By 1997 that figure had nearly doubled, to 311,000. That is equal to only 0.7 percent of married couples in which both partners are white, but it is a more significant 8.4 percent of married couples in which both partners are black. And new marriages are even more biracial: 12.1 percent of new marriages by African-Americans in 1993 were to partners who were members of other races.

"It's amazing how much change we've made," observes Boston   14
University sociologist Alan Wolfe, author of *One Nation, After All*. "In
1967 the Supreme Court ruled Virginia's miscegenation law uncon-
stitutional. If that law were still on the books, Clarence Thomas
would be in jail rather than on the Supreme Court."

Which Box Do I Check?

The most certain, though possibly least significant, consequence of   15
growing intermarriage is that it will play havoc with Census Bureau
racial breakdowns. An increasing number of multiracial Americans—such as, most prominently, golf star Tiger Woods—have
balked at the racial classification boxes on survey and other government and business forms. The Clinton administration has now decided that in the year 2000 census, people will be allowed to check
more than one racial box. Government racial statistics may never be
the same—and as the numbers become blurred, the now heated
controversies over affirmative action and other race-centered issues
may lose some of their force.

But intermarriage and the increasing ease of interracial dating   16
among young people are a signal of a far deeper change in U.S. society. One of the biggest reasons for optimism about the 21st century, according to American Enterprise Institute fellow Dinesh
D'Souza, author of *The End of Racism,* is "the very healthy attitude of
young people, who are in general much less haunted by the specter
of old-fashioned racism."

Interracial marriages (and, to a lesser degree, dating) do not af-   17
fect just the two people involved. Such relationships cannot help but
have a ripple effect on each partner's family and circle of friends.
Stephan Thernstrom notes, "My cousin is married to a black woman,
and that certainly had an enlightening impact on my aunts and my
mother and father and my uncle. It had many reverberations
throughout the whole extended family."

Of course, intermarriage and interracial dating are only an indi-   18
rect signal of narrowing economic and social differences. Public
opinion polls tell the same story, however. In particular, an unpublished poll by the Gallup Organization last year suggests that
African-Americans' lives have improved since midcentury. Seventy-
nine percent of black respondents last year said they were satisfied
with their standard of living; only 45 percent answered that question
the same way in 1963. Eighty-four percent were satisfied with their

jobs, compared with only 61 percent of those who responded to a similar question in 1963.

19   About half of both blacks and whites polled rated race relations as "very" or "somewhat" good, and 83 percent of whites and 80 percent of blacks thought relations between the races had gotten better or at least remained the same over the past year. (The poll, updating a 1997 Gallup study, was based on telephone interviews with 2,004 adults, roughly half of whom were white and half black. Responses from the black and white subgroups could have a sampling error of plus or minus 4 percentage points.)

20   Although both blacks and whites appeared to believe race relations are improving, the Gallup poll revealed a dramatic gap in their perception of today's reality: whites think race relations are better than blacks do. For example:

- Forty-three percent of blacks, but 76 percent of whites, thought blacks and whites are treated about the same in their communities. Fifty percent of blacks, but only 19 percent of whites, thought blacks are treated "not very well" or "badly."
- Forty-two percent of blacks, but only 9 percent of whites, thought blacks are treated less fairly on the job. Fifty percent of blacks, but 83 percent of whites, thought blacks are treated "the same or better."
- Fifty-five percent of blacks, but only 29 percent of whites, thought blacks are treated less fairly by the police, such as in traffic incidents.

21   Moreover, in responses that offer some measure of daily slights and insults, 46 percent of blacks said that within the past 30 days they had been treated unfairly in a store, in the workplace, at a restaurant, bar, theater or other place of entertainment, by the police or while using public transportation. Fifty-four percent of black males reported such unfair treatment, adds Jack Ludwig, vice president and research director of Gallup's Social Audits Division.

22   Still, by most measures, the 1960s civil-rights-movement goal of all races together is closer today than ever before—with one horrific exception: urban poverty.

23   "I think it's clear that if we were ever to 'solve' the race problem, we'd have a tremendous class problem and that really the race problem is becoming a class problem," says Wolfe, whose 1998 book reported that the views and outlooks of suburban, middle-class whites and blacks are more united by class than they are divided by race.

His view is widely shared. "Urban poverty and education are at the top of the want list, the need list, of this country," Franklin declares. Rainbow/PUSH Coalition president Jesse Jackson warned in a 1997 PBS interview that "while there's a focus on the race gap, the bigger gap today is the class gap." 24

The long U.S. economic expansion of the 1990s has brought a few tentative hints of improvement. Crime rates have dropped for most of the decade. Black unemployment rates and births to teenage unwed mothers have also dipped. But the country has barely begun to scratch the surface of this problem. 25

When Gallup asked its 2,004 black and white respondents last year whether U.S. race relations would ever be solved, the answer was grim. Fifty-eight percent of blacks and 57 percent of whites said race relations "will always be a problem." 26

But 100 years is a long time, and there is no reason to think that the 21st century will not bring changes as dramatic as those of the 20th. "We have made enormous progress since 1899, when they were running my grandpa out of Mississippi," Wilkins notes. "They were going to lynch him." 27

And in 1899, Stephan Thernstrom says, "if you had asked what will be the racial future in the 20th century, people would not have used our racial categories. They would have said, 'Well, let's talk about the Jewish race and the Mediterranean race and the Nordic race,' and that way of thinking has become entirely discredited." Thernstrom believes such "utterly unscientific, 19th-century anthropological concepts [are] not likely to have sway over the American public a century hence." 28

✦ Framing the Context

1. What purposes can Agnew assume that readers have for subscribing to *Scientific American*?

2. What assumptions might Agnew make about his readers' relationship to the subject of race relations?

✦ Point of View

3. What point of view does Agnew choose to use?

4. Describe the relationship that level of visibility establishes between Agnew and his readers.

✦ *Shape of Ideas*

5. Outline Agnew's article and describe the structure he uses to present his ideas.

6. In what way does the structure Agnew uses help the readers to answer the question in the title of the article?

✦ *Choosing Voice*

7. How does the formality level of Agnew's writing voice complement his point of view?

8. What effect does paragraph 2 have on Agnew's voice and his relationship to his readers? Explain how that effect is created.

✦ *Credibility*

9. Identify the techniques (presented in Chapter 5) Agnew uses for incorporating his sources.

10. In what way does the range of sources contribute to Agnew's credibility?

Social Saturation and the Populated Self

Kenneth J. Gergen

✦ ✦ ✦

The selection that follows is a chapter excerpted from author Kenneth J. Gergen's book, The Saturated Self: Dilemmas of Identity in Contemporary Life *(1991), a text that explores the consequences of the bombardment of fragmented images from multiple sources on our understanding of who we are. Although this is a long selection, Gergen clearly divides his ideas into sections for a better understanding of the cultural changes that have produced this effect.*

Random moments from contemporary life: 1

- You find your mailbox stuffed with correspondence—advertisements for local events, catalogues from mail-order houses, political announcements, offers for special prizes, bills, and, just maybe, a letter.
- You return from a weekend away to find your answering machine overflowing with calls to be returned.
- You try to arrange a meeting with a business colleague in New York. She is attending a meeting in Caracas. When she returns next week you will be in Memphis. When all attempts to arrange a mutually convenient meeting place fail, you settle for a long-distance phone meeting in the evening.
- An old friend calls, passing through on business, and wants to meet for a drink or dinner.
- You think about planning a New Year's Eve party, but most of your good friends are away in Colorado, Mexico, or other vacation spots.
- You are away for the evening, but you program your VCR so that you won't miss a favorite program.
- You are in Montreal for a few days, and are surprised to meet a friend from back home in Atlanta.

Most of these events are commonplace in contemporary life, 2
scarcely worth comment. Yet none of them were commonplace

473

twenty years ago, and several have only entered our lives within the past five years. Such events are manifestations of a profound pattern of social change. The change is essentially one that immerses us ever more deeply in the social world, and exposes us more and more to the opinions, values, and lifestyles of others.

3   It is my central thesis that this immersion is propelling us toward a new self-consciousness: the postmodern. The emerging common-places of communication—such as those just cited—are critical to understanding the passing of both the romantic and modern views of self. What I call the *technologies of social saturation* are central to the contemporary erasure of individual self. This chapter will explore the ways in which social saturation has come to dominate everyday life. However, we shall also see that as we become increasingly conjoined with our social surroundings, we come to reflect those surroundings. There is a *populating of the self,* reflecting the infusion of partial iden-tities through social saturation. And there is the onset of a *multi-phrenic* condition, in which one begins to experience the vertigo of unlimited multiplicity. Both the populating of the self and the mul-tiphrenic condition are significant preludes to post-modern con-sciousness. To appreciate the magnitude of cultural change, and its probable intensification, attention must be directed to the emerging technologies.

The Technologies of Social Saturation

> *Communication . . . defines social reality and thus influences the organization of work . . . the curriculum of the educational system, formal and informal re-lations, and the use of "free time"—actually the basic social arrangements of living.*
>
> —Herbert I. Schiller, *Communication and Cultural Domination*

4   In the process of social saturation the numbers, varieties, and intensities of relationship increasingly crowd the days. A full appre-ciation of the magnitude of cultural change, and its probable inten-sification in future decades, requires that one focus first on the technological context. For in large measure, an array of technologi-cal innovations has led to an enormous proliferation of relationships. It is useful to survey two major phases in technological development, specifically what may be roughly called *low-tech* and *high-tech* phases.

Preliminary advice to the reader is in order. Read the following section on technological change as rapidly as possible, for an experiential immersion in the enormity of the whole.

Life in Low Tech

Perhaps the most dramatic aspect of the low-tech phase is the simultaneity of its many developments. Here we are speaking of no less than seven sweeping and overlapping developments within the century, each of which casts us further into the social world. Consider their impact on social life: [5]

1. *The railroad* was one of the first significant steps toward social saturation. The first surge in rail travel began in the mid-1800s. In 1869 it became possible for Americans to cross the continent by train.[1] Although rails are less used in the United States than other modes of transportation, most nations continue to improve their systems. Major new track lines are being laid in Russia and China. Fast rail systems have been installed in Japan, France, Italy, and Sweden, and an under-Channel system will soon link London and Paris. The number of rail passengers in Europe reached an all-time high in 1988, almost doubling the volume in 1970.[2] At the same time, urban mass transit—including elevated and underground rail—moves a steadily increasing volume of persons. Underground systems now operate in such diverse cities as Cairo, Prague, Minsk, and Beijing. More than sixty major cities around the world are now expanding their urban rail systems, and twenty-five new systems have opened in the last two years. With the recent development of the "maglev" (or "flying train"), capable of carrying 1,000 passengers at a speed of over 300 mph, rail transportation may be facing a renaissance. [6]

2. Although *public postal services* were available in the eighteenth century, they did not truly begin to flourish until the advent of railroads in the nineteenth century and then airlines in the twentieth. In the early 1800s there were only about two thousand miles of postal routes in the United States;[3] by 1960 the figure had jumped to over two million miles. The volume of mail is also expanding rapidly; Americans receive almost three times more mail now than in 1945. At present the volume of mail is so great that the U.S. Postal Service is considered the largest single [7]

business in the world. In the early 1980s it employed over 700,000 workers, and it now moves over eighty billion items a year—nearly four hundred pieces of mail for every citizen of the nation.

8   **3.** At the beginning of this century *the automobile* was virtually unknown. Less than 100 cars had ever been produced in the entire world. Production increased only slowly until the assembly line was perfected in the 1920s. By 1930 world production of motor vehicles had reached the four-million mark, with more than three quarters of them produced in the United States. Fifty years later, in 1980, the annual production figure had jumped to almost 40 million—of which approximately a fifth were made in the States.[4] Improvements in roads have also expanded the number of locations within reach. At the turn of the century there were only a hundred miles of hard-surface roads in the United States; by 1970 there were over two million miles of paved roads. Within recent decades the superhighways—more than 44,000 miles of them—have added new dimensions to long-distance travel.[5] Because of the expanding number of cars and people's increased dependency on them, traffic has become a major policy issue. Highway congestion is now so intense that the average speed on the Los Angeles freeways has dropped to 35 mph. In the next twenty years the volume of traffic is expected to rise by another 42 percent.[6]

9   **4.** *The telephone* made its entry into daily living at the turn of the century; within five decades there were some 90 million phones in the United States;[7] in the next decade, the number of phones almost doubled. There are now about 600 million telephones in the world (even though two-thirds of the world's population still has no access to telephones). And the miles of telephone wire continue to expand (from 316 million miles of wire in 1960 to 1,290 million miles in 1984). The pattern of telephone relationships is also changing. Most dramatic is the shift in the function of the telephone from a community, to a national, to an international resource. The number of overseas calls from the United States in 1960 was approximately 3 million; by 1984 this figure had multiplied by almost 130 times, to almost 430 million calls.[8] And, within the 1980s, international telephone calls increased sixfold. As we shall see, high tech is in the process of sending this figure upward by untold magnitudes.

5. *Radio broadcasting* began in the United States and Great Britain   10
   in 1919. Since that time it has insinuated itself into virtually all
   aspects of social life. It has altered social patterns in living rooms,
   dining rooms, bedrooms, automobiles, beaches, workshops,
   waiting rooms, and city streets. In 1925 there were 600 stations
   in the world. This figure doubled in the next ten years, and by
   1960 there were over 10,000 stations.[9] With miniaturization and
   mass production radios became increasingly affordable. By the
   mid-1980s there were some two billion radios in the world. In
   recent years "personal audio" has also become a major cultural
   phenomenon. There are now more than 12 million personal
   stereos moving about the globe, some to the very edges of civilization: An anthropologist visiting hill tribes along the Burmese
   border recently reported that the tribespeople offer to trade local
   handicrafts for personal stereos.

6. At the turn of the century *motion pictures* scarcely existed. The   11
   first moving pictures were shown in scattered music halls. With
   improvements in photography, projection, and sound recording,
   however, motion pictures became increasingly popular. Even
   during the depression, box-office receipts remained relatively
   high. By the 1950s the weekly film audience in the United States
   alone reached 90 million.[10] Although film attendance at theaters
   has declined substantially as a result of television, both television
   and videocassettes continue to expose vast numbers of people to
   commercial films. (Over 60 percent of those American households with television also own a videocassette recorder.) In 1989
   more new films were made in the United States than ever
   before—and even more were produced in India.

7. *Printed books* have been disseminating ideas, values, and modes of   12
   life for over 400 years. By the mid-1700s, for example, England
   produced some 90 titles a year; a century later, it produced
   600.[11] With the development of the rotary printing press and
   factory production systems, commercial publishing has become
   a dominant force in the twentieth century. Particularly in the
   1950s, with the emergence of paperback books, ownership of
   books became possible for vast segments of the population: by
   the 1960s English publishers printed over 20,000 titles a year,
   and by the 1980s, five nations (Canada, England, West Germany,
   the United States, and the USSR) were publishing between
   50,000 and 80,000 titles a year.[12]

13   So we find seven technologies of social saturation—rail, post, automobile, telephone, radio, motion pictures, and commercial publishing—all rapidly expanding within the twentieth century. Each brought people into increasingly close proximity, exposed them to an increasing range of others, and fostered a range of relationships that could never have occurred before.

High Life in High Tech

14   The seven low-tech alterations only began the saturation process. The past two decades have added untold potential for relatedness. We must briefly consider, then, the second, or high-tech, phase in the technology of social saturation, specifically developments in air transportation, television, and electronic communication.

Air Headings

Airport Gridlock Near, Aviation Experts Warn

—Headline, *New York Times*

15   The stories are told with increasing frequency: An executive flies from Washington, D.C., to Tokyo to represent his firm at a cocktail party; he returns the next day. Frankfurt couples fly to New York for the weekend to watch Boris Becker play in the U.S. Open. A New York executive flies to San Francisco to spend the day in consultation, and returns that night to Scarsdale on "the redeye." University officials wish to meet with candidates for an executive position; all are flown from locations across the continent for a single afternoon of meetings in an airport hotel. For a family reunion, eighteen people fly to St. Louis from five states across the nation.

16   For steadily increasing numbers air travel is becoming a casual matter. Businesses routinely think in terms of global expansion. Multinational corporations are so powerful that their budgets exceed that of many nations. Large cities are increasingly dependent on revenues from conference centers, international fairs, and tourism. For many academics, global conference-going is now a way of life. The reader of the Sunday *New York Times* in the 1930s would find no travel section. Today the section typically offers low-budget escapes to more than two hundred exotic locations. A high-school class reunion in North Carolina can pull graduates of over thirty years from as far away as Hawaii. Americans of Irish, Italian, German, and

Scandinavian descent go to Europe in large numbers to locate relatives they have never met.

Such dramatic changes in social pattern have occurred only   17
within the lifetime of most readers. Passenger travel by air was
scarcely available before 1920. By the year 1940, however, there were
approximately 3 million passengers in the United States.[13] Within
ten years this figure jumped by six times. By 1970 the number of passengers reached almost 160 million. That figure again doubled in the
next ten years. Almost eight of ten Americans have now flown. And,
even though air traffic approaches gridlock, the FAA estimates
1990's total at 800 million passengers.[14] The number of passengers
boarding planes in such cities as Dallas, Denver, Memphis, and
Washington is expected to double by the year 2000. The Concorde
now reaches speeds of Mach 2, transporting passengers from London to New York in less than four hours; a new generation of SSTs
may bring Tokyo as close.[15]

Vistas of Video

> *A timid appearing junior college student meets a tall, blond, drug-using*
> *housepainter . . . and invites him to dinner. He gets amorous and rapes her*
> *in the bedroom of her apartment. She files charges but less than a month later*
> *she posts his bail and moves in with him and plans to be Mrs. Rapist. . . .*
> *When asked how she could marry [him] after what he did to her, she referred*
> *to a soap opera in which one character rapes another and later marries her.*
> *"It's like Luke and Laura on 'General Hospital,' " [she] said. . . . In keeping with the . . . TV flavor of the whole affair, [he] asked her to marry him*
> *while they were watching the Oprah Winfrey show, and they are considering an invitation to appear on the Phil Donahue show . . .*
>
> *– Philadelphia Daily News*

The year 1946 is a watershed, the first year of commercial tele-   18
vision. In 1949 over a million television sets were sold in the United
States. Two years later there were ten million; by 1959, fifty million.[16]
By the early 1980s there were some 800 million television sets in use
throughout the world. And they are watched. In the United States
the average television set brings the outside world into the home for
seven hours a day.

All that is well known. But two more subtle issues deserve at-   19
tention, both significant to the understanding of social saturation.

20   First, it is important to consider a phenomenon with beginnings in the low-tech period of radio, film, and commercial publishing, but which becomes paramount in the high-tech era of television. This is the phenomenon of *self-multiplication,* or the capacity to be significantly present in more than one place at a time. In the face-to-face community one's capacities to carry on a relationship or to have social impact were restricted in space and time. Typically one's identity was manifest to those immediately before one's eyes, though books and newspapers made "multiples" of powerful individuals. With the development of radio and film, one's opinions, emotions, facial expressions, mannerisms, styles of relating, and the like were no longer confined to the immediate audience, but were multiplied manifold. Insights murmured into a microphone in Denver's Brown Palace Hotel could be heard by thousands in St. Louis, Minneapolis, and Grand Rapids. Manners of courting, arguing, deceiving, or playing the hero in a Hollywood studio were available for small-town millions across the country.

21   Television has generated an exponential increase in self-multiplication. This is true not only in terms of the increased size of television audiences and the number of hours to which they are exposed to social facsimiles, but in the extent to which self-multiplication transcends time—that is, in which one's identity is sustained in the culture's history. Because television channels are plentiful, popular shows are typically rebroadcast in succeeding years. The patient viewer can still resonate with Groucho Marx on *You Bet Your Life* or Jackie Gleason and Audrey Meadows on *The Honeymooners.*

22   Further, the VCR has made video-rental libraries possible— perhaps 500,000 throughout the country. Now people need not wait for a given film to be screened or televised; it lies waiting close by for the further duplication of its personages. People can choose the actors they wish to identify with or the stories that will bring fantasies to life. Increasingly this also means that in terms of producing a sense of social connection, any given actor may transcend his or her own death; viewers can continue their private relationships with Marilyn Monroe and James Dean long after the physical demise of the performers. With television, a personage may continue a robust life over eternity.

23   A second issue follows quickly from the first. I am proposing that the media—especially radio, television, and the movies—are vitally expanding the range and variety of relationships available to the population. Yet, the critic may reasonably respond, do such exposures

count as *real* or important relationships? After all, there is no give-and-take, no reciprocal interchange. The answer to this challenge depends largely on what one counts as "real or important." Surely face-to-face encounter is not a requirement of what most people would consider "real and important" relationships. Some of the world's most intense affairs of the heart (Héloïse and Abelard, Elizabeth Barrett and Robert Browning) were carried on largely by written word. Nor does reciprocal interchange seem essential for significant bonding; consider people's relationships with religious figures such as Jesus, Buddha, and Mohammed. If palpable presence is not essential to such relationships, then one must be prepared for the possibility that media figures do enter significantly into people's personal lives.

There is good reason to believe so. Social researchers have long been concerned with the impact of televised violence on the attitudes and behavior of the young. Numerous instances of people acting out what they've seen on television have been documented, even when the models engage in theft, torture, and murder.[17] More directly, Richard Schickel's *Intimate Strangers* explores the manner in which the media generate an illusionary sense of intimacy with celebrity figures.[18] Not only are famous people available to us on television, in the movies, in autobiographies, and in celebrity magazines, but often these media furnish intimate details of their personal lives. We may know more about Merv, Oprah, Johnny, and Phil than we do our neighbors. At one point, according to a national survey, newsman Walter Cronkite was the "most trusted man in America." And, because such figures do become so well known, people absorb them into their cast of significant others—loving, sympathizing with, and loathing them. It is thus that David Letterman sought a court injunction against a woman who claimed to be his wife, John Lennon was killed by an unknown fan, President Reagan was shot by John Hinckley, and the television star Rebecca Schaeffer was killed by a fan who had written unanswered letters to her for two years. The columnist Cynthia Heimel argues that because celebrity figures are known by so many people, they serve as forms of social glue, allowing people from different points of society to converse with each other, to share feelings, and essentially to carry on informal relations. "Celebrities," she proposes, "are our common frames of reference, celebrity loathing and revilement crosses all cultural boundaries. Celebrities are not our community elders, they are our community."[19]

25   Also relevant are the immense amounts of time, money, and personal effort that go into maintaining media relationships. Millions are spent each year on magazines, books, posters, T-shirts, towels, and photographs bearing likenesses of the favored idol. When *Batman* opened, a crowd of 20,000 stood for hours to glimpse celebrities for a few seconds in person. How many of one's neighbors elicit such dedication? It may also be ventured that with the advances in film technology, the movies have become one of the most powerful rhetorical devices in the world. Unlike most of our acquaintances, films can catapult us rapidly and effectively into states of fear, anger, sadness, romance, lust, and aesthetic ecstasy—often within the same two-hour period. It is undoubtedly true that for many people film relationships provide the most emotionally wrenching experiences of the average week. The ultimate question is not whether media relationships approximate the normal in their significance, but whether normal relationships can match the powers of artifice.

26   For many, the powers of artifice may indeed be in the superior position. So powerful are the media in their well-wrought portrayals that their realities become more compelling than those furnished by common experience. The vacation is not *real* until captured on film; marriages become events staged for camera and videotape; sports fans often prefer television because it is more fully lifelike than the eyeball view from the stands. It is to the media, and not to sense perception, that we increasingly turn for definitions of what is the case.

Electronic Innovation and the Proliferation of Relationships

> *Tomorrow's executives will have to feel as "at home" in Sapporo as Strasbourg as San Francisco . . . asserts Lester Thurow, Dean of MIT's Sloan School of Management. . . . "To be trained as an American manager is to be trained for a world that is no longer there."*
>
> —*U.S. News and World Report*

27   Two of the greatest impediments to communicating, and thus relating, over long distances are slowness and expense. In the 1850s it was possible to convey a message across the American continent, but the speed of transmission was approximately ten miles an hour. The Pony Express required nine days to carry mail from Missouri to California, and the cost for half an ounce was $5.[20] The telegraph system later increased the speed of transmission by an enormous

magnitude, but it was still expensive. In recent decades, electronic transmission has cut sharply into these two barriers, and current developments stagger the imagination.

In the late 1950s the development of the digital computer brought great advantages: it could store immense amounts of information in a relatively small space, and could process and transmit this information very quickly. The computer has now become a mainstay for most businesses of any magnitude. With the development of the microchip in the late 1970s, the efficiency of information storage, processing, and transmission increased by an additional magnitude. In the space required by a single handwritten letter, the equivalent of 500 books—two good-sized bookcases—can now be stored on a microchip.[21] With the perfection of laser processing, the microchip will be replaced by a process enabling a single disk on a home computer to store the entire works of Shakespeare several times over. In a single suitcase could be deposited the entire contents of the Library of Congress. Where days might be required to transmit the contents of a single book by telegraph or even phone, microprocessing enables such contents to be transmitted within a matter of seconds. Further, the microchip has meant that computers could be cheap enough for home use; the personal computer business is now a major growth industry in many countries. In 1981 there were slightly over 2 million personal computers in America.[22] By 1987 the figure jumped to almost 38 million, some 10 percent of which allows laptop work to continue in trains, planes, and hotel rooms. And sales continue to rise . . .

With low-cost electronic printing equipment (including home printers and copy machines), every computer owner is now a potential book publisher. Through desktop publishing, computer owners become direct agents of their own self-multiplication. Proponents of electronic communication had expected use of paper to dwindle in the 1990s, but largely because of desktop publishing, more paper is now used than ever before. With the development of the modem, any computer could be linked via existing phone cables to any other computer with a modem. This development, in turn, gave birth to electronic mail, computer teleconferences, and on-line databases (or information services).

Electronic mail first served mainly those within one city or organization. Most large cities offer bulletin-board services, which allow individuals to place an announcement of their interests on a file open to all users of the system. In this way computer conversations develop, and fanciful subcultures spring to life, sharing interests—at any time of day or night—in areas ranging from African art to aphrodisiacs, backgammon to banjos, philately to fellatio. There is almost always someone "out there" to talk to. Many local bulletin boards are also connected to national routing services that transmit messages overnight and free of charge from one board to another across the country. Many participants speak of the warm and accepting relations that develop within these contexts—much like a corner bar, where there are always old buddies and new friends. Estimates are that up to a billion messages a year are now being transmitted in the United States by electronic mail.[23]

31   Teleconference services enable groups of persons from across the country simultaneously to converse with one another. Over a half million Americans also make use of national, on-line information services or videotex—CompuServe, Dow Jones, or the Source—with databases that rapidly inform their users of airline schedules, movie reviews, world weather, the national news, and more. In France there are over 3,000 such home services available, including home banking, shopping, real-estate listings, and magazine contents.

32   In the 1960s rockets made it possible to place communication satellites into orbits that keep them in a fixed position relative to points on earth. While in orbit, they can bounce continuous electronic transmissions from one point on earth to another over almost one-third of the planet's surface. At present these satellites transmit radio signals, telephone communication, digital data, and the like instantaneously to the far corners of the globe. Governments rely on such services to carry out their foreign policies, multinational corporations to conduct business, and individuals to sustain friendships. In poor rural areas in Mexico, satellite dishes allow Mexican families to receive as many as 130 TV channels from at least seven nations and in five languages. Satellite television reception is only in its infancy. In the mid-1980s it involved 130 satellites; twice as many are anticipated by the early 1990s.[24] To help business and government take advantage of the satellite capabilities, new companies are springing to life. These enterprises, some now boasting over 100,000 employees, install globe-spanning communications networks.

33   Worldwide electronic linkages, in combination with computer and telephone, have enabled the development of further social linkages via fax machines, which can convey printed matter rapidly and inexpen-

sively throughout the world. A letter written by a political figure in Iran can, within seconds, be received in embassies around the globe. And with the aid of photocopy and mail, the same message can be in the hands of thousands the following day. Fax machines are rapidly gaining the capacity to transmit complex visual materials (such as maps and photographs), and the cost is dropping enough for fax services to be offered in hotels, in airports, and on trains. Low-cost, personal fax facilities are now advertised in flight magazines; the next step is clear.

These developments—computers, electronic mail, satellites, faxes—are only the beginning. Innovations now emerging will further accelerate the growth in social connectedness. At the outset is the digitization of all the major media—phonograph, photography, printing, telephone, radio, television. This means that the information conveyed by each source—pictures, music, voice—is becoming translatable to computer form. As a result, each medium becomes subject to the vast storage and rapid processing and transmission capabilities of the computer.[25] Each becomes subject to home production and worldwide dissemination. We now face an age in which pressing a button will enable us to transmit self-images—in full color and sound—around the globe.

Fiberoptic cables increase the amount of information that can be received a thousandfold. This opens the possibility for a virtual infinity of new television and radio bands. Further, fiberoptic cable will allow the transmission of a television picture of twice the fidelity of what is now available (approximating 35mm motion picture film). Digital phone services can be carried on the cable, not only reproducing the voice with fidelity, but also enabling subscribers to see the other person. So much information can be carried on the cable that all these various services could be taking place while subscribers were simultaneously having their utility meters read and their electronic mail collected. With a home fax receiver, one could also have an instant *Los Angeles Times* or *National Geographic* at one's fingertips.[26] Plans are now under way for people to designate the kinds of news they wish to see, and for computers to scan information services and compose individualized newspapers—to be printed on reusable paper.[27]

Over a hundred nations (including the USSR) are now involved in linking all the world's phone systems. Simultaneously, the development of the cellular phone is mobilizing possibilities for communication. With the development of point-to-point contact around the world, the 12 million cellular phones now in use will represent but a bare beginning. One could be anywhere—from a woodside walk in Maine to a hut in the Malaysian jungle—and speak with a loved one or colleague on the other side of the globe. Plans are now afoot for the world system to carry *all* electronic signals—including phone, television, recorded music, written text. This would enable a user to plug into the system anywhere from Alabama to Zaire and immediately transmit and receive manuscripts, sound recordings, or videotapes. The process of social saturation is far from complete.

The Process of Social Saturation

> *Monocultural communication is the simplest, most natural, and—in the contemporary world—most fragile form of communication. At its best, it is a rich, satisfying, and effortless way of communicating; at its worst, it can be narrow-minded and coercive.*
>
> —W. Barnett Pearce, *Communication and the Human Condition*

37   A century ago, social relationships were largely confined to the distance of an easy walk. Most were conducted in person, within small communities: family, neighbors, townspeople. Yes, the horse and carriage made longer trips possible, but even a trip of thirty miles could take all day. The railroad could speed one away, but cost and availability limited such travel. If one moved from the community, relationships were likely to end. From birth to death one could depend on relatively even-textured social surroundings. Words, faces, gestures, and possibilities were relatively consistent, coherent, and slow to change.

38   For much of the world's population, especially the industrialized West, the small, face-to-face community is vanishing into the pages of history. We go to country inns for weekend outings, we decorate condominium interiors with clapboards and brass beds, and we dream of old age in a rural cottage. But as a result of the technological developments just described, contemporary life is a swirling sea of social relations. Words thunder in by radio, television, newspaper, mail, telephone, fax, wire service, electronic mail, billboards, Federal Express, and more. Waves of new faces are everywhere—in town for a day, visiting for the weekend, at the Rotary lunch, at the church social—and incessantly and incandescently on television. Long weeks in a single community are unusual; a full day within a single neighborhood is becoming rare. We travel casually across town, into

the countryside, to neighboring towns, cities, states; one might go thirty miles for coffee and conversation.

Through the technologies of the century, the number and vari-   39
ety of relationships in which we are engaged, potential frequency of contact, expressed intensity of relationship, and endurance through time all are steadily increasing. As this increase becomes extreme we reach a state of social saturation. Let us consider this state in greater detail.

Multiplying Relationships

In the face-to-face community the cast of others remained relatively   40
stable.[28] There were changes by virtue of births and deaths, but moving from one town—much less state or country—to another was difficult. The number of relationships commonly maintained in today's world stands in stark contrast. Counting one's family, the morning television news, the car radio, colleagues on the train, and the local newspaper, the typical commuter may confront as many different persons (in terms of views or images) in the first two hours of a day as the community-based predecessor did in a month. The morning calls in a business office may connect one to a dozen different locales in a given city, often across the continent, and very possibly across national boundaries. A single hour of prime-time melodrama immerses one in the lives of a score of individuals. In an evening of television, hundreds of engaging faces insinuate themselves into our lives. It is not only the immediate community that occupies our thoughts and feelings, but a constantly changing cast of characters spread across the globe.

Two aspects of this expansion are particularly noteworthy. First   41
there is what may be termed the *perseverance of the past*. Formerly, increases in time and distance between persons typically meant loss. When someone moved away, the relationship would languish. Long-distance visits were arduous, and the mails slow. Thus, as one grew older, many active participants would fade from one's life. Today, time and distance are no longer such serious threats to a relationship. One may sustain an intimacy over thousands of miles by frequent telephone raptures punctuated by occasional visits. One may similarly retain relationships with high-school chums, college roommates, old military cronies, or friends from a Caribbean vacation five years earlier. Birthday books have become a standard household

item; one's memory is inadequate to record the festivities for which one is responsible. In effect, as we move through life, the cast of relevant characters is ever expanding. For some this means an ever-increasing sense of stress: "How can we make friends with them? We don't even have time for the friends we already have!" For others there is a sense of comfort, for the social caravan in which we travel through life remains always full.

42   Yet at the same time that the past is preserved, continuously poised to insert itself into the present, there is an *acceleration of the future*. The pace of relationships is hurried, and processes of unfolding that once required months or years may be accomplished in days or weeks. A century ago, for example, courtships were often carried out on foot or horseback, or through occasional letters. Hours of interchange might be punctuated by long periods of silence, making the path from acquaintanceship to intimacy lengthy. With today's technologies, however, it is possible for a couple to maintain almost continuous connection. Not only do transportation technologies chip away at the barrier of geographic distance, but through telephone (both stable and cordless), overnight mail, cassette recordings, home videos, photographs, and electronic mail, the other may be "present" at almost any moment. Courtships may thus move from excitement to exhaustion within a short time. The single person may experience not a handful of courtship relationships in a lifetime but dozens. In the same way, the process of friendship is often accelerated. Through the existing technologies, a sense of affinity may blossom into a lively sense of interdependence within a brief space of time. As the future opens, the number of friendships expands as never before.

Bending the Life-Forms

> *Our private sphere has ceased to be the stage where the drama of the subject at odds with his objects . . . is played out, we no longer exist as playwrights or actors, but as terminals of multiple networks.*
> —Jean Baudrillard, *The Ecstasy of Communication*

43   New patterns of relationship also take shape. In the face-to-face community one participated in a limited set of relationships—with family, friends, storekeepers, clerics, and the like. Now the next telephone call can thrust us suddenly into a new relationship—with a Wall Street broker, a charity solicitor, an alumni campaigner from the

old school, a childhood friend at a nearby convention, a relative from across the country, a child of a friend, or even a sex pervert. One may live in a suburb with well-clipped neighbors, but commute to a city for frequent confrontation with street people, scam merchants, panhandlers, prostitutes, and threatening bands of juveniles. One may reside in Houston, but establish bonds—through business or leisure travel—with a Norwegian banker, a wine merchant from the Rhine Pfalz, or an architect from Rome.

Of course, it is television that most dramatically increases the variety of relationships in which one participates—even if vicariously. One can identify with heroes from a thousand tales, carry on imaginary conversations with talk-show guests from all walks of life, or empathize with athletes from around the globe. One of the most interesting results of this electronic expansion of relationships occurs in the domain of parent-child relationships. As Joshua Meyrowitz proposes in *No Sense of Place,* children of the preceding century were largely insulated from information about the private lives of adults.[29] Parents, teachers, and police could shield children from their adult proceedings by simply conducting them in private places. Further, books dealing with the misgivings, failings, deceits, and conflicts of the adult world were generally unavailable to children. Children remained children. Television has changed all that. Programming systematically reveals the full panoply of "backstage" trials and tribulations to the child. As a result the child no longer interacts with one-dimensional, idealized adults, but with persons possessing complex private lives, doubt-filled and vulnerable. In turn, parents no longer confront the comfortably naive child of yesteryear, but one whose awe is diminished and whose insights may be acute. 44

The technology of the age both expands the variety of human relationships and modifies the form of older ones. When relationships move from the face-to-face to the electronic mode, they are often altered. Relationships that were confined to specific situations—to offices, living rooms, bedrooms—become "unglued." They are no longer geographically confined, but can take place anywhere. Unlike face-to-face relationships, electronic relationships also conceal visual information (eye movement, expressive movements of the mouth), so a telephone speaker cannot read the facial cues of the listener for signs of approval or disapproval. As a result, there is a greater tendency to create an imaginary other with whom to relate. One can fantasize that the other is feeling warm and enthusiastic or 45 cold and angry, and act accordingly. An acquaintance told me that he believed his first marriage to be a product of the heavy phoning necessary for a long-distance courtship. By phone she seemed the most desirable woman in the world; it was only months after the wedding that he realized he had married a mirage.

46   Many organizations are now installing electronic-mail systems, which enable employees to carry out their business with each other by computer terminals rather than by traditional, face-to-face means. Researchers find that employee relations have subtly changed as a result. Status differences begin to crumble as lower-ranking employees feel freer to express their feelings and question their superiors electronically than in person. Harvard Business School's Shoshana Zuboff suggests that the introduction of "smart machines" into businesses is blurring the distinctions between managers and workers. Managers are no longer the "thinkers" while the workers are consigned to the "doing."[30] Rather, out of necessity the workers now become managers of information, and as a result, they considerably augment their power.

Relating in New Keys

47   Of the new forms of relationship that the saturation process has helped create, two are of special interest. First is the *friendly lover* relationship. For the essential romanticist, the object of love was all-consuming. He or she possessed value of such immense proportion that a lifetime of steadfast commitment could be viewed merely as preparation for an eternity of spiritual communion. The belief in marriage for "true love" is still pervasive, but as the social world is increasingly saturated, such relationships become unrealistic. Rather, men and women (especially professionals) are often in motion—traveling to business meetings, conferences, sales campaigns, consultations, vacations, and so on. Murmurings of "I can't live without you" lose their authenticity when one must add, "except until next Tuesday, and possibly again until the following Wednesday." And because many attractive members of the opposite sex are encountered along the way—providing professional benefits and companionship as well—a multiplicity of low-level, or "friendly," romances is invited. To illustrate, a single professional woman from Maryland disclosed that she was "seeing" a local lawyer (unhappily married) because it was fun and convenient. At the same time, he took a back seat when a favorite "old friend" in her profession came in from Oklahoma.

However, especially during the summer, she was keen to spend her weekends with a Boston consultant (relevant to her line of work) whose boat was moored at Martha's Vineyard. Each of these individuals, in turn, had other friendly lovers.

A second interesting pattern, the *microwave relationship,* is found increasingly on the domestic front. The ideal family unit has traditionally included a close, interdependent "nucleus," composed of a father-provider, a caretaking mother, and children whose lives are centered in the home until early adulthood. Social saturation has cut deeply into this traditional view. Husband and wife are now both likely to have work and recreational relations outside the family; daycare and babysitting facilities are increasingly required; children's social activities may be scattered across city and countryside; evening obligations or indulgences are frequent both for parents and for children over the age of six; and family members are typically drawn into outside activities—sports, religious, community, hobbies, visits—on the weekends. Differing television needs often thrust various family members into different trajectories even when they are at home together. In many families the crucial ritual of interdependence—dinner together—has become a special event. (In some households the dining-room table, once a family center, is strewn with books, papers, letters, and other objects dropped there by family members "passing through.") The home is less a nesting place than a pit stop.

At the same time, however, many parents are loath to give up the traditional image of the close-knit family. As a result, a new form of relationship emerges in which family members attempt to compensate for the vast expanses of nonrelatedness with intense expressions of bondedness. As many understand it, quantity is replaced by quality. The microwave oven is more than a technological support for those living a socially saturated life. It is also a good symbol of the newly emerging form of relationship: in both cases the users command intense heat for the immediate provision of nourishment. The adequacy of the result is subject to debate in both cases.

Intensifying Interchange

> *Modern society is to be distinguished from older social formations by the fact that it affords more opportunities both for impersonal and for more intensive personal relationships.*
>
> —Niklas Luhmann, *Love as Passion*

50   Interestingly, technology also intensifies the emotional level of many relationships. People come to feel more deeply and express themselves more fully in an increasing number of relationships. This proposal may seem suspect. If persons pass through our lives in increasing numbers and speeds, wouldn't the outcome be a sense of superficiality and a disinclination to get involved? The attractive stranger you meet in Seattle is regrettably from Omaha; the fascinating new neighbors are returning in the spring to London; the absorbing seatmate on the plane is flying on to Bombay. What is there to do but keep it light and cool? To be sure, the vast share of the passing parade remains simply that. However, consider two aspects of the traditional, face-to-face community.

51   First, as relationships continue over a period of years they tend toward normalization. People choose to do things that reliably give them satisfaction. Changes in pattern mean risking these satisfactions. Thus, relationships over time tend toward a leveling of emotional intensity. As many married couples put it, "Exciting romance is replaced by a comfortable depth."

52   Second, the face-to-face community lends itself to a high degree of informal surveillance. People tend to know what the others are doing most of the time. They see each other across a room, through their windows, passing in the street, and so on. And where the social world remains stable, and new information is scant, the smallest details of one's life become everyone's topics of conversation. Petty gossip and strong community norms walk hand in hand. The intensity generated by the new, the novel, and the deviant is in scarce supply.

53   In the present context of saturation, neither of these conditions prevails. Because all relationships are constantly being disrupted, it is more difficult for any given relationship to normalize. The evening at home, once quiet, relaxed, and settling, is now—by dint of telephone, automobile, television, and the like—a parade of faces, information, and intrusions. One can scarcely settle into a calming rut, because who one is and the cast of "significant others" are in continuous motion. Further, because relationships range far and wide, largely through various electronic means, they cannot easily be supervised by others who care. One can find the intimacy of "telling all" to a close friend in Chicago, because those who would be horrified in Dallas or Topeka will never know. One can let the internal fires rage in Paris, because the folk in Peoria will never see the glow. One academic colleague spoke of his conversation with a woman

while waiting in a check-in line for a return journey to the United States. The plane was to stop over in Iceland, and passengers had the choice of continuing the journey directly or remaining in Iceland and catching the next plane two days later. The professor found himself attracted to the lady and emboldened by the anonymity of the situation. Suddenly he found himself stammering a proposal to the woman to remain with him in Iceland for two days. Her complex smile gave him no answer. They silently approached the baggage carts on which travelers had to place their bags for either the direct flight or the layover. To his speechless amazement, she maneuvered her bag into the latter cart. After two days of bliss they parted company, never to communicate with each other again.

The press toward intensity is not limited to normalization and the 54 breakdown of surveillance. There are also factors of fantasy and fleetingness at play. As the romanticists were well aware, little inspired the pen so much as the absence of the adored one. In the other's absence, one's fantasies were free to roam; one could project onto the favored person all virtues and desires. In this respect, nineteenth-century romanticism can be partially attributed to the combination of a cultural morality that discouraged a free play of relationships and the number of individuals educated in writing. Although standards of morality have liberalized since then, the increased possibility for relationships at a distance has had much the same effect as it did on the romantics. Relations at a distance can thus glow more brightly, and interchanges remain more highly charged.

The occasional meeting is intensified, finally, by its shortness. If 55 it is agreed that the other is a "good friend," "very close," or a "special person," then the short periods of meeting must be similarly expressive. One must somehow demonstrate the significance of one's feelings and the high esteem in which the relationship is held. And, because there is little time, the demonstrations must be loud and clear. The result may be an elegantly prepared dinner, reservations at an unusual restaurant, entertainments or excursions planned, selected guests invited for sharing, and the like. Friends living in a central European city recently complained of what amounted to a delirium and exhaustion. So frequently did visiting friends require a "display of significance" that both spirits and pocketbooks were depleted. Couples in frequently visited cities such as New York and Paris speak of the measures they take to ensure they have no spare bedrooms. With frequent visitors, no time remains for their nurturing capacities; spare rooms risk the evisceration of their private relationship.

Populating the Self

> *The very din of imaginal voices in adulthood—as they sound in thought and memory, in poetry, drama, novels, and movies, in speech, dreams, fantasy, and prayer . . . can be valued not just as subordinate to social reality, but as a reality as intrinsic to human existence as the literally social.*
>
> —Mary Watkins, *Invisible Guests*

56   Consider the moments:

- Over lunch with friends you discuss Northern Ireland. Although you have never spoken a word on the subject, you find yourself heatedly defending British policies.
- You work as an executive in the investments department of a bank. In the evenings you smoke marijuana and listen to the Grateful Dead.
- You sit in a café and wonder what it would be like to have an intimate relationship with various strangers walking past.
- You are a lawyer in a prestigious midtown firm. On the weekends you work on a novel about romance with a terrorist.
- You go to a Moroccan restaurant and afterward take in the latest show at a country-and-western bar.

57   In each case individuals harbor a sense of coherent identity or self-sameness, only to find themselves suddenly propelled by alternative impulses. They seem securely to be one sort of person, but yet another comes bursting to the surface—in a suddenly voiced opinion, a fantasy, a turn of interests, or a private activity. Such experiences with variation and self-contradiction may be viewed as preliminary effects of social saturation. They may signal a *populating of the self,* the acquisition of multiple and disparate potentials for being. It is this process of self-population that begins to undermine the traditional commitments to both romanticist and modernist forms of being. It is of pivotal importance in setting the stage for the postmortem turn. Let us explore.

58   The technologies of social saturation expose us to an enormous range of persons, new forms of relationship, unique circumstances and opportunities, and special intensities of feeling. One can scarcely remain unaffected by such exposure. As child-development specialists now agree, the process of socialization is lifelong. We continue to incorporate information from the environment throughout our lives. When exposed to other persons, we change in two major ways. We increase our capacities for *knowing that* and for *knowing how.* In

the first case, through exposure to others we learn myriad details about their words, actions, dress, mannerisms, and so on. We ingest enormous amounts of information about patterns of interchange. Thus, for example, from an hour on a city street, we are informed of the clothing styles of blacks, whites, upper class, lower class, and more. We may learn the ways of Japanese businessmen, bag ladies, Sikhs, Hare Krishnas, or flute players from Chile. We see how relationships are carried out between mothers and daughters, business executives, teenage friends, and construction workers. An hour in a business office may expose us to the political views of a Texas oilman, a Chicago lawyer, and a gay activist from San Francisco. Radio commentators espouse views on boxing, pollution, and child abuse; pop music may advocate machoism, racial bigotry, and suicide. Paperback books cause hearts to race over the unjustly treated, those who strive against impossible odds, those who are brave or brilliant. And this is to say nothing of television input. Via television, myriad figures are allowed into the home who would never otherwise trespass. Millions watch as talk-show guests—murderers, rapists, women prisoners, child abusers, members of the KKK, mental patients, and others often discredited—attempt to make their lives intelligible. There are few six-year-olds who cannot furnish at least a rudimentary account of life in an African village, the concerns of divorcing parents, or drug-pushing in the ghetto. Hourly our storehouse of social knowledge expands in range and sophistication.

This massive increase in knowledge of the social world lays the groundwork for a second kind of learning, a *knowing how*. We learn how to place such knowledge into action, to shape it for social consumption, to act so that social life can proceed effectively. And the possibilities for placing this supply of information into effective action are constantly expanding. The Japanese businessman glimpsed on the street today, and on the television tomorrow, may well be confronted in one's office the following week. On these occasions the rudiments of appropriate behavior are already in place. If a mate announces that he or she is thinking about divorce, the other's reaction is not likely to be dumb dismay. The drama has so often been played out on television and movie screens that one is already prepared with multiple options. If one wins a wonderful prize, suffers a humiliating loss, faces temptation to cheat, or learns of a sudden death in the family, the reactions are hardly random. One more or less knows how it goes, is more or less ready for action. Having seen it all before, one approaches a state of ennui.

60   In an important sense, as social saturation proceeds we become pastiches, imitative assemblages of each other. In memory we carry others' patterns of being with us. If the conditions are favorable, we can place these patterns into action. Each of us becomes the other, a representative, or a replacement. To put it more broadly, as the century has progressed selves have become increasingly populated with the character of others.[31] We are not one, or a few, but like Walt Whitman, we "contain multitudes." We appear to each other as single identities, unified, of whole cloth. However, with social saturation, each of us comes to harbor a vast population of hidden potentials—to be a blues singer, a gypsy, an aristocrat, a criminal. All the selves lie latent, and under the right conditions may spring to life.

61   The populating of the self not only opens relationships to new ranges of possibility, but one's subjective life also becomes more fully laminated. Each of the selves we acquire from others can contribute to inner dialogues, private discussions we have with ourselves about all manner of persons, events, and issues. These internal voices, these vestiges of relationships both real and imagined, have been given different names: *invisible guests* by Mary Watkins, *social imagery* by Eric Klinger, and *social ghosts* by Mary Gergen, who found in her research that virtually all the young people she sampled could discuss many such experiences with ease.[32] Most of these ghosts were close friends, often from earlier periods of their lives. Family members were also frequent, with the father's voice predominating, but grandparents, uncles, aunts, and other relatives figured prominently. Relevant to the earlier discussion of relations with media figures, almost a quarter of the ghosts mentioned were individuals with whom the young people had never had any direct interchange. Most were entertainers: rock stars, actors and actresses, singers, and the like. Others were religious figures such as Jesus and Mary, fictitious characters such as James Bond and Sherlock Holmes, and celebrities such as Chris Evert, Joe Montana, Barbara Walters, and the president.

62   The respondents also spoke of the many ways the social ghosts functioned in their lives. It was not simply that they were there for conversation or contemplation; they also served as models for action. They set standards for behavior; they were admired and were emulated. As one wrote, "Connie Chung was constantly being used as a role model for me and I found myself responding to a question about what I planned to do after graduation by saying that I wanted to go into journalism just because I had been thinking of her." Or, as

another wrote of her grandmother, "She showed me how to be tolerant of all people and to show respect to everyone regardless of their state in life." Ghosts also voiced opinions on various matters. Most frequently they were used to bolster one's beliefs. At times such opinions were extremely important. As one wrote of the memory of an early friend, "She is the last link I have to Christianity at this point in my life when I am trying to determine my religious inclinations." Still other respondents spoke of the way their ghosts supported their self-esteem: "I think my father and I know that he would be proud of what I have accomplished." Many mentioned the sense of emotional support furnished by their ghosts: "My grandmother seems to be watching me and showing that she loves me even if I am not doing so well."

In closely related work, the psychologists Hazel Markus and 63 Paula Nurius speak of *possible selves,* the multiple conceptions people harbor of what they might become, would like to become, or are afraid to become.[33] In each case, these possible selves function as private surrogates for others to whom one has been exposed—either directly or via the media. The family relations specialists Paul Rosenblatt and Sara Wright speak similarly of the *shadow realities* that exist in close relationships.[34] In addition to the reality that a couple shares together, each will harbor alternative interpretations of their lives together—interpretations that might appear unacceptable and threatening if revealed to the partner. These shadow realities are typically generated and supported by persons outside the relationship—possibly members of the extended family, but also figures from the media. Finally, the British psychologist Michael Billig and his colleagues have studied the values, goals, and ideals to which people are committed in their everyday lives.[35] They found the typical condition of the individual to be internal conflict: for each belief there exists a strong countertendency. People feel their prejudices are justified, yet it is wrong to be intolerant; that there should be equality but hierarchies are also good; and that we are all basically the same, but we must hold on to our individuality. For every value, goal, or deal, one holds to the converse as well. Billig proposes that the capacity for contradiction is essential to the practical demands of life in contemporary society.

This virtual cacophony of potentials is of no small consequence 64 for either romanticist or modernist visions of the self. For as new and disparate voices are added to one's being, committed identity becomes an increasingly arduous achievement. How difficult for the romantic to keep firm grasp on the helm of an idealistic undertaking when a chorus of internal voices sing the praises of realism, skepticism, hedonism, and nihilism. And can the committed realist, who believes in the powers of rationality and observation, remain arrogant in the face of inner urges toward emotional indulgence, moral sentiment, spiritual sensitivity, or aesthetic fulfillment? Thus, as social saturation adds incrementally to the population of self, each impulse toward well-formed identity is cast into increasing doubt; each is found absurd, shallow, limited, or flawed by the onlooking audience of the interior.

Multiphrenia

> *Modern man is afflicted with a permanent identity crisis, a condition conducive to considerable nervousness.*
> —Peter Berger, Brigitte Berger, and Hansfried Kellner, *The Homeless Mind*

65   It is a sunny Saturday morning and he finishes breakfast in high spirits. It is a rare day in which he is free to do as he pleases. With relish he contemplates his options. The back door needs fixing, which calls for a trip to the hardware store. This would allow a much-needed haircut; and while in town he could get a birthday card for his brother, leave off his shoes for repair, and pick up shirts at the cleaners. But, he ponders, he really should get some exercise; is there time for jogging in the afternoon? That reminds him of a championship game he wanted to see at the same time. To be taken more seriously was his ex-wife's repeated request for a luncheon talk. And shouldn't he also settle his vacation plans before all the best locations are taken? Slowly his optimism gives way to a sense of defeat. The free day has become a chaos of competing opportunities and necessities.

66   If such a scene is vaguely familiar, it attests only further to the pervasive effects of social saturation and the populating of the self. More important, one detects amid the hurly-burly of contemporary life a new constellation of feelings or sensibilities, a new pattern of self-consciousness. This syndrome may be termed *multiphrenia,* generally referring to the splitting of the individual into a multiplicity of self-investments. This condition is partly an outcome of self-population, but partly a result of the populated self's efforts to exploit the potentials of the technologies of relationship. In this sense, there is a cyclical spiraling toward a state of multiphrenia. As one's

potentials are expanded by the technologies, so one increasingly employs the technologies for self-expression; yet, as the technologies are further utilized, so do they add to the repertoire of potentials. It would be a mistake to view this multiphrenic condition as a form of illness, for it is often suffused with a sense of expansiveness and adventure. Someday there may indeed be nothing to distinguish multiphrenia from simply "normal living."

However, before we pass into this oceanic state, let us pause to consider some prominent features of the condition.[36] Three of these are especially noteworthy.   67

Vertigo of the Valued

> *Because of the constant change and feeling "off balance," it is essential for men and women to develop . . . coping skills. First, understand that you will never "catch up" and be on top of things and accept this as all right. . . . Put a high priority on spending time relaxing and enjoying life, in spite of all that needs to be done.*
>
> —Bruce A. Baldwin, *Stress and Technology*

With the technology of social saturation, two of the major factors traditionally impeding relationships—namely time and space— are both removed. The past can be continuously renewed—via voice, video, and visits, for example—and distance poses no substantial barriers to ongoing interchange. Yet this same freedom ironically leads to a form of enslavement. For each person, passion, or potential incorporated into oneself exacts a penalty—a penalty both of *being* and of *being with*. In the former case, as others are incorporated into the self, their tastes, goals, and values also insinuate themselves into one's being. Through continued interchange, one acquires, for example, a yen for Thai cooking, the desire for retirement security, or an investment in wildlife preservation. Through others one comes to value whole-grain breads, novels from Chile, or community politics. Yet as Buddhists have long been aware, to desire is simultaneously to become a slave of the desirable. To "want" reduces one's choice to "want not." Thus, as others are incorporated into the self, and their desires become one's own, there is an expansion of goals— of "musts," wants, and needs. Attention is necessitated, effort is exerted, frustrations are encountered. Each new desire places its demands and reduces one's liberties.   68

69   There is also the penalty of being with. As relationships develop, their participants acquire local definitions—friend, lover, teacher, supporter, and so on. To sustain the relationship requires an honoring of the definitions—both of self and other. If two persons become close friends, for example, each acquires certain rights, duties, and privileges. Most relationships of any significance carry with them a range of obligations—for communication, joint activities, preparing for the other's pleasure, rendering appropriate congratulations, and so on. Thus, as relations accumulate and expand over time, there is a steadily increasing range of phone calls to make and answer, greeting cards to address, visits or activities to arrange, meals to prepare, preparations to be made, clothes to buy, makeup to apply . . . And with each new opportunity—for skiing together in the Alps, touring Australia, camping in the Adirondacks, or snorkling in the Bahamas—there are "opportunity costs." One must unearth information, buy equipment, reserve hotels, arrange travel, work long hours to clear one's desk, locate babysitters, dogsitters, homesitters . . . Liberation becomes a swirling vertigo of demands.

70   In the professional world this expansion of "musts" is strikingly evident. In the university of the 1950s, for example, one's departmental colleagues were often vital to one's work. One could walk but a short distance for advice, information, support, and so on. Departments were often closeknit and highly interdependent; travels to other departments or professional meetings were notable events. Today, however, the energetic academic will be linked by post, long-distance phone, fax, and electronic mail to like-minded scholars around the globe. The number of interactions possible in a day is limited only by the constraints of time. The technologies have also stimulated the development of hundreds of new organizations, international conferences, and professional meetings. A colleague recently informed me that if funds were available he could spend his entire sabbatical traveling from one professional gathering to another. A similar condition pervades the business world. One's scope of business opportunities is no longer so limited by geography; the technologies of the age enable projects to be pursued around the world. (Colgate Tartar Control toothpaste is now sold in over forty countries.) In effect, the potential for new connection and new opportunities is practically unlimited. Daily life has become a sea of drowning demands, and there is no shore in sight.

The Expansion of Inadequacy

> *Now You Can Read the Best Business Books of 1989 in Just 15 Minutes Each!*
>
> —Advertisement, *US Air Magazine*

> *Information anxiety is produced by the ever-widening gap between what we understand and what we think we should understand.*
>
> —Richard Saul Wurman, *Information Anxiety*

It is not simply the expansion of self through relationships that hounds one with the continued sense of "ought." There is also the seeping of self-doubt into everyday consciousness, a subtle feeling of inadequacy that smothers one's activities with an uneasy sense of impending emptiness. In important respects this sense of inadequacy is a by-product of the populating of self and the presence of social ghosts. For as we incorporate others into ourselves, so does the range of proprieties expand—that is, the range of what we feel a "good," "proper," or "exemplary" person should be. Many of us carry with us the "ghost of a father," reminding us of the values of honesty and hard work, or a mother challenging us to be nurturing and understanding. We may also absorb from a friend the values of maintaining a healthy body, from a lover the goal of self-sacrifice, from a teacher the ideal of worldly knowledge, and so on. Normal development leaves most people with a rich range of "goals for a good life," and with sufficient resources to achieve a sense of personal well-being by fulfilling these goals. 71

But now consider the effects of social saturation. The range of one's friends and associates expands exponentially; one's past life continues to be vivid; and the mass media expose one to an enormous array of new criteria for self-evaluation. A friend from California reminds one to relax and enjoy life; in Ohio an associate is getting ahead by working eleven hours a day. A relative from Boston stresses the importance of cultural sophistication, while a Washington colleague belittles one's lack of political savvy. A relative's return from Paris reminds one to pay more attention to personal appearance, while a ruddy companion from Colorado suggests that one grows soft. 72

Meanwhile newspapers, magazines, and television provide a barrage of new criteria of self-evaluation. Is one sufficiently adventurous, clean, well traveled, well read, low in cholesterol, slim, skilled in cooking, friendly, odor-free, coiffed, frugal, burglarproof, family-oriented? 73

The list is unending. More than once I have heard the lament of a subscriber to the Sunday *New York Times*. Each page of this weighty tome will be read by millions. Thus each page remaining undevoured by day's end will leave one precariously disadvantaged—a potential idiot in a thousand unpredictable circumstances.

74   Yet the threat of inadequacy is hardly limited to the immediate confrontation with mates and media. Because many of these criteria for self-evaluation are incorporated into the self—existing within the cadre of social ghosts—they are free to speak at any moment. The problem with values is that they are sufficient unto themselves. To value justice, for example, is to say nothing of the value of love; investing in duty will blind one to the value of spontaneity. No one value in itself recognizes the importance of any alternative value. And so it is with the chorus of social ghosts. Each voice of value stands to discredit all that does not meet its standard. All the voices at odds with one's current conduct thus stand as internal critics, scolding, ridiculing, and robbing action of its potential for fulfillment. One settles in front of the television for enjoyment, and the chorus begins: "twelve-year-old," "couch potato," "lazy," "irresponsible" . . . One sits down with a good book, and again, "sedentary," "antisocial," "inefficient," "fantasist" . . . Join friends for a game of tennis and "skin cancer," "shirker of household duties," "underexercised," "overly competitive" come up. Work late and it is "workaholic," "heart attack–prone," "overly ambitious," "irresponsible family member." Each moment is enveloped in the guilt born of all that was possible but now foreclosed.

Rationality in Recession

> *A group of agents acting rationally in the light of their expectations could arrive at so many outcomes that none has adequate reasons for action.*
> —Martin Hollis, *The Cunning of Reason*

> *Latin Debts: Lack of Consensus*
> *Washington Awash in Arguments, Dry on Agreements*
> —Headlines, *International Herald Tribune*

75   A third dimension of multiphrenia is closely related to the others. The focus here is on the rationality of everyday decision making—instances in which one tries to be a "reasonable person." Why, one

asks, is it important for one's children to attend college? The rational reply is that a college education increases one's job opportunities, earnings, and likely sense of personal fulfillment. Why should I stop smoking? one asks, and the answer is clear that smoking causes cancer, so to smoke is simply to invite a short life. Yet these "obvious" lines of reasoning are obvious only so long as one's identity remains fixed within a particular group.

The rationality of these replies depends altogether on the sharing of opinions—of each incorporating the views of others. To achieve identity in other cultural enclaves turns these "good reasons" into "rationalizations," "false consciousness," or "ignorance." Within some subcultures a college education is a one-way ticket to bourgeois conventionality—a white-collar job, picket fence in the suburbs, and chronic boredom. For many, smoking is an integral part of a risky life-style; it furnishes a sense of intensity, offbeatness, rugged individualism. In the same way, saving money for old age is "sensible" in one family, and "oblivious to the erosions of inflation" in another. For most Westerners, marrying for love is the only reasonable (if not conceivable) thing to do. But many Japanese will point to statistics demonstrating greater longevity and happiness in arranged marriages. Rationality is a vital by product of social participation. 76

Yet as the range of our relationships is expanded, the validity of each localized rationality is threatened. What is rational in one relationship is questionable or absurd from the standpoint of another. The "obvious choice" while talking with a colleague lapses into absurdity when speaking with a spouse, and into irrelevance when an old friend calls that evening. Further, because each relationship increases one's capacities for discernment, one carries with oneself a multiplicity of competing expectations, values, and beliefs about "the obvious solution." Thus, if the options are carefully evaluated, every decision becomes a leap into gray vapors. Hamlet's bifurcated decision becomes all too simple, for it is no longer being or nonbeing that is in question, but to which of multifarious beings one can be committed. T. S. Eliot began to sense the problem when Prufrock found "time yet for a hundred indecisions / And for a hundred visions and revisions, / Before taking of a toast and tea."[37] 77

The otherwise simple task of casting a presidential vote provides a useful illustration. As one relates (either directly or vicariously) to various men and women, in various walks of life, and various sectors of the nation or abroad, one's capacities for discernment are multiplied. 78

Where one might have once employed a handful of rational standards, or seen the issues in only limited ways, one can now employ a variety of criteria and see many sides of many issues. One may thus favor candidate *A* because he strives for cuts in the defense budget, but also worry about the loss of military capability in an unsteady world climate. Candidate *B*'s plans for stimulating the growth of private enterprise may be rational from one standpoint, but the resulting tax changes seem unduly to penalize the middle-class family. At the same time, there is good reason to believe that *A*'s cuts in defense spending will favor *B*'s aims for a stimulated economy, and that *B*'s shifts in the tax structure will make *A*'s reductions in the military budget unnecessary. To use one criterion, candidate *A* is desirable because of his seeming intelligence, but from another, his complex ideas seem both cumbersome and remote from reality. Candidate *B* has a pleasing personality, useful for him to garner popular support for his programs, but in another sense his pleasant ways suggest he cannot take a firm stand. And so on.

79   Increasing the criteria of rationality does not, then, move one to a clear and univocal judgment of the candidates. Rather, the degree of complexity is increased until a rationally coherent stand is impossible. In effect, as social saturation steadily expands the population of the self, a choice of candidates approaches the arbitrary. A toss of a coin becomes equivalent to the diligently sought solution. We approach a condition in which the very idea of "rational choice" becomes meaningless.

80   So we find a profound sea change taking place in the character of social life during the twentieth century. Through an array of newly emerging technologies the world of relationships becomes increasingly saturated. We engage in greater numbers of relationships, in a greater variety of forms, and with greater intensities than ever before. With the multiplication of relationships also comes a transformation in the social capacities of the individual—both in knowing how and knowing that. The relatively coherent and unified sense of self inherent in a traditional culture gives way to manifold and competing potentials. A multiphrenic condition emerges in which one swims in ever-shifting, concatenating, and contentious currents of being. One bears the burden of an increasing array of oughts, of self-doubts and irrationalities. The possibility for committed romanticism or strong and single-minded modernism recedes, and the way is opened for the postmodern being.

Notes

1. Although rail transportation in the United States accounts for a smaller proportion of public travel, the number of rail passengers continues to mount. The U.S. Department of Transportation's *15th Annual Report, Fiscal Year 1981* (Washington: U.S. Government Printing Office, 1981) reports that from 1972 to 1981, the number of passengers increased from 13.7 million to 20.6 million. See also F. D. Hobbs, "Transportation," in *Encyclopaedia Britannica* (1988).
2. *International Herald Tribune*, 15 May 1990.
3. See Andrew C. Brix, "Postal Systems," in *Encyclopaedia Britannica* (1988). The *Annual Report of the Postmaster General, 1986* (Washington: U.S. Government Printing Office, 1986) says that the annual volume of mail continues to increase at a steady and substantial rate for all classes, including priority, express, second-class, and third-class. The volume within the latter two classes jumped from a total of 45 billion in 1982 to 65 billion by 1986.
4. John B. Rae, *The American Automobile Industry* (Boston: Twayne, 1984).
5. *U.S. News and World Report*, 23 July 1990.
6. Hobbs, "Transportation."
7. Ivan Stoddard Coggeshall et al., "Telecommunications Systems," *Encyclopaedia Britannica* (1988). Calvin Sims. "U.S. Phone Companies Prospering as Costs Fall," *International Herald Tribune*, 23 May 1989, reports that long-distance services are expected to be "the growth industry of the 1990s."
8. *Statistical Abstracts of the United States, 1987* (Washington: U.S. Government Printing Office, 1987).
9. Coggeshall et al., "Telecommunications."
10. For a detailed account, see Tino Balio, ed., *The American Film Industry* (Madison: University of Wisconsin Press, 1985). Also see Elizabeth Weis et al., "Motion Pictures," *Encyclopaedia Britannica* (1988).
11. Philip S. Unwin, George Unwin, and Hans Georg Artur Viktor, "Publishing," *Encyclopaedia Britannica*, (1988).
12. *UNESCO Statistical Yearbook*, 1989, and R. R. Bowker Data Services, New York.
13. *Air Transport 1987* (Washington: Air Transport Association of America, 1987). See also F. D. Hobbs, "Transportation."
14. *Statistical Abstracts;* also see Robert Bailey, "Industry Rides Wave of Expansion," *International Herald Tribune*, 11 June 1989.
15. Mark Frankel, "Jets of the Future," *Newsweek*, 3 July 1989, 38–39.
16. Cobbet Steinberg, *TV Facts* (New York: Facts On File, 1985).
17. See, for example, G. Comstock et al., *Television and Human Behavior* (New York: Columbia University Press, 1978) and L. D. Eron, "Prescription for Reduction of Aggression," *American Psychologist* 35 (1980): 244–52.

18. Richard Schickel, *Intimate Strangers: The Culture of Celebrity* (New York: Doubleday, 1985).
19. Cynthia Heimel, *Village Voice,* 2 Jan. 1990.
20. Glenn D. Bradley, *The Story of the Pony Express* (Chicago: McClurg, 1913).
21. Tom Forester, *High-Tech Society* (Cambridge, Mass.: MIT Press, 1987).
22. *USA Today,* 4 May 1989.
23. Stewart Brand, *The Media Lab: Inventing the Future at MIT* (New York: Viking, 1987), p. 24.
24. Ibid., pp. 36–39.
25. The capacity for digitizing information enables TV cameramen to shoot video in Tiananmen Square, for example, and (via live satellite transmissions) have it readied for viewing in the U.S. within five minutes,
26. Brand, *The Media Lab.*
27. Joe Bernard, "Tomorrow's Edition," *TWA Ambassador* (July 1990): 38–40.
28. A useful description of communication in the traditional or "monocultural" community is furnished by W. Barnett Pearce in *Communication and the Human Condition* (Carbondale: University of Northern Illinois Press, 1989).
29. Joshua Meyrowitz, *No Sense of Place* (New York: Oxford University Press, 1985). A similar thesis is developed by Neil Postman in *The Disappearance of Childhood* (New York: Delacorte, 1982).
30. Shoshana Zuboff, *In the Age of the Smart Machine* (New York: Basic Books, 1988).
31. Bruce Wilshire describes the process by which humans come to imitate each other as *mimetic engulfment.* See his "Mimetic Engulfment and Self-Deception," in Amelie Rorty, ed., *Self-Deception* (Berkeley: University of California Press, 1988). Many social scientists believe that such tendencies are innate, appearing as early as the first two weeks of life.
32. Mary Watkins, *Invisible Guests: The Development of Imaginal Dialogues* (Hillsdale, N.J.: Analytic Press, 1986); Eric Klinger, "The Central Place of Imagery in Human Functioning," in Eric Klinger, ed., *Imagery, Volume 2: Concepts, Results, and Applications* (New York: Plenum, 1981); Mary Gergen, "Social Ghosts, Our Imaginal Dialogues with Others" (paper presented at American Psychological Association Meetings, New York, August 1987). See also Mark W. Baldwin and John G. Holmes, "Private Audiences and Awareness of the Self," *Journal of Personality and Social Psychology* 52(1987):1087–1198.
33. Hazel Markus and Paula Nurius, "Possible Selves," *American Psychologist* 41(1986): 954–69. Closely related is Barbara Konig's fascinating novel, *Personen-Person* (Frankfurt: Carl Hanser Verlag, 1981). The narrator realizes that she may be soon meeting an attractive man. The entire volume is then composed of a dialogue among her many inner voices—the residuals of all her past relations.

34. Paul C. Rosenblatt and Sara E. Wright, "Shadow Realities in Close Relationships," *American Journal of Family Therapy* 12 (1984): 45–54.

35. Michael Billig et al., *Ideological Dilemmas* (London: Sage, 1988).

36. See Peter Berger, Brigitte Berger, and Hansfried Kellner, *The Homeless Mind* (New York: Random House, 1973), for a precursor to the present discussion.

37. T. S. Eliot, "The Love Song of J. Alfred Prufrock," in *The Waste Land and Other Poems* (New York: Harvest, 1930).

✦ ✦ ✦

✦ Framing the Context

1. Describe the characteristics (i.e., age, education, profession) of the reader likely to read Gergen's book, *The Saturated Self: Dilemmas of Identity in Comtemporary Life,* from which the selection was excerpted.

2. What does the opening list of bulleted moments indicate about Gergen's assumed relationship to his readers?

✦ Point of View

3. What point of view does Gergen choose to present his ideas?

4. How does this point of view affect his relationship to his readers and his readers' relationship to the subject?

✦ Shape of Ideas

5. This excerpt represents a full chapter from Gergen's book. Using the headings and subheadings, make an outline of the chapter and describe the structure Gergen uses.

6. How does the progression of the headings and subheadings connect the readers to Gergen's purpose?

✦ Choosing Voice

7. What level of formality does Gergen use in his writing voice and how does it complement his point of view and purpose?

8. Explain how paragraph 25 illustrates Gergen's level of formality.

✦ Credibility

9. Identify five different types of sources Gergen uses to construct his credibility.

10. Gergen positions an italicized quote under his headings and subheadings. What purpose do these quotes serve and how do they contribute to Gergen's credibility?

Politics on the Internet

Doug Bailey

✦ ✦ ✦

America's voting record is at an all-time low. Despite efforts to increase voter registration, each year fewer people go to the polls to vote. Doug Bailey, founder and publisher of National Journal's The Hotline, *a daily on-line briefing on American politics, believes that condition is likely to change in the near future when video-on-demand becomes a primary channel for conducting campaigns. Bailey's article appeared in the August/September 1999 issue of* Civilization, *the magazine of the Library of Congress.*

1   The jukebox classically embodies a corollary to the general law of supply and demand: When the people pick the music, they're much more likely to listen to it.

2   So while some of us may dread the prospective democratization of democracy via the Internet—and some may cringe at the thought that an on-line campaign by core supporters helped lift Jesse Ventura off the mat and into the Minnesota governor's chair—make no mistake: The full interactive potential of the Internet offers a real chance to restore some purpose to our politics by restoring some power to our people.

3   Of course, there already have been a number of well-publicized abuses of democracy on-line—and there will be plenty more. E-mail campaigns organized by interest groups will clog congressional computers. Politicians will scarcely be in a position to restrain themselves from spewing e-mail spam—it being as free as the franking privilege. Phony sites will fool the gullible. Some members of congress will even use the web to raise campaign contributions the night before a big floor vote. All that, and more, is inevitable.

4   Individual empowerment, of course, is most likely to give advantage to those who seek it—including relatively small-scale but highly motivated, true-believing interests. And even the most ubiquitous availability of technology is unlikely to empower those on the bottom rungs in a free-enterprise economy. It's a new millennium, not nirvana.

But the convergence of television and online capability is open- 5
ing up extraordinary new opportunities in entertainment, communications, and education, and it will likely also mean a welcome fresh
start for our politics. Interactive video-on-demand will not just let
you instantly replay Leno one-liners, choose optional database reports to accompany the news, and view a ball game from the camera
angle of your choice. It will also enable voters to dial up candidates
they want to hear from—on issues they want to hear about—all at
times they choose themselves.

Even in the absence of a fully two-way conversation, it will be 6
the voters who ask the questions and control the conversation. The
voters in control! Hmmmm. What a revolutionary idea.

The contrast with today's world of 30-second TV spots could 7
not be greater. No one watches TV for the ads; the challenge to admakers, both commercial and political, is to be entertaining enough
or confrontational enough or bizarre enough to keep the viewer
from clicking elsewhere or going for a beer. For the most part, only
negative ads make contact—so that's what we get.

And for any TV audience, even on today's niche channels, the 8
demographics are still broad enough that a campaign risks boring
the public, or worse, by making ads issue-specific instead of taking
up the character issue or other emotionally charged themes. There's
a reason why elevator music bores its captive audience: Muzak
doesn't connect because it's for everyone and thus for no one.

That has been the politics of passive television. Everything 9
changes in the Wurlitzer world of video-on-demand, in which the
subject is chosen by the voters themselves—not by candidates, consultants, or admakers. When you click to see candidate Giuliani's position on police brutality, you want Giuliani, not marching bands.
And you want his comments on police brutality, not on Hillary Rodham Clinton's role in Whitewater. And if you don't get what you
want, you and your vote may just go elsewhere.

Video-on-demand is just another example of people on-line tak- 10
ing charge of their lives. They trade the stocks they want; the middleman is out. They order their own airline tickets; the middleman is out.
They deliver their own mail; the middleman is out. With video-on-
demand, the voters will set the agenda, the candidates will respond,
and the middleman consultant will be out—or at least humbled.

Is it a panacea? Of course not. Will it change things? Count on it. 11

12   The 30-second television ad won't disappear. Not a chance. But pretaped direct answers to FAQs (that's e-speak for "frequently asked questions") on the issues will be more important. Fundraising may still be a crucial part of most campaigns, but when it comes to financing, the on-line playing field is as level as they come. There are few lower overheads in campaign strategy than the cost of going on-line.

13   Voting may even increase a little. When we can pick the music, we're also more likely to dance. At the very least, those who vote are likely to know more about who they are voting for, and why.

14   Every day, more Americans are on-line, and most who are on-line vote. Every day, each computer sold has greater capacity for video streaming. Every day, more broadband options are available for quicker and clearer video images on-line. This convergence is about to rock our world with a cultural change nearly as great as television itself.

15   And video-on-demand will be only the beginning. Video e-mail is around the next corner. And users will become their own Peter Jenningses, downloading their own nightly news reports directly to their computers, uniquely tailored to their own interests, needs, and whims. On-line registration and on-line voting, each with video-imprint safeguards, seem inevitable.

16   There's enough time—and good reason—to ponder and worry about all that. But video-on-demand in simple forms is already with us now, and is sure to produce some winners in 2000.

17   And politics so loves a winner that by the campaign of 2004, it seems certain to be dancing to an interactive beat—with the people calling the tune.

✦ ✦ ✦

✦ *Framing the Context*

1. What can Bailey assume about the readers' purposes for reading *Civilization*?

2. How do the first two paragraphs indicate the assumptions Bailey makes about his readers' relationship to the subject?

✦ *Point of View*

3. Bailey has the expertise to write from a subjective point of view but chooses not to. What point of view does he use and how does it affect his relationship to his reader?

4. Had Bailey chosen to write from a subjective point of view, how would his relationship to his readers change?

✦ *Shape of Ideas*

5. Visually Bailey's article is presented in two sections. How do those sections define the structure he uses?

6. How does the structure reveal and connect the readers to Bailey's purpose?

✦ *Choosing Voice*

7. Using paragraph 2 as an example, explain how Bailey's language choices (sentence structure, diction, punctuation) convey the level of formality in his writing voice.

8. Describe the tone of Bailey's voice and select six examples that illustrate that tone.

✦ *Credibility*

9. How does Bailey's professional expertise contribute to his credibility?

10. Instead of outside sources Bailey incorporates examples to achieve his purpose. Explain how his selection of examples affects his credibility.

MBA.com/Do MBAs
Really Matter?

*Susan Moran with Justin Kitch
versus Steve Jurvetson*

✦ ✦ ✦

A main feature in the October 1999 issue of Business 2.0 *addresses the changing role of education as preparation for the top positions in today's increasingly e-commerce world. In "MBA.com," the first of the series of articles that follow, Susan Moran, senior editor at* Business 2.0, *explains how and why business graduate schools (B-Schools) are redesigning their MBA programs. Moran's article—and a detailed review of the top-ten B-School graduate programs (not included here)— is followed by two opposing views on the value of earning an MBA degree. Justin Kitch, founder and CEO of Homestead.com, presents the view against the MBA in "Look, Mom, No MBA"; Steve Jurvetson, managing director at venture capital firm Draper Fisher Jurvetson, presents the view for earning the MBA degree in "I Want My MBA."*

MBA.com

1   Those who feel that getting a head start in the Information Age starts with prenatal exposure to mathematics and computer science won't be surprised to learn that business schools are overhauling their curricula to give students a competitive edge in the New Economy.

2   It's no wonder. The Internet is dramatically altering the way people communicate and do business, so universities that want to remain intellectual gene pools of future leaders must keep abreast of the changes. There's also a financial incentive: Large corporations and Internet startups alike are showing increasing willingness to sponsor ecommerce programs at business schools. And students— eager to catch the dot-com boom—are spurring graduate schools to offer more ebusiness courses and other activities.

3   "It's definitely the topic du jour. It's very hot," says Milton Blood, managing director of the AACSB International Association for Management Education, about ecommerce programs at B-schools.

"What's driving this trend is simply the observation of huge amounts of money now being transferred in electronic commerce. Those schools that can establish their place early on are counting on having more of an advantage in terms of being able to attract the best students and the best employers." 4

We chose 10 business schools that are taking the lead in preparing students for the New Economy, based on course work, non-academic activities, networking ties to high-tech companies, student and recruiter feedback, and the number of graduates who have started their own ventures or are working in Internet-related executive positions. While many B-schools offer executive MBA programs with ecommerce certificates, we've focused on standard full-time programs. All stand out because they have initiated innovative ecommerce tracks or research institutes. The ecommerce offerings range from a separate master's degree in ecommerce (Carnegie Mellon University) to course-work emphases or concentrations. Some schools prefer not to offer students specialties in ecommerce, but have expanded and centralized their ebusiness-related courses and independent studies, and have strengthened their ties to the high-tech and venture communities. 5

Also, many offer campus-wide business plan contests, which have become a springboard for many Internet entrepreneurs. 6

Many did not make the cut, but are worth mentioning for their various initiatives in the ecommerce area. They include the Fuqua School of Business at Duke University, Georgia State University, the University of Washington Business School (Seattle), New York University, Columbia University, and the Jesse H. Jones Graduate School of Management at Rice University (Houston). 7

With record amounts of money chasing Internet-related start-ups, MBAs are in demand like never before. Venture-backed investments reached a record $7.7 billion in the second quarter of this year. Of that, half went to Internet-related companies, according to a PricewaterhouseCoopers MoneyTree survey. In fact, business students are growing increasingly restless, some crafting business plans and wooing venture capital months before graduating. 8

In either case, MBAs are in the catbird's seat, many of them shunning consulting or corporate jobs for the entrepreneurial challenge—and chances of fortune—that Net startups offer. . . . Otherwise high-flying tech companies are having a tougher time luring B-school grads. "We're definitely seeing a lot of competition from startups that 9 we hadn't really seen before," laments Lisa Weathersby, manager of corporate business recruiting for Intel. "This year there are a whole lot more students who are willing to take their chances with start-ups. . . . It makes it a little more difficult to recruit."

10   Intel is trying to persuade new MBAs that they can satisfy their entrepreneurial itch by joining Intel's (nonsemiconductor) product development group or new business group, where they would work with Internet startups that Intel has invested in.

11   Even Excite@Home is having trouble netting MBAs who are leaning toward younger ventures that hold the stock option carrot out to applicants. "They have expectations, given how many pre-IPO companies there are out there," says Aida LaChaux, staffing manager at the Redwood City, Calif.-based company. "A lot of MBAs are looking at what companies can give them today, and more financially. . . . We try to accommodate their needs as best we can."

12   Some recruiters caution that MBAs obsessed with following the high-risk, high-reward path may be risking too much, including their spirit. "The problem is [MBAs] in the past wouldn't go to start-ups because they had a distorted sense of risk. Now their vision is distorted, but this time they're seeing too little risk," says Mike Maples, a co-founder of Motive Communications of Austin, Texas, whose software and Web service automate technical support for companies. He is also a Harvard Business School MBA from the Class of '94. "A lot of MBA programs create a dangerous atmosphere where people get caught up in the track of the moment and forget to follow their passion. . . . Anyone who's not passionate about a job has flunked the cosmic IQ test."

Do MBAs Really Matter?

Look, Mom, No MBA

1   Does an MBA make sense for an aspiring entrepreneur? It depends. Aspiring entrepreneurs fall into two categories: Type I and Type II. The first is fascinated with the abstract idea of business, and looking for a perfect scam in the market to attack. This person should get an MBA, and almost always does, because a business degree is as much about contacts, business plans, and fundraising as it is about academic study. Two years of case studies, cocktail parties, and business

plan competitions is a perfect catalytic state for the "great idea" and/or a naive investor. If you are this type of entrepreneur, you should stop reading this article immediately and apply to business school.

The Type II entrepreneur is fanatical about a specific revolutionary technology, product, or idea. This person usually doesn't have the foggiest idea about business and has little interest in generic business principles. They are often suffering under the delusion that they can "change the world" and, as one might suspect when embarking on such a task, time is the scarce commodity—especially in the Internet world.

2

Who's Got the Time?

It has been said that Internet time is roughly the equivalent of dog years: Seven Internet years equal one normal year. This means that while you are squandering two years in business school, someone else is already out in the Internet world implementing *your* big ideas.

3

No matter which type of entrepreneur you are, there are two major skills required to get your idea off the ground: vision and communication. Business school doesn't focus on either of these things. It doesn't matter how many business principles or well connected people you know; if you can't inspire other people to believe in your vision—or you don't have one in the first place—someone else will get there first.

4

Type I entrepreneurs are often great at communication—luckily for them it is one of the major screening criteria for MBA programs—but they usually lack in vision. It is common for Type I people to go to business school in search of this vision. While you may get inspired with a vision while attending business school, you won't learn to be visionary there. That visionary inspiration is impossible to teach or force—it just has to come—and it is tough to succeed as an entrepreneur without it. Other, more basic, human needs usually take over long before success, such as rational thought and sleep.

5

In contrast, Type II entrepreneurs are visionary by definition but often are short on communication skills. They work day and night on the prototype of their collapsible Internet defibrillator, or whatever it is, until they suddenly realize that they need to raise money—the ultimate test of communication skills. Alas, having a vision is not the same as pitching one, and many great visions get lost in the chasm between the two.

6

Don't Talk, Do

7   Unfortunately, business school is rarely an answer for Type IIs who lack the necessary communication skills, even if they realize their deficiency in time. First, they have to decide to go to business school, which means putting their vision on hold. Nothing is more blasphemous to Type IIs than postponing their vision. Two years is equivalent to four complete re-designs, 18 product releases, 200 all-nighters, and more than 1,000 bowls of ramen. Secondly, even if they decide to go, they have to get in, which is quite hard to do without the aforementioned communication skills. Finally, business school is less about teaching communication skills than it is about using them.

8   If you are an aspiring entrepreneur mostly interested in business for the sake of business, an MBA might be a great way to set the stage for your success. You might even discover your vision—or a visionary—while you are there. However, if you are an entrepreneur already feeling the visionary juices bubbling to the surface, then an MBA is a waste of precious time. With a lot of hard work and a little luck, you will soon realize the ultimate irony that comes with being a hard-charging entrepreneur lacking an MBA: You spend a lot of time recruiting, pitching to, raising money from, and pleasantly ignoring the advice of people who have one.

I Want My MBA

1   There comes a time when you look back on your life and realize that of all the myriad potentials you envisioned as a child, your life has tracked a path of progressive narrowing. In many ways, business school reopens that field of view. Rather than trundle along a path that may look like a rut in retrospect, there is a child-like rush of myriad horizons open anew.

Brain Food

2   It is an academic program after all. Many applicants have gone through academic withdrawal, and they yearn for a revival of that undergraduate spirit. In any academic curriculum there is a balance of short-term tactics and long-term frameworks, between depth and breadth. Most of the value is in the higher-level analytical frameworks and self-awareness rather than in the details of corporate finance or

accounting. The MBA coursework is like a Chinese menu of delights: Interpersonal Dynamics, Business Strategy, High-Tech Entrepreneurship, and Brand Marketing. Most business schools teach with the case method. Most of the lessons are learned by reading a summary of a real business situation and hashing out the implications and strategic counter-moves in class. The classes are highly participatory. Often the CEO or protagonist from the case would jump in to debrief the class in the last 10 minutes of an hour-long debate.

Business judgment, especially in evaluating new business ventures, is fundamentally an exercise in pattern recognition—what elements of the market, team, and strategy were correlated with success. Rarely would a direct comparison suffice; rather, a new business is often the complex composite of several successful business elements. The corpus of MBA cases is like a highlight reel of a lifetime of business experience. Although no substitute for direct experience, they nevertheless provide a stable of mental triggers, analogies, and frameworks for learning quickly in future business contexts.

And then there are the classes that go on across the street at the University. You can catch up on that engineering seminar. Or take an introduction to computer programming. The amazing variety of the undergraduate and graduate schools is open once again.

Network of Contacts

Business school is unique in that it is one of the few academic programs where you are likely to get a job from one of your classmates. Unlike engineering grad school, medical school, or law school, MBA students have made a three- to five-year run at a career *before* coming to business school. It is a fundamental difference; you are more likely to find your career by getting to know your classmates than by anything the Career Placement Center can do. It is the background for the "Great Job Swap"—most of the bankers want to leave banking and most of the consultants want to get out of consulting. Many of them end up swapping jobs. Whether it is from this subtle realization, or the prior predilection of a bunch of gung-ho business types, "networking" is on the brain. There are more parties and networking events per year than many of us have had in our entire lives. Welcome to the blurring of work and play, endemic to the Information Age.

The network of contacts are the students, faculty, and guest speakers from Silicon Valley. Each is learning from the others. The case method requires teams of students to band together; almost everything is a group project.

7   And then there are the clubs. I spent as much time working on the "High-Tech Club" as I did on academics. Under the Stanford brand, I emailed invitations to technology executives to speak to the school, and it proved to be very effective. Jim Clark spoke to us back before Netscape Communications was even a company. Steve Jobs gave a fireside chat at my house. The High Tech Club had at least one great speaker every week, for two years.

8   Long after graduation, the classmates constitute a business development and partnership network, as well as a security-blanket employment network. A couple of years after graduation, when several of them are looking for new jobs, they often turn to their classmates for leads and introductions. One of the most important jobs of the venture capitalist is to serve as matchmaker—for corporate partnerships, team building, customer contacts, and follow-on financing. Business school contacts prove invaluable.

A Time to Dream

9   School is refreshing; it provides a time to think, a time to reflect, and a time to interview. For me, the transition into venture capital took 60 interviews across 15 firms, and countless informational interviews and background research. It was a process I might not have undertaken while employed elsewhere. Business school provides a spectacular opportunity to pursue the career of your dreams.

10   If you are an Internet executive or an entrepreneur with a great idea, I would not advise stepping out of the market for two years to get an MBA. The opportunity cost is too great. But if you are looking to break into the industry or explore new careers, business school can open doors and accelerate the process. To find your calling in life is priceless.

✦ ✦ ✦

✦ Framing the Context

1. How are the three authors of these articles likely to relate differently to the readers of *Business 2.0*? Explain why.

2. Define the occasion that generated the need for this set of articles.

✦ *Point of View*

3. What point of view does Moran choose to use and how is it similar to or different from the point of view Kitch and Jurvetson use?

4. Identify the similarities and differences these writers establish in their relationship to the readers.

✦ *Shape of Ideas*

5. How does the structure Moran uses prepare readers for the debate that follows?

6. Kitch and Jurvetson both want readers to accept their respective claim as valid, but they use different structures to achieve their purpose. Describe each structure and explain the difference in how those structures connect with the readers.

✦ *Choosing Voice*

7. Explain and illustrate how the difference in the way Kitch and Jurvetson use the dash conveys the character and tone of their writing voices.

8. On a scale of one to ten, with ten being the most formal, rate the level of formality for each writer and identify the language choices that create that level.

✦ *Credibility*

9. Moran quotes directly from four sources. What do these sources have in common and how to do they contribute to Moran's credibility in achieving her purpose?

10. Neither Kitch nor Jurvetson quote from sources. What sources do they use to support their claims and how will those sources affect their individual credibility with the readers?

The Y1K Problem

Daniel Radosh

✦ ✦ ✦

While most current articles speculate on how technology will affect the new century, this article, which appeared in the October/November 1999 issue of Civilization, *the magazine of the Library of Congress, presents a look into the last millennium using today's technology. Daniel Radosh, a New York–based freelance writer asks the question: "What insights can the technology of 1999 deliver about the world as it was a millennium ago?" To answer that question, Radosh researched the entire essay on the Internet as an experiment. As he explains, "I was utterly ignorant about the subject [researching on the Internet] when I began—which is indeed the point of this exercise." What results is two journeys, both filled with unexpected insights. Daniel Radosh writes regularly about the media for* The Nation *and has been published in* GQ, Playboy, Esquire, *and* Salon.

1   Centuries later, it would be called the Dark Ages, but life at the turn of the second millennium had far more vivid colorations than popular imaginings tend to ascribe to it.[1] Individual lives could be nasty, brutish, and short, but collectively, the 300-odd-million people who populated Earth in the year 1000 forged a period of history that was anything but gloomy.[2]

2   The crossroads of the world is Constantinople; with more than a million inhabitants, it is far more populous than any city in Europe.[3] Emperor Basil II will be remembered as the Slayer of the Bulgarians, but Byzantium's fame rests less on military might than on arts and culture.[4] Ideas, icons, and affluence flow between the emerging Christian nations to the west and the flourishing Islamic world to the east.

3   Byzantium is starting to use a revolutionary product introduced from China, where it has been in use for a millennium already. It's called paper.[5] (It won't reach Spain for another 200 years—around the time it will be rejected as too Muslim by Holy Roman Emperor Frederick II.) Christians and Muslims are not yet really at each other's throats (except for endless skirmishes in Spain[6]). Islam's fiercest

battles are in Hindu northern India, where a Turkish ruler named Mahmud ("The Sword of Islam") leads 17 plundering expeditions in two decades.[7]

Christianity's major running battle has been with paganism, but Pope Sylvester II has helped the Latin church shake off a long slump.[8] Newly Christianized lands include Denmark, Hungary, and Kievan Rus', where Prince Vladimir I allegedly chooses Orthodoxy over Islam because, among other things, he knows Russians will never accept a prohibition on alcohol.[9] Throughout Europe, a new cult of the Virgin Mary is catching on. Even Iceland converts, though its small wooden churches are still festooned with pagan idols.[10] Christianity, through its monasteries, is keeping education alive on a continent that has largely forsaken it.[11] Europeans are more interested in farming, especially since cutting-edge technologies such as horseshoes and heavy plows have produced huge yields.[12]

In contrast, the Islamic world is devoted to scholarship, and Sylvester II learns what he can from the East, where science is enjoying a golden age without parallel since ancient Greece; in medicine, master surgeon Al-Zahravi is being justly compared to the Greek physician Galen.[13] The de facto capital of Islam is Baghdad, which exceeds even Constantinople in size and splendor. Visitors gasp at its marble palaces, gardens, menageries, aqueducts. The river teems with every kind of craft, from old Assyrian rafts of inflated skins to the newest, smartest Chinese junks.[14]

Chinese civilization is so advanced that it has already perfected bureaucracy and urban sprawl.[15] Nearby, Japan is entering the age of the samurai.[16] In Africa, the empire of Ghana is fabulously wealthy: Even the king's dogs wear collars of precious metal, and gold is so plentiful that private mining is prohibited, lest inflation render it worthless.[17] Across the Atlantic, Mayan civilization, its glory days behind it, is migrating northward to the Land of Turkey and Deer, now known as Yucatán.[18]

Slowly, the world is shrinking. In 1000, the Viking explorer Leif Eriksson reaches the Americas. His sister plans to import New World timber, but she has a falling-out with her partners and hacks them to death with a battle axe.[19] But most of Leif's countrymen live in turf-covered houses and eat bread made from pine bark when wheat is scarce—which would surprise folks in England, where the only Scandinavians they tend to meet are in raiding parties.[20] King Aethelred II, the Unwise, will mint nearly 40 million pennies trying to buy off the invaders and then attempt, unsuccessfully, to exterminate those Danes already settled in England.[21]

8   Throughout Europe, families gather around the fire in their one-room dwellings at night—with their livestock—cooking dishes such as small-bird-and-bacon stew with walnuts.[22] When relieving themselves, they grab a handful of moss to clean up as they head out the door.[23] Most people wear a simple tunic and cloak, changing and washing only their undergarments. Fashions haven't changed much—and won't—for centuries.[24] Rich folks wear jewelry, but the stones are lackluster, since gem cutting won't be invented for another 400 years. The Church frowns on recreational sex but, as always, that doesn't stop anyone. Pregnancy is warded off with potions, prototype condoms, even a woolen contraceptive sponge soaked in astringent.[25]

9   But wait: Doesn't the turn of the millennium resonate with apocalyptic fears? Apparently not.[26] Some would-be prophets noted the arrival of Halley's comet ten years earlier and wrote millennial tracts that rattled the Church hierarchy. But many Christian lands—never mind others—have yet to adopt an *anno domini* convention for dates, so few fixate on the calendar.[27] Only a few monks and acolytes study biblical prophecy, anyway. Christians believe that the end could come at any time—but they have believed this, and will, for centuries. With little fanfare, the date passes quietly into history.

Notes

1. Unsure even what historical period I'm looking into, I go to Yahoo! <www.yahoo.com>, the most popular web index—a place where people are constantly compiling, categorizing, and writing brief descriptions of web sites. But a search for "year 1,000" turns up "listings to over 1000 televised soccer matches each year" and other miscellany. I try "ancient history" and turn up an index at the University of Evansville, Exploring Ancient World Cultures <eawc.evansville.edu/eawcindex.htm>, that offers an interactive global chronology: When I enter 1000, I learn that "the early Middle Ages begin in 600 C.E. and last until 1050."

2. When you want to find a specific piece of information, a web index is less useful than an automated search engine such as Alta Vista, Lycos, or Infoseek, which will scan every web page it can find. I start at Inference Find <www.infind.com>, which searches many such engines and collates the results. Searching for *population, world,* and *medieval,* I find a pair of estimates in the same ballpark.

3. From Lands' End <beyond.landsend.com/viking/lore/vi_trade.html>. (See footnote 19.)

4. A virtual "gallery walk" at New York's Metropolitan Museum of Art <www.metmuseum.org/htmlfile/education/byzantium/byzhome.html> lets you view its Byzantine collection by chronology, theme, or historical context.

5. From the American Museum of Papermaking <www.ipst.edu/amp/index.html> at the Institute of Paper Science and Technology, an accredited research university in Atlanta, Georgia. Finding such sites is one of the true delights of searching the web.

6. From the promotional site of the Spanish Ministry of Foreign Affairs <www.SiSpain.org/SiSpain/english/index.html>, which I stumbled onto by following links; in web research, serendipity rules.

7. Posted excerpts from a 1997 history textbook used at Stetson University in De Land, Florida <www.stetson.edu/~psteeves/classes/ghazni.html>. Conveniently, many professors now post required readings online.

8. So argues James Reston, Jr., according to Amazon's synopsis of his recent book, *The Lost Apocalypse: Europe at the Year 1000 A.D.* <www.amazon.com>. Like browsing at a bookstore, searching an online bookseller is a painless way to do basic research.

9. From the Russian National Tourist Office's official site <www.interknowledge.com/russia>.

10. From *The Catholic Encyclopedia,* the entire text of which is available online <www.knight.org/advent/cathen>.

11. At About <www.about.com>, experts are available to guide you into virtually any conceivable subject. Its medieval history section <historymedren.about.com> offers original essays, including one on monastic life, and well-chosen links.

12. From a University of Kansas syllabus <www.ukans.edu/kansas/medieval/108/syll97.html>.

13. Web sites' reliability can be hard to evaluate. Poor spelling, grammar, and even design are handy red flags, but skepticism is *always* advisable. Fortunately, the *Encyclopedia Britannica's* web site <www.britannica.com> only links to sites that meet its scholarly standards. A British article on medieval Islamic science makes the cut <www.ummah.org.uk/science/islscience.htm>. Other material here is drawn from an erudite personal page at a Muslim web site <www.muslimsonline.com/~azahoor>.

14. For hundreds of documents, including a vivid firsthand description of Baghdad in 1000 C.E., Fordham University's Medieval Sourcebook <www.fordham.edu/halsall/sbook.html> is invaluable.

15. From an informed amateur's History of China page <www.chaos.umd.edu/history/toc.html>.

16. From a site purportedly run (not written) by a ten-year-old, World Surfari <www.supersurf.com/japan/history.htm>. Its Japan page, at least, is a *Britannica* link.

17. From a contemporaneous account posted by the City College of New York History Department <www.humanities.ccny.cuny.edu/history/readercont.htm>.

18. From "The Mystery of the Maya," an extensive multi-media exhibit posted by the Canadian Museum of Civilization <www.civilization.ca/membrs/civiliz/maya/mmc10eng.html#yucatan>.

19. An account of a 1998 recreation of Leif Eriksson's voyage, with plenty of background material, is posted at its sponsor's site <beyond.landsend.com/viking>.

20. At the home page of the Jorvik Viking Centre, a reconstructed tenth-century village <www.jorvik-viking-centre.co.uk>, you can hear 32 seconds of reenacted viking conversation and see what a viking woman really looked like, based on computer-generated cranial reconstruction.

21. From the Viking Network <viking.no> and an amateur Anglo-Saxon history page <www.chem.mtu.edu/pchares/anglousa/anglosaxonI.html>; Old English can also be heard read aloud <www.kami.demon.co.uk/gesithas/readings/readings.html>.

22. Carnegie Mellon University in Pittsburgh, Pennsylvania, lists medieval recipes <www.cs.cmu.edu/People/mjw/recipes/ethnic/historical/med-anglosaxon-coll.html>; other material from the University of Kansas (see footnote 12).

23. From a recent review in *Salon* <www.salon.com> of another book, *The Year 1000*, by Robert Lacey and Danny Danziger.

24. From "What was it really like to live in the Middle Ages?," an exhibit posted by the Corporation for Public Broadcasting <www.learner.org/exhibits/middleages>, and material from a student page <library.advanced.org/12834/text/distaffside.html>.

25. Undergraduates love to write papers on such stuff. Posted by Millersville University in Millersville, Pennsylvania <www.millersv.edu/~english/homepage/duncan/medfem/contra.html>.

26. The Center for Millennial Studies <www.mille.org> has a thorough exploration of millennialism past and present.

27. From *The Catholic Encyclopedia* (see footnote 10).

✦ ✦ ✦

✦ *Framing the Context*

1. What experience are the readers of *Civilization* likely to have in relationship to Radosh's experiment with researching on the Internet?

2. What relationship can Radosh assume the readers will have to the subject of the article?

✦ *Point of View*

3. How does Radosh's point of view in the article differ from the point of view he uses to report his Internet research experience?

4. Describe the relationship Radosh establishes with the readers in each section.

✦ *Shape of Ideas*

5. Although Radosh presents the chronology of the last millennium, how does he structure the presentation of his ideas within that chronology?

6. How does that structure connect the readers to his purpose in the article?

✦ *Choosing Voice*

7. Although Radosh uses different points of view in the article and the research experience, he establishes a similar level of formality in both. Describe that level of formality and identify three examples of language in both to illustrate your description.

8. Explain the effect this level of formality has on how the readers interact with both sections.

✦ *Credibility*

9. How does Radosh use his commentary in reporting his research process to establish credibility?

10. Radosh uses the same technique for incorporating sources throughout the article, but at the end he tells readers they can access those sources on-line via hyperlinks. How is this strategy for using sources likely to affect Radosh's credibility with his *Civilization* readers?

Coda
The Faustian Pact
Sven Birkerts

✦ ✦ ✦

In The Gutenberg Elegies, The Fate of Reading in an Electronic Age *(1994), critic Sven Birkerts reflects on the complex pleasures of reading and his fears that we will sacrifice too much of ourselves and our literary culture by embracing the technology of the electronic age. The last chapter of the book presented here brings together those two worlds in a final, decisive battle for Birkerts. Sven Birkerts, awarded the National Book Critics' Circle Citation for Excellence in Reviewing and Lila Wallace–Reader's Digest Foundation and Guggenheim Fellowships, is the author of three books of criticism, including* American Energies: Essays on Fiction. *His essays and reviews have appeared in the* New York Times Book Review, *the* Atlantic Monthly, Harper's, *and the* New Republic.

1   I've been to the crossroads and I've seen the devil there. Or is that putting it too dramatically? What I'm really saying is that I've been to the newsstand, again, to plunk down my money for *Wired*. You must have seen it—that big, squarish, beautifully produced item, that travel guide to the digital future. To read the magazine and to look it (one does spend a great deal of time *looking* at *Wired*, checking out the ads, turning it this way and that to follow the little typographic trails) is almost to be persuaded that the future is here and that it can work. That ingenuity, design intelligence, and the capabilities of the microchip will soon liberate the world entirely from its sooty industrial roots. *Wired* gives us our old planet repackaged as a weightless environment, more dream than matter—information moving through cyberspace at the speed of thought (*intelligent* thought), with interactive resources putting people in control, allowing them to tailor the "fit" of their experience; digitally programmed words and visuals and sounds coalescing in ever-fresh multimedia combinations; pools of the like-minded gathering into networks, establishing grassroots power bases via Internet; virtual re-

ality opening up realms of sensation, dazzling retreats just adjacent to our own ever more depleted world . . . and so on.

The ads and the graphics are finally more seductive than the excitable proselytizing of the writers. We are taken most by the *look* of it all—the compact, crisp, high-resolution design that inspires confidence, that allows us to revere the near-mystical power of the concealed microprocessors. Bold colors, sans serif type fonts, unexpected layouts. Everything orchestrated to say: *That was then, this is now.* Alongside *Wired*, dominantly print-driven vehicles like *The New Yorker* or even *The Paris Review* look dowdy, Victorian. Unbroken columns of print suddenly seem like visual molasses.

Yes, I've been to the crossroads and I've met the devil, and he's sleek and confident, ever so much more "with it" than the nearest archangel. He is casual and irreverent, wears jeans and running shoes and maybe even an earring, and the pointed prong of his tail is artfully concealed. Slippery fellow. He is the sorcerer of the binary order, jacking in and out of terminals, booting up, flaming, commanding vast systems and networks with an ease that steals my breath away. I don't hate him—I admire and fear him, and I wonder, as I did in high school when confronted with the smooth and athletic ones, the team captains and class presidents, whether I would not, deep down, trade in all this doubting and wondering and just be him.

I have heard pornographic books and magazines referred to as "masturbation aids." *Wired* is, for me, of that ilk—except that it does not get me thinking dirty thoughts, it just gets me thinking. But I use it as one might use something from the aforementioned category: to put me on a very specific mind-track. I buy the magazine and read it and study it in order to engage myself in what I think of as the argument of our time—the argument between technology and soul. Every time I open the covers and find myself slipping into that most beguiling reverie of the near future, I have to ask: Is this what we want? Do we know what we're doing? Do people understand that there might be consequences, possibly dire, to our embrace of these technologies, and that the myth of the Faustian bargain has not become irrelevant just because we studied it in school?

To me it is very clear that the process is well underway and that it is not likely to stop. From our president on down people are smitten, more than they have been with anything in a very long time. I can't open a newspaper without reading another story about Internet or the information highway. The dollar, not the poet, is the antenna of the race, and right now the dollar is all about mergers and acqui-sitions, as seen in the bidding war for Paramount, the fierce battles being waged for control of the system that will wire us each to each and will allow us, soon enough, to cohabit in the all-but-infinite in-formation space. If we are separate on earth because of geography and physics (two bodies cannot inhabit the same space), we will be piled together like transparent wafers in cyberspace. The dollar is smart. It is betting that the trend will be a juggernaut, unstoppable; that we are collectively ready to round the corner into a new age. The dollar is betting, as it always does, against the soul.

6   *Soul*—a vast, elusive word, and I need to be careful not to use it indiscriminately. What do I mean by it? Although I don't want to rule out its religious sense, I am not using it, as believers have for cen-turies, to designate the part of ourselves that is held to be immortal. My use of soul is secular. I mean it to stand for inwardness, for that awareness we carry of ourselves as mysterious creatures at large in the universe. The soul is that part of us that smelts meaning and tries to derive a sense of purpose from experience. It is the *I* that speaks when we say, "I've always believed . . . " as opposed to the *I* we refer to when we say "I went to get the car fixed this morning." I don't know that I can get more precise about it—I don't know that preci-sion is called for. Soul is our inwardness, our self-reflectiveness, our orientation to the unknown. Soul waxes in private, wanes in public. We feel it, or feel through it, when we are in sacral spaces, when we love, when we respond to natural or artistic beauty. Soul may be elicited in many ways. We comprehend it unthinkingly—we either know it as a resonance, a presence, or we deduce it, negatively, from a feeling of absence. When we cannot get clear, cannot feel the im-portance of something we know to be important; when we harken to images that take us from the present that we feel trapped in: im-ages of childhood, of isolated retreat in nature. Except in situations we deem communal, where we have communion with other souls, soul is private. Solitary. Said Emily Dickinson, "The soul selects its own society." And as I write this I think that, yes, there is something Dickinsonian, something tremulous and antiquated about it all. I hear ticking clocks and footsteps in empty houses. The inward self collects around a center, defines itself in its separation from others. What an odd notion. I see Old Nick winking and I find myself won-dering if we might not indeed be ready to push onto something new, to put behind us once and for all this melancholy business of iso-lated selves trudging through a vale of tears.

This is where I often end up when I start thinking about these
things—I feel as though a train has gone racing by, leaving me on the
platform watching the swirl of candy wrappers. Yet, were the train to
stop for me, I would not get on. Something holds me back, a fear not
unlike what I've known on the brink of certain relationships. Then I
held back because I sensed that to plunge would be to change myself
as a person. Not a bad thing necessarily, but just not what I wanted
then. The disinclination I feel about the digital future is stronger,
more certain, but the fear grows from the same root. I see the situation in Faustian terms, as an either/or. To embrace the microchip and
its magic would be to close myself off from a great many habits and
attitudes, ones that define me to myself, I would have to reposition
myself on the space-time axis. I would have to say good-bye to a certain way of looking at the world because that way is bound up with a
set of assumptions about history and distance, and difficulty and solitude and the slow work of self-making—of which go against the
premises of instantaneousness, interactivity, sensory stimulation and
ease that make the world of *Wired* attractive to so many.

I think, then, in terms of a face-off, a struggle, a war. But it is to
a large degree a war inside myself. In the larger societal sphere there
is no great contest. We already know that technological ingenuity
will set the agenda and that Americans, never that deeply entrenched
in tradition, will follow. We are accustomed to taking up interesting
offers. And the nature of the whole electronic system is such that
recalcitrance is discouraged. Think of the incursion of the tele-
technologies—phone and TV—and, more recently, of the telephone
answering machine. Our society exerts pressures that make it very
hard not to play the game. The game underway now is the game
called "on-line" and, bitter it is to say it, I am still on the platform
watching the dance of the candy wrappers.

I know which way the future is going, but I cannot find it in myself to get in step. At times I take this situation, this refusal, very
seriously—I think of it as a crisis at the very core of my life. At other
times, though, it seems comic. I see myself as one of the histrionically
gesturing actors in the movie *Singin' in the Rain*—a man from the era
of silent films who cannot believe that the newfangled talkies are
really going to carry the day. But with this difference: That in my heart
I know that the change is already taking place. The question I face is
not, as some would have it, whether I should get myself a computer,
find myself a network, do whatever one does to be in step. To me it is
more a question of how I want to position myself as history makes a

swerve, not only ushering in new circumstances and alignments, but changing its own deeper nature as well. For once the world goes fully on-line, there will be no more history of the old kind. History as we all studied it in school depended not just on the idea of chronological sequence, but also on fixed coordinates of space and time. X did such and such a thing here at such and such a time. No more. Most events of significance—most displays of force—will take place off the space-time axis. In cyberspace, among numbers. Binary codes don't live in time in the same way that people do, yet it will be their movement and interaction that will determine movements in the outer scape. The slow conventions of narrative will be overwhelmed by simultaneity. The time line, that organizing fiction that served us for so long, will go the way of Ptolemaic reckoning; we will have it only as a vestige.

10   Dire prognostications. What is it that I envision? Not a revolution—this is not a revolutionary scenario. I see instead a steady displacement of old by new, a generational pressure that escalates, its momentum gathering as the members of the old dispensation age and die off. Gone are those crusty individualists, those Jason Robards figures who still tickle us in movies; disappearing are the ideals they once espoused. As they move off the stage, they are not being replaced by chosen successors, but by people who have come up shaped by radically different stimuli. Not that generations haven't since time immemorial shouldered their predecessors aside. But this time there is a difference. The rate of change, social and technological, has surpassed exponentially the gradually escalating rates of previous periods. There is a ledge, a threshold, a point after which everything is different. I would draw the line, imprecisely, somewhere in the 1950s. That was when television worked its way into the fabric of American life, when we grew accustomed to the idea of parallel realities—one that we lived in, the other that we stepped into whenever we wanted a break from our living. People born after the mid-1950s are the carriers of the new; they make up the force that will push us out of our already-fading rural/small-town/urban understanding of social organization. The momentum of change has already made those designations all but meaningless. And many think it is a good thing.

11   I see the wholesale wiring of America. I see ever more complex and efficient technological systems being interposed between the individual and the harsh constraints of nature. This electronic mesh is already changing absolutely the way we deal with information. In fact,

it is changing our whole idea of what information is. Former scales and hierarchies are being renovated. The medium shapes the message. If it can't be rendered digitally, it can't be much good. Software codes are a sorting hopper; they determine what flies through the circuits and what doesn't. We will see how the movement and control, the shaping of data will become a more central occupation. We will all (except the poor and the refuseniks) spend more and more of our time in the cybersphere producing, sending, receiving, and responding, and necessarily less time interacting in a "hands-on" way with the old material order. Similarly, we will establish a wide lateral interaction, dealing via screen with more and more people at the same time that our sustained face-to-face encounters diminish. It will be harder and harder—we know this already—to step free of our mediating devices. There will be people who will never in their lives have the experience that was, until our time, the norm—who will never stand in isolated silence among trees and stones, out of shouting distance of any other person, with no communication implement, forced to confront the slow, grainy momentum of time passing. The ways of being that ruled individuals since individuals first evolved are suddenly, with a finger-snap, largely irrelevant. This is more astonishing than we generally admit. Where do those reflexes go, those codes inscribed in the chips of our cells, spooled and spun in our DNA? What happens to all of the genetic information we outgrow?

But back to *Wired* and its can-do boosterism, its fervid embrace   12
of the future, its covert assumption of the inevitability of complete social transformation. The remarkable thing about *Wired* is that it presents a fully self-contained order, a closed circuit. Nowhere in its pages do we find any trace of the murky and not-so-streamlined world that we can still see outside our windows. No ice on the mittens, no fumbling for quarters while the bus (late) toils toward us through morning traffic. Everything is clean as a California research park. No sense of getting from here to there.

And what is wrong with this picture? What, apart from the obvi-   13
ous fact that the world has so many steps to take before it becomes the high-resolution place willed by the editors of the magazine? I am most struck by the assumption on the part of all concerned of a continuum and the lack of what might be called existential questioning. There is what feels like a collective trust that we will all slide along smoothly from A, the present, to B, the future, without having to understand the

world anew. But of course we will. For the change from A to B is not, as many historical changes have been, one of degree. Here is a change of kind, a paradigm shift, a plummet down the rabbit hole.

14   The editors of *Wired* like to tap innovative and unorthodox minds, whether for more off-the-wall explorations (William Gibson, Douglas Coupland) or more practically-oriented discussions, like Mitchell Kapor's "Democracy and the New Information Highway," in which the guru thoughtfully and pragmatically addresses the vital issues of access and control. I would like to make a few observations about Kapor's article, not because he makes any points that I disagree with, but because I see operative in his presentation certain assumptions that I would never dream of making, but which underscore my point, that so many of the believers think that we are moving along a simple continuum, that we are merely replacing some tired old tools with some sensationally effective ones.

15   Kapor's teasing first paragraph (I am quoting from an adapted version of his piece that appeared in the *Boston Review*) is worth giving in full because it summarizes the fantasy, the vision that inspires the hundreds of thousands of workers in the high-tech vineyards and which percolates throughout the pages of a journal like *Wired*. It is, let me emphasize, a rhetorical ploy, a scenario Kapor blocks out so that he can get to his real opening point, which is that the struggle for the control of the system that will deliver this nirvana to us has created massive gridlock. Writes Kapor:

> *The visionaries sketched it out, the computer literati caught onto it, and now it's all over the mainstream media: a high-speed, fiber optic, "new information highway" carrying an expanding universe of information and entertainment into the home and the workplace. Thousands of movies, mail-order catalogues, newspapers and magazines, educational courses, airline schedules, and other information databases will be available with a few clicks of a remote control. Two-way video conferencing will revolutionize business meetings, visits to the doctor, and heart-to-heart talks.*

A nice touch, that last phrase—but never mind. After showing us the bureaucratic and political impediments that have arisen to stall the realization of this best of all possible worlds, Kapor makes an interesting move. He sets up as his goal in matters electronic, "a decentralized democracy, founded on the primacy of individual liberty and committed to pluralism, equality, and community." He then identifies his ideal as Jeffersonian, and lets the identification stand without any deeper inquiry into the implications of such an identification.

I read Kapor's article with some interest, and I found that so long as my reaction stayed within the general thought-circuit of the piece, I was nodding in agreement. But I was also aware of a gradually mounting sense of disquiet, the source of which, I realized (and this is often true with the essays I read in *Wired*) was not to be found in what the work itself said, but outside, in the realm where assumptions and unstated issues reside. 16

First, I was troubled—obliquely, then more overtly—by Kapor's ready conflation of terms, those pertaining to the new information highway and those invoking the Jeffersonian vision of a participatory democracy. It is not that the discourses cannot be connected, but I understood Kapor as suggesting that the information highway can actually serve and enhance a Jeffersonian egalitarianism. And with that we part company. As I see it, the techno-web and the democratic ideal are in opposition. Our whole economic and technological obsession with getting on-line is leading us away—not from democracy necessarily, but from the premise that individualism and circuited interconnection are, at a primary level, inimical notions. Warring terms. Let me make what looks like a digression before returning to this idea. 17

In the later chapters of his intellectual autobiography, *The Education of Henry Adams*, Adams reports on the revelation he experienced at the Great Exposition of 1900. In the chapter entitled "The Dynamo and the Virgin," he adduces the two great forces that, in a manner of speaking, divide the world between them. One is the dynamo, the apotheosis of applied mechanics, of which he writes: 18

> *The planet itself seemed less impressive, in its old-fashioned, deliberate, annual or daily revolution, than this huge wheel, revolving within arm's-length at some vertiginous speed, and barely murmuring—scarcely humming an audible warning to stand a hair's-breadth further for respect of power—while it would not wake the baby lying close against its frame.*

The other force, the Virgin, the force of faith and inwardness, "was still felt at Lourdes, and seemed to be as potent as x-rays," but in rude America her influence was almost negligible. Still, it would be between dynamo and Virgin, those representative centers of opposing force, that our personal and societal fortunes would be sorted out. 19

20   Adams's formulation, construed metaphorically (maybe more metaphorically than he intended) has been in my thoughts often, first as an explanatory trope for our present-day situation, later as the template for a new trope, one more suited to our transformed culture. These days I don't think in terms of dynamo and Virgin, I think of circuit and therapist. The terms are less grand than Adams's, but they lend themselves better to the facts of our case. As the dynamo brought industrialism to its zenith in the middle of our century, so now has the microscopic mazework of the silicon chip extended the promise of a computerized future. And where the Virgin was once the locus of spirit and care, the protectress of the interior life, the new site of power, now secular, is the office of the trained therapeutic specialist.

21   Like Adams's two forces, mine are symbolic orders in opposition. But unlike his, mine connect; they are not mutually exclusive. Where the circuit makes possible, maybe inevitable, a life lived significantly through mediated interactions (e-mail, ATM banking, home shopping), often leading to an obscure sense of subjective dissolution, of unreality (once called "anomie"), the therapist is the agent of repair and reconstitution. The electronic involvement leaches out traditional meaning and a sense of self by shattering the basic space-time coordinates we have always oriented ourselves by; the therapeutic involvement looks to develop narratives that, if they cannot restore wholeness, can at least offer some compensation for its loss.

22   To put it yet another way, being on-line and having the subjective experience of depth, of existential coherence, are mutually exclusive situations, thus creating a link between circuit and therapist. Electricity and inwardness are fundamentally discordant. Electricity—and the whole circulatory network predicated upon it—is about immediacy; it is in the nature of the current to surmount impedances. Electricity is, implicitly, of the moment—*now*. Depth, meaning, and the narrative structurings of subjectivity—these are *not* now; they flourish only in that order of time Henri Bergson called "duration." Duration is deep time, time experienced without the awareness of time passing. Until quite recently, people on the planet lived mainly in terms of duration time. Time not artificially broken, but shaped around natural rhythmic cycles; time bound to the integrated functioning of the senses, the perceptions.

23   We have destroyed that duration. We have created invisible elsewheres that are as immediate as our actual surroundings. We have

fractured the flow of time, layered it into competing simultaneities. We learn to do five things at once or pay the price. We have plunged ourselves into an environment of invisible signals and operations; we live in a world where it is as unthinkable to walk five miles to visit a friend as it was once unthinkable to speak across that distance through a wire.

The hardwiring of the nation is well underway. The infrastructure is being set into place; the control battles are now joined. The face-off between Viacom and QVC over the purchase of Paramount is only the most eye-catching instance of what is going on at all levels of the communications industry. We are not about to turn from the millennial remaking of the world—indeed, we are all excited to see just how much power and ingenuity we command. By degrees— it is happening year by year, appliance by appliance—we are wiring ourselves into a gigantic hive. Life in the near future will take place among an exciting and maddening and deeply distracting hum of signals. When everyone is on-line, when the circuits are crackling, the impulses speeding every which way like thoughts in a fevered brain, we will have to rethink our definitions of individuality and our time-honored ideals of subjective individualism. And of the privacy that has always pertained thereto. It may already be time. But to undertake such a reconsideration of ourselves—our private and collective selves—we will have to dispense with certain illusions. One of the deepest and most fiercely held may be that proposed by the Jeffersonian paradigm. 24

I have no trouble, then, with anything *in* Mitchell Kapor's presentation. But what alarms me, not just about his essay but in general, is that the terms of this most massive change are bandied about and accepted with no debate. No one is stepping forth to suggest that there might be something at stake, that the headlong race to wire ourselves might, in accordance with the gain-loss formulae that apply in every sphere of human endeavor like the laws of physics, threaten or diminish us in some way. To me the wager is intuitively clear: we gain access and efficiency at the expense of subjective self-awareness. I am not ready to trade, and I wonder how the man from Monticello would vote if we could get him back for a moment from the informationless realm of the dead. 25

My assessment is not optimistic. The devil may himself be at the crossroads, but we have already picked our direction and started 26 toward it. There was not, however, a moment of choosing; no pact was signed with the blood of a virgin. We have—subtly, at times all but imperceptibly—been conditioned; our preliminary technologies had us moving down that road before anyone even knew where it might lead. The electronic future was not there in an envelope that we could either open or ignore; we have made it inevitable through countless acts of acquiescence.

27   When we look at the large-scale shift, looking as if at a motion study, we can see not only how our situation has come about, but also how it is in our nature that it should have. At every step—this is clear—we trade for ease. And ease is what quickly swallows up the initial strangeness of a new medium or tool. Moreover, each accommodation paves the way for the next. The telegraph must have seemed to its first users a surpassingly strange device, but its new-fangledness was overridden by its usefulness. Once we had accepted mechanical transmission over distances, the path was clear for the telephone. Again, a monumental transformation: turn select digits on a dial and hear the voice of another human being. And on it goes, the original inventions coming gradually, one by one, allowing the society to adapt. We mastered the telephone, the television with its few networks running black and white programs. And while no law required citizens to own or use either, they did in a remarkably short time achieve near-total saturation.

28   We are, then, accustomed to the trade; we take the step that will enlarge our reach, simplify our communication, and abbreviate our physical involvement in some task or chore. We do not as readily streamline our pleasures. Indeed, it is in the name of pleasure that we accept so many of these changes—we want more time for the pursuit of what we most enjoy.

29   The difference between the epoch of early modernity and the present is, to simplify drastically, that formerly the body had time to accept the graft, the new organ, whereas now we are hurtling forward willynilly, assuming that if a technology is connected with communications or information processing it must be good, we must need it—and that we had better get it lest we find ourselves stranded by the wayside, on some windy platform watching the express rattle by. I never cease to be astonished at the contemplation of what a mere two decades has brought us. Consider the evidence. Since the early 1970s we have seen the arrival—we have accepted, deemed all but indispensible—of personal computers, laptop computers, phone an-

swering machines, calling cards, fax, cellular phones, VCRs, modems, Nintendo games, e-mail, voice mail, camcorders, CD players, smart environments, virtual reality technologies . . . Very quickly, with almost no pause between increments, these circuit-driven tools and entertainments have moved into our lives, and with minimum ruffling of the waters, really—which of course makes them seem natural, even inevitable. Marshall McLuhan called improvements of this sort "extensions of man," and this is their secret. We embrace them because they seem a part of us, an enhancement. They don't seem to challenge our power so much as add to it.

I am startled, though, by how little we are debating the deeper philosophical ramifications. We talk up a storm when it comes to policy issues (who should have jurisdiction, etc.), and there is great fascination in some quarters with the practical minutiae of functioning, compatibility, and so on. But why do we hear so few people asking whether we might not ourselves be changing and whether the changes are necessarily for the good? Maybe because our overall American bewitchment with technology is based on the assumption that improvements in the material sphere are intrinsically good. If this is so, it reveals that there is for us a fatal split, a great divide, between the so-called objective world and the private, subjective, existential realm. If we did not have this split we could not refrain from asking at every turn whether our outer decisions and deeds did not have significant inner consequences. We don't ask—at least not often, and not in any public way that I am aware of. But of course the connection is there. Of course the inner and outer are on a continuum; events in one sphere necessarily impinge on the other.

My explanation for this blithe indifference to inward consequences is simple. I believe that we are—biologically, neuropsychologically—creatures of extraordinary adaptability. We greet change and disturbance by reorganizing the internal economy; we assess the odds and play what our calculations tell us will be the winning hand. We fit ourselves to situations, whether of privation or beneficent surplus. And in many respects this is to the good. The species is fit because it knows *how* to fit.

But there are drawbacks as well. The late Walker Percy, whose prescience, concern, and humor I admire tremendously, made it his work to explore the terms of the great trade off. Over and over, in his fiction as well as his speculative essays, he asks the same basic questions. As he writes in the opening of his essay "The Delta Factor,"

30
31
32

"Why does man feel so sad in the twentieth century? Why does man feel so bad in the very age when, more than in any other age, he has succeeded in satisfying his needs and making over the world for his own use?" Why are we "lost in the cosmos?" Why do we feel so deeply, if unconsciously, disconnected? One of his answers is that the price of adaptation is habit, and that habit—of perception as well as behavior—distances the self from the primary things that give meaning and purpose to life. We are cut off from beauty, from love, from true passion, and from the spiritual.

33   In "The Loss of the Creature," Percy explored this paradox with great resourcefulness and nudged his reader with illuminating anecdotes:

> *A man in Boston decides to spend his vacation at the Grand Canyon. He visits his travel bureau, looks at the folder, signs up for a two-week tour. He and his family see the tour, see the Grand Canyon, and return to Boston. May we say that this man has seen the Grand Canyon? Possibly he has. But it is more likely that what he has done is the one sure way not to see the canyon.*

Percy's point here is that under these circumstances, true seeing is most unlikely, "because the Grand Canyon, the thing as it is, has been appropriated by the symbolic complex which has already been formed in the sightseer's mind." By habit. And it is just possible that this person at some level feels a lack, a sense of distance from authentic experience. Percy then asks how his sightseer might recover the experience that habits of thought and perception have denied him. "The tourist leaves the tour, camps in the back country. He arises before dawn and approaches the South Rim through a wild terrain where there are no trails and no railed-in lookout points. In other words, he sees the canyon by avoiding all the facilities for seeing the canyon."

34   The tourist—the contemporary individual—lives his life in the circuit of habit, and so long as he remains within that circuit he is unconscious of anything outside. He is unaware, to paraphrase Percy's beloved Kierkegaard, that he is in despair, cut off from the sources of authentic selfhood. For it is the nature of adaptation to keep us sane and functional through the exclusion of the whole class of deeper questions and doubts about meaning, permitting them, at most, a subthreshold presence which manifests itself as an occasional wistfulness, sadness, homesickness. But when that same person faces something as magnificent and challenging as the Grand Canyon, the tension is exacerbated. He feels his lack as an inchoate sort of failure.

All of which is to say that we accept these gifts of technology, these labor-saving devices, these extensions of the senses, by adapting and adapting again. Each improvement is, at bottom, an order of abstraction that we accommodate ourselves to. Abstraction is, however, a movement away from the natural given—a step away from our fundamental selves, selves rooted for millennia in an awe before the unknown, a fear and trembling in the face of the outer dark. We widen the gulf, and if at some level we fear the widening, we respond by investing more of our faith in these systems we have wrought.

We sacrifice the potential life of the solitary self by enlisting ourselves in the collective. For this, even more than the saving of labor, is finally what these systems are all about. They are not only extensions of the senses, they are extensions of the senses that put us in touch with the extended senses of others. The ultimate point of the ever-expanding electronic web is to bridge once and for all the individual solitude that has heretofore always set the terms of existence. Each appliance is a strand, another addition to the virtual place wherein we will all find ourselves together. Telephone, fax, computer-screen networks, e-mail, interactive television—these are the components out of which the hive is being built. The end of it all, the *telos*, is a kind of amniotic environment of impulses, a condition of connectedness. And in time—I don't know how long it will take—it will feel as strange (and exhilarating) for a person to stand momentarily free of it as it feels now for a city dweller to look up at night and see a sky full of stars.

Whether this sounds dire or not depends upon your assumptions about the human—assumptions, that is, in the largest sense. For those who ask, with Gauguin, "Who are we? Why are we here? Where are we going?"—and who feel that the answering of those questions is the grand mission of the species—the prospect of a collective life in an electronic hive is bound to seem terrifying. But there are others, maybe even a majority, who have never except fleetingly posed those same questions, who have repressed them so that they might "get on," and who gravitate toward that life because they see it as a way of vanquishing once and for all the anxious gnawings they feel whenever any intimations of depth sneak through the inner barriers.

In his justly celebrated essay, "The Work of Art in an Age of Mechanical Reproduction," Walter Benjamin sets forth the idea, now almost commonplace, that the copying and disseminating of, say, a painting robs it of its aura. "Even the most perfect reproduction of a work of art is lacking in one element: its presence in time and space, its unique existence at the place where it happens to be." This is common sense, and the viewer of the reproduction at some level accepts it as part of the bargain. A few paragraphs on, however, Benjamin introduces a more devastating formulation: "The situations into which the product of mechanical reproduction can be brought may not touch the actual work of art, *yet the quality of its presence is always depreciated*" (emphasis mine). This he explains by arguing that the reproduction compromises the "historical testimony" of the work—its material witness to time—a compromise that saps its authority.

39   Benjamin's full argument would require patient elaboration. I only wish to borrow its ruling assumption—that technological abstraction changes the status of the thing abstracted—and his key notion of "aura." Aura, like soul, is one of those terms that are easy to intuitively catch the sense of, but very hard to define satisfactorily. The aura is the uniqueness, the presence, the natural emanation of a thing—its spirit. The aura is there when we stand in front of the original of a painting, and is absent when we are before the copy— even if the copy is so faithful as to be nearly identical. The copy is not the actual record of the brush and paint, does not hold as a part of its history the artist's actual physical engagement with materials. Many will shrug and say, "So what? I enjoy the beauty and can supply the rest in my imagination." And they are not wrong, but their response does not obviate the distinction between the thing and its surrogate. That distinction, elusive though it may be, is what underwrites our value systems, aesthetic and otherwise. Moreover, it is a distinction that will soon enough become a live issue (it is already in the philosophy of Jean Baudrillard and others) as the relative value of "real" and "virtual" experiences is contested.

40   Benjamin writes lyrically but also with a certain slipperiness about aura. He attempts to distinguish between aura as it applies to historical objects (works of art) and the aura that belongs to natural objects. "We define the aura of the latter as the unique phenomenon of a distance, however close it may be. If, while resting on a summer afternoon, you follow with your eyes a mountain range on the horizon or a branch which casts its shadow over you, you experience the aura of those mountains, of that branch." The uniqueness, or presence, then, is understood as a separateness, a resistance—the quality of being-in-itself, the "otherness" that all things manifest.

41   But now Benjamin speaks of "the desire of contemporary masses to bring things 'closer' spatially and humanly, which is just as ardent

as their bent toward overcoming the uniqueness of every reality by accepting its reproduction. Every day the urge grows stronger to get a hold of an object at very close range by way of its likeness, its reproduction."

Benjamin, in his analysis, concentrates on objects of human perception—man-made objects as well as natural ones. He does not direct much focus upon the subjects, the perceivers themselves. That is, he acknowledges how changed aesthetic engagement—made possible by film, for instance—alters the ways in which we see and understand reality. But he does not take the next big step and examine the aura—the uniqueness—of the individual himself; he does not ask how that aura may be affected by the individual's engagement with various technologies. This is a whole other subject, one that may not have been as pressing for Benjamin as it is for us, because in his time the forces of mediation—the technologies abstracting and deflecting natural human interactions—had not yet attained critical mass.

But the time has come and it may be worthwhile to apply some of Benjamin's terms to our own situation. To put it in simple terms: Do we each, as individuals, have an aura, a unique presence that is only manifest on site, in our immediate space-time location? And if we do, how is this aura affected by our myriad communications media, all of which play havoc with our space-time orientation?

These are uncomfortably loose and difficult questions. Although we all know what it is to feel the human presence of another person, who is going to argue for presence as an essential attribute? There is no verifying, quantifying, or analyzing it. How then would we begin to theorize about the change or depletion of presence, of aura? Only in the most bumbling fashion, I'd say.

I am taking it as a given that every person is blessed with aura, that he or she gives off the immediate emanation, or "vibes," of living. At any and every moment, our actions, our emotional disposition, our thoughts, our will all combine into what another person might experience as our presence. At earlier stages of history, before the advent of the sense-extending technologies, human interactions were necessarily carried out face to face, presence to presence. Before the telephone and the megaphone, the farthest a voice could carry was the distance of a shout. We could say, then, that all human communication is founded in presence. There was originally no severance between the person and the communication.

The telephone obviously altered that. It eliminated the need for a spatial proximity while keeping the time link intact. "It's raining here," says one person; the other, bemused by the miracle of distance surmounted, allows that the sun is shining where he sits. Bring in the answering machine, the voice mail, and the time link is cut. "This is Bill. It's about three o'clock and I wanted to ask you . . ." Add to this the possibility that Bill's friend is not even picking up the message at his home, but has punched in digits from the office, maybe even from the car phone, and you begin to see what a dispersal of presence contemporary communication involves.

47   But the telephone and answering machine are only a small part of the picture. A comparable set of transformations has taken place on every front. Hand-written letters gave way to typed letters, which became word-processed letters, a great many of them structured in advance by the software. And now e-mail chatter is making rapid inroads on the tradition of paper, envelope, and stamp. Photographs, home movies, camcorder records of the stages on life's way. Every set of technological advances, every extension of the senses, involves some distortion of the time-space axis—the here and now—that used to be the given.

48   And who can say what the effect of all these changes and enhancements will be? Where is there a platform, an unaffected point of vantage, from which one can make a disinterested assessment? The only procedure I can think of is the comparative one: to look at the state of things in the present and then draw comparison with what we know about various periods in the past. Which can be done readily enough. But if one then wishes to make value judgments, to calculate gain/loss formulas, all sorts of problems arise. Who is to say that any historical period is better than any other? Communications cannot be compared in isolation from everything else. And to argue for the nineteenth century, or the seventeenth, is preposterous. Sure, village life had its benefits—certain kinds of intimacy and cohesion—but village life also knew brutality, idiocy, and the horrors of disease. And so on.

49   Still, one has to hazard something about the times and their tendencies. Taking my cue from Benjamin, I would say that the net effect of all of our mediations of the real—of our abstracting and fragmenting of a formerly more direct engagement with the world—can be compared to that wreaked upon the original work of art by reproduction. That is, our various improvements not only mark a diminution of the function improved upon (as the telephone leached the power and immediacy from all human dialogue), but they also work to dissolve some of the fundamental authority of the *human* itself. We are ex-

periencing the gradual but steady erosion of human presence, both of the authority of the individual and, in ways impossible to prove, of the species itself. The same processes that are bringing this depletion about are also making inevitable a most peculiar compensation: It is getting easier and easier to accept the idea of electronic tribalism—hive life. Subjective individualism is now not the goal but the impedance factor, but as that gets leveled, the movement of the impulse through the circuit gains force. Subjective individualism, what remains of it, is like aura—we now must think of it in terms of resistance, or, to cite Benjamin, "the unique phenomenon of a distance."

My core fear is that we are, as a culture, as a species, becoming shallower; that we have turned from depth—from the Judeo-Christian premise of unfathomable mystery—and are adapting ourselves to the ersatz security of a vast lateral connectedness. That we are giving up on wisdom, the struggle for which has for millennia been central to the very idea of culture, and that we are pledging instead to a faith in the web. What *is* our idea, our ideal, of wisdom these days? Who represents it? Who even invokes it? Our postmodern culture is a vast fabric of competing isms; we are leaderless and subject to the terrors, masked as the freedoms, of an absolute relativism. It would be wrong to lay all the blame at the feet of technology, but more wrong to ignore the great transformative impact of new technological systems—to act as if it's all just business as usual.

There is, finally, a tremendous difference between communication in the instrumental sense and communion in the affective, the soul-oriented, sense. Somewhere we have gotten hold of the idea that the more all-embracing we can make our communications networks, the closer we will be to that partaking that we long for deep down. For change us as they will, our technologies have not yet eradicated that flame of a desire not merely to be in touch, but to be, at least figuratively, embraced, known and valued not abstractly but in presence. We seem to believe that our instruments can get us there, but they can't. Their great power is all in the service of division and acceleration. They work in—and create—an unreal time that has nothing to do with the deep time we thrive in: the time of history, tradition, ritual, art, and true communion.

The devil no longer moves about on cloven hooves, reeking of brimstone. He is an affable, efficient fellow. He claims to want to help us all along to a brighter, easier future, and his sales pitch is very smooth. I was, as the old song goes, almost persuaded. I saw what it could be like, our toil and misery replaced by a vivid, pleasant dream. Fingers tap keys, oceans of fact and sensation get downloaded, are dissolved through the nervous system. Bottomless wells of data are accessed and manipulated, everything flowing at circuit speed. Gone the rock in the field, the broken hoe, the grueling distances. "History," said Stephen Dedalus, "is a nightmare from which I am trying to awaken." This may be the awakening, but it feels curiously like the fantasies that circulate through our sleep. From deep in the heart I hear the voice that says, "Refuse it."

✦ ✦ ✦

✦ Framing the Context

1. What different purposes might readers have for reading a book on "the fate of reading in an electronic age"?

2. How does the first paragraph in this last chapter of Birkerts's book indicate the assumptions he makes about his readers' relationship to the subject?

✦ Point of View

3. What effect does Birkerts's point of view have on his relationship to his readers?

4. How does the point of view affect the readers' relationship to the subject?

✦ Shape of Ideas

5. How does Birkerts use "the Faustian pact" as a metaphor for structuring his chapter?

6. This final chapter, the fifteenth, is Birkerts's last opportunity to achieve his purpose. What is that purpose and how does the structure of the chapter make the final connection with the readers?

✦ Choosing Voice

7. Birkerts frequently poses questions. What quality do those questions contribute to his writing voice?

8. Birkerts uses both formal and informal language. Identify two examples of each and explain what effect each level of formality has at that point in the chapter.

✦ *Credibility*

9. Birkerts does not define or describe most of the sources he includes. How will his assumption that his audience is familiar with those sources affect his credibility?

10. How does Birkerts construct credibility in presenting information about technology?

✦ *Suggestions for Writing about the New Century*

1. How is the profession you plan to enter changing? What role will it play as society's needs change? Will your education prepare you for those changes? Will past changes in that profession help you to predict change? Research the historical evolution of that profession and current predictions for its future role. Present your analysis with a guide to others preparing to enter that profession.

2. Demographics are used to predict change, needs, and patterns of behavior in our society, but how are these demographics determined? How are the data collected, by whom, and how often? Who analyzes and presents that data for interpretation? Who uses demographics and for what purposes? Research the field and apply what you learn to a specific issue.

3. How conscious is your acceptance and use of the newly emerging technologies? Have they changed the range of people you communicate with, the frequency of your communication, the content of your communication? Analyze how your current habits in using technology affect your relationships with other people, and from that analysis develop a portrait of your "social self."

4. With literally millions of Web sites available, what criteria do you use for determining the value of a site? The last part of the URL identifies a general context for using the site, for example .org, .edu, .com, .gov. Consider how that context affects your expectations. Visit a site you have never used before and evaluate its value as a resource for its intended purpose.

5. When the stock market crashed in the late 1980s, thousands of Wall Street stockbrokers who lost their jobs decided to leave "the rat race" and move to rural settings. Is it possible that the bombardment of information technology makes possible and the displacement of people who don't work in technology will have a similar backlash effect? Will people who choose not to be a part of the technological revolution create alternative, perhaps more traditional lifestyles? Investigate society's responses to major changes in the past, research current predictions on the future of technology, and present an argument on what the alternative response to the Information Age might be.

6. It's easy to spend hours on the Internet looking for information, clicking from one link to the next, drilling down through layers of

information. Try duplicating Radosh's experiment by writing a short Web-based essay on an unfamiliar topic, including a commentary on the sites you use.

7. Will interactive enhancement of the Internet, such as the video-on-demand Bailey describes, actually increase political involvement and heighten our tenets of democracy? Consider this issue first on a personal level. Analyze your current involvement as a voter. Would the ability to select information on candidate's views at your convenience and to interact with them on-line increase your participation in the democratic process? Explore the possibilities in a personal essay.

8. Education is enhanced by technology in many ways, from Web-based courses and on-line class discussions to distance education and "virtual" degrees. How far do you think the impact of technology will extend? Will everyone eventually become home schooled on-line? Using your own experience, interviews with educators and students with on-line course experience, and research, formulate an opinion on the future impact of technology on getting an education and present a well-documented argument.

Acknowledgments *(continued from p. ii)*

Chapter 1

Kathleen Burge, "Woman of the Year: Jody Williams," from *Ms.* Magazine, January/February 1998. Copyright © 1998 by Ms. Magazine. Reprinted by permission of Ms. Magazine.

Emily Gest, "Woman of the Year: Donna Shirley," from *Ms.* Magazine, January/February 1998. Copyright © 1998 by Ms. Magazine. Reprinted by permission of Ms. Magazine.

Chapter 2

Paul Saffo, "Neo-Toys," from *Civilization*, October/November 1998. Copyright © 1998 by Civilization. Reprinted by permission of the author.

Hannah Nyala, "Revenge and Reconciliation" from *Civilization*, December 1999/January 2000. Copyright © 1999 by Civilization. Reprinted by permission of the author.

Chapter 3

William Gibson, "The Net Is a Waste of Time . . . and That's What's Good about It." Copyright © 1996 by William Gibson. Reprinted by permission of the author and Martha Millard Literary Agency.

Max Frankel, "Let's Be Chromatically Correct" from *New York Times,* December 6, 1998. Copyright © 1998 by the New York Times. Reprinted by permission.

Chapter 4

James D. Watson, "All for the Good" from *Time,* January 11, 1999. Copyright © 1999 by Time Inc. Reprinted by permission.

Robert Wright, "Who Gets the Good Genes?" from *Time,* January 11, 1999. Copyright © 1999 by Time Inc. Reprinted by permission.

Chapter 5

Linda Mooney, "The Cancer Your Doctor May Miss" from *Prevention.com*, May 1999. Copyright © 1999 by Rodale Inc. Reprinted by permission of Prevention Magazine. All rights reserved.

pcusa.org, "Proposed New Labeling Implies Wine Has Health Benefits," November 16, 1998. Reprinted by permission of Presbyterian Church (USA), Washington Office, www.pcusa.org/pcusa/nmd/wo, and the Alcohol Policies Project at the Center for Science in the Public Interest, 1875 Connecticut Avenue, NW, Suite 300, Washington, DC 20009-5728, http://www.csinet.org/booze.

Chapter 6

Alan Edelstein, "No More Heroes," from *Everybody Is Sitting on the Curb: How and Why America's Heroes Disappeared.* Copyright © 1996. Reprinted by permission of Greenwood Publishing Group, Inc., Westport, CT.

Alexander Melendez, "A Long Time Ago in a Galaxy Not So Far Away." Copyright © 1999. Reprinted by permission of author/student.

Richard Reynolds, "Living in the New Middle Ages," from *Super Heroes: A Modern Mythology.* Copyright © 1994. Reprinted by permission of Chrysalis Books Group.

Barbara Ehrenreich, "GreatWomen, Bad Times," from *Time,* April 13, 1998. Copyright © 1998 Time Inc. Reprinted by permission.

Andrew Bernstein, "The Soul of a Champion: A Letter to Michael Jordan" from *Central Florida Future,* January 20, 1999. Copyright © 1999. Reprinted by permission of the College Press Exchange.

548

Reprinted by permission of Bonnie Bucqueroux, executive director of the Michigan Victim Alliance.

Chapter 9

Bill Tonelli, "Steak in the Heart: Chewing the Fat with a Cardiac Surgeon" from *Men's Journal*, November 1999. Copyright © 1999 by Men's Journal Company, LP. Reprinted by permission. All rights reserved.

Kari Watson, "The Brain's Balancing Act" from *Natural Health,* September/October 1998. Copyright ©1998 by Natural Health. Reprinted by permission of Natural Health. For a trial issue of Natural Health, call 800-526-8440.

Jim Thornton, "Filtering the Flood" from *Cooking Light* Magazine. Copyright ©1999 by Cooking Light® Magazine. Reprinted by permission of Cooking Light Magazine.

Michael D. Lemonick, "Designer Babies" from *Time,* January 11, 1999. Copyright © 1999 by Time Inc. Reprinted by permission.

Natalie Angier, "Drugs, Sports, Body Image and G.I. Joe" from *The New York Times,* December 22, 1998. Copyright © 1998 by The New York Times. Reprinted by permission.

Kathy Gay, "Journey of a Latent Vegetarian" from www.vegsource.org. March 1997. Reprinted by permission of VegSource Interactive, Inc.

Jill Kramer, "Dialing Up Angels" from *Natural Health,* September/October 1998. Copyright © 1998 by Natural Health. Reprinted by permission of Natural Health. For a trial issue of Natural Health, call 800-526-8440.

Stacey Mihm, "Hospitals Were Made for Recovery." Copyright © 1999. Reprinted by permission of student/author.

Chapter 10

Corbett Trubey, "The Argument against TV," from *Lotus* Magazine, April 1999. Reprinted by permission of Lotus Magazine.

Paul Levinson, "Millenial McLuhan: Clues for Deciphering the Digital Age," from *The Chronicle of Higher Education,* October 19, 1999. Copyright © 1999 by The Chronicle of Higher Education. Reprinted by permission of the author.

James Poniewozik, "Will RealAudio Kill the Radio Star?" from Salon.com, May 24, 1999. Copyright © 1999. Reprinted with permission.

Ellen Goodman, "Culture of Thin Bites Fiji Teens," from *The Boston Globe,* May 28, 1999. Copyright © 1999 by The Boston Globe Newspaper Co./Washington Post Writers Group. Reprinted by permission.

Hoag Levins, "How Newspapers Don't Get It about Cyberspace," from www.mediainfo.com, March 28, 1998. Copyright © 1998. Reprinted by permission of the author.

Michael Mattis, "Your Wireless Future" from *Business 2.0* Magazine, August 1, 1999. Copyright © 1999. Reprinted by permission of Business 2.0 Magazine.

Greg Lindsay, "Hey Kids, Let's Put on a Show," from *Time Digital,* October 4, 1999. Copyright © 1999 by Time Inc. Reprinted by permission.

Netaid.org, "World Wide Web Helps War on Poverty," from www.netaid.org, October 9, 1999. Reprinted by permission of Netaid.org.

Neil Postman, "Future Schlock," from *Conscientious Objections: Stirring Up Trouble about Language, Technology, and Education.* Copyright © 1988 by Neil Postman. Reprinted by permission of Alfred A. Knopf, a Division of Random House, Inc.

Chapter 11

Jocelyn Bartkevicius, "The Land" from *Out of the Garden.* Copyright © 1999. Reprinted by permission of author.

550

Chapter 12

index of authors and titles

◆ ✦

553

subject index

◆ ✦